Economics
of
TRANSPORTATION

Economics

of

TRANSPORTATION

RUSSELL E. WESTMEYER, Ph.D.

PROFESSOR OF BUSINESS ADMINISTRATION
COLLEGE OF BUSINESS ADMINISTRATION
UNIVERSITY OF ARKANSAS

New York PRENTICE-HALL, INC. *1952*

Copyright
1952
by
PRENTICE-HALL, INC.
70 Fifth Avenue, New York

PRINTED IN THE UNITED STATES OF AMERICA

L.C. Cat. Card No.: 52-9966

PREFACE

In keeping with the recent rapid development of motor, domestic water, and air transportation, the present writer has deemed it proper to treat them more extensively than has been customary. Also, the growth of freight forwarding and the ever increasing complexity and perplexity of the railroad labor problem seem to make a somewhat detailed consideration of these matters almost imperative. To keep the book within reasonable limits, some phases of railroad transportation which are no longer as significant as formerly are treated in much less detail than has been traditional. This is particularly true of railroad competition, discrimination, unification, and the rate base and rate-of-return problem. Competition, discrimination, and unification are discussed in Chapter 4, "Some Economic Characteristics of Railroad Transportation," and are considered in historical perspective in the chapters on regulation. The rate base and rate-of-return problem are taken up in Chapter 10, "General Level of Railroad Rates." Those wishing a more detailed consideration of any of these subjects will, of course, have no difficulty in supplementing the text.

The Suggested Readings given at the end of each chapter are not intended to constitute an exhaustive list of references. Their purpose, rather, is to aid in obtaining additional information on various subjects from readily available sources.

Part One of the book covers the place of improved transportation in the economic scheme of things, and the early history of domestic transportation in the United States. Part Two covers railroad transportation. More space is devoted to the railroad than to any other single agency of transportation, which is not unreasonable because the railroads have a much longer history and are presently hauling more traffic than all other agencies combined. Much of the material in this section deals with the development and present status of carrier regulation and provides the necessary background for studying the regulation of the newer agencies. In a larger sense,

PREFACE

therefore, a good deal of the material in Part Two applies not just to railroads but to all forms of transportation.

Parts Three, Four, and Five deal with motor, domestic water, and air transportation, and Part Six deals with other forms of domestic transportation. While none of these parts is as long as Part Two, this does not mean that the newer agencies have been neglected. Their shorter history, smaller scale of operations, and the fact that their regulation is based largely on earlier experiences with railroad regulation make it unnecessary to devote as much space to any one of them as to railroads.

Part Seven takes up the very important matter of interagency relationships and the place of each in a sound national transportation system. Each form of transportation has its advocates who are interested in promoting it and it alone; the theme of Part Seven is that the public interest requires the development of a sound national transportation system using all forms of transportation to their best advantage.

Special thanks for many helpful suggestions are due to Professor C. S. Dunford of Michigan State College who read the original draft of the manuscript; to Professor Virgil Cover of Syracuse University who read the final draft; to Professor Stanley Berge of Northwestern University who read the section on air transportation; and to Professor Harry Jenkins of the University of Arkansas for his criticisms of specific aspects of the work. The author, however, assumes full responsibility for any errors of omission or commission. Special thanks also are due to Dean Paul W. Milam of the College of Business Administration, University of Arkansas, for adjustment of teaching load and for his patience and understanding during difficult periods. In addition, the Bureau of Business and Economic Research of the College was most helpful in providing stenographic assistance. Finally, the author wishes to acknowledge his debt to his wife, Mildred Palmerton Westmeyer, who gave unselfishly and unsparingly of her time in the final preparation of the manuscript and book.

Fayetteville, Arkansas   R.E.W.

CONTENTS

PART ONE: INTRODUCTION

PART TWO: RAILROAD TRANSPORTATION

CONTENTS

PART THREE: HIGHWAY TRANSPORTATION

PART FOUR: DOMESTIC WATER TRANSPORTATION

PART FIVE: AIR TRANSPORTATION

PART SIX: OTHER TRANSPORTATION AGENCIES

PART SEVEN: NATIONAL TRANSPORTATION PROBLEMS AND POLICIES

Part One

INTRODUCTION

The Importance
of
IMPROVED TRANSPORTATION

THE SUBJECT MATTER OF TRANSPORTATION

Importance of improved transportation. An efficient and economical transportation system is something which the average individual tends to take for granted. If he thinks of transportation at all, it is probably in terms of passenger trains, automobiles, and airplanes—instrumentalities which permit him to travel conveniently from one place to another. These things are important, of course, but the significance of improved transportation as a means of moving goods should not be overlooked, for without economical and efficient methods of transporting goods, present-day civilization simply could not exist. It is, therefore, no exaggeration to say that the maintenance and further development of an economical and efficient transportation system is a matter of the utmost importance to the nation, and the informed citizen should be sufficiently familiar with the transportation system and basic transportation problems to enable him to pass judgment on the transportation policies of the government and of the carriers themselves. As an introduction to the study of transportation, the following pages are devoted to a brief consideration of the various ways in which improved transportation has contributed to the development of modern society.

Various approaches to the study of transportation. Transportation as a field for serious study may be approached from various points of view. In the first place, transportation may be studied as an engineering problem, with attention devoted to the construction and maintenance of railroads, highways, airports, and the like; or to the designing of ships, locomotives and cars, motor vehicles, barges and tugs, and airplanes. Transportation also may be studied as a problem in business administration, either from the point of view of the sellers of transportation services or from the point of view of the buyers of these services. Again, transportation may be studied as an economic problem, since efficient and economical transportation is recognized as being basic to the success of any modern economy. Finally, transportation may be studied as a public utility, an industry functioning in that shadowy area intermediate between those activities which are clearly recognized as legitimate fields for government action and those activities which are clearly reserved for private enterprise. This book concerns itself primarily with the economic and public utility aspects of transportation.

In studying the economic and public utility aspects of transportation it is common to draw a sharp line of distinction between the transportation of goods in foreign trade by ocean, on the one hand, and rail, motor, domestic water, pipe line, and air transportation on the other. There is good reason for this. Ocean transportation differs markedly in many ways from other forms of transportation, both in methods of operation and in the economic and regulatory problems confronting the industry and its shippers. Furthermore, ocean carriers do not compete directly with other forms of transportation except, to a limited extent, with the international operations of domestic airlines. Rail, motor, domestic water, pipe line, and air transportation also may be studied individually since each type of transportation has problems peculiar to itself. All of these forms of transportation, however, have many similarities and many common problems, and since they compete directly with one another and constitute integral parts of a national transportation system, it is useful to study all of them under the one broad heading of inland or domestic transportation. A distinction also may be made between intercity transportation—the movement of passengers and property between towns, and local transportation—the movement of people and property within an urban area. This book deals with all forms of domestic intercity transportation.

ECONOMIC SIGNIFICANCE OF IMPROVED TRANSPORTATION

Basic importance of improved transportation in the United States. The importance of improved transportation to the United States may be shown in a simple way by attempting to imagine what this country would be like today if there had been no improvement in transportation facilities beyond the primitive roads and vehicles which existed at the time of our Revolution. It seems reasonable to suppose that a thin population, at least by present standards, would be spread over those areas where climatic conditions and natural resources made a self-sufficient economy possible, with larger populations along the sea coasts and in the interior along the banks of navigable streams. It is possible that the United States would still be confined to the Atlantic seaboard area. California and the west coast might constitute a separate nation or part of some colonial empire. And the Mississippi River and its tributaries might constitute the backbone of one or more other nations. Manufacturing probably would be in the handicraft stage with goods produced locally for local markets. Large-scale production would be out of the question, and luxuries and such present day necessities as automobiles, cheap radio and television sets, and vacations in Yellowstone Park would be unknown.

The importance of improved transportation to the United States is no new discovery. It was known to the founding fathers at the very beginning of the national period, and by the very early 1800's they already were trying to do something about it, although their interest probably was more political than economic. When Charles Carroll, the last surviving signer of the Declaration of Independence, laid the first rail of the Baltimore and Ohio Railroad in 1828, he declared that he considered this act to be second in importance only to his signing of the Declaration of Independence if, indeed, it was second to that. If, indeed, it was second to that! It is interesting to speculate about what Mr. Carroll might say on this subject if he were to come to life today—when distances are measured in hours and minutes rather than in miles—and address the nation over a coast-to-coast network.

The dependence of the people of the United States upon improved transportation has been demonstrated strikingly on various occasions in recent years. During World War II, transportation "know how" made it possible to send fighting men and war materials to remote corners of the earth and to meet the enemy in his own back yard. The nationwide strikes of coal miners which occurred at intervals during the postwar years sometimes necessitated sharp reductions in the schedules of railroads using coal burning locomotives, and shippers and the traveling public experienced immediate and severe hardships. The brief strike of enginemen and trainmen in May, 1946, created a national emergency of the first magnitude. Had that strike continued more than a few days vast quantities of perishables would have been ruined, and the food problem would have become serious in the densely populated areas of the East. The epidemic of "sickness" which struck railroad workers in the terminal areas of St. Louis, Chicago, and elsewhere in the latter part of 1950 brought further difficulties and threatened a creeping paralysis of the industrial mechanism.

Transportation and large production. The inhabitants of the United States enjoy the highest standard of living found anywhere on earth because of their ability to produce an enormous volume and variety of low priced goods and services, in part through the utilization of the techniques of large production. And it is not at all difficult to demonstrate that large production as it exists today could not have been developed without an efficient and economical system of transportation. In the first place, efficient and economical transportation makes possible the accumulation of the vast quantities of raw materials without which modern large production could not function today. Many of the basic raw materials of industry are located in sparsely settled areas and must be shipped long distances to factories or primary markets located in or near the great centers of population in the East, the Middle West, and the Far West. Copper, cattle, coal, iron, grain, and wood pulp are a few such basic commodities. Obviously, large production could not possibly exist without some means of transporting raw materials cheaply, promptly, and in large quantities to manufacturing areas.

An adequate supply of raw materials is not the only thing necessary for the successful operation of large production. Just as important as an adequate supply of raw materials is a market for the product, and the greater the volume of production the wider must be the market in which the product is sold. For example, the great meat packing enterprises in Chicago and Kansas City could not have grown to their present size if the market for their products had been confined to the area immediately surrounding the packing plants. The same thing is true of automobiles, tires, steel, and other mass production industries. In many cases the output of a single plant is sold over the entire United States and even over the whole earth. In other cases it has been recognized that the economies of such large-scale production have their limits and regional plants have been established, but even these regional plants sell their product over rather wide areas. Clearly, without economical and efficient transportation such distribution could not be achieved.

Transportation and geographical specialization. By providing for the low cost movement of large quantities of raw materials from source of supply to factory, and for the low cost movement of finished products over a wide market area, improved transportation makes it possible for individual plants to achieve the economies of specialization and the division of labor characteristic of modern large production. But improved transportation also makes possible a division of labor on a geographical or territorial basis which has contributed importantly to increased production and higher standards of living. It is a well known fact that some regions are better suited to the production of certain things than they are to the production of others, these special advantages accruing from the availability of natural resources, favorable climatic conditions, cheap power, cheap labor, skilled labor, or some other peculiar characteristic. And economists have recognized for many years that if the people of each country, or each section of a country, will specialize in the production of those things for which they or their region are best fitted, the result of such specialization will be the production of a greater total volume of goods.

Geographical specialization is practical only to the extent that it is possible for the people of each region to exchange their surplus products for the surplus products of other regions in order that all may have the things they want or need. Here again efficient and economical transportation enters the picture. If the surplus products cannot be transported safely from one region to another, or if transportation costs are so high that they more than absorb the savings achieved through geographical specialization, then there is no point in specializing on a geographical basis. In brief, the economies of geographical specialization are entirely dependent upon the availability of efficient and economical transportation.

The development of motor freight transportation and, to a lesser extent, air transportation, has contributed importantly to the further development of certain kinds of geographical specialization. Many kinds of fruits and vegetables can be produced in the South, some over an extended period of time. These products have been, and still are, shipped to northern markets by railroad, although the cost of packing and refrigeration has added to the cost of the product on the market, and it has been possible to sell some of the more perishable products in distant markets only at the expense of considerable deterioration. The motor freight carrier has enlarged the opportunities for specialization of this sort by making possible a substantial reduction in the cost of packing and often eliminating the need for refrigeration, thus lowering the cost of the product on the market. The airplane makes possible the long distance movement of perishables without refrigeration, but as yet the service is too costly to be practical on a large scale.

Transportation and rent. Land rent varies with the productivity or usefulness of each individual plot of land. In the case of agricultural, mineral, and forest land, productivity depends in part upon the natural qualities of the land itself and in part upon its location with reference to markets or centers of population. There was, for example, during the nineteenth century a good deal of land in the interior of the United States which was more fertile than land then being cultivated in the East, but the rental value of the western land was very low because there was no way of bringing its products to market. The construction of railroads greatly reduced the cost of transportation, brought this land closer to the market, and increased the rental value of the land. In some cases, no doubt, the development of this new land had an adverse effect on the rental value of some of the older lands in the East. For the most part, however, the eastern lands acquired values of an entirely different sort as they were taken over for use as sites for factories and urban dwellings.

In the case of urban land, rental value depends largely upon location, but improved transportation also has played its part here. Improved transportation makes the areas surrounding large population centers available for suburban factory and home sites with an attendant increase in the rental value of the land in these areas. The western migration of population which was facilitated by improved transportation has led to the establishment of new population centers in the interior and increased rental values in the newer areas. In some cases older population centers suffered a diminution of population and a decline in land values. In other cases, however, immigration and a rising birth rate have more than filled the gaps and held urban rental values up.

Transportation and labor. Improved transportation, to the extent that it has contributed to vastly increased production, has contributed to lower prices and higher real wages. Improved transportation also tends to reduce sharp differences in wages between different sections of the country by making it possible for workers to migrate from low wage areas to areas of high wages. For many years this sort of migration took place only in a slow and halting fashion because workers who had been born and raised in a certain area did not readily pull up stakes and move to strange places, especially if they were already married and were raising a family. The development of low priced automobiles, however, has made traveling commonplace, and people are not as averse to trying their luck in greener pastures as was formerly the case. During World War II, labor migrations were very extensive, the rural areas in the South in particular losing population to industrial centers. Such migrations are bound to reduce somewhat regional disparities in wage rates, and improved transportation in the form of cheap automobiles has certainly played a part in this process.

Transportation and the location of markets. Probably no better illustration of the economic significance of transportation can be found than in the role it has played in the location of market centers. It is no accident that many of the world's great commercial centers developed at or near points where navigable rivers entered the ocean or at the confluence of two rivers or other bodies of water. London, Rotterdam, Hamburg, Constantinople, Cairo, and Shanghai are but a few of such Old World points which come to mind. In the United States this same relationship between transportation and the development of great commercial centers is evident. New York City, established where the Hudson River enters the ocean, and later to be connected with the Great Lakes by way of the Erie Canal, became the nation's foremost commercial center. St. Louis, located on the west bank of the Mississippi, north of the mouth of the Ohio and just below the mouths of the Missouri and the Illinois, became very early an outfitting and trading point, and from these beginnings the city developed into one of the great commercial centers of the interior. Chicago, originally a frontier outpost at the head of navigation on Lake Michigan, became a focal point for railroads building west from the eastern seaboard. This in turn made it the logical eastern terminus for railroads building into the West. Hence Chicago became the greatest railroad center on earth and one of the world's greatest commercial and industrial areas.

Transportation and the location of industry. Although transportation is only one of a variety of factors which enter into the determination of the location of a given industry, it is often the dominant consideration, and changes in the quality, quantity, or price of transportation service can completely alter the pattern of industrial location. Of course, some industries have little or no choice in matters of location. Thus retail establishments and the so-called service industries must locate where there is a market for their goods or services. The raising of certain crops often is limited to certain areas by climatic conditions. Industries requiring large amounts of power often locate near sources of cheap hydroelectric power; and lumbering, mining, and other types of extractive industries must locate where the materials they extract exist. In these latter cases, however, transportation does play some part because, unless some very cheap means of transportation is available, supplies of raw materials in remote areas are not likely to be exploited until supplies nearer to the centers of population are exhausted or become too expensive to produce.

Where considerations other than transportation are unimportant, industry tends to locate in such a way as to minimize transportation charges, and this in turn commonly necessitates a choice between locating in or near the market where the finished product is sold, locating at the source of raw materials, or locating at some point intermediate between the two. The actual location of any given industry, to the extent that transportation costs are the basic factor, will tend to be fixed on the basis of two separate but closely related considerations. One of these is the extent to which the raw material is completely utilized in the manufacturing process, and the other is the relationship of the freight rates on the raw materials to the freight rates on the finished product. If all or a large part of the raw material is utilized in the process of manufacture, as in the case of the milling of wheat into flour, then it should not make too much difference whether the manufacturing takes place at the source of the raw material or in the market, assuming that differences in freight rates between the two products do not exist. If, however, the industry is one which makes use of the so-called weight-losing materials, a different situation exists. In the case of the ores of such metals as gold, silver, and copper, a large amount of waste material is left over after the metal has been extracted, and to process such weight-losing materials in the market would involve the payment of freight charges for the transportation of a great deal of useless material. Hence it is common to process weight-losing materials at the source of supply and ship the finished or partially finished product to market.

In many cases, whether loss of weight in the manufacturing process is involved or not, the relationship between the freight rates on the raw material and on the finished product must be considered in determining the location of an industry. If the cost of transporting the raw materials is low relative to the cost of transporting the finished product, which is often true, there will be a tendency for the industry to locate near the market. This was the case for many years in the petroleum industry. All parts of the crude oil are utilized in one way or another, and the cost of transporting crude oil by pipe line is extremely low as compared with the cost of shipping the finished products by railroad or motor carrier. Hence many of the nation's great refineries were located in or near markets for the finished products. Tankers have so reduced the cost of transporting refined liquid petroleum products, however, that great oil refineries are now found along the Gulf coast near oil producing areas, and the finished products are shipped by water to eastern markets.

Many other illustrations of the influence of transportation costs on the location of industries may be cited. An industry making use of materials which are found almost everywhere will naturally tend to locate near the market for its product. The manufacture of soft drinks and common building bricks are often cited as illustrating this point. Industries which use large quantities of two or more basic raw materials will tend to gravitate to points where these resources are found in close proximity. If the resources involved are widely separated, however, a careful balance must be reached between the transportation costs involved before a decision can be reached on where the industry should locate.

This last situation suggests the possibility of a location intermediate between the sources of raw materials or between the raw materials and the market. Indeed, an intermediate location may be a possibility even where only a single major raw material is involved. One difficulty with the intermediate location is the fact that freight rates do not increase proportionately with distance (for reasons which are explained in a later chapter). Hence the rates charged for two short hauls will be higher than the rate charged for a single haul covering the same distance as the two short hauls. If, for example, a flour mill is located half way between a terminal grain market and an urban flour market, and assuming that both wheat and flour move under the same rate, it will cost more to ship the wheat from the elevator to the mill and the flour from the mill to the market than it will cost to ship the wheat from the grain market to a mill located in the flour market or to ship the flour from a mill in the grain area to the market. In a good many cases this disadvantage of the intermediate location has been offset by the establishment of special concessions known as transit arrangements which make the over-all transportation charge about the same regardless of where the manufacturing process takes place.

Improved transportation and industrial location. Technical improvements in transportation which lead to lower charges, better service, or both may bring about the relocation of industry, although such relocations are not likely to take place overnight. The construction of railroads over the Appalachian Mountains, previously mentioned in connection with the effect of improved transportation on land rent, led to a shift in agricultural production from the eastern seaboard to the fertile lands of the Ohio Valley. At one time live poultry was shipped to market in special railroad cars, but improved methods of refrigeration, expedited transportation by railroad and truck, and the more recent development of quick freezing has led to the growth of an extensive poultry processing industry right in the producing areas.

The development of the motor vehicle and motor transportation has had a significant impact on the location of industry. For example, the railroad is not well adapted to the movement of small shipments, and for years this service was slow and expensive. The motor carrier, on the other hand, is particularly well adapted to the economical movement of small shipments, over relatively short distances, and a number of industries have taken advantage of this fact by establishing branch plants or warehouses at strategic locations all over the United States. Subassemblies or finished products are shipped to these locations by railroad in carload lots at low rates, and the finished product is then shipped in smaller lots throughout the area by motor vehicle. Sometimes improved transportation leads to the development of new industries, as in the case of the shipment of orchids from Hawaii and cut flowers from California by air to all parts of the United States.

Discriminatory freight rates and the location of markets and industry. The location of commercial and industrial centers may be determined, or at least influenced, by the practice of fixing rates to and from certain points arbitrarily higher or lower than those charged to and from other points. This was a common complaint against the railroads in the days before they were subjected to effective regulation, and there can be little doubt that such artificial freight rate advantages did promote the development of some points at the expense of others. More recently the South, and to a lesser extent the Southwest and Middle West, have objected that the general level of freight rates in these areas has been higher than in the East and that this has retarded the development of industry outside of the East.

IMPROVED TRANSPORTATION

TRANSPORTATION AND SOCIAL WELFARE

Production and social welfare. It will be apparent at once that transportation, to the extent that it has contributed to increased production, gives rise to great possibilities in the direction of improving social well-being. After the United States was hit by the full impact of the Industrial Revolution, production increased tremendously, and this great increase in production was accompanied over the years by a rising standard of living. In addition to contributing to an improved standard of living in the sense of making available a larger quantitative supply of goods per capita, improved transportation also has helped to enrich the general standard of living by making available to large numbers of people a much wider variety of goods and services than they would otherwise enjoy. Healthful fresh fruits and vegetables are available the year round in almost all parts of the United States. Similarly, improved transportation has provided the people of this country with bananas, cocoa, coffee, rubber, hemp, coconut oil, pineapples, tin, and many other products of foreign soils at prices which make their utilization in one form or another possible to almost everyone.

Cultural development and the broader outlook. Transportation has been responsible, too, for certain gains of a less material nature. Improved transportation has made it possible for people to travel from one section of the country to every other section of the country and to foreign countries. Good roads and inexpensive automobiles have played an especially important role in this connection. By bringing the people of all parts of the United States into contact with one another and with the peoples of other countries, there is an opportunity for all to benefit from a comparison of ideas and practices and from an understanding of each other's problems. Cheap transportation has made possible, too, the wide diffusion of ideas through newspapers and magazines, although some may be inclined to argue that this has had harmful as well as beneficial results. Similar statements may be made with regard to the movies and the radio which are devices for transporting ideas.

TRANSPORTATION AND POLITICAL UNITY

The Pacific railroad. In addition to promoting social unity improved transportation has been, at various times and places, an important factor contributing to the creation of the political unity of an area. In the United States the construction of the Union Pacific-Central Pacific transcontinental railroad project in the 1860's played an important role in binding California and the Pacific coast to the states and territories east of the

Missouri River. Prior to the construction of a railroad to the Pacific the only means of communication between the eastern states and California consisted of a long ocean journey by way of Cape Horn, a dangerous trip across the Isthmus of Panama, or the slow and sometimes dangerous trek across the prairies and mountains in prairie schooners or in primitive stage-coaches. The railroad to the Pacific provided relatively easy access to California, no doubt played its part in holding that state to the Union, and contributed enormously to the development of the intermediate territory.

Australian government railroad. The government-owned railroad which links the railroad systems of Australia's east and west coasts is perhaps one of the most striking examples of a railroad built to promote political unity. At the turn of the present century a strong movement developed to join the various British colonies which had been established in Australia into a single commonwealth. The crown colony of Western Australia, however, with its own ports and separated by a great waterless plain from the concentration of eastern colonies, saw nothing to be gained from such a union. In order to get the people of Western Australia to agree to the commonwealth idea it was necessary to commit the proposed new government to the construction of a transcontinental railroad which would link the two coasts, and such a railroad was built. A full 800 miles of route ran through uninhabited country, so barren and arid that along the entire line there was no natural surface water available. Surveys were made with camels and water, labor, supplies, and even firewood, had to be hauled from the starting point of the line as construction progressed. At the time that it was built there was no need for this railroad in the sense that development of the area traversed was handicapped for lack of transportation facilities. Water transportation existed for such through movements as might be necessary between the east and west coasts, and there was no local traffic in the intermediate area. Nonetheless, the line was built and played its part in the unification of Australia under a single government.

TRANSPORTATION AND MILITARY NEEDS

Military railroad systems. In some parts of the world military considerations have played an important part in laying out railroad systems. The German railroad system, as it was ultimately developed, took the form of a wagon wheel or spider web, with the outer circumference skirting the German border and with lines radiating in all directions from Berlin to this outer circumference. This arrangement made it possible for Germany to shift men and supplies from one front to another with considerable facility during World War I. Large forces would be concentrated on the western front for a big push. After the push took place, the army would dig in, enough men would be left to hold the trenches, and the remaining soldiers and equipment would be shifted to some other front for another push. And while the German railroad system contributed to German successes during World War I, Hitler's failure to maintain the railroads adequately and the subsequent breakdown of transportation is said to have been a contributing factor to the ultimate defeat of the Germans in World War II.

The railroad which runs all the way across Siberia, linking Russia's eastern provinces with European Russia, is another example of a railroad built at least partly for military purposes, and the fact that it was not altogether completed at the time of the outbreak of the Russo-Japanese War no doubt contributed to the defeat of the Tsar's forces in the land fighting in the Far East. The Berlin to Bagdad railroad and the Cape to Cairo railroad, both very much in the news at one time, are other illustrations of railroad projects motivated by military considerations. Although there was never a Berlin to Bagdad railroad in the sense of a single system under common ownership or management, and although there is no such thing, even today, as a continuous railroad running north and south through Africa, both of these projects were steeped in military significance.

World War II demonstrated beyond question the dependence of the United States upon railroad transportation in time of war. Much of the material produced for the armed forces, because of its weight and bulk, could be transported from factory to factory and from factory to port or training center only by the railroads. The tanker fleet, which before the war had transported a large tonnage of liquid petroleum products from Gulf coast refineries to the East, had to be withdrawn from this service as a result of the submarine menace and because it was needed to supply overseas fighting forces; but the railroads managed to carry this added burden until relieved somewhat by the completion of the Big Inch and Little Inch pipe lines. Similarly, troop movements could be handled, practically speaking, only by railroad. All the various carriers were plagued by equipment shortages, but the railroad plant proved to be the more expansible, and the railroads were called upon to handle an ever increasing proportion of the total volume of traffic during the years of maximum war effort.

Highway and air transportation. While the armed forces of all major powers made considerable use of motor vehicles during World War I, it remained for Nazi Germany to grasp the military significance of motor transportation, and in the interval between wars the Germans developed a fine system of hard surfaced highways, obviously laid out with military use in mind. In this country the motor vehicle played an important part in local movements of goods, and the volume of intercity traffic handled by commercial carriers increased even though their relative share of this business declined sharply. In the actual theaters of war motor vehicles, of course, played a vital role in the movement of supplies and personnel to the fighting fronts. Although domestic airlines handled only an insignificant amount of tonnage, their services were of great value in moving emergency shipments and in the high speed transportation of passengers at a great saving of time. As a fighting machine the airplane has, of course, occupied a dominant position in modern warfare, but aside from this, it has proved of incalculable value in supplying troops at the front and in moving men and supplies at high speed over long distances and across otherwise inaccessible terrain.

EVILS ARISING FROM IMPROVED TRANSPORTATION

Evils of modern industry. Although improved transportation has contributed importantly to economic, social, and political progress, it has not been without its attendant evils. If the railroad, for example, is to be given credit for the part it has played in the development of modern large-scale production and the division of labor, then it must also bear its share of the responsibility for the monotony of assembly line production and for the evils of city life. The motor vehicle in its turn has contributed importantly to the number of accidental deaths and has played a part in the spread of crime, in juvenile delinquency, and in a general loosening of public morals.

Antisocial policies. It must be recorded, too, that some of the railroad magnates of the last century were responsible for corrupting legislators and public officials—a development that is not pleasant to relate. Discrimination in rates, before this practice was outlawed effectively, promoted the development of some communities at the expense of others, brought industrial success to a favored few and failure to many others, and played an important part in developing some of the great nineteenth century monopolies. Jay Gould and Jim Fisk, two speculators of this period, made use of economically desirable transportation systems as convenient vehicles for the issuance of stocks and bonds, the proceeds of which went to fatten their own purses while the railroads themselves faced bankruptcy. Fortunately, standards of public and business morals have risen somewhat since the nineteenth century, and such antisocial policies which still remain are of a much less open and arrogant nature. This situation is the result in part of legislation brought about by the very excesses described, in part by higher standards of business ethics, and in part by a realization that policies designed to exploit wide segments of the public may in the long run do more damage than good to the individuals and to the businesses practicing them.

THE TRANSPORTATION SYSTEM OF THE UNITED STATES

General. Although each of the various forms of transportation is discussed in some detail in the chapters which follow, it will be useful by way of introduction to present a bird's-eye view of the transportation system of the United States as it exists today. This system is composed of an extensive network of railroads, highways, waterways, airways, and pipe lines, together with the necessary terminal facilities. While it is proper to speak of these various networks as the transportation system of the United States, it is important to understand that they do not constitute an *integrated* system. Each network was developed independently of the others and pretty much without regard to its effect on the others. It is true that a certain amount of internetwork coordination has come about as a result of cooperation between different types of carriers, sometimes through voluntary action and sometimes by compulsion, but at present the lack of coordination is far more significant than its presence. Some of the consequences of this lack of coordination are discussed in Chapters 32 and 33.

Railroads. In 1950 the railroad network of the United States consisted of 223,779 miles of line and 375,296 miles of track.[1] About 95 per cent of the network is operated by Class I line haul railroads, railroads having annual revenues in excess of $1 million and operating trains across country between cities and towns. The balance of the network is operated by the smaller line-haul railroads and by switching and terminal lines. The latter usually operate in and around industrial areas and seaports, switching cars from one railroad to another and between line-haul railroads and the sidings of industrial and commercial concerns, and performing various other terminal area services. The railroad companies and the railroad lines of the United States are privately owned and operated almost without exception and are devoted to the transportation of passengers and property for the public at large. In 1950 the railroads carried 596,940 million ton miles of freight and other goods traffic, or 58.69 per cent of the total

---

[1] Miles of line, or *mileage,* are computed on the basis of distances spanned. Thus a railroad operating between two points one hundred miles apart has one hundred miles of line even though it may be double tracked and have extensive switching facilities and sidings. Total number of miles of track, or *trackage,* includes all tracks. Unless otherwise noted, all traffic data in this section are from the *Annual Report* of the Interstate Commerce Commission for 1951.

volume of intercity movement of property by all means of transportation; and 32,481 million passenger miles, or 8.12 per cent of all intercity passenger miles, including those traveled in private automobiles.[2]

In addition to the railroads described in the preceding paragraph, some railroad facilities are owned and operated by private industries for their own use. Logging companies and mining companies sometimes have their own private railroad facilities, and many large industrial concerns have their own tracks and equipment for intraplant transportation and switching. Statistics on such private facilities are not available, but it is unlikely that, in the aggregate, they add greatly to total mileage and trackage.

Highways. The highway system of the United States consists of more than 3 million miles of rural roads, more than half of which are surfaced in one way or another, including gravel as a type of surface. Approximately 13 per cent of the surfaced highway mileage is Portland cement concrete or bituminous concrete.[3] Unlike the railroad network, the highway system is publicly owned and maintained. A very few publicly-owned roads and bridges are operated on the toll principle, with a direct charge being assessed against each motor vehicle operator for each time the facility is used, and recent difficulties encountered in financing highway construction suggest that additional toll roads may be built in the future. By and large, however, the public highways are and will continue to be freely available to motor vehicle operators without the assessment of direct user charges, and their construction and maintenance is likely to continue to be financed by motor fuel taxes and other direct charges levied on motor vehicle owners, and by contributions from the general tax revenues.

Many different kinds of transportation operations are carried on over the rural highways. Some motor carriers provide a "for-hire" service to the general public similar to that provided by the railroads, except that the service is usually much more restricted concerning the types of com-

---

[2] A ton mile is the equivalent of one ton of freight hauled one mile and is the standard unit for measuring traffic density. One ton of freight hauled one hundred miles equals one hundred ton miles. Similarly, one hundred tons of freight hauled one mile also equals one hundred ton miles. Passenger miles are computed in the same way. It is important in interpreting traffic statistics not to confuse *tons* with *ton miles*. For example, it was stated in a public advertisement that the trucking industry moved more tonnage in 1950 than all other agencies of transportation combined, and, presumably for that reason, motor transport was the nation's No. 1 carrier. No statistics are available to check the validity of the assertion, although if all trucks of all kinds, including farm trucks and local delivery trucks, are included, it might well be true. But to base traffic statistics on tons rather than on ton miles is to give the same weight to a haul of one mile as is given to a haul of a thousand miles, and this, to say the least, is misleading.

[3] Figures on highway mileage and surface adapted from U.S. Department of Commerce, Bureau of Public Roads, *Highway Statistics*, 1949.

modities transported. Other motor carriers do not offer their services to the general public, preferring to transport goods for a limited number of shippers on a contract basis. In addition to the services performed by motor carriers operating on a "for-hire" basis, many commercial and industrial concerns carry their own products over the road in their own trucks. And, of course, extensive use is made of the highways by operators of privately-owned cars, by farmers, by school buses, and the like. In 1950 motor vehicles of all kinds, including private trucks as well as those offering their services for hire, are estimated to have carried 125,995 million ton miles of freight and other goods traffic, or 12.39 per cent of the total volume of intercity movement of property by all carriers. Also in 1950, motor carriers for hire generated 20,912 million passenger miles or 5.23 per cent of total intercity passenger traffic, and the private automobile was estimated to have produced 337,339 million passenger miles, or 84.34 per cent of the total.

Domestic waterways. The domestic waterway system of the United States does not constitute a single interconnected network of waterways over which traffic can move freely, as it does in the case of the railroad and highway systems. Instead, there are three distinct types of waterway systems, and the three are interconnected only in a very limited sense. To begin with, there are the coastal and intercoastal shipping lanes, along which ocean-going boats move between Atlantic and Gulf coast ports, between Pacific coast ports, and between the east and west coasts by way of the Panama Canal. Because ocean vessels are not limited to narrowly defined routes and because the routes they follow often are quite roundabout, it would be meaningless to attempt to calculate the number of route miles of shipping lanes. Unlike railroads and motor carriers, coastal and intercoastal shipping does not require the construction and maintenance of a right of way. Various aids to navigation, however, such as harbors and deep water channels constructed to connect inland cities with the ocean, are built, maintained, and owned by the public, and these facilities are provided free of charge to the users. Port facilities are commonly provided and maintained from public funds, although charges may be levied against shipping concerns to cover a part of their cost. Because of indefinite and roundabout routes, ton mile statistics are not very significant, but they have been estimated at 221,448 million for 1949. This figure is not included in the total intercity ton miles on which the various percentages given in this section are computed. Much of the coastal traffic is handled privately by the large oil companies and other industrial enterprises in their own boats.

The Great Lakes constitute a second major waterway system. Navigation on the Great Lakes does not require the construction and maintenance of expensive right-of-way facilities, except at three points where it has been necessary to construct and maintain canals and channels in order to make maximum use of the Lakes. These facilities have been built and are maintained and owned by the United States and Canadian governments without cost to the carriers using them. In addition, harbor and port facilities are provided from the public funds, although some shippers have their own private docks. It may be noted at this point that expenditures of public funds on the Great Lakes have been small relative to expenditures on other waterways and in terms of cost per ton mile of traffic moved. The Interstate Commerce Commission does not separate Great Lakes from river and canal traffic in its annual reports, but as a rough estimate it may be said that domestic transportation on the Great Lakes accounted for 10 per cent or more of total intercity goods traffic in 1949.[4] There is some transportation of passengers in Great Lakes boats but the amount is insignificant. A large part of the freight moving on the Great Lakes consists of iron ore and coal hauled in specially designed boats owned or contracted for by private industries. Relatively little traffic is moved for the general public.

Navigable rivers and canals comprise the third type of waterway system in the United States. The principal river and canal system is made up of the Mississippi River system—the Ohio, the Illinois, the Missouri, and various tributary streams. Other systems include the Intercoastal Canals, the New York State Barge Canal, the Warrior River system, and various minor waterways. All told there are some 27,000 miles of navigable rivers and canals in the United States, although much of this mileage is navigable only by vessels of very shallow draft. As in the case of the highway system, navigable rivers and canals are built, maintained, and owned by the public, primarily by the Federal Government. Unlike the highway system, however, no direct charges, taxes, licenses, or other payments are assessed against the users of these facilities to help meet the costs incurred. In 1949 river and canal carriers transported approximately 5 per cent of the total volume of intercity goods traffic.[5] A substantial volume of freight moved on rivers and canals is transported by industrial concerns in their

---

[4] In its 1950 annual report the Interstate Commerce Commission gives a preliminary estimate of all domestic inland waterway traffic, including rivers and canals along with the Great Lakes, of 132,262 million ton miles or 15.2 per cent of the total intercity movement of property by all forms of transportation. In his annual report for 1950 the Chief of Engineers, U.S. Army, shows total inland waterway traffic for 1949 to be 139,396,230,000 ton miles of which 97,503,348,000 ton miles is attributed to domestic traffic on the Great Lakes.

[5] See footnote 4. The Chief of Engineers, U.S. Army, figures that 41,892,882,000 ton miles of freight were handled by river and canal transportation in 1949.

own vessels, some by contract carriers, and several operators offer a service to the general public.

Airways. In essence an airway is a path through the air between two airports. Markers on the surface of the earth aid the pilot of a plane in keeping on his course, and intermediate landing fields are provided for emergency landings. Major airways also are equipped with beacons for night flying and with various electronic devices which increase safety of operation. According to the Civil Aeronautics Administration, there were 57,368 miles of civil airways in the United States on January 1, 1949. Airways, like waterways, are built, maintained, and owned by the Federal Government, and no charge is made for their use. Airports generally are provided by municipalities, often with federal assistance, and in many cases some charge is made for their use.

Most of the air transportation in the United States is provided by a few large companies which operate on schedule between points which are generally a considerable distance apart. For the most part their service is limited to the larger centers of population. In addition, a number of smaller companies have been authorized to perform a scheduled local or feeder service which provides a substantial number of smaller communities with direct air transportation service and connections with the major lines. There are also a number of operators offering an irregular or non-scheduled air transportation service. For the most part, the air transportation service is offered to the public at large, or at least to that part of the public which is so located as to be able to make use of it, although there is some contract flying. Air transportation by commercial or industrial concerns for their own account probably is of little present significance. In 1950 domestic airlines transported 308 million ton miles of property, including mail, or .03 per cent of the total volume of intercity transportation of property. In the same year these airlines generated 8,030 million passenger miles or 2.01 per cent of total intercity travel.

Pipe lines. In 1949 there were 63,639 miles of trunk pipe line and 47,212 miles of local or gathering lines handling crude petroleum in the United States. In addition, there were 14,133 miles of gasoline pipe line. Practically all of the pipe line mileage is owned by the large refining companies or by companies affiliated with them, and while theoretically the lines are available for the general public use, in practice service is confined almost wholly to petroleum to be used by the owning company. In 1950 the pipe lines handled 129,174 million ton miles of crude petroleum and its products or 12.70 per cent of the total volume of property moved by all carriers in that year.

Indirect carriers. Before concluding this brief survey of the transportation system of the United States, mention should be made of the services performed by what, for lack of a better name, are here called indirect carriers. The indirect carrier undertakes to provide transportation for the general public but relies on one or more of the carriers described previously to perform the actual transportation between point of origin and destination. The freight forwarder, for example, collects small shipments from various individuals or business concerns which it undertakes to transport to specified destinations. These small shipments are consolidated into large lots which are then moved to destination by existing carriers at the lower rates which commonly prevail for large lot shipments. Freight forwarders make use of all forms of transportation except pipe lines, and frequently they use the services of more than one type of carrier in getting a shipment to destination. The Railway Express Agency is another example of an indirect carrier. It makes use of the services of railroads and airlines, and other agencies to a lesser extent, in performing an expedited transportation service. The Post Office Department and the Pullman Company are other examples of indirect carriers.

Comparative importance of different types of transportation. Since 1937 the Interstate Commerce Commission has published statistics of the annual volume of traffic by different agencies of transportation, and the figures are given in Table I. Reference will be made to them from time to time as the discussion progresses.

Table I

VOLUME OF INTERCITY TRAFFIC HANDLED BY VARIOUS
AGENCIES OF TRANSPORTATION [6]

Freight and Other Goods Traffic
(in millions of ton miles)

Year	Railroads		Motor Carriers		Inland Waterways [1]		Pipe Lines		Air Lines	
	Volume	*% Total Traffic*	*Volume*	*% Total Traffic*	*Volume*	*% Total Traffic*	*Volume*	*% Total Traffic*	*Volume*	*% Total Traffic*
1937	363,614	61.82	44,000	7.48	110,127	18.73	70,400	11.97	9	[2]
1938	292,510	63.49	37,000	8.03	66,746	14.49	64,423	13.99	10	[2]
1939	336,100	62.20	43,000	7.96	96,249	17.81	65,015	12.03	11	[2]
1940	379,161	61.96	51,003	8.33	118,057	19.29	63,745	10.42	14	[2]
1941	481,748	63.62	57,123	7.55	140,454	18.55	77,818	10.28	16	[2]
1942	645,262	70.23	50,207	5.47	148,565	16.17	74,730	8.13	33	[2]
1943	734,715	71.97	48,199	4.72	141,652	13.87	96,257	9.43	52	.01
1944	747,168	69.25	49,308	4.57	150,112	13.91	132,336	12.26	71	.01
1945	691,116	68.20	56,155	5.54	142,756	14.09	123,293	12.16	92	.01
1946	602,099	68.19	64,300	7.28	123,973	14.04	92,490	10.48	77	.01
1947	664,422	66.89	77,918	7.84	146,714	14.77	104,153	10.48	153	.02
1948	647,267	64.39	87,640	8.72	150,530	14.97	119,597	11.90	223	.02
1949	534,694	60.56	93,653	10.61	139,396	15.79	114,916	13.02	235	.02
1950	596,940	58.69	125,995	12.39	164,642	16.19	129,174	12.70	308	.03

[1] Including Great Lakes.
[2] Less than .01%.

[6] Interstate Commerce Commission, *Annual Report*, various years.

IMPROVED TRANSPORTATION

Passenger Traffic

(in millions of passenger miles)

Year	Railroads		Motor Carriers		Private Autos		Inland Waterways [1]		Air Lines	
	Volume	% Total Traffic	Volume	% Total Traffic	Volume	% Total Traffic	Volume	% Total Traffic	Volume	% Total Traffic
1937	25,652	9.56	12,673	4.72	228,364	85.08	1,309	.49	407	.15
1938	22,656	8.59	[2]		239,134	90.67[3]	1,487	.56	476	.18
1939	23,669	8.71	[2]		245,891	90.49[3]	1,486	.55	678	.25
1940	24,766	8.71	[2]		257,346	90.46[3]	1,317	.46	1,041	.37
1941	30,583	9.81	[2]		277,962	89.17[3]	1,821	.58	1,370	.44
1942	55,073	19.70	21,515	7.70	199,635	71.42	1,860	.67	1,418	.51
1943	89,865	33.53	27,416	10.23	147,131	54.91	1,927	.72	1,632	.61
1944	97,704	34.90	26,548	9.48	151,251	54.03	2,187	.78	2,264	.81
1945	93,535	30.60	26,927	8.81	179,837	58.82	2,056	.67	3,362	1.10
1946	66,262	18.74	25,576	7.23	253,570	71.70	2,327	.66	5,910	1.67
1947	46,752	13.30	23,948	6.81	272,958	77.64	1,845	.52	6,075	1.73
1948	41,894	11.62	23,529	6.53	287,423	79.74	1,670	.46	5,941	1.65
1949	35,975	9.38	22,411	5.85	316,774	82.63	1,402	.37	6,770	1.77
1950	32,481	8.12	20,912	5.23	337,339	84.34	1,190	.30	8,030	2.01

[1] Including Great Lakes.
[2] Separate figures for motor carriers and private automobiles not shown.
[3] Includes motor carrier traffic.

History of Transportation
in
THE EARLY UNITED STATES

RECOGNITION OF THE NEED FOR ECONOMICAL TRANSPORTATION

Colonial civilization. The important centers of population in Colonial North America were concentrated along the Atlantic seaboard, particularly that part of it stretching from Delaware north to New England, and including such cities as New York, Boston, Philadelphia, and Baltimore. Each of these cities, in addition to being a center of political and cultural life, was a trading center associated with a more or less definite section of the hinterland stretching as far back as the Allegheny Mountains. To the west of the Alleghenies the country was quite fertile, but these mountains and their associated ranges to the south proved to be an effective barrier to migration from the East. As if this physical handicap were not enough in itself, England discouraged migration into the transmountain area, and in 1763 white settlement was limited to the region east of the mountains.

At this time transportation and communication and travel between the Atlantic seaboard cities and interior points on the coastal plain depended upon rivers and trails and one or two very crude roads, while the eastern centers themselves were connected with each other principally by coastwise sailing vessels. It has been said that the cities along the Atlantic coast were closer to England than they were to some of the more remote settlements of the interior, and in view of the superior transportation afforded by ocean-going vessels this seems to be altogether reasonable.

Movement into the West. Although the mother country sought to restrict the migration of colonists west of the mountains, it does not appear that the hardy pioneer spirits of the time paid too much attention to these restrictions, and for some years prior to the Revolution settlers were finding their way increasingly over or around the mountain barrier. During the Revolution, however, the Indians seized the opportunity to reclaim their lands with the result that not many settlers moved west, and many of those already established found it necessary to return to the East. But this condition did not endure for long; after the Revolution a great migration began to take place over the mountains.

EARLY TRANSPORTATION

The reasons for the westward movement of the population after the Revolution were varied. For one thing, the eastern seaboard area was rapidly filling up, and no doubt this concentration of population—although very sparse by present-day standards—led many a hardy pioneer to pack up his belongings and seek new land to conquer and freer air to breathe. As early as 1760 the westward movement of population had reached the mountain barrier, where it was slowed down but not halted by the terrain and by English prohibitions on further movements. A second explanation of the westward movement is found in the generous grants of western lands made to the soldiers of both armies by the Continental Congress and the Colonies during the course of the war. Such land had been offered to soldiers in the American army as part payment for their services and to the soldiers of the enemy as an inducement to desert. Finally, the successful conclusion of the Revolution made it possible for the people to deal more effectively with the Indian opposition, and of course independence brought an end to the earlier British restrictions.

The Wilderness Road. As a result of these and possibly other considerations a great migration began to take place over the mountains into the Ohio Valley country. Those who traveled west from Philadelphia and Baltimore followed various water courses and trails to low passes over the mountains in southern Pennsylvania. West of the passes other streams led to the Ohio River and the promised land. Although this route was followed by many, by all odds the most famous and widely used route to the West was the Wilderness Road. As originally laid out by Daniel Boone in 1775 it was not a road at all in the modern sense but a blazed trail through the Cumberland Gap into the heart of Kentucky. Thousands of settlers migrated to Kentucky and then north to the Ohio River over this route, and this traveling host wore the blazed trail into a path and then into a pack horse trail. Eventually the Wilderness Road became the basis of a wagon road to Kentucky, but this was not to come for many years.

Need for improved transportation. With the migration over the mountains that followed the successful conclusion of the Revolutionary War came the first great need for improved transportation. It was not unduly hard for the settlers to make their way over the mountains, for as pointed out above there existed a number of trails over which travelers and pack trains could and did move in substantial numbers. But once a settler had cleared a piece of land and begun its cultivation the lack of satisfactory wagon roads made it practically impossible for him to move his surplus corn or other produce back to the eastern markets where it could be exchanged for iron and salt and the few items of manufactured goods needed on the frontier.

EARLY TRANSPORTATION

Early attempts to solve the transportation problem. The farmers of western Pennsylvania attempted to solve their transportation problem by distilling their grain into whiskey. Because whiskey was a product of high value in relation to its bulk, they could afford to transport it by pack horse over the trails to the East. It has been said that at one time nearly every farmer in western Pennsylvania, Virginia, and North Carolina distilled whiskey, and it is not surprising that when the Federal Government placed an excise tax on whiskey in 1791, the farmers in this area went into open rebellion. They were afraid that such a tax would make the manufacture and sale of whiskey unprofitable and so would constitute a threat to the only product that they could successfully transport to the East. In addition to whiskey, some furs and skins were transported over the mountains by means of pack trains. Obviously, however, such movements were no solution to the western farmers' transportation problems.

THE OHIO RIVER

Ohio River traffic. The western settlers had come from the East, and the natural market for their products was in the East, but the difficulties of transporting goods over the mountains were so great that it is not surprising that settlers made maximum use of the natural waterways in the Ohio River Valley. Products were moved down the Ohio and Mississippi rivers on flatboats, arks, and rafts to New Orleans where they were sold for local consumption or shipped by ocean-going vessels to the eastern seaboard cities and to foreign countries. Some attempts were made to construct ocean-going vessels on the upper Ohio for the purpose of moving goods down the Ohio and Mississippi and up the coast to the Atlantic seaboard centers without the necessity of transshipment at New Orleans. Pittsburgh and Marietta both boasted shipyards at one time, and some of the boats built on the Ohio River carried goods as far as the West Indies and even to Europe. The construction of ocean-going vessels, however, required an amount of capital which rarely was available on the frontier, and the difficulties of navigating ocean-going boats on narrow inland bodies of water and the impossibility of a return trip to the home port, made the construction of ships on the Ohio River somewhat impractical.

Unsatisfactory nature of early water transportation. While river transportation made possible the movement of bulky products that could not have been shipped by land, it was far from being a solution to the settlers' problems. It was slow, a month being the usual time required for the trip from Pittsburgh to New Orleans. It was dangerous because of the presence of hostile Indians. It was uncertain because of the many obstacles to navigation. For a number of years it was a one way movement only because the necessity of depending upon the river current made a return trip impossible. Finally, the route was closed at times because of the presence in New Orleans of European powers not always friendly in their attitude toward the Americans.

When a boat or a raft reached New Orleans and its lading had been sold, the owner was faced with the problem of selling his craft and getting himself, his crew, and his purchases back home. This last usually involved a long and dangerous overland journey on which few of the things the settlers needed could be carried. The construction of barges and keel boats made a return trip by water possible, but the prospect of such a trip was hardly one to be looked forward to with pleasure. Sails were used when the wind was right, and oars could be used where the current was slight. If neither sails nor oars could be used, which must have been the case frequently, poles and tow ropes were employed. Another scheme involved fastening one end of a long rope to the prow of the boat, passing the other end of this rope around a tree or river snag upstream, and then returning it to the boat. The men in the boat would then haul in on the loose end, thus pulling the boat upstream. When the tree or snag was reached, another rope was passed around another tree or snag farther upstream and the process repeated. It is said that the trip upstream from New Orleans to Pittsburgh took as long as four months to accomplish.

Not until the coming of the river steamboat could the Ohio and Mississippi rivers develop as important arteries of travel and transportation. In the meantime the people of the western country had to look to some other solution of their transportation problem. Some discussion of the steamboat and the part it played in opening up the West, however, may be in order at this point.

THE STEAMBOAT

The power of steam. Every school boy is familiar with the story of James Watt watching the steam lift the lid from his mother's teakettle, thus discovering the power of steam and eventually leading to his construction of the first steam engine. But James Watt, like a number of other men of science, did not discover the thing that made him famous. More than two hundred years before the birth of Christ and something like 2000 years before the birth of James Watt, Hero of Alexandria, a Greek scientist, invented a simple device which utilized the power of steam ejected into the atmosphere to make a metal ball revolve. Hero's *aeolipile*, however, was hardly more than a toy, and he did not put it to any practical use. In the years that followed, various other individuals experimented with steam, and during the seventeenth century some really important discoveries were made with regard to its use, but it was not until 1705 that the power of steam was put to any truly practical use. In that year Thomas Newcomen, an Englishman, made use of principles already discovered to develop a pump designed to draw water from English coal mines. Newcomen's engines were very inefficient from the point of view of fuel consumption because the cylinder had to be alternately heated and cooled, but they did work and were widely used in English mines for fifty years.

In the meantime James Watt had watched his mother's teakettle. He very early displayed mechanical abilities and in due course became a mechanical instrument maker in Glasgow, Scotland. It was here that he was called upon to repair a model of one of Newcomen's engines, and while engaged in this work, he observed the obvious inefficiency of alternately heating and cooling the cylinder. He set to work to devise an engine in which the cylinder would always be kept hot, and after a considerable period of experimentation he succeeded, thus making possible a considerable saving of fuel. Although James Watt did not discover the power of steam, nor did he develop the first steam engine, it was his work that made the modern industrial system and the modern transportation system possible.

The steamboat. The use of steam to propel boats through the water antedated James Watt's work on the steam engine by many years. As early as 1707 the Frenchman, Papin, used steam power to propel a boat, but his experiments met with considerable public disfavor and his boat was seized and destroyed by river boatmen when he attempted to navigate it. Other experiments were conducted in England and France, both before and more or less contemporaneously with Watt's work on improving the steam engine. Credit for originating the steamboat in the United States must be given to John Fitch. In 1785 Fitch made a working model in the form of a small boat equipped on the side with paddles attached to an endless chain, the device being somewhat reminiscent of a treadmill with upright boards set on it at intervals. This was followed by a skiff with a series of vertical oars on each side which were connected with a steam engine by a cranklike device. A third boat was propelled by a series of flat paddles at the rear and was large enough to carry passengers. Fitch had considerable difficulty in financing his activities and ultimately dropped out of the picture.

Robert Fulton. Fitch was followed by a number of other experimenters, both in England and in the United States. Between 1787 and 1807 a sort of jet propulsion was attempted, both side and rear paddle wheels had been tried, and even a screw propellor was developed. But none of these early experimenters was to achieve the success that was attained by Robert

Fulton. Fulton was a farm boy who had come to Philadelphia where he worked as an apprentice jeweler and studied art on the side. In 1786 he went to London to study under the American painter, Benjamin West, and here he became interested in engineering and the steamboat. In 1801 he met Robert Livingston, the American minister to France, and this was the beginning of a long and close business association. Livingston himself had built a steamboat in 1789, and he greatly encouraged Fulton to pursue his studies and activities along these lines. After some not too successful experiments in France, Fulton returned to the United States where he proceeded to build his famous steamboat, the *Clermont*. Unlike his predecessors Fulton did not attempt to build the boat himself. He had the hull made by a New York shipbuilder according to his specifications, and the engine was built by highly qualified machinists in England.

The *Clermont*, propelled by side paddle wheels, made its maiden trip on August 17, 1807, covering the one hundred fifty miles between New York and Albany in thirty hours. It was a real boat, about one hundred feet long as compared with the forty-five feet of Fitch's rear paddle vessel. It operated regularly up and down the Hudson River and is said to have attained a speed of twenty miles per hour. It was followed by other and still larger boats built by Fulton and Livingston and firmly established the steamboat as an accepted phase of American life.

The steamboat and the opening of the West. Fulton and Livingston were not unaware of the prospects for the use of steamboats on the rivers west of the mountains, and in 1810 they sent Nicholas Roosevelt to explore the possibilities for steamboat navigation on the Ohio and Mississippi. Roosevelt reported favorably on the project with the result that work was soon started on a one hundred and sixteen foot boat, the *New Orleans*, and late in 1811 this boat descended the Ohio and Mississippi rivers from Pittsburgh to New Orleans. The successful completion of this voyage may be said to mark the beginning of a new era in the opening up of the West, but for various reasons the possibilities of the steamboat in this area were not fully realized for a number of years. In the first place, the falls in the river at Louisville made through movements by steamboat difficult except at times of high water. A second difficulty arose from the fact that there were a number of different claimants of patent rights on steamboats who were constantly issuing warnings against infringements of their rights. Under the circumstances would-be boat builders hesitated to build steamboats as long as such construction might expose them to attacks in the courts. Still another difficulty was the existence of certain unpopular but nevertheless effective navigation rights enjoyed by Livingston and Fulton.

Livingston and Fulton had obtained from the State of New York exclusive rights to operate steamboats on the waters of that state, and prior to the construction of the steamboat *New Orleans* at Pittsburgh, they had obtained a similar monopoly from the State of Louisiana. Since New Orleans was the only available market for the produce of the Ohio Valley and since the Mississippi River at New Orleans was wholly within the State of Louisiana, the effect of the Louisiana grant was to give Livingston and Fulton control over steamboat movements on the Mississippi north of Louisiana and on the rivers of the Ohio Valley. The Livingston-Fulton monopoly functioned to retard the free movement of commerce, and it was obvious that something would have to be done if the people were to realize the full advantages of this new and promising form of transportation. Fortunately, in 1818, the district court of Louisiana held that the State of Louisiana had no right to grant the Livingston-Fulton monopoly, and in 1824 the Supreme Court held in *Gibbons v. Ogden* that the New York laws granting exclusive navigation rights to Livingston and Fulton were in conflict with certain federal statutes regulating commerce between the states. Under such circumstances, said the Court, the federal law takes precedence over state law. This meant the end of state attempts to regulate commerce on navigable streams and marked the beginning of a fifty-year period of steamboat prosperity on the Ohio and Mississippi rivers.

EARLY HIGHWAYS

Demand for improved land transportation. It may be assumed that the settlers in the Ohio Valley would have been more than willing to ship their goods overland to the East if any practical method of transportation had been available, and eastern interests in their turn were not unaware of the potential value of this western trade. It is not surprising, therefore, to find various schemes being proposed for opening a route across the mountain barrier to connect the eastern seaboard cities with the Ohio River and the West. Of all the schemes proposed, the first to be completed were cross-mountain roads, the relatively low cost of road construction probably accounting for the early concentration on this means of transportation.

Colonial road building. In early colonial days people traveled on trails, either on foot or on horseback; in boats on the many navigable streams; or in coastwise sailing vessels. Such roads as existed were extremely primitive and seldom extended beyond the environs of the towns. They were little more than cleared strips of ground, full of stumps in the wooded sections and quagmires during wet weather. For many years bridges were practically unknown, and if a stream happened to be too high to ford, the traveler had to go up and down the bank until he came to a ferry or just sit down and wait for the water to go down. With the passage of time, however, colonial roads were improved and extended beyond the immediate environs of the towns, some bridges were built, and during the first half of the eighteenth century companies were organized which undertook to move goods and passengers between various towns on more or less regular schedules. By the end of the eighteenth century intercity passenger coaches and freight wagons were operating on schedule and in considerable numbers, and a passenger could make the trip from Boston to New York in four days and from New York to Philadelphia in a day and a half.

Post-revolutionary roads. After the Revolution, the construction of toll roads or turnpikes was undertaken in various parts of the United States. A road was cleared and improved after a fashion, and a toll or charge was made for its use, the amount of the charge depending upon the nature of the use and the distance traveled. Some of these projects were financed by state and county governments, but generally they were private business ventures. At intervals along the road swinging gates called turnpikes barred the path of the user until he had gone to the adjacent toll house and paid the necessary toll. The toll roads were an improvement over the earlier free public roads, but some of them must have been very poor roads indeed if the accounts of early travelers are to be believed. Some, however, were well built and maintained and even had macadamized surfaces. The toll roads not only were superior to the earlier free roads but also their construction contributed in some measure to a general improvement of all roads in the United States.

National Pike. In 1806 Congress provided for the construction of a road by the Federal Government from Cumberland, Maryland, to a point on the Ohio River near Wheeling in what was then Virginia. The selection of Cumberland as the eastern terminus seems to have been dictated in some measure by expediency. At the time Pennsylvania was engaged in building turnpikes which would connect Philadelphia with Pittsburgh and that part of the state west of the mountains. At the same time Maryland was interested in building roads west from Baltimore and the District of Columbia, but it had no particular interest in extending these roads into the small mountainous section of Maryland west of Cumberland. And it could not have built a road to the Ohio River even if it had wanted to because its territory did not extend that far. Since Pennsylvania was going to build a road to the Ohio River anyway, and since Maryland could not be expected to extend its roads beyond Cumberland, the logical procedure seemed to be to make the federal road an extension of the Maryland road west of Cumberland.

Work on the National Pike, or the Cumberland Road as it was first called, began in 1808, and the road was opened for traffic to Wheeling on the Ohio River in 1818. The cost of the completed project was in excess of $1,500,000, no doubt a substantial sum in those days, but the road was well built and its use resulted in a considerable reduction in the cost of transporting goods to and from the Ohio Valley. Many connecting roads were built, and the completion of the road from Cumberland to Baltimore substantially increased the trade of that city with the West. And fears expressed by the people of Philadelphia concerning the effect of the National Pike on their trade with the West were realized. Wheeling on the western end, as well as Baltimore on the eastern, benefited greatly from the completion of the road.

Contemporary accounts testify to the extensive use that was made of the National Pike. A number of stage coach companies operated four horse coaches, the fastest coaches making the one hundred and thirty mile trip between Wheeling and Cumberland in twenty-four hours. The drivers of the brightly painted coaches engaged in frequent contests of speed in which their passengers were considerably shaken up. Picturesque brightly colored Conestoga wagons, forerunners of the famous prairie schooner of a later period, hauled large quantities of freight. Pack trains of horses and mules also played an important part in the movement of goods. Emigrant families moving westward and solitary travelers on foot or on horseback completed the picture. At frequent intervals along the road taverns and wagon stands were encountered where horses could be changed or stabled for the night and where travelers and wagon drivers could secure food, drink, and shelter.

Roads in the Ohio Valley. Five per cent of the net proceeds from the sale of public lands in Ohio was to be used for the improvement of roads in, to, and through Ohio, with three-fifths of the money obtained in this way to be used within the state itself. The funds derived from this source were not too large, however, and were used primarily to lay out a road system. The resulting roads were not sufficiently improved to be of much use as important arteries of transportation and travel, and the state began to authorize the construction of turnpikes. The first charter granted to a private turnpike company was issued in 1809, and for a good many years thereafter the state depended largely upon turnpike companies for its improved roads. The toll roads usually were well built and maintained, a condition which may have been the result of a common charter provision specifying that no tolls could be collected if the roads were not kept in good repair.

In 1820 Congress appropriated $10,000 as a first step toward extending the National Pike from Wheeling to the Mississippi River, and in the years that followed the road was extended onward through Ohio, Indiana, and into Illinois. Original plans called for the construction of a first-class road, but money was not available, and the western section of the road was not nearly as well constructed as the section east of Wheeling. In some cases specifications permitted the leaving of stumps up to fifteen inches in height in the central section of the roadway, and the last sections of the project consisted of nothing more than dirt roads. Work on the National Pike ceased in 1838, at which time the road had been extended west as far as Vandalia, Illinois. This was still short of the original goal, but the demonstrated superiority of canals and railroads had made it clear that highway vehicles could not hope to compete successfully with these newer forms of transportation. Although it outlived its usefulness before it reached its ultimate goal, the National Pike played an important part in the development of the country west of the Alleghenies.

Plank roads. The plank road consisted of heavy wooden planks about eight feet long laid side by side on two parallel rows of heavy wooden stringers, very much like an oversized old fashioned sidewalk. The first plank road in the United States was built in New York State in 1837, and during the succeeding twenty years or so, numerous similar roads were built, many of them in the area west of the mountains. Plank roads were inexpensive to build and offered a smoother surface for highway vehicles than was true of ordinary roads. They provided improved transportation for sections of the country not yet sufficiently developed to justify the construction of railroads, and in a few cases they even competed with early railroads. They appear to have been built generally by private companies and operated as toll roads. Although the construction and utilization of plank roads proved to be but a transitory phase in the development of improved transportation in the United States, these roads were of considerable importance during the relatively short period in which they were used, especially to farmers.

CANALS

Early canal projects. The value of the canal as an aid to inland water transportation was recognized as early as the beginning of the eighteenth century, but the colonists had no resources with which to construct such costly projects. Toward the end of the century a few short canals were dug in order to circumvent natural obstacles to river traffic or to connect an inland area with the ocean. Although not many canals were built, a large number of canal and river improvement projects were put forward, and a good many canal companies were incorporated. Many of these proposals were nothing more than grandiose daydreams which never got beyond the paper stage. Others had merit but were foredoomed to failure because of chronic lack of funds.

EARLY TRANSPORTATION

Canals and the opening of the West. It may be taken for granted that the possibility of constructing canals to link the Ohio River with the Atlantic seaboard cities was not overlooked, but the obstacles encountered were too great to justify such construction. Not the least of these obstacles was the heavy original cost of building locks and digging channels with the primitive hand methods available at that time. Although the actual cost of moving traffic over a canal was very low as compared with the cost of moving the same traffic by land vehicles, the initial cost of canal construction was far in excess of the cost of building roads. This fact determined that highways be used as a means of reaching the West until such time as a sufficient volume of traffic developed to make canal construction profitable.

The heavy initial cost of construction, however, was not the only factor that retarded canal development to the West. Equally as formidable as the financial requirements were the natural obstacles to construction found in the terrain separating the Ohio River country from the coastal plain. Those who might seek to open up the West by means of canals were faced with the necessity of crossing a stretch of mountainous country 1,300 miles long and 300 miles wide, certainly not an encouraging prospect for would-be canal builders. In all that 1,300 mile stretch of mountainous country there was only one point where a canal to the West was genuinely feasible. This was in the northern part of the State of New York where there occurred an almost complete break in the chain of the eastern mountains. And so it was perhaps inevitable that as soon as sufficient traffic was in prospect to justify a canal link with the West such a canal would be built across the State of New York.

Erie Canal. During the latter part of the eighteenth century and the early part of the nineteenth century, the people of the State of New York had been actively engaged in the construction of turnpikes to provide the back country with access to the eastern seaboard. By about 1810 such progress had been made that even the western parts of the state had roads, and a new grain-growing area was beginning to develop which required some cheaper means of transportation to New York City than was then available. To transport grain by wagon from the Great Lakes to New York City in the year 1817 is said to have cost three times as much as the market price of wheat in New York City and six times as much as the market price of oats. It was plain to be seen that the new grain-growing regions could not be developed satisfactorily as long as such heavy transportation charges prevailed.

A canal across the northern part of New York to connect the Great Lakes with the Hudson River had been suggested as early as 1800, but it does not appear that the proposal met with universal approval. The farmers in the eastern part of the state were afraid that a canal would bring an influx of agricultural products from the West which would have a depressing effect on the favorable market they enjoyed in New York City. Likewise the residents of the tier of counties in the southern part of New York were opposed to the expenditure of the state's money for a canal which would have been of little direct benefit to them. On the other side of the picture the advantage of the canal to the farmers in western New York was obvious. But perhaps even more important than this was the advantage that would accrue to the people of New York City. It was clear from the first that a canal connecting New York City with the Great Lakes would make the whole country west of the mountains and north of the Ohio tributary to New York City, thus giving that city a tremendous advantage over Philadelphia, Baltimore, and other rival trading centers.

One of the principal problems involved in planning the construction of the canal concerned the matter of financing, but it was believed that the resources of the state were sufficient to allow construction to begin. In 1812 an act was passed by the state legislature to examine the matter further, but war with England made it necessary to postpone action. In 1816 a new law was passed looking toward the construction of the canal, and in 1817 some attempt was made to obtain aid from the Federal Government and from some of the states in the interior which would benefit from the project. No aid was forthcoming from these sources, however, and so on April 15, 1817, the legislature passed a law authorizing the construction of the canal solely by the State of New York.

Thus was born the Erie Canal, by all odds the best known and the most important of the early canal projects. Started in 1817 and completed in 1825 the canal traversed the State of New York from Buffalo on Lake Erie to the Hudson River at Albany. Between Albany and New York City the Hudson River, long a major artery of travel and transportation, was utilized to carry canal traffic to the coast. The Erie Canal as originally constructed was 363 miles long, 40 feet wide at the top, 28 feet wide at the bottom, and contained 4 feet of water. A branch canal of similar construction 64 miles long connected the main project with Lake Champlain.

The State of New York put $10 million into the construction of the Erie Canal and the branch canal to Lake Champlain, but the instant success of the project more than justified this expenditure and more than vindicated the claims of those who had urged its construction. Each year the canals moved more goods. Tolls were reduced, but even with these reduced tolls the canals made money, and in ten years' time had paid for themselves. In fifteen years enlargement was necessary to take care of the expanding traffic. The Erie Canal offered the West what it had wanted and needed for so long a time, cheap transportation. And it made New York City the chief American port on the Atlantic, a position which it has never lost.

Pennsylvania Public Works. Work on the Erie Canal had hardly gotten under way when a movement developed in Pennsylvania for the improvement of transportation facilities between Philadelphia and the Ohio River at Pittsburgh. At this time a series of turnpikes stretched all the way from Philadelphia to Pittsburgh, and these improved roads had given Philadelphia an early advantage in the trade with the West. The recently finished National Pike to the south, however, had completely changed this picture. The National Pike brought Baltimore ninety miles nearer than Philadelphia to the Ohio Valley, a not inconsiderable distance at a time when land travel and transportation was either by foot or by horse or ox drawn vehicles. Furthermore, the National Pike was partly toll free whereas tolls were charged over the entire route between Philadelphia and Pittsburgh. In view of the advantages already enjoyed by the southern route the prospect of a new all-water route from New York west must have been quite disconcerting to Philadelphia businessmen.

Speeches were made and figures were quoted to prove that Philadelphia had natural advantages over New York, and speed was urged to retain for Pennsylvania its early advantage in the western trade. But speeches and figures could not overcome the fact that a Pennsylvania canal would have to be built through an extensive mountain barrier, a problem that the New York canal builders did not have to face at all. This was a problem that required considerable thought, and it was not until 1826, a year after the completion of the Erie Canal, that work was started on the construction of the Pennsylvania Public Works. As finally completed, the project was a canal only in part, the difficulties of canal construction through the mountains having necessitated a liberal use of inclined plane and horse railroads to connect the various navigable sections.

Those Pennsylvanians who had advocated the construction of a canal to the West expected that the Pennsylvania Public Works would compete successfully with the Erie Canal, but their expectations were never realized. The necessity of changing back and forth between cars and boats was inconvenient and time consuming, as was the necessity of passing through a large number of locks on the canal sections of the project. By the same token it must have been a fairly expensive route for shippers and travelers to utilize. There is no doubt that the Pennsylvania Public Works provided a useful route to the West, but the Erie Canal was by all counts the more important of the two. Indeed, it is said that businessmen in Philadelphia found it preferable to ship their goods to New York and thence west via the Erie Canal instead of using the Pennsylvania Public Works.

Western canals. While the people of New York and Pennsylvania were actively engaged in building canals to the West, the westerners themselves had not overlooked the possibility of canal construction within their own area. Of the many projects proposed, two deserve special mention at this point. One was a canal to bypass the Falls of the Ohio at Louisville which had long been a deterrent to navigation on the Ohio River. This canal was built in 1828 with the assistance of the Federal Government and was a great aid to navigation on the Ohio. The other was a canal running north and south across Ohio and connecting Lake Erie with the Ohio River, a natural concomitant of the Erie Canal. The construction of such a canal would make possible an uninterrupted water movement from New York City clear into the Mississippi Valley and at the same time provide interior Ohio with an economical transportation route over which goods could be moved east to New York or south to the Ohio River and New Orleans. Construction of the Ohio Canal, which was to span the state between Cleveland and Portsmouth, was started in 1825 and completed in 1832. This canal and some others built in the state proved of considerable value to the people of Ohio prior to the development of railroad transportation.

EARLY RAILROADS

The first railroads. Who first conceived of the idea of running cars on rails probably never will be known. Such cars were used in England as early as the seventeenth century, generally to move coal downhill from a mine to nearby rivers or canals. The track consisted of parallel strips of wood or rows of stone, at first laid directly on the ground, later fastened in one way or another to the ground or to each other. Wherever possible, gravity provided the motive power. Otherwise, the cars were drawn by horses. These primitive railroads were gradually improved and their use extended until by the opening of the nineteenth century they were found in many sections of the British Isles. It was not until the development of a practical steam locomotive, however, that the railroad entered its real stage of development.

The steam locomotive. One of the first practical applications of the steam engine to a land vehicle was made by William Murdock, an assistant to James Watt. In 1784 Murdock devised a small steam-propelled vehicle, but he was discouraged by his employer who could see no future in such a line of activity. In 1803 another Englishman, Richard Trevithick, built a steam carriage, and in 1804 also built a steam locomotive which ran on rails. In the same year Oliver Evans, an American, exhibited a peculiar contraption in the form of a steamboat mounted on wheels which he ran through the streets of Philadelphia. Other men worked on the principle of steam as applied to land vehicles, but the development of a truly successful locomotive had to wait for the appearance of George Stephenson. As a young man Stephenson had worked with steam engines in English coal mines, first as a fireman and later as an engineer, and it was while doing this work that he became interested in the idea of developing a steam locomotive to pull coal cars along the rails from the mines to port areas. In 1814 he succeeded in building such a locomotive and during the next ten years a number of similar locomotives were put into use by English coal mines.

In 1825 the Stockton and Darlington Railroad, with George Stephenson as its chief engineer, was opened for traffic in England. The primary purpose of this ambitious twelve-mile undertaking was to move coal from the mines at Stockton to the river port of Darlington, but it was also intended to haul other freight and to move passengers. Stephenson designed a locomotive for this line which attained a speed of fifteen miles per hour and hauled a load of ninety tons. In 1829 the directors of the Liverpool and Manchester Railroad, an even more ambitious undertaking than the Stockton and Darlington, held a contest for locomotive builders, and Stephenson's entry, the *Rocket*, exceeded all expectations. Operating at a maximum speed of 29.5 miles per hour it convinced even the most skeptical of the success of the steam railroad. Stephenson generally is given credit for inventing the locomotive, but Stephenson's success story is much the same as that of James Watt and Robert Fulton. Murdock's little machine preceded Stephenson's first effort by thirty years, and both Trevithick and Evans were ten years ahead of Stephenson. Furthermore, it has been said that there was very little about Stephenson's *Rocket* that he had not borrowed from other inventors. Nevertheless, Stephenson deserves credit for the way in which he utilized the best developments of his time in producing a really successful locomotive.

First American railroads. The use of tracks on which cars could be drawn came much later in America than in England. There is some evidence of such a track having been used in Boston in 1795 in connection with a brick kiln, and there is definite evidence of a car track having been built on Beacon Hill in Boston in 1807 by Stephen Whitney. In 1809 Thomas Leiper built a line three-quarters of a mile long to connect his stone quarries in Pennsylvania with tidewater, and during the following years, other similar lines were built. The stone used in the construction of the Bunker Hill monument was moved from the quarry to tidewater over a line of rails about three miles long. All of these early enterprises were private projects used to move a single commodity and in one direction only. None could be said to have been a railroad in the modern sense of the word.

Although there is no evidence that the builders of these early lines looked upon them as anything more than adjuncts to private business undertakings, there were some people in the United States who had visions of railroads as a means of transportation in the modern sense. John Stevens of New Jersey was thinking along these lines as early as 1811, and just a year later he was advocating a railroad in preference to a canal to link New York City with the Great Lakes. Stevens wanted Congress to build and operate railroads, but Congress was not interested. He obtained permission to build a railroad in New Jersey and later one in Pennsylvania, but in neither case was he able to obtain the financial support necessary to undertake construction. In 1825 Pennsylvania interests, concerned with the establishment of an improved route to the West from Philadelphia, sent an American engineer named Strickland to England to study and report on English internal transportation facilities, including railroads. And the Pennsylvania Public Works when finally completed made liberal use of simple railroads operated by horses or stationary engines.

The Baltimore and Ohio Railroad. The year 1825 saw the completion of the Erie Canal, connecting New York City with the West, and in the following year Pennsylvania started work on what was originally intended to be a canal to the Ohio River. The good citizens of Baltimore, viewing with alarm the way in which the rival ports of New York and Philadelphia were struggling for control of the western trade, began in their turn to call for the construction of a canal from Baltimore westward to the Ohio River. Unfortunately, however, Baltimore was very poorly situated for such a project. New York had already built a canal around the mountains, and Pennsylvania was embarking on a canal project which was expected to make its way through the mountains, but west of Baltimore the canal builders found themselves faced with three mountain ranges, the Blue Ridge, the Shenandoahs, and the Alleghenies. Here was poor country, indeed, for canal construction.

In 1827, without any extended period of preliminary agitation, Baltimore interests decided upon the bold project of a railroad which would stretch all of the way from Baltimore to the Ohio River. In some measure the choice must have been one of necessity, but at the same time it must be recognized that there was considerable popular interest in railroads in this country. Stevens had built a miniature steam railroad in 1820. The success of the Stockton and Darlington opened in England in 1825 was well known. And the report of the American engineer, Strickland, on

English railroads, published in 1826, had aroused considerable interest in the possibilities of railroads in the United States.

So it was that in February and March of 1827 the states of Maryland and Virginia issued charters incorporating the Baltimore and Ohio Railroad and granting it authority to build a line from Baltimore to some point on the Ohio River. Ground was broken for the new railroad on July 4, 1828, by Charles Carroll of Carrollton, last surviving signer of the Declaration of Independence, with the statement previously mentioned that he considered this act to be second only in importance to the signing of the Declaration of Independence, if even it was second to that.

The Baltimore and Ohio Railroad was faced with hard sledding from the first. It was only natural to rely upon English experience in connection with the actual construction of the line, but American engineers were not long in discovering that the sharp curves and steep grades made necessary by the nature of the terrain and the necessity of conserving finances presented them with problems unknown to their English contemporaries and predecessors. Time and money were lost on the Baltimore and Ohio, as well as on other early American lines, because the early railroad builders had to learn by experience. Furthermore, rival canal companies and associated interests desirous of developing a parallel route along the Potomac River placed obstacles in the way of the extension of the Baltimore and Ohio. And finally, as was the case with all early American internal improvements, financial problems were not inconsiderable.

Several short lines were constructed out of Baltimore, including one that reached Washington, D. C., in 1835, and these lines were operated successfully. But one thing or another delayed the extension of the line westward, and it was not until 1853 that the Baltimore and Ohio reached the Ohio River at Wheeling. The completed project cost something more than $7,500,000 to build. It contributed importantly to the development of Baltimore, but it did not give that city the expected preeminence over its rivals to the north. Long before the Baltimore and Ohio Railroad reached Wheeling the significance of the railroad and its superiority to road and canal transportation was realized, and both New York interests and Pennsylvania interests had turned to railroad building. As a result the Baltimore and Ohio was the fourth, not the first, railroad to reach the country west of the mountains.

EARLY TRANSPORTATION

SUGGESTED READINGS

Ambler, Charles H., *A History of Transportation in the Ohio Valley*. Glendale, California: Clark, 1931.

Dunbar, Seymour, *A History of Travel in America*, Vols. I-III. Indianapolis: The Bobbs-Merrill Company, 1915. This four-volume work contains many fine reproductions, some of them in color, of contemporary pictures of early transportation instrumentalities. There are some discrepancies in dates and minor details between this work and other similar works, and some of the author's conclusions would not be accepted by students of transportation. Nevertheless, this is a very valuable source of information on transportation in the United States up to the time of the completion of the first transcontinental railroad.

Hulbert, A. B., *Historic Highways of America*. Cleveland: Clark, 1902-05. This sixteen-volume work is a valuable source of information although rather detailed for general reading.

MacGill, Caroline, and staff, *History of Transportation in the United States before 1860*. Washington: The Carnegie Institution, 1917. Prepared under the direction of Balthasar H. Meyer, long-time member of the Interstate Commerce Commission. This appears to be the standard work on the subject.

Wood, Frederick J., *The Turnpikes of New England*. Boston: Marshal Jones Company, 1919.

Part Two

RAILROAD TRANSPORTATION

3.

Development
of
RAILROAD TRANSPORTATION

Development of railroad net, 1830-1950. Table II shown below tells more eloquently than words the story of the development and present status of the railroad network of the United States.

Table II

DEVELOPMENT OF RAILROAD NET, 1830-1950

Year	Total Mileage	Increase During Decade
1830	23	
1840	2,818	2,795
1850	9,021	6,203
1860	30,626	21,605
1870	52,922	22,296
1880	93,262	40,340
1890	163,597	70,335
1900	193,346	29,749
1910	240,293	46,947
1920	252,845	12,552
1930	249,052	− 3,793
1940	233,670	−15,382
1950	223,779	− 9,891

Although ground was broken for the Baltimore and Ohio Railroad in 1828, only 23 miles of railroad were in operation by 1830, but in the next two decades 9,000 miles were added. This period from 1830 to 1850 has been aptly described as the period of infancy of the American railroads, a period in which the railroad builders were feeling their way along, experimenting, and generally laying the foundation for the remarkable growth yet to come. After 1850, the railroad infant really began to grow, and the United States experienced an enormous expansion of railroad mileage between the years 1850 and 1910, with the years 1850 to 1890 in particular being looked upon as the great era of railroad building. Each decade during this period witnessed a growth in mileage greater than that which had taken place during the preceding decade, with the decade of 1881-90 alone accounting for the construction of

70,335 miles of railroad. Although considerable mileage was laid down after 1890, at no time did construction even closely approach the record of the 1880's. A marked decline in construction took place in the decade 1910-20, and since then railroad abandonments have consistently exceeded new construction.

PERIOD OF INFANCY, 1830-50

Early difficulties. The reasons for the slow growth of the railroad net prior to 1850 are not difficult to determine. In the first place, railroads were new, and because there was an almost complete lack of knowledge of how railroads should be built and operated, progress was necessarily slow. It was early discovered that English techniques were not always well adapted to conditions in the United States, and experience had to be gained by the slow and painful process of trial and error. In the second place, the country was new and sufficient traffic had not yet developed to justify more extensive railroad building. And in the third place, various special interests were opposed to railroad construction. Naturally the canal and stage coach companies, together with innkeepers and other interests closely associated with these companies, did what they could to restrict railroad operations, and they sometimes succeeded in inducing legislatures to attach onerous restrictions to the construction of new railroads. As late as 1853 business interests in Erie, Pennsylvania, fought a proposal to establish a uniform gauge for two lines which entered that city from opposite directions. Although a single gauge would have obvious advantages to the shipping and traveling public, uniformity was opposed on the ground that it would destroy the business of Erie teamsters and others who profited from the fact that passengers and goods could not be transferred directly from one line to the other.

Lack of capital. Another factor which held back railroad construction was a persistent lack of capital. Railroads were new, and only the most enthusiastic or foolhardy would put up the money necessary for their construction. Then, too, there was the fact that capital for almost any purpose was scarce in the early days of the United States. This country had plenty of land and natural resources to contribute to internal improvements but had to rely upon foreign sources for capital, and the amount of capital obtainable from foreign investors was an uncertain quantity. At the outset a considerable supply of foreign capital was made available by British interests, but for some time after the financial collapse of 1837, with its accompanying losses to investors, English and European capitalists lost interest in investments in the United States.

DEVELOPMENT OF RAILROADS

PERIOD OF GREAT EXPANSION, 1850-1910

Factors underlying development. The factors underlying the tremendous growth of the railroad net between the years 1850 and 1910 are varied. In the first place, large amounts of capital became available and continued to be available, with some brief interruptions, throughout a large part of this period. Second, the westward movement of the population, which sometimes preceded and sometimes followed railroad construction, created a demand for new railroad transportation facilities. Third, state and local governments, along with numerous private citizens and business concerns, offered financial incentives to promote the construction of railroads in their vicinities. Fourth, the Federal Government also aided railroads in various ways, its principal contribution being a grant of approximately 130 million acres of public land to the railroad builders. Fifth, the demand for the construction of a railroad to the Pacific coast, which appeared almost as soon as did the railroad itself, led ultimately to the construction of not one but several such lines. Sixth, bold operators saw and took advantage of speculative opportunities inherent in railroad construction. And seventh, the growth of trade and industry during the latter half of the nineteenth century was both a cause of and caused by railroad construction. Because this was the great period of railroad building, each of these factors will warrant some further discussion.

AVAILABILITY OF NEW CAPITAL

Renewed interest of foreigners in American internal improvements. The early period of European interest in internal improvements in the United States ended with the panic of 1837 as already noted, but after the discovery of gold in California there was a renewal of interest in American railroads on the part of English and European investors. For many years the Illinois Central was controlled by foreign interests, and so much Dutch capital was invested in the Chicago & Northwestern that it had at one time a foreign representation of two directors on its board. The panic of 1873 and the manipulations of such financial operators as Jay Gould and his crowd once again brought disrepute to investments in American internal improvements, but in a few years' time foreign interest had revived. As a matter of fact a large part of the tremendous growth in railroad mileage that took place during the 1880's was financed abroad. Many foreign investors were forced to liquidate their investments following the severe panic of 1893, but as late as 1899 foreigners still held over $3 billion in American securities, mostly in railroad stocks and bonds.

DEVELOPMENT OF RAILROADS

Decline of foreign investments. In 1898 the United States entered a period of marked prosperity, and American investors not only absorbed new issues of railroad securities but also bought up a considerable part of those held abroad. In the early years of the twentieth century there was some revival of interest in American railroads on the part of European investors, but a series of bankruptcies and revelations of fraudulent financial practices soon terminated this interest. By this time, however, the American railroad net was approaching its point of maximum growth. While the railroads felt the need of additional capital for the purpose of improving existing property, the foreign market for capital had served its purpose as far as contributing to the tremendous growth of the railroad net was concerned.

WESTWARD MOVEMENT OF THE POPULATION

Acquisition of land in the West. The original thirteen states comprised a land area which extended to the Mississippi River. In 1803 the Louisiana Purchase added the area lying between the Mississippi and the Rocky Mountains, and the cession of Florida by Spain in 1819 added further to the domain of the new nation. All of these acquisitions were made prior to the development of the railroad and numerous settlements were made as far west as the Mississippi, both before and during the period of the railroad's infancy. More or less coincidental with the beginning of extensive railroad growth came further large acquisitions of land. Texas came into the Union in 1845; title to the Oregon Territory was established in 1846; in 1848 an immense area in the West was acquired from Mexico following the victorious conclusion of the Mexican War; and in 1853 the Gadsden Purchase completed the present land area of the United States.

The western migration. The discovery of gold in California in 1849 was the signal for hardy adventurers and fortune seekers to move west, and in the 1850's a considerable migration to the West took place. During the Civil War, of course, people in the East and South were occupied with other matters, but the period immediately following the war was characterized by a substantial amount of homesteading in the West, and this interest of the people in the western lands provided a strong stimulus for railroad construction. In many cases, particularly in the Mississippi Valley and in the mining regions in the western mountains, settlement preceded the coming of the railroads, but probably in most cases settlement was impractical until the railroad had provided an access to land and an outlet for crops. In any event the land was there and people wanted to settle it, and this proved a powerful stimulus to railroad construction.

PRIVATE, LOCAL, AND STATE AID TO RAILROADS

Private aid to railroads. The people of the United States, and particularly those who resided in the more recently acquired sections of the country, were quick to realize the advantages of railroad transportation, and in many cases provided direct inducements to railroad promoters to build through their communities. As far as individual citizens were concerned this aid commonly took the form of subscriptions to the securities of proposed railroad projects, and stories are told of farmers even mortgaging their farms in order to obtain funds to buy such securities. In some cases land was donated for right of way and for other purposes. Corporations and other business concerns also contributed in one way or another to railroad construction, hopeful that such construction would increase the value of their lands or their business enterprises.

Local governmental aid. More important than the contributions of private citizens was the aid received by railroad builders from various governmental bodies. Counties and municipalities purchased the stocks and bonds of railroads projected to serve their citizens. They also made direct contributions in the form of money, securities, land for yard and station facilities, building lots, equipment, material, and labor. Some made direct loans to railroads and some guaranteed bonds issued and sold by the railroads themselves. In many cases this flow of financial aid was encouraged by railway promoters who played one community off against another in an effort to get all that they could. It must also be recorded that once the aid had been received, railroad promoters were not always meticulously careful in keeping their part of the bargain and might locate their lines as they saw fit, regardless of earlier promises. As a result local governments, and private individuals as well, sometimes got little or nothing for their contributions. In later years some local governmental units sought to repudiate their commitments, but in general the courts held that such commitments were valid and would have to be met.

State aid. In addition to local aid the railroads received a substantial amount of financial assistance from state governments, particularly from states in the South and West. State governments purchased railroad stocks and bonds, made direct loans, guaranteed principal and interest on railroad-issued bonds, donated money and labor and the like, provided tax exemption in one form or another, and made some grants of public land. There was a good deal of fraud and corruption in connection with state aid to railroads, and in later years a number of states repudiated some of their obligations made in connection with railroad construction. Because of the corruption involved and because of the heavy tax burden the people were asked to bear to meet the states' promises, it later became common for state constitutions to prohibit the investment of state money in any private enterprise. Somewhat later local governmental bodies were similarly prohibited from investing the taxpayers' money in private undertakings.

FEDERAL LAND-GRANT POLICY

Why land grants were made. Although state and local aid was of some value to a number of different railroads, the chief public contribution to railroad construction was made by the Federal Government during the years 1850-71 in the form of donations of public land. Congress recognized the need for railroad construction if the early settlement of the West was to be achieved, but the risk involved in undertaking construction in undeveloped country was obviously too great to attract private capital. It would be years before sufficient traffic could be developed to pay a satisfactory return on the heavy capital outlay required if, indeed, such traffic ever developed. Since there was a demand for railroads and since private capital could not be expected to build the desired lines under existing conditions, Congress had two alternatives. It could build the railroads itself as public projects, or it could offer to subsidize their construction by private enterprise. In view of the widely voiced opposition to government in business it is not surprising that Congress adopted the latter alternative. And since the Federal Government held title to large areas of land in the West, gifts of land in aid of railroad construction suggested themselves as an economical method of subsidization.

Characteristics of federal land grants. The first of these land grants was made in 1850 to the Illinois Central Railroad. Actually the land was granted first to the state and then by the state to the railroad, this roundabout procedure being the result of some uncertainty about the constitutionality of the grants. Beginning in 1862, however, Congress made grants directly to the railroad corporations themselves. Most of these later grants were made in territories rather than in states, and the question of states' rights did not enter to complicate matters. The Illinois Central Railroad was given a strip of land 200 feet wide through the public domain on which to build its tracks. And in addition to this necessary land for right-of-way purposes, it was given alternate sections of land on each side of the right of way extending for a distance of six miles outward from the track. The remaining alternate sections and the land beyond the six-mile strip were retained by the Government for general settlement. Some of the later grants, especially those made to the more westerly lines, were much more extensive in scope, providing for a right of way up to 400 feet wide and alternate sections of land which in some cases extended as much as twenty-four miles out from the right of way.

The idea behind the granting of land in amounts far in excess of the needs of the railroad for actual construction purposes was an interesting one. It was intended that the railroad would sell the alternate sections of land that it had received from the Government and use the money thus obtained to help finance construction. In this way Congress could subsidize railroad construction in the West without any cash outlay on its part. The larger grants that were made to the more westerly lines were justified on the ground that the value of land adjacent to the right of way was less than in the areas farther east. Also, it was believed that the heavier construction costs typical of rough mountainous country necessitated larger subsidies.

In the event that a land-grant line was projected through an area in which some or all of the land had already been taken up by settlers the railroad was entitled to additional sections of land elsewhere along its right of way to make up for the loss. A time limit was placed on construction, the railroad being required to commence construction by a certain date or forfeit its land-grant claims, but these time limits were not always scrupulously observed. Finally, the terms of the land grants provided for the free transportation of government property and troops. In 1876, however, the Supreme Court held that this meant free use of the right of way only and that the railroad was entitled to some compensation for the actual movement of troops and government property.[1] Although the logic of the Court's reasoning has been questioned, the continued transportation of government troops and property without charge might well have bankrupted certain railroads. In any event the Government enjoyed and continued to enjoy substantial reductions in the rates it paid by virtue of the terms of the land grants.

Justifications of the land-grant policy. Justifications of the land-grant policy are suggested in what has been said above, but it may be well to summarize them here. First, the railroad network in the West could not have been built at the time without outside aid. It is probably true, as some critics have pointed out, that the railroads would have been built eventually without government aid, but the land-grant policy does deserve credit for an earlier opening up of the West than would other-

---

[1] *Lake Superior and Mississippi Railroad Co.* v. *U.S.*, 3 Otto 442.

wise have been the case and no doubt played some part in binding the newer sections to the older parts of the nation. Second, the railroads built into the Great Plains region were useful to the Government in maintaining order and protecting settlers from hostile Indians. Third, the people stood to gain financially from the increase in value of the alternate sections of land retained by the Government. Without railroad transportation much of this land was practically worthless, but its value was bound to increase substantially after railroad transportation made it accessible for practical settlement. Finally, the Government was entitled to reduced rates on land-grant railroads, a concession that over the years proved to be of very real value.

Objections to the land-grant policy. The idea of granting public land to private corporations for the purpose of building railroads was not without its critics, among the earliest of whom were the representatives of the original thirteen states. These states had abandoned their earlier claims to the western lands in favor of the Federal Government, and their representatives felt that if Congress granted land in the newer states for the purpose of constructing railroads in those states, it should grant an equal amount of western public land to aid in the construction of railroads in the older states where no public land existed. In addition, there was some doubt of the constitutionality of such grants of land. Grants were made, however, and as these grants proved to be successful in promoting railroad construction the objections died away. There was also more than a suspicion of corruption involved in the changed attitude that some of the representatives in Congress took toward the land-grant question. Eastern capital was beginning to appreciate the possibilities of gain that might lie in large grants of public land. It became increasingly interested in the development of western railroads and its influence may have had something to do with the changed views of some legislators.

Termination of the land-grant policy. Between 1850 and 1871 some 155 million acres of land were granted by Congress to aid railroad construction, of which slightly more than 130 million acres were eventually actually patented to various railroads. After 1871 no further grants of land were made, although construction continued after that date under the provisions of land grants made in earlier years. The reasons for the termination of the land-grant policy are clear enough. In the first place, there was a growing feeling that the public lands of the United States ought to be reserved for actual settlement and that bona fide settlers ought not to have to buy this land from private corporations. In the second place, there was the feeling, not without foundation, that some of the land grants were essentially nothing more than swindles, by means of which private corporations had been able to obtain public lands without cost and without regard for the public interest. Finally, there was a rapidly growing feeling of hostility toward railroad management because of various practices which were considered inimical to the public interest. The precise nature of these complaints is considered in Chapter 5, but in general they involved high rates, high-handed methods, and an arrogant attitude on the part of some railroad magnates.

THE PACIFIC RAILROADS

Early plans. The railroad had hardly made its appearance in the United States before the idea of building a railroad across the country to the Pacific Ocean was voiced. As early as 1834 one Dr. Barlow was writing in favor of such a line to be built by the Government. The idea grew rapidly until by 1850 it was generally accepted that a Pacific railroad would be built in the not-too-distant future. Such a line would bind the west coast to the United States, aid in the western migration of the population, serve the armed forces, and would give this country a substantial advantage in the Asiatic trade. Not only would the country benefit from direct trade with the Orient, but also it would benefit by virtue of the fact that a transcontinental railroad would function as a part of a through route between the Orient and Europe.

Of the various schemes for building a railroad to the Pacific coast the earliest and best known were those which Asa Whitney presented to Congress at various times from 1848 on. According to Whitney's later proposals the Government would sell him a strip of land sixty miles wide from Lake Michigan or the Mississippi River to the Pacific Ocean. Whitney was to pay 10¢ an acre for this land, and he would finance the construction of a railroad out of the proceeds of its sales. Various other proposals were made for the construction of a line by private interests or by the Federal Government. Throughout the 1850's Congress entertained a variety of bills looking toward the construction of a Pacific railroad, but except for an appropriation of $150,000 made in 1853 for the purpose of surveying the route, nothing was done.

It is interesting to note why Congress was unable to make headway toward the construction of a Pacific railroad even though the value of such a line was almost universally recognized. One difficulty faced was constitutional. It was recognized that the railroad could not be built without public assistance, but there were those in Congress who insisted that the Federal Government had no right to make appropriations for internal improvements. The principal difficulty, however, arose out of sectional differences over the location of the proposed line. There were, in fact, three practical routes: a northern route, a central route, and a southern route. Construction over the northern route would have made the Pacific coast and the intervening territory tributary to the business interests of the North, and it was believed that the South would benefit but little from such a route. To a considerable extent this was also true of the central route. For a similar reason the southern route, which was the shortest and simplest, was objectionable to northern interests.

Construction of the first Pacific railroad. With the outbreak of war between the North and South and the withdrawal of the southern representation in Congress, the way was clear for the passage of a Pacific railroad act, since the principal constitutional objections had come from southern advocates of states' rights. At the same time the withdrawal of the southern representation ended the dispute over routes. In 1862 Congress passed a law providing for the construction of a railroad to the Pacific coast over the central route. Two separate corporations were to be chartered, the Union Pacific to build from a point on the western border of Iowa to the western boundary of Nevada Territory; and the Central Pacific, a California corporation, to build from Sacramento to a connection with the Union Pacific, on the Nevada-California border. Curiously, neither of the termini selected had any existing railroad connections, but at this time railroads were building westward across Iowa toward the Missouri River, and Sacramento had river boat transportation to San Francisco.

The Act of 1862 provided for federal aid in the form of land grants and loans of government bonds, but at the same time it placed some rather severe limitations on other methods of financing. As a result investments in the project proved to be unattractive to private capital, and no progress was made in construction. Since the purpose of Congress was to get a railroad built and since the railroad was not being built, it was found necessary to amend the original act in various respects in 1864 and again in 1865 and 1866. The amendments greatly liberalized the financial provisions of the original act and, among other things, specified that the two lines, the Union Pacific and the Central Pacific, could disregard the original junction on the California-Nevada border and build until they met.

Construction on the Central Pacific got under way in 1863, and the following year the Union Pacific started building westward from Omaha. The construction of these two railroads is a saga of man's determination to overcome vast distances and tremendous mountain barriers, replete with Indian warfare, labor shortages, honky-tonks, and physical violence. Also it involved a gigantic race between the two railroads to see which could build the most line, for every mile of line built meant a prize in land grants and other government assistance. The two lines finally were joined at Promontory Point, Utah, on the northern shore of the Great Salt Lake on May 10, 1869.

Other Pacific railroads. The joining of the Union Pacific and the Central Pacific at Promontory Point gave the nation its first through rail route to the Pacific coast, but even as the ceremonies in Utah were taking place, work was progressing on other lines destined to span the country both south and north of the original route. A number of lines built by various companies and later acquired by the Union Pacific greatly expanded the original scope of that company's line from Omaha to Ogden, Utah, over the central route. Independent lines built into the central area include the Missouri Pacific and the Rock Island lines to the Rocky Mountains, the Denver and Rio Grande Western from Denver to Salt Lake City, and the Western Pacific from Salt Lake City to San Francisco. Two major transcontinental railroads were built to the south of the original route, the Southern Pacific, which runs between Portland, San Francisco, and New Orleans; and the Atchison, Topeka, and Santa Fe, which now extends from Chicago to San Francisco. The first transcontinental line to be built over the northern route was the Northern Pacific, running from a point near Duluth, Minnesota, to the north coast of the Pacific and completed in 1883. Ten years later the Great Northern completed its line from St. Paul to Puget Sound to become the most northerly transcontinental line in the United States, and the Puget Sound extension on the Chicago, Milwaukee, and St. Paul, opened in 1909, gave that railroad a through line from Chicago to the north Pacific coast.

SPECULATIVE ACTIVITIES

The construction company. During the latter half of the nineteenth century a number of bold financial buccaneers awoke to the possibilities of the railroad as a means of enlarging their personal fortunes. The construction company was a favorite device utilized to this end, the technique being well described by Ripley [2] in the following hypothetical case.

A knot of promoters planning an enterprise, first formed a railroad corporation and authorized, let us say, capital stock to the amount of $1,000,000. This consisted of 10,000 shares, par value $100. The stock was issued to themselves part paid ($10 per share)—$100,000 in all being temporarily borrowed by them individually for the purpose. A glowing prospectus then offered for sale two millions of bonds with the proceeds of which the road was to be built. These bonds were sold at $80, with perhaps a bonus of stock thrown in, thus realizing

---

[2] W. Z. Ripley, *Railroads, Finance & Organization.* New York: Longmans, Green & Company, 1923, p. 18.

$1,600,000 in cash. From this the promoters reimbursed themselves for the $100,000 already advanced, by charging a 5 per cent commission for marketing the bonds. This enabled them to pay off their personal loans. It left $1,500,000 cash in the treasury of the railway corporation as well as a controlling portion of its own capital stock. The next step was the organization by these same directors of a construction company, which built the road for an actual outlay of $1,200,000. The railway directors now voted to pay their construction company $1,500,000 in cash for this work and in addition the remainder of the share capital of the road. A profit to themselves of $300,000 plus the prospective value of the capital stock, which had cost them nothing, obviously resulted. If the enterprise were henceforth profitably operated, all well and good. If not, it might fail even to pay interest on its bonds. If bankruptcy ensued, a receiver, possibly representing the old stockholders rather than the bondholders, was appointed. In any event the promoters had realized 300 per cent on their first investment, itself borrowed, from the profits of the construction company. Moreover, they still controlled the railroad through its capital stock. Thus were the foundations of a number of large fortunes laid....

With fortunes to be made out of *building* railroads, it is not surprising that railroads were built, even though some lines were projected considerably in advance of the need for them and bondholders and the railroads themselves suffered from the financial indiscretions of the builders.

Other speculative opportunities. Railroad building offered other speculative opportunities which were not overlooked by individuals more concerned with lining their pockets with gold than with buildng up a sound and useful transportation system. Promoters of a railroad sometimes decided upon a location and then bought up or pre-empted desirable lands along the right of way. Some of this land was sold to the new railroad for station sites and the like at high prices, and some of it was sold to the public. Still another technique was the construction of "hold up" lines. A group of promoters would build a line of railroad closely paralleling an existing line solely to force the established line to buy up the new line, at a substantial profit to the promoters, in order to suppress potential competition. Best known examples of this sort of promotion are the West Shore, which paralleled the New York Central lines up the Hudson River, and the Nickel Plate, which ran side by side with the Lake Shore and Michigan Southern for a considerable distance across northern Ohio.

GROWTH OF TRADE AND INDUSTRY

One other consideration worth mentioning in connection with the growth of the American railroad net after 1850 is the great development of trade and industry which took place in this country, especially after the Civil War. In addition to this industrial development there was a very heavy growth of export traffic to Europe in the form of grain, cattle, and beef. There may be some question in particular instances whether railroad construction resulted from the growth of trade and industry or whether the growth of trade and industry resulted from the construction of railroads, but the matter is beside the point here. There can be no question that the existence of industrial traffic, either real or potential, necessitated and encouraged railroad development.

DECADE OF DECLINING GROWTH, 1910-20

Peak mileage reached in 1916. Because the railroad pattern of the United States was laid out during the years 1850-1910, much of the preceding discussion has been devoted to the events of that period. For the present purpose a somewhat briefer consideration of subsequent events will suffice. The years 1910-20 were noteworthy for a sharp decline in construction activity, the decade showing a net increase in mileage of only 12,552 miles as compared with 46,947 miles in the preceding decade and 70,335 miles in the 1880's. Also of significance is the fact that in 1916, just past the middle of the decade, the American railroad net reached its point of maximum growth with a total mileage of 254,037. The causes of this decline in construction activities are noted briefly in the pages that follow. Although discussed separately, it should be pointed out that they are not independent and isolated phenomenon but are closely interrelated.

Overexpansion. One obvious explanation of the decline in construction activity is found in an overexpansion of the railroad network. The activities of speculators and others interested in railroad construction had led to the building of much mileage considerably in advance of the needs of the people in the areas involved. When railroad construction was halted temporarily by the panic of 1893, the main outlines of the network were already in existence. Subsequent construction consisted primarily of filling in gaps and carrying to completion work which had been planned prior to 1893 but which had been halted by the financial difficulties accompanying the panic. When this work was finished, new construction was bound to slow down until such time as traffic had caught up with the existing plant.

Lack of capital. During this general period, moreover, the railroads were finding it increasingly difficult to obtain new capital, and without new capital new lines could not be built. In view of the expansion of the railroad net during earlier periods, new lines might not have been built even if new capital had been available, but the lack of capital was felt severely by the railroads in a number of other ways. Normal increases in traffic necessitated the purchase of new and better equipment, and improvements in right of way, including the multiple tracking of some lines, were indicated where traffic was too heavy for existing tracks and structures. The inability of the railroads to make these needed improvements was particularly marked during World War I and accounts in part for the car shortages and traffic tieups that characterized rail transportation during that war.

The inability of the railroads to obtain needed capital resulted from a variety of circumstances, some of them indigenous to the transportation industry and some the result of factors completely outside the industry. Of these indigenous circumstances two may be mentioned at this point. One of these was the unenviable record of failures with attendant financial losses which had resulted from overbuilding, financial manipulation, and fraud. The early years of the twentieth century witnessed the failure of a number of well established companies, and investigations of these failures revealed such shocking financial irregularities and, in some cases, ignorance and inefficiency, that it is small wonder that railroad securities fell into ill repute.

The other factor was a general decline in the net earnings of railroads in the early years of the twentieth century. This decline in earnings was caused in part by increased costs of operation arising out of a rising price level, in part by higher taxes, and in part by the failure of regulatory bodies to allow rate increases commensurate with higher costs of operation. Regulation is discussed elsewhere, but it may be pertinent here to note that the regulation of railroad rates was generally ineffective prior to 1906 and very effective after that time.

In addition to these difficulties, there were two elements external to the railroad industry that led to a decline in available capital. One of these was the First World War. This war wiped out what was left of the European market for American railroad securities since investors in the belligerent countries were putting their funds into the wartime issues of their own governments. Many of them also sold their remaining holdings in railroad securities, and these securities were purchased by American investors who otherwise might have been inclined to invest in new railroad issues. The other factor was the increasing popularity of securities being sold by commercial and industrial enterprises. Many of these offered higher returns than the railroads could pay and coupled these returns with a fairly good record for safety. The Government, too, with its Liberty and Victory bonds paying up to 6 per cent interest, attracted many investors who under different circumstances might have been customers for railroad securities.

DEVELOPMENT OF RAILROADS

Construction since 1920. There was, of course, little construction during and immediately following the war years, but in the early 1920's there was a brief rise in railroad building. The Great Northern and the Western Pacific together built a line in northern California, giving that area some railroad competition for the first time and also providing an entry for the Great Northern into the San Francisco area. In the Texas Panhandle a number of lines were built to serve the growing agriculture and industry of that region, and there was also some construction in and into the Texas Rio Grande Valley to serve newly developed fruit and vegetable growing areas. Except for these few cases, however, such construction as has taken place has been to relocate existing lines, provide cutoffs, and provide short extensions to serve new industries or new industrial areas. Since March 1, 1920, all new construction projects, with a few insignificant exceptions, must be approved by the Interstate Commerce Commission, and in its *Annual Report* for 1951 that body reported that it had authorized the construction of 10,925 miles of new railroad, of which 7,818 miles had actually been built.[3] The great bulk of construction authorization, some 9,500 miles, was made before October 31, 1930. The small amount of construction completed since 1920, and particularly since 1930, is a reflection in part of long periods of business stagnation and inadequate earnings, and in part of the rise of newer forms of transportation, especially the motor vehicle.

Abandonment of mileage. A decline in the construction of new railroad mileage is in itself no necessary indication of a decline in the importance of railroad transportation. It should be perfectly obvious that the rate of construction carried on during the latter half of the nineteenth century could not be maintained indefinitely. After all, there is no point in building railroad facilities which are in excess of the needs of the people. But since 1916 railroad abandonments have consistently exceeded new construction with the result that by the end of 1950 total railroad mileage in the United States was 223,779 as compared with the 254,037 miles of 1916, a decrease of 30,258 miles. A substantial part of the mileage abandoned since 1920 has consisted of railroads originally built to serve some special purpose, which purpose no longer exists. For example, many railroads were built originally to serve mining areas, and after the veins of ore or coal were exhausted there was no further need for the line. Such abandonments are natural and become noticeable only when new construction fails to offset them. On the other hand, a substantial volume of

---

[3] p. 156.

railroad abandonments in recent years is traceable in whole or in part to the development of hard surfaced highways and the growth of highway transportation. The reasons for this development and its possible effects on the railroads and on the life of the American people must be left for later discussion.

Capital improvements. Statistics of railroad mileage may be deceptive as an index of railroad development because railroads develop intensively as well as extensively, and mileage figures do not show this intensive development. As noted previously there has been a steady improvement in railroad equipment and facilities, and in recent years the advances made along these lines have been marked. Thus while railroad mileage declined from 254,037 miles in 1916 to 223,779 miles in 1950, during this same period investment in plant and equipment increased from $17,842,777,000 to $30,174,312,000. It is interesting to note that in some measure these improvements have been brought about by one of the factors which has contributed importantly in recent years to the decline in railroad mileage, namely, the competition of newer forms of transportation.

GENERAL EXTENT OF PUBLIC AID TO RAILROAD TRANSPORTATION

Problem stated. In the period following the close of World War I the United States experienced a remarkable development of highway and air transportation and a revival, after a long period of stagnation, of river and canal transportation. None of these newer forms of transportation could have developed to its present size and scope had it not been for substantial aid from the public purse and, with the possible exception of highway transportation, all continue to be heavily dependent upon public aid of one sort or another.[4] The railroads, operating today without benefit of subsidy, have been quite outspoken in their objections to the policy of subsidizing competing forms of transportation, but the other side has been quick to point out that the railroads themselves received substantial public assistance during their earlier years, and some rather startling statements have been made about the extent of this aid. That subsidies played an important part in the development of the railroad network is not to be denied. That they were as large in amount and as broad in scope as is sometimes claimed is another matter. Since railroads are not now subsidized a discussion of public aid to railroad transportation would seem to have little present-day significance, but its injection into current controversies

---

[4] Public aid to highway transportation is discussed in Chapter 18; to water transportation in Chapter 22; and to air transportation in Chapter 26. The effect of subsidies on the transportation system as a whole is discussed in Chapter 32.

over subsidies to the newer forms of transportation makes it necessary to give the matter more consideration than it probably deserves.

Studies of public aid. Most of the statements made and conclusions reached with regard to public aid to railroad transportation are based on a study sponsored by the Federal Government and made by the staff of the Federal Coordinator of Transportation as of the early 1930's, hereafter referred to as the Coordinator's study.[5] The Coordinator's staff went back to the beginning of railroad transportation and sought to place a money value on every aid granted to railroads from that time up to the time of the completion of the study. These aids were found to total $1,503 million in round numbers, from which was deducted $60 million representing benefits derived by government, primarily from reduced rates, leaving a net amount of public aid to railroads of $1,443 million.

A later study, also under the auspices of the Federal Government, was made by the staff of the Board of Investigation and Research in 1940, referred to hereafter as the Board's study.[6] This study does not give a figure for gross public aid, but an examination of the various items included indicates total public aid to railroads of something more than $600 million, or considerably less than half of the amount found in the Coordinator's study. For one reason or another the Board's study appears to have been largely ignored.

The great difference between the Coordinator's results and the Board's results is due principally to three factors. In the first place, the Coordinator's staff, as noted above, went back to the very beginning of railroad transportation in calculating public aid to railroads, but in calculating public aid to highway transportation it ignored all road expenditures prior to 1921. Similarly, it ignored all waterway expenditures prior to the modern period. The Board's staff, on the other hand, took the position that a study of public aid should be confined to those aids which have some present-day significance, and it applied this principle to railroads as well as to other types of transportation. This point alone accounts for a substantial part of the difference between the two studies. In the second place, the two studies differ in the method of measuring the amount of public aid contained in certain items. And in the third place, the Coordinator's staff employed a most unusual definition of public aid, and this led to the inclusion of several items which are not public aid in any commonly

---

[5] Federal Coordinator of Transportation, *Public Aid to Transportation*, Vol. II. For an explanation of the nature and purpose of the office of Federal Coordinator of Transportation see pp. 150-151.

[6] Board of Investigation and Research, *Public Aids to Domestic Transportation.* 79th Congress, 1st Session, House Document 159. The Board of Investigation and Research is described on p. 165.

accepted sense. An item by item comparison of the two studies is given in Table III.

Table III
PUBLIC AIDS TO RAILROAD TRANSPORTATION

Nature of Public Aid	Coordinator's Study	Board's Study
Land Grants:		
Net proceeds from land-grant land sold	$439,721,218	$434,806,671
Estimated value of land-grant land still held for sale (as of date of study)	49,615,981	60,684,032
Land used for right of way and other carrier purposes	86,807,630	2,000,000
Lands donated for right of way by counties, municipalities, individuals, associations, and private corporations, including apparent aids	232,000,000	97,160
Other Direct Contributions:		
Contributions of cash, material, equipment, labor, and securities by states, local governments, individuals, associations, and private corporations	63,000,000	
Loans:		
Pacific railroad loans	48,000,000	74,319,783
Loans by state and local governments	46,000,000	24,467,333
Guaranty or endorsement of bonds by state and local governments	25,000,000	
R.F.C. loans	114,560,000	
P.W.A. loans	46,130,000	
Subscriptions to railroad securities:		
Subscriptions to railroad stocks and bonds by state and local governments	50,000,000	
Collective subscriptions to railroad stocks by citizens and communities	87,000,000	
Rights in the public domain:		
Street vacations	77,000,000	22,000,000
Street occupancies	118,000,000	
Other aids:		
Tax exemptions	12,600,000	
Expense of federal surveys	75,000	13,386
Remission of import duties on railway iron	5,996,840	
Banking privileges granted to railroads	1,000,000	
Total	1,502,507,205	624,385,205

DIRECT AIDS

Land grants. Contrary to popular belief, only a few railroads were built with land-grant aid, more than two-thirds of this aid having gone to five present-day railroads or their predecessors. Sales of land netted the railroads $439,721,218 according to the Coordinator and $434,806,671 according to the Board. The small amount of land-grant land still retained by the railroads was valued at $49,615,981 by the Coordinator as of December 31, 1930, and at $60,684,032 by the Board as of January 1, 1940. The land-grant railroads also received land for right-of-way and other carrier purposes, of which approximately 650,000 acres remain in their possession. The Coordinator's staff estimated the market value of this land as of December 31, 1930, at $86,807,630, and used this as the measure of public aid involved. The Board, however, reasoned that the carriers could not realize this value except by selling the land, which they could not do and still operate. Furthermore, it stated that the land was received initially on the implied condition that it would revert to the Government if it ceased to be used for carrier purposes. The Board concluded that the railroads could have bought the right-of-way land without difficulty for one or two million dollars at the time that it was given to them and that this was the proper measure of public aid.

The Coordinator's study includes $232 million of public aid in the form of "lands donated for right of way by counties, municipalities, individuals, associations and private corporations, including apparent aids." The term "apparent aids" refers to legal conveyances of title under a nominal consideration, i.e., one dollar and other valuable considerations. In some cases substantial sums were paid for the land involved, while in other cases nominal and real consideration were identical. There is no way, however, of distinguishing between the two types of conveyances at this late date. The Coordinator determined the amount of public aid contained in these items on the basis of the December 31, 1930, value of the land still held, plus amounts received by the railroads from land previously sold. This procedure resulted in a figure of $4,583,515 for land conveyed by county and municipal governments; $104,646,277 for land conveyed by individuals and business concerns; and $122,656,848 for apparent aids; or a total of $232 million in round numbers.

The Board, measuring public aid in terms of what the railroads would have had to pay for the land at the time of its acquisition, estimated that land donations by county and municipal governments accounted for only $97,160 of public aid. It reached the altogether reasonable conclusion that lands donated by individuals, associations, and private corporations do not represent public aid in any normally accepted sense of the term, and rejected this item *in toto*. It concluded that the Coordinator's estimate of apparent aids would reduce to $10,435,040 if value at time of acquisition were used as a base. Since, however, there was no way of determining what part of this represented aid from local and municipal governments, which is public aid, and what part represented land obtained from private sources, which is not public aid, the Board concluded that there was no adequate basis for determining how much actual public aid was involved. If value at time of acquisition is adopted as a reasonable criterion of public aid, the amount involved obviously could not have been large.

Other direct contributions. The Coordinator's study shows an item of public aid in the form of "contributions of cash, material, equipment, construction, labor, and securities in aid of railroad construction by states, local governments, individuals, associations, and private corporations" amounting to about $63 million. The Board was unable to segregate the private from the public aid and did not attempt to do so. The railroads have estimated that public aid from this source represented at most $22,425,092.[7]

OTHER AIDS

Loans. Some of the Pacific railroads received loans from the Federal Government in the form of United States bonds which were sold by the railroads to the public at a considerably lower rate of interest than would have been the case if the railroads had sold their own bonds. The Coordinator estimated that this saving in interest payments represented public aid in the amount of $48 million. The Board, on the other hand, concluded that public aid should be measured by the amount lost by the Government through default of interest and principal payments, and on this basis arrived at a figure of $74,319,783. A number of states also made loans in aid of railroad construction which resulted in a saving of $46 million in interest charges according to the Coordinator. The Board was unable to find adequate information to determine the amount of loss experienced by the states on these loans but gave an incomplete figure of $24,467,333. It noted, however, that most of these loans were made to southern railroads before the Civil War and that in many cases portions of track and much equipment were destroyed by the opposing armies. To some extent, then, it would appear that this item is of little significance insofar as present-day railroad transportation is concerned.

Instead of making direct loans, some state and local governments sought to aid railroad construction by guaranteeing or endorsing railroad bonds, enabling the railroads to save approximately $25 million in interest charges according to the Coordinator. The Board noted that most of these guarantees were made in the South prior to the Civil War and during the Reconstruction period and that defaults were influenced by abnormal conditions. It did not believe that the amount was significant with regard to current transportation policy.

---

[7] Association of American Railroads, *What is Public aid to Transportation?* Washington: 1940, pp. 36-37.

DEVELOPMENT OF RAILROADS

During the depression a number of railroads borrowed from the Reconstruction Finance Corporation, and the Coordinator estimated that they saved $114,560,000 by such borrowing. The Board was unable to determine what loss, if any, was suffered by the Government as a result of default in interest and principal because the loans still were outstanding at the time its study was made. It noted, however, that they were secured by collateral which the R.F.C. considered adequate in most cases.

During the depression the Government also offered loans to railroads to carry on maintenance and equipment improvement programs, largely for "pump priming" and unemployment relief. The Coordinator estimated that the railroads enjoyed a saving of about $46,130,000 as a result of being able to make these loans from public rather than private sources. According to the Board, it was expected that these loans would be liquidated without any overall loss to the Government. Considering the circumstances under which these depression loans were made, the propriety of computing public aid as the difference between the cost of borrowing from private as compared with public sources is open to question. It seems reasonably certain that many of these loans would not have been made at all if borrowing had been confined to private sources, and the Coordinator acknowledged that some of the carriers had to be urged to borrow, even from public sources. To the extent that loans were urged upon the carriers for pump priming and work relief programs, there would seem to be little justification for calling them public aid even if the Government had lost money on them.

Subscriptions to railroad securities. State and local governments at one time aided in the construction of railroads in their areas through the purchase of railroad stocks and bonds. These securities usually were sold at par to governmental bodies whereas sales to private investors frequently had to be made at a discount, and the Coordinator estimated that this additional revenue resulted in public aid in the amount of $50 million. The Board was unable to calculate the amount of loss incurred by governments through the purchase of railroad stocks and bonds and concluded that these early aids had little bearing on present transportation policies. The Coordinator also included public aid in the amount of $87 million representing collective subscriptions to railroad stocks by citizens of communities. It may be doubted that this represents public aid in any customary use of the term.

Rights in the public domain. Railroads have received right-of-way grants from municipalities in the form of the exclusive use of certain public thoroughfares, usually dead-end streets and alleys. The Coordinator estimated these street vacations to represent public aid in the amount of $77 million, based on the value of the land as of December 31, 1930. The

Board, believing that value at time of acquisition should be used, placed the amount at $22 million. In addition to these exclusive street occupancies the railroads share streets or portions of streets with the general public. Sometimes this occurs when it is necessary to run a track longitudinally along a city street, but most of these occupancies occur at grade crossings. The Coordinator estimated public aid derived from such joint use of streets at $118 million, but the Board was of the opinion that there was no adequate basis for concluding that these rights conferred public aid on the railroads. It has been pointed out that in many cases municipalities developed or expanded after the railroad was built and that streets were built along or across railroad property instead of the railroads being built on public property.

Other aids. In an effort to encourage railroad construction some state and local governments exempted early railroads from taxation for varying numbers of years, and the Coordinator estimated that this represented public aid in the amount of $12,600,000. In 1824 Congress authorized surveys of routes for canals and roads, and between 1828 and 1838 a number of railroad surveys were made under the provisions of this act, representing public aid in the amount of $75,000, according to the Coordinator. Between 1830 and 1843 the high duty on imported iron products was remitted in whole or in part insofar as iron rails were concerned, and the Coordinator estimated this to represent a benefit of $5,996,840. During the 1830's certain railroads were granted charters which permitted them to operate banks as well as to construct a line of railroad, an arrangement which had been used earlier in connection with canal companies. Many of these combined enterprises issued substantial amounts of worthless paper money without building any railroads at all, and some of the states and their citizens suffered financial loss in this way. The Coordinator calculated that $1 million of public aid was involved in this situation. In general, the Board took the position that none of these early concessions were of any present-day significance.

CONCLUSION

Offsets. As noted previously, the land-grant lines were required to move government traffic at reduced rates, and the resultant savings in transportation charges constituted a legitimate offset against the value of the grants themselves. Furthermore, competing railroads which had not received land grants found it necessary to offer similar rate reductions in order to secure a share of government traffic, and since the Government would have routed all of its traffic over the land-grant lines in the absence of such concessions, it seems reasonable to include these savings as an offset to the value of the land grants. In addition, the terms of the Illinois Central grant provided that the grantee was to pay 7 per cent of the gross receipts from its charter lines in lieu of state taxes on the land involved, a provision which has resulted in the payment by the carrier of substantially larger amounts than would have been the case if ordinary property taxes had been assessed.

The Coordinator recognized that the savings accruing to the Government from land-grant rate reductions constituted a legitimate offset against the value of the land grants, but only to the extent that such savings occurred on the land-grant lines themselves. After a somewhat complicated set of adjustments the Coordinator concluded that $60 million represented a liberal allowance for these savings and for the extra revenue accruing to the State of Illinois. This amount deducted from gross benefits of $1,503 million produced the final figure of $1,443 million, which is the figure commonly quoted as representing the value of public aid to the railroads.

The Board concluded that $34,600,000 of extra revenue had accrued to the State of Illinois as of December 31, 1941, and that the Federal Government had saved $580 million in freight rates up to June 30, 1943. This last figure includes savings derived from the voluntary rate reductions, and it is also affected by the increased amount of traffic which resulted from the defense and war activities of the Federal Government. After June 30, 1943, there was a continued large movement of government traffic and further large increases in the savings enjoyed by the Government from land-grant rate reductions. The total amount of these savings is not known, but it has been estimated to have run as high as $1,500 million as of October 1, 1946, on which date the Federal Government abandoned all claim to further land-grant rate reductions.

Conclusion. In bringing this brief discussion of public aids to railroad transportation to an end, certain observations are in order. In the first place, enough has been said about the techniques employed by the Coordinator to suggest that his widely-used figures on public aid to railroad transportation are at least of debatable validity. Of course, a similar statement may be made of the Board's study as well. Second, contrary to widely-held opinion there was no general policy of land-grant aid to railroad construction, and only a small number of railroads were the direct beneficiaries of such aid. The amount of mileage constructed with land-grant aid was large, however, including a substantial part of the present railroad network west of the Mississippi. And third and most important, the land grants involved a *quid pro quo* which may have saved the Government up to $1,500 million and which is very often ignored in discussions of the land-grant question. It should be pointed out, however, that these savings cannot be set off directly against the money value of the land grants because the railroads obtained prompt benefits from the land they received whereas the benefits to the Government stretched thinly over a long period of time, with the major benefits of very recent origin. Nevertheless, the fact that dollars and cents savings to the Government may have amounted to as much as three times the money value of the land grants is not without significance. While it is obviously impossible to reach a definite conclusion on the point, it is perhaps not too unrealistic to assume that the money value of the land-grant rate reductions was sufficient to equal the money value of public aids to railroads in its entirety, even after allowing for the time element, variations in price levels, and other incalculables.

SUGGESTED READINGS

Board of Investigation and Research, *Public Aids to Domestic Transportation*. 79th Congress, 1st Session, House Document 159, pp. 105-188.

Davis, J. P., *The Union Pacific Railway*. S. C. Griggs and Co., 1894.

Dunbar, Seymour, *A History of Travel in America*. Indianapolis: The Bobbs-Merrill Co., 1915. Volumes III and IV contain much interesting material on early locomotives, equipment, and railroad operating problems.

Federal Coordinator of Transportation, *Public Aids to Transportation*, Vol. II. pp. 3-103.

Haney, Lewis Henry, *A Congressional History of the Railways in the United States*. Madison, Wisconsin: Democrat Printing Company, 1908, 1910. Volume I recounts early plans for a Pacific railway. Volume II gives considerable data on the congressional history of the Union Pacific and other Pacific railroads.

Henry, Robert Selph, *This Fascinating Railroad Business*. Indianapolis: The Bobbs-Merrill Company, 1946. This book is devoted to a description of the railroad's physical plant and to the problems of railroad operation. Well written and an excellent source of information. The author is both historian and assistant to the president of the Association of American Railroads.

Locklin, D. Philip, *Economics of Transportation*, 3rd Ed. Chicago: Richard D. Irwin, Inc., 1947. Chapter V. contains a brief discussion of the development of the railroad net, land-grant problems, etc.

Magill, Caroline, and staff, *History of Transportation in the United States before 1860*. Washington: The Carnegie Institution, 1917.

Miller, Sidney L., *Inland Transportation*. New York: McGraw-Hill Book Company, Inc., 1933. Part II contains an excellent description of the railroad history of the United States.

Ripley, William Z., *Railroads, Rates and Regulation* and *Railroads, Finance and Organization*. New York: Longmans, Green & Company, 1912, 1915. These two volumes are classics in the field of railroad transportation. The second volume is especially useful for its extended discussion of fraud in connection with early railroad construction and finance.

Stevers, Martin D., *Steel Trails*. New York: Minton, Balch & Co., 1933. Similar to the book by Robert S. Henry but not as detailed.

Van Metre, T. W., *Trains, Tracks and Travel*. New York: Simmons-Boardman Publishing Co., 1931. A simplified account of railroad plant and equipment and operations. For "children from seven to seventy."

4.

Some Economic Characteristics
of
RAILROAD TRANSPORTATION

RAILROAD COSTS

Constant and variable costs. The costs incurred in running a railroad, like the costs incurred in running any kind of a business, may be divided into *constant costs* and *variable costs*, and it is important that these two concepts be clearly understood. Variable costs include all those costs which vary directly with the volume of traffic moved, rising in total amount as traffic increases and declining as traffic falls off. Constant costs are those costs which are incurred irrespective of the volume of traffic handled. They do not rise and fall with variations in the volume of traffic, at least in the short run. Few, if any, of the costs incurred in running a railroad are completely variable or completely constant, but locomotive fuel consumed may be cited as an example of an expense which is largely variable, and interest on the investment in a passenger terminal will serve to illustrate an expense or cost which is constant, at least over a relatively long period of time.

For many years there was general agreement that the business of railroad transportation involved a substantial element of constant cost, various students estimating that from one-half to two-thirds of railroad costs were constant. Some students now hold that this is no longer true and that railroad costs under present conditions are largely variable. Others still accept the earlier thesis, although probably most would agree that the proportion of constant costs is not as large as was formerly the case. Regardless of the present situation, however, it does appear to be correct to say that until fairly recent times railroad costs were constant to a very considerable extent, at least in the short run, and this fact has had considerable influence on rate making and various other economic aspects of railroad transportation. The reasons for the existence of this large element of constant cost are worth noting briefly.

Traditional short-run analysis of railroad costs. The construction of a railroad of any consequence requires a very large capital investment because of the heavy costs incurred in laying track, building bridges, providing terminal and right-of-way facilities, and purchasing locomotives, rolling stock, and other equipment. During the heyday of railroad build-ing this large initial investment characteristically resulted in the construc-tion of railroads which initially possessed considerable unused capacity. For example, thousands of miles of railroad were built into new and undeveloped areas and into areas already served by existing lines, and each of these railroads had to have a right of way and track even though, to begin with, there might not be more than enough traffic to justify the operation of more than one or two trains a day. Consequently, if traffic developed as anticipated, the increased traffic could be handled without any increase in capital investment except to the extent that it might be necessary to purchase additional motive power and rolling stock. Under these circumstances the capital costs incurred in connection with original construction represented a substantial element of constant costs.[1]

In addition, students have commonly found a substantial element of constant cost in railroad operating expenses. Maintenance of way and structures, which is a major item of expense, is made necessary largely because of the action of the elements, and the need for maintenance does not rise and fall to any great extent with variations in the volume of traffic. To a lesser extent this is also true of the maintenance of equip-ment. A box car, for example, spends far more time standing idle on sidings than it does in moving over the road as part of a freight train. A train requires a minimum crew of operating employees whether few cars or many are hauled. And a minimum of employees must be maintained to operate yards, stations, and offices. Until recently, railroad tax accruals, which always have taken a significant "bite" out of revenues, were trace-able primarily to the property tax, a tax which varies with the needs of government rather than with variations in the volume of traffic.

Long-run analysis of railroad costs. It is recognized that few, if any, costs are constant over a long period of time. Although the original in-vestment in a railroad right of way and track produces considerable excess capacity, a continued increase in traffic will eventually result in the optimum capacity of the plant being reached and passed, and management

---

[1] The railroads obtained much of their permanent capital through the sale of bonds and other types of fixed interest-bearing obligations rather than through the sale of stock, for reasons which are discussed in Chapter 14. Some writers consider that only interest on this part of the capital investment represents a constant cost because the railroad is under no legal obligation to pay stock dividends. Other writers look upon dividends on stock as well as interest on funded debt as representing a constant cost, recognizing the economic principle that a return on the investment in an enterprise is a cost of production which must be met if the enterprise expects to survive and prosper. In either case a substantial element of constant cost is involved.

may find it expedient to double track or make such other improvements as may be possible, thus increasing investment and capital costs.[2] In the past, however, it has been difficult to make capital improvements in small enough increments to take care of the needs of the immediate future, and expansion programs frequently put the railroad once more in possession of substantial unused capacity. For example, at a given time existing traffic might exceed the optimum capacity by 10 per cent, with double tracking the only practical means of increasing capacity. But a double-tracked line can handle several times the traffic handled by a single-track line, thus bringing about another condition of unused capacity.

Eventually, of course, the optimum capacity of the expanded facilities might be reached and passed, with a subsequent further increase in investment and capital costs. Thus, in the long run, capital costs increase with increased traffic and are properly considered to be variable. In the long run, too, capital costs should decline with declining traffic. Since much of the railroad plant is more or less permanent in nature, it does not shrink readily with declining traffic, but in time unprofitable branches may be abandoned and written off, and if there is a general decline in traffic over a period of years, bankruptcy proceedings may shrink the capital investment, and such proceedings are almost certain to result in a reduction in fixed charges. A similar process of reasoning may be applied to capital in the form of motive power and rolling stock, although here capital costs respond to traffic trends somewhat more quickly. Also, maintenance of way, structures, and equipment will vary with volume of traffic over a long period of time.

While it is not unimportant that railroad costs are variable in the long run, this fact has not influenced railroad practices and railroad economics to the same extent as has the fact that costs in the short run have been considered to be largely constant. Hence the discussion which follows is confined to the short-run analysis.

Constant costs and increasing returns. Where a part of the cost of operating a business is constant in nature, the business is said to operate under conditions of increasing returns until such time as optimum output is reached. This means that, assuming optimum output is not reached, an increase in production will not be accompanied by a proportionate increase in total cost of production, since only the variable costs increase, and as a result there will be a decline in the per unit cost of production. To put the same thing in a different way, the constant costs will be

---

[2] Optimum capacity is reached when the average total cost per unit of output is at a minimum.

spread out over a larger number of units of output, thus decreasing the cost of each unit. And if this reduction in unit costs is not offset by a reduction in the selling price of the product or by an increase in the cost of marketing it, the result of an increase in output will be a more than proportionate increase in profits. Conversely, a decline in production will not be accompanied by a corresponding reduction in costs, and assuming that an offsetting price increase is not possible, a decline in production will result in a more than proportionate reduction of profits or even in a loss.

If constant costs are relatively unimportant, their effect on unit costs of production will be slight, but if a substantial portion of the cost of operating a business is constant, even small variations in the volume of business may have a significant effect on unit cost of production and on profits. This has been the case with the railroads in the past, and it is still true according to many students.

Effect of traffic variations illustrated. The effect of traffic variations on the profitability of railroad transportation, assuming a substantial element of constant cost, may be illustrated by examining the operations of an imaginary railroad which handles only freight. For the present purpose it may be assumed that the railroad is not operating up to the point of maximum profit and that it can handle more traffic without acquiring additional plant and equipment. Furthermore, in order not to complicate the explanation unduly, it may be assumed that a more or less stable price level and rates of wages exist. Suppose, first, that the railroad hauls 150 million ton miles of freight a year at an average charge of 1.1¢ per ton mile, that its constant costs come to $1 million, and that its variable costs equal $500,000. Under these conditions results of operation will be as follows:

Revenue (150,000,000 ton miles @ 1.1¢ per ton mile)		$1,650,000
Expense:		
Constant	$1,000,000	
Variable	500,000	
Total expense		1,500,000
Profit		$ 150,000

Now suppose that the railroad, without any change in its average charge of 1.1¢ per ton mile, experiences a 10 per cent increase in traffic, bringing its total annual volume of traffic to 165 million ton miles. Assuming that the increased traffic is still within the optimum capacity of the existing plant and equipment, what effect will it have on profitability of operations? Constant costs will, of course, remain the same as before, but the increase in traffic will necessarily be accompanied by an increase in variable costs. If, for the sake of simplicity, it is assumed that variable costs increase in the same proportion as traffic, i.e., 10 per cent, the results of operation will be as follows: [3]

```
Revenue (165 million ton miles @ 1.1¢ per ton mile)      $1,815,000
Expenses:
    Constant              $1,000,000
    Variable                 550,000
               Total expense                                1,550,000
                     Profit                                $  265,000
```

Here a 10 per cent increase in traffic has resulted in an increase in profit of almost 77 per cent, this increase being attributable to the fact that the carrier is making a more complete utilization of facilities for which it must pay whether they are used or not.

Equally startling results will follow from a 10 per cent decline in traffic from the original 150 million ton miles, again assuming that total variable costs vary in the same ratio as volume of traffic. Thus:

```
Revenue (135 million ton miles @ 1.1¢ per ton mile)      $1,485,000
Expenses:
    Constant              $1,000,000
    Variable                 450,000
               Total expense                                1,450,000
                     Profit                                $   35,000
```

Here a 10 per cent decline in traffic has caused profits to decline to a point where they are less than one-fourth of their former level. And a 15 per cent decline in traffic will result in an actual loss of $22,500 as a simple calculation will show.

These illustrations show the importance to a railroad of getting additional traffic when its plant and equipment are being operated at less than optimum capacity. They also show the unhappy results which may follow upon even a relatively small decline in traffic. It may be noted now that this phenomenon has been of importance not only to railroad management and railroad investors but also to the public in general. Suppose, for example, that the railroad finds that it can obtain a 20 per cent increase in traffic by lowering its average rate to 1¢ per ton mile. Or suppose that it has obtained a 20 per cent increase in traffic and that it has been ordered by some regulatory body to reduce its average charge to 1¢. In either

---

[3] The increase in variable costs might be either more or less than 10 per cent. For example, if a 10 per cent increase in traffic required the employment of additional labor, opportunities might arise for a greater degree of specialization, and variable costs might not increase by 10 per cent. On the other hand, traffic may increase to the point where it can be handled with the existing plant and equipment only with a more than proportionate increase in total variable costs.

event, and assuming that action by a regulatory body is not followed by a further increase in traffic, the result will be as follows:

Revenue (180,000,000 ton miles @ 1¢ per ton mile)		$1,800,000
Expense:		
Constant	$1,000,000	
Variable	600,000	
Total expense		1,600,000
Profit		$ 200,000

Under these circumstances a 20 per cent increase in traffic has reacted to the advantage of both the railroad and the public, the railroad enjoying an increased profit and the public enjoying a lower rate. Hence the desirability of promoting increased traffic when the railroad plant is not being utilized up to the point of maximum profit.

Conversely, anything which results in a reduction in traffic will react unfavorably on the public as well as on the railroads as long as plant and equipment are not being utilized beyond the point of maximum profit. Faced with sharply declining profits railroad managements in the past have skimped on maintenance and reduced service to the disadvantage of the shipping public. And they have raised rates wherever shippers could stand higher rates and where lack of competition made rate increases possible. In recent years railroads generally, faced with declining traffic and rising costs of operation, have sought to increase their rates, more especially on those commodities which cannot be handled readily by other forms of transportation.

Sources of increased traffic. It is easy enough to increase the imaginary traffic of an imaginary railroad by 10 or 20 per cent or any other figure which comes to mind, but in actual practice such increases are not so simply obtained. Railroads as a whole have enjoyed a substantial increase in traffic over the years as a result of the increase in population and the growth of trade and industry, but individual railroads quite naturally prefer to obtain more immediate results by making use of more direct methods. One of these is to create new traffic. Many railroads employ agricultural experts and livestock experts to work with the farmers they serve to improve the quantity and quality of crops and cattle. Some employ geologists and other types of experts to aid in the development of industry along their lines.

Railroads always have sought to increase their traffic by the obvious policy of taking traffic away from competing lines. Today such efforts take the form of energetic traffic solicitation, improved service, the creation of good will, and the like. But in the latter half of the nineteenth century, before the railroads were subject to effective regulation, rate cutting was a favorite method of obtaining an additional share of existing traffic. Traffic increases resulting from general economic growth, from the development of new business, and from improved service have all led to an improvement in the general public well-being. But attempts to capture a larger share of existing traffic by cutting rates at times have had almost disastrous results on the railroads and have reacted unfavorably on the public. Why this has been true will be indicated presently.

Causes of declining traffic. An understanding of the factors which cause railroad traffic to decline is just as important, and perhaps more important, than is an understanding of the means available for increasing traffic. Recurring periods of general economic stagnation are invariably accompanied by a sharp decline in railroad traffic. Every depression of any duration has had disastrous effects on railroad earnings and innumerable bankruptcies have resulted from the inability of railroad management to meet constant costs in the form of fixed charges.[4] The periods of business stagnation which began in 1873, 1884, 1893, 1907, 1920, and 1929 were all accompanied by numerous railroad bankruptcies with severe losses to security holders and poor service to the public. On July 31, 1939, ten years after the stock market crash of 1929, there were 108 railroads with a total mileage of 76,703 in the hands of the courts. In addition to general business stagnation, hard times in a particular industry or industries will be reflected in the traffic statistics of certain railroads. A good example of this sort of thing is found in the effect on traffic of the depression in agriculture after World War I. Individual railroads also suffer traffic declines as a result of technological changes and exhaustion of natural resources. For such traffic declines there is often no solution short of complete abandonment.

In recent years newer forms of transportation have sprung up to dispute the transportation field with the railroads. To some extent these newer agencies have created new traffic, but they have also obtained traffic at the expense of the railroads. Prior to the outbreak of war in 1939 these newer forms of transportation were beginning to make their competition felt, but during the war traffic was so heavy that the services of all were needed. Since the end of World War II this competition has become exceedingly keen and has contributed generally to a downward trend of railroad traffic. The various ramifications of this problem are discussed at another point.

Variability of operating expenses under present conditions. The idea that a large proportion of railroad costs is constant and that railroad earnings are, therefore, quite susceptible to variations in the volume of

---

[4] If the railroads had relied less on the sale of bonds as a means of obtaining capital, however, fewer bankruptcies would have taken place.

traffic was advanced and gained general acceptance during the era of extensive railroad construction in the latter half of the nineteenth and the first decade of the twentieth centuries. At this time billions of dollars were being invested in the construction of thousands of miles of railroad to serve new and undeveloped areas and older areas already served by existing lines, and the inevitable result was the creation of a network of railroads which possessed a carrying capacity far in excess of the needs of the times. This meant that increased traffic could be handled without a proportionate increase in cost and, conversely, that a decrease in traffic was not accompanied by a corresponding decline in costs. Hence the presence of constant costs was obvious. The era of extensive railroad construction came to an end in the early years of the twentieth century, however, and with its passing a new school of thought has appeared which holds that under present conditions railroad costs are largely variable. The conclusion is applied primarily to main line operation, and an exception is made for railroads with unusually light traffic.

The conclusion that railroad costs are largely variable is based in part on studies of the operating ratio, i.e., the ratio of operating expenses to operating revenues, made prior to World War II. These studies sought to show that railroad operating expenses can be made to vary closely with variations in the volume of traffic, it being assumed that operating revenues are a rough measure of traffic volume.[5] Other things being equal, and this is a major qualification as will be noted presently, if operating expenses contain any substantial element of constant costs, the operating ratio will be quite sensitive to variations in volume of traffic as expressed in terms of operating revenues—falling with an increase in revenues and rising as revenues decline. If, on the other hand, operating expenses are largely variable, they will tend to rise and fall somewhat in proportion with the rise and fall of revenues, and the operating ratio should not vary greatly from year to year. The year by year variations in operating revenues, operating expenses, and the operating ratio since 1921 are shown in the first three columns of Table IV.

In some respects the above figures appear to confirm the existence of an element of constant cost in operating expenses. For example, a year by year analysis shows that for the most part the operating ratio has varied inversely with operating revenues, falling with an increase in

---

[5] A direct comparison of expenses with volume of traffic is difficult because of the variety of traffic handled by the typical railroad. Railroads handle freight, passengers, mail, express, and miscellaneous traffic, and it is not easy to reduce these items to a common denominator. Nor is there a completely satisfactory way of allocating the many common costs incurred in handling the various types of traffic.

revenue and rising with a decrease in revenue. The decline in revenue which took place at the outset of the depression was accompanied by a noticeable increase in the operating ratio. The large increases in revenue which took place after the outbreak of World War II were accompanied by a substantial decline in the operating ratio, except in the years 1943 and 1944 when the railroads were called upon to handle a record volume of business with inadequate and worn-out equipment and some inexperienced labor. Since the end of World War II every decline in revenue has been accompanied by an increase in the operating ratio and every increase in revenue by a lowered operating ratio.

Table IV

OPERATING REVENUES, OPERATING EXPENSES, AND CAPITAL INVESTMENT, CLASS I RAILROADS, 1921-1950 [6]

Year	Operating Revenues	Operating Expenses	Operating Ratio	Operating Revenues	Investment in Plant and Equipment
	(in millions of dollars)			(1921—100%)	
1921	$5,516,598	$4,562,668	82.71	100	100
1922	5,559,093	4,414,522	79.41	101	101
1923	6,289,580	4,895,167	77.83	115	105
1924	5,921,496	4,507,885	76.13	108	109
1925	6,122,510	4,536,880	74.10	111	112
1926	6,382,940	4,669,337	73.15	116	115
1927	6,136,300	4,574,178	74.54	111	118
1928	6,111,736	4,427,995	72.45	111	121
1929	6,279,521	4,506,056	71.76	114	124
1930	5,281,197	3,930,929	74.43	96	127
1931	4,188,343	3,223,575	76.97	76	127
1932	3,126,760	2,403,445	76.87	57	127
1933	3,095,404	2,249,232	72.66	55	126
1934	3,271,567	2,441,823	74.64	59	125
1935	3,451,929	2,592,741	75.11	62	125
1936	4,052,734	2,931,425	72.33	73	124
1937	4,166,069	3,119,065	74.87	74	125
1938	3,565,491	2,722,199	76.35	64	125
1939	3,995,004	2,918,210	73.05	73	125
1940	4,296,601	3,089,417	71.90	78	126
1941	5,346,700	3,664,232	68.53	97	126
1942	7,465,823	4,601,083	61.63	136	126
1943	9,054,724	5,657,461	62.48	165	128
1944	9,436,790	6,282,063	66.57	172	130
1945	8,902,248	7,051,627	79.21	162	132
1946	7,627,651	6,357,415	83.35	139	133
1947	8,684,918	6,797,265	78.27	158	135
1948	9,671,722	7,472,035	77.26	176	140
1949	8,580,142	6,891,819	80.32	156	143
1950	9,473,093	7,059,276	74.52	172	146

[6] Adapted from Interstate Commerce Commission, *Statistics of the Railways of the United States,* various years.

SOME ECONOMIC CHARACTERISTICS

On the other side of the picture, attention has been called to the fact that after the first two years of the depression decline in traffic, the railroads were able to reduce their operating ratio in the face of continued declining traffic in 1932 and 1933. While they were unable to do this in succeeding years, they did maintain operating ratios which were lower than would be expected in comparison with earlier years. Furthermore, if operations during the early 1920's are discounted,[7] the variations in the operating ratio up to World War II are relatively small considering the rather wide variations in volume of traffic as measured by operating revenues.

It should be pointed out that the operating ratio does not constitute a satisfactory measure of the variability or lack of variability of railroad operating expenses because it reflects variations in the general level of rates, variations in wage rates, and variations in the general price level, as well as variations in volume of traffic. Changes in wages and prices no doubt explain in part the reduction in expenses in 1932 and 1933 and the increases in succeeding years, and they most certainly have influenced the operating ratio in the years following the end of World War II. Also, railroad management has been able to reduce expenditures in lean years by deferring certain types of maintenance work until more prosperous times. A part of the decline in the operating ratio in 1932 no doubt is traceable to such a policy. But simply to defer maintenance does not eliminate it as a cost properly chargeable to the year in which it was deferred, and clearly such a policy could not be maintained for long in the face of a prolonged decline in traffic.

Finally, it is worth noting that railroad management has been active over the years in increasing operating efficiency, a policy which tends to exert a downward pull on the operating ratio. This has helped to hold the operating ratio down during periods of declining traffic, but it does not necessarily follow that increased efficiency is accompanied by an increase in the relative importance of variable costs. In general, then, it may be said that studies based on the operating ratio cannot be accepted as providing convincing proof that operating expenses are almost wholly variable in the short run. There is some tendency to agree, however, that they are more variable than was formerly thought to be the case.[8]

---

[7] The Government operated the railroads from December 28, 1917, to March 1, 1920, as a wartime measure, and private operation in the early 1920's reflects in some respects adjustments from the period of government control.

[8] A fairly recent study of the operating expenses of the South African Railways reaches the conclusion that they were about 25 per cent constant during the year ending March, 1938. W. A. Timmerman, *Railway Expenditures and the Volume of Traffic.* New York: Manhattan Publishing Company, p. 7.

Variations in capital costs under present conditions. In addition to the claim that operating expenses are now largely variable, it has been contended that capital costs also show a considerable degree of short-run variability, at least during periods of increasing traffic. In this connection attention may be called to columns four and five in Table IV which show relative changes in operating revenues and investment in plant and equipment, using 1921 as a base. Of course, it is not satisfactory to use operating revenues for comparative purposes since they reflect variations in the general level of rates as well as variations in the volume of traffic. In defense of the use of operating revenues, however, it may be said that there is a rough correlation between operating revenues and freight ton miles hauled, although this correlation is much less marked when a comparison is made with revenue passenger miles.

Bearing in mind this limitation, it will be noted that the generally upward trend of operating revenues from 1921 to 1929 was accompanied by a steady increase in investment in road and equipment. To some extent this may represent postwar rehabilitation and to some extent it may reflect improvements which contributed to the steady decline in operating expenses which took place during this period. But it also took place during a period when there was a rather substantial increase in the volume of revenue ton miles of freight handled. The depression years, however, were not accompanied by any corresponding decline in investment, the investment account proving to be quite unresponsive to the sharp and prolonged decline in traffic. The tremendous volume of traffic generated by World War II was handled without any substantial increase in investment in plant and equipment, the figure for the peak year of 1944 not being much greater than it was for the early years of the depression. It is, of course, a well-known fact that the railroads were unable to obtain the labor and materials necessary for making improvements, a condition which is reflected in the sharp expansion of investment after the war in the face of declining revenues. This postwar expansion also may be explained in part in terms of the efforts of the railroads to improve their service to meet the competition of newer forms of transportation.[9]

What conclusions may be drawn from the figures with reference to the variability of capital costs? To begin, the figures reveal the long run tendency of investment in plant and equipment to increase with increased traffic as previously noted. But they also show a strong tendency for capital costs to increase in the short run with increased traffic. Although the increase in investment which occurred from 1921 to 1929 may be

---

[9] Should the railroads be successful in increasing their traffic in this way, then the increased investment would be the cause of increased traffic rather than the other way around.

explained, in part, in terms of factors other than increased traffic, the fact remains that traffic did increase during this time. And it seems reasonable to suppose that if government regulations had permitted, a substantial part of the increase in investment following World War II would have taken place during the war years. Under present conditions, then, it would appear that increased capital costs follow closely along with increased traffic.

In this connection it may be pointed out that prospects for increased traffic in modern times have not been sufficient to justify such expensive expansion activities as the construction of new lines or the multiple tracking of old ones. Furthermore, in those areas where traffic is heaviest, high land values make extensive developments prohibitive. Hence investment in plant and equipment tends to take the form of improvements designed to increase the capacity of existing facilities, including such things as the use of more powerful locomotives capable of hauling heavier trains, installation of heavier rail and easing curves for high-speed operation, and adoption of automatic block signals, centralized train control, hump switching, and various other devices and techniques which can be expanded unit by unit to meet the needs of increased traffic.

While there appears to be a rather close correlation between increased investment in plant and equipment and increased traffic, in the short run as well as in the long run, the same cannot be said when traffic is on the decline. Thus investment in plant and equipment in 1938 and 1939 was practically identical with investment in 1929 in spite of a much smaller volume of traffic. It may be objected that a period of ten years is hardly long enough to allow those forces which bring about a decline in investment to come into full play, and this is probably correct. But the important point to note here is that no matter how variable capital costs may be in the short run during periods of increased traffic, they are almost completely constant in the short run in face of declining traffic. In view of the rapid growth of newer forms of transportation in recent years and the keen competition for available traffic, this inability to reduce capital costs rapidly to meet declining traffic may prove to be far more significant than the ability to increase them with increased traffic.

Comparisons of individual railroads. A comparison of the operating ratios of individual railroads shows that many light traffic lines have higher operating ratios than many heavy traffic lines, suggesting the presence of constant costs. But there are many exceptions to this. For example, in 1949, the eastern railroads as a group had the highest traffic density per mile of line and also had the highest operating ratio of any major group of railroads in the United States. The operating revenues of different railroads, however, are influenced significantly by differences in operating conditions. Hence the operating ratio by itself cannot have too much significance as a measure of the presence or absence of constant costs. Attempts also have been made to show that investment in road and equipment varies closely with density of traffic, with the light traffic lines having a lower investment per mile of railroad than heavy traffic lines. This condition, however, is quite consistent with the acknowledged variability of capital costs in the long run and hardly can be considered significant as a short-run phenomenon.

Conclusion. The more recent statistical analyses of railroad costs involve too many variables to justify any definite conclusion that railroad costs today are largely variable. They do suggest, however, that costs are more variable than was formerly thought to be the case, at least in the sense that they tend to increase more nearly in proportion to increases in the volume of traffic. But during periods of declining traffic no such conclusion can be reached. On the contrary, it would seem that railroad costs are relatively unresponsive to declining traffic and, as noted above, this may prove to be a matter of considerable significance. Some practical consequences of this latter conclusion are noted in a later chapter.

COMPETITION

The growth of competition. There was little competition between railroads before 1850 because not many competitive lines were built. Building a railroad was a risky undertaking and once built the railroad needed all the traffic available. Consequently new railroads were built to serve areas and communities not yet favored with railroad transportation. Most of these lines were quite short, although in some cases they linked communities together in such a way as to make fairly long journeys possible. For example, it was possible to make a journey by rail from New York to Buffalo by way of Albany, a distance of 435 miles, but the trip required the use of twelve different railroads.

The 1850's, however, witnessed the beginning of more ambitious undertakings. Communities which had formerly been connected by a series of short lines now enjoyed through service over a single line of railroad. Obviously the short independent lines could not hope to compete with these new through lines, and they were forced to consolidate into single through systems. Indeed, in some cases, the advantages of such consolidations were recognized and unions effected even before a through line was built in the area involved. This construction of through lines and the consolidation of short local lines into through systems, coupled with the activities of promoters who sometimes built mileage in excess of the needs of the area served, laid the groundwork for a period of keen competition which began in the late sixties and continued to the close of the nineteenth century.

Destructive competition. Not only was competition keen, but in the course of time it became exceedingly destructive wherever it was allowed to operate without restriction. The explanation of this phenomenon is found in the fact previously mentioned that a substantial part of the costs of railroad operation were, and probably still are, constant in nature. If a railroad which was not operating at the point of maximum profit could get additional traffic without reducing its rates, its earnings would improve substantially, since its costs would increase only by the amount of variable expense incurred in handling the additional traffic. Indeed, it would be worthwhile for such a carrier to go after additional traffic even if it could be obtained only at reduced rates. If existing traffic yielded revenues sufficient to cover variable costs and constant costs in full, then anything the carrier could get over the variable costs of handling the additional traffic would represent a clear profit. And if existing traffic did not yield revenues sufficient to meet constant costs in full, then anything it could get from the additional traffic over and above variable costs would be helpful to it in meeting its constant costs.

During the latter half of the nineteenth century many areas were oversupplied with railroad transportation facilities, and rival railroads were under constant temptation to battle each other for traffic which could exercise a choice of routes. A railroad could afford to offer reduced rates to shippers using a competing line because, as pointed out above, anything it received over and above variable costs on such traffic represented a clear gain, but obviously such a program could not be carried on without inviting retaliation. The other railroad, also faced with costs which were largely constant in nature, could not afford to permit its traffic to be diverted in this way. Hence the second line was bound to meet the new rate and might even cut it further in an effort to draw some business from the first line. The original line would then be forced to lower its rates again, and a rate war was on.

Some examples of nineteenth century rate wars. Just as soon as railroads began to compete with one another for traffic which could exercise a choice of routes, rate cutting appeared, but the real era of rate wars began in 1869. In 1869 the charge for moving first class freight from Chicago to New York was $1.88 per hundred pounds, but in the following year the charge was forced down to a minimum of 25¢ for all classes of freight. In the early eighties immigrants were carried from New York to Chicago at a cost of $1.00 a person, and the eastbound grain rate fell to a low of 8¢ per hundred pounds. At one time freight was moved from New York to San Francisco for as little as 30¢ per hundred pounds and in 1894 every railroad in the South was involved in a rate war, with the first class rate from New York to Atlanta falling from $1.14 to 50¢.

Consequences of destructive competition. The consequences of the rate wars of the latter part of the nineteenth century were not inconsiderable. Among the happier results may be mentioned the eventual establishment of a permanently lower level of freight rates. These lower rates promoted industrial development with attendant benefits to industry and to the public in general, and the increased traffic resulting from industrial development was helpful to the railroads as well. It has been said, also, that the rate wars contributed in some degree to greater operating efficiency as railroad managements sought to offset reduced revenues with lower operating costs.

Unfortunately, the undesirable consequences of destructive competition were more numerous and more significant than the desirable ones. The rapid succession of rate wars, peace agreements, and more rate wars introduced an element of uncertainty into business activity, since businessmen found it difficult to plan ahead or to quote prices for future delivery when they did not know in advance what freight rates they would have to pay. Another none-too-happy consequence of the rate wars was the fact that rate cuts were not applied uniformly to all communities and to all shippers, with sometimes disastrous results to the less favored communities and shippers. Rate cutting was a contributing factor to the bankruptcy of a number of lines with attendant losses to railroad security holders. It also contributed to the decline of river and canal transportation. Boat line operators found it impossible to meet the deep cuts in rates, and the railroads discovered that it was worth while to carry much low grade freight which formerly had been left to the water carriers. Finally, the excesses of competition led to serious attempts to bring it under control and ultimately to a movement toward monopoly.

DISCRIMINATION

Place discrimination. One consequence of destructive competition which merits further consideration was discrimination in rate making. Rate wars were naturally confined to those points where competition existed, and the carriers saw no need for extending the low rates existing at competitive points to those communities along their lines where no competition existed. Not only did they fail to extend the benefits of rate cuts to these less fortunate points, but also they were under some temptation to raise rates at noncompetitive points in order to make up in some measure for the losses incurred where competition was severe. Competition between rail and water carriers also was an important cause of place discrimination. River cities like Vicksburg, Memphis, and New Orleans enjoyed lower rates than did intermediate points where steamboats could not penetrate. Rates from the East were lower to Mobile than to intermediate points because of the existence of coastwise shipping. Place discrimination of this type was widespread at one time in the South.

In some cases place discrimination was forced upon the carriers by competition between rival industrial or commercial centers. The way in which such discrimination might arise is shown in Figure 1.

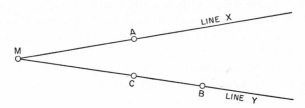

FIGURE 1. *Illustration of Place Discrimination Forced by Market Competition.*

A is a commercial center which serves, among various points, the market at M. B is also a commercial center and the business interests of B desire an opportunity to compete with A for a share of the market at M. In order to compete in M, however, shippers located at B must have rates to M comparable with those charged from A to M, and in the days before effective regulation pressure from shippers at B, coupled with its own self-interest, might induce the railroad on which B is located to reduce the rate from B to M, equalizing it with the A to M rate. Since, however, the same pressure and the same self-interest did not exist at noncommercial points intermediate between B and M, the carrier would not be likely to make a proportionate reduction in the rate from C and other intermediate points to M.

Consequences of place discrimination. As long as competition continued free of any control, either private or public, it is difficult to see how place discrimination could be avoided. Where railroads had to battle each other or to compete with water carriers for traffic at competitive points, rates were forced to artificially low levels, and they could not afford to extend these low rates to points where it was not necessary to fight for traffic. At the same time, however, it is perfectly clear that low rates at competitive points helped to build up certain communities at the expense of communities not so fortunate as to be located where keen competition existed. Many communities which had been favored with low railroad rates because they were ports of call for water carriers continued to enjoy these low rates after water transportation ceased to exist as a serious competitive threat. And it is sometimes difficult to say whether low rates to certain points were necessary because these points were commercial centers or whether these points became commercial centers because of low rates. To enable one community to develop at the expense of others under the artificial stimulation of favorable railroad rates was clearly contrary to American ideas of fair play, and it was an important contributing factor to the development of a demand for railroad regulation.

Regional place discrimination. In fairly recent years a new type of place discrimination has occupied considerable attention as a result of the complaint that rates in certain sections of the country were on a higher level than was true of similar rates in other sections. Southern interests in particular complained that rates between points in the South and from the South to the North and East were higher than those charged for movements of similar distances between northern and eastern points. This problem is considered in some detail in Chapter 13.

Personal discrimination. Personal discrimination exists when certain shippers are granted concessions which are not also made available to their competitors. It could and did exist at the same time and along with place discrimination. The technique of personal discrimination was simple. A certain shipper was selected and offered a favorable rate if he would agree to make all shipments over the line making the concession, the shipper benefiting from the lower rates and the railroad benefiting from the increased traffic. These rate concessions were invariably kept secret. To have made them public would have caused a general outcry because of their obvious unfairness and also would have invited retaliation from rival railroads, especially at points where competing lines were endeavoring to maintain some sort of an agreed scale of rates. But most important of all, secrecy resulted from the desire of the carrier involved to build up the favored shipper at the expense of his competitors so as to obtain an increased volume of traffic.

Methods employed. Prior to 1887 the most common method of granting rate concessions was through the use of some form of rebate. When this plan was followed, the railroad charged the favored shipper the same rate as was paid by his competitors on identical hauls, and later refunded or rebated a part of the amount paid. In this way it would appear to anyone who came in contact with freight bills and related documents that the shipper in question had actually paid the regular rate. The rebate might be in cash, in free transportation, in "presents," or in the form of some other valuable consideration.

Perhaps one of the most curious and at the same time one of the most flagrant of the earlier discriminatory devices was the drawback. In 1885 the Cleveland and Marietta Railroad moved crude oil for the Standard Oil

Company from Macksburg to Marietta, Ohio, at a rate of 10¢ a barrel, although it charged other shippers 35¢ a barrel for the same service. The fact that competitors were required to pay a 250 per cent higher rate in itself constituted a major discrimination. In this case, however, the Standard Oil Company not only received a rate that was 25¢ below that paid by its competitors, but it also received 25¢ from the railroad for every barrel of oil its competitors shipped out of Macksburg. Such a payment, known as a drawback, illustrates the extremes to which personal discrimination sometimes went. The Standard Oil Company, by threatening to build a pipe line to carry its oil, practically forced the management of the railroad to acquiesce to the arrangement.

In 1887 personal discrimination was prohibited by law and railroads were required, among other things, to make annual reports of receipts and expenses. Under the circumstances it became difficult to make rebates and drawbacks because they could not be shown on the books except by falsification. But various other discriminatory devices were developed which, although sometimes just as unlawful as the rebate and drawback, were not so easily detected. It was many years before this evil was brought under control.

Consequences of personal discrimination. The principal evil arising out of personal discrimination, aside from its obvious unfairness, was the encouragement it gave to the development of industrial monopolies. The development of the great industrial monopolies late in the nineteenth century coincides closely with the period of great personal discrimination in railroad rates, and there can be no doubt that rate concessions played an important part in the growth of monopoly power in this country. It is safe to say that the public has never approved of uncontrolled monopoly, and this is especially true when monopolies have been permitted to develop by the use of such artificial devices as favoritism in rate making. From this point of view alone personal discrimination stood condemned.

In addition to public concern over the evils of unregulated monopoly, the practice of personal discrimination did not always react favorably on the railroads themselves. It sometimes happened that a railroad, by granting secret rebates, helped a preferred shipper to build up a monopolistic position in his industry, only to discover that it had created a Frankenstein monster. For once a shipper had gained control of all of the traffic of a given type in his area he was in a position to secure further rate concessions by threatening to give his business to another railroad. Sometimes, too, individual railroads failed in their attempts to build up one shipper to a monopolistic position. It was not always easy to keep the agreements secret, and if other railroads found out about a rebating agreement, they might make similar reductions to other selected shippers. The shippers would once again compete on even terms and the railroads would divide the traffic as before, but at lower rates.

COOPERATION

Cooperation an outgrowth of competition. Another consequence of railroad competition that warrants some further consideration is cooperation. The rate wars of the latter part of the nineteenth century proved to be costly to the railroads, and it is not surprising that railroad managements sought to get together in an effort to raise rates to a profitable level and avoid the competitive excesses of the time.

Gentlemen's agreements. Probably the earliest, simplest, and least effective method of cooperation was the "gentlemen's agreement." Railroad managements, frightened by the disaster facing them as the result of a bitter rate war, sometimes would confer, work out a new and higher scale of rates, and each agree to abide by it. Such an informal agreement is commonly referred to as a gentlemen's agreement, but unfortunately for the success of such arrangements, gentlemen were not always gentlemen. When the management of some particularly needy or greedy carrier thought that it might gain some advantage by a rate cut or by a rebating arrangement, it broke the agreement and a new rate war was precipitated.

Traffic pools. The traffic pool was an attempt to avoid competition through an agreement designed to assure each railroad in the pool a certain percentage of the competitive traffic between specified points. The percentage was not necessarily the same for each carrier, and it could be revised from time to time to meet changed conditions. Since each carrier presumably was guaranteed enough of the competitive traffic to make its participation worthwhile, some of the temptation to solicit traffic by cutting rates was eliminated. As a result, the traffic pool met with somewhat greater success than the gentlemen's agreement.

One difficulty faced by the managers of a traffic pool involved the problem of seeing that each carrier received no more than its proper share of traffic once the percentages had been agreed upon. Usually no great differences arose between the assigned percentages and the actual traffic received, but in order to maintain the proper division of traffic, one or two large shippers would be selected at competitive points. In exchange for rate concessions these shippers would agree to shift their competitive business back and forth between the different members of the pool in order to maintain the percentages at approximately the agreed upon level. Such shippers were known as "eveners."

The money pool. The money pool allowed each member carrier to haul all traffic that came to it without recourse to traffic diversions or eveners.

In one type of money pool each member carrier kept its entire receipts from noncompetitive traffic but only a certain percentage of the revenue derived from traffic which could exercise a choice of routes. The percentage of revenue retained on competitive traffic, usually 40 to 50 per cent, was supposed to represent the actual out-of-pocket cost of moving the traffic. The remaining 50 or 60 per cent was then pooled, and periodic distributions of the pooled funds were made in accordance with previously agreed upon percentages. Not all money pools operated in exactly the same way, but the type here described will serve to illustrate the general principle.

The money pool had certain advantages over the traffic pool as far as the railroads were concerned. It eliminated the need for eveners and so the need for granting certain shippers reduced rates. Furthermore, the managers of these pools customarily had in their possession a certain amount of money belonging to all of the carriers, and any carrier which withdrew or broke the agreement forfeited its share of this money. On the other hand, the money pool was not without its weaknesses. Since each carrier was free to carry all of the traffic that came to it, there was a tendency in some cases for a carrier to seek to increase its traffic by rebates and the like so as to be able to claim a larger percentage of the pooled profits when periodic revisions of the pooling agreement came up.

Exclusive field of operation agreements. This somewhat awkward term is used here to designate a variety of arrangements in which certain areas of activity were reserved exclusively to specified carriers. For example, traffic at competitive points might be divided between the rival carriers according to the nature of the traffic, each carrier soliciting only certain specified types of traffic. In some cases a division of territory was effected, with each carrier being assigned an exclusive territory and each agreeing not to construct lines into territory assigned to the others.

Legal status of cooperation. Under the common law, pooling agreements were not unlawful, but they could not be enforced at law. As a result, pooling agreements survived only as long as the individual carriers who were parties to such agreements found it to their interest to continue them. Many pools were short-lived. In 1887 railroad pools were specifically prohibited by law, and thereafter many of the railroads organized traffic associations in which they met and agreed to fix rates but in which they were very careful, openly at any rate, not to divide competitive traffic or to pool earnings. In 1897 in the Trans-Missouri Freight Association case and in 1898 in the Joint Traffic Association case, the Supreme Court ruled that organizations of this type violated the Sherman Act and were, therefore, illegal. Since, however, it was necessary for the traffic officials of different railroads to meet from time to time to discuss numerous matters of common interest, the traffic associations were continued; and there was, perhaps, more than a suspicion that they continued to be used to limit rate competition.

Results of cooperation. It is difficult to pass final judgment on the over-all effect of the pools and other cooperative devices described in this section. The public was understandingly alarmed by evidence of the existence of agreements designed to restrict competition in rates and was aroused to action by the revelation of agreements among carriers not to invade each others' territories. On the other hand, pooling was not an unmixed evil. The dangers to the railroads and the public alike which arise when competition in rate making is allowed free play have been pointed out. Fluctuating rates, railroad bankruptcies with attendant losses to security holders, and the evils of place and personal discrimination are all traceable to the uncontrolled rate wars that broke out in the 1870's. The pool served successfully in some cases to prevent suicidal rate wars and to introduce an element of stability into railroad rates at a time when regulation was either ineffective or nonexistent. In some cases, too, pools achieved stability without at the same time maintaining rates at an artificially high level.

MONOPOLY

Nature of railroad transportation monopoly. Enough has been said about competition in the railroad field to leave, perhaps, the impression that railroad transportation is a naturally competitive industry, but this is by no means true. Railroad transportation presents an unusual combination of both competitive and monopolistic elements. In some cases monopoly has arisen because the nature of the terrain through which a line runs makes it physically impossible for more than one railroad to be built. Such a situation is said to give rise to a natural monopoly, and an outstanding example of a natural monopoly is found in the lines of the Denver and Rio Grande Western Railroad serving southwestern Colorado. The only natural break in the Colorado Rockies that is suitable for the construction of a railroad is the Royal Gorge, so narrow in places that there is room for only a single railroad track. Thus when the Denver and Rio Grande Western built through this gorge it achieved a virtual monopoly in the country to the west.

Such examples of natural monopoly are not too common. A much more common cause of monopoly in the field of railroad transportation is economic in nature and arises out of the fact that there never has been enough traffic available for every city and town in the United States to receive service from more than one railroad. There are, of course, many communities which enjoy the services of two or more railroads, and at these points competition always has existed, but strung out between these competitive points are literally thousands of cities and towns which never have been and probably never will be served by more than one railroad. To and from these thousands of communities railroad transportation is just as monopolistic as it is competitive at other points. The growth of motor transportation in recent years has given these communities the benefit of competitive transportation, although the railroad still has a monopoly on certain types of traffic.

Quite apart from the more or less inevitable types of monopoly described above, railroad magnates have at times created monopolies by artificial means. Agreements to divide up territory have been mentioned. On a much larger scale were the monopolies built up by a few individuals or large railroad companies toward the close of the nineteenth century. During a few short years in the nineties and in the first decade of the twentieth century, a large portion of the railroad mileage of the United States was divided up into a half dozen huge systems. In the West, E. H. Harriman gained a virtual monopoly of traffic moving over the central and southern transcontinental routes while the northern route was controlled by the Hill-Morgan group. In the general area north of the Ohio and east of the Mississippi, two great combinations were developed. One of these, controlled by the Vanderbilts, was built around the New York Central Railroad, and the other was built around the Pennsylvania Railroad. For a time these two groups worked in close cooperation in securing control of lesser lines in the area.

In the South, the Southern Railway, controlled by the Morgans, worked in harmony with the Louisville and Nashville and the Atlantic Coast Line, the three major railroads of the area. The New York, New Haven, and Hartford acquired an almost complete monopoly over the provision of all kinds of transportation in New England, a monopoly characterized by financial improvidence, dishonesty, wholesale bribery, falsification of accounts, and the like. Finally, the Goulds attempted to string together a system stretching from the Atlantic to the Pacific. But the Gould lines were none too strong financially, the heavy expense of linking them together with new construction was more than the system could stand, and it collapsed before it could be completed.

Legal status of monopolistic combinations. The first successful attack on monopolistic railroad combinations culminated in 1904 when the Supreme Court held that control of the Great Northern and the Northern Pacific by the Northern Securities Company, a holding company, constituted a violation of the Sherman Anti-Trust Act.[10] The Court, how-

---

[10] 193 U.S. 197.

ever, permitted the Great Northern and Northern Pacific stock, which was held by the Northern Securities Company, to be distributed *pro rata* to Northern Securities Company stockholders, the net effect of this method of distribution being to leave control of the two railroads unchanged. Late in 1912 the Supreme Court held that Union Pacific ownership of 46 per cent of the stock of the Southern Pacific was a combination in restraint of trade,[11] and in this case it refused to sanction a *pro rata* distribution of the Southern Pacific stock to Union Pacific stockholders. In 1914 the Government, after an earlier and unsuccessful attempt at dissolution of the New Haven combine, obtained an agreement from the New Haven management to dispose of the component parts of the monopoly it had built up. In view of the decisions handed down by the Supreme Court there was little else that the New Haven could do. Since 1920, as will be pointed out presently, effective control over railroad combinations has passed into the hands of federal regulatory authorities, and the dangers of uncontrolled monopoly no longer exist.

Consequences of monopolistic railroad combination. It is not easy to pass judgment on the consequences of the monopolistic railroad combinations which were effected during the late nineteenth and early twentieth centuries. The Gould lines suffered from the fact that men like Jay Gould made their money out of building railroads and manipulating their securities rather than out of efficient operation and management. Harriman used his power to exact monopolistic rates from the shipping public, and rate competition was eliminated between the Great Northern and the Northern Pacific under Hill-Morgan control, even though these two lines were in direct competition at many points.

On the other hand, while monopolistic control may have led to higher rates than were necessary, it did achieve some stability in the rate structure, and the dangers of personal and place discrimination were reduced somewhat. Furthermore, men like Hill and Harriman must be given credit for building up first class railroads and offering adequate service to the public. Jim Hill did a great deal to develop the country served by his Great Northern Railroad, and it is no misnomer to refer to him as an empire builder. Finally, many of the railroads which came into the New Haven system were connecting rather than competing lines, and to this extent some good came out of even the unfortunate New Haven monopoly.

Perhaps it may be fair to say that some of the combinations effected during the late nineteenth and early twentieth centuries were economically sound in the sense that they resulted in the establishment of well

---

[11] 226 U.S. 61.

integrated, well built, and well operated railroad systems, and certainly any reduction in destructive competition and unfair discriminatory practices was economically and socially desirable. The trouble arose from permitting combinations to be built up by individuals motivated by personal gain without taking steps to restrain their corresponding power to fleece the public. In other words, in the railroad business it was not the existence of monopoly that was bad, but rather the existence of uncontrolled monopoly. This fact is now recognized and incorporated into the law.

SUGGESTED READINGS

Most of the following books contain discussions of the various matters taken up in this chapter. The older books are particularly useful for illustrative material on pools, monopoly, and discriminatory practices.

Bigham, Truman C., *Transportation, Principles and Problems.* New York: McGraw-Hill Book Company, Inc., 1946.

Daggett, Stuart, *Principles of Inland Transportation,* 3d Ed. New York: Harper and Brothers, 1941.

Hadley, Arthur Twining, *Railroad Transportation.* New York: G. P. Putman's Sons, 1885.

Healy, Kent T., *The Economics of Transportation in America.* New York: The Ronald Press Company, 1940. Chapter II contains a vigorous exposition of the variability of railroad costs.

Johnson, Emory R. and Thurman W. Van Metre, *Principles of Railroad Transportation.* New York: D. Appleton and Company, 1920. Part III in particular is interesting and useful.

Jones, Eliot, *Principles of Railway Transportation.* New York: The Macmillan Company, 1927.

Larrabee, William, *The Railroad Question.* Chicago: The Schulte Publishing Company, 1898.

Locklin, D. Philip, *Economics of Transportation,* 3d Ed. Chicago: Richard D. Irwin, Inc., 1947.

Miller, Sidney L., *Inland Transportation.* New York: McGraw-Hill Book Company, Inc., 1933.

Timmerman, W. A., *Railway Expenditures and the Volume of Traffic.* New York: Manhattan Publishing Company.

5

Regulation
of
RAILROAD TRANSPORTATION TO 1887

THE RAILROAD A COMMON CARRIER

Duties and obligations of common carriers. Railroads are "common carriers," and it will be desirable at this point to describe briefly the common carrier business. This can be done best by outlining the duties and obligations of a common carrier as they have been developed over the years by the courts. First of all, a common carrier is one which hauls passengers or goods belonging to others. Second, it offers its services for hire. Third, it must undertake to serve all who may apply for its services. Fourth, it must serve without discrimination all those who are similarly circumstanced. Fifth, it must offer its services at reasonable rates. And sixth, it is expected to use more than ordinary care to assure the safe arrival of passengers and freight at destination.

Duties and obligations not unlimited. The duties and obligations of a common carrier are not without limit. The carrier may establish reasonable rules and regulations with regard to the conditions under which it renders its services, although it may not establish such rules to favor some users of its services over others. A carrier may limit its service in some degree by refusing to carry certain types of goods. It may even limit its services to a single type of commodity as in the case of a motor truck line equipped only with tank trucks for moving petroleum products. It may not, however, refuse to haul certain types of products for some shippers while at the same time accepting these products from others. Finally, a common carrier is required to move people or goods by the methods of its business only, and generally only over those routes or in those areas in which it professes to operate.

COMMON LAW JUSTIFICATION OF REGULATION

Laissez faire. The people of the United States have generally looked with favor on a system of free enterprise with a minimum of interference with business by government. This general attitude traces back to a philosophy of social organization called liberalism which appeared in the seventeenth and eighteenth centuries and which was based on the concept of the freedom of the individual. Under this philosophy governments would interfere with the freedom of the individual only to the extent necessary to protect the equal freedom of others. Liberalism found political expression in the concept of a democratic state, and in the course of time it found economic expression in the doctrine of *laissez faire*. Put very briefly, the idea behind laissez faire is that the individual should be allowed maximum freedom of action in the process of making a living, society interfering with the economic activities of the individual only to the extent necessary to prevent force and fraud.

This is not the place to discuss economic philosophies, but a brief resumé of the principal features of a laissez faire economy may be in order at this point. First of all, advocates of laissez faire believe that business should be carried on by private individuals rather than by government. This is consistent with their belief in individual freedom of action. In addition they believe that private ownership and operation of business is more efficient than public or government ownership. Second, the advocates of laissez faire believe that the best interests of society are promoted when each individual pursues his own personal interests. The basis for this contention is the belief that individual businessmen will seek to produce those things which are easiest to sell or those things which offer the largest profit, and it is assumed that these are the things that people want the most. Third, the advocates of laissez faire believe in competition because they contend it promotes maximum efficiency in production and at the same time protects the public from exploitation. Competition, according to the true advocate of laissez faire, guarantees the public the best possible goods at the lowest possible prices.

Although government must not engage in business itself, it plays an important part in any laissez faire economy. First, it must protect property rights because without such protection a system of private enterprise cannot function. Second, it must provide certain aids to business which by their very nature cannot be provided by business itself; a sound monetary system, for example. Third, it is supposed to protect the whole people by taking steps to encourage competition and prevent the growth of monopoly. Finally, government must provide all of those services which for one reason or another are impractical or impossible for private enterprise to provide at a profit. Such services include the provision of lighthouses, schools, roads, and public parks, to mention a few typical examples.

It was under such a laissez faire concept of economic life that England experienced that most remarkable development known as the Industrial Revolution. In a few short years in the late eighteenth and early nineteenth centuries more advances were made in developing the productive mechanism than had been made in all previous history. Unfortunately, the industrialists of the time, apparently gone mad in the search for profits and freed from all legal and social restraints, exploited the men, women, and children of England who labored in their factories and mills to the point where the whole future of the English race was endangered, and government was forced to step back into the picture with restrictions designed to protect the health and welfare of the people. Such interference, however, was held to a minimum, and the basic outlines of the laissez faire economy continued to be accepted in England and spread to the United States and the nations of Western Europe. Only in very recent times has the overriding superiority of the laissez faire system been challenged seriously. Here, then, is the source of the idea that has prevailed for so long in this country, that business should be carried on privately without interference on the part of the state.

Necessity for justifying regulation. As suggested above, a certain minimum of government interference with business in general has come to be accepted as necessary, but in the case of a few industries this interference has, for one reason or another, grown to very extensive proportions. Included in these industries are the railroads and other agencies of transportation. Also included are the so-called public utility enterprises, such as light and power plants, telephone and telegraph companies, gas companies, water works, and the like; and banks, insurance companies, and other types of financial institutions. In view of the widespread acceptance of the laissez faire concept of the relationship of government to business, how is it possible to justify the extent to which railroads, along with certain other industries, have been subjected to public control?

An historical development. To some extent it might be argued that regulation is a hangover from concepts developed by the courts in times prior to the widespread acceptance of the laissez faire doctrine. In the Middle Ages, for example, there developed the concept of a "common calling." Thus there were common carriers, common barbers, common tailors, common millers, common surgeons, and the like. The use of the term "common" in those days, however, seems to have meant nothing more than that the individuals so designated offered their peculiar services to the public at large as distinguished from those other craftsmen who worked for private account. For some reason that is not entirely clear certain of these common callings, including the services of innkeepers, wharfingers, ferrymen, and carriers, were singled out for special consideration by the courts, and a body of court decisions grew up limiting the freedom of action of individuals engaged in these businesses. Although acceptance of the laissez faire philosophy released business in general from governmental restrictions, it was probably not unnatural that the body of common law previously built up by the court decisions continued to be applied to those industries which had already been singled out for special consideration.

The agency principle. As mentioned previously, there are a few activities of a semicommercial nature which have come to be regarded as governmental prerogatives. Governments are expected to provide these services, but they may if they see fit delegate their performance to private companies. When this happens, the private company may be said to be acting as an agent of government and so subject to control by government. One of the best expositions of this point of view is found in an 1837 judicial opinion in which the Supreme Court said in part:

> That railroads, though constructed by private corporations and owned by them, are public highways, has been the doctrine of nearly all the courts ever since such conveniences for passage and transportation have had any existence....
> Whether the use of a railroad is a public or a private one depends in no measure upon the question who constructed it or who owns it. It has never been considered a matter of any importance that the road was built by the agency of a private corporation. No matter who is the agent, the function performed is that of the State. Though the ownership is private the use is public.[1]

In substantiation of the agency principle reference is sometimes made to the fact that railroads and certain other types of businesses have been granted the right of eminent domain. This is the power of the state to take property from an individual where such property is essential to some public purpose. The state may take the property in question even though the individual does not wish to part with it, although the state must pay the owner its reasonable worth. The right of eminent domain does not justify taking property for private use, and the fact that states had granted this right to railroads to enable them to obtain necessary right of way for their facilities was recognized by the Supreme Court as evidence of the public nature of the business.[2]

One difficulty with the agency principle is that the industries subject to regulation have increased in number with the years, and some of the industries regulated today hardly can be said to act as agents of government. Take the light and power industry, for example. The manufacture and sale of electricity is recognized as being subject to regulation, yet the

---

[1] *Olcott* v. *The Supervisors*, 16 Wall. 678, 694-695.
[2] *Ibid.*

provision of light has never been regarded as a peculiar function of government. Governments never attempted to regulate the manufacture and sale of candles or of lamps and kerosene, but they do regulate the activities of electric service companies. Likewise with gas: gas is used extensively for heating and cooking, and the companies engaged in its distribution and sale are subject to regulation. Coal, wood, and various petroleum products are not subject to regulation, at least to the degree that is true of gas companies. This situation does not deny the significance of the agency principle as a justification of regulation, but it does suggest the existence of some other element in the regulatory picture.

Monopoly in a field of great public interest. It may be said with some logic that all business in a laissez faire economy exists by consent of the people. The people are the customers of business, and in a free society they have the right to withdraw their patronage from business at any time they see fit, and without such patronage no business can long exist. More important than this is the fact that business as it is carried on today could not exist without the protection of property offered to it by government. The vast accumulations of property required by such present-day industrial giants as railroads, steel mills, automobile plants, and the like, could not be built up and held were it not for the protection of property guaranteed by the government. In a democratic state the people control the government, and so it may be fairly said that it is the people who provide protection for business.

Since the people make business, in the modern sense, possible, it would seem reasonable to suppose that they have the right to act to prevent business from exploiting them by charging high prices, by giving poor or discriminatory service, or by establishing arbitrary rules and regulations. To prevent such exploitation they depend upon competition which, as previously mentioned, is intended to be the great regulator in a laissez faire economy. Businessmen compete with one another for the patronage of the public, either by cutting prices, by improving the quality of their product, or by giving superior service. Thus competition is said to protect the public from exploitation by assuring the manufacture and sale of the highest quality products at the lowest prices and with the best service.

But competition cannot always be relied upon to protect the public from exploitation at the hands of business because sometimes it is impossible or impractical to have competition. There are, for example, natural monopolies. Then there are the so-called economic monopolies. The construction of a light and power plant and the erection of poles and other transmission facilities involves a tremendous investment, and the company must have all of the business it can get if it is to operate profitably. The construction of a competing plant in the same community might easily result in both companies failing. Furthermore, competition in a situation like this would involve a tremendously wasteful and unsightly duplication of facilities. Similar conditions exist in water supply companies, street railways and bus lines, telephone and telegraph companies, and the like. In the case of the telephone, public service would be greatly handicapped by competition since the subscriber to the services of one company would be able to talk only to those individuals who were on that company's lines.

Since competition does not always exist, people cannot rely entirely upon it to protect themselves from exploitation, and they must, therefore, seek some other method of protection. Here they have but two alternatives, government ownership and operation of the monopoly or private ownership under public control. In some countries the first alternative has been adopted either in whole or in part, but in England, until recent times, and in the United States, the hold of the laissez faire philosophy was so great that government ownership and operation was quite generally rejected. Thus there was left only regulation as a means of protecting the people from exploitation when competition did not exist.

It should be noted that the mere absence of competition does not of itself justify regulation. A person might, for example, obtain a monopoly of the manufacture and sale of an expensive food delicacy, but it is hardly likely that his business would be subjected to public regulation except insofar as all food processing industries, monopolistic or otherwise, may be subject to pure food and drug laws. The point is, of course, that so few people would be interested in buying such a delicacy that regulation would cost more than it would be worth. On the other hand, the services offered by a railroad or a light and power plant are invested with a very great public interest because practically everyone makes use of these services. Consequently when a monopoly exists in such a business, regulation is essential for the protection of the public well-being. Regulation is justified, then, when a monopolistic situation exists in a business involving great public interest.

It may be objected that transportation today is not monopolistic since a substantial amount of competition exists both within and between the different transportation agencies. Railroad competition, however, always has been confined to a limited number of points as was pointed out in Chapter 4, and the majority of communities throughout the United States have never had the benefit of railroad competition. Even the rise of motor transportation has not completely eliminated this monopolistic situation since there are certain commodities which it is impractical for motor carriers to handle. It would be impossible, of course, to justify the regulation of air, water, and motor carriers on the grounds that these forms of transportation are essentially monopolistic in nature, for such is not the case. There are other bases for regulation, to be mentioned presently, however, which justify control over the newer agencies of transportation. In any event, it would be impossible to regulate the rates and other activities of the railroads without at the same time applying some measure of similar regulation to their competitors.

CONSTITUTIONAL BASIS FOR REGULATION

Regulation by statutory law. The right to limit the freedom of action of businessmen engaged in certain callings was established many years ago in the English courts. The nature of these limitations and the extent to which they may be applied to different kinds of business has been developed over the years in a long series of court decisions in both England and the United States. Because of this fact it has become common to speak of the application and enforcement of these court-made limitations as regulation under the common law. But the judiciary is not the only body possessed of powers to place limitations on business. Legislatures also possess this power, and today practically all regulation in the United States is carried on under the provisions of statutes enacted by various legislative bodies. Such statutory law regulation takes precedence over common law regulation. The common law, however, may be applied to any situation which is not covered by statute law.

Constitutional limitation on regulation under statutory law. A significant limiting feature to regulation under statutory law in the United States is the fact that legislatures in this country must act within the framework of the state and national constitutions. In other words, a legislative body cannot regulate railroads or other types of businesses without having some constitutional basis for such action, and so it is necessary to inquire into the constitutional basis for regulation in the United States. The Federal Government, being a government of enumerated powers, may engage only in those activities delegated to it by the Constitution of the United States. About the only really specific authority that it has to regulate business is found in the commerce clause of the Constitution which gives Congress the right to regulate interstate and foreign commerce, but Congress has been successful in using certain other of its enumerated powers to achieve regulatory ends, including the power to levy taxes, and authority to control money and coinage and the carrying of the mails. In addition, the promise of subsidies to states which will pass laws in accord with certain congressional wishes has been used in recent years to extend the regulatory powers of Congress.

The police power. The constitutional basis for state interference with business is somewhat different from the basis for interference in the case of the Federal Government. The states' activities are limited, of course, by certain provisions of the Federal Constitution. They may not interfere with the prosecution of interstate and foreign commerce nor may they deprive a person of life, liberty, or property without due process of law, to mention two of the more common limitations on state authority. After making allowance for the various limitations of state sovereignty found in the Federal Constitution, however, there still remains a broad constitutional basis for the regulation of business by the states. The state's power to regulate business need not take the form of a specific constitutional declaration of such a right, but rather it is a part of that authority of a sovereign state which has come to be known as the police power. The police power includes all of those remaining powers which are said to reside inherently in the American state by virtue of its being a sovereign body. It may be defined succinctly as the power of the American state to restrain and regulate the use of liberty and property for the purpose of protecting the public health, safety, morals, and general welfare. It is worth noting that the use of the police power by a sovereign state is quite consistent with that basic tenet of liberalism that governments may interfere with the freedom of action of the individual where such interference is necessary to protect the equal freedom of other individuals.

A few illustrations of the police power may be in point here. Under its power to protect the public health a state may regulate the food and drug industry within its confines and may require a railroad to install sanitary drinking facilities in its passenger cars. For the protection of public safety many laws have been passed requiring manufacturing establishments to install guards for belts and flywheels. Railroads and other carriers have been required to install safety devices and to comply with rules and regulations devised by the state for the safety of its citizens. The protection of the public morals has led some municipalities, acting under police power delegated to them by the state, to outlaw indecent theatrical performances and the sale of salacious literature. Protection of the public welfare lies behind many state laws designed to restrict or prohibit the sale of liquor to minors, the outlawing of horse racing and other gambling devices, restrictions on the sale and use of firearms, and the like. More important for the present purpose is the fact that protection of the public welfare is considered a valid basis for the regulation of the rates charged and the services rendered by railroads, other common carriers, and certain other types of business.

EARLY REGULATION OF RAILROADS IN THE UNITED STATES

Initially no problem of regulation. Such railroad legislation as was enacted in the early years of the industry was designed to promote railroad construction rather than to restrict the activities of existing lines. Communities and states vied with each other in their efforts to secure new railroad lines, and states passed general railroad laws which permitted promoters to build lines wherever they chose without the necessity of obtaining special permission from state legislatures. Coupled with this desire for more railroads was the dominant laissez faire philosophy of the time. Furthermore, the many abuses which characterized railroad transportation during its period of expansion were not immediately apparent at the outset, and so there appeared to be no reason for departing from the policy of government noninterference with business.

Judicial regulation. Back in the days when the ideas of the people and their legislatures were dominated by the philosophy of laissez faire, such regulation of railroads and similar enterprises as existed was carried on under the common law and through the courts. The procedure was simple in principle; an individual with a real or fancied grievance simply brought suit in court to recover damages. In practice, however, this so-called regulation by law suit was far from satisfactory. The basic weakness of the method is found in the fact that effective regulation ought to function to anticipate and prevent abuses from developing, whereas the court procedures of the time functioned to remedy wrongs *after* they had been committed. Also, the amounts involved in individual complaints were often too small to justify the expense of court action although in the aggregate such complaints might involve substantial sums of money. Finally, the procedure was too slow to be useful. This was particularly true in the case of railroad regulation. The industry was growing rapidly and sometimes conditions changed so fast that a particular court decision no longer had any significance by the time it was handed down.

Charter regulation. Railroads were organized as corporations and as such could not operate without obtaining a charter from a state government, and some attempt was made to include regulatory provisions in these charters. In practice, however, charter regulation proved to be quite unsatisfactory. In the first place, individual charters varied widely, both within a state and as between different states, leading to wide differences in the degree of regulation applied to different railroads. Second, some of the early charters contained no provision for their amendment to meet changing conditions. Third, in some cases little effort was made by the states to see to it that the carriers complied with the provisions of their charters. And finally, the regulatory provisions were generally very poorly drawn, leaving loopholes which often rendered them ineffective.

THE GRANGER MOVEMENT

Development of demand for more effective regulation. Before 1870 there was no great public demand for effective regulation of the railroads. Such major abuses as discrimination and the elimination of competition did not become major threats to the public well-being until after the Civil War, and the public seemed to be content to rely upon competition for protection from high rates. Furthermore, the principal railroad problem, particularly in the Middle West, was to get more railroads because railroads were essential to the development of new country. Under the circumstances the people were not disposed to take any action which might discourage the construction of new mileage. On the contrary, every effort was made to encourage construction. As previously noted, Congress made enormous grants of public land while individuals and state and local governments offered inducements in the form of donations, loans, and stock and bond subscriptions. In such an atmosphere it is not surprising that there was little demand for railroad regulation.

But times have a way of changing, and shortly before 1870 a strong demand developed in the Middle West for effective railroad regulation. Overexpansion of agriculture had resulted in a sharp decline in the price of wheat in the immediate postwar period, and many farmers could not get an acceptable price for their grain on the basis of existing freight rates. On the other hand, the railroads were overexpanded, too, and apparently not in a position to make a general reduction in rates. This situation was aggravated by the fact that rates were low at competitive points and very high at noncompetitive points, a phenomenon which the farm population naturally found difficult to understand.

In addition to the foregoing basic difficulties, other factors entered into the demand for regulation. Financial manipulation had ruined some lines with attendant losses to investors. Railroads were corrupting legislators and public servants by giving them free passes and selling them stock at less than market value. There were signs of efforts to eliminate competition. And finally, the railroads of the Middle West, under the control of absentee owners, appear to have been managed without too much regard for the needs of the country, and their local agents must have done a remarkably good job of spreading ill will among the farmers of the area.

The Granger movement. The rural unrest which accompanied the decline in agricultural prices after the Civil War led to the organization in 1866 of a national secret society, the Patrons of Husbandry, among farmers in the South and West. Each lodge was called a Grange and from this developed the custom of speaking of the activities of this group as the Granger movement. The stated purposes of the Granges were to improve the conditions of farm life and to make farming more productive. Naturally they became interested in reduced railroad rates as a means of making farming more profitable, and in due course they became the focus of the demand for railroad regulation. Although nonpolitical in concept, they exercised considerable influence on state legislatures, especially in the Middle West, and so significant was this influence that the numerous regulatory measures enacted in this area in the early 1870's are commonly referred to as the Granger laws.

Maximum rate laws. The first concrete legislative result of the Granger movement was the enactment in several midwestern states of a series of maximum rate laws. The first of these laws, adopted by the State of Illinois in 1871, fixed maximum passenger fares and specified that freight rates were not to exceed those in effect in 1870. The law also prohibited place discrimination by specifying that no railroad could charge as much for a shorter haul as it charged for a longer haul involving the same kind of traffic. In the same year a somewhat similar law was passed in Minnesota, and in 1874 both Iowa and Wisconsin adopted laws which established fixed schedules of maximum charges for moving goods and passengers. In succeeding years other states in the Middle West and West enacted railroad regulatory measures.

These early laws were not the answer to the regulatory problem, principally because legislative bodies by their very nature are not suited to handle the detailed problems involved in rate making. The members of such bodies, charged with the solution of a wide variety of legislative problems, cannot devote the time or acquire the complex knowledge of operating and traffic conditions that go into the determination of specific rates. Also, the fixing of rates by legislative action is too inflexible. Conditions arise which necessitate rate changes, yet such changes could not even be initiated, at least in an upward direction, until such time as the legislature happened to be in session and happened to find time to consider the matter.

There was always the danger, too, that legislators, anxious to help their farmer constituents and no doubt irked by the sometimes arrogant attitude of railroad management, would be tempted to fix rates at destructively low levels. This attitude may account for the low level of rates established in Iowa and Wisconsin where fixed schedules of maximum rates were established directly by the legislatures. And, in conjunction with a lack of understanding of the economics of rate making, this attempt to fix rates at destructively low levels probably also entered into the framing of laws designed to prevent place discrimination which made no distinction between those rate differentials which were unreasonable and those which were quite proper and economically sound.

Commission regulation. The idea of handling certain railroad regulatory matters through a small body of public servants working outside of the legislature is almost as old as the railroad itself. The first such commissions were established in New England, and out of them developed the so-called advisory commission, of which the Massachusetts commission established in 1869 is probably the best known. The advisory commissions investigated railroad activities to determine whether or not the carriers were living up to the terms of their charters and such laws as might be applicable to them. These commissions could hear complaints and could initiate investigations on their own account. After a hearing they could publish their findings and make recommendations, but the railroads were not required to comply with these recommendations. If the commission felt that a given situation could be resolved only by legislation, it proposed such legislation to the governing body of the state.

At first blush the advisory commission would appear to offer a peculiarly innocuous type of regulation since it had no power to do anything other than report and recommend. Nevertheless, in the areas in which it originated, the advisory commission worked fairly well. In Massachusetts, for example, the commission dealt with a railroad system that had achieved a degree of stability and had outgrown many of the abuses incident to a period of rapid growth. Furthermore, the eastern railroads were largely locally owned, and their stockholders and managers were friends and neighbors of the people who used the railroads for moving goods or for personal travel. Hence railroad management was much more sensitive to public opinion than might otherwise have been the case.

While the advisory commission seems to have worked well enough in the East, it was not acceptable to western advocates of railroad regulation. In this part of the country the railroads were still in the expansion stage, and all of the abuses characteristic of such a stage of development were present. Furthermore, absentee ownership was common, and the owners of the lines, many of whom lived in the East and in Europe, were not amenable to the pressure of public opinion. Consequently the Middle West gave birth to mandatory commissions possessing positive powers of control. The principle of the mandatory commission was simple enough. The legislature enacted some general piece of legislation, such as a statement to the effect that all rates must be just and reasonable, and then proceeded to establish a commission with the power to decide in each individual case whether or not a given rate was just and reasonable.

Laws establishing mandatory commissions appeared contemporaneously with the maximum rate laws discussed above. Indeed, they were as much a part of the Granger legislation as the maximum rate laws themselves. Illinois, for example, established a railroad and warehouse commission as early as 1871, although this commission was organized somewhat along the lines of the earlier New England advisory commissions. Two years later, however, Illinois repealed its maximum rate law and vested the power to fix maximum rates in its railroad commission. Similarly, the Minnesota maximum rate law was repealed in 1874 and the fixing of maximum rates, as well as certain other regulatory matters, was placed in the hands of a commission of the mandatory type. The Wisconsin legislation combined a maximum rate law with a commission empowered to lower but not to raise the rates above the statutory limits. Iowa, alone, failed to adopt the commission technique.

Decline of the Granger movement. After a few years the widespread and outspoken demand for control of railroad activities died down, and the Granger laws were repealed in the principal states involved, with the exception of Illinois which retained its legislation. In 1875 Minnesota abandoned the mandatory commission it had set up only a year before and substituted a single commissioner operating on the advisory principle. In 1876 Wisconsin also substituted a single commissioner with no real power, and in 1878 Iowa abandoned its maximum rate law in favor of an advisory commission.

The repeal of the Granger laws must be attributed in no small measure to the activities of the railroads themselves. They carried on an extensive propaganda campaign designed to show that the laws were harmful to both business and agriculture, and they sought to comply with the laws in such a way as to bring about a public demand for their repeal. In their campaign to discredit the Granger laws the railroads were aided in some measure by economic conditions. The panic of 1873 naturally resulted in a decline in railroad construction, but the railroads took advantage of the situation to claim that their financial difficulties and the cessation of construction were the consequences of the Granger laws.

Revival of positive control. The repeal of the Granger laws and the substitution of innocuous commission regulation of the advisory type did not, of course, eliminate the evils out of which the original demand for regulation developed, and in a few years a strong demand developed for a revival of positive control. Minnesota led off in 1885 with a new commission with power to fix rates. States which had abandoned more effective means of control for advisory commissions switched over to the mandatory commission. States undertaking regulation for the first time adopted mandatory commissions, and even the eastern states abandoned their advisory commissions in favor of the mandatory type. By

1887, the year in which the Federal Government established a national mandatory type commission, twenty-five states had established regulatory commissions. Today every state has a regulatory body of some kind.

CONSTITUTIONALITY OF REGULATION

Granger laws contested in the courts. It is not to be supposed that railroad managements accepted without a fight the principle of regulation embodied in the Granger laws. On the contrary, they took the attitude that railroad transportation was a private business enterprise carried on for profit and that the public had no more right to regulate the railroad business than it had to regulate any other kind of a private business undertaking. It is true that occasionally they chose to accept a regulatory law, but this was only because they saw an opportunity to discredit it in the eyes of the people by placing the worst possible interpretation on it. For the most part they contested the laws, with the result that much of the Granger legislation was promptly tied up in the courts. The issues involved were finally resolved by the Supreme Court in 1876 in favor of the people in a series of cases known as the Granger cases, involving legislation enacted by the states of Illinois, Iowa, Minnesota, and Wisconsin.[3]

Right to regulate. The fundamental issue of the right of the people to regulate certain callings was raised in *Munn* v. *Illinois*, the first of the Granger cases to be decided. Munn and Scott were operators of huge terminal grain storage elevators in Chicago, and they had contested the validity of an Illinois statute fixing maximum rates to be charged for storing grain. Munn and Scott contended, among other things, that the legislative fixing of rates acted to deprive them of property without due process of law and was, therefore, repugnant to the recently adopted Fourteenth Amendment to the Constitution.

The Supreme Court, however, rejected the idea that legislative price fixing necessarily constituted taking property without due process of law. It found that the business in question was clothed with a public interest and was, therefore, subject to control by the public for the common good, although the Court was not clear on just how it was determined that a business was clothed with a public interest. The Court did point out that the elevation and storage of grain in Chicago was an essential part of the movement of grain from producing areas to its ultimate destination. It also

---

[3] *Munn* v. *Illinois*, 94 U.S. 113; *Chicago, Burlington and Quincy Railroad Company* v. *Iowa*, 94 U.S. 155; *Peik* v. *Chicago and Northwestern Railway Co.*, 94 U.S. 164; *Chicago, Milwaukee, and St. Paul Railroad Company* v. *Ackley*, 94 U.S. 179; *Winona and St. Peter Railroad Company* v. *Blake*, 94 U.S. 180; *Stone* v. *Wisconsin*, 94 U.S. 181.

noted that the Chicago elevators were controlled by a few firms which got together each year to fix the rates to be charged for their services.[4] Although the Court did not say so, it will be obvious that here was a situation involving monopolistic control of a business affected with a great public interest. While the railroads were not involved in this particular case, the principle established was equally applicable to them and was so applied by the Court in other Granger cases.

Judicial review. It was also argued in the Granger cases that the owner of property was entitled to a reasonable compensation for its use, even though the property was clothed with public interest, and that the determination of what was a reasonable compensation was a matter for the courts, and not legislatures, to decide. The Supreme Court rejected this contention on the ground that if a state legislature had the power to regulate at all, it had the power to regulate rates. The Court recognized that this was a power which might be abused, but concluded that for protection from legislative abuse the people must resort to the polls rather than to the courts.[5]

It is a little difficult for one not schooled in the niceties of the law to understand the logic of the Court's position on this point, for it would seem obvious that the judiciary must have some final word in the fixing of rates charged by regulated enterprises. Otherwise, the only check on the power of a legislature to fix destructively low rates would be the legislature's own realization of the ultimate effect of such rates on the ability of regulated enterprises to continue to offer service. And certainly to say that the remedy for such legislative abuse was recourse to the polls was somewhat less than realistic. It would be hard to conceive of Illinois farmers, for example, going to the polls and voting into office a candidate who had campaigned on a platform of higher freight rates. In a later case the Court reached the conclusion that the power to regulate was not the power to destroy and that a state could not require a railroad to carry persons or property without just reward.[6]

Power to regulate interstate commerce. A third point raised in the Granger cases involved the extent to which the states could exercise jurisdiction over interstate commerce. For example, a shipment moving between a point in Iowa and a point in Illinois was interstate commerce without question, but could the states involved regulate those parts of the movement which took place within their respective boundaries? On this

---

[4] *Munn v. Illinois,* 94 U.S. 113.
[5] *Ibid.*
[6] *Stone v. Farmers' Loan and Trust Company,* 116 U.S. 307 (1886).

point the Supreme Court held, in effect, that *until Congress undertook to regulate interstate commerce* a state could regulate that part of an interstate movement which took place within its own borders to the extent necessary to protect its own citizens.[7]

Contractual nature of railroad charters. At the time the Granger laws were enacted most of the railroads involved operated under charters which gave them the right, either directly or by implication, to fix their own rates. These charters, they contended, were contracts entered into between the states and the railroad corporations, and any attempt on the part of the states to fix rates constituted a violation of Article I, Section 10 of the Constitution, which prohibits the states from passing any law impairing the obligation of contracts.[8] On this point the Supreme Court held, in effect, that the right of the states to regulate railroads was firmly established at the time the charters were granted, even though it had not been exercised, and the mere fact that a charter had been granted which authorized a railroad to fix its own rates did not carry with it a renunciation of the state's own superior right to regulate unless such renunciation was specifically included in the terms of the charter.[9]

Constitutionality of commission regulation. One point remains to be settled, and that has to do with the constitutionality of the mandatory commission as an instrument of regulation. The establishment of commissions with regulatory powers was promptly challenged as an unconstitutional delegation of legislative power on the ground that the constitutions of the various states and of the Federal Government vested legislative power in the hands of elected legislatures, and these bodies could not abdicate this power without doing violence to the constitutions involved. In various cases, however, the Supreme Court held that commissions were no more than administrative boards created by the states for carrying into effect the will of the state as expressed by its legislature. In other words, a legislature may not delegate its power to make a law, but it can delegate the power to administer a law to a regulatory commission.[10]

---

[7] *Chicago, Burlington and Quincy Railroad Company* v. *Iowa*, 94 U.S. 155 (1876).

[8] This contention was based on an 1819 decision of the Supreme Court in the Dartmouth College Case (4 Wheat. 518) holding that a charter is a contract, the obligation of which cannot be impaired without violating the Constitution.

[9] *Chicago, Burlington and Quincy Railroad Company* v. *Iowa*, 94 U.S. 155 (1876).

[10] See *Railroad Commission Cases*, 116 U.S. 307 (1886); *Field* v. *Clark*, 143 U.S. 649 (1892); *Reagan* v. *Farmers' Loan and Trust Co.*, 154 U.S. 362 (1894).

SUGGESTED READINGS

Barnes, Irston R., *The Economics of Public Utility Regulation.* New York: F. S. Crofts and Company, 1942. Useful in connection with the judicial development of regulation.

Cooley, T. M., *A Treatise on Constitutional Limitations.* Boston: Little, Brown & Company, 1903. The police power.

Daggett, Stuart, *Principles of Inland Transportation,* 3rd Ed. New York: Harper and Brothers, 1941. Contains a brief account of the development of the Granger laws.

Glaeser, Martin G., *Outlines of Public Utility Economics.* New York: The Macmillan Company, 1931. One of the best accounts of the development of the common law basis for regulating carriers and other utilities.

Hadley, Arthur Twining, *Railroad Transportation.* New York: G. P. Putnam's Sons, 1885. An early text on transportation.

Healy, Kent T., *The Economics of Transportation.* New York: The Ronald Press Company, 1940. Brief textbook account of the development of railroad regulation.

Johnson, Emory R. and Thurman W. Van Metre, *Principles of Railroad Transportation.* New York: D. Appleton and Company, 1916. Development of Granger laws.

Jones, Eliot, *Principles of Railway Transportation.* New York: The Macmillan Company, 1927. Development of regulation in the United States.

Larrabee, William, *The Railroad Question.* Chicago: The Schulte Publishing Company, 1893. An interesting account of the development of regulation with particular reference to Iowa. By a governor of Iowa who played an active part in regulatory legislation.

Thompson, C. Woody and Wendell R. Smith, *Public Utility Economics.* New York: McGraw-Hill Book Company, Inc., 1941. Judicial development of regulation.

6

Federal Regulation

of

RAILROAD TRANSPORTATION (I)

THE ACT TO REGULATE COMMERCE

Appearance of demand for federal regulation of railroads. The seemingly high and certainly discriminatory freight rates which, along with other factors, contributed importantly to the demand for state regulation of railroads also contributed to a demand for federal regulation. The farmers of the Middle West were not slow to appreciate the price advantage which would accrue to them if they could dispose of their surplus grain in a wider market, and such a market appeared to exist in the East and in Europe. But in order to sell grain at a profit at these more distant points they had to have lower rates to the East. Here was a situation that could not be solved by the individual legislatures of the Granger states. The Iowa farmers, for example, might count on the Iowa legislature to provide or attempt to provide low rates on grain as far as the Iowa-Illinois boundary, but they had no control over the rates charged by the railroads across Illinois, Indiana, Ohio, Pennsylvania, and New York. Federal control over such rates was the only solution, and the need for such control was soon recognized in Washington.

Failure of Congress to act. The right of Congress to regulate interstate commerce was clear, but Congress was slow to exercise this right. In 1874 the Windom Committee reported to the Senate that the defects and abuses of transportation at that time were insufficient facilities, unfair discrimination, and extortionate charges; and recommended, among other things, federal regulation of the railroads. No action was taken on the Windom Committee report, nor was any action taken on regulation during the ensuing twelve years, although the matter continued to be debated. During this twelve-year period the primary complaint against the railroads shifted from high rates to discrimination, and particularly to personal discrimination. Dissatisfaction with the apparent inability of Congress to enact legislation to bring objectionable railroad practices under control led to political repercussions, and several western congressmen lost their seats because of indifference or enmity to railroad regulation. In 1885 the Senate appointed the Cullom Committee to investigate and report on railroad regulation, and in 1886 this committee recommended that steps be taken to prevent discrimination and to establish a commission to enforce the law.

Wabash decision. Sharp differences existed between the House and the Senate on the subject of railroad regulation, and these differences might have continued to delay action had it not been for a decision handed down by the Supreme Court in the Wabash case.[1] In this case the Court, reversing its earlier stand in the Granger cases, held that the states could not regulate any part of an interstate movement, not even that part which took place wholly within the boundaries of a single state. This decision was of critical importance because approximately three-fourths of railroad traffic at this time was interstate in the sense that it crossed a state boundary. This meant that three-fourths of all traffic would go unregulated unless Congress acted. The consequences of further delay were too clear to be ignored. The House and Senate promptly resolved their differences and the Act to Regulate Commerce became law on February 4, 1887.

The Act to Regulate Commerce. The Act to Regulate Commerce contained twenty-four sections, the more important provisions of which are summarized below.

Section 1 specified that the act was to apply only to interstate and foreign commerce by railroad or by a combination of rail and water movement under common control, management, or arrangement. The section also provided that all rates were to be reasonable and just, and prohibited every unjust and unreasonable charge.

Section 2 forbade rebates, and personal discriminations of every sort were forbidden.

Section 3 prohibited undue preferences in matters other than rates, thus being in a sense an extension of Section 2. It declared it to be unlawful for any carrier to give any undue or unreasonable preference to any particular person, company, locality, or description of traffic in any respect whatsoever.

Section 4 made it "unlawful for any common carrier subject to the provisions of the act, to charge or receive any greater compensation in the aggregate for the transportation of passengers or like kind of property, under substantially similar circumstances and conditions, for a shorter than for a longer distance over the same line, in the same direction, the shorter being included within the longer distance. . . ." The Interstate Commerce Commission, which was provided for in a later section of the act, was

---

[1] *Wabash, St. Louis, and Pacific Railway Company* v. *Illinois,* 118 U.S. 557 (1886).

given authority, after an investigation, to permit departures from this provision.

This part of the act came to be known as the long and short haul clause. It represented an effort on the part of Congress to make a distinction between unwarranted place discrimination and differences in rates for which some sound economic justification existed. For example, some of the early state laws prohibited a railroad from charging as much for a short haul as it charged for a longer haul anywhere else on its line, but such prohibitions were unsound in that they failed to take into consideration differences in the nature of the terrain, in operating costs, and in traffic densities. How the long and short haul clause was designed to avoid these difficulties may be shown by means of a simple illustration (Figure 2).

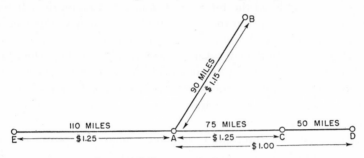

FIGURE 2. *Long and Short Haul Clause Discrimination.*

Assume that a rate of $1.00 has been established for the 125 mile haul from A to D. Charging a rate of $1.15 for the 90 mile haul from A to B would not violate the law because the haul is not over the same line, nor would a charge of $1.25 between A and E be a violation because the shorter distance EA is not within the longer distance AD. Nor would a rate of $1.00 from A to D prevent the charging of a higher rate from C to A. Here the movement is over the same line and the shorter is included in the longer, but it is not in the same direction. But assuming substantially similar circumstances and conditions the law would not permit a higher charge from A to C than that charged from A to D or a higher charge from C to A than charged from D to A.

Section 5 declared all agreements for pooling freight or for dividing earnings to be unlawful.

Section 6 stated that all rates and fares were to be printed and posted for public inspection and filed with the Interstate Commerce Commission. Ten days' advance notice was required before any rate increase could go into effect and in 1889 the act was amended to provide for three days' notice of any rate decrease. All charges other than those published were prohibited. The purpose of these prohibitions was to prevent discrimination. Before this time few shippers ever saw printed rate sheets, and this made it fairly easy for carriers to practice personal discrimination. The actual posting of rates and giving notice in advance of rate changes, together with the requirement that the rates posted must be the ones charged, was supposed to make it difficult for carriers to discriminate against smaller shippers by keeping them in ignorance of actual rates.

Section 10 provided for a maximum fine of $5,000 for each violation of the act upon conviction of the offending party in the courts. In 1889 this section was amended to include imprisonment for certain violations, and this penalty was extended to include the shipper as well as the carrier where rebates were obtained by means of falsifications of various kinds.

Section 11 established the Interstate Commerce Commission. It was to consist of five members, no more than three of whom were to be from any one political party. Members were to be appointed for six-year terms by the President with the approval of the Senate. No commissioner could engage in any other employment nor could he have any financial interest in any common carrier organization. Originally the Commission was to report to the Secretary of the Interior, but in 1889 it was made an independent agency.

Section 12 gave the Interstate Commerce Commission power to require witnesses to testify and to demand the production of books and documents of all sorts which might bear on any matter being investigated. The testimony or evidence a witness might give was not to be used against him in any subsequent criminal action in which the witness might be the defendant.

Section 13 provided that complaints received by the Commission were to be forwarded to the carrier or carriers involved, and if the matter was not settled in this way, the Commission was to conduct an investigation. The Commission was also given the right to conduct investigations on its own volition.

Section 14 declared that after making an investigation the Commission was to make a report in writing, which was to relate its findings concerning the facts involved and its recommendations on the disposition of the case. The Commission's findings were to be *prima facie* evidence in all subsequent judicial proceedings concerning the facts of the case. The framers of the act had in mind here that the work of investigating and deciding upon the facts of each case would be done by the Interstate Commerce Commission and that in any subsequent judicial proceedings the courts would confine themselves to a review of questions of law. Thus the courts would accept the Commission's report as a true and complete statement of the facts involved, but they might question the Commission's interpretation of the law or the constitutionality of the law itself.

Section 15 stated that if the Commission found that a carrier had violated the act, it was to order the carrier to desist from further violation, and if the complaining party had suffered damage, the carrier was to make reparation to that party. If the carrier obeyed the order, the matter was closed.

Section 16 declared that if a carrier refused to obey an order of the Commission, the Commission or some other interested party could apply to a federal court for an enforcing order. The court was to hear the matter promptly and if it found that the order had been violated, it might issue an injunction requiring obedience.

Section 20 authorized the Commission to require annual reports and empowered it to prescribe a uniform system of accounts for all carriers coming under its jurisdiction.

EMASCULATION OF THE ACT TO REGULATE COMMERCE

General. President Cleveland appointed able men to the new Interstate Commerce Commission, and it went about its duties in an atmosphere of conciliation and cooperation. Rate changes were made in conformity with the long and short haul clause, pools were abandoned, tariffs simplified and published, and substantial improvements made in statistical and accounting practices. But the success of the Commission was short-lived. The law under which it operated was admittedly tentative in nature. It was in part a compromise between the conflicting views of different groups, and compromises are often satisfactory to nobody. Thus the difficulties in which the Commission soon found itself were due in some measure to inherent defects in the law, but at the same time it is hard to escape the conclusion that they also were the result of a rather narrow interpretation of the law by the courts. In any event, after two or three years of success, the Commission was in trouble, and ten years after its passage the Act to Regulate Commerce was practically a dead letter.

Refusal of witnesses to testify. The law prohibited rebating, and the Commission undertook a vigorous prosecution of this evil. But rebates were by nature secret arrangements, and the only way their existence could be proved was through the testimony of those who had participated in them or witnessed the actual proceedings. In 1890 a shipper declined to say whether or not he had received a rebate on the ground of self-incrimination. His defense was the Fifth Amendment to the Constitution of the United States which states that no person shall be compelled to be a witness against himself in any criminal case. It is true that the law specified that any testimony a witness might give could not be used against him in a subsequent action in which he was the defendant, but the Supreme Court agreed that once a shipper admitted having received a rebate, it would not be too difficult for the Government to gather other evidence to convict him in a later action.[2] In 1893 Congress passed the Compulsory Testimony Act which provided that no witness should be prosecuted for anything about which he might testify in connection with an alleged violation of the Act to Regulate Commerce, and in 1896 the Supreme Court held that this provided full immunity to witnesses.[3]

Court delay. The Commission was handicapped in its activities by the seemingly interminable delay of court procedures. It reported two cases before the courts for five years, another for six, and still another for nine. Under the circumstances the railroads found it advantageous to ignore the Commission's orders, and shippers found it less and less worth while to use the Commission's services. Contributing importantly to the delay was the practice followed by the courts of rehearing the facts of cases appealed from the Commission. It had been supposed that the courts would confine themselves to questions of law, accepting the Commission's findings as *prima facie* evidence of the facts involved in a given case, but this the courts did not do. Indeed, not only did they rehear the evidence, but also permitted the carriers to introduce evidence not previously presented to the Commission. Thus it sometimes happened that the Commission issued an order based on a given set of facts, which was later rejected by the courts on the basis of a more complete set of facts. There is more than a suspicion that carriers deliberately withheld evidence from the Commission, for if the Commission were reversed frequently enough, it would be discredited in the public mind.

Rate-making powers. The Act to Regulate Commerce did not give the Interstate Commerce Commission specific power to fix rates. In actual practice the railroads fixed their own rates, but if after a hearing the Commission found a rate unreasonable, it determined the reasonable rate to be used as a basis for awarding reparations to injured shippers, and this became the rate for the future. In 1897, however, in the Maximum Freight Rate case the Supreme Court held that the Commission's authority was limited to determining whether or not a given rate was reasonable and that it had no power to specify a rate to take the place of one declared unreasonable.[4]

---

[2] *Counselman* v. *Hitchcock,* 142 U.S. 547 (1892).
[3] *Brown* v. *Walker,* 161 U.S. 591.
[4] *Interstate Commerce Commission* v. *Cincinnati, New Orleans and Texas Pacific Railway Company,* 167 U.S. 479.

FEDERAL REGULATION

The effect of this decision was disastrous. It left the Commission with the power to declare a rate unreasonable and order its reduction, but without any power to say what the reasonable rate would be in the future. It meant that once the Commission had found a rate unreasonable and had ordered its reduction, the carrier could lower the offending rate a fraction of a cent and fully comply with the order. Of course, a second investigation could be instituted and the new rate found unreasonable and ordered reduced, but again all the carrier needed to do was to reduce it another fraction of a cent. Under such circumstances any effective control over interstate freight rates was nonexistent.

Long and short haul clause. The original long and short haul clause was a peculiar combination of the specific and the vague. The statement that a carrier should not charge more for a short haul than for a long haul over the same line, in the same direction, the shorter being included in the longer, was so definite that it left no room for interpretation. But this prohibition applied only "under substantially similar circumstances and conditions," a statement as indefinite as the first one was definite. In one of its very first cases the Interstate Commerce Commission outlined its views on the circumstances and condition which might or might not justify a lower charge to the more distant point.[5] It recognized that a lower charge might be justified at points where carriers subject to its jurisdiction were in competition with carriers not subject to its jurisdiction, e.g., water carriers and intrastate railroads, but otherwise only under rare and peculiar circumstances.

The Commission specifically refused to recognize that competition between carriers which were subject to its jurisdiction justified a departure from the long and short haul principle. Suppose, for example, that two carriers, X and Y, operated between A in one state and B in another, with C a point on X intermediate between A and B. Here the Commission would not recognize competition at A and B as justifying a lower rate from A to B than was charged from A to C, for both railroads were subject to its jurisdiction. The Commission's views here are understandable since this was exactly the kind of discrimination that the law was designed to prevent. The Commission also refused to recognize the desire to encourage manufacturing or to build up trade centers as sound reasons for permitting departures from the long and short haul clause.

The question of the validity of the Commission's interpretation of the long and short haul clause was raised before the Supreme Court in the Alabama Midland case, decided in 1897.[6] In the course of its opinion in

[5] *In re Louisville & Nashville R.R. Co.*, 1 I.C.R. 31 (1887).

[6] *Interstate Commerce Commission* v. *Alabama Midland Railway Company*, 168 U.S. 144. See also 181 U.S. 1 (1901).

this case the Court declared, in effect, that competition between railroads and competition between trading centers must be given due consideration in determining the similarity or dissimilarity of conditions at different points. Since this sort of competition was largely responsible for the place discriminations the law was designed to prevent, the result of the decision in the Alabama Midland case was to destroy the whole purpose of the long and short haul clause. The combined effect of this decision and the decision in the Maximum Freight Rate case was to leave the Commission powerless to do very much other than make reports and issue protests. The Commission itself remarked that by virtue of judicial decision, it had ceased to be a body for the regulation of interstate carriers, and "The people should no longer look to this Commission for protection which it is powerless to extend." [7]

Personal discrimination. Section 2 of the Act to Regulate Commerce prohibited rebates and personal discrimination of every sort, a provision which was so simple and clear that it could not be attacked in the courts. Carriers and favored shippers proved adept at evading the intent of the law, however, and the list of discriminatory devices adopted appears to be almost endless. With the carrier's knowledge, a shipper might mis-describe a shipment on the bill of lading, or the wrong rate might be applied, and if the discrepancy were detected, either or both parties could plead that the error was unintentional. A tariff might contain a typographical "error" which would be "corrected" as soon as it had served its purpose. Some important shippers were sellers of railroad supplies, and by paying favored shippers higher than market prices for such supplies, railroads in effect granted them rebates. The big meat packers owned fleets of refrigerator cars which they rented to the railroads for excessive sums, the effect again being that of granting a rebate. Sometimes favoritism took the form of granting certain shippers free services, and sometimes the railroads allowed shippers excessive sums for services performed for the railroads.

Many industrial concerns own trackage in and about their plants, which trackage connects with the lines of one or more railroad companies so that freight in carloads may be switched to and from the plant for loading and unloading. In the late 90's and early 1900's some companies proceeded to incorporate these privately-owned switching tracks as railroad companies, all of the stock of the railroad being owned by the industry it served. As independent railroads these new companies were entitled to establish joint rates with connecting lines and to share in the division of such rates. In some cases these so-called industrial railroads received as

---

[7] Interstate Commerce Commission, *Annual Report,* 1897, p. 51.

much as twenty-five per cent of the joint through rate even though their lines might be only a few hundred or a few thousand feet long. Since the profits enjoyed by the industrial railroads were returned to the industrial concerns owning them, the result was a clear discrimination in favor of such businesses.

THE ELKINS ACT

Demand for more effective regulation. No doubt the Supreme Court was technically correct in its interpretation of the Act to Regulate Commerce, but the fact remains that with the Commission stripped of all effective authority the abuses which it had been hoped would be checked or eliminated continued unabated. In addition to the obvious need for a rehabilitation of the Act to Regulate Commerce, certain new developments contributed to a rising demand for further legislation at the turn of the century. One of these was the spread of consolidation referred to in Chapter 4. The people still had faith in the efficacy of competition, and they did not relish the prospect of being placed at the mercy of huge railroad combines subject to no effective public control. A second new development was the growth of the antitrust movement. Various revelations had been made of how discriminatory freight rates had contributed to the growth of some of the great monopolies of the time, and the people demanded action to bring this sort of thing to an end. Finally, rising freight rates must be mentioned. Rising freight rates were in part a reflection of the spread of consolidation and of cooperation in rate making, and they gave the people a prevue of what might be expected if monopoly were permitted to grow unchecked and unregulated.

Elkins Act. The first important legislative attempt to strengthen the Act to Regulate Commerce was the Elkins Act of 1903, its sole purpose being to eliminate personal discrimination as far as possible. The Elkins Act was sponsored by the railroads themselves, for the railroads had come to realize that rebating and rate cutting was leading to a serious depletion of revenues without any over-all offsetting advantages. The Elkins Act made railroad corporations as well as their officers and agents liable in the event of a violation of the law. Formerly the individual or individuals responsible for granting a rebate could be punished if found guilty, but the railroad corporation which might benefit from such acts remained untouched. Second, the penalty of imprisonment was dropped because it was believed that witnesses tended to be reluctant to testify if their testimony might lead to the accused being sent to jail. Third, any departure from a published rate was an offense. Formerly it had been necessary to show that one shipper received a lower rate than others in order to prove discrimination, and this was sometimes difficult to do. Fourth, receivers of rebates were made liable as well as the carriers giving such rebates. Under the earlier law the shipper was liable only in the event of a falsification on his part, and this had made it possible and profitable for large shippers to bring pressure on railroads to grant rebates since they could not be prosecuted if caught. Finally, the new law made some improvements in the methods of enforcing obedience through judicial processes.

THE HEPBURN ACT

Congressional history of the act. The railroads would have been more than content to let matters rest with the Elkins Act, but there was a growing public demand for more positive action. The railroads sought to counteract this development with a widespread propaganda campaign employing the most devious and dubious methods, but fortunately the public had at this time a powerful advocate in the person of President Theodore Roosevelt, who in 1904 and again in 1905 demanded congressional action on railroad regulation. A breakdown of railroad service, investigations of financial scandals, revelations of propaganda techniques, and a number of flagrant violations of the law all contributed to the demand for a new law. The need for action was so clear that both Houses of Congress approved the Hepburn bill which became law on June 29, 1906.

Provisions of act. The provisions of the Hepburn Act may be summarized conveniently as follows: (1) The scope of the Act to Regulate Commerce was extended to include express companies, sleeping car companies, industrial railroads, private car lines, and pipe lines other than those engaged in moving water and gas. (2) The Interstate Commerce Commission was given the power to fix maximum rates, and to establish joint routes, together with the maximum joint rates to be applied, and the division of such rates where carriers could not agree on a division. It could also determine switching charges and the division of rates where industrial and terminal railroads were involved. It could establish reasonable charges for facilities or services provided for the railroads by shippers and reasonable charges for icing and storage and various other services and facilities provided by railroads for shippers. (3) Thirty days' notice was required for any rate change, up or down. (4) Passes were prohibited except for railroad employees and certain other limited groups. (5) The penalty of imprisonment was restored and the maximum fine fixed at $20,000. In addition, the receiver of a rebate was liable to a sum equal to three times the value of rebates received by him during the six years prior to the commencement of action against him. (6) A "commodities clause" described below was included. (7) Enforcement procedures were strengthened somewhat. (8) Accounting procedures and the like were strengthened. (9) The number of commissioners was increased to seven, the term of office to seven years, and individual salaries were raised to $10,000 a year.

Enlargement of rate-making powers. Probably the most important single provision of the Hepburn Act was that which gave the Interstate Commerce Commission power to fix maximum rates after determining that an existing rate was unreasonable. Some of the members of Congress wanted to keep rate-making matters in the hands of the judiciary in spite of, or perhaps because of, the weaknesses of judicial rate regulation, but those who fought for really effective regulation were successful in conferring this power upon the Commission. No longer was the Commission to be hampered by possessing only the purely negative power to say that a rate was unreasonable.

Personal discrimination. One of the most striking features of the Hepburn Act was the multiplicity of provisions it contained which were designed to strike directly or indirectly at personal discrimination. Inclusion of private car lines and industrial railroads, together with the provisions for fixing switching charges and the division of joint rates, struck at two favorite discriminatory devices. The power of the Commission to fix reasonable charges for services performed by shippers and for special services provided by railroads also struck a blow at potentially discriminatory devices. The prohibition of free passes eliminated a means of favoring shippers and prevented the use of passes to influence legislators, judges, and newspapermen. Finally, it was hoped that the extreme penalties assessed for giving and receiving rebates would be sufficient to deter further law breaking.

Commodities clause. One other provision of the law designed to strike at personal discrimination of a somewhat different type was the commodities clause. A number of railroads owned coal mines which competed with independently-owned mines along their lines, and such railroads often discriminated in various ways against the independent mine owners. By denying the independent owners adequate car supplies or railroad sidings, and by charging them exorbitant rates, the railroad mine owners were in a position to force the independents out of business. To prevent this sort of thing the law provided that no railroad might engage in interstate or foreign transportation of "any article or commodity other than timber and the manufactured products thereof, manufactured, mined, or produced by it, or under its authority, or which it may own in whole or in part, or in which it may have any interest, direct or indirect, except such articles or commodities as may be necessary and intended for its use in the conduct of its business as a common carrier."

It will be noted that the law did not directly forbid railroad ownership of mining or manufacturing facilities. The railroads used large quantities of coal for locomotive fuel and for other purposes and no good purpose would have been served by preventing them from mining their own coal. Similarly, many railroads engage in car and locomotive manufacturing work for themselves. Hence the law does not prohibit railroad ownership of mining and manufacturing facilities, but a railroad may not transport its own products to sell to others. The exception made for timber and manufactured products thereof was made in the interests of the lumber industry which operated many small railroads primarily to move timber from logging areas to mills. Such railroads might perform an incidental common carrier service of value to the area, and to apply the commodities clause to them would have done more harm than good.

Enforcement of Commission's orders. Some changes were made in the judicial procedures in connection with the enforcement of the Commission's orders. Under the old procedure if a carrier refused to obey an order of the Commission, the Commission had to apply to the courts for an injunction to compel obedience, thus placing the burden of proof on the Commission. The Hepburn Act specified that Commission orders, except those involving money payments, were to become effective after thirty days, and after the effective date of such an order, the carrier was liable for a fine of $5,000 a day for every day it refused to obey the order. The effect of this provision was to force the carrier to take the initiative in seeking relief, although the Commission could still appeal to the courts in the event the carrier did not. The earlier law *authorized* the courts to enforce obedience, but the new law *directed* the courts to enforce obedience if they found the order was regularly made and duly served. The courts could suspend an order of the Commission but only after a hearing. Either party might appeal from the decision of the initial court, but the appeal was directly to the Supreme Court and the case was to have priority on the Supreme Court's docket. In general it may be said that the advantage of the new procedure was found in the effort made to speed up court action on Commission cases.

Publicity of accounts. The original Act to Regulate Commerce had authorized the Commission to require annual reports, to demand additional information if needed, and to prescribe a uniform system of accounts for all carriers. Unfortunately the enforcement powers of the Commission proved weak, and it experienced difficulty in getting data for annual reports and other information that it needed. The Hepburn Act provided for annual reports, and more frequent ones if the Commission desired, to be made under oath, and heavy penalties were provided for falsification or for delay in filing reports. All accounts were to be kept in accordance with forms prescribed by the Commission, no accounts other than those specified by the Commission were to be permitted, and the Commission was to have access to the books of any carrier at any time. To this end it could employ special examiners to keep track of the carriers' accounting activities.

Professor Ripley,[8] writing only a few years after the passage of the Hepburn Act, considered these accounting provisions to be among the most important in the act. A uniform and policed system of accounts makes certain kinds of rebating dangerous because the lower rates charged can be shown on the books only by falsification, a procedure punishable by fine and imprisonment. Similarly, open books tend to bring to light financial manipulations detrimental to investors. Third, an accurate understandable system of accounts is useful in determining profits and hence the justification or lack of justification for rate increases. Without some such control a carrier might reflect in its books a loss and use this as the basis of a request for increased rates, when in fact the carrier actually operated at a profit. Finally, a uniform system of accounts is useful to railroad management itself, since it facilitates comparison of the results of operations of different railroads and so makes it possible for management to determine weak spots and correct them.

Judicial interpretation. The commodities clause was soon attacked in the courts, but its constitutionality was fully upheld by the Supreme Court in the Delaware and Hudson case.[9] Of more far reaching significance was a series of opinions involving the question of the power of the courts to review orders of the Interstate Commerce Commission.[10] The effect of these opinions was to confine the courts to questions of law in hearing appeals from orders of the Commission. In brief, an order of the Commission was considered final unless it exceeded its statutory power, was based on a mistake of law, or the law itself was unconstitutional. Furthermore, the courts were not to consider the facts of a case unless an order of the Commission was clearly inconsistent with the facts.

---

[8] William Z. Ripley, *Railroads, Rates and Regulation.* New York: Longmans, Green and Co., 1912, pp. 515-520.

[9] *United States* v. *Delaware and Hudson Railroad, etc.,* 213 U.S. 257 (1909). See also 220 U.S. 257 (1911).

[10] *Interstate Commerce Commission* v. *Illinois Central Railroad Co.,* 215 U.S. 452 (1910); *Interstate Commerce Commission* v. *Chicago, Rock Island and Pacific Railway Company,* 218 U.S. 89 (1910); *Interstate Commerce Commission* v. *Union Pacific Railroad Company,* 222 U.S. 541 (1912).

FEDERAL REGULATION

THE MANN-ELKINS ACT

Need for further legislation. Although the Hepburn Act represented a definite step forward, further revision of the law was soon necessary. The general price level was rising, and the railroads were filing literally thousands of notices of rate increases each year. The Commission obviously could not act promptly on each and every complaint arising out of these increases, yet thirty days after notice had been filed the new rate went into effect and stayed in effect until such time as the Commission might order its reduction. Also a number of court decisions had gone against the Government, indicating the necessity of further clarification of the law, or for reforms in the judicial processes. And the long and short haul clause, effectively emasculated in the Alabama Midland case, still remained a dead letter. These and other minor considerations led to the passage of the Mann-Elkins Act which became law on June 18, 1910.

Power to suspend rates. One of the most significant provisions of the new act was that which gave the Commission the power to suspend rate changes. Under the law as it stood in 1906 the Commission could, after a hearing, declare a rate to be unreasonable and fix the rate to be charged in its place, but in the nature of the case it could not act until *after* the offending rate had gone into effect. Under the procedure then followed the carrier or carriers filed notice of a rate increase with the Commission, and this increase went into effect thirty days later. After a shipper had paid the higher rate, he could bring a complaint before the Commission, the Commission would hold hearings, and if it held the rate unreasonable, it fixed the correct rate.

This method of handling rate increases was unsatisfactory for at least two reasons. In the first place, if a shipper had contracted to sell his product for future delivery at an established price, his profits might be jeopardized by the necessity of paying higher rates during the time in which a rate case was making its way slowly through the machinery of the Commission. It is true that he could sue for the difference between the rate he paid and the rate held to be just, but this was obviously a clumsy, time consuming, and wholly unsatisfactory solution to the problem. Furthermore, whenever it was possible to do so, the individual or firm which paid the freight charge in the first instance passed the higher charge on to the buyer in the form of higher prices. Thus whoever paid the higher rates in the first instance lost nothing unless the product involved happened to be one for which the demand was highly elastic, and those who really bore the burden of the increased rates were not in a position to recover.

FEDERAL REGULATION

This weakness in the law had been known for some time, and two possible remedies suggested themselves. One was to require carriers to give bond that they would make refund in the event that a rate increase was rejected, but the carriers objected to the financial burden entailed by such a scheme. Furthermore, it would not have solved the problem where shippers passed higher rates on to others. The other solution suggested was to grant the Commission power to prevent a rate increase from going into effect until it could decide whether or not the new rate was reasonable. The railroads had successfully opposed this sort of thing in the past on the ground that if the rates in question were held to be reasonable, they would be deprived unjustifiably of revenue during the intervening period. But obviously it was just as unfair to compel shippers to pay higher rates which were later held to be unreasonable. Furthermore, the railroads were protected in the event of a demand for a decrease in an established rate because the existing rate remained in effect until after a hearing had been held and a decision reached. It would seem to be reasonable similarly to protect shippers from rate increases.

While railroad regulation was being discussed in Congress a number of railroads filed notice of rate increases to go into effect on June 1, 1910. This move was blocked by an injunction obtained on the grounds that the carriers acted in concert in violation of the Sherman Act, but it served to point up to Congress the need for legislation. As a result the new law gave the Commission the power to suspend any new rate or regulation from taking effect for 120 days after the date it would normally go into effect. If at the end of that time, the Commission had not yet disposed of the case, it could suspend the change for an additional six months. The wording of this provision made it possible for the railroads to put into effect numerous minor changes in rates, to which little or no objection was likely to develop, with the usual thirty days notice; but at the same time it reserved to the Commission the right to hold up more significant changes until it had time to investigate them. The law also provided that the burden of proof that an increased rate was necessary rested with the carrier.

Commerce Court. In an effort to speed up the adjudication of Commission cases before the courts and at the same time provide a court specialized in interstate commerce matters, President Taft suggested the establishment of a special court, and such a court, the Commerce Court, was provided for in the Mann-Elkins Act. This court was to be made up of five judges designated by the Chief Justice of the Supreme Court, each of whom was to serve for five years. It was to sit continuously to hear certain types of interstate commerce cases, and appeals could be taken from its decisions directly to the Supreme Court.

Long and short haul clause. It is perfectly clear that Congress intended to limit place discrimination when it inserted the long and short haul clause in the original Act to Regulate Commerce. The clause was still in the law, but it was to all intents and purposes inoperative because of limitations placed upon the Commission by the Supreme Court. Violations of the principle were quite common in the South, and merchants and others in the interior cities of the West suffered severely as a result of lower rates to Pacific coast points than were granted to intermediate points. The influence of western Independent Republicans finally forced the issue, and four changes were made to strengthen the clause.

The first of these changes was the elimination of the phrase "under substantially similar circumstances and conditions," thus leaving it entirely up to the Commission to decide when a departure was justified. A second change specified that the movement was to be over the same line *or route*, making it clear that the clause applied to through movements over the lines of two or more railroads as well as over the lines of a single carrier. Third, it was specified that once a railroad had reduced a rate to meet water competition it could not subsequently raise the rate simply by showing that water competition no longer existed. This was to prevent railroads from using the law to force water carriers out of business and then raise rates to cover earlier losses. A final change specified that no higher rate could be charged for a through haul than the sum of the rates charged for the intermediate hauls making up the through haul.

Other provisions. The Commission was authorized to institute hearings on its own motion with regard to rates without waiting for a complaint to be filed. Where individual shippers brought complaints the Commission's activities were confined to the individual matters complained of, but sometimes carriers announced general rate changes which involved increases in a large number of rates, and obviously it would save time and lead to a more equitable decision if the whole schedule could be examined as a unit. The Commission had actually followed this practice, but some question had been raised about its power to do so. Another change gave the shipper the right to designate the railroads over which a shipment would move in the event that a joint haul over two or more lines was necessary. Again, carriers were prohibited from disclosing information about a shipper's goods to a competing shipper. Finally, the Mann-Elkins Act gave the Commission authority over the interstate operations of telephone, telegraph, and cable companies. In 1934, however, the regulation of these means of communication was turned over to a newly established Federal Communications Commission, and no further consideration will be given to this passing phase of the Commission's activities.

FEDERAL REGULATION

Results of the Mann-Elkins Act. Events of the time revealed that the additional powers conferred upon the Interstate Commerce Commission by the Hepburn Act and the Mann-Elkins Act had greatly increased the effectiveness of that body. The tendency of the carriers to increase rates, which had been evident for some years, was effectively checked. The Commission used its power to suspend rates to prevent further important rate increases from going into effect prior to a determination of their reasonableness. In these cases the carriers were handicapped by the fact that they had to bear the burden of proof to justify any increased rate. Possibly as a result of this requirement, the Commission rejected applications for general rate increases in several important cases.

The Commerce Court was established and began to function, only to come to a short and tragic end. This court, instead of serving to speed up adjudication of legal problems, seemed to look upon itself as a sort of superior Interstate Commerce Commission. In spite of the statements of the Supreme Court to the effect that the courts were to confine themselves to matters of law, the Commerce Court inquired into the Commission's findings on facts, reviewed the cases themselves, and in a number of cases reversed the Commission. When the Supreme Court in its turn reversed the Commerce Court and upheld the Commission, it became apparent that the Commerce Court was actually an obstruction. Moreover, one of the judges of the court was tried and found guilty of corruption and was impeached. Two bills to abolish the court were vetoed by President Taft, but late in 1913 a new Congress and a new President cooperated to end its existence.

The amendments to the long and short haul clause brought about a marked change in the application of that part of the law. In the first ten months after the amendments went into effect the Commission received nearly 6,000 applications for relief from the long and short haul restriction, a figure considerably in excess of the total number of all formal cases filed prior to that time. The Commission took the attitude that Congress intended the prohibition against a higher charge for the shorter haul to be the rule rather than the exception and that it was to permit departures only in unusual cases. Furthermore, it held that the carrier must prove the need for a departure and that such departures must not do injustice to intermediate points.

In general the Commission allowed departures for the following reasons. First, when water competition existed, but such water competition had to be real and significant. Second, it sometimes allowed relief where two points were served by more than one carrier and one carrier's route was quite circuitous. If the circuitous line was to get any through traffic, it had to establish a through rate comparable with that charged by the shorter line, and it could not always afford to extend correspondingly low rates to intermediate points. Third, it occasionally allowed a departure because of the force of market competition. For example, California orange growers had to have a rate to eastern points comparable with the rate over the much shorter haul from Florida, and the railroads could hardly afford to extend this low rate inland.

OTHER REGULATORY MEASURES

Panama Canal Act. Over the years the railroads had adopted with considerable success various techniques for driving competing water carriers out of business. These techniques included such things as cutting rates, buying up competing water lines and discouraging their use by means of high rates, control of water front facilities, and refusal to interchange goods which might move partly by rail and partly by water. Some fear was expressed that when the Panama Canal was opened, the railroads would gain control of the water lines that might use it, thus stifling at the outset any possible water competition for transcontinental traffic. In order to encourage water transportation in general and Panama Canal traffic in particular the completion of the canal was made the occasion for further legislation.

The Panama Canal Act, adopted in 1912, contained a specific prohibition against any railroad owning or controlling a common carrier by water with which it competed or might compete. In the case of Panama Canal traffic the prohibition was made absolute, but elsewhere the Commission could permit continued operation of a water carrier by a railroad if such operation was in the public interest and if water competition was not reduced or prevented thereby. The Commission was also given the power to require physical connections between rail and water carriers to facilitate interchanges of traffic, and to establish through routes and maximum joint rates. The Commission followed a rather flexible policy in administering this new phase of its duties. It ordered the Trunk Line railroads, i.e., those operating in the area between Chicago and New York, to relinquish their control over boat lines on the Great Lakes. These railroads had dominated shipping on the Great Lakes and discouraged it by high rates. On the other hand, it permitted common control at other points where joint operation appeared to be in the public interest.

Valuation Act of 1913. The original Act to Regulate Commerce specified that all rates were to be reasonable and just, but Congress did not set forth any definition or rule on just how a reasonable and just rate could be determined, and no official definition of such a rate existed until 1898. In that year in the case of *Smyth v. Ames* [11] the Supreme Court held that the basis for the determination of reasonable rates was the fair value of the property used, and that a railroad was, in effect, entitled to charge rates which would bring it a fair return on the fair value of its property. This gave the Commission a basis for determining reasonable rates, but this fact meant little at the time because it had been shorn of all power to fix rates anyway. But the Hepburn Act and the Mann-Elkins Act had considerably extended the powers of the Commission in matters of rate making, and the problem of obtaining a sound base for determining the reasonableness of rates became a matter of importance.

The Interstate Commerce Commission urged upon Congress the need for obtaining an adequate valuation of the railroads as a basis for the determination of rates, and Congress complied in 1913 with the Valuation Act, directing the Commission to ascertain the value of each railroad in the United States. The Commission estimated that it would take three years to do the work, but the task proved to be one of tremendous magnitude, and it took twenty years to complete the valuations *as of 1913*. Further years of work faced the Commission to obtain the values of lines built since 1913 and to bring the 1913 figures up to date, but subsequent changes in the law rendered this work less significant.

Other acts. In order to enable the Commission to handle its increased duties the Commission Divisions Act was passed in 1917. This increased the number of commissioners to nine and authorized the Commission to organize its members into divisions of not less than three members each, each division to handle a particular phase of the work. Thus there was established what might be called a series of little commissions within the larger body. These divisions heard cases and issued orders just as did the Commission, but their decisions could always be appealed to the full Commission. Also in 1917 came the Esch Car Service Act. This gave the Commission control over the rules and regulations established by the carriers for the movement, distribution, exchange, interchange, and return of freight cars.

FEDERAL CONTROL OF RAILROADS, 1918-20

Effort to operate privately. After the United States went to war in April 1917, the amount of railroad traffic increased enormously. The railroads were unable to get the equipment they needed to handle this great volume of traffic, and as the war progressed a substantial number of railroad employees were drawn into the armed forces or left the rail-

---

[11] 169 U.S. 466.

roads for employment at higher rates of pay in various war industries. The situation demanded a coordination of railroad facilities so that they could be operated as a single system, particularly in the great industrial area east of the Mississippi River, and in an effort to promote maximum efficiency in an all out program to help win the war the railroads promptly established the Railroads' War Board.

The Railroads' War Board attempted, partly by persuasion and partly by coercion, to increase the average load per freight car, the speed of loading and unloading, and the speed of car movements, all in an effort to utilize available cars more efficiently. It also prevailed upon individual railroads to cut down on passenger service, thus releasing men and equipment for the more vital freight service. In these and other ways the Board functioned to help move the war traffic in the face of equipment and labor shortages. Its problems were particularly difficult in the East because the bulk of the freight for Europe moved through a few eastern ports. Terminal facilities were inadequate, as were shipping facilities, and cars of freight were sent East without much regard to the ability of available port and shipping facilities to handle the goods. As a result loaded cars piled up on sidings and a serious car shortage threatened. The railroads also were handicapped for a time by the requests of government departments for preferred treatment when preferred treatment was unnecessary.

Federal operation. In spite of its best efforts the Railroads' War Board was unable to solve the problems confronting it, and a serious breakdown of railroad service threatened in the East. There are some who feel that if the Board had been given requisite authority, it could have handled the situation, but others believe that motives of self-interest made it impossible at that time for the railroads to achieve the necessary coordination by voluntary means. In any event the Government took over the railroads on December 28, 1917. Under the law federal control could continue for a period not to exceed twenty-one months after the ratification of peace, but it could be terminated earlier. Control of any individual railroad could be relinquished at any time before July 1, 1918, and actually a large number of short line railroads were released from federal control before that date.

During the period of federal operation, the Government guaranteed each railroad under its control an annual rental payment which was not to exceed the line's average annual operating income for the three years ending June 30, 1917, and railroad properties were to be maintained by the Government in such a way as to return them in substantially the same condition as they were when taken over. Such improvements or additions as might be necessary were to be made by the Government, but the owners of the railroads were to pay for these improvements upon the return of their property, except as it could be shown that the improvements were made solely for war purposes.

Results of federal operation. President Wilson appointed William G. McAdoo to be Director General of Railroads, and he served until shortly after the end of the war when he was succeeded by Walker D. Hines. Under Mr. McAdoo an organization was established to operate the railroads as a unit, and acting with the authority of the Government behind him, he was able to accomplish much. Numerous steps were taken to increase the efficiency of utilization of equipment, a greater coordination of rail and ocean shipping facilities was achieved, and the threat of a breakdown of railroad service was averted. Wages were increased as of January 1, 1918, a step which was essential if the railroad workers were to be kept on the job, but no further wage increases were made. Rates, too, were increased once, the increase going into effect in June, 1918. Financially the results were not too happy, the loss suffered by the Government during the period of federal control being variously estimated at something more than a billion dollars.

During the 1920's the results of wartime operation were the subject of considerable debate because of their possible bearing on the question of the efficiency of government operation of business as contrasted with private operation. Naturally some criticisms arose out of inconveniences suffered by individuals, some of them perhaps unnecessarily, during the period of federal operation. Other criticisms were made of the way in which government policy had promoted the development of unionism among railroad employees and of the poor condition in which the railroads found their property at the termination of federal control. But the principal criticism was based on the heavy losses incurred by the Government as a result of its operations.

On the other hand, it was argued that there was no reason to believe that the railroads could have done any better, if indeed they could have done as well, if left under private control. Certainly the situation was deteriorating at the time the Government assumed control. It would be difficult, too, to establish emergency control over an industry of such magnitude without inconveniencing many people and without inefficiencies creeping in. While government control promoted the growth of unions, the Government was able to simplify its labor problems by being able to treat with workers by groups rather than individually. Finally, it was argued that the heavy losses were due principally to the Government's failure to raise rates as a rising price level increased railroad costs. Some argued, too, that the method of calculating the rental payments for the use of the railroads led to excessive payments, but this was vigorously denied by others.

FEDERAL REGULATION

Looking at the matter from the vantage point of the years, it may be doubted that the financial results of federal wartime operation of the railroads prove very much with regard to the success or failure of government in business. There now seems to be little doubt that the deficit was due in no small part to the failure of the Government to raise rates to meet rising costs, yet if the Government had raised rates it would have contributed to the already existing evil of rapidly rising prices. It is, perhaps, not without significance, that the Interstate Commerce Commission allowed very substantial rate increases shortly after the Government returned the railroads to their owners. But quite apart from all of this was the fact that the Government did not take over the railroads to make money. If that had been its purpose, it might just as well have taken over all of the grocery stores, steel mills, and church bazaars. The Government took over the railroads because it thought that such a move was necessary in order to prosecute a war successfully. It had to see that the goods were put through and that the troops were put through, and it succeeded in doing this even though at times economy and efficiency of operations had to be subordinated to the urgency of the need for moving the men and materials of war.

SUGGESTED READINGS

Daggett, Stuart, *Principles of Inland Transportation*, 3rd Ed. New York: Harper and Brothers, 1941.

Johnson, Emory R. and Thurman W. Van Metre, *Principles of Railroad Transportation*. New York: D. Appleton and Company, 1916.

Jones, Eliot, *Principles of Railway Transportation*. New York: The Macmillan Company, 1927. A good account of the development of federal regulation.

Larrabee, William, *The Railroad Question*. Chicago: The Schulte Publishing Company, 1893.

Locklin, D. Philip, *Economics of Transportation*, 3rd Ed. Chicago: Richard D. Irwin, Inc., 1947. Good account of place and personal discrimination.

Miller, Sidney L., *Principles of Inland Transportation*. New York: McGraw-Hill Book Company, Inc., 1933.

Ripley, William Z., *Railroads, Rates and Regulation*. New York: Longmans, Green & Company, 1912. One of the best accounts of the development of federal regulation.

7

Federal Regulation
of
RAILROAD TRANSPORTATION (II)

THE TRANSPORTATION ACT, 1920: CONGRESSIONAL HISTORY

Necessity for legislation to provide temporary financial assistance to carriers. The end of the war with Germany and the prospective return of the railroads to their owners necessitated legislation to provide some degree of financial assistance during the changeover period. Rates would have to be increased once the railroads were returned to private control, but major rate adjustments are not effected over night, and it was certain that some little time would elapse between the return of the railroads to private operation and the approval of rate increases by the Interstate Commerce Commission. If the carriers were to bridge this gap, they would have to have some financial assistance.

Other serious financial problems faced the carriers. Equipment and employees were scattered all over the country, and in various other ways individual operating organizations were disrupted. Some railroads owed the Government substantial sums for improvements made to their lines during the war, and they were in no position to meet these obligations immediately. New capital was needed for improvements deferred during the war, and this capital could not be obtained from private sources on reasonable terms. Finally, labor was dissatisfied with the failure of the Railroad Administration to raise wages to meet increased living costs, and it was clear that demands for higher wages were in the offing. For all of these various reasons the need for some sort of financial aid to help the railroads over the transition period was quite apparent.

Need for permanent changes in regulatory policy. In addition to the need for temporary financial aid there was a recognized need for certain major changes in regulatory concepts and techniques. Perhaps the most serious problem facing the railroads and public alike was the progressive decline in railroad earnings which had begun before the war and promised to continue unless positive steps were taken to reverse the trend. This decline in earnings, along with other factors, had seriously weakened railroad credit, and unless the confidence of investors in railroad securities was restored, the railroads would find it impossible to obtain the funds necessary to make the improvements required to meet the needs of the public.

Another difficulty requiring solution was the so-called strong and weak line problem. Although railroad earnings taken as a whole were not good, some railroads were much worse off than others, and this made an extremely touchy situation at points where financially weak carriers were competing with strong lines. The rates charged by both would, of course, have to be about the same, but a scale of rates which would permit the weak lines to operate might be excessive for the strong lines, while a scale of rates adequate for the strong lines might bankrupt the weak. Then, too, there were many carriers operating in light traffic areas where shippers and receivers of freight could not afford to pay rates sufficiently high to enable the carrier to stay in business. Such carriers could neither raise rates nor continue to operate on the basis of existing rates. Something had to be done to keep these lines operating, for to abandon them would deprive thousands of communities and hundreds of thousands of individuals of the only means of transportation available to them.

Other needed changes in regulatory policy were indicated. For a number of years there had been a growing demand for some sort of regulation of railroad security issues, principally to prevent overcapitalization and other unsound financial practices. There was also a growing feeling that the policy of enforcing competition among carriers was a mistake, and that the evils arising from competition in the railroad field more than offset any advantages that might be gained thereby. Car shortages and periodic breakdowns of railroad service both before and during the war pointed up the need for more effective and positive regulation of railroad service. And the threat of possible tieups arising out of labor difficulties, a point which had received peculiar emphasis during the war, indicated the need for machinery which would bring about the settlement of labor disputes without resorting to strikes or lockouts.

Adoption of Transportation Act, 1920. After the end of the war, President Wilson made it quite clear that he wanted to terminate federal control as soon as possible. He also indicated that he thought the country's regulatory program needed overhauling, but he made no specific suggestions concerning what changes should be made. Hearings on railroad legislation got under way early in 1919 but progress was slow, and it was not until November that the House passed the Esch bill, and it was December before the Senate adopted its own Cummins bill. There were marked differences between the two bills, the House bill generally providing for an extension and expansion of existing regulatory procedures in accordance with past experience, while the Senate bill contained a number of new and untried measures.

It was clear that the differences between the two bills would require some time to iron out, and so President Wilson, who had previously announced his intention of relinquishing control of the railroads on January 1, 1920, extended the date to March 1, 1920. A conference committee was appointed, but its work was handicapped by the haste required to meet the March 1st deadline, and under the circumstances it is not surprising that the more radical and untried features of the Senate bill gave way to the less controversial provisions of the House bill. In a few cases compromises were worked out, one or two of which proved quite unsatisfactory. The compromise bill was reported out on February 18, 1920, passed the House on February 21, the Senate on February 23, was signed by the President on February 28, and became law on March 1st.

TRANSITIONAL PROVISIONS

Nature of provisions. Perhaps the most important of the transitional provisions was the offer of the Government to guarantee the railroads, for the first six months of private operation, earnings equal in amount to what they would have received if federal control had continued over that period; an offer which almost all of the carriers chose to accept. A second provision allowed the carriers ten years to pay for improvements made to their properties by the Government during the period of federal control. Third, Congress established a loan fund from which the carriers could borrow for periods up to fifteen years to meet maturing obligations, obtain new equipment, or make other additions and improvements to their plants. Finally, financial assistance was extended to the large number of short lines which had not been operated by the Government during the war, many of which had suffered severely. All of these provisions were temporary in nature, and since they have long passed out of existence, no further consideration will be given to them.

RULE OF RATE MAKING

A new concept of rate making. Reference has been made to the serious problem which faced the country as a result of the progressive decline in railroad earnings. This decline was due to various factors, but without question one of the most important causes was the restrictive policy that the Interstate Commerce Commission had followed with regard to rate increases after it had acquired positive control over rates. The Commission functioned to protect the public from unreasonably high and discriminatory rates, but it did not assume any particular responsibility for protecting the railroads from inadequate rates. Its attitude is understandable in view of the fact that regulation itself arose out of a demand for the protection of the public from high and discriminatory freight rates, but without adequate earnings the railroads could neither give the service the people wanted nor expand their facilities to meet the growing needs of commerce and industry. It seemed clear, then, that a new concept of rate making was needed, one which would direct the Commission to establish rates which were not only reasonable to shippers but which also were sufficiently high to enable the carriers to provide adequate service.

Rule of rate making. In an effort to restore railroad earnings, and thereby railroad credit, Congress wrote into the Transportation Act, 1920, a rule of rate making to guide the Interstate Commerce Commission in fixing rates. The Commission was directed to prescribe such rates as would permit the carriers as a whole or "as a whole in each of such rate groups or territories as the Commission may from time to time designate" to earn, "under honest, efficient and economical management" a fair return on the fair value of railroad property held for and used in the service of transportation. Five and one-half per cent was fixed as the fair rate of return for the first two years, after which the Commission was to determine the fair rate of return. Authority already existed under the Valuation Act of 1913 for the Commission to determine the fair value of the carriers involved. It will be noted that this rule of rate making was based on the rule established by the Supreme Court in 1898 in the case of *Smyth v. Ames.*[1]

Not a guarantee of earnings. In the years immediately following the passage of the Transportation Act, 1920, the rule of rate making became something of a political football, and it was widely misinterpreted, especially by advocates of farm relief, as constituting a government guarantee of earnings to the railroads. But the rule was not a guarantee of earnings because the Government was under no financial obligation to the owners of the railroads in the event that actual earnings failed to equal a fair return on the fair value of their property. Indeed, in only one year did the railroads even approximate a fair return on the fair value of their property under the rate levels permitted by the Interstate Commerce Commission, and in no case were they reimbursed for failure to earn a fair return.

Rule not applicable to individual rates. It should be noted that the rule of rate making did not require the Commission to fix rates in such a way that the charge made for moving each specific commodity would

---

[1] See page 127.

be sufficient to meet all the costs of moving that commodity plus something by way of a fair return on the fair value of the property. For one thing, it would have been impossible to apply such a rule. A railroad uses the same tracks, motive power, rolling stock, and other equipment to move hundreds of different commodities, and there is no way of determining what part of the cost of providing these facilities is attributable to each individual commodity shipped. Again, costs vary from day to day, from train to train, and even from car to car, depending upon the total volume of goods shipped. Thus the cost of hauling a 100 pound shipment of a given commodity in a car containing 40,000 pounds of other freight is less than would be the case if it were shipped in a car containing 30,000 pounds of other freight.

Finally, the value of the commodity must be taken into consideration. If heavy or bulky low grade commodities like sand and gravel were assessed rates sufficiently high to meet their full share of all costs plus something by way of a fair return, their prices at destination would be so high that people would be unable to buy them. Yet it is essential to the public well-being that such commodities be made available for use. It is, therefore, common to place low rates on such commodities and make up the difference by charging higher rates on more valuable items of traffic. All that the Commission was expected to do was to fix rates on individual commodities in such a way that all of them, one taken with another, would bring a fair return on the fair value of the property.

Rule not applicable to individual carriers. Perhaps the most unusual feature of the rule of rate making was the fact that it did not apply to individual railroads. Instead the Commission was directed to fix rates which would in the aggregate enable the carriers *as a whole*, or as a whole by sections of the country, to earn a fair return on the fair value of their property. Wide variations existed in the earning capacities of different carriers which meant that if the rule were applied to individual lines, some would have to have a higher level of rates than others. But in a great many cases the high cost lines either competed directly with strong lines for traffic between common points or served industries which competed with similar industries located on strong lines, and the existence of this competition made it impossible to establish separate scales of rates which would meet the needs of each type of carrier for a fair return on the fair value of its property.

Recapture of excess earnings. To solve this problem two possibilities suggested themselves. One was to fix the rates at a level which would enable the strong lines to earn a fair return on the fair value of their property, and if the weak lines could not meet these rates, then they would have to go out of business. This, of course, is what would happen under conditions of competition to a concern that could not meet the prices charged by its rivals, but such a solution is out of the question as far as the transportation industry is concerned because at noncompetitive points it would deprive hundreds of thousands of people of transportation services vital to their very existence. The other possibility that suggested itself was to fix the level of rates high enough to permit the weaker carriers to earn a fair return on the fair value of their property, but such a scheme would be wholly unsatisfactory from the point of view of the shipping public. After all, the bulk of traffic was moved by a relatively small number of large railroad systems, most of which could be classified as strong lines, and it hardly seemed fair to require the bulk of shippers to pay excessive rates for the sole purpose of keeping a number of weak lines in business.

In seeking a way out of this apparent impasse Congress hit upon the expedient of instructing the Interstate Commerce Commission to fix rates which would yield the carriers as a whole, or as a whole by sections of the country, a fair return on the fair value of their property. In other words, the Commission was to strike a sort of an average in fixing the general level of rates, an average which would yield some carriers a fair return, some more than a fair return, and some less than a fair return. But the matter did not end here. If a carrier earned more than a fair return on the fair value of its property in any one year, it was to divide that excess equally between itself and the Government. The carrier was required to put its share of such excess earnings in a reserve fund out of which it could pay interest, dividends, and rentals in any year in which its earnings failed to equal a fair return on the fair value of its property. The carrier was to continue to place excess earnings in this fund until the fund equaled 5 per cent of the value of its property, after which it could use its share of further excess earnings for any lawful purpose. The Government's share of excess earnings was to be placed in a contingent fund out of which the Interstate Commerce Commission could make loans at 6 per cent interest to carriers in need of loanable funds and which could provide some assurance of repayment. Money from this fund could also be used by the Commission to buy equipment and facilities to lease to needy carriers.

Objections to recapture clause. At the time the recapture clause was being debated in Congress considerable disagreement developed over its constitutionality, and once the law was passed the carriers were not long in taking this particular provision to the courts. In 1924, however, the Supreme Court upheld the constitutionality of the recapture clause in the

Dayton-Goose Creek case.[2] In this case the carrier argued that the rates it charged were of long standing, that in many cases their reasonableness had not been questioned, and that some had been approved and even fixed by the Commission. Its contention was, in effect, that earnings derived from reasonable rates belonged to the carrier and could not be taken away from it. The Court held, however, that no railroad was entitled as a constitutional right to more than a fair return on a fair value of its property. The fact that some railroads earned more than a fair return was due to the method of rate making adopted by Congress, and so Congress had a right to appropriate earnings in excess of a fair return which resulted from the rate-making procedure.

Aside from the question of constitutionality, certain other objections to the recapture clause developed very early in its history. In the first place, if some carriers earned more than a fair return solely because of the rate-making technique adopted by Congress, then it might be argued that this same rate-making technique was responsible for the deficits suffered by other less fortunate carriers. Therefore, it would seem to be more logical for the Government to give rather than to lend the less favored carriers the money that it had obtained from the prosperous lines. Such an argument is not wholly valid in that the rate-making technique was not altogether responsible for the plight of many weak railroads. There were many lines which could not earn a fair return regardless of the rates charged for the simple reason that a high level of rates would have destroyed what little traffic they had. Nevertheless, it soon became clear that the law could not be of much benefit to the weak lines, since all that it did was to offer them an opportunity to borrow money at 6 per cent interest, and such lines as could provide the necessary security to qualify for loans from the recapture fund could borrow from private sources on the same or lower terms.

Various other objections were raised to the recapture of excess earnings. The results of each year's operations were considered independently for the purpose of recapturing earnings, and this worked a hardship on lines which for various reasons experienced a considerable fluctuation of earnings. Such lines might make excess profits one year and suffer a deficit the next, but this circumstance was not taken into account in the recapture procedure. This difficulty could have been avoided by making the provisions of the law apply over a period of years rather than by treating each year separately. It also was argued that railroad stocks would become less attractive as investments if earnings were limited to 6 per cent, but on the other hand, the rule of rate making, plus the fact that a carrier

---

[2] *Dayton-Goose Creek Railway* v. *U.S.*, 263 U.S. 456.

could retain half of its excess earnings, offered the possibility of a certain stability of earnings which ought to improve the attractiveness of railroad stocks. Finally, the success of the rule of rate making and the recapture of excess earnings depended in no small degree upon the ability of the Interstate Commerce Commission and the carriers under its jurisdiction to agree upon the fair value to be applied to each individual railroad involved. As will be brought out presently, the carriers and the Commission were unable to agree on these valuations, and in the last analysis this proved to be the biggest stumbling block to the successful administration of this part of the law.

OTHER RATE PROVISIONS

Power to fix minimum rates. The law conferred upon the Commission the power to fix minimum as well as maximum rates for both single line hauls and joint through hauls. Authority to fix minimum rates had been requested by the Commission as early as 1893, and the reasons for extending this authority should be noted briefly. In the first place, the Commission had discovered that discrimination can arise out of rates which are unreasonably low as well as rates which are unreasonably high. Unduly low rates at competitive points burden the rates charged at noncompetitive points, except in those cases where the long and short haul clause applies, and unduly low rates on certain commodities may place a burden on rates charged for moving other commodities. It is true that the Commission could move indirectly against low rates which burdened other traffic by ordering a reduction in the higher noncompetitive rates, thus possibly forcing the offending carrier to increase unduly low rates. But it might not always be possible for the Commission to reduce the noncompetitive rates, and carriers might, for reasons of their own, persist in charging unduly low rates to certain points or on certain commodities. And in any event this was a much less satisfactory method than a direct approach to the offending rates themselves.

Other reasons suggest themselves for granting the Commission authority over minimum rates. It made it possible to prevent cutthroat competition with all of its attendant damage to railroad service and credit. It made it possible for the Commission to act against carriers applying unduly low rates at certain points for the sole purpose of forcing water carriers out of business. It is possible, too, that the power to fix minimum rates was necessary to a proper control of the rule of rate making. If the Commission was to fix individual rates in such a way that they would, in the aggregate, bring a fair return on the fair value of the property, it would seem to be essential that it have the power to prevent the application of rates which were too low. Otherwise, rates which were too low would necessitate increases elsewhere in order for the carriers to earn a fair return.

Power to fix exact rate. The new law specified that if after a hearing the Commission found a rate, regulation, or practice unreasonable, it was authorized to determine and prescribe the proper rate, regulation, or practice. As far as rates were concerned this added nothing to the Commission's power. With the power to fix both maximum and minimum rates, it automatically possessed the power to fix exact rates.

Changes in the long and short haul clause. Three changes were made in the long and short haul clause, all of which made mandatory on the Commission the adoption of certain policies which, in general, it was already following. The first of these instructed the Commission, when making exceptions to the clause, not to permit the establishment of a rate to the more distant point that was not reasonably compensatory. It should be noted here that a railroad may find it profitable to establish a lower rate to a more distant point if by so doing it can utilize facilities which might otherwise be idle, but clearly the public interest would not be served by permitting a carrier to establish a rate that was so low that it did not even meet the variable operating costs incurred in handling the additional traffic. If such a rate were necessary to enable the carrier to compete with other carriers for a share of the business at hand, it would be better to relinquish the traffic altogether than to carry it at an actual out-of-pocket loss. Clearly the only reason that a carrier might want to establish such a rate would be to drive a rival carrier, probably a water carrier, out of business.

A second change in the long and short haul clause had to do with its application to intermediate points on circuitous lines or routes. If a railroad, or combination of railroads, serving two points by means of a circuitous line were permitted to lower its rates between those points to the level charged by a rival carrier having a more direct line, no higher rates could be charged to and from intermediate points on the circuitous line which did not involve a haul greater in length than that of the direct line between the competitive points. This provision, which is of debatable validity, was subsequently repealed, and need not be discussed further.

A third change in the long and short haul clause specified that the Commission was not to authorize any departure from its provisions because of merely potential water competition. For several years before the passage of the Transportation Act, 1920, the Commission had refused to grant relief because of potential water competition, but at an earlier period it had been much more liberal in this respect. This provision made it impossible for railroads to strive to stifle water competition before it could develop, and it made it impossible to use the threat of imaginary water competition to justify departures that could not be defended on other grounds.

Power to suspend rate changes. The Commission's power to suspend rates had proved to be of real value, but the extended suspension period permitted by the Mann-Elkins Act tended to work a hardship on the carriers, especially during periods of rising prices. Consequently the Transportation Act, 1920, changed the rate suspension period to 120 days and 30 days, a period which was again changed in 1927, this time to seven months. If at the end of the rate suspension period the Commission had not reached a decision, the new rates were to go into effect and were to remain in effect until such time as the Commission was able to dispose of the matter. To protect shippers in the event that the Commission ultimately refused to sanction the new rates, the Commission was authorized to require the carriers to keep accurate accounts of the additional amounts received by them from these rates and refund overpayments with interest. In actual practice the carriers have simply refrained from putting proposed rate increases into effect until they have been passed on by the Commission, even though more than seven months may have elapsed.

RAILROAD INTERCORPORATE RELATIONSHIPS

Plan of consolidation. The Transportation Act, 1920, contained a number of provisions dealing with railroad intercorporate relationships which reveal a marked departure from earlier beliefs in the desirability of competition as at least a partial regulator of railroad rates and services. Without question the most startling change in this respect was the congressional mandate to the Interstate Commerce Commission to take steps looking toward the consolidation of the railroads of the continental United States into a limited number of systems. To this end the Commission was to work out a tentative plan in which each and every railroad under its jurisdiction would be allocated to a specified railroad system. Insofar as possible these railroad systems were to be planned in such a way that a uniform scale of rates would bring each substantially the same rate of return on the value of its property. Also insofar as possible, existing routes and channels of trade were not to be disturbed. Finally, Congress revealed that it had not completely abandoned the old faith in competition, for it specified that the systems were to be arranged to preserve competition as fully as possible.

After having prepared a tentative consolidation plan, the Commission was to hold hearings on it at which all interested parties could file or present objections, and following such hearings the Commission was to prepare and publish a final plan. The Commission was authorized to modify its final plan from time to time if, in its opinion, such modification was required in the public interest. Once the final plan had been published, two or more carriers could consolidate their properties providing the proposed consolidation was in harmony with the over-all plan, that it met with the approval of the Commission, and that the par value of the stocks and bonds of the new corporation did not exceed the combined value of the consolidated properties. No carriers were required to consolidate, but those wishing to effect consolidations were required to make their plans conform with the Commission's master plan except as it might be modified by the Commission itself.

The consolidation provisions of the Transportation Act, 1920, take on meaning only as they are related to the rule of rate making. In fact, they are an integral part of that rule, and their consummation was essential to its ultimate success or failure. Congress, it will be recalled, had been unable to work out a method of rate making which would assure to each carrier a fair return on the fair value of its property. Competition between carriers and between communities necessitated the adoption of a more or less uniform scale of rates, but because of wide variations in the earning capacities of different carriers, any practical scale of rates adopted would bring some carriers more and other carriers less than the fair return to which each was entitled.

The actual rule adopted, with its averaging of rates and its taking from the strong to lend to the weak, was clumsy and awkward when taken by itself. If, however, the Commission succeeded in consolidating all of the railroads into a limited number of systems, each of such a nature that, to quote the actual wording of the law, they "can employ uniform rates in the movement of competitive traffic and under efficient management earn substantially the same rate of return" the rate problem would be solved. A scale of rates which would bring a fair return to one system would bring a fair return to all. As progress was made toward such a goal there would come to be less and less need for the awkward recapture provisions and conceivably this aspect of the law might ultimately pass out of existence.

Quite apart from the matter of rates and rate making, consolidation had been advocated for various other reasons. For example, the combination of one or more weak lines with a strong line offered a possible part solution to the strong and weak line problem. Of course, the Commission would have to avoid saddling a strong line with so many weak lines that the stability of the whole system was endangered, even though in some cases reduced operating costs and better management might improve the earning power of weak sections. Just how the strong could be expected to take over the weak under a scheme of voluntary consolidation was not quite clear. It was widely believed, too, that consolidation would bring about many economies which would benefit the carriers and the public alike. These included the elimination of circuitous routes, elimination of duplication of service, elimination of interchange of through traffic between connecting lines, elimination of numerous competitive expenses, more efficient use of terminal facilities, and the like. While undoubtedly some economies would result from unified operation, it may be doubted that these economies would be as great as many believed.

Acquisition of control. The law further provided that the acquisition of control of one carrier by another through lease, stock ownership, or any means short of actual consolidation, could be effected only after obtaining the approval of the Interstate Commerce Commission. Some such provision as this was necessary in order to prevent carriers from achieving virtual consolidations in their own interests without reference to the master plan of consolidation. The provision also made it possible to approve combinations which appeared to be in the public interest during the period before the adoption of the final plan. One weakness of this section of the law was its restriction to the acquisition of control of one carrier by another carrier. Because of this wording, acquisitions by holding companies were completely beyond the Commission's jurisdiction, a loophole in the law which was not overlooked in succeeding years.

Interlocking Directorates. The law provided that "it shall be unlawful for any person to hold the position of officer or director of more than one carrier, unless such holding shall have been authorized by order of the Commission, upon due showing that neither public nor private interests will be adversely affected thereby." The lodging of discretionary power with the Commission made it possible for it to prevent the use of interlocking directorates as a means of unifying competing lines without, however, denying to complementary lines the privilege of operating under a common management. This particular section of the law also contained a provision designed to prevent representatives of investment bankers and of railroad equipment manufacturers from sitting on the board of directors of carriers which might use their facilities.

Permissive pooling. It will be recalled that the original Act to Regulate Commerce contained an absolute prohibition against pooling. The prohibition against pooling was continued, but the Commission was authorized to permit the pooling of traffic or earnings if such would be in the interest of better service or economy in operation and would not unduly restrain competition. In view of the extent of the Commission's control over rates there was no longer any likelihood of pooling agreements being used for antisocial purposes, and an absolute prohibition against pooling might work a hardship on carriers under certain circumstances. For example, two centers of population might be served by four railroads, each offering through passenger service with a morning and evening departure from each city, a total of eight trains each way. If patronage were light the carriers might wish to pool their traffic, providing one train in the morning, one at noon, and one in the evening. The railroads would benefit from the elimination of the expense of operating five trains each way, and the public would benefit from more frequent service.

OTHER PROVISIONS

Regulation of security issues. The new law prohibited carriers from issuing securities or from assuming any obligation in respect of the securities of any person or corporation without first obtaining the consent of the Interstate Commerce Commission. Before it could grant such permission the Commission was required to find that the proposed issue or assumption of obligation was for some lawful object within the carrier's corporate purposes, that it was compatible with the public interest, and that it was reasonably necessary and appropriate for the purpose intended. The regulation of railroad security issues had been advocated for a number of years by the Commission and others, and the House had three times passed bills providing for such regulation, but each measure failed to pass the Senate. It was argued that security regulation would make impossible a recurrence of the financial scandals of the early 1900's, would improve railroad credit by preventing unwise or irresponsible actions on the part of certain railroad managements, and would protect investors.

In making provision for the regulation of security issues Congress recognized that emergencies may arise which require prompt action. When a carrier needs funds in a hurry, it would be greatly embarrassed if it had to make application to the Commission and then wait for the machinery of the Commission to grind out an authorization. To handle such emergency requirements carriers were permitted to issue short term notes of two years' duration or less without obtaining the consent of the Commission. To eliminate the possibility of this provision being used to evade the purpose of the law it was further provided that the total amount of such notes was not to aggregate more than 5 per cent of the par value of all of an applicant carrier's securities then outstanding.

Service. The act contained a number of provisions having to do with the utilization of cars and locomotives which gave the Commission powers of a managerial nature. The act stated that it was the duty of the carrier to furnish safe and adequate car service and to establish, observe, and enforce just and reasonable rules and practices with respect thereto. The Commission itself was authorized to establish reasonable rules, regulations, and practices with respect to car service. In case of an emergency the Commission was authorized to suspend any or all rules, require the joint use of terminals, and establish preferences, embargoes, and the like. It could even reroute freight in disregard of a shipper's instructions.

Through routes and joint rates. When service is offered between two points over a combination of two or more railroads, the combination is called a through route and the rate covering the through movement is known as a joint rate. Congress first gave the Interstate Commerce Commission authority to establish through routes in the Hepburn Act, which act also gave the Commission the power to determine the way in which the joint through rate would be divided among the participating carriers in the event that the carriers themselves were unable to agree upon such a division. In the Transportation Act, 1920, the Commission was given the power to act on its own authority to establish equitable divisions of joint rates, a provision that is traceable to the strong and weak line problem. The Commission could now prevent strong lines from forcing inequitable divisions of joint through rates on weak connecting lines.

The law specified that the Commission in the exercise of its authority to fix the divisions of joint rates "shall give due consideration, among other things, to the efficiency with which the carriers concerned are operated, the amount of revenue required to pay their respective operating expenses, taxes, and a fair return on their railway property held for and used in the service of transportation, and the importance to the public of the transportation services of such carriers; and also whether any particular participating carrier is an originating, intermediate, or delivering line, and any other fact or circumstance which would ordinarily, without regard to the mileage haul, entitle one carrier to a greater or less proportion than another carrier of the joint rate fare or charge." It seems quite clear from the wording of the law that Congress had in mind the possibility of aiding weak lines through favorable divisions of joint rates.

Construction and abandonment. An entirely new provision in the law gave the Commission extensive powers over the construction and abandonment of railroad mileage. No carrier in interstate commerce might extend or abandon all or any part of its lines without first obtaining from the Commission a certificate specifying that the public convenience and necessity required such extension or abandonment. Furthermore, the law permitted the Commission to order a carrier to extend its lines and to provide itself with safe and adequate facilities for performing its car service. Before it could require a line extension, however, the Commission had to find that the extension was reasonably required in the interest of public convenience and necessity, and before it could require either an extension or the provision of additional facilities it had to find that the expense involved would not impair the ability of the carrier to perform its duty to the public. The Commission's authority did not extend to spur, industrial, team, switching, or side tracks located or to be located wholly within one state, or to street, suburban, and interurban electric railroads not operated as a part of a general steam railroad system of transportation.

These provisions of the law were designed to serve various purposes. In the first place, the abandonment provisions protected dependent communities from the indiscriminate abandonment of nonpaying branches by larger railroad systems, while at the same time they protected carriers, both weak and strong alike, from unreasonable restrictions placed on the abandonment of lines by state laws and commissions. Control of construction enabled the Commission to prevent construction of lines into areas which could hardly support existing mileage. Furthermore, by preventing the construction of ill-conceived railroad projects, the Commission could act to prevent the addition of new weak lines to the already existing excessive number of such lines. The compulsory provisions of the act, those calling for extensions of lines and the provision of safe and adequate facilities, were the subject of some controversy concerning their constitutionality. The Commission has had little occasion to exercise these latter powers, however, except insofar as safety regulation is concerned.

Jurisdictional matters. The fact that a large number of railroads carried both interstate and intrastate traffic at the same time was bound to lead to conflicts between state and federal authorities because experience had shown time and again that it was impossible neatly to set off the intrastate activities of a carrier from its interstate activities in such a way that the one would not interfere with the other. This problem had been particularly vexing with regard to rates, and the Transportation Act, 1920, provided that whenever, after a full hearing, the Commission found that any rate, regulation, or practice prescribed for intrastate commerce caused any undue or unreasonable advantage, preference, or prejudice as between persons or localities in intrastate commerce, on the one hand, and interstate commerce on the other, the Commission was to prescribe such rates or practices as would remove the discrimination. In other words, the Commission was to have the final word in the event of a jurisdictional conflict.

The possibility of conflicts between state and federal regulatory measures was recognized in other sections of the act. For example, federal regulation of security issues was to take precedence over state laws and practices, even though such regulation might at times do violence to the provisions of state constitutions. The same was true of federal regulation of railroad construction and abandonments. The law, however, also provided for cooperation where possible. The Commission was required to notify state authorities of hearings dealing with matters in which the states in question might have a direct interest, and the Commission was further authorized to confer with state regulatory bodies and even to hold joint hearings with such bodies.

Other provisions. Congress recognized the heavy burden of added powers and duties that it had placed upon the Commission and sought to offset this burden in part by increasing the number of commissioners from nine to eleven and raising the salary of each to $12,000 per year. Detailed machinery for the settlement of railroad labor disputes was established, this machinery to be administered by agencies which were entirely independent of the Interstate Commerce Commission. The nature of this machinery and subsequent developments are discussed in Chapter 17. The Transportation Act, 1920, also provided that the Act to Regulate Commerce, as amended, could be cited as the Interstate Commerce Act, by which name it is now commonly known.

RESULTS OF THE TRANSPORTATION ACT, 1920

Transportation Act, 1920, not entirely satisfactory. The Transportation Act, 1920, was hailed by some as the solution of the railroad problem, but if they actually believed that to be the case, they were soon disappointed. First to fall were the provisions of the act having to do with the peaceful settlement of labor disputes. These were repealed in 1926 and an entirely new procedure established. The rule of rate making, which to many constituted the very heart of the Transportation Act, 1920, was abandoned in 1933, and in 1940 the consolidation provisions of the act were drastically modified. The reasons for these major failures will be brought out as the discussion proceeds. Except for some minor changes, the remaining provisions of the act survived the test of time and are all still a part of the law of the land. These provisions also will be considered further as the discussion proceeds.

HOCH–SMITH RESOLUTION

Postwar depression in agriculture. In 1920, following on the heels of World War I, the country suffered a sharp depression which, fortunately, was short-lived. Agriculture, however, did not recover along with other industry, and farmers continued to suffer from the generally low level of prices of agricultural commodities. The situation in agriculture was due primarily to the postwar loss of foreign markets, although other factors also were involved. Farm interests blamed the unprofitable nature of agriculture partly on high freight rates, and they appealed to the Interstate Commerce Commission for lower rates, arguing that agriculture could not thrive under existing rates and that this in turn would harm business generally. But the Commission was unable to find that the rates assailed were on the whole unreasonable. Nor was it convinced that depressed conditions in agriculture were due to high freight rates, and it refused to accept as valid the idea that rates which were otherwise reasonable should fluctuate with the economic conditions of an industry.[3]

Hoch-Smith Resolution. Unable to make any headway with the Commission, agricultural interests appealed directly to Congress. Here they met with greater success, the result of their efforts being the adoption in 1925 of the Hoch-Smith Resolution, which stated in part that "it is hereby declared to be the true policy in rate making to be pursued by the Interstate Commerce Commission in adjusting freight rates, that the conditions which at any given time prevail in our several industries should be considered in so far as it is legally possible to do so, to the end that commodities may freely move."

Having made this general statement of principle, Congress went on to direct the Commission to undertake an investigation of the rate structure to determine the extent to which rates were unreasonable and the extent to which they gave undue advantage to various localities, parts of the country, and kinds of traffic; and to make such changes as might be necessary to correct any defects found to exist. In making such changes the Commission was to give due regard to the general and comparative levels in the market value of various kinds of commodities, to a natural and proper development of the country as a whole, and to the maintenance of an adequate transportation system. In the concluding paragraph of the resolution, the Commission was directed to fix rates on products of agriculture affected by depressed conditions at the lowest lawful level compatible with the maintenance of adequate transportation service.

Objections to Hoch-Smith Resolution. There are a number of objections to fixing rates on the basis of the economic condition of a given industry. In the first place, as early as 1893 the Supreme Court had declared that the right of a railroad to charge a given rate did not depend at all upon whether its customers were making or losing money.[4] Second, application

---

[3] *National Live Stock Shippers' League* v. *A.T. & S.F. Ry.*, 63 I.C.C. 107 (1921); *Rates on Grain, Grain Products, and Hay,* 64 I.C.C. 85 (1921).

[4] *Union Pacific Railway Co.* v. *Goodridge,* 149 U.S. 680. See also *Northern Pacific Railway Co.* v. *North Dakota,* 236 U.S. 585 (1915).

of this principle would require constant readjustments of the rate structure as first one industry and then another suffered varying degrees of hardship. This in turn would make it impossible to establish any degree of stability in rate relationships between commodities and between different parts of the country. Third, the Hoch-Smith Resolution did not repeal the rule of rate making. The railroads as a whole were not earning the fair return they were supposed to have, and a reduction in the rates on agricultural commodities would further decrease their earnings unless the rates charged for moving the products of more prosperous industries were raised. Yet it seems reasonable to suppose that the industries singled out for increased rates would find this action just as objectionable as agricultural interests had found the Commission's refusal to lower rates on agricultural commodities.

Judicial interpretation. Some uncertainty existed on the legal effect of the Hoch-Smith Resolution because of the way in which the principle embodied in it was hedged in by various restrictions. For example, the Commission was to apply it "in so far as it is legally possible to do so . . ." and to give due regard to the maintenance of an adequate transportation system. In 1927 the Commission, acting on the basis of the Hoch-Smith Resolution, ordered a reduction in the rates on deciduous fruits from California to the East, although two years previously it had held these rates to be reasonable. The carriers challenged this order in the courts, and in 1930 the Supreme Court rejected the Commission's action. In referring to the statements in the resolution regarding agriculture the Court said: "They are more in the nature of a hopeful characterization of an object deemed desirable if, and insofar as, it may be attainable, than of a rule intended to control rate making." [5] In this way the Court effectively disposed of the Hoch-Smith Resolution as a positive factor in rate making.

Significance. The Hoch-Smith Resolution is not without significance to students of transportation because it is a prime example of political rate making. The Resolution may be regarded either as a political sop thrown out to agriculture or as an expression of congressional displeasure with the Commission's refusal to heed the demands of the farmers. In either event it was adopted with little regard to its effect on the rate structure or on orderly processes of rate making. The regulation of transportation agencies vitally effects the whole economy, and it is neither fair to the carriers nor proper to the development of the economy to permit railroad rates and practices to be influenced by special interests. In the Interstate Commerce Commission the nation has a nonpartisan and nonpolitical body of experts which functions continuously in the interests

---

[5] *Ann Arbor R.R. Co.* v. U.S. 281 U.S. 658, 669.

of the whole people, and it is obvious that no such body can operate effectively if its actions are subjected to pressure from special interests.

EMERGENCY RAILROAD TRANSPORTATION ACT OF 1933

Effect of 1929 depression on the railroads. The stock market collapse which occurred late in 1929 ushered in a period of grave hardship for the nation's railroads. Industrial stagnation meant declining traffic, and declining traffic had a disastrous effect on railroad earnings. Because approximately 60 per cent of railroad capitalization was in the form of funded debt, the interest on which was due and payable without regard to earnings, many carriers faced bankruptcy. Even those carriers which were not in imminent danger of becoming insolvent found their credit impaired by shrinking earnings. Railroad security holders were becoming panicky, and investors in general were growing pessimistic about the future of the railroads.

Attempts to safeguard the railroads. In June, 1931, the carriers sought relief from their difficulties by applying for a general 15 per cent increase in freight rates, basing their case largely on the contention that the rule of rate making required the Commission to establish rates which would yield a fair return on the fair value of their property. The Commission, however, rejected this interpretation of the law and refused to sanction the proposed increase. It pointed out that the law from the beginning had provided that all rates must be just and reasonable, a requirement which had not been repealed by the rule of rate making, and it quoted from several Supreme Court decisions to the effect that the public could not be expected to pay more than the services rendered by the carriers were reasonably worth. It pointed out that prices in general had fallen sharply without any corresponding decline in freight rates, and noted that it would be difficult to argue that transportation services were now worth more to shippers than had formerly been the case.

Furthermore, the Commission pointed out that an increase in freight rates did not necessarily mean an increase in earnings. Indeed, there were many factors in the situation which seemed to suggest that the reverse might be true. For one thing, industries already facing disaster might find it impossible to survive if freight rates were increased, thus completely eliminating them as a source of traffic. Also, increased rates at this time would encourage the diversion of freight to the rapidly expanding motor carrier industry, to water carriers, and to pipe lines. Higher rates would encourage the decentralization of industry, with industries establishing branch plants and warehouses at strategic points near sources of raw materials and markets. Similarly, high railroad freight rates on certain commodities encouraged the substitution where possible of commodities not involving similarly high charges.

Proposals of the Commission. Although rejecting the proposed 15 per cent rate increase, the Commission was not unmindful of the immediate difficulties faced by the carriers, and it permitted the adoption of some increases, particularly on commodities where there was little likelihood of competition from other carriers. These increases took the form of surcharges added to existing rates, and the increased revenue resulting therefrom was to be pooled and lent to needy carriers to enable them to meet fixed charges. The carriers organized the Railroad Credit Corporation to administer the pooled funds, and during its short life this organization helped many carriers to meet their fixed charges. The surcharges were in effect from January 4, 1932, to September 30, 1933, although during this last six months the additional funds were retained by the carriers who received them in the first instance.

Continued decline in earnings. The additional income derived from the surcharges was not as great as the carriers had anticipated, and earnings continued to decline as the depression deepened. Earnings for 1931 were substantially less than those of 1930, and a net deficit was incurred in 1932. In its report on the 15 per cent rate increase case the Interstate Commerce Commission had recommended certain legislative changes, and Congress now proceeded to take action by passing the Emergency Railroad Transportation Act of June 16, 1933. Some of the provisions of this act were of a purely temporary nature to help the carriers in the depression-created emergency, and some were in the nature of permanent changes in the Interstate Commerce Act.

TEMPORARY PROVISIONS

Federal Coordinator of Transportation. The Emergency Railroad Transportation Act of 1933 provided for the establishment of a Federal Coordinator of Transportation, to be appointed by the President by and with the advice and consent of the Senate or to be appointed by the President from the membership of the Interstate Commerce Commission. The carriers in turn were to establish regional coordinating committees, one each in the East, the South, and the West. The purposes to be achieved by the office of Federal Coordinator and by the regional committees were to encourage and promote or require carrier cooperation to avoid unnecessary duplication of services and facilities and otherwise cut down on expenses, to promote financial reorganization of the carriers so as to reduce fixed charges, and to study other means of improving conditions surrounding transportation in all of its forms and to prepare plans to this end.

The railroad employees of each of the three designated regions were to select regional committees, and carrier committees and the Coordinator were required to consult with these regional labor committees before taking any action which would affect the interests of workers. Furthermore, no action could be taken under the terms of the emergency provisions which would result in a reduction in employment, and no action could be taken which would worsen the position of an employee with respect to compensation. The carriers were to bear the cost of property losses and expenses incurred by employees as a result of any transfers made necessary by actions under the emergency provisions of the law.

Results of emergency provisions. The emergency provisions of the Emergency Railroad Transportation Act of 1933 remained in effect until June 16, 1936, after which time Interstate Commerce Commissioner Joseph B. Eastman, who had been appointed Federal Coordinator of Transportation, returned to his duties with the Commission. They were not, on the whole, particularly successful. At the time the law was passed the railroads were in a difficult financial position, but rate increases were either impractical or impossible because shippers, too, were in financial difficulties and because of competition from unregulated carriers. Consequently emphasis was placed on reducing expenses by encouraging railroad management to cooperate in the joint use of facilities, eliminating competitive activities, and the like.

But it was not easy for those in charge of normally competitive railroad enterprises to agree to cooperative action without keeping in mind the competitive positions of their respective properties. Furthermore, no scheme of cooperation could be put into effect if it involved a reduction in employment, but it is hard to see how any substantial economies could be achieved in this way without involving a reduction in employment. Under the circumstances it is not surprising that little or nothing was accomplished along these lines. In one respect, however, the emergency provisions did bear some fruit. A great deal of research was carried on under the direction of the Federal Coordinator of Transportation, and a number of valuable studies were published, including the one on public aid referred to in Chapter 3.

NEW RULE OF RATE MAKING

Objections to 1920 rule. The Emergency Railroad Transportation Act of 1933 repealed the 1920 rule of rate making, together with the recapture of excess earnings clause, and substituted an entirely new rule. The Commission's experiences in attempting to apply the 1920 rule of rate making had not been too happy, the principal difficulty arising out of the fact that the rule sought to stabilize railroad earnings without regard to fluctuations in general economic conditions. On this point the Commission said:

> Railroad earnings reflect general economic conditions very closely, and to the extent that such conditions fluctuate railroad earnings will fluctuate, and it is impracticable to avoid these fluctuations by moving railroad charges up and down. To attempt this would mean higher rates in times of depression and lower rates in times of prosperity. Perhaps it was assumed, when the present section 15a was devised, that we had reached an era when economic conditions would remain stable; but if so, no such thought is any longer entertained. Another important factor which was then unanticipated or disregarded was the competition of other transportation agencies which has developed so rapidly in recent years to the detriment of railroad earnings.[6]

Other objections to the rule of rate making may be noted. There was, for example, the difficulty of reconciling the injunction that all rates must be just and reasonable with the provision that rates were to be fixed to yield the carriers a fair return on the fair value of their property. With regard to the recapture provisions the Commission observed that their enforcement imposed heavy expenditures of time and money on both the Government and the railroads. There was the constant threat of litigation arising out of disagreements about proper accounting procedures and disagreements about what constituted the fair value of railroad properties. The possibility of the Government recapturing excess earnings encouraged extravagant expenditures by prosperous companies in good times so as to avoid the payment of excess earnings, and payments due on account of excess earnings made in earlier years hung like a cloud over the credit of many carriers when times were bad. Finally, many carriers which might need loans from the fund could not meet the requirements covering security and reasonable prospect of repayment, and those which could meet these requirements could borrow money at lower rates of interest elsewhere.

New rule of rate making. The new rule of rate making adopted by Congress followed closely recommendations made to it by the Commission. It read quite simply as follows:

> In the exercise of its power to prescribe just and reasonable rates the Commission shall give due consideration, among other factors, to the effect of rates on the movement of traffic; to the need, in the public interest, of adequate and efficient railway transportation service at the lowest cost consistent with the

---

[6] Interstate Commerce Commission, *Annual Report*, 1932, pp. 16-17. Section 15a contained the rule of rate making.

furnishing of such service; and to the need of revenues sufficient to enable the carriers, under honest, economical, and efficient management, to provide such service.

The recapture clause was repealed, the repeal being made retroactive to March 1, 1920, and all recaptured earnings were ordered returned to the carriers from whom they had been received. The Commission had estimated that recapturable earnings amounted to well over $300 million but this exceeded by far the carriers' own calculations. Actually they had paid in as of November 1, 1932, only $9,882,277.94 as the Government's half of excess earnings, and since most of even this small amount had been paid under protests of one sort or another, no loans had ever been authorized from the fund. The total amount in the fund, including interest, came to $12,882,403.87.

Conclusion. Thus came to an end one of the major experiments in regulation initiated by Congress in the Transportation Act, 1920. The whole experiment had been costly both to the carriers and to the Government, involving as it did the tremendous expense of obtaining and keeping up to date the valuation figures and the continuing expense of litigation. It had been productive of numerous disputes over valuations and accounting procedures to be followed in determining earnings. The new rule, by relieving the Commission of the necessity of fixing rates in conformity with the fair return on fair value base, greatly simplified its work in connection with the establishment of the general level of rates. It would be a mistake, however, to look upon the provisions of the 1933 Act as constituting a return to pre-1920 conditions of rate regulation because the new rule definitely requires that rates established by the Commission be fair to carriers as well as to shippers. Obviously the carriers cannot offer adequate and efficient railroad transportation service unless they receive revenues sufficient to maintain their properties and to attract the capital necessary to improve and extend their service and facilities.

CONSOLIDATION

Avoidance of consolidation requirements. In 1929 the Commission had published its final plan of consolidation as required by the Transportation Act, 1920, but numerous practical difficulties had militated against the consummation of the consolidations contemplated in that plan. In the first place, the original law provided one set of conditions for complete consolidation and another set of conditions for acquisitions of control of one carrier by another by means short of actual consolidation, a circumstance which was somewhat confusing. Second, the Commission's consolidation plans had been sidestepped neatly in some cases by means of the use of holding companies. A third difficulty arose out of the requirement that the capitalization of the consolidated companies must not exceed the combined value of the properties as determined under the Valuation Act, and extensive delay was involved in obtaining and bringing up to date the necessary valuation figures.

Provisions of the law. The Emergency Railroad Transportation Act of 1933 sought to solve these difficulties by providing that all combinations or unifications irrespective of how achieved required the approval of the Interstate Commerce Commission, and holding companies were specifically mentioned. The separate standards for acquisitions of control and for complete consolidations were eliminated, and all such unifications were henceforth to be in harmony with the plan of consolidation, and also to be of such a nature as to promote the public interest, before they could obtain the approval of the Commission. The capitalization requirements of the original measure were dropped. There was no danger of over-capitalization resulting from the abandonment of this provision because the Commission had complete authority under the security regulation provisions of the Transportation Act, 1920, to control the securities issued by the consolidated corporation.

Conclusion. The provisions of the Emergency Railroad Transportation Act relative to consolidation were designed to encourage consolidations in accordance with the final plans of the Commission by eliminating some of the obstacles in the path of such consolidations. Unfortunately, the new law took cognizance of only a part of the difficulties involved and further amendments were necessary.

MOTOR CARRIER ACT, 1935

Change in organization of Interstate Commerce Act. The regulation of interstate motor carrier transportation is discussed elsewhere, but it should be noted here that passage of the Motor Carrier Act, 1935, brought about a change in the organization of the Interstate Commerce Act. All of the existing provisions of that act were made Part I of the Interstate Commerce Act, with a Part II added to cover the regulation of interstate motor carriers.

SUGGESTED READINGS

Daggett, Stuart, *Principles of Inland Transportation*, 3rd Ed. New York: Harper and Brothers, 1941.

Locklin, D. Philip, *Railroad Regulation Since 1920.* New York: A. W. Shaw, 1928.

FEDERAL REGULATION

Locklin, D. Philip, *Economics of Transportation*, 3rd Ed. Chicago: Richard D. Irwin, Inc., 1947.

MacVeagh, Rogers, *The Transportation Act, 1920*. New York: Henry Holt and Company, 1923. Contains complete text of Transportation Act, 1920, together with debates and statements preceding its passage.

Miller, Sidney L., *Principles of Inland Transportation*. New York: McGraw-Hill Book Company, Inc., 1931.

Sharfman, I. L., *The Interstate Commerce Commission*, Four Volumes. New York: The Commonwealth Fund, 1931-1937. This monumental work traces the Commission's work down to the middle 1930's.

8.

Federal Regulation
of
RAILROAD TRANSPORTATION (III)

Unfavorable financial status of railroads. Railroad earnings had fallen sharply down through 1934, in which year the ratio of net income to capital stood at only .10 per cent. In 1935 this figure rose to .24 per cent and in 1936 to 1.01 per cent, but the recession in business conditions in the latter part of 1937 wiped out a substantial part of even this modest gain. The year 1938 was a very poor one, with an over-all deficit of $87,468,000, and by the end of 1938 railroad companies operating about 31 per cent of the total mileage of the country were bankrupt or in receivership. Earnings improved somewhat in 1939 as Europe drifted toward war, but it was realized that any war induced increase in traffic would be temporary and would not solve the underlying causes of railroad difficulties.

Basic causes of continuing difficulties. In its annual report for 1938 the Interstate Commerce Commission called attention to the growing seriousness of the railroad problem and to insistent demands that Congress do something about it. The problem, the Commission declared, was the product of railroad poverty precipitated by an abrupt and continued decline in traffic that was unparalleled in severity and duration. The immediate and primary cause of this decline in traffic was the depression, but this was far from being the whole story because the improvement in general business conditions that had taken place since 1933 was not accompanied by a corresponding improvement in railroad traffic. In this connection the Commission quoted figures showing that industrial production in 1936 was 105 per cent of 1923-25 while railroad freight ton miles were only 83.6 per cent and passenger miles only 61.6 per cent. Such figures showed clearly that railroad traffic losses were not altogether a product of the depression. In varying degrees these losses reflected the growing tendency of industry to decentralize; the substitution of gas, hydroelectric power, and fuel oil for coal, and improvements in the utilization of coal itself; the substitution of such products as cement which involve relatively short hauls for such characteristically long haul products as steel, stone, and lumber; the decline in export and import traffic; and above all, the great increase during the depression years of competition from other forms of transportation.

A transportation revolution. Whether it realized it or not, said the Commission in 1938, the country had experienced a transportation revolution in a very short space of time. Common carrier motor vehicles were carrying large numbers of passengers and an increasing amount of freight. The Panama Canal and the continued construction and improvement of inland waterways were adding greatly to the sum total of water transportation. Pipe lines were being extended and used to move natural gas and gasoline as well as petroleum. And air transportation was born and "grew like Jack's bean stalk." On top of this there had been a vast growth of private transportation of persons and property by highway and water. This growth, the Commission pointed out, could not have been accomplished without the expenditures of vast sums of money by state and federal governments in highway improvements, waterway improvements, and in various aids to air transportation.

This vast increase in the supply of transportation facilities was accomplished largely as the result of government action, without plan or anticipation of the consequences. Not only were the railroads suffering from inadequate earnings and extensive bankruptcies but so also were motor carriers, water carriers, and air carriers. Only the pipe lines had remained prosperous. Instead of each type of carrier confining its activities to those operations for which it was best fitted, with competition existing only in those areas where two or more types of carriers could compete on comparatively equal terms, all were engaged in a savage fight for business without much regard for the cost of providing the service. The Commission found that keen competition between rival agencies existed in innumerable cases even though one form of transportation had a clear, and often a large, advantage in cost, with results disastrous to all.

Other factors contributing to railroad distress. While the two factors, the depression and the rise of competition, were unquestionably basic to the railroads' difficulties, these difficulties were enhanced to a greater or lesser degree by certain other elements in the situation. One of these, already mentioned in connection with the earlier depression years, was the extent to which the railroads had been financed by means of borrowed money. This had driven a number of carriers into receivership and had driven others to curtail expenditures with an attendant deterioration of the physical properties. Another difficulty was found in the financial abuses of the past which still hung like a cloud over the destiny of certain lines. Other difficulties included the failure of railroad management to appreciate the impending danger of competition from other forms of transportation, inability to modernize equipment because of lack of credit, construction of expensive passenger terminals, improvident planning of some of the early lines, and increased wages.

Recommendations of the Interstate Commerce Commission. In its annual reports for 1938 and 1939 and in a special report submitted to Congress on March 20, 1939, the Interstate Commerce Commission made a number of recommendations for further legislation. For one thing, the Commission recommended that its regulatory activities be extended to include the regulation of water carriers. It proposed changes in the consolidation provisions of the law to encourage consolidation or other forms of coordination to eliminate or reduce unnecessary competitive expenses. It recommended certain minor changes in procedure which would enable it to speed up its work. It believed that Congress should provide for an examination of the relative economy and fitness of the various types of carriers with a view to encouraging the use of each to perform those transportation services for which it was best suited, at the same time avoiding such uses as would be merely harmful to agencies better suited to the work. Such a study also might discover and lead to the development of many opportunities for the joint and cooperative use of all. It expressed approval of proposals to eliminate land-grant rate reductions on government traffic, to relieve the railroads of disproportionate burdens of the cost of grade crossing eliminations, and the cost, in excess of direct benefits derived, of bridge changes necessitated by inland waterway improvements.

Along what might be called nonlegislative lines the Commission expressed the belief that an improvement in general business conditions could do more than anything else to improve railroad revenues. Some limited opportunities might exist for increasing revenues by raising rates, but it did not look with particular favor on this sort of remedy. At one point it remarked:

Transportation success can never be the product of high rates and restricted service. As the makers of low-priced automotive vehicles fully demonstrated, there is no fixed amount of transportation to be performed, but rather an amount capable of indefinite expansion, provided the public can be offered sufficiently attractive service at a price which it is able to pay.[1]

Steps should be taken, continued the Commission, to press the reorganization of bankrupt railroads to an early completion, and the possibility of voluntary readjustment of the financial structures of some lines not in bankruptcy was suggested. Expenses might be reduced by wage reduc-

---

[1] Interstate Commerce Commission, *Annual Report,* 1938, p. 22.

tions, but this was a matter outside the jurisdiction of the Commission.

The Commission's position with regard to transportation legislation is summed up in a broad and statesmanlike way in the following quotation from its 1938 report:

The essence of the situation is that a virtual revolution in transportation has occurred within a comparatively short period of time. No more extraordinary development of transportation facilities has ever been seen than has taken place in this country in the past 20 years. The results of this revolution have not been consolidated, and the revolution still progresses with attendant confusion and disturbance. There is need for readjustments between and within the different branches of the transportation industry, for consideration of present tendencies and their probable results, for the avoidance of uneconomic and wasteful practices, and in general for the determination, creation, and protection of the conditions most favorable to the development of a transportation system which will best serve the public interest. There is a field here both for continuing study and research and for active, aggressive, and consistent leadership on the part of the Government which has never been occupied. The real problem is to fill that void in the best possible way.[2]

Transportation Act of 1940. Transportation legislation was under discussion in Congress throughout 1938 and 1939 and a good part of 1940. The result of this discussion was the Transportation Act of 1940, approved by the President on September 18, 1940. It contained a declaration of a national transportation policy applicable to all modes of transportation subject to the jurisdiction of the Interstate Commerce Commission, and made certain amendments to Parts I and II of the Interstate Commerce Act. In addition, it created a new Part III bringing domestic water transportation partly under the jurisdiction of the Commission. The following discussion is confined to those provisions of the law having a direct bearing on the regulation of railroads.

ESTABLISHMENT OF A NATIONAL TRANSPORTATION POLICY

Declaration of policy. The Transportation Act of 1940 began with the following declaration of a national transportation policy:

It is hereby declared to be the national transportation policy of the Congress to provide for fair and impartial regulation of all modes of transportation subject to the provisions of this Act, so administered as to recognize and preserve the inherent advantages of each; to promote safe, adequate, economical, and efficient service and foster sound economic conditions in transportation and among the several carriers; to encourage the establishment and maintenance of reasonable charges for transportation services, without unjust discriminations, undue preferences or advantages, or unfair or destructive competitive

---

[2] Interstate Commerce Commission, *Annual Report*, 1938, pp. 24-25.

practices; to cooperate with the several States and duly authorized officials thereof; and to encourage fair wages and equitable working conditions;—all to the end of developing, coordinating, and preserving a national transportation system by water, highway, and rail, as well as other means, adequate to meet the needs of the commerce of the United States, of the Postal Service, and of the national defense. All of the provisions of this Act shall be administered and enforced with a view to carrying out the above declaration of policy.

Significance of declaration of policy. For almost a hundred years improved transportation had meant railroad transportation. The writings of earlier students of transportation are full of references to the railroad problem, for the railroad problem was the transportation problem. State legislatures and Congress passed laws to regulate railroad transportation and established railroad commissions to apply and administer them. The Transportation Act, 1920, was a railroad regulatory measure, identifying transportation with railroad transportation. But with the rapid rise of motor, water, and air transportation in the 1930's, the transportation problem and railroad problem were no longer synonymous. The railroad problem had become a part of a larger transportation problem, and recognition of this fact is implicit in the declaration of a national transportation policy. With this declaration Congress committed itself to a policy of developing, coordinating, and preserving a national transportation system.

In the declaration of policy Congress recognizes the justice of the complaint of railroad management that the closely regulated railroads cannot compete on even terms with unregulated or inadequately regulated agencies of transportation. The declaration of policy also takes cognizance of the chaotic conditions and the economic consequences which may result from a policy of permitting all types of carriers to compete for all types of traffic regardless of cost or efficiency of service. It is recognized that each type of carrier has certain peculiar advantages, and the Commission was told to administer regulation in such a way as to recognize and preserve the inherent advantages of each. The Commission was further admonished to administer regulation so as to encourage the establishment and maintenance of reasonable charges for transportation, without unjust discrimination, undue preferences or advantages, or unfair or destructive competitive practices. All of this seems to suggest that the Commission should encourage each type of carrier to operate only in those areas where it had a clear advantage or where competition on even terms was possible.

The declaration of policy also may be interpreted as a directive to the Commission not to regulate motor and domestic water transportation in the interests of the railroads. Thus Congress stated that it wanted to provide for the fair and impartial regulation of all modes of transportation subject to the act, and the Commission was directed to administer the law so as to recognize and preserve the inherent advantages of each and to avoid unfair or destructive competitive practices.

It may be well to point out that the 1940 declaration of policy is significant only to the extent that Congress by legislation and the Interstate Commerce Commission by interpretation are prepared to carry it through to its logical conclusion. Unfortunately, it has not always been possible to reconcile the declaration of a national policy on transportation with other congressional policies, as will be pointed out in later chapters.

CONSOLIDATION

Difficulties encountered in grouping railroads into systems. After making several unsuccessful attempts to get Congress to relieve it of the necessity of preparing a consolidation plan, the Interstate Commerce Commission issued its plan late in 1929. A part of the Commission's reluctance to prepare a consolidation plan may be traced to difficulties inherent in any attempt to divide railroads into systems in such a way as to secure general approval of all of the parties at interest. There were, for example, a number of short independent railroads of considerable strategic value which could not be placed in one system without doing damage to another. Conversely, there were numerous weak lines which were not wanted by any of the major carriers. Many cities and towns protested specific consolidation proposals because of the elimination or reduction of competition which would result. Some which had enjoyed an advantage by virtue of the fact that they were terminal points on certain railroads objected to prosposals which would reduce them to just another town on a through system. Still others objected to specific proposals for fear that they would lose railroad shops or other employment-creating facilities. Finally, railroad labor was particularly skittish because of the prospective loss of jobs inherent in any consolidation proposal.

Weaknesses of 1920 law. In addition to the purely practical difficulties encountered by the Commission in working out a plan of consolidation, certain characteristics of the law itself contributed to make it unworkable. For one thing, the law required that the systems be worked out in such a way that each would earn, under a uniform scale of rates on competitive traffic, substantially the same rate of return; and in addition, competition was to be preserved as fully as possible and existing channels of trade maintained. No human agency could work out a grouping of lines which would meet these requirements and at the same time provide an equitable allocation of strategic short lines, preserve a large number of weak lines, satisfy the diverse interests of numerous cities and towns, and safeguard the jobs of railroad workers.

But probably the principal weakness in the law was the concept of voluntary consolidation according to a fixed plan. Any plan worked out by the Commission in the broad public interest inevitably would run counter to the individual self-interest of the major railroads involved, especially in connection with the disposition of weak lines. The law did not require consolidation in accordance with the Commission's plan, but since no consolidations could be effected that did not conform with the plan, or some modification thereof, the choice was between consolidating according to the plan or not consolidating. Under the circumstances it is not surprising that no major consolidations were effected.

Present requirements. In 1940 the fixed plan idea was dropped completely and an entirely new procedure adopted which may be summarized briefly as follows. (1) Carriers are permitted to combine according to their own plans, either through consolidation or by use of the acquisition of control technique, subject to approval by the Interstate Commerce Commission. (2) The Commission can require, as a condition to obtaining its approval, the inclusion of one or more railroads in the area to be served by a proposed combination, if such railroads request to be included and if such inclusion appears to be consistent with the public interest. (3) The Commission is not to approve any guarantee or assumption of payment of dividends or fixed charges unless it finds that such is not inconsistent with the public interest, or any transaction which would result in increased fixed charges unless it is not contrary to public interest. (4) During a period of four years following a consolidation, no employee's position can be worsened, except that an employee of less than four years' duration need not be protected for a period longer than his actual period of employment. Other arrangements, however, may be made by agreement between the carriers and the unions involved. (5) If consolidation of a railroad with a motor carrier is proposed, the Commission is required to find that the combination will be consistent with the public interest, that the railroad will be able to use motor vehicle service to public advantage, and that such operation will not unduly restrain competition. (6) Detailed provisions are included to make the law applicable to holding companies and to all other devices or techniques which might be employed to evade its intent.

The authority of the Commission to require the inclusion of other lines in the area to be served by the consolidated system should be useful in inducing major carriers to include certain weak but publicly important lines in their consolidation plans. The provisions for protecting labor are an indication of the strength of the labor vote in 1940. These provisions are not likely to handicap consolidation activities so long as a labor shortage exists, but they might prove a retarding factor should a labor surplus develop. So far the results of the new law have not been spectacular. It had been in operation scarcely more than a year when the United States was plunged into war, and during the ensuing years the railroads were preoccupied with the burdens of war transportation. Since the close of World War II, a number of combined operations have been undertaken under the terms of the 1940 law, the most important of these being the Chesapeake & Ohio-Pere Marquette combination and the combination of the Gulf, Mobile, and Ohio with the Chicago and Alton.

OTHER AMENDMENTS

Changes in Commission organization and procedure. Congress had long recognized that every expansion of the Commission's duties increased the burden of its work. At first Congress sought to cope with this problem by adding more commissioners and by 1920 the number had expanded from the original five to eleven. But the addition of more commissioners beyond a certain number was no solution to the problem because as regulatory bodies get larger they become unwieldy. As early as 1917 Congress authorized the Commission to organize its members into divisions of not less than three members each, each division to handle a particular phase of the work of regulation. These "little commissions" had been organized and no doubt helped considerably in getting the work done. But with the addition of motor carriers in 1935 and water carriers in 1940, even this division of the larger group into smaller units was not enough, and further steps had to be taken to make it possible for the Commission to comply with the provisions of the law.

The Transportation Act of 1940 provides that duties may be assigned to Commission divisions, individual commissioners, or to boards of employees. It is provided, however, that if a single commissioner, employee, or board of employees takes testimony at a public hearing, any finding or report issued by such individual or individuals has to be accompanied by a statement of the reasons therefor and a recommended order, all of which is to be filed with the Commission and served upon the interested parties. The recommended order is to become the order of the Commission unless exceptions to it are filed in twenty days or it is stayed by action of the Commission or a division of the Commission. In the event that exceptions are filed or the order is stayed the matter is then to be determined by the Commission or by one of its divisions. Further to conserve its time, the Commission is given authority to limit requests for rehearings to cases involving matters of general transportation importance. It may be noted here that it has become the general practice today for hearings to be held and reports made by individual employees called examiners. Major cases, of course, are handled directly by the Commission.

Discrimination. Certain changes were made in Section 3 of the act, that section which originally declared it to be unlawful for any carriers to give any undue or unreasonable preference to any particular person, company, locality, or description of traffic in any respect whatsoever. This section was amended to specify that its provisions are not to be construed as applying to discrimination, prejudice, or disadvantage to the traffic of other types of carriers. The prohibition against discrimination also is extended to regions, this change being a recognition of complaints from the South and West that rates were higher in those areas than in the East. One other change which might be mentioned in connection with discrimination has to do with the establishment of export rates on agricultural products. The practice had developed of charging somewhat lower rates for hauling manufactured goods intended for export than were charged for hauling the same goods to the same ports if the goods were intended for domestic consumption. The Transportation Act of 1940 declares it to be the policy of Congress that farm commodities intended for export are to be granted export rates on the same principles as were applicable to industrial products intended for export.

Rates. The Transportation Act of 1940 contains a number of provisions dealing with rates in addition to those mentioned above in connection with discrimination. The 1933 rule of rate making which specified that the Commission was to give due consideration, among other things, to the effect of rates on the movement of traffic was amended to provide that due consideration be given to the effect of rates on the movement of traffic *by the carrier or carriers for which the rates are prescribed.* The rest of the rule remains unchanged. The purpose of this change was to prevent the Commission from fixing rates for one type of carrier for the purpose of protecting the traffic of another type of carrier. The Commission has interpreted this provision to mean that no carrier shall be required to maintain rates to protect the traffic of another carrier if the rates in question would be unreasonable by other standards.

In 1910 the Mann-Elkins Act provided that the burden of proof was on the carrier to show the reasonableness of any proposed increase in rates, a provision which strengthened the hand of the Commission in dealing with such proposals. The Transportation Act of 1940 expanded this principle by placing the burden of proof on the carrier to justify any proposed change in rates, fares, charges, classifications, rules, regulation, or practices. Not only is the carrier required to prove that changes proposed in matters other than rates are just and reasonable, but also he is expected to prove that rate reductions as well as increases are just and reasonable. The first change extends the rule to matters related to the rate-fixing process as well as to rates themselves, and the second increases the authority of the Commission to deal with rate reductions designed to meet or beat competition.

Board of Investigation and Research. Following a recommendation of the Interstate Commerce Commission, Congress provided for the establishment of a three member Board of Investigation and Research to be appointed by the President by and with the advice and consent of the Senate to investigate (1) the relative economy and fitness of different types of carriers to determine the service for which each type of carrier was especially fitted or unfitted, and the methods by which each type should be developed so as to provide an adequate national transportation system; (2) the extent to which right-of-way or other transportation facilities had been or were being provided from public funds without adequate compensation, direct or indirect; and (3) the extent to which taxes were being imposed upon such carriers by the various agencies of government.

The Board also was authorized to investigate any other matters it might deem important for the improvement of transportation and to effectuate the national transportation policy. It was to have a life of two years, but the President could extend its life for an additional two years. Inasmuch as the President failed to appoint the Board until some months after the passage of the law, it was necessary to extend its life for the additional two years. The Board no doubt was handicapped in obtaining adequate personnel because of the brief period of its existence and because of its being engaged in "nonessential" work during a period of active warfare. It issued a number of reports having to do with rail, motor, and water transportation, and to some extent with air transportation. Detailed references to some of its work appear elsewhere in this volume.

Repeal of land-grant rate reductions. In the discussions that had preceded the adoption of the Transportation Act of 1940 there had been considerable support for a relinquishment of the Government's right to reduced rates by virtue of the fact that it had granted land to aid in the construction of early railroads. These reductions were depriving the carriers of not insignificant amounts of revenue at a time when they needed revenue badly, and it was believed by some that the Government had been more than repaid for the land it had given to the railroads. Consequently the Transportation Act of 1940 released the land-grant railroads from the duty of transporting government traffic at reduced rates, except for the transportation of military or naval property and personnel on official duty. Unfortunately for the railroads involved, preparations for war and actual warfare itself soon led to the movement of an enormous volume of military and naval traffic so that, relative to the total volume of traffic hauled, the repeal of the land-grant rates meant little. After World War II Congress took action to terminate land-grant rate reductions in their entirety on October 1, 1946.

WARTIME OPERATION AND REGULATION

Impact of World War II. The impact of World War II on the railroads was noticeable long before Pearl Harbor. The national defense program and the demands of the lend lease act had the effect of revitalizing an American industrial mechanism that was only slowly recovering from a long period of stagnation. Thus preparations for war and war itself brought to the railroads the increased traffic and revenues they had needed for so long, although it was clear that this represented no permanent solution to the railroads' difficulties. And even as they were enjoying an unprecedented increase in the volume of traffic, the railroads were facing new problems.

The traffic losses and inadequate earnings the railroads had experienced as a result of the depression and the competition of rival transportation agencies had led railroad management to permit the supply of cars and locomotives to decline materially, with the result that on December 31, 1941, just after this country's entrance into World War II, there were 25 per cent fewer freight cars, 30 per cent fewer passenger cars, and 32 per cent fewer locomotives than were in existence on December 31, 1916, just a few months before the United States entered World War I. Offsetting this decline in the number of cars and locomotives in operation was the fact that both freight car capacity and locomotive power had increased substantially in the intervening years. Thus there was a decline of only 7 per cent in the carrying capacity of freight cars and actually a small increase in the tractive effort of locomotives. Furthermore, the track system was better in 1941 than it had been in 1916. Although total miles of road owned had declined, there had been an important increase in multiple tracked mileage and in yards and sidings, all factors contributing to a more intensive use of the existing railroad network. Thus, in spite of a sharp decline in the number of cars and locomotives available, the carrying capacity of the railroads was roughly the same in 1941 as in 1916.

But with the above facilities the railroads were called upon to move an enormously greater volume of traffic than they handled during World War I. In 1944, for example, the railroads moved 747,168 million ton miles of freight as compared with 408,778 million ton miles moved in 1918. And during the active war years, the War Production Board failed to allocate sufficient materials to enable the railroads to do much more than replace worn out equipment, with the result that there were only about 2.7 per cent more freight cars and 4.3 per cent more locomotives in 1944 than existed in 1941.

Railroad equipment difficulties were augmented by the equipment problems of rival transportation agencies. Before the war a susbtantial volume of traffic had been handled by coastwise steamers, particularly petroleum products moved from the Gulf coast to the North Atlantic area, but the activities of German submarines soon drove these ships from the seas. Furthermore, available ships were diverted wherever possible to moving war materials to the fighting fronts. The heavy burden of handling this water-borne domestic traffic was thrown almost entirely upon the railroads until somewhat later in the war when the completion of the Big Inch and the Little Inch pipe lines removed a part of the burden. While motor freight carriers moved a somewhat greater volume of traffic than they had handled before the war, they were handicapped by shortages of new trucks, parts, and tires, and a considerable number of trucks had to be laid up. As a result the relative amount of freight moved by motor carriers declined steadily until the end of the war period. Goods movement by air, including air mail and express, increased both absolutely and relatively, but the total volume was so small as to be insignificant from a tonnage point of view. In the passenger field gasoline and tire rationing brought a large reduction in the volume of traffic moving by private automobile. This decline in traffic by private automobile placed a burden on the railroads that they found most difficult to bear.

Private operation. One of the most striking features of wartime operation of the railroads was the fact that the 1917 experiment in federal control and operation was not repeated, and the railroads were operated throughout the war period as private enterprises by their individual owners. Railroad managements understandably have made much of the war record of the railroads under private management as compared with the record of federal control during World War I. Without wishing to detract in any way from the remarkable accomplishments of railroad management, however, it should be pointed out that conditions existing in the two war periods were not exactly parallel.

For one thing, in 1917 the railroads were not well organized for cooperative action; in 1941 they were. In the early 1920's the carriers had taken definite steps to improve the utilization of freight cars by organizing a car service division within the American Railway Association (now the Association of American Railroads), and this body had been given extensive authority over the distribution of cars. They also organized, in cooperation with shippers, thirteen shippers' regional advisory boards, each active in a different section of the country. Each board met once every three months, and at these meetings representatives of shippers sought to estimate their individual needs for the ensuing period. Armed with such data the carriers were able to shift the nation's car supply back and forth between various parts of the country in anticipation of fluctuating needs. There is no doubt that this organization was useful in enabling the carriers to secure maximum use of equipment and to assure the best service possible.

Other differences between the two wars should be mentioned. In World War I the general movement of goods was toward the East, necessitating a large empty car mileage westbound. In World War II, however, there was an extensive movement of goods west as well as east, resulting in a more efficient utilization of equipment through a reduction in empty car miles. And there were available more extensive port and warehouse facilities than was true at the time of World War I. Nor had the lessons of World War I gone unheeded. The conflicting priorities issued by various government departments in 1917 were largely avoided. As a result of wartime difficulties, the Transportation Act, 1920, had extended the Interstate Commerce Commission's control over railroad service, and it had been given sweeping powers over car service in times of emergency. Steps were taken to prevent a repetition of the disastrous practice of permitting cars to be loaded and sent to port areas without reference to the ability of port and shipping facilities to handle the goods at destination. And finally, it may be assumed that railroad management wanted no repetition of government control with its postwar confusion and possibilities of government ownership. It seems reasonable to suppose that management was ready to exhaust all efforts to make private control work.

Office of Defense Transportation. Regardless of how effectively the carriers might organize themselves to maximize the utilization of equipment, no private organization could be given the power to ration transportation and exercise such other compulsion as might be necessary. To this end the President established by executive order the Office of Defense Transportation, placing at its head Joseph B. Eastman, a veteran member of the Interstate Commerce Commission and the same man who had served as Federal Coordinator of Transportation from 1933 to 1936. In the performance of its duties the Office of Defense Transportation was to collaborate with existing agencies, and it sought to maximize the utilization of transportation equipment by cooperation rather than compulsion wherever possible. It issued various orders designed to increase the utilization of freight cars, to coordinate rail movements with port facilities and ship departures, to minimize the less important uses of equipment, and in various other ways to promote the war effort as far as transportation was concerned. Its orders were not subject to judicial review.

Results of wartime operation. The war demonstrated effectively the dependence of the nation upon railroad transportation. The accomplishments of the railroads in carrying a load almost double that carried in the earlier war, with plant capacity certainly no greater than existed in 1917, is little short of amazing. Also, most of the railroads made money during the war, many of them for the first time in years, and a number of lines were able to reduce their fixed charges or otherwise make substantial improvements in their financial status. The inability to secure new equipment during the war, however, coupled with the deterioration of existing equipment under heavy wartime use, posed serious problems of car supply in the postwar years. And the rising cycle of wages and prices necessitated demands for higher rates which in turn contributed to further price and wage increases. Caught in this vicious circle the position of the railroads was not a happy one. This matter is discussed more fully in Chapter 32.

REED-BULWINKLE ACT AND OTHER RECENT LEGISLATION

Rate bureaus. The Interstate Commerce Act gives the carriers the right to initiate rates by filing them with the Interstate Commerce Commission. Where a general rate increase is involved, the Commission exercises its suspension powers and conducts hearings, but where individual rate changes are proposed, either by carriers or by shippers, the proposal usually goes first to what is known as a rate bureau or conference. This is a cooperative organization composed of the carriers in a given geographical area which provides a means of contact between the shippers and carriers of the area and between the carriers and the various regulatory bodies. Any railroad or shipper may propose a change in rates, and such proposals are publicized and public hearings held by the bureau involved if requested. At these hearings interested shippers have an opportunity to express their views, but the public is not present when the carriers decide whether or not to make the proposed change. Although individual member carriers are not bound to abide by the decision of the bureau, they usually do so. If a decision necessitates a change in rates, new tariffs are filed with the Interstate Commerce Commission and state regulatory bodies. Any carrier or shipper who is not satisfied with the action taken by the bureau may take separate action before the Commission.

Advantage to public. Rate bureaus have been operating in all parts of the country for many years and have met with almost universal approval from shippers, railroads, and regulatory bodies. And as the newer forms of transportation have developed they also have adopted similar rate-making procedures. One of the principal advantages claimed for the practice of initiating rate changes through rate bureaus is that it gives the carriers an opportunity to confer with shippers and ascertain their wishes and needs before deciding what action they should take with reference to a given rate proposal. As a result the bureau procedure has operated to reduce greatly the number of requests for the suspension of rate tariffs filed with the Commission and to reduce the number of formal complaints lodged against rates already in effect. Obviously the procedure functions to speed up the rate-making processes and to lighten the burden of regulatory bodies. And shippers have testified that rate bureaus are helpful in that they can present a problem to all of the carriers involved at one time instead of having to carry out separate conferences with each.

Need for cooperative action. In order to conform with the requirements of the Interstate Commerce Act it is necessary for the railroads to confer and cooperate with each other on a wide variety of matters, including certain aspects of rate making. For example, the law requires the establishment of through routes which permit freight to move from origin to destination over the lines of two or more railroads without interruption and under a single through rate. Obviously such routes and rates cannot be established unless the participating carriers have some means of getting together to work out the rates to be charged and the amount to be received by each carrier. Also, the law provides that rates must be just and reasonable and free from undue preference or prejudice, but freight rates are so interrelated that it frequently is impossible for a railroad, acting unilaterally, to change a rate between two points without affecting rates at many other points not on its line. This point is very well expressed in the following brief quotation from a statement by the late Commissioner Joseph B. Eastman.

Where there is more than one route between two points, as a practical matter the rates must ordinarily be the same over all the routes. Even in the case of rates from widely separated origins to a common market, a change in one of the rates may impel changes in them all. A change in the rate basis on one commodity between certain points may even force changes in the rates on other commodities between different points.

It must be evident to any reasonable man that the carriers cannot respond to all the duties imposed by law, if each individual carrier acts in a vacuum. It is a situation, under all the conditions, which plainly calls for consultation, conference, and organization and for many acts of a joint or cooperative character....[3]

---

[3] Testimony given in 1943 before the Senate Committee on Interstate Commerce on S. 942, pp. 830-831.

By cooperating with each other through rate bureaus and other organizations the carriers are able to take into consideration all the possible consequences of a proposed rate change before reaching a decision on a course of action. Of course, since these conferences are not open to the public, there is always the danger of collusion among the carriers, but shippers are well organized, and if they are not satisfied with the outcome, they can and will take their case to the Commission. Apparently shippers as a whole have felt no cause for alarm on this score.

Attitude of Department of Justice. In 1942 the Antitrust Division of the Department of Justice took public notice of the activities and practices of carrier rate bureaus, and in 1944 the Department of Justice instituted a suit against the western railroads and others in which it attacked the legality of the rate bureaus. The basis of the Department's complaint was that when railroads conferred and agreed among themselves before filing rates with the Interstate Commerce Commission, they were violating the antitrust laws. Spokesmen for the Department of Justice also have contended that the dominant carriers bring pressure to bear to prevent individual railroads from taking independent action.

Reed-Bulwinkle Act. The attitude of shippers and regulatory bodies was that collusion or coercion should not be tolerated, but that destructive competition and chaos would result if the bureaus were eliminated and the initiation of rates left to each railroad acting independently. Since the Department of Justice apparently intended to pursue its attack, an appeal was made to Congress to legalize rate bureaus, subject to control by the Interstate Commerce Commission. Congress responded with the Reed-Bulwinkle bill which was vetoed by President Truman, but under the urging of shippers, his veto was overridden, and the bill became law on June 17, 1948. The law is quite simple. It permits the establishment of agreements among carriers covering rates and related matters, subject to approval by the Interstate Commerce Commission. Before giving its approval the Commission must find that the agreement accords each party the free and unrestrained right to take independent action if it wishes to do so. The parties to an approved rate agreement are specifically relieved from the operation of the antitrust laws.

Since the adoption of the Reed-Bulwinkle Act the railroads and other carriers subject to the jurisdiction of the Interstate Commerce Commission have filed a considerable number of rate bureau agreements with the Commission. They have been approved by the Commission, which has not hesitated to require changes where changes appeared to be in order. Although shippers, carriers, and commissions are in almost universal agreement that the rate bureaus are essential, the Department of Justice has continued its opposition to them in their present form. It has appeared in opposition to specific agreements in hearings before the Commission, and late in 1950 it announced that it was going to file suit to set aside the orders of the Commission approving two agreements, including one covering the western railroads. The suit instituted in 1944 against the western railroads was to be held in abeyance pending the disposition of the later suit.

Railroad labor legislation. As previously noted, the provisions of the Transportation Act, 1920, dealing with the settlement of labor disputes were short-lived, being replaced in 1926 by the Railway Labor Act of that year. This in turn was amended in various respects in 1934. In addition, there have been laws and proposed laws dealing with retirement benefits, unemployment insurance, and other aspects of social security as applied to railroad workers. All of these matters are discussed in Chapter 17.

Railroad reorganization. The numerous financial difficulties arising out of the depression which began in 1929 led Congress to adopt new regulations designed to promote the reorganization of properties in financial difficulties. The first such legislation was passed by Congress in 1933 in the form of an amendment to the Federal Bankruptcy Act, known as Section 77. Section 77 in turn was amended in certain respects in 1935. Dissatisfaction with the results accomplished under Section 77 led to demands for further legislation which took the form of Public Law 478, adopted in 1948. The subject of railroad reorganization is discussed in Chapter 15.

Reconstruction Finance Corporation. Brief mention should be made of the relationship of the Reconstruction Finance Corporation to the railroads. This corporation extended loans to a number of railroads during the early years of the depression, loans which enabled them to avoid receiverships, at least temporarily. Such loans required the approval of the Interstate Commerce Commission. The Emergency Railroad Transportation Act of 1933 specified that the Interstate Commerce Commission was not to approve a loan to any carrier which, in its opinion, was in need of financial reorganization.

Defense Transport Administration. With the Korean War and the revival of defense activities President Truman delegated authority with respect to priorities and allocations for transportation services to the Interstate Commerce Commissioner responsible for supervision of the Commission's Bureau of Service. This happened to be Commissioner James K. Knudson who had been sworn in as a commissioner only a few months before. On October 4, 1950, Mr. Knudson announced the formation of the Defense Transport Administration to carry out the functions assigned to him. There has been some interchangeability of employees between the Interstate Commerce Commission and the Defense Transport Administration. At the time of writing the activities of the Administration have been minor in nature, but it does provide the machinery for priorities and allocations in the event of an all-out war effort.

THE INTERSTATE COMMERCE ACT TODAY

Need for summary. The nation has gone a long way in the regulation of railroads since the passage in 1887 of the Act to Regulate Commerce. Some of the provisions of the orginal law remain unchanged, some have been dropped, and others have been amended and reamended. New provisions have been added over the years, and some of these in turn have been amended, reamended, or dropped. Even the name of the law has been changed. It would, therefore, seem desirable to summarize the present provisions of the Interstate Commerce Act before proceeding to other matters. Unless otherwise noted all of the provisions summarized below are from Part I except, of course, the preamble which applies equally to all parts. Numerous highly detailed and technical provisions of the law have been omitted as being of no broad general significance. It will be instructive to compare this summary of the provisions of the present law with the summary of the provisions of the original Act to Regulate Commerce given on pages 110 to 113 inclusive.

Preamble. It is the policy of Congress to provide for fair and impartial regulation of all forms of transportation subject to the Interstate Commerce Act, so administered as to recognize and preserve the inherent advantages of each; to promote safe, adequate, economical, and efficient service and foster sound economic conditions in transportation and among the several carriers; to encourage the establishment and maintenance of reasonable charges for transportation services, without unjust discriminations, undue preferences or advantages, or unfair or destructive competitive practices; to cooperate with the several states; and to encourage fair wages and equitable working conditions—all to the end of developing, coordinating, and preserving a national transportation system. All the provisions of the act are to be administered and enforced with a view to carrying out this policy.

Section 1. (3) The provisions of Part I apply to interstate commerce and foreign commerce by railroad, pipe line, express, and sleeping car companies. The provisions of certain following sections cover holding companies, voting trusts, and the like, as well as actual operating companies.

(4) Carriers must provide service, establish through routes with like types of carriers, and railroads must establish reasonable joint routes with water carriers.

(5) All charges shall be just and reasonable, and every unjust and unreasonable charge is prohibited.

(7) Free passes are prohibited except for officers and employees and certain other enumerated groups. Both giver and receiver of an unlawful pass are subject to a fine of not less than $100 or more than $2,000.

(8) (Commodities clause) No railroad may transport in interstate commerce any article or commodity, other than timber and the manufactured products thereof, in which it has any interest, except for its own use.

(11) Railroads must provide safe and adequate car service without unreasonable rules and regulations.

(15-17) The Interstate Commerce Commission is given broad powers over the use of railroad facilities in times of emergency.

(18-22) Railroads must secure the consent of the Interstate Commerce Commission before they can build or abandon any line. The Commission may order a carrier to provide safe and adequate facilities and to extend its lines, provided that the expense involved will not impair the ability of the carrier to perform its duty to the public. None of these provisions apply to spur, industrial, team, switching or side tracks, located wholly within one state, or to street, suburban, or interurban electric railroads not operated as a part of a general steam railroad system.

Section 2. Rebates and personal discriminations of every sort are forbidden.

Section 3. (1) It is unlawful for carriers to discriminate in any way whatsoever. This applies to personal and place discrimination, and to discrimination in connection with different types of traffic. Place discrimination includes regions or territories as well as cities and towns.

(1a) It is declared to be the policy of Congress to grant export rates on agricultural products on the same principles as are applicable to rates on industrial products for export.

(4) Carriers must provide for the interchange of passengers and goods and must not discriminate as between connecting lines.

(5) The Interstate Commerce Commission may compel the joint use of terminal facilities if this can be done without substantially impairing the ability of the owning carrier to handle its own business.

Section 4. (1) No carrier shall charge more for a short haul than for a longer haul over the same line or route in the same direction, the shorter being included in the longer, or to charge more for a through haul than the aggregate of the intermediate rates. The Interstate Commerce Commission may authorize departures from this provision, but it shall not permit the establishment of any charge to or from the more distant point that is not reasonably compensatory, nor shall it grant any such departure on account of merely potential water competition.

(2) When a railroad reduces a rate to or from points where it is in competition with a water carrier, such rates may not be increased unless the Commission finds that the increase rests upon changed conditions other than the elimination of water competition.

Section 5. (1) Pooling agreements are unlawful unless approved by the Interstate Commerce Commission.

(2) Approval of the Interstate Commerce Commission is required to effect consolidations or acquisitions of control. A person not a carrier must also obtain approval before he can acquire control of two or more carriers by stock ownership or otherwise.

All proposals for railroad consolidation or acquisition of control must be consistent with the public interest, and if one of the parties is a motor carrier it must also be shown that services by motor will be in the public interest and that competition will not be unduly restrained. No transaction involving increased fixed charges shall be approved unless it can be shown that such an increase would not be contrary to the public interest. The interests of displaced workers must be protected.

(3) When a noncarrier is authorized to acquire control of one or more carriers, the noncarrier is required to comply with those parts of the law dealing with accounts, reports, and the like.

(11) Commission approval of a consolidation or acquisition relieves the parties from the antitrust laws and from the necessity of obtaining approval of state authorities.

(14-16) No railroad may have any interest in any water line with which it might compete. The Interstate Commerce Commission is authorized to make exceptions to this rule except insofar as it relates to vessels operating through the Panama Canal.

Section 5a. Agreements among carriers covering rates and related matters are permitted, subject to approval by the Commission. The right of individual carriers to take independent action must be protected.

Section 6. (1-2) All rates, fares, and other charges must be filed with the Commission and posted in stations.

(3) Thirty days notice to the Commission and to the public is required for any rate change. For good cause the Commission may allow changes on lesser notice.

Section 10. Violations of the law by a carrier or its agent are subject to a fine not to exceed $5,000 for each offense. Where unlawful discrimination is involved imprisonment not to exceed two years may be added. Willful falsifications by either carrier or shipper are subject to a fine of $5,000 for each offense, a maximum of two years in the penitentiary, or both.

Section 11, 24.[4] The Interstate Commerce Commission consists of eleven members, with terms of seven years, and each to receive $12,000 per year. Appointments are made by the President, by and with the advice and consent of the Senate. No more than six shall be of any one political party, and no commissioner may engage in any other employment or have any interest in any common carrier subject to the act.

Section 12. (1) The Interstate Commerce Commission is authorized to inquire into the business of common carriers and report thereon. It may require carriers to provide information.

(2) Attendance of witnesses at court proceedings is required.

(3) No person shall be excused from testifying on the grounds that such testimony may incriminate him, but such testimony shall not be used against him in a subsequent criminal proceeding. (This provision is modified considerably by the Compulsory Testimony Act of 1893 which provides that no witness may be prosecuted because of any matter concerning which he might testify before the Commission or in a court case dealing with the Interstate Commerce Act.)

Section 13. (1) Complaints received are to be forwarded to the carrier involved. If the carrier or carriers involved do not satisfy the complaint or there appears to be reasonable ground for investigation, it is the duty of the Commission to investigate.

(2) The Commission has power to institute an investigation on its own authority.

(4) If the Commission finds that a rate, fare, charge, classification, regulation or practice causes any undue advantage or prejudice as between intrastate commerce on the one hand and interstate or foreign commerce on the other, it shall prescribe the rate, fare, charge, and the like, which will remove the discrimination.

Section 14. The Commission is required to make a report in writing of each investigation and may provide for the publication of its reports.

Section 15. (1) If the Commission finds that a rate, regulation, or practice is unjust, unduly discriminatory, or in some other way violates the act, it is authorized to prescribe the rate, regulation, or practice to be adopted. This includes fixing a maximum or a minimum rate or both.

(3-4) The Commission is authorized to establish through routes and joint rates after full hearings and it may establish temporary through routes without hearings in the event of an emergency.

----

[4] Section 11 contains the provisions governing the original organization of the Commission. Its present composition is found in Section 24.

(6) The Commission may prescribe the divisions of joint rates.

(7) The Commission is authorized to suspend any change in rates, fares, charges, classification, regulation, or practice for a maximum period of seven months beyond the date on which it normally would go into effect. If the proceeding has not been concluded at the end of seven months from the effective date, the change goes into effect, but if a rate increase is involved, the Commission may order the carrier or carriers to keep accurate records for possible refund with interest in the event the rate increase is not approved.

At any hearing involving a change in rates, regulations, and the like, the burden of proof is on the carrier to show that the proposed change is just and reasonable.

(8) If a shipment moves over two or more railroads to get to its destination, the shipper has the right to designate the connecting line or lines where a choice of such lines exists.

(10) If the shipper does not specify the connecting carrier, the Commission may direct the routing of the traffic.

(11) It is unlawful for any carrier, its officers, or its employees to divulge information about the traffic of a shipper or consignee which might be of benefit to a competitor. It is also unlawful for a person or corporation to solicit or knowingly receive such information.

Section 15a. In the exercise of its power to prescribe just and reasonable rates the Commission shall give due consideration, among other factors, to the effect of rates on the movement of traffic by the carrier or carriers for which the rates are prescribed; to the need, in the public interest, of adequate and efficient railroad transportation service at the lowest cost consistent with the furnishing of such service; and to the need of revenues sufficient to enable the carriers, under honest, economical, and efficient management to provide such service.

Section 16. (2) If a carrier does not comply with an order for the payment of money, the complainant may file complaint in the courts, and in such a procedure the findings and order of the Commission shall be prima facie evidence of the facts.

Section 17. (1, 2, 4) The Commission may divide its members into divisions, each division to consist of not less than three commissioners. Functions may be assigned to divisions, to individual commissioners, or to boards of employees. Such divisions, individual commissioners, and boards have the same jurisdiction, powers, duties, and obligations as the whole Commission.

(5) Any finding, report, or requirement of an individual Commissioner or board involving the taking of testimony at a public hearing, shall be accompanied by a statement of the reasons therefor and a recommended

order. If no exceptions are filed, the recommended order becomes the order of the Commission. The Commission, or a duly designated division thereof, upon its own motion may, and where exceptions are filed it shall, reconsider the order of an individual commissioner or board.

(6) Applications for rehearing, reargument, or reconsideration of a decision, order, or requirement may be made, and the Commission may grant such rehearing, and so forth, if there appears to be sufficient reason. The Commission may limit such rehearings, and the like, to issues of general transportation importance.

Section 19a. The Commission is to determine the value of the railroads.

Section 20. (1) The Commission is authorized to require annual and other reports from the carriers.

(3) The Commission may prescribe a uniform system of accounts.

(4) Falsification of records or accounts is punishable by a maximum fine of $5,000, as much as two years in prison, or both.

Section 20a. (2) A railroad or a corporation organized for the purpose of engaging in transportation by railroad may not issue securities or assume any obligation with respect to securities issued by others without first obtaining the consent of the Interstate Commerce Commission. The Commission shall give its consent only if it finds that the issue or assumption of an obligation is for some lawful object, is compatible with the public interest, is necessary or appropriate to the service of the applicant, will not impair its ability to serve the public, and is reasonably necessary and appropriate for such purpose.

(9) Authority of the Commission is not required for the issuance of short term notes of two years duration or less and aggregating not more than 5 per cent of the par value of all of the applicant's outstanding securities.

(12) No person may be an officer or director of more than one carrier without the consent of the Interstate Commerce Commission. No officer or director of a carrier may receive for his own benefit any money in connection with the sale of securities issued by the carrier.

Section 20b. This section deals with financial readjustments. It is discussed in Chapter 15.

SUGGESTED READINGS

Britton, Lewis W., ed., *Transportation in 1948* and *Transportation in 1949.* Washington: The Traffic Service Corporation, 1949 and 1950. Events of these years as taken from the files of *The Traffic World.*

Drayton, Charles D., *Transportation Under Two Masters.* Washington: National Law Book Company, 1946. In opposition to the position of the Department of Justice on rate bureaus. See the book by Wiprud.

FEDERAL REGULATION

Interstate Commerce Commission, *Annual Report,* various years.

Locklin, D. Philip, *Economics of Transportation,* 3rd Ed. Chicago: Richard D. Irwin, Inc., 1947.

Railway Age.

Traffic World.

Wiprud, Arne C., *Justice In Transportation.* New York: Prentice-Hall, Inc., 1945. Essentially the position of the Department of Justice on rate bureaus. Read in connection with the book by Drayton.

9.

State

vs.

FEDERAL REGULATION

THE PROBLEM OF JURISDICTION

Dual regulatory authority. One final problem needs to be resolved before leaving the subject of railroad regulation; namely, the line of demarcation between the jurisdiction of state regulatory bodies and the jurisdiction of the Interstate Commerce Commission. It must not be thought that the passage of the Act to Regulate Commerce in 1887 brought an end to state activity in the field of railroad regulation, for such was not the case. On the contrary, the scope of state regulation of railroads expanded year by year, and many of the later provisions of the Interstate Commerce Act, including such things as security regulation and the control of construction and abandonment, were introduced originally by the states. And as state regulation expanded in scope it also expanded in area as state after state adopted regulation in one form or another. Thus there exists a dual regulatory authority, and the necessity for a clear line of demarcation between the jurisdiction of state bodies and the jurisdiction of the Interstate Commerce Commission is obvious.

Constitutional distribution of authority. The Federal Government is said to be one of delegated powers—it may exercise only such powers as are delegated to it by the Constitution of the United States, either specifically or by implication. Other powers are reserved for the states unless prohibited by the Constitution. Since the Constitution specifically delegates to the National Government the power to regulate commerce among the states and does not specifically prohibit the states from regulating commerce within their respective boundaries, it would seem reasonable to suppose that federal regulation of railroads would be confined to movements of goods and passengers which cross state lines and that the states would have exclusive jurisdiction over movements taking place entirely within state boundaries. But the problem is not as simple as it sounds because railroad corporations by their very nature cannot compartmentalize their activities, making a nice distinction between those activities which are purely interstate and those which are purely intrastate. Both interstate and intrastate goods and passengers are carried side by side in the same cars, hauled by the same locomotives, manned by the same train crews, and over the same roadbed. Hence it is frequently impossible to regulate one type of movement without at the same time regulating or interfering with the other.

Position of the courts. This problem of the division of power between the nation and the states is not confined to the regulation of railroads but permeates the whole fabric of government in the United States. In delineating the division of powers between the states and the Federal Government the Supreme Court has recognized over the years three zones of authority. In one zone federal power is absolute and may not be invaded by the states. In a second zone state power is exclusive and may not be interfered with by the Federal Government, although in recent years this zone has been narrowed somewhat by the willingness of the Court to accept a broad interpretation of the nature of the powers delegated to Congress in the Constitution. Finally, there is a third zone in which federal and state powers are concurrent. In this zone the Court recognizes the existence of both state and federal authority, but it is important to note that this does not mean that both authorities can exercise power over the same thing at the same time. In this field the states can act in the absence of federal action, but if at any time Congress decides to assume jurisdiction, federal authority replaces state authority. In other words, the states may assume jurisdiction until or unless Congress asserts its authority, in which event state action must give way.

In the field of railroad regulation the Supreme Court has not held consistently to any one of these three zones of authority. Rather its decisions have varied with the nature of the particular regulatory problem involved in whatever case happened to be before it. In some of its decisions the existence of an exclusive federal power to regulate interstate commerce has been clearly recognized, the Wabash decision being an outstanding example of this. In a few cases the exclusive jurisdiction of the state has been accepted. And in still other cases, including some of the most important in recent times, the Court has recognized the existence of concurrent powers. The Minnesota and Shreveport cases, presently discussed, fall in this category. Where concurrent powers are found to exist the Court's decision will, of course, hinge upon whether or not Congress has acted to assume jurisdiction. If it has, then the Federal Government has exclusive jurisdiction. If it has not, the states may exercise the power in question until such time as Congress chooses to act. It is impossible, therefore, to establish any hard and fast over-all line of demarcation between state and federal authority. Rather the problem must be related to specific areas or subjects of regulation.

STATE *vs.* FEDERAL REGULATION

Granger cases. The question of conflicting jurisdictions, insofar as it relates to railroad regulation, first came before the Supreme Court in 1876 in the Granger cases. In these cases the Court recognized that state regulation might involve some incidental interference with interstate commerce, and it also recognized that Congress had authority under the Constitution to regulate interstate commerce. A majority of the Court, however, held that until Congress enacted the necessary legislation to make its authority effective, the states could take such steps as were necessary to protect their own citizens, even though in so doing interstate commerce might be affected. In other words, it was the opinion of the Court that here was a situation that came within the zone of concurrent powers. As a practical matter this decision meant that a state could regulate the rates charged by railroads on that part of an interstate movement which took place wholly within its borders, but that it could exercise this power only so long as Congress failed to act to implement its own superior power.

Wabash decision. Perhaps it was a good thing for the people that the Court took the position that it did in the Granger cases, but the logic of its position may be questioned, and it did not hold to it. In 1886 in the Wabash case a reconstituted court held that a state could not regulate any part of an interstate movement, not even that part which took place within its own boundaries. In this case the majority held that the power to regulate interstate commerce was one which was reserved exclusively to the Federal Government, and the fact that Congress had not acted actually to regulate interstate commerce was irrelevant to the issue. The Wabash decision was followed promptly by the passage of the Act to Regulate Commerce and the establishment of the Interstate Commerce Commission, and from that date down to 1913 a clear line of demarcation existed between the jurisdictions of state and federal authorities. Any movement which took place wholly within the boundaries of a single state was intrastate commerce and within the exclusive field of jurisdiction of the states, and any movement which crossed a state line or an international boundary was interstate or foreign commerce and within the exclusive field of jurisdiction of the Interstate Commerce Commission. If, as often happens, a movement between two points in the same state crossed and recrossed the state line or an international boundary, it was considered to be interstate commerce by the courts and subject to the jurisdiction of the Interstate Commerce Commission.

Problem not solved by Wabash decision. While the line of demarcation set up by the courts following the Wabash decision seemed clear enough, it did not eliminate the possibility of conflict between state and federal authorities. This fact was recognized by the Interstate Commerce Commission as early as 1889, when it noted that there were a great many railroads in the country which did not extend beyond the limits of a single state, but these railroads connected with roads which were interstate in the sense that they crossed state lines, and all participated to some extent in interstate traffic. Furthermore, the interstate railroads also did an intrastate business. State traffic and interstate traffic were taken on the same trains, under the same management; the freight and passage money were received into the same treasury; the expenses of transportation were paid by the same officers from the same fund; and it would be impossible to determine with accuracy the cost or the profit of the state business as distinguished from the interstate.[1]

Minnesota Rate Cases. As long as the Interstate Commerce Commission was impotent to fix rates the jurisdictional issue remained more or less academic, but after the passage of the Hepburn Act in 1906 the Commission was vested with real rate-making power, and the problem of jurisdiction became significant. This was the question before the Supreme Court in the Minnesota Rate Cases, decided in 1913.[2] The Minnesota Rate Cases involved the validity of certain orders of the Railroad and Warehouse Commission of Minnesota and certain acts of the Minnesota legislature, the effect of which was to bring about substantial reductions in passenger fares and freight rates between points entirely within the State of Minnesota.

But even though the rates prescribed were solely between points within the state they necessitated important changes in various interstate rates. For example, the cities of Duluth and Superior, both located at the head of Lake Superior, are adjacent to each other, but Duluth is in Minnesota and Superior is in Wisconsin. Both cities competed for trade over a broad area in Minnesota, and the railroads serving the two cities had recognized this competition by establishing the same rates between them and various Minnesota points. Consequently when the railroads were ordered to reduce their rates between Duluth and other Minnesota points, they promptly reduced the rates between Superior and Minnesota points.

A similar situation existed at other border points, and by a peculiar combination of circumstances the reduction in the Minnesota intrastate rates affected rates over a wide area beyond the state as far west as the Pacific coast. Substantial reductions in passenger rates led travelers to buy tickets from points of origin in Minnesota to border points at the low

---

[1] Interstate Commerce Commission, *Annual Report*, 1889, pp. 73-74.
[2] *Simpson* v. *Shepard*, 230 U.S. 352.

intrastate rates, and then at the border points to buy an interstate ticket to destination, in this way effecting an over-all reduction in interstate passenger rates.

The stockholders of three railroads, the Northern Pacific, the Great Northern, and the Minneapolis and St. Louis, brought suit to restrain the orders of the Railroad and Warehouse Commission of Minnesota and the acts of the Minnesota legislature on various grounds, including the assertion that these orders and acts had resulted in an unconstitutional interference with interstate commerce. The Supreme Court, however, made a sharp distinction between the type of interference with interstate commerce involved in the Wabash case and the type of interference involved in the cases then before it. In the Wabash case the interference was direct, the state actually having fixed a part of an avowedly interstate rate. This, according to the Court, the state could not do because the Constitution of its own force, and without the necessity of action by Congress, established the essential immunity of interstate commerce from the direct control of the states. But in the Minnesota Rate Cases no such direct interference with interstate commerce was involved. Every rate established was between points within the state, and every rate involved was, therefore, an intrastate rate. It was the railroads, not the state, which reduced the interstate rates to conform with the Minnesota intrastate rates.

The Court did not deny that an interference with interstate commerce existed, and went on to say that if a situation became such, by reason of the interblending of the interstate and intrastate operations of interstate carriers, that adequate regulation of their interstate rates could not be maintained without imposing requirements with respect to their intrastate rates which substantially affected the former, it was for Congress to determine the measure of regulation it should supply. Congress had not yet seen fit to exercise this power, however, and until it did so the state was free to fix rates even though an interference with interstate commerce was involved.

Shreveport Rate Cases. In the early years of the twentieth century the Railroad Commission of Texas established an unusually low level of rates on movements within that state. It did this partly to help Texas shippers and partly to encourage the growth of commercial and manufacturing centers in the state, the contention being that existing interstate rate relationships gave out-of-state business interests an advantage over business interests within the state. One consequence of these low intrastate rates was to give such Texas commercial centers as Houston and Dallas an advantage over Shreveport, Louisiana, in the northeast Texas market, since Shreveport jobbers had to pay the interstate rates to get their goods into Texas. The difference in rates was substantial and undeniably was injurious to the commerce of Shreveport. For example, a rate of 60¢ would carry 100 pounds of first class freight 55 miles west into Texas from Shreveport, while the same rate would carry 100 pounds of first class freight 160 miles east from Dallas. Marshall, Texas, which was 42 miles from Shreveport and 148 miles from Dallas, enjoyed a rate on wagons from Dallas which was almost 20¢ a hundred pounds lower than the rate charged from Shreveport to Marshall. Similar discriminations existed in favor of Houston in the competition for business in northeast Texas.

In 1911 the Railroad Commission of Louisiana filed a complaint with the Interstate Commerce Commission, alleging that certain interstate carriers maintained unreasonable rates from Shreveport to various Texas points and that these carriers were unjustly discriminating against Shreveport in favor of Texas points in connection with the rates charged to northeast Texas. In a report handed down in 1912 the Interstate Commerce Commission failed to find that the interstate rates from Shreveport west into Texas were unreasonable, but it did find that the complaint of the Railroad Commission of Louisiana with regard to the existence of unjust discrimination was valid.

In an order issued in connection with the 1912 report the Commission required the railroads, among other things, not to charge any more for hauling certain commodities west from Shreveport than they charged for hauling those same commodities an equal distance east from Dallas or north from Houston. The railroads could have complied with this order by lowering the Shreveport interstate rate on the commodities involved to the same level as the Texas intrastate rates, but this they refused to do on the ground that they could not be required to reduce rates which were admittedly reasonable for no other purpose than to equalize them with the unusually low intrastate rates. In this the railroads were supported by the Commerce Court which held that the railroads could comply with the equalization order of the Interstate Commerce Commission by raising the Texas intrastate rates even though the Railroad Commission of Texas had ordered these rates established.

With the issue thus squarely joined, the case found its way in due course to the Supreme Court.[3] Here it was argued by the State of Texas that Congress had no power to fix the intrastate charges of an interstate carrier; and that even if Congress did have such power, it had not exercised it, and so the Interstate Commerce Commission's order could not be interpreted as permitting the railroads to raise the intrastate rates in question. In answer to the first contention the Supreme Court merely repeated the doctrine enunciated in connection with the Minnesota Rate Cases.

---

[3] *Houston, East & West Texas Railway* v. *United States*, 234 U.S. 342 (1914).

Wherever the interstate and intrastate transactions of carriers are so related that the government of one involves the control of the other, it is Congress, and not the state, that is entitled to prescribe the rate.

With regard to the contention that Congress had not acted to assume jurisdiction the Court pointed to the fact that Congress had, in Section 3 of the Act to Regulate Commerce, made it unlawful for any common carrier subject to the provisions of the act to make or give any undue or unreasonable preference or advantage to any locality in any respect whatsoever. The Commission, acting as an agent of Congress, had ordered the discrimination eliminated, and when the Commission acted, Congress had acted. Thus the Shreveport decision established beyond the shadow of a doubt the supremacy of the Interstate Commerce Commission in connection with intrastate rates which affected interstate commerce.

It is instructive to note the small thread of difference between the Minnesota Rate Cases and the Shreveport Rate Cases which led to a decision in favor of the state in the first instance and against the state in the second. The Interstate Commerce Commission was not involved in the Minnesota Rate Cases since the stockholders of the railroads involved had taken their complaint directly to the courts. Hence the Supreme Court held that Minnesota had the authority to establish the disputed rates because Congress had taken no action to assume jurisdiction. But in the Shreveport Rate Cases the controversy was initiated when the Railroad Commission of Louisiana filed a complaint with the Interstate Commerce Commission, and when the Interstate Commerce Commission acted to prohibit the discrimination complained of, it was the same thing as if Congress itself had acted because the Interstate Commerce Commission was acting as an agent of Congress.

Illinois Passenger Fare Case. The Minnesota and Shreveport decisions clearly established the right of the Federal Government to exercise control over intrastate rates which interfered with interstate commerce, but neither decision established a clear line of demarcation between intrastate rates which did interfere with interstate commerce and intrastate rates which did not interfere with interstate commerce. In the Illinois Passenger Fare Case, decided in 1918, the Supreme Court held that the power of the Commission to fix intrastate rates was dominant only to the extent necessary to remove an existing discrimination against interstate traffic, and it could not be extended to cover intrastate rates which did not affect interstate commerce.[4] Before the effect of this decision could be evaluated, however, new developments made it obsolete.

---

[4] *Illinois Central Railroad Company* v. *Public Utilities Commission of Illinois,* 245 U.S. 493.

STATE *vs.* FEDERAL REGULATION

Wisconsin Passenger Fares Case. In 1920, not long after the Government had relinquished control of the railroads, the Interstate Commerce Commission ordered a broad general increase in freight rates and passenger fares and charges. The interstate railroads operating in Wisconsin promptly applied to the railroad commission of that state for similar increases in intrastate rates, but the Wisconsin commission, while allowing the freight rate increases, refused to sanction increased passenger fares and charges on the ground that such increases would be a violation of a state statute prescribing a maximum charge of 2¢ per mile for carrying passengers by rail in Wisconsin. The refusal of the Wisconsin commission to sanction increased passenger fares and charges came before the Interstate Commerce Commission which, after an investigation, ordered the railroads serving the state to raise their intrastate fares and charges to the same level as had been applied to interstate movements of passengers.

This sweeping order, overriding the Wisconsin commission and Wisconsin laws, was justified by the Interstate Commerce Commission on the ground that the newly adopted rule of rate making placed upon it the affirmative duty of fixing interstate rates which would yield the carriers as a whole, or by sections of the country, a fair return on the fair value of their property. The Commission believed that the interstate passenger fares it had established were necessary to enable the carriers to achieve a fair return and that if the 2¢ fare named in the state statute were sustained, it would mean a loss in revenue to the interstate carriers serving Wisconsin of $6 million per year. Clearly if intrastate rates and fares were insufficient to meet their fair share of the burden of costs and pay something by way of a fair return, the Commission would be obligated to raise interstate rates to make up the difference, and so any intrastate rate that did not meet cost plus a fair return constituted a burden on interstate commerce.

In 1922 the Supreme Court sustained the Commission's line of reasoning in the Wisconsin Passenger Fares Case, holding that the effective operation of the Interstate Commerce Act reasonably and justly required that intrastate traffic pay a fair proportionate share of the cost of maintaining an adequate railroad system.[5] Thus the Court gave sanction to an enormous extension of federal authority over intrastate rates, since any intrastate rate could now be challenged if it appeared to be too low to bear its fair share of the total burden of cost and profit.

Subsequent developments. In a long series of orders stretching out over the years the Interstate Commerce Commission has repeatedly exercised

---

[5] *Railroad Commission of Wisconsin* v. *Chicago, Burlington & Quincy Railroad Company,* 257 U.S. 563.

its power to modify intrastate rates, sometimes on the basis of the Shreveport principle when discrimination is direct, and sometimes on the broader basis of inadequate revenues from intrastate rates. The mere fact that a given intrastate rate is lower than a comparable interstate rate, however, does not necessarily mean that the two must be brought into a condition of equality, and the same is true of levels of rates. In a number of cases the Commission refused to permit carriers to raise intrastate rates that were below the interstate level on the ground that the resultant loss of revenue was insufficient to work an injury on interstate commerce. And even if the Commission feels that an increase in intrastate rates is necessary, it must still reckon with the Supreme Court. Thus in 1944 the Commission ordered an increase in the one way motor bus fares prevailing in four southern states from 1.65¢ to 2.2¢, the latter being the interstate rate and the intrastate rate in the remaining forty-four states. A year later, however, the Supreme Court set aside the order in a five to four decision on the ground that the evidence failed to show prejudice against interstate passengers or interstate commerce.[6]

It should be noted, perhaps, that the repeal of the rule of rate making in 1933 did not in any way restrict the power of the Interstate Commerce Commission to exercise control over intrastate rates. Although the law no longer calls upon the Commission to fix rates which will yield a fair return on the fair value of railroad property, the new rule of rate making specifies that in fixing rates the Commission shall give due consideration, among other things, to the need of revenues sufficient to enable the carriers, under honest, economical, and efficient management to provide adequate and efficient service. Thus the Commission is still under the affirmative duty of establishing rates which are adequate, and low intrastate rates may still place a burden on interstate commerce if permitted to stand.

CONSTRUCTION AND ABANDOMENT

Extent of problem. Prior to the passage of the Transportation Act, 1920, about half of the states exercised control of one sort or another over either railroad construction, abandonment, or both. In a number of cases, however, the degree of control exercised was quite limited so that the jurisdictional issue when it arose was confined to a very few states. Nevertheless, the matter is of some importance since it provides further evidence of the expanding power of Congress and the Interstate Commerce Commission over state governments and regulatory bodies in the field of railroad transportation.

---

[6] *North Carolina* v. *United States*, 325 U.S. 507.

STATE *vs.* FEDERAL REGULATION

Jurisdiction of the Interstate Commerce Commission in abandonment proceedings. One of the first cases to come before the Interstate Commerce Commission under the abandonment provisions of the Transportation Act, 1920, involved the Eastern Texas Railroad, a thirty mile line located wholly within the State of Texas. This little line had been built originally to serve a lumbering area, but when the timber had been logged off, the railroad suffered a severe decline in traffic and claimed that it had been operating at a loss for several years. Although the physical properties of the Eastern Texas Railroad did not extend outside the boundaries of the state, it was an interstate carrier in the sense that it handled freight which had or would move in interstate commerce by way of connecting lines, and so it applied to the Interstate Commerce Commission for a certificate of convenience and necessity which would permit it to abandon its line. After holding hearings on the matter the Commission issued such a certificate late in 1920, and the State of Texas promptly took the matter to the courts. Texas had a law exercising control over railroad abandonments and, in addition, the Eastern Texas, in common with all other Texas railroads at that time, was incorporated under Texas laws.

The State of Texas argued that the Interstate Commerce Commission's jurisdiction in a case like this was limited to permitting abandonment of operation as an interstate carrier, and with this argument the Supreme Court agreed. It was not, reasoned the Court, as if the road were a branch or extension whose unremunerative operation would or might burden or cripple the main line and thereby effect its utility or service as an artery of interstate and foreign commerce. On the contrary, its continued operation solely in intrastate commerce could not be of more than local concern.[7]

It is clear from this decision that if the owners of a railroad located wholly within a single state wish to abandon their property, the Interstate Commerce Commission's authority is limited to permitting abandonment of operation in interstate commerce. Presumably then it is up to the state to decide whether or not the line must continue to operate to move freight which has not come from or will not go beyond the borders of the state. It will be obvious that this limitation on the authority of the Interstate Commerce Commission is of no real significance, however, because if a line cannot operate successfully when it is carrying both interstate and intrastate commerce, it certainly cannot operate successfully moving intrastate commerce alone. To require it to continue to do so would result in the state depriving its owners of property without due process of law. This was the opinion of the Supreme Court which subsequently per-

---

[7] *State of Texas* v. *Eastern Texas Railroad Co.,* 258 U.S. 204 (1922).

mitted the owners of the Eastern Texas Railroad to abandon their property completely.[8]

The opinion of the Supreme Court in the Eastern Texas case suggested that the Commission's authority might be considerably broader in the event of an abandonment involving a branch line or a portion of a main line, even though the line to be abandoned was wholly within a single state, since the continued operation of a portion of a line at a substantial loss might result in an undue burden on the interstate operations of the rest of the line. Acting on this assumption the Commission issued a certificate to the Colorado and Southern Railroad, a Colorado corporation operating a railroad partly in Colorado and partly in other states, permitting it to abandon a branch line located entirely within the State of Colorado. The State of Colorado took exception to this action by the Commission, but in 1926 the Supreme Court affirmed the right of the Commission to assume jurisdiction in full.[9] If in a case like this the Interstate Commerce Commission's jurisdiction had been limited to permitting only the abandonment of operations in interstate commerce, the state could have required the Colorado and Southern to continue to operate the branch in intrastate commerce, and the resultant losses incurred might have placed an undue burden on the interstate operations of the rest of the property. Although the Colorado and Southern was an interstate carrier in the sense that its lines extended into more than one state, the opinion of the Court in the Colorado and Southern case was sufficiently broad to cover branch lines or parts of the main line of railroads whose entire mileage lies within a single state, providing that the railroad is an interstate carrier in the sense that it handles goods which have moved or will move in interstate commerce.

The decisions quoted above essentially nullify any state control over railroad abandonments. The Commission may order the complete abandonment of a branch or a portion of the main line of a carrier operating in interstate commerce, and this gives it practically unlimited power because almost every railroad operating in the United States carries goods in interstate commerce. It is true that the Commission may not order the complete abandonment of a railroad located wholly within a single state but must confine its activities in such cases to permitting only the abandonment of operations in interstate commerce. As mentioned previously, however, this limitation on its authority does not mean that the states can require the continued operation of such lines in intrastate commerce

---

[8] *Railroad Commission of Texas* v. *Eastern Texas R.R. Co.*, 264 U.S. 79 (1924).
[9] *Colorado* v. *United States*, 271 U.S. 153.

since such a requirement would in all probability result in taking property without due process of law.

Jurisdiction of the Commission in construction cases. Very little conflict has developed between state and federal authorities with reference to the construction of railroads. If the Interstate Commerce Commission refuses to grant a certificate permitting the construction of a line for operation in interstate commerce, there is nothing that a state can do to compel it to reverse its decision. It is true, of course, that a state can grant permission for a line to be built to operate in intrastate commerce, but if the Interstate Commerce Commission has already refused its projectors the right to operate in interstate commerce, there is little likelihood that they would build it anyway, except under the most unusual circumstances. And if the Commission grants permission to build a line of railroad, a state would not be likely to protest, again except under the most unusual circumstances. In any event there have been so few applications for permission to build new lines of railroads in recent years that the question of jurisdiction is largely academic.

SAFETY AND SERVICE

Regulation of safety by the states. The whole field of safety regulation is one which lies peculiarly within the zone of concurrent powers. When Congress undertook the regulation of interstate commerce, it did not at first concern itself with safety legislation, and in case after case the courts sustained state laws designed to promote safety of operations as a valid exercise of the police power even though such legislation often did indirectly affect interstate commerce. Thus a state could specify the speed at which a train might move through towns in the state even though the train was operating in interstate commerce, and it could license and examine engineers employed in operating interstate trains through the state.[10] Similarly, state laws designed to protect the public health also have been upheld as a valid exercise of the police power.

Assertion of federal jurisdiction. Beginning with the Safety Appliance Act of 1893, Congress began to assert its authority over interstate commerce in the field of safety regulation. This act required, among other things, that all locomotives used in the movement of interstate traffic must be equipped with power brakes. Likewise, a certain number of cars in each train had to be equipped with power brakes controlled from the engine cab. And all cars used in moving interstate commerce were required to be equipped with automatic couplers. In 1903 an amendment

---

[10] *Smith* v. *Alabama*, 124 U.S. 465 (1888).

made these and other requirements applicable to all vehicles used on any railroad engaged in interstate commerce, thus extending the law to include locomotives and cars used in intrastate service by carriers which also operated in interstate commerce. The Hours of Service Act passed in 1907 limited to specified maxima the hours of work for employees operating the trains of carriers engaged in interstate commerce. The Boiler Inspection Act of 1911 was designed to prevent the use of locomotives with defective boilers. And the Transportation Act, 1920, authorized the Interstate Commerce Commission to require any carrier subject to its jurisdiction to install automatic train stop or train control or other safety devices.

Judicial interpretation. Every one of these congressional enactments involved an interference with intrastate commerce and conflicted to a greater or lesser extent with state safety legislation. Since locomotives and cars are used interchangeably for the movement of both interstate and intrastate commerce, it would be impossible to provide them with one set of brakes and couplers to conform with federal law and other sets which would conform with the possibly different requirements of various state laws. Similarly, the same employees handle both interstate and intrastate commerce, and they cannot work under one set of rules established by Congress and another set established by the legislature of the state in which they happen to reside or work. The courts have consistently held to the doctrine already mentioned that congressional action in such fields supersedes state action.[11]

Car service. The Interstate Commerce Act gives the Commission power to establish reasonable rules and regulations with respect to car service by railroads subject to its jurisdiction, and in times of emergency it may suspend such rules and regulations, direct the utilization of locomotives, cars, and other vehicles, require joint use of terminal facilities, and establish embargoes, and the like. Here again there is a real possibility of interference with intrastate commerce because again the same equipment is used to serve both interstate and intrastate shippers. The only limitation on the Commission's authority is found in the statement in the law that "nothing in this part shall impair or affect the right of a State, in the exercise of its police power, to require just and reasonable freight and passenger service for intrastate business..." but the significance of this exception is immediately negatived by the addition of the words "except insofar as such requirement is inconsistent with any lawful order of the Commission made under the provisions of this part."

---

[11] *Southern Railway Co.* v. *R.R. Commission of Indiana,* 236 U.S. 439 (1915).

STATE *vs.* FEDERAL REGULATION

Accounts and reports. The original Act to Regulate Commerce, together with subsequent amendments, empowered the Interstate Commerce Commission to prescribe a uniform system of accounts and to require such regular and special reports as it felt necessary. Here again was a source of conflict between federal regulations and state laws. The fact that a given railroad employed the same men, equipment, right-of-way, and other facilities in carrying both interstate and intrastate commerce made it impossible to establish any truly accurate separation of the two types of business.

Furthermore, if each railroad maintained two entirely separate sets of records, with the intrastate records not open to inspection by the Interstate Commerce Commission, the way would be opened for concealing discrimination and other unlawful practices. Moreover, the earnings of carriers on intrastate operations may be a factor in the determination of the over-all reasonableness of their interstate rates. It might also be noted that the Commission was in a position to gather and publish some extremely valuable statistical data, and the value of such data would be substantially reduced if it did not cover intrastate as well as interstate operations. From the beginning, the Commission has required rail carriers subject to its jurisdiction to report on all of their operations, and in this it has been sustained by the courts.[12]

Security regulation. The Transportation Act, 1920, made it unlawful for any carrier subject to the act to issue securities or to assume any obligation or liability in respect of the securities of any person or corporation, *even though permitted by the state creating the carrier corporation,* without obtaining the permission of the Interstate Commerce Commission. Furthermore, the law specified that the jurisdiction of the Interstate Commerce Commission was exclusive and plenary, and a carrier might issue securities and assume obligations or liabilities in accordance with the provisions of the law without securing the approval of state authorities.

The only limitation placed on the Commission's authority, insofar as the jurisdictional question is concerned, was the requirement that the issue in question must be for some lawful object within the carrier's corporate purpose. This requirement would seem to indicate a certain limited degree of authority remaining in the hands of the state in which a particular railroad happens to be incorporated, but even this authority may be more apparent than real. For one thing, the law stated, as already noted, that the jurisdiction of the Commission was exclusive and plenary, and for

---

[12] *Interstate Commerce Commission* v. *Goodrich Transit Co.,* 224 U.S. 194 (1912).

another thing it is difficult to see how the *interstate* activities of an interstate carrier could be limited by the statutes of the state issuing its charter.

In the early 1920's some opposition developed on the part of state authorities to the disregard of state laws inherent in the security regulation provisions of the Transportation Act, 1920. It was contended that a railroad corporation is a creature of the state in which it was organized and that the issuance of securities by such a corporation is a matter of primary interest to the state. The Commission, however, has held consistently that a corporation operating as a common carrier in interstate commerce is subject to its jurisdiction. Although it has given considerable weight to the requirements of various state laws in connection with various orders, the Commission has refused to withhold its approval of an issue of securities until such time as the applicant obtained the consent of some state authority, and it has refused to make its approval of security issues contingent upon susbequent approval by a state body. Although the jurisdictional question has not been passed on by the Supreme Court, the authority of the Interstate Commerce Commission has been upheld in the lower courts. Furthermore, certain Supreme Court decisions dealing with other matters suggest a recognition on the part of that body of the superior jurisdiction of the Commission.[13]

Intercorporate relationships. The provisions of the law dealing with consolidations and with acquisitions of control short of actual consolidation confer exclusive and plenary authority on the Interstate Commerce Commission. Once the Commission has given its approval, the carriers or corporations involved have full authority to carry the transaction into effect without state approval, and they are relieved from the operation of the antitrust laws and of all other restraints, limitations, and prohibitions of law, federal, state, or municipal, insofar as it may be necessary to carry out their plans. And any power granted to any carrier or corporation in this part of the act is deemed to be in addition to and in modification of its powers under its corporate charter or under the laws of any state. Only one minor limitation is included. The law specifies that to give effect to the combination a majority of the voting stockholders is required, unless a different vote is required under applicable state law. The scope of the Commission's authority under the Transportation Act of 1940 seems to be clear enough although it has never been passed upon by the Supreme Court.

---

[13] *Pittsburgh & West Virginia Ry.* v. *I. C. C.*, 293 Fed. 1001 (1923); *Whitman* v. *Northern Central Ry. Co.*, 146 Md. 580, 127 Atl. 112 (1924); *R. R. Commission* v. *Southern Pacific Co.*, 264 U.S. 331 (1924); *Venner* v. *Michigan Central R. R. Co.*, 271 U.S. 127 (1926).

STATE *vs.* FEDERAL REGULATION

COOPERATION

Desirability of cooperation. Almost from its very inception the Interstate Commerce Commission recognized the evils that might flow from a system of divided jurisdiction, and early in 1889, just two years after its creation, members of the Commission met with representatives of the various state commissions in an effort to work out a system of cooperation between the two groups. Sincere efforts were made in the years that followed to bring about some uniformity of regulation, but unfortunately many obstacles presented themselves to the achievement of any degree of uniformity. The various state commissions, like the Interstate Commerce Commission itself, were not free agents, but had to act within the framework of constitutional limitations, state laws, and judicial interpretations, all of which placed a severe handicap on their ability to cooperate. In one field, however, that of accounting and statistics, a noticeable degree of cooperation was achieved, the Commission reporting in 1909 that the situation in this field was wholly satisfactory.[14]

After the decisions of the Supreme Court in the Minnesota and Shreveport cases, the matter of cooperation between state and federal bodies became less important since these decisions recognized the superiority of Congress over state bodies in the event of a conflict between interstate and intrastate commerce. But it should not be assumed from this that the Interstate Commerce Commission followed a policy of running roughshod over state laws and state commissions once it was vested with authority to control intrastate rates and practices that interfered with interstate commerce. On the contrary, it frequently recognized the rights and interests of the states and sought from time to time to encourage the cooperation of state commissions. All such cooperative action was purely voluntary as far as the Interstate Commerce Commission was concerned, however, since it was neither required nor authorized by law. Cooperation was finally authorized and to some extent required by the Transportation Act, 1920, and the nature of this phase of the 1920 act is discussed briefly below.

Rates. The law provided that whenever an investigation involved any rate, fare, charge, classification, regulation, or practice of any state, the Commission should cause the state or states interested to be notified of the proceeding. It also authorized the Commission to confer with the authorities of any state having regulatory jurisdiction over the carrier involved with respect to the relationship between rate structures and

---

[14] Interstate Commerce Commission, *Annual Report,* 1909, p. 57.

practices of carriers subject to the jurisdiction of both the state body and the Interstate Commerce Commission. And to that end the Commission was authorized and empowered to hold joint hearings with any state regulatory body on any matter wherein the Commission had power to act and where the rate-making authority of a state would or might be affected by the action taken by the Commission. The Commission was also authorized to avail itself of the cooperation, services, records, and facilities of such state authorities in the enforcement of any provision of Parts I or III of the Interstate Commerce Act.

In spite of the clear intent of the law, the Interstate Commerce Commission and the state commissions, the latter acting through the National Association of Railroad and Utilities Commissioners, were unable to get together immediately on a program of cooperative action. The Commission itself was unwilling to undertake joint hearings in cases where the state rates involved were the result of state laws which the state commissions were unable to modify, or in cases where the difference between the interstate and intrastate rates was the result of the action of state commissions themselves, which commissions would normally appear as litigants in favor of the rates. The state commissions, on the other hand, took the position that to eliminate all such cases from joint consideration would make cooperation useless. In 1922, however, the Supreme Court, in connection with its decision in the Wisconsin Passenger Fares Case, urged the importance of conferences between state commissions and the Interstate Commerce Commission as a means of dispensing with rigid federal control over state rates, and thereafter the Interstate Commerce Commission and the state commissions got together on a plan of cooperative action. Since that time the Commission has held numerous joint hearings and consultations with state regulatory bodies, although it should be understood that final authority rests with the Interstate Commerce Commission and not with representatives of state commissions.

Construction and abandonment. The Transportation Act, 1920, provided that the Interstate Commerce Commission, upon receiving a request for a certificate of public convenience and necessity permitting the construction or abandonment of a line of railroad, was to notify the governor of each state involved and that each state had the right to be heard in connection therewith. In some cases the Commission has held joint hearings with state commissions and in a number of cases the hearings have been held before state bodies acting for the Interstate Commerce Commission. Again it should be noted that final authority rests with the Commission. No state body has the power to issue an order although the Commission has at times followed the recommendation of a state body.

Security regulation and consolidations. The Transportation Act, 1920, also specified that upon receipt of an application for authority to issue securities the Commission was to cause notice thereof to be given to the governor of each state in which the carrier operated. The railroad commissions, public service or utility commissions, or other appropriate state authorities involved had the right to make such representations as they might deem just and proper for preserving and conserving the rights and interests of their people. Similarly, the Commission was required to notify the governor of each state involved in the event of a consolidation proposal coming before it.

SUGGESTED READINGS

Daggett, Stuart, *Principles of Inland Transportation,* 3rd Ed. New York: Harper and Brothers, 1941.

MacVeagh, Rogers, *The Transportation Act,* 1920. New York: Henry Holt and Company, 1923.

Shaffman, I. L., *The Interstate Commerce Commission,* Vol. II. New York: The Commonwealth Fund, 1931.

10

General Level
of
RAILROAD RATES

THE RATE PROBLEM

Railroad problems further considered. The underlying purpose of the preceding five chapters has been to present a chronological survey of the development of railroad regulation in the United States. In the course of this survey a number of specific transportation problems were introduced and developed to the extent necessary to show their influence on the course of railroad regulatory legislation and procedures. But some of the problems introduced in this way happen to be of sufficient importance in their own right to justify a more detailed examination than seemed wise to apply in connection with a general survey of the development of railroad regulation. It is the purpose of this and succeeding chapters to examine in some detail the more important of these problems.

The rate problem. Of the various transportation problems that have been introduced up to this point none commands more universal attention and interest than the rate problem. Regardless of the point of view from which railroad transportation is approached, whether it be that of the railroad, the shipper, or the general public interest, rates are of fundamental importance. It may be somewhat misleading, however, to speak of a rate *problem* because actually there are several more or less distinct rate problems, each of which is of no little significance. The broadest of these rate problems, and the one which has been given the most consideration in the preceding discussion, has to do with the general level of rates. How much in the aggregate should the railroads receive for the services they render, and how much in fact do they receive?

A second rate problem has to do with the determination of the relationships which should exist between the rates charged for hauling different kinds of traffic. For example, how should the rates charged for hauling coal compare with the rates charged for hauling coffee? Should the rate on lard be more or less than the rate on lard substitutes, or should they both be the same? A third rate problem involves the determination of the rates to be charged for hauls between different cities and within and between different sections of the country. Finally, there has developed in recent years a new rate problem, that of determining the proper relationships that should exist between the rates charged by different types of carriers.

The first of these rate problems, that having to do with the general level of rates, constitutes the subject matter of the present chapter. The problems involved in the determination of the rates to be charged for moving different kinds of traffic, and the techniques utilized in establishing rate relationships as between different cities and within and between different sections of the country are taken up in succeeding chapters. The fourth rate problem, that of determining what the relationships should be between the rates charged by different kinds of transportation services, involves broad questions of public policy. These questions, along with other related matters, are considered in the closing section of this book dealing with public policy and with the transportation system as a whole.

THE DOCTRINE OF JUST AND REASONABLE RATES

Munn v. Illinois. The statement that all rates must be just and reasonable has become axiomatic over the years, but it is an axiom which has been subject to widely different interpretations. There hardly can be any doubt that the proponents of the Granger laws had in mind rates which were just and reasonable to *shippers,* since the Granges had been crying out against what they considered to be high and discriminatory freight rates. It is clear, of course, that rates established in this way might not be fair to the railroads involved, but in *Munn v. Illinois* the Supreme Court held that the fixing of rates was a legislative function with which it could not interfere, even though it recognized that this was a power which might be abused by legislatures.[1]

Stone v. Farmers' Loan and Trust Co. As was indicated in an earlier chapter the Supreme Court's reasoning on the above point was open to question. If the judiciary had no final word on the determination of just and reasonable rates, the only check on the power of the legislature to fix destructively low rates would be the legislature's own realization of the ultimate effect of such rates on railroad service, and the result of unduly low rates could be disastrous to railroads and public alike. In 1886 a reconstituted court held in the case of *Stone v. Farmers' Loan and Trust Company* that the power to regulate was not the power to destroy. Under the pretense of regulating rates, said the Court, a state could not require a railroad to carry persons or property without reward. It could

---

[1] 94 U.S. 113 (1876).

not do that which in law amounted to taking private property for public use without just compensation, or without due process of law.[2] In 1894 this doctrine was reaffirmed and further refined in the case of *Reagan v. Farmers' Loan and Trust Co.* in which the Court played with the idea of rates which would, under certain circumstances at least, pay a return on a company's stocks and bonds.[3] Thus at a fairly early date the Court established the principle that rates as a whole must not be so low as to cause carriers to operate at a loss or without just compensation for their services.

Just and reasonable rates in interstate commerce. The original Act to Regulate Commerce provided the Interstate Commerce Commission with no positive instructions with reference to fixing rates other than the rather vague directive that all rates "shall be reasonable and just," but in view of the widespread public hostility toward the railroads at this time, it seems safe to assume that the people wanted the Commission to fix rates which were reasonable and just to shippers. Any power which the Interstate Commerce Commission might have had to establish such rates, however, was to all intents and purposes removed by the Supreme Court in its decision in the Maximum Freight Rate case.

As a result of the decision in *Stone v. Farmers' Loan and Trust Co.*, the carriers were guaranteed a floor under rates, while as a result of the decision in the Maximum Freight Rate case any ceiling on rates was effectively removed. Rates could not be so low as to be confiscatory, but the upper limit on rates, at least as far as interstate commerce was concerned, was held down only by competition or by the limits of what the traffic would bear. Since the Wabash decision had made state regulation ineffective as far as the bulk of traffic was concerned, the net result was that the railroads were protected on all traffic from rates that were too low while on a large part of the traffic the public had little or no real protection from rates that were too high. This, of course, was exactly the opposite of the original intent of regulatory legislation.

Smyth v. Ames. In 1898 the Supreme Court, in the case of *Smyth v. Ames,* enunciated one of the most significant and at the same time one of the most controversial principles in the history of railroad and public utility regulation. Said the Court:

We hold ... that the basis of all calculations as to the reasonableness of rates to be charged by a corporation maintaining a highway under legislative sanction must be the fair value of the property being used by it for the convenience of the public. ... *What the company is entitled to ask is a fair return upon the*

---

[2] 116 U.S. 307.
[3] 154 U.S. 362.

value of that which it employs for the public convenience. On the other hand, what the public is entitled to demand is that no more be exacted from it for the use of a public highway than the services rendered by it are reasonably worth.[4]

What the Court was saying, in effect, was that a railroad was entitled to charge rates which in the aggregate would bring it an income sufficient to meet all of its expenses plus a profit of a certain percentage, representing a fair rate of return on the fair value of its property. The profit, of course, would constitute a return to those who had invested their capital in the railroad enterprise. By basing the fair return on the fair value of a railroad rather than on its capitalization the Court was protecting the public from the necessity of paying rates sufficiently high to yield a return on the watered stocks of an overcapitalized company.

In *Stone v. Farmers' Loan and Trust Company* and in *Reagan v. Farmers' Loan and Trust Company* the Court had placed a floor under rates equal to cost of service plus some sort of a hazily stated return to investors. The decision in *Smyth v. Ames* now defined this floor more specifically as cost plus a fair return on the fair value of the property. The rule no doubt had some effect on intrastate rates, but it did not alter the situation so far as interstate commerce was concerned because the Interstate Commerce Commission had no positive control over rates. With the passage of the Hepburn Act, however, this situation changed radically. The Commission was now clothed with clear authority to fix maximum rates, and it could make the minimum rates guaranteed by *Smyth v. Ames* the maximum rates as well. At long last the law provided the people with a ceiling on rates to go along with the floor previously established by the courts.

Subsequent developments. The practical application of the *Smyth v. Ames* rule to the fixing of a railroad rate depended upon the availability of figures reflecting the fair value of the various railroad enterprises, but the Valuation Act was not passed until 1913, and it was many years after that before valuations, even as of 1913, were determined. In the meantime there was considerable complaint about the inadequacy of rates fixed by the Commission during the years 1906-20 and many students came to realize that the country could not maintain an adequate transportation system unless rates were sufficiently high to enable the carriers to operate at a reasonable profit. Increasingly it came to be realized that rates must be just and reasonable to the carriers as well as to the shippers, and recognizing the soundness of this position, the formulators of the Transportation Act, 1920, systematized the *Smyth v. Ames* doctrine into

---

[4] 169 U.S. 466, 546. Italics supplied.

a statutory rule of rate making. But the 1920 rule proved to be unworkable and it was replaced in 1933 by a new rule which, in effect, simply directed the Interstate Commerce Commission to fix rates which were fair to both shippers and carriers.

FAIR VALUE

What is fair value? For many years the courts had wrestled with the problem of placing some limitation on the power of legislatures to fix the rates to be charged by regulated enterprises, and finally a solution was worked out in the form of the fair return on the fair value doctrine enunciated in *Smyth v. Ames.* But unfortunately the Supreme Court in the process of solving one problem had created two new ones—what is a fair value and what is a fair rate of return? As to fair value the Court was not very helpful in its *Smyth v. Ames* opinion, saying that

> ...in order to ascertain that value, the original cost of construction, the amount expended in permanent improvements, the amount and market value of its bonds and stock, the present as compared with the original cost of construction, the probable earning capacity of the property under particular rates prescribed by statute, and the sum required to meet operating expenses, are all matters for consideration, and are to be given such weight as may be just and right in each case.[5]

And, as if the Court were afraid that it might have left something out, it added: "We do not say that there may not be other matters to be regarded in estimating the value of the property." In other words, everything which might have anything to do with the determination of value was to be taken into consideration. On the face of it this seems to be a reasonable requirement, but as a purely practical matter many of the criteria of value mentioned by the Court are directly contradictory, and it would be difficult, indeed, to give much weight to any one of them without at the same time doing violence to the others. The Court, however, was pioneering a new field and a more precise definition hardly could be expected at the time.

Valuation controversy. In the years that followed the enunciation of the *Smyth v. Ames* doctrine, an extended controversy developed over the proper procedure to follow in determining the value of a railroad or other public utility enterprise for rate-making purposes. The issue was important because the stakes involved were large as the following simple illustration will show. Suppose that a regulatory commission has placed a value of $10 million on the property of a certain public utility and that

---

[5] 169 U.S. 466, 546 (1898).

it considers 6 per cent to be a fair rate of return. In effect, then, the commission has sanctioned a scale of rates which will yield revenues sufficient to meet all of the utility's expenses and leave it a profit of $600,000. Actually, however, the rates being charged yield a profit of $800,000, and the commission takes steps to lower them. But the utility protests that the commission erred in placing the value of its property at $10 million and that actually the property is worth $15 million. A 6 per cent return on $15 million should bring a profit of $900,000 which is more than the utility is actually earning, and so it claims that the commission should raise rather than lower the rates. Under such circumstances it is not surprising that valuation for rate-making purpose became the subject of much litigation.

Railroad valuation since 1933. Congress abandoned the fair return on fair value principle in 1933 in favor of a more flexible rule of rate making, and so railroad valuation for rate-making purposes is no longer the vital issue that it was during the 1920's. While, however, there is no justification today for an extended discussion of railroad valuation, the subject does warrant some brief consideration. Technically the rule of rate making enunciated in *Smyth v. Ames* is still the basis of all rate making, although recent decisions of the Supreme Court to be discussed presently have rendered it largely inoperative. But a more important reason for giving some brief consideration to valuation is found in the fact that the present rule of rate making calls upon the Interstate Commerce Commission to fix rates which will provide revenues sufficient to enable the carriers, under honest, economical, and efficient management, to provide adequate and efficient transportation service; and it is almost axiomatic that rates fixed in this way will have to be sufficient to yield railroad security holders an adequate return of some sort on the value or worth of their investment. If it were not so, railroad owners would be unable to improve their properties from earnings, nor would they be able to attract new capital for better equipment and improved facilities. Thus, although valuation is no longer a major issue as far as the railroads are concerned, it is still a factor which enters into the determination of reasonable rate levels.

THEORIES OF VALUE

Market value. In *Smyth v. Ames* the Supreme Court set forth a long list of factors to be taken into consideration in valuing a railroad for rate-making purposes, but the valuation controversy soon settled around three concepts of value—market value, original cost, and cost of reproduction. The market value of a business, simply stated, is what its owners can get for it if they offer it for sale. Of course, the price they can get may be influenced by a variety of factors, but basically the market value of a business is a reflection of its earning capacity. If a given business enterprise has present and prospective earnings of $12,000 a year and if the market rate of interest on investments of similar risk is 6 per cent, a prospective buyer will not pay more than $200,000 for the business, because $200,000 invested elsewhere will bring him an equal return. While earning capacity may be acceptable as a method of determining value for purposes of purchase and sale, it does not provide an acceptable method of determining value for rate-making purposes. This is because the earning capacity of a regulated enterprise is determined in part by the general level of rates already in existence. Hence, if earning capacity is used as a basis for determining a reasonable level of rates, there immediately arises the problem of how to determine whether or not existing rates are reasonable.

A variation of the market value theory seeks to express the value of a utility for rate-making purposes in terms of the market value of its stocks and bonds. In the last analysis, however, the market value of stocks and bonds reflects the earning capacity of the corporation issuing them, and so this theory is open to exactly the same objection as the earning capacity theory. In addition, the value of stocks may be manipulated, and the market value of bonds reflects differences between the contract rate of interest and the market rate. Thus this theory would tend to give weight to factors external to the company and which are not directly related to its value for rate-making purposes.

Original cost. Original cost has been variously defined, and a number of problems arise in connection with the calculation of value according to this method, but it is doubtful that the present importance of valuation for railroad rate-making purposes justifies any extended discussion of the methods and problems which characterize any particular valuation theory. According to one definition original cost is determined by taking the actual cost of the original property less depreciation, adding to this the cost of any additions and improvements, and deducting the cost of any abandoned property. According to another school of thought, the same procedure is used, but all expenditures are carefully scrutinized, and if any costs are inflated because of dishonesty or gross inefficiency, they are scaled down accordingly. This latter method is commonly spoken of as the actual prudent investment theory, and it has the support of numerous economists and public authorities. Insofar as possible, original cost is determined from the books of record, but in the case of some older properties, particularly those which have changed hands one or more times, book records no longer exist, and it is necessary to estimate what the properties originally cost or what they should have cost.

Cost of reproduction. The cost of reproduction method determines value for rate-making purposes on the basis of present as contrasted with original cost of construction, and like original cost it gives rise to a number of problems. In the first place, value may be based on the cost of building a plant identical with the one in operation, less depreciation, or on the cost of building a substitute plant, taking into consideration the fact that if a new plant were being built, it would incorporate all of the technical developments made since the existing plant was constructed. Second, it may be based on the cost of reproducing a plant under the conditions existing at the time that it was originally built, or on the basis of what it would cost under present conditions. For example, if a railroad had been built originally through a forest which has long since disappeared, should the cost of felling nonexistent trees be included in determining cost of reproduction? Finally, it may be based on cost of reproduction using construction methods employed at the time the plant was built, or it may be based on cost using modern methods of construction.

Relative merits of valuation theories. The market value method may be dismissed as unsound. Generally speaking, original cost valuations can be determined more accurately because they may be obtained from the books of record whereas cost of reproduction must be estimated. Also, original cost valuations are more easily and more accurately kept up to date. Both of these statements, however, may be and have been disputed by advocates of cost of reproduction. Something may be said for cost of reproduction on the ground that it will assure investors a return which is in line with the general movement of prices, although the desirability of this has been disputed. Numerous arguments for and against original cost and cost of reproduction have been analyzed and criticized in great detail by competent students, but none of them touch on the main issue. The real point at issue, to put the matter succinctly, is simply a matter of "whose ox is being gored." Utilities will tend to support whichever theory brings the highest valuations because the higher the valuation the greater the income they receive. Conversely, the public will tend to support that theory which brings the lowest valuation because low valuations mean low rates.

JUDICIAL INTERPRETATION

Position of Supreme Court. In *Smyth v. Ames* the Supreme Court failed to set forth any usable standard of value, and this fact led inevitably to a long series of cases in which the pros and cons of valuation theory were argued in great detail. In the first of these cases, coming only a year after the *Smyth v. Ames* opinion, the Court held in susbtance that a company was entitled to demand a fair return upon the reasonable value of the property at the time it was being used for the public benefit, thus giving support to the cost of reproduction theory of valuation.[6] In succeeding cases the Court held pretty consistently to this theory, although it did not deny that cost might be a factor to be taken into consideration.

In its first decision involving an Interstate Commerce Commission valuation under the 1920 rule of rate making, the Supreme Court rejected the Commission's valuation of the St. Louis and O'Fallon Railroad because all property constructed prior to 1914 had been valued on the basis of 1914 prices without regard to subsequent higher prices. The Court held that the Commission had erred in failing to give consideration to cost of reproduction, but it gave no indication of how much consideration had to be given to it.[7]

The insistence of the Court that consideration be given to cost of reproduction peculiarly complicated the work of the Commission in connection with the recapture of excess earnings required by the Transportation Act, 1920. If cost of reproduction had to be considered, a revaluation of every railroad would have to be made each year because the law required that excess earnings be recaptured on an annual basis. Fortunately, the repeal of the rule of rate making in 1933 relieved the Commission of this arduous task.

Abandonment of fair value as a rate base. The tendency of the Supreme Court to insist that consideration be given to cost of reproduction also made the valuation problem difficult for rate-making authorities other than the Interstate Commerce Commission. In fixing public utility rates the various commissions found it difficult and costly to determine just what the cost of reproduction value should be in any particular case, and it was difficult to keep such valuations up to date. In 1942, however, the Supreme Court departed from its earlier position in a way which seemingly has revolutionized the whole rate making procedure. In that year the Court handed down its opinion in the Natural Gas Pipeline case in which it said in part:

> The Constitution does not bind rate-making bodies to the service of any single formula or combination of formulas. ... Once a fair hearing has been given, proper findings made and other statutory requirements satisfied, the courts cannot intervene in the absence of a clear showing that the limits of due process have been overstepped. If the Commission's order, as applied to the facts before it and viewed in its entirety, produces no arbitrary result, our inquiry is at an end.[8]

---

[6] *San Diego Land & Town Co. v. National City*, 174 U.S. 739 (1899).
[7] *St. Louis & O'Fallon R. v. United States*, 279 U.S. 461 (1929).
[8] *Federal Power Commission v. Natural Gas Pipeline Co.*, 315 U.S. 575, 586.

This position was reaffirmed two years later in the Hope Natural Gas case.[9]

The opinions of the Supreme Court in the Natural Gas Pipeline and Hope Natural Gas cases appear to permit rate-making authorities to adopt any method they see fit in determining a basis on which to establish a reasonable level of rates so long as the resulting rates do not produce an arbitrary result. But how is the Court to decide whether or not a given scale of rates will produce an arbitrary result in any particular case? The answer to this question is suggested in the Hope Natural Gas case in which the Supreme Court remarked that earnings should be sufficient to bring stockholders a return similar to that which is being paid on other investments of comparable risk. Also, a utility should be able to earn enough to assure the confidence of investors in its financial integrity and to permit it to maintain its credit and attract new capital. All of this suggests that a new rule of rate making is in the process of being developed, a rule which will require the establishment of rates high enough to yield a return sufficient to enable a regulated enterprise to pay its security holders, prospective as well as present, an acceptable return on their investments. Some of the implications of this principle, and some of its limitations, will be noted presently.

THE FAIR RETURN PROBLEM

Meaning and significance. The rule of rate making enunciated by the Supreme Court in *Smyth v. Ames* called for the establishment of a general level of rates which would bring a carrier a fair return on the fair value of the property used by it in the service of the public. In other words, rates were to be sufficiently high to yield the carrier a fair return, to be determined by applying a certain percentage figure called a fair rate of return to a rate base equal to the fair value of the property. Up to this point attention has been focused on the rate base aspect of this rule, but a moment's reflection will reveal readily enough that the determination of what constitutes the fair rate of return to be applied to the rate base is just as important as the rate base itself.

Take, for example, the illustration used earlier in this chapter to show the importance of the valuation figure in the determination of rates. If a 6 per cent rate of return is assumed to be fair, a $10 million valuation applied to a given utility will justify a scale of rates netting it $600,000, but if a $15 million valuation is insisted upon, rates which net the utility $900,000 will be in order. Exactly the same problem arises in connection

---

[9] *Federal Power Commission* v. *Hope Natural Gas Co.*, 320 U.S. 591.

with the rate of return. Conceivably the management of the utility involved might accept the $10 million valuation as correct but insist that 9 per cent rather than 6 per cent is a fair rate of return. A 6 per cent rate of return on a $10 million valuation will justify rates which net $600,000 as indicated above, but a 9 per cent rate of return on a $10 million valuation will justify rates which net $900,000. Hence under the fair return on the fair value rule the stakes involved in determining a fair rate of return are just as great as they are in the case of determining the valuation to be used.

Although fair value was abandoned by Congress in 1933 as a basis for determining railroad rates, the determination of a fair return is still a vital factor in the rate-making process. In fixing railroad rates, for example, the law requires the Interstate Commerce Commission to consider, among other things, the need of revenues sufficient to enable the carriers, under honest, economical, and efficient management, to provide an adequate transportation service; and to do this it is necessary for the Commission to determine what kind of a return the rates must bring in order to make it possible for the carriers to offer such a service. Similarly, other rate-making bodies must fix rates so as to yield the utilities under their jurisdiction a fair return according to one standard or another in order to comply with the Supreme Court requirement that the rates adopted must not produce an arbitrary result.

Definition of fair return. If it is assumed that the people of the United States want a continuation of improved railroad transportation service under private enterprise, then it may be set down as a general principle that a fair return must be one which is sufficient to attract capital to the railroad industry. In any dynamic society transportation companies must expand and improve their facilities to provide for the growth of trade and industry and to meet the demands of a higher standard of living. But it is axiomatic that investors will not provide the funds necessary to make possible this expansion and improvement of faciles unless they have some reasonable assurance of obtaining what they consider to be an adequate return on their investments.

In other words, a fair return must be sufficient to enable the railroad industry to maintain its credit by making regular payments at acceptable rates of interest on its fixed obligations, and if there is any expectation of financing improvements by the sale of stock, an acceptable rate of dividends must be paid as well. This, it will be noted, is the same as the test of a fair return suggested by the Supreme Court in the Hope Natural Gas case. Of course, there is always the possibility that a given type of transportation agency may be unable to charge rates which will be sufficient to enable it to maintain interest and dividend payments because of the existence of competition from other types of transportation agencies which are more efficient or which are subsidized by the Government. Under such circumstances the question of a fair return is largely academic, and eventually the less efficient or less favored agency will have to pass out of existence, be subsidized, or be taken over by the Government.

Elements in fair rate of return. If a fair return is one which will attract capital to the railroad industry, how can regulatory authorities apply this rule to the practical determination of how much a railroad should be permitted to earn? Or how much do investors have to expect to receive in order to induce them to put their savings into railroad securities? The rate of return which an investor must receive in order to induce him to make an investment depends upon three considerations— the rate of pure interest, investment expense, and risk.

Pure interest, according to a common definition, is the amount of money that must be paid to induce a person to forego the present enjoyment of goods by saving a part of his income and making this saved income available for use by others. The rate of pure interest is believed to differ with different individuals and with different circumstances, but it has nothing to do with the type of investment contemplated. It will be the same for all types of investments and so will not affect the investor's decision whether he should put his money into railroads or into any one of a hundred other industries.

The second element in the rate of return, investment expense, involves all of those expenses incurred in making investments and in managing them after they are made. These expenses will not vary greatly as between different types of investments, at least as far as major industries are concerned. Thus as far as pure interest and investment expenses are concerned one investment is about the same as another. In the case of the risk element, however, the situation is quite different.

Importance of risk. Every investment involves at least some risk, and investors expect to receive more than a mere payment for pure interest and investment expense to offset this risk. Naturally, the amount that the investor must be paid to induce him to take a given risk will be great or small depending upon the degree of risk involved. This factor contributes importantly to determine the minimum rate of return which investors feel they must have for investing in different kinds of securities, in different companies, and in different industries. Thus, since bond interest must be paid before stock dividends, the rate of return on a good bond is less than the return on a good stock issued by the same corporation. Similarly, an old established concern with a long record of satisfactory earnings will be able, other things being equal, to obtain capital at a lower rate of interest than a newly organized competitor.

Demand for capital. What has been said up to this point relates specifically to the supply of capital that is made available for industrial or other use. It seeks to show how pure interest, investment expense, and risk function to determine the minimum rate of return which investors must have in order to induce them to save and invest their savings in various ways. But there is also a demand side to the picture which must not be overlooked. Directly or indirectly the users of capital compete with one another for the available supply. Industrial users compete with commercial users, producers with consumers, and governments with nongovernmental users. At any given time there are some industries which are more profitable than others, and if they are in an expanding stage, they may be able to pay investors more for the use of their capital than the minimum which it is presumed that investors must have. When this happens, an increasing amount of capital is attracted to these industries, and other industries will have to offer higher rates of return if they expect to obtain additional capital.

Determination of fair rate of return. It may be said, then, that a return which will attract capital to a given industry must be sufficient to enable that industry to pay interest and dividends equal to those which are paid by other industries involving a similar degree of risk. This principle, which is applicable to all users of capital, provides a practical rule for determining a fair return for the railroad transportation industry. If the people of the United States want a continuation of improved railroad transportation under private ownership, regulatory commissions must be prepared to permit the railroads to earn, insofar as it is possible for them to do so, a return sufficient to enable them to pay interest and dividends comparable with payments made by other users of capital where a similar degree of risk is involved. If it be objected that a regulated industry like railroad transportation cannot be compared with industries and commercial establishments operating under conditions of competition, insofar as risk is concerned, it may be pointed out that investors do make these comparisons, and their judgments are reflected in their willingness or unwillingness to invest in railroad securities at the rates of return existing at any given time.

FACTORS INFLUENCING DETERMINATION OF FAIR RETURN

Overcapitalization. Certain qualifications must be made to the principle outlined above in using it to determine a fair rate return for the railroad transportation industry. In the first place, should the principle be applied to an industry without regard to the legitimacy of its existing capitalization? If the railroads taken as a whole are overcapitalized as is sometimes claimed, the use of this rule would justify rates high enough to pay interest and dividends on securities which in part do not represent property employed in the service of the public. In this connection, however, it must be remembered that rates are supposed to be just and reasonable to shippers as well as to carriers, and it would be difficult to defend as just and reasonable a scale of rates which required shippers to pay interest and dividends on securities which exceeded the worth of the company. Fortunately, in spite of irresponsible statements sometimes made to the contrary, it has been demonstrated repeatedly that the railroads are not overcapitalized. It will be sufficient here to note that total capital outstanding in 1950 was only $18,273,631,000 for line-haul railroads, as compared with a reported property investment less depreciation reserve of $23,542,162,000.[10] These figures hardly suggest the existence of overcapitalization.

Proper accounting procedures. In deciding whether or not a given scale of rates will enable the railroads to pay investors a rate of return equal to that paid on other investments of similar risk it is necessary to assume the existence and honest use of correct accounting procedures. In unregulated business enterprises it is possible to disguise profits, at least for a period of time, by the use of questionable methods of accounting for depreciation. Fortunately, the extensive control which the Interstate Commerce Commission has exercised for so many years over railroad accounting procedures and the issuance of railroad securities makes it difficult to apply such practices to the railroad transportation industry.

Responsible and efficient management. In applying the fair return standard outlined above it also is necessary to assume the existence of responsible and efficient management. In earlier years irresponsible railroad managements diverted funds for their own use by making use of construction companies and other devices. In addition, inefficient managements have at times incurred expenses far in excess of what such expenses reasonably should have been. All such activities inflate costs and tend to increase the rate of return which investors will demand to offset the increased risk involved. Today, of course, the Interstate Commerce Commission has full authority to prevent the revenue depleting activities once favored by irresponsible and dishonest managements, but it cannot guarantee to protect investors and the public from the results of inefficient management. Clearly a fair return should be based on the amount necessary to attract capital to those railroads which are operated by responsible and reasonably efficient managements.

Degree of risk. It is often assumed that a fair return for a regulated

---

[10] Interstate Commerce Commission, *Annual Report*, 1951, pp. 168, 169.

enterprise like railroad transportation need not be as large as the returns which are sometimes found in the field of competitive enterprise. This is true because an investment in a regulated enterprise involves a lesser degree of risk than is often the case where competition prevails. A railroad is protected from unnecessary competition on the part of other railroads. Destructive competition is minimized by the Interstate Commerce Commission's power to fix minimum rates. The Commission's jurisdiction over accounting procedures and the issuance of securities protects investors in railroad securities to a somewhat greater extent than is true of industry in general. Furthermore, the Supreme Court held many years ago that a railroad was entitled to a fair return on the fair value of its property, and the present law places upon the Interstate Commerce Commission the affirmative duty of fixing rates which will be fair to the carriers as well as to the shippers.

On the other hand, certain contrary forces must be taken into consideration. The extent to which the railroad business is characterized by constant costs may lead to wide fluctuations in earnings with variations in business conditions. The railroads have complained that the Interstate Commerce Commission has failed to grant rates sufficiently high to make railroad securities attractive investments. The machinery for the settlement of labor disputes is entirely separate and distinct from the machinery for fixing rates, and there may be extended lags between wage increases and rate increases. Although railroads are protected from competition to some extent as far as other railroads are concerned, the government policy of building hard surfaced highways and improved waterways, together with the policy of providing airways, airports, and airmail subsidies, has encouraged the development of an increasing amount of competition from other forms of transportation. All of these considerations go a long way to explain why investments in railroad securities, with the exception of equipment obligations, are not considered attractive today.[11]

Capital structure. About one-half of the over-all capitalization of the railroads of the United States is in the form of bonds and other types of funded debt, and this fact may have some bearing on the determination of the return necessary to attract capital to the railroad industry. Because bondholders have a preferred claim on earnings, the interest rate on bonds can be placed at a lower level than the dividend rates expected or anticipated by stockholders. Hence it is believed that the rate of return necessary to attract capital to the railroad industry need not be as large as in the case of an industry financed wholly or in large part by the sale of stock.

---

[11] The special status of equipment obligations is discussed in Chapter 14.

On the other hand, the more extensively an industry is financed through the sale of bonds, the greater becomes the risk incurred by the purchasers of its preferred and common stocks. With one-half of railroad capital in the form of bonds and other similar securities, the owners of which have a first claim on earnings, the risk taken by investors in railroad stocks is obvious. To offset this risk the over-all return would have to be large enough to meet the relatively low interest rates paid on funded debt and at the same time offer the possibility of a susbtantial reward to stockholders. In view of the generally low rates of return earned by railroads on their outstanding capital in recent years it is not surprising that railroad stocks are poorly regarded by investors today.

Need for stable earnings. Railroads, like most other types of business enterprises, must expect low returns or no returns at all during hard times, but unlike competitive business enterprises they have no assurance under the law that they will be able to make up for these low earnings or losses when business is good. This means that if railroad securities are to become attractive investments, a fair return must be calculated on the basis of earnings over a period of years and not for each year considered separately. The railroads must be permitted to earn enough during good years to enable them to establish reserves to take care of interest and dividends when traffic is slack.

APPLICATION TO INDIVIDUAL RAILROADS

Capitalization problem. The concept of a fair return as one which will yield railroad security holders a rate of return comparable with that obtained from other investments of similar risk must be thought of in terms of the railroad industry as a whole, for it by no means follows that each individual railroad can charge rates which will bring it such a return. Individual railroads, as distinguished from the industry as a whole, may be overcapitalized, and it would not be fair to shippers to permit an overcapitalized railroad to charge rates high enough to support its excessive capitalization, even if the competitive situation permitted. The stockholders of an overcapitalized line should take drastic steps to reduce its capitalization, and if this seems to be impossible, the line should be reorganized and the overcapitalization eliminated. Also, it would seem reasonable to base a fair return on the amount necessary to attract capital, assuming an average ratio of stocks to funded debt.

Of course, it might be objected that the above policy would encourage stockholder owners to finance improvements through the sale of bonds, since the higher the ratio of bonds to stocks, the greater will be the return to common stockholders. While this is true, it is also true that the higher the ratio of bonds, the greater is the risk assumed by stockholders. In any event, the control over the issuance of railroad securities now exercised by the Interstate Commerce Commission can be relied upon to limit the sale of bonds and other types of funded debt should the sale of other securities be possible.

Weak lines. There are many railroads in the United States so situated that they cannot possibly earn enough to attract capital, regardless of the scale of rates that they might be permitted to charge. Most of these are short lines located in light traffic areas or in areas where the motor vehicle has cut deeply into the traffic. For these lines the whole question of rates that will attract capital is largely academic because in the very nature of the case they have no need for additional capital, and sooner or later most of them probably will be abandoned. Then there are other and more important railroads which cannot expect to charge rates sufficient to bring a return necessary to attract capital partly because they are in competition with more favorably situated carriers. If a genuine public need is shown for such a railroad, its continued operation will have to depend upon consolidation with a stronger line or on some sort of public subsidy. It is difficult to see how any scheme of rate making could be devised which would bring some needy but needed railroads a fair return according to the principle outlined above.

Reward for efficiency. As already pointed out, a return which is fair to the railroad industry as a whole should be based on the amount necessary to attract capital to those railroads which are operated by responsible and reasonably efficient management. From this it follows that a railroad which is not operated efficiently must suffer the consequences which result from a return that is less than necessary to attract capital until such time as steps are taken to substitute more efficient management. A somewhat different problem is presented by the railroad corporation with an unusually efficient management. Since competition between carriers necessitates a good deal of uniformity of rates, it will be apparent that a scale of rates designed to bring a fair return to those carriers operating in a reasonably efficient manner will bring something more than a fair return to the unusually efficient. But this is as it should be, and any scheme which had the effect of depriving such a line of the fruits of efficient management would discourage progress, and this in turn would be bad for the railroads and the public both. The somewhat higher returns enjoyed by a railroad favored with an unusually efficient management should prove an incentive to greater efficiency on the part of other railroads.

GENERAL LEVEL OF RAILROAD RATES

General level of rates, 1920-40. In closing this chapter a brief review of Interstate Commerce Commission policy in attempting to fix rates in conformity with statutory rules of rate making is in order. In 1920, with the newly established rule of rate making and the obvious revenue needs of the railroads in mind, the Commission authorized susbtantial increases in the general level of rates, ranging from an increase of 25 per cent in the South to a 40 per cent increase in the East. These increases were calculated to net the railroads a 6 per cent return on an estimated valuation of $18,900 million but this return was never realized because of the sharp postwar depression which developed in the fall of 1920 and continued on into 1921 and 1922. Traffic fell off sharply, and there were demands for rate reductions from harassed shippers, particularly in the agricultural areas. The railroads reduced a number of important rates, either voluntarily or as a result of Interstate Commerce Commission orders, and in 1922 there was a general reduction in rates not previously reduced.

Throughout the rest of the 1920's the Interstate Commerce Commission refused to permit any further changes in the general level of rates, although only in 1926 did the railroads come close to earning a return of 6 per cent on valuation, but early in 1932 some increases were allowed in an effort to maintain railroad credit. Other increases were granted from time to time in the 1930's, the last one coming in 1938, but the difficulties faced by shippers and the threat of competition from other forms of transportation placed a distinct limit on the extent to which the general level of rates could be raised. It was recognized by the carriers as well as by the Commission that it was impossible to achieve a satisfactory return under the conditions then existing, and no attempt was made to establish rates on such a basis.

General level of rates since 1940. In 1941 wage increases added $382 million to the annual railroad wage bill, and at the same time rising prices of materials and supplies added further to the costs of railroad operation. In order to protect their revenues the carriers applied for a general 10 per cent increase in rates, and early in 1942 the Commission granted an increase which, after making allowances for numerous specific exceptions, averaged about 4.7 per cent. These increases were mostly suspended in 1943, however, because of substantial increases in railroad revenues resulting from the heavy volume of war traffic. Although wage increases amounting to $354 million were granted in 1943, no further increases in the general level of rates were made during the balance of the war period. The peak of wartime traffic was reached in 1944 and began to decline in 1945. New wage increases, the rising cost of railroad materials and supplies, and declining traffic led the railroads to apply for a general 25 per cent increase in rates in April 1946. In June the Interstate Commerce Commission, realizing the urgency of the carriers' need for more revenue, allowed an interim increase of 6 per cent on most traffic, with smaller increases permitted on the balance. In December the Commission authorized a general 20 per cent increase in rates to take the place of the earlier interim increases, but since the increase did not apply equally to all traffic, the new rates were estimated to raise carrier revenues by 17.6 per cent.

The same combination of higher wages, rising costs of materials and supplies, and declining traffic led to further applications for rate increases, and the Commission granted an increase of about 22.6 per cent in July 1948, and a further increase of 9.1 per cent in August 1949. In each case smaller interim increases were granted before the announcement of the final decision. Early in 1951 another general rate increase was proposed by the carriers, and in August, 1951, an average increase of 6.6 per cent was granted. The over-all effect of these various increases was to raise freight rates 67.7 per cent over the 1939 level according to a railroad spokesman. Taking into consideration changes in the composition of traffic and the average length of haul, along with the fact that the increases did not apply equally to all kinds of traffic, carrier revenue per ton mile of freight hauled was estimated to have increased by only 47.8 per cent.[12] The railroads believed that the 1951 increase would not cover much more than half of the cost increases incurred since the last rate increase, but the Commission felt that the prevailing upward trend of traffic at the time would compensate in part for the higher costs.[13] Dissatisfied with the results of the 1951 rate increase, the railroads soon applied for an additional increase, and in April 1952 a further increase, estimated to bring rates 78.9 per cent above the June 1946 level, was granted.

Conclusion. The figures shown in Table V indicate clearly the extent to which the railroads have failed to produce earnings sufficient to attract new capital to the industry. Even for a regulated enterprise the rates of return on outstanding capital and on net property investment have been low. The holders of 26 per cent of all railroad stocks received no dividends in 1950, the best record achieved in many years. Even in the case of stocks on which dividends are paid, the average rate has been quite modest as compared with other industries of no greater, if as much, risk as railroad transportation. The failure of the railroads to earn a return

---

[12] Statement by Walter S. Franklin, quoted in *Traffic World*, August 18, 1951, p. 29.
[13] *Traffic World*, August 11, 1951, pp. 15, 21.

Table V

SELECTED STATISTICS ON RATE OF RETURN AND STOCK DIVIDENDS, LINE HAUL RAILROADS AND LESSOR SUBSIDIARIES [14]

Year	Total Railroad Capital Actually Outstanding	Net Income	Ratio of Net Income to all Capital Outstanding	Proportion of Stock Paying Dividends	Average Rate of Dividends on:		Rate of Return on Net Property Investment
					Dividend Paying Stock	All Stock	
1921	$20,247,686,000	$350,540,000	1.73%	56.92%	9.02%	5.13%	2.99
1922	20,463,595,000	434,459,000	2.12	59.38	6.37	3.78	3.75
1923	21,057,513,000	632,118,000	3.00	62.09	7.30	4.53	4.57
1924	21,680,783,000	623,399,000	2.88	64.97	6.37	4.14	4.49
1925	21,734,095,000	771,053,000	3.55	66.70	6.52	4.35	5.07
1926	21,748,806,000	883,422,000	4.06	69.12	7.32	5.06	5.35
1927	21,848,928,000	741,924,000	3.40	70.25	8.47	5.95	4.64
1928	22,025,588,000	855,018,000	3.88	73.65	7.12	5.25	5.01
1929	22,306,752,000	977,230,000	4.38	76.23	7.47	5.70	5.24
1930	22,782,889,000	577,923,000	2.54	76.93	7.83	6.02	3.59
1931	22,747,229,000	169,287,000	.47	73.20	5.48	4.01	2.20
1932	22,831,547,000	−121,630,000		32.85	4.57	1.50	1.38
1933	22,656,920,000	26,543,000	.12	31.11	5.09	1.58	2.03
1934	22,412,057,000	23,282,000	.10	34.26	6.21	2.13	1.99
1935	22,079,551,000	52,177,000	.24	34.39	5.94	2.04	2.16
1936	21,961,035,000	221,591,000	1.01	36.20	6.45	2.33	2.88
1937	21,694,645,000	146,351,000	.67	39.64	5.85	2.32	2.56
1938	21,428,320,000	−87,468,000		32.07	4.34	1.39	1.62
1939	21,193,501,000	141,134,000	.67	32.64	5.62	1.84	2.56
1940	21,047,280,000	243,138,000	1.16	38.29	5.79	2.22	2.94
1941	20,707,778,000	557,672,000	2.69	40.65	6.20	2.52	4.28
1942	20,471,191,000	992,843,000	4.85	56.37	4.74	2.67	6.34
1943	19,913,582,000	946,150,000	4.75	57.97	4.83	2.83	5.75
1944	19,402,593,000	733,461,000	3.78	58.46	5.29	3.09	4.73
1945	18,681,292,000	502,250,000	2.69	57.13	5.49	3.13	3.77
1946	18,449,437,000	334,966,000	1.82	55.50	5.42	3.01	2.75
1947	18,050,122,000	537,405,000	2.98	56.20	5.41	3.04	3.41
1948	18,249,091,000	767,949,000	4.21	69.75	5.20	3.63	4.24
1949	18,342,568,000	496,103,000	2.70	64.24	5.18	3.33	2.86
1950	18,273,631,000	854,951,000	4.68	73.70	5.15	3.80	

[14] Figures in last column are from Association of American Railroads, *Railroad Transportation, A Statistical Record, 1911-1949*, Washington, 1950. All other figures are taken or adapted from annual reports of Interstate Commerce Commission.

sufficient to attract new capital is by no means entirely due to an inadequate general level of rates but is due in part to the competitive situation in transportation. Some of the implications of low railroad earnings are discussed in the concluding chapters of this volume.

SUGGESTED READINGS

The literature on valuation is extensive, but since the problem is of little significance today as far as railroad transportation is concerned and is becoming somewhat less important in the over-all field of public utility regulation, there does not seem to be much point in detailing it here.

Barnes, Irston R., *The Economics of Public Utility Regulation*. New York: F. S. Crofts & Co., 1942. Chapters 11-17 contain a detailed consideration of the valuation and rate of return problem.

Bigham, Truman C., *Transportation, Principles and Problems*. New York: McGraw-Hill Book Company, Inc., 1946. Chapters 9-11.

Jones, Eliot, *Principles of Railway Transportation*. New York: The Macmillan Company, 1924. Chapters 15 and 16.

Locklin, D. Philip, *Economics of Transportation*, 3rd Ed. Chicago: Richard D. Irwin, Inc., 1947. Chapters 15 and 16. Chapter 16 includes a useful bibliography on valuation and the rate of return.

Railway Age and Traffic World are useful sources of current information on matters dealing with the general level of rates.

Ripley, William Z., *Railroads, Finance and Organization*. New York: Longmans, Green & Company, 1915. Chapters 15-16.

Sharfman, I. L., *The Interstate Commerce Commission*, Vol. III B. New York: The Commonwealth Fund, 1936. Chapter 14.

Thompson, C. Woody and Wendell R. Smith, *Public Utility Economics*. New York, McGraw-Hill Book Company, Inc., 1941. Chapters 13-20.

11.

Determination of Rates

on

SPECIFIC COMMODITIES

INTRODUCTORY

Problems presented in this chapter. Chapter 10 was given over to an examination of the principles underlying the determination of the general level of rates, and to pointing up the fact that the railroads, if they are to continue to operate under a system of private ownership, must be able to charge rates which will enable them to earn enough to pay interest and dividends to railroad security holders comparable with the interest and dividend payments received by investors in other industries of similar risk. But this does not mean that the rate charged for each and every haul must be sufficient to cover the full cost of the haul and make a prorata contribution to the return necessary to attract investors. Indeed, for reasons that will be brought out in this and succeeding chapters, it would be impossible to work out and put into practice such a system of rate making, and in actual practice rates are found to vary considerably between different kinds of commodities and between different shipping points. This chapter is devoted to a consideration of the principles involved in determining the rates charged for moving different kinds of traffic, while the problems involved in the determination of the comparative level of rates between different points constitute the subject matter of the two chapters that follow.

Passenger fares. The method of quoting passenger fares is quite simple. A basic rate in terms of so many cents per mile per passenger is established, and the actual charge made for a given trip is computed by multiplying this basic rate by the number of miles traveled. Of course, if two or more lines compete with one another in offering service between the same points, competition will lead to the establishment of a uniform charge even though the distance may not be the same by all lines. Two basic types of service are offered, first class and coach. Coach service, which is the cheaper, is offered in the familiar chair car with two rows of seats, each seat providing space for two passengers. First class service is offered in Pullman cars and in parlor cars of one sort or another. The passenger who travels first class must pay a higher rate per mile than the coach passenger and in addition must pay for the use of the seat or sleeping space that is reserved for him. The amount of this latter charge varies with the length of the trip and the nature of the space used, i.e., chair, berth, roomette, or room.

In addition to these basic types of passenger service, some railroads serving large cities offer a commuter service at low rates for people living in suburban areas. Some railroads offer excursion trips on special occasions at very low charges, and some western railroads provide a tourist sleeper service intermediate in charge between first class and coach. And some high-speed trains are operated at an additional charge over and above the regular fare.

The higher fares charged for first class service are justified because of the greater cost of rendering the service. A Pullman car or parlor car costs more to build than a typical coach. Furthermore, Pullman cars are heavier and cost more to pull. Moreover, the seating capacity of Pullman cars and parlor cars is much less than that of an ordinary coach, and so the cost of providing and hauling the equipment must be spread over a smaller number of passengers. Finally, observation-lounge cars, reading materials, and other special services usually are provided for first class passenger, all of which adds to the cost. Differences in fares also may reflect in some degree differences in what the traffic will bear. Some people are willing to pay more for the prestige of riding in superior equipment or for the privilege of enjoying a reserved seat or for the privilege of not having to be crowded. On the other hand, there are many people who are price conscious. These people are bound to be attracted by low bus fares and by the low out-of-pocket cost of travel by private automobile when two or more are traveling together. Clearly this is a factor that must be taken into consideration by the railroads in establishing the level of coach rates.

Charges for hauling freight: Class rates. The railroads have found it convenient to group all of the multitudinous commodities shipped by freight into a small number of classes, and rates are then quoted for moving classes of freight rather than for moving individual items. Such rates are commonly referred to as class rates. To determine the rate charged for moving a specified item of freight between two points, it is necessary to consult first the Consolidated Freight Classification which lists all of the numerous items shipped by railroad freight, together with the group or class assigned to each. The group or class number assigned to any given item is called its rating. Having determined the correct rating, resort must next be had to a tariff or rate sheet showing rates between various points. This tariff gives the actual rates in terms of cents per hundred pounds for hauling each class of freight between different stations. In this way the correct class rate is determined.

The importance of the practice of classifying freight is found in the fact that railroad freight rates, unlike passenger fares, cannot be quoted on the basis of so many mills or so many cents per ton mile, with the charge determined by multiplying a rate per ton mile by the number of miles hauled. This means that railroad freight tariffs quote rates on a point to point basis, but to quote a separate rate between every pair of points in the United States on each of the approximately ten thousand items listed in the Consolidated Freight Classification would present an impossible publishing task.[1] By grouping these items into a small number of classes and quoting rates on the basis of classes of freight instead of on individual items, the publishing problem is greatly simplified.

Commodity rates. In addition to class rates the railroads publish a large number of commodity rates which apply directly to the movement of specific commodities. Class rates apply to the movement of all commodities between all points in the country, while commodity rates apply only to specified items of freight, and their application is limited to specifically named points or areas. Generally speaking commodity rates apply to important commodities which move in large quantities, items such as grain and coal and cotton, and to bulky low grade commodities like sand and gravel which cannot stand high rates. Commodity rates almost always are lower than comparable class rates, and when a commodity rate is published it takes the place of and supersedes the class rates which would normally apply. In some cases, however, tariffs provide for the alternative use of class or commodity rates, the shipper paying whichever of the two will result in the lower charge. At the present time most small or less-than-carload shipments move under class rates, as do also some carload shipments of high grade freight, while the heavy lower grades of freight move under commodity rates.[2]

Exception ratings. Similar in nature to commodity rates are the exception ratings frequently employed in connection with the shipment of railroad freight. It sometimes happens that it is desired to accord certain items of freight lower ratings than those shown in the Consolidated Freight Classification, but only under certain special conditions. For example, it may be desired to apply a reduced rating on a certain item

---

[1] This does not mean that ten thousand different commodities are listed in the Classification. The same commodity may be classified in two or more different ways depending upon its nature or the way in which it is packed.

[2] Students sometimes are inclined to think of commodity rates as applying only to basic commodities such as are dealt with on commodity exchanges. This is not the distinction made above, however, and many items of freight which are not traded on organized exchanges move on commodity rates.

when shipped over the lines of some particular railroad or group of railroads without having the reduced rating apply generally to all railroads. Such limited changes in the Classification are called exception ratings or exceptions to the Classification. They have been used in certain areas to meet motor competition and for other special purposes.

Importance of classification. The great bulk of railroad freight moves under commodity rates or exception ratings and not under the ratings shown in the Consolidated Freight Classification. Nevertheless an examination of the principles of freight classification and the problems arising out of such classification is a matter of importance because these same principles also enter into the determination of commodity rates and exception ratings. Furthermore, exception ratings are based directly on the Consolidated Freight Classification and a great many commodity rates also are closely related to the classification ratings. For these reasons, and others, an understanding of freight classification and the problems related thereto is necessary to an understanding of the problem of determining rates on specific commodities.

THE CLASSIFICATION OF FREIGHT

Origin of classification. Early railroads were conceived of as passenger carrying enterprises, but as soon as they began to move freight they found it advantageous to group the various items offered for shipment into a small number of classes and to establish rates for classes of freight rather than for individual items. The idea of classification probably originated with the highway carriers of the prerailroad era, these early freighters having established a technique of computing charges for hauling light and bulky articles on the basis of space occupied while at the same time using a weight basis for heavier and more compact shipments. Some of the early railroads also used this dual system of computing charges, but for the most part railroads grouped their freight into classes and assessed charges exclusively on the basis of weight. This is the system in use on the railroads today, although it is interesting to note that the space-weight system still survives in ocean transportation and in a modified form in air transportation.

Development of regional classification. Originally each railroad worked out its own system of classification without reference to the classifications used on other lines. This worked all right in the early days when railroads were largely disjointed in nature and a shipper could ship only to those points located on the railroad serving his community. As the railroad network expanded, however, railroads began to accept shipments for through movements via connecting lines, and the multiplicity of classifications became confusing. A given railroad might have its own classification which applied to shipments between points on its own lines and at the same time be a party to several other classifications applicable to movements in conjunction with other lines. Classifications might even differ with the direction of movement, with one classification applying to westbound movements and a different one to eastbound movements. It has been said that at one time there were 138 different classifications in the area between Chicago and New York alone.

The first important step toward achieving some order out of this chaotic situation was taken in 1882 when a number of railroads running west out of Chicago adopted a Joint Western Classification, which was later adopted by many other western lines. In 1887 a large number of eastern carriers adopted what they called the Official Classification, and by 1889 the southern lines had adopted the Southern Railway and Steamship Association Classification, later called the Southern Classification. Not only did these three classifications replace numerous individual line and joint classifications, but in the course of time they also replaced a number of state classifications which had been established to govern intrastate freight movements.

CONSOLIDATED FREIGHT CLASSIFICATION

Origin of Consolidated Freight Classification. In 1919, during the period of government operation of the railroads, the three regional classifications were combined to form the Consolidated Freight Classification. This classification provided a single set of rules and regulations applicable to all three classification territories, and uniformity also was achieved in commodity descriptions and in the minimum number of pounds of freight required to obtain the benefit of the lower ratings usually applied to carload lot shipments. But uniformity was not achieved on the actual ratings applied to the various individual items listed.

Present classification territories. The Official Classification is used by those railroads whose lines lie predominantly in that part of the United States bounded on the north by Canada; on the east by the Atlantic Ocean; on the west in a general way by a line drawn down the west shore of Lake Michigan to Milwaukee, thence roughly southwest across Wisconsin to the Mississippi River, and down the Mississippi to the mouth of the Ohio; and on the south by a line drawn eastward along the Ohio River to Cincinnati, thence to Kenova, West Virginia, and from Kenova through Roanoke and Suffolk to Norfolk, Virginia. Southern Classification applies in the area south of the above line and east of the Mississippi, and Western Classification applies to the vast area lying west of Official and Southern Classification territories. In simpler terms, Official Classification may be said to apply roughly east of the Mississippi and north of the Ohio, Southern Classification east of the Mississippi and south of the Ohio, and Western Classification west of the Mississippi.

In Illinois the eastern divisions of the railroads using the Western Classification interlace with the western divisions of the railroads using the Official Classification, with a few lines also using Southern Classification. In order to avoid confusion and possible discrimination, intrastate shipments in Illinois are governed by a separate Illinois Classification which also has a limited application to certain interstate shipments. The Illinois Classification is printed along with the Official, Southern and Western Classifications as a part of the Consolidated Freight Classification.

Interterritorial shipments. A shipment moving between two points located in the same classification territory will move under the classification applicable thereto, but when a shipment moves between points in two different classification territories, an obvious complication arises. In order to avoid confusion and to prevent misunderstandings and possible discrimination, agreements have been reached on the classifications to be applied in connection with various interterritorial movements. Where joint through rates are quoted on movements between Official Classification and Southern Classification territories, the Southern Classification usually applies. Between Western Classification Territory and Southern and Official Classification Territories the Western Classification commonly applies, although there are a number of important exceptions to this rule. Any confusion that might result is eliminated, however, by the requirement that every tariff must specifically state the classification to be used in conjunction with it.

Classification committees. The railroads in each of the three classification territories have a classification committee to handle classification matters for them, and these committees are responsible for such additions and changes as are made from time to time in the classifications. In addition to the three regional committees, there is a Consolidated Classification Committee which handles changes in rules and regulations and in other aspects of classification where uniformity exists. This committee also publishes the Consolidated Freight Classification. Shippers may apply to these various committees for changes in classification, and their reasons for requesting such changes will be heard. If shippers object to changes initiated by the classification committees, or if a committee refuses to make changes requested by shippers, an appeal may be made to the Interstate Commerce Commission. Since a change in the rating applied to a commodity will affect the charge that is made for hauling that commodity, the Interstate Commerce Commission or the proper state regulatory body obviously will have final jurisdiction.

Class designations. Official Classification provides seven major classifications which are designated as 1, 2, 3, Rule 26, 4, 5, 6. Southern Classification has twelve consecutively numbered classifications, and Western Classification has five numbered and five lettered classes, 1, 2, 3, 4, A, 5, B, C, D, E. In determining the actual rates to be applied to each of these various classifications a first class rate is established, and the rate for each lower class is fixed as a percentage of this first class rate. The percentage relationship of each class to the first class rate is shown in Table VI.

Table VI
CLASSIFICATION RATINGS

Official Classification		Southern Classification		Western Classification	
1	100%	1	100%	1	100%
2	85	2	85	2	85
3	70	3	70	3	70
Rule 26	55	4	55	4	55
4	50				
		5	45	A	45
		6	40		
				5	37½
5	35	7	35		
				B	32½
		8	30	C	30
6	27½				
		9	25		
		10	22½	D	22½
		11	20		
		12	17½	E	17½

It will be noted that in all three classifications the second class rate is fixed at 85 per cent and the third class rate at 70 per cent of the first class rate. From this point on, however, the classifications are not uniform in the percentage relationships of the various classes to the first class rate. In addition to the major classes, there are a considerable number of multiple, fractional, and percentage classifications. There is, for example, a rating of 1¼ which means that the items to which it is applied are charged for on the basis of 1¼ times the first class rate. Similarly, a rating of 1½ means a rate equal to 1½ times the first class rate. D1 means double the first class rate and 3t1 means three times the first class rate. A rating of 40 means 40 per cent of the first class, and a rating of 50 means 50 per cent of first class. Indeed, any number in excess of 12, which is the lowest class rating for Southern Classification, indicates a percentage of the first class rate.

25705–25860

Item	ARTICLES	Less Carload Ratings	Carload Minimum (Pounds)	Carload Ratings
25705	Ivory, animal, scrap or shavings, in barrels or boxes.	3	24,000R	R26-4-4
25710	Ivory, nut or vegetable, meal, scrap or shavings, in bags, barrels or boxes	4-50-4	36,000	6-6-5
25715	Ivory, nut or vegetable, other than meal, scrap or shavings, in bags, barrels or boxes	3	36,000	5-6-5
25721	Jewelers' lappings, plate scrap, polishings, stonings or other jewelers' refuse of extraordinary value. Not taken.			
25722	Jewelry—Not taken.			
25724	Jugs or pails, insulated and jacketed, in barrels or boxes	2	24,000R	4
25725	Kettles, stills or tanks, iron or steel, 2 gauge or thicker, glass enameled, steam jacketed or not jacketed, not mounted on bolsters or frames, returned for reenameling, loose or on skids	2	24,000R	40-6-A
25727	Kettles, stills or tanks, not mounted on bolsters or frames, iron or steel, glass enameled or glass lined, steam jacketed or not jacketed:			
	SU, LCL, in boxes or crates, except tanks may be shipped loose or on skids; CL, loose or in packages	1	20,000R	4
	KD, LCL, in boxes or crates; CL, loose or in packages	2	20,000R	4
25730	Kindling, fire, composition, in bags, barrels, boxes or crates	4-50-4	30,000	6-9-C
25733	Kits, electric fence equipment, consisting of steel fence post fixtures, lightning arrestors, fence testers, wire insulators, insulated copper wire, composition and steel handles, flat metal signs or store display stand, in boxes	2	24,000R	R26-4-4
25736	Kits, metal polishing, consisting of liquid cleaner, steel wool and sponges, in boxes	2	30,000	R26-4-4
25739	Kits, repair, internal combustion engine circulating or fuel pump, in boxes	1	24,000R	3
25742	Knee protectors, in packages	1	20,000R	3
25745	Knit goods, noibn, in boxes or in packages 88 or 849	1	12,000R	2
25751	Knobs or pulls, door or drawer, noibn, in bags, barrels, boxes, or barrels with cloth tops	3	30,000	4
25754	Labels, paper and foil combined, cut or not cut, prepaid, in packages	2	30,000	R26-4-4
25757	Laces, corset, horse net or shoe, in bales, barrels or boxes	1	20,000R	3
25760	Lacquered ware, noibn, in barrels, boxes or crates	1	20,000R	3
25763	Ladders, aluminum or aluminum and wood combined, see Note 1, item 25775, in packages	1½	10,000R	1

25766	Ladders, noibn, steel, see Note 1, item 25775, loose or in packages	3	36,000	37½-6-5
25770	Ladders, noibn, wood, or wood and steel combined, see Notes 1 and 2, items 25775 and 25780, loose or in packages	2	12,000R	3
25775	Note 1.—Ladders or ladder sections exceeding 24 feet in length, LCL, will be subject to minimum charges of 1,000 lbs. at first class rate for entire shipment.			
25780	Note 2.—CL rating includes 1 steel scaffold bracket for each ladder in shipment.			
25782	Ladders, collapsed, wood and metal bracing, feet or fittings, see Note 3, item 25783, in packages	2	30,000	R26-4-4
25783	Note 3.—Ratings apply only on ladders having side pieces and rungs collapse and compactly folded to sides.			
25784	Ladders, magnesium metal or magnesium metal alloy, in packages	D1	10,000R	1
25785	Ladders, rolling shelf, wooden, without track or track fixtures, with or without ladder fixtures, in packages	1	20,000R	3
25790	Ladders, rope, or rope with metal or wooden rungs, in packages	1	20,000R	3
25795	Ladders, step, other than step stools, other than aluminum, magnesium metal or magnesium metal alloy, loose or in packages	1	12,000R	3
	Lahn (lame), copper:			
25796	Plain, in boxes	3	30,000	4
	Other than plain, in boxes	1	24,000R	R26-4-4
25798	Laminated plastics, in rods, sheets or tubes, see Note, item 25799, in boxes or crates	2	30,000	4
25799	Note.—Ratings apply on rods, sheets or tubes of paper, fabric, rubber or fibre soaked in liquid plastic material with heat and pressure applied.			
	LAMPS, LANTERNS OR LIGHTING FIXTURES, OR PARTS NAMED:			
25800	Bases, fluorescent lamp, filled or not filled with insulating material, in barrels or boxes	1	20,000R	3
25803	Bases, incandescent lamp, filled or not filled with insulating material, in barrels or boxes	2	30,000	4-5-A
25805	Burners, lamp, in barrels or boxes	1	16,000R	3
25810	Carbide of calcium lights, in cans in boxes	1	20,000R	3
25815	Lamp arms, in barrels or boxes	2	30,000	R26-4-4
25817	Lamp canopies, chimneys, globes or shades, mica, in boxes	D1	10,000R	1
25820	Lamp shades or reflectors, cellulose, cloth, paper or pulpboard: Other than flat or nested, in boxes	D1	10,000R	1
25825	Flat or nested, in boxes	1	20,000R	3

* Used and adapted by permission of Consolidated Classification Committee.

RATES ON SPECIFIC COMMODITIES

Commodity descriptions. The contents of a typical page from a recent issue of the Consolidated Freight Classification is reproduced in part on pages 226-227. Special attention should be called to the minute detail with which the various items are described. It will be noted, too, that some commodities are listed more than once, these multiple listings usually reflecting differences in the nature of the commodity itself or differences in methods of packing. Note that ladders are given eight different listings. The letters "noibn" are an abbreviation of "not otherwise indexed by name" and designate a miscellaneous classification used when a more specific description cannot be found to fit a given item. Sometimes a distinction is made between an item that is shipped fully assembled or "set up" (SU) and the same item shipped partially or wholly unassembled or "knocked down" (KD). The terms LCL and CL are abbreviations of "less than carload" and "carload." The item numbers shown to the left of the listings are used in connection with an index printed in the front of the Classification.

Rating columns. The first column on the right-hand side of the page gives the ratings applicable to less-than-carload lots, and the third column gives the ratings on carload shipments. Note that the carload lot ratings are lower than the less-than-carload ratings. If a given item of freight is classified the same in all three territories, only one classification symbol is shown in the rating columns. Where three figures are shown in a rating column, the first figure is the rating used in connection with Official and Illinois Classifications, the second for Southern Classification, and the third for Western. Wherever the Illinois Classification differs from the Official Classification, four symbols are used, the first being the Official Classification rating, the second the Illinois, the third the Southern, and the fourth the Western.

Carload minimum weights. The figures shown in the Carload Minimum column indicate the minimum weight in pounds which a shipper must offer in order to be entitled to the lower carload ratings. If the weight of a given shipment does not come up to the specified minimum, a shipper may still take advantage of the carload rating by paying the freight charges on the minimum weight shown instead of on the actual weight of the shipment. Note that the minimum weights are not the same for all items. These differences are due in part to differences in loading characteristics. For example, a shipper would have no difficulty in loading 50,000 pounds of coiled iron or steel wire rods in a car, but it might be impossible to get 50,000 pounds of lamp shades in an ordinary box car. To establish a carload rating based on a minimum weight which is in excess of the number of pounds that can be loaded in a car is the equivalent of having no carload rating at all.

RATES ON SPECIFIC COMMODITIES

Carload minimum weights also are affected to some extent by trade practices. If trade practices are such that the maximum amount of a given commodity purchased at any one time is 20,000 pounds, then there would be no point in establishing a carload rating with a minimum weight of 40,000 pounds. It will be noted that carload ratings tend to vary inversely with the minimum weights established for various commodities. Carload shipments of aluminum ladders, for which a carload minimum weight of 10,000 pounds is provided, are rated first class. Knit goods with a carload minimum weight of 12,000 pounds are rated second class. Steel ladders, noibn, with a carload minimum weight of 36,000 pounds are rated 37½-6-5, and so on. In this way the carriers attempt to equalize, insofar as possible, the revenue derived from each of their cars.

The letter R means that the minimum weight varies with the size of car used according to a scale given in the Classification. It will be noted that all of the items for which relatively low carload minimum weights have been established are subject to this provision. The carriers, while willing in many cases to establish low carload minimum weights to accommodate shippers, are not willing to apply these weights to shipments made in cars which are capable of carrying large and heavy loads. Occasionally the letters AQ appear in the carload minimum weight column. This is an abbreviation for "any quantity" and indicates that no carload rating has been established.

Exceptions to the classification. Individual railroads and groups of railroads may publish exceptions to the classification ratings, and such exceptions take precedence over the ratings shown in the Consolidated Freight Classification as far as the lines publishing them are concerned. In some cases classification exceptions apply only between specified points or in a certain area or are in some other way limited in their application, but in other cases they may have widespread application. In addition to the exceptions published by individual railroads and groups of railroads, the Consolidated Freight Classification itself is amended from time to time by the publication of supplements, and when this is done, the material in the supplements takes precedence over the main classification. From time to time, too, as these supplements accumulate, it becomes necessary to publish a new edition of the Consolidated Freight Classification incorporating all changes made since the preceding edition.

UNIFORM FREIGHT CLASSIFICATION

Attempts to establish a uniform classification. Even a casual acquaintanceship with the technique of publishing and quoting freight rates will reveal the complications arising out of the necessity of using three separate classifications. The desirability of having a single uniform classification was recognized many years ago, but no real progress was made toward this end until the adoption of the Consolidated Freight Classification in 1919. While this was definitely a step in the right direction, it failed to achieve uniformity in the all important matter of ratings. With the passing of the years an increasing number of individual ratings were made uniform, but there continued to be extensive differences in ratings, particularly on those applicable to shipments in carload lots.

Obstacles to achieving uniformity. For various reasons the achievement of uniformity is no simple matter. In the first place, adoption of a uniform rating on any given item must result in a reduced rating on that item as far as some railroads are concerned, unless the new rating is as high as or higher than the highest former rating. Hence it is not simple to get general railroad acceptance of uniform ratings except on a basis which is unacceptable to shippers. Second, if an industry in a given area is able to compete with similar industries in other areas only because of a more favorable classification rating, uniformity may well sound the death knell for that industry. In the long run, of course, this weeding out of the less efficient would be a good thing, but the immediate consequences of such action on industry and on the area in which it is located cannot be ignored completely. Third, certain commodities move much more extensively in some areas than in others, and this is said to justify differences in classification ratings. Fourth, it can be shown that it costs more to handle certain items in some parts of the country than in others. And finally, for many years the general level of class rates was higher mile for mile in the South and West than in Official Territory, and it would appear that in some cases lower classification ratings were established to offset this difference in class rates.

Uniform classification order. Although the difficulties encountered in attempting to work out a uniform classification are real, the consensus of opinion has been that they are not insurmountable. In 1939 the Interstate Commerce Commission instituted an investigation of classifications and class rates and in 1945 ordered the establishment of a single uniform classification. A single scale of class rates applicable to most of the country was ordered established at the same time.[3] The railroads set up a committee of experts to formulate a new classification. This committee held numerous public hearings, and in due course a tentative classification was filed with the Commission "as information."

---

[3] *Class Rate Investigation, 1939,* 262 I.C.C. 447. Note that the working out of a uniform classification is another example of the need for intercarrier cooperation of the type authorized by the Reed-Bulwinkle Act.

After further hearings on the matter of a uniform classification and a uniform scale of class rates, the Commission adopted a report on July 26, 1951, ordering the railroads to file a uniform classification within four months. Subsequently the railroads requested the Commission to extend the filing date to February 1, 1952, and on that date Uniform Freight Classification No. 1 was filed, to become effective May 30, 1952. Since it was almost inevitable that some of the changes in ratings would mean higher rates for some shippers, numerous requests for suspension were filed, but late in May the Commission ordered the new classification into effect.[4]

FACTORS AFFECTING RATE DETERMINATION ON SPECIFIC COMMODITIES

Legal aspects of problem. In establishing the exact ratings to be applied to each item of freight moving under class rates, or in establishing the exact rate on an item which moves under a commodity rate, the carriers and the Interstate Commerce Commission must be guided by certain legal requirements. Paragraph 5 of Section 1 of the Interstate Commerce Act specifies that all charges must be just and reasonable, and Paragraph 6 extends this requirement to include classifications of freight as well as rates themselves. Obviously a just and reasonable classification of freight is essential to the establishment of just and reasonable charges, at least as far as class rates are concerned.

Section 3, Paragraph 1, makes it unlawful for carriers to give any undue or unreasonable preference to any particular description of traffic in any respect whatsoever. This provision, however, may be modified to the extent that the Commission is able and sees fit to aid depressed industries under the provisions of the Hoch-Smith Resolution. Finally, there is the rule of rate making which specifies that the Commission is to give due consideration, among other factors, to the effect of rates on the movement of traffic and to the need of the carriers for revenues sufficient to enable them to provide satisfactory service. While the rule of rate making is generally understood to apply to rates as a whole, it must enter indirectly into the determination of individual rates as well.

Economic aspects of problem. While the ratings applied to the various items listed in the Consolidated Freight Classification must conform with the legal requirements mentioned above, it is important to understand that the problem of determining ratings is basically one of economics rather

---

[4] The railroads asked that requests for suspension be denied, pointing out that numerous ratings had been reduced and that it was not reasonable to expect them to maintain these reductions if the proposed increases were denied.

than of law. As pointed out at the beginning of this chapter, class rates are calculated by finding the rating applicable to the item being shipped and then assessing the rate applicable to that class of freight from and to the points involved. Taken by itself a rating is not a rate, but it is an essential part of the rate-making process, and the economic factors involved in determining ratings cannot be separated from the economics of rate making itself.

Railroad freight rates are prices, and like any prices they are determined by the interaction of the forces of supply and demand. On the supply side this means that no railroad, except under special circumstances, will haul any commodity at a rate which does not cover the cost of the service rendered. And on the demand side the buyer of transportation will not pay any more than the service is worth to him. Thus the rate charged for moving any commodity from any point to any other point by railroad reflects the influence of cost on the one hand and value of the service on the other.

Cost of service. It is necessary to qualify the statement that no railroad will haul any commodity at a rate which does not cover the cost of the service rendered. In the first place, it is impossible to determine the exact cost of hauling any particular commodity because of the extent to which common costs are encountered in railroad transportation. Take, for example, the costs incurred in providing and maintaining the right of way, road bed, and track. On most railroads this track structure is used by both passenger and freight trains, and there is no way in which the costs involved can be allocated scientifically between passenger service and freight service—or between the numerous items of traffic handled by each.

Costs such as these are called common costs and include, in addition to the ones mentioned, the cost of providing and maintaining signal systems, communications systems, and structures along the way; administrative expenses; and various others. It is true, of course, that some costs can be allocated directly to passenger service and some to freight service, but allocating these costs to individual items of traffic within a given service is not so simple. Thus the cost of providing and maintaining box cars can be charged directly to the freight service, but when an attempt is made to allocate box car costs to each of the different kinds of commodities shipped in box cars the problem of common costs is again encountered.

Attention should also be called to the fact that unit cost of production is not static in the railroad business because of the extent to which railroad costs are constant. As long as a railroad is operating under conditions of increasing returns unit costs will decline with an increase in traffic and increase with a decline in traffic. As pointed out in Chapter 7, costs vary from day to day, from train to train, and even from car to car. Thus the cost of transporting a 100 pound shipment of canned goods in a car containing 40,000 pounds of other freight will be less than if it were transported in a car containing 30,000 pounds of other freight. And it will be less if it is transported in a train of forty cars than in one of thirty cars. Here, again, difficulties are encountered in attempting to allocate costs.

Finally, it should be noted that cost of service has more than one meaning in railroad transportation. It may refer to a rate which is sufficiently high to cover variable or out-of-pocket cost plus a full share of the burden of constant costs, including an adequate return. It may refer to a rate which covers only the out-of-pocket costs. Or it may refer to a rate which covers out-of-pocket costs plus some contribution, great or small, toward other costs. Other things being equal, it is safe to say that no railroad will establish any rate which does not cover the out-of-pocket costs attributable to any given type of traffic. Three qualifications must be made to this statement. In the first place, it is impossible to determine precisely what these costs are for the reasons already given. Second, rates may fall below out-of-pocket cost should the carriers become engaged in a destructive rate war. And third, very low developmental rates have been established in the past to encourage the development of a new industry or a new producing area, and it is possible that some such rates temporarily may have been below out-of-pocket cost.

Value of service. Since in the last analysis railroad rates are determined by the interaction of the forces of supply and demand, consideration must be given to the nature of the demand for transportation service. Transportation charges represent a cost of doing business as far as the shipper or receiver of freight is concerned, and this means that what he is willing to pay for any given transportation service depends upon what he can get for the goods or services he is manufacturing or selling. In other words, the demand for transportation is a derived demand and cannot be separated from the demand for the goods or services into the cost of which transportation enters.

If the demand for a given product is elastic, an increase in transportation charges will tend to lower the sales of that commodity and hence reduce the volume of traffic. On the other hand, a decline in the sales of one commodity may be accompanied by an increase in the sales of another commodity which may or may not bring about an increase in traffic related to the latter. If the demand for the commodity is inelastic, increased freight rates should not unduly affect its sale, but there may be a decline in sales and volume of traffic in other commodities. In addition to the effect of freight rates on the sale of a given commodity, individual transportation companies must take into consideration the availability of alternative means of transportation in judging the demand for their particular type of service.

Application to classification. There are a considerable number of factors which affect the cost of moving different articles by railroad, and a somewhat smaller number affecting the demand for service, and consideration is given to the more important of these in the following discussion. Although each factor is considered separately, the actual rating applied to any given item commonly reflects the influence of more than one factor, and in numerous cases it will represent some sort of balance between conflicting considerations. As pointed out previously, it is not possible to determine the precise cost of handling any particular item of freight. It is possible, however, to apply the various cost factors to individual commodities in such a way as to approximate the relative cost of handling each. In other words, commodities can be rated more or less accurately in terms of one costing more or less than another to handle even though exact costs cannot be ascertained. With this in mind, attention now may be directed to the various factors which enter into the determination of classification ratings.

COST AS A DETERMINANT OF CLASSIFICATION

Size of shipment. Mention has been made of the fact that the ratings provided for carload shipments are lower than those applying to less-than-carload shipments of the same commodity. Most business concerns find it possible to offer a lower unit price on quantity orders because selling, accounting, and billing expenses need not be appreciably more for large orders than for small ones, and to this general principle the railroad business is no exception.

But far more important than this is the fact that the railroad does not ordinarily assume responsibility for loading and unloading carload shipments. The railroad will switch cars to and from the private sidings of shippers and receivers of carload freight, or to and from a convenient public team track if they have no private sidings, and the work of loading or unloading is done by the employees of the shipper or receiver. Less-than-carload freight, on the other hand, is loaded and unloaded by the railroad's own employees. In view of the expense involved in providing freight houses and freight handling equipment, not to mention all of the labor that is required for handling small shipments, it is not surprising that the ratings on less-than-carload shipments are substantially higher than the carload ratings.

RATES ON SPECIFIC COMMODITIES

Handling loose shipments. The Consolidated Freight Classification permits the shipment of a good many items of freight in a loose or unpackaged form. Where such goods are shipped in carload lots and loaded and unloaded by shipper and consignee they constitute no problem for the railroad, but when items of small size are shipped loose in less-than-carload lots they constitute a special problem because of the added handling costs involved. As a general rule the carriers do not accept small items for shipment unless they are packaged in one way or another, but in a few cases, usually involving relatively heavy items that are not easily damaged, loose less-than-carload shipments are accepted under certain circumstances. As might be expected, higher ratings may be applied when a given item is shipped loose instead of being packaged. For example, rough iron castings weighing less than fifteen pounds are rated second class when shipped loose and 4-50-4 when shipped in packages.

Weight in relation to bulk. The preceding discussion explains why it costs the railroads more, pound for pound, to handle freight in less-than-carload lots than it costs to handle the same freight in carload lots, and it explains why it costs more to handle loose less-than-carload shipments than it costs to handle the same shipments when packaged. But what has been said up to this point applies equally well to all commodities, and it does not explain why it costs more to handle some commodities than others. Of all of the factors which contribute to the cost of handling different types of commodities, weight is probably the most obvious. A carload of iron castings packed in barrels will weigh a great deal more than a carload containing the same number of barrels of fireworks packed in sawdust, and it will clearly require more fuel and pulling power to move a carload of iron castings than it will take to move a carload of fireworks. And in handling less-than-carload freight a railroad must provide itself with more loading contrivances and more manpower to handle heavy articles than are necessary to handle light weight shipments.

Since railroad freight rates are quoted almost always in terms of cents per hundred pounds, however, the charge for hauling a heavy item is automatically higher than the charge for hauling a lighter one, assuming that all other cost factors are the same. Hence weight taken by itself need not enter into the determination of ratings except to the extent that unusually heavy items may require special handling equipment or special rolling stock.

But the question of bulk or size in relation to weight is not taken into consideration by the practice of calculating freight rates on the basis of weight, and bulk constitutes a factor of considerable importance in the classification of freight. For example, if a wheeled hand plow is shipped fully assembled in a crate, it is charged for at one and one-half times the first class rate; but if the wheels and the plowshare are removed and packed in a crate along with the frame, a third class rating applies. The reason for this is quite simple. Although the weights on the two shipments will be very nearly the same, the fully assembled plow takes up substantially more space in a freight car than does the same plow shipped knocked down. Thus the railroad is deprived of space in its cars which it might use for the shipment of other freight, and so it is justified in putting a higher rating on assembled plows.

Value of the commodity. Except in certain specifically enumerated situations, such as acts of God, the carriers are liable for the loss of or damage to goods entrusted to their care. Partly because of this fact it is almost always true that the greater the value of a given commodity the higher will be the rating assigned to it. Thus a billiard ball made of composition is rated first class while a billiard ball made of ivory moves at three times the first class rate. Both weigh the same and both occupy the same amount of space, but if a shipment of ivory balls is lost or damaged the carrier will be out a great deal more than would have been the case if composition balls had been shipped.

So important is the value factor in the case of a few commodities that the Interstate Commerce Commission has permitted the establishment of ratings which vary directly with the value of the shipment as declared by the shipper. Such ratings have been applied to commodities such as rugs which have a wide range of market values and to commodities such as paintings where wide differences of opinion might exist about their value. It should be emphasized that ratings which vary with value are very uncommon. In the overwhelming majority of cases the carriers may not limit their liability in the event of loss or damage.

Risk of loss or damage. The fact that carriers are liable for the loss of or damage to goods entrusted to their care influences costs in still another way because some items of freight are more easily lost or damaged than others. For example, experience has shown that small articles are more frequently lost, stolen, or damaged than large ones. And, of course, some commodities are much more easily damaged than others, and this means more damage claims. Since the payment of claims constitutes one of the costs of conducting a transportation business it follows naturally that, other things being equal, railroads must place higher ratings on goods that are easily damaged than on goods that are not subject to much damage.

Some items which in themselves may or may not be subject to much damage are of such a nature that damage to them is likely to damage or ruin other articles shipped in the same car. A smashed can of paint, for example, can result in damage claims running into hundreds of dollars.

Also, there are some items which move in commerce which can cause serious damage to railroad equipment. In all of these cases it is clear that the risk element must be taken into consideration in establishing the ratings to be used. In a class by themselves are explosives, which move under high ratings and for which detailed regulations have been prescribed to govern their movement.

Nature of packaging. Closely related to the risk factor, and in fact a special aspect of it, is the nature of the outside packing employed by the shipper. An examination of the Consolidated Freight Classification reveals a large number of cases in which two or more ratings are quoted for moving the same commodity, the difference in ratings being due to the nature of the outside container. A plow set up and crated is rated at one and one-half times first class as already noted, but the same plow shipped uncrated is charged for at double the first class rate. Although an uncrated plow weighs slightly less than the same plow crated and, if anything, will take up less room, the possibility of the uncrated plow being damaged or doing damage to other goods in the car is greater. In a number of cases goods which are packed in barrels or boxes enjoy a lower rating than the same goods packed in bags or bales.

Other cost factors. A variety of other factors influence, either directly or indirectly, the cost of moving various commodities and hence affect the rating which is applied to them. These factors include such things as the over-all volume of traffic expected from a particular commodity or group of commodities, whether the traffic is seasonal or continues regularly throughout the year, the need for providing special services or facilities, the type of equipment required, the speed with which the goods must be moved, and the like. Some of these considerations are more significant in connection with the establishment of commodity rates than they are in determining classification ratings, and further consideration will be given to them presently.

DEMAND AS A DETERMINANT OF CLASSIFICATION

Value of the commodity. The value of a commodity as a determinant of classification is peculiar in that it has both a cost aspect and a demand aspect. As noted in the preceding section, a carrier is liable for the loss of or damage to goods entrusted to his care, and he must assign higher ratings to the more valuable commodities in order to cover the greater financial liability incurred in handling them. But quite apart from this is the fact that shippers of valuable commodities can, as a general rule, afford to pay higher rates pound for pound than is true of shippers of low grade commodities. This is because the higher the value of a commodity *in relation to its weight or bulk* the less will be the effect of transportation charges on its final selling price.

The importance of the value factor may be illustrated by taking two such ordinary products as baseballs and coal. Suppose, for the purpose of illustration, that baseballs sell at the factory for $1.00 each while coal sells at the mine for $10.00 a ton and that dealers in baseballs and coal expect to sell their respective products at a common destination for a price which will cover transportation charges plus a 50 per cent markup over cost at origin. What would be the effect on the retail selling price of these two commodities if both moved similar distances under identical rates, say 50¢ per hundred pounds? A baseball packed for shipment will weigh approximately one-half pound which means that a rate of 50¢ per hundred pounds will add ¼¢ to the retail price of the baseball. Hence a retail price of $1.50¼ will cover transportation charges and a 50 per cent markup over cost. In the case of coal, on the other hand, a rate of 50¢ per hundred pounds is the equivalent of $10.00 per ton, and the coal dealer will have to sell his coal for $25.00 a ton if he expects to recover transportation charges and get a markup of 50 per cent over cost. Putting the same thing in somewhat different terms, in this hypothetical situation transportation charges constitute approximately 1/60 of 1 per cent of the retail price of the baseballs, an amount so small that it can be ignored, but in the case of coal they make up 40 per cent of the retail price, and the coal dealer might find it difficult to sell his coal.

The foregoing imaginary situation clearly illustrates the important role that the value of a commodity may play in the rate-making process. The dealer in sporting goods can afford to pay a rate several times 50¢ per hundred pounds on baseballs. Even a rate four times 50¢ would add only 1¢ to the retail price of his balls, an amount which would have no measurable effect on the sale of baseballs. But a rate of 50¢ a hundred pounds would be a matter of major concern to the coal industry because such a rate would so add to the price of coal as materially to reduce its sale. Also, it would be a matter of major concern to the whole people because of the basic importance of coal for household and industrial uses. By charging higher rates than are necessary to meet all costs for moving high value commodities, the carriers may be able to establish other rates sufficiently low to make it possible to move socially desirable products which could not move in quantity if they had to bear their full load of all costs.[5]

---

[5] It is not intended to imply that low rates on low grade freight are in all cases based on this principle. In some cases the cost of handling low grade freight is very low and if enough such traffic is handled, it may be quite profitable to move it at low rates.

RATES ON SPECIFIC COMMODITIES

Not only is it in the general public interest to take the value of a commodity into consideration in fixing rates, but it is also in the carrier's interest. If carriers sought to fix rates in such a way that each commodity moved bore its full share of all costs, constant as well as variable, the rates established for certain low grade commodities would be so high that these commodities would not move in any quantity. Thus the consequence of such a scheme of rate making would be a sharp reduction in total volume of traffic carried. Because of the important part played by constant costs in the railroad industry, it is well worth while for the railroads to move low grade traffic at reduced rates rather than to forego moving it altogether, providing the rates established are sufficient to meet something more than out-of-pocket costs. This "something more" can be applied to meeting constant costs, or if existing traffic already covers the constant costs, the "something more" is profit.

Value of the commodity as a determinant of classification is not without its limitations. For one thing, it does not follow necessarily that every commodity that has a high value can stand an equally high rate. Again, there are a number of commodities which exist in a variety of different qualities, with a considerable spread in value between the highest and the lowest in quality. Full utilization of the value of the commodity principle would suggest a series of ratings for such commodities, high ratings for the most valuable and progressively lower ratings for the less valuable, but while such ratings have been established in a few cases, neither the law nor the Interstate Commerce Commission have looked with favor on such a scheme of rate making. To establish ratings based on actual values declared by shippers would lead to evasion and discrimination, and to permit carriers to limit their liability on goods in general would not be in the interest of the shipping public. Finally, there are some commodities which are subject to frequent fluctuations in value, and if major reliance were placed on value in such cases, frequent changes in ratings would be necessary.

Stage of manufacture. A special aspect of the value of the commodity as a determinant of classification is found in the relationship that often exists in the ratings applied to a given product as it passes through various stages in the manufacturing process. For example, crude iron ore takes a twelfth class rating in the Southern Classification. Pig iron is rated tenth class, while such a crudely finished product as a sash weight is rated sixth class. Corset stays are rated fourth class, and such finely finished products as surgical instruments are rated first class. Such ratings, of course, are explainable in terms of the greater dollars and cents liability involved in handling the more valuable goods, but they also reflect in some measure greater ability to pay as a product progresses step by step toward completion.

Another factor that has to be taken into consideration in this connection is the fact that many raw materials are subject to shrinkage as they pass through various manufacturing processes, but as they are progressively refined the amount of waste on which buyers must pay freight tends to become less. Obviously the more the waste material involved the lower the rate the shipper can afford to pay. It by no means follows, however, that manufactured products always take higher rates than the raw materials from which they are made. For example, by-products of manufacturing processes commonly move under lower ratings than are applied to the raw materials from which they are derived. It sometimes happens, too, that small quantities of a relatively valuable raw material are combined with other less valuable materials in the manufacture of a given product, and in this case it is quite possible that the raw material will move under a higher rating than the finished product.

Product relationships. In a number of cases the ratings on certain products are influenced by competitive conditions existing in business and industry. Butter and oleomargarine must be given the same rating even though transportation costs and other considerations are not identical. Similarly, lard and lard substitutes are rated the same. In other cases competitive conditions must be taken into consideration even though the ratings established are not identical. This is true in the building industry where products made of wood—window frames, for example—compete with similar products made of iron or steel. Similarly, brick, tile, and concrete blocks compete to some extent with cement, sand, gravel, and reinforcing iron. Wall board competes with lath and plaster, and numerous other examples will come to mind readily enough. In these cases ratings are not identical because of differences in relative weights and in quantities used, but a balance of some sort is struck to avoid giving one item a substantial advantage over another in so far as that is possible. Where keen product competition exists any change in the rating applied to one product is sure to be followed by adjustments in the established ratings on competing products.

Value created by advertising. An interesting problem arises when a manufacturer creates by means of branding and skillful advertising a market value for his product which is considerably in excess of the value it would have if it were sold under the ordinary name of its component parts. In one case a manufacturer of patent medicines claimed that the value of his product, made principally of herbs and water with 10 per cent to 25 per cent alcohol, was no greater than that of ale, beer, and mineral water and so should not bear a higher transportation charge, even though as a result of skill in advertising the medicine sold for four times the price of beer and mineral water.[6] In another case the manufacturer of a cheap soap similar to laundry soap described and sold his product as toilet soap but objected to the carriers rating it as toilet soap.[7] The Commission has never been impressed by such arguments, holding that when a manufacturer describes an article to the public for the purpose of marketing it, he also describes it for purposes of carriage.[8]

Use to which a product is put. In some cases it has been argued that the use to which a product is put should be taken into consideration in computing freight charges, thus recognizing the fact that certain commodities are more valuable in some uses than in others. It has been argued, for example, that a distinction should be made between coal used for manufacturing purposes and coal that is shipped for domestic use.[9] Such a proposal, of course, is open to the objection that it would encourage evasion through misrepresentation of the use to which a given commodity was to be put. The Commission has not accepted this principle as a proper basis for framing rates, although in a few cases it has taken the use principle into consideration, especially where it has been possible to establish some distinction in the product itself when intended for different uses.

Influence of competition. The development of rival forms of transportation in recent years has had a definite influence on the demand for railroad transportation service. This has been especially noticeable in connection with the competition of motor freight carriers for the movement of the higher grades of freight, the kind of freight that most commonly moves under classification ratings. While it cannot be said that the intrinsic value of transportation service has declined because of the appearance of competition, the value of railroad transportation service to shippers has declined wherever rival transportation agencies can offer equal service at lower rates or better service at the same rates. This factor has had an increasing influence on classification ratings.

COMMODITY RATES

Types of commodity rates. Commodity rates as previously noted are rates quoted directly on specific commodities rather than on classes of commodities. Sometimes they are published in separate tariffs, and sometimes they are published in tariffs containing both class and commodity

---

[6] *Warner v. The New York Central & Hudson River R. Co.*, 3 I.C.R. 74 (1890).
[7] *Andrews Soap Co. v. The Pittsburgh, Cincinnati & St. Louis R. Co.*, 3 I.C.R. 77 (1890).
[8] *Ibid.*, p. 80.
[9] *Re Louisville & Nashville R. Co.*, 4 I.C.R. 157 (1892).

rates. Commodity rates do not have the universal application of classification ratings but apply only between the points specified in a particular tariff. There are some important commodities that move almost entirely under commodity rates while in other cases commodity rates are extremely limited in their application. There is some tendency to relate commodity rates to class rates by making them certain percentages of the class rates. In some cases commodity rates, while not related directly to class rates, are related to each other in accordance with some more or less definite plan. In still other cases commodity rates are published without any definite relationship either to class rates or to other commodity rates.

Factors underlying the establishment of commodity rates. All of the factors which enter into the determination of classification ratings also are involved in the determination of commodity rates. Often, however, some one of these factors is present in an exaggerated form and so necessitates a departure from the classification procedure. For example, some commodities have such a low value in relation to their weight or bulk that they cannot move even under the lowest classification ratings, and if they are to move at all, a commodity rate lower than the lowest class rate must be established. Then there are some low grade commodities such as sand and gravel that might move short distances under classification ratings but cannot stand such ratings on a haul of any length. Under such circumstances a classification rating might be used for local movements, but a commodity rate would have to be applied to the longer hauls.

Volume of traffic is another consideration that may lead to the establishment of commodity rates. Between certain points or on certain lines the volume of traffic in a certain commodity may be so large that the carrier or carriers involved can move it in solid trainloads, and the lower cost per car resulting from such movements may be reflected in a commodity rate lower than the rate which would result from the use of the ratings provided in the Classification. This does not mean that the commodity rate is confined to individual shippers who can ship the product in trainload lots. On the contrary such rates apply to all shippers who can ship the commodity involved between the points or over the line on which the rate applies.

In some cases commodity rates have been established where shippers are able and willing to load cars considerably in excess of the carload minimum weights provided in the Classification. Thus the Classification might specify a minimum weight of 30,000 pounds as a prerequisite to obtaining a carload rating on a given commodity, but under certain circumstances heavier loading might be encouraged by establishing a commodity rate applicable in connection with a substantially higher minimum weight or even with maximum car capacity. Special trainload lot rates have been proposed from time to time, but the Commission has not looked with favor on such rates because of the belief that they tend to concentrate business in the hands of the few large shippers who can take advantage of them. Somewhat related to quantity of shipment as a justification for establishing commodity rates is regularity of shipment. If a carrier can depend upon a steady volume of certain types of goods over a certain line or into or out of a certain area, he can make more efficient use of his equipment, and it may be worth while to establish a commodity rate if by so doing continued regularity can be assured.

Competition between rival producing areas and the railroads serving them has led to the establishment of numerous commodity rates. This has been true particularly of the rates on coal from differently located coal fields to important consuming centers and export points. In the case of coal a matter of just a few cents a ton in freight rates may determine whether or not a given field and the railroad or railroads serving it can compete in a given market. Such differentials, involving as they do a single commodity in a single situation, cannot be provided for within the framework of classifications and class rates. A commodity rate, or in some cases an exception rating, is the only solution.

Competition, although of a different sort, has been recognized as justifying a trainload lot rate on molasses. In this case a large company was moving molasses up the Mississippi River in multiple barge lots at a cost substantially below the railroad carload rate. The Commission permitted the railroad to establish a reduced rate on trainload lots between specified points in order to meet this competition.[10] In December 1946, the Texas Railroad Commission allowed a special rate covering the intrastate movement of unfinished gasoline between two points in lots of twenty cars or more. The alternative to this rate would have been the construction of a pipe line and loss of the traffic to the railroad.[11] Such volume rates are, however, exceptional.

CONCLUSION

Early importance of value of service. Before the development of effective regulation, and for a considerable period thereafter, railroad traffic officials placed primary emphasis on the value of the service or "what the traffic will bear" in fixing the rates and ratings applied to individual commodities. When effective regulatory commissions were established they quite naturally refused to sanction the application of exhorbitant rates simply because shippers could afford to pay them, for the law required

---

[10] *Molasses From New Orleans, La., To Peoria And Pekin, Ill.,* 235 I.C.C. 485 (1939).
[11] *Railway Age,* Vol. 122, May 3, 1947, p. 903.

all rates to be reasonable and just, but apart from this limitation value of the service continued to play a major role in the determination of rates and ratings. The high rates that were charged for moving commodities that could stand high rates were justified on the ground that they made possible the lower rates which were necessary for the movement of other commodities.

As a result of the development of newer forms of transportation, and more particularly the development of motor freight transportation, the railroads are no longer as free as formerly to place primary emphasis on value of service in the determination of rates and ratings. To apply a rate or rating to a given commodity which is substantially in excess of the cost of moving that commodity is to invite competition from carriers which are not wedded to the principle of fixing rates on the basis of value of service. As soon as shippers discovered that they could ship high grade less-than-carload freight cheaper by motor truck than they could by rail, the railroads were compelled to revise their rates and ratings downward to meet this competition. In this connection the Interstate Commerce Commission observed in 1945:

Development of competitive transportation agencies with flexible service, and a disregard of the element of value by the competitive agencies in the determination of their charges, have reacted upon the policies of the classification committees with the result that generally weight density is now the dominant consideration in determining classification ratings. This does not mean that value and other principles of classification are completely eliminated from consideration; but it does mean that value of an article does not control the rating to the extent it formerly did.[12]

Importance of cost. It stands to reason that a railroad will not want to establish a rating or rate on any commodity which will not cover the estimated cost of handling that commodity, but this does not mean that each commodity shipped must bear its full share of all of the costs of running a railroad. Indeed, some commodities could not move under such a system of rate making. If the ratings or rates on some commodities are not sufficient to bear their prorata share of all costs, however, the ratings or rates on other commodities will have to more than cover these costs if the railroad is to remain solvent.

As mentioned previously, no railroad will establish any rating or rate which does not promise to at least cover out-of-pocket cost, except on a temporary basis for developmental purposes or to force a weaker competitor out of business. Thus the railroads might be able to drive the truckers off the highways, as they drove the steamboats off the water in

---

[12] *Class Rate Investigation, 1939*, 262 I.C.C. 447, 482.

the latter half of the nineteenth century, by a judicious use of rate cutting. The Interstate Commerce Commission, however, through its power to fix minimum rates, can prevent such rate cutting, and the Commission has not looked with favor on the dissipation of carrier revenues that may result from such destructive competition. Furthermore, Congress has declared it to be the national transportation policy to preserve the inherent advantages of all forms of transportation subject to the Interstate Commerce Act, and it would be inconsistent with this policy to permit cutting of rates below cost in order to drive motor carriers out of business.

Although a rating or rate which does not cover out-of-pocket costs is not profitable, anything that the carrier can get over and above such costs is worth while. A rating which will move traffic and contribute something toward constant costs is to be preferred to a rating which will not move the traffic at all and so not contribute anything toward constant costs. It is interesting to note that carriers, with the consent of regulatory bodies, are free to establish rates on individual commodities which do not meet costs in full, but the Supreme Court has held that they cannot be compelled to move goods at rates that are less than cost or virtually at cost, cost including the fixed or overhead expenses apportionable to the traffic in question as well as out-of-pocket costs.[13]

SUGGESTED READINGS

Bigham, Truman C., *Transportation, Principles and Problems*. New York: McGraw-Hill Book Company, Inc., 1946. Chapter 15.

Consolidated Freight Classification. Chicago: Consolidated Classification Committee.

Daggett, Stuart, *Principles of Inland Transportation*, 3rd Ed. New York: Harper and Brothers, 1941. Chapter 17.

Interstate Commerce Commission, *Class Rate Investigation, 1939*, 262 I.C.C. 447. Contains considerable information on the subject of classification.

Jones, Eliot, *Principles of Railway Transportation*. New York: The Macmillan Company, 1924. Chapter 8.

Locklin, D. Philip, *Economics of Transportation*, 3rd Ed. Chicago: Richard D. Irwin, Inc., 1947. Chapters 8 and 18.

Ripley, William Z., *Railroads, Rates and Regulation*. New York: Longmans, Green & Company, 1912. Chapter 9.

Sharfman, I. L., *The Interstate Commerce Commission*, Vol. 3-B. New York: The Commonwealth Fund, 1936. Chapter 15.

Wilson, G. Lloyd, *Freight Classification and Rate Making*. Chicago: The Traffic Service Corporation, 1940.

---

[13] *Northern Pacific Railway Co.* v. *North Dakota*, 236 U.S. 585 (1915).

12

Principles

of

RATE MAKING

INTRODUCTORY

Cost v. what the traffic will bear. The present chapter is devoted to a consideration of the principles involved in determining the rates to be applied between different shipping points in contrast with the problem of determining the ratings on specific commodities discussed in Chapter 11. Rates between points, like ratings on specific commodities, represent a compromise between the cost of rendering the service on the one hand and "what the traffic will bear," i.e., what shippers are willing and able to pay, on the other. Used in this way the term "cost of service" may have more than one meaning. It may refer to a rate which covers the variable cost plus its full share of constant costs, including a fair return, or it may refer to a rate which covers only the variable or out-of-pocket costs incurred on a given haul. Or it may refer to a rate which covers variable costs plus some contribution, great or small, toward meeting constant costs.

Other things being equal, it stands to reason that no railroad will establish a scale of rates which does not cover at least the variable or out-of-pocket costs involved. On the other hand, no railroad can charge more than what the traffic will bear because to do so would be to pinch off traffic and destroy the very source of its income. It will be clear that the nature of the system adopted for determining the rate relationships between different shipping points will be influenced powerfully by the relative weight accorded these two rate-making principles.

If cost of service is given dominant weight by the railroads or by rate-making authorities, the rate relationships between different shipping points will be determined by differences in operating costs, traffic densities, and relative lengths of haul. Where operating costs are high, as in mountainous areas, rates will be higher mile for mile than in areas where lower operating costs prevail. Similarly, higher rates may be justified in light traffic areas than in areas of heavier traffic. And, of course, in either case rates based on cost will be higher for long hauls than for short ones.

If, on the other hand, what the traffic will bear is given dominant weight in determining rates between different points, no simple or consistently logical procedure for establishing rate relationships is possible. Where no competition exists shippers are charged as high a level of rates as they can pay without putting them out of business, while at other points a railroad will charge whatever is necessary to enable it to secure business in competition with other railroads or other kinds of carriers.

The history of railroad transportation in the United States in the days prior to the development of effective regulation reveals a strong tendency on the part of railroad traffic officials to fix rates on the basis of what the traffic will bear, and a brief survey of the more important rate systems which grew out of this practice will serve to illustrate certain common principles of rate making. As might be expected these systems were characterized by numerous violations of the long and short haul clause, although all of them gave some consideration to distance as a factor in rate making; and in one outstanding case distance was the dominant consideration. Although rates today are based primarily on distance, some of these early rate systems became so firmly intrenched that it took years for the Interstate Commerce Commission to remove the inequities inherent in them and place rates on a more logical basis.

SOME EARLY RATE STRUCTURES

Trunk line rate structures. The so-called trunk line rate structure was worked out in the 1870's by those railroads serving that part of the United States which lies roughly east of the Mississippi and north of the Ohio and Potomac rivers. This area was divided up into the New England region, comprising the New England states; Trunk Line Territory, covering the area between the New England states on the east and Buffalo and Pittsburgh on the west; and Central Freight Association Territory, covering the area between Buffalo and Pittsburgh on the east and the Mississippi River on the west. The trunk line rate structure merits consideration because it is an early example of the *distance principle* of rate making, according to which rates increase progressively with the length of haul rather than with what the traffic will bear. The rate adjustments discussed below were worked out specifically to cover shipments between points in Central Freight Association Territory on the one hand and Trunk Line Territory on the other, but other rates in the general area also were fixed in accordance with the distance principle.

Historical background. In the early 1870's there were several railroads and combinations of railroads over which freight could move between the Chicago and New York areas, and these railroads competed keenly with one another for traffic, especially for east bound grain traffic which constituted a major source of revenue. In addition to competing among themselves, the railroads had to contend with competition from water carriers, a substantial amount of grain moving east by way of the Great Lakes and the Erie Canal. In those days the bulk of the grain traffic originated east of the Mississippi River in Central Freight Association Territory along the lines of a number of independent short line railroads running north from the Ohio River and south from the Great Lakes. These north-south lines crossed some or all of the main east-west trunk lines, which made it possible for the grain to move over several different routes, and so it is not surprising that the big trunk lines fought each other for this traffic. To make matters worse, some of the north-south carriers had been built by interests committed to the building up of certain river and lake ports, and in addition, the north-south lines usually could get a longer haul on the grain by interchanging it with water carriers rather than with the trunk line railroads.

Elimination of competition and adoption of trunk line rate system. After some bitter rate wars, the east-west carriers got together to seek some means of eliminating this destructive competition among themselves and with the water carriers. The result was an agreement which brought railroad competition under control by the adoption of a uniform system of rate making based on the distance principle. Thus originated the trunk line rate system. Adopted in 1876 and modified periodically it proved to be so satisfactory that it continued in effect until 1931. Under this system a basic rate was established for movements between Chicago and New York by the shortest practical railroad route, and all rates between points in Central Freight Association Territory and points in Trunk Line Territory were based on percentages of this Chicago-New York rate, being less for shorter distances and more for longer distances.

The rates adopted were not exactly proportionate with distance because it was recognized that every freight shipment required handling at points of origin and destination, and these terminal handling costs were about the same for all shipments regardless of the length of the haul. Furthermore, it was found desirable to establish a number of zones running in a generally north and south direction, and all points in a given zone were accorded the same rate. If at any time water competition necessitated a change in the Chicago-New York rate, a similar change took place in all other east-west rates, since all were calculated as percentages of the Chicago-New York rate.

The rates charged between any two points were figured on the basis of distance via the shortest practical route, but they applied equally to all lines or combinations of lines which could provide service between any given points regardless of differences in length of haul. Naturally the carrier or carriers with the shortest haul enjoyed some advantage, but this was an advantage enjoyed by different carriers at different points. The elimination of competition between the east-west lines was disadvantageous to the independent north-south railroads, although there still remained the possibility of cooperation between the latter and the water carriers. But the trunk lines threatened to refuse to turn over westbound freight for delivery to points on the north-south lines unless the latter cooperated by turning over their east bound grain traffic to the trunk line railroads. Since the westbound traffic in manufactured goods and the like was of a type that could not be handled readily by the water carriers, the north-south lines were forced to acquiesce. They did not fare very well as a result of the elimination of competition among their connections, and many failed and were taken over and operated as branches of the big railroads.

Southern rate system and the basing point principle. The southern railroads made extensive use of the *basing point principle* of rate making prior to the days of effective regulation, especially in connection with rates between points in the South and points in other parts of the country. Under this system low through rates were granted to certain cities and towns in the South called basing points, and the rate to any other point was determined by taking the through rate from the point of origin to the nearest basing point and adding to it the local rate from the basing point to the point of final destination. Since local rates in the South were very high, because the sparse population made for a light volume of local traffic which in turn meant high unit costs of operation, this system of figuring rates accorded those towns which had been fortunate enough to be designated as basing points a considerable advantage over nonbasing points in obtaining the trade of the countryside.

Basing point system illustrated. In Figure 3 A represents the point at which a given shipment originates, B is a basing point, and C and D are nearby communities without basing point status. Under the basing point system, the through rate from A to C was computed by adding the A to B rate of $1.00 to the 50¢ local rate in effect from B to C, thus giving a through rate, A to C, of $1.50. Since the rates at C were very high relative to the rates at B, country people were encouraged to sell their cotton and do their trading at B rather than at C.

FIGURE 3. *Basing Point Principle of Rate Making.*

The situation described in the preceding paragraph, unreasonable as it seems to be, was nothing as compared with the situation that existed when the destination point was intermediate between the point of origin and the nearest basing point. In a case like this the rate was figured in the same way, i.e., the through rate from point of origin to the nearest basing point plus the local rate from basing point to destination. Thus the rate from A to D, like the rate from A to C, was $1.50, being made up of the through A to B rate of $1.00, plus the local B to D rate of 50¢. In this situation, and there were many like it in the South at one time, merchants located in D actually paid a higher rate from A than did merchants located in B, even though D was intermediate between A and B and shipments from A to B had to pass through D to get to their destination. Under the circumstances it is not surprising that the southern rate structure was characterized by numerous violations of the long and short haul clause, and it was not until 1910 that Congress gave the Interstate Commerce Commission sufficient power to deal with such obviously discriminatory situations.

Selection of basing points. The basing point system was not confined to the South, but it found its most extensive development there, the principal reason advanced for its adoption being the extent to which the southern railroads had to contend with water competition. The railroads competed keenly with coastwise vessels for traffic between the East and various southern seaports, and rates at these points were forced to a low level. The same situation existed with reference to shipping on inland waterways. Bounded on the west by the Mississippi and on the north by the Ohio and pierced by numerous streams which were navigable by shallow draft vessels, the South had long depended upon the river steamboat as a means of transportation, and railroad rates at river ports had to be made with this steamboat competition in mind.

The railroads found it worth while to cut rates to meet or beat water competition as long as the reduced rates were sufficient to cover variable costs and pay anything at all on constant costs, but if rates all over the South were based on the same depressed levels that existed at water points, the railroads might bankrupt themselves. To overcome this difficulty various ocean, gulf, and river ports were designated basing points, and rates to nearby interior towns were made by adding the water determined basing point rate to the railroad rate from the port to the interior destination point. Even though the interior destination happened to be intermediate between the point of origin and the basing point as far as a rail haul was concerned, the railroads could justify their action on the ground that the rate charged to the interior point was no higher than would be the case if the goods came by water and were then shipped by rail from the port to destination.

It is not so easy to justify the rather substantial number of cities and towns which were made basing points even though they were not located on the coast or on navigable inland waterways. Some cities were made basing points because they had already developed as important trade centers before railroads were built, and it was said to be necessary to grant them favorable rates in order to enable them to continue as established distributing and jobbing points in competition with distributing centers in the North. A number of towns were made basing points because they were served by two or more railroads. Finally, some towns were made basing points by arbitrary decisions of railroad officials who saw some advantage to their particular railroad in such a procedure.

Later history of basing point system. It was difficult to justify much of the discrimination that arose where basing points were created solely as a result of railroad competition or the arbitrary decision of railroad officials, and at many points the necessity for reduced rates to meet water competition disappeared as water carriers were brought under control or forced out of business. The Mann-Elkins Act of 1910 clothed the Interstate Commerce Commission with sufficient authority to take action against violations of the long and short haul clause, but the Commission had to move slowly because the comprehensive revision of a long standing rate system is a difficult procedure and one which must be undertaken with a view to avoiding sudden disruption of economic relationships.

In 1916 the Commission acted to eliminate most of the long and short haul discriminations except where water competition was a factor. A further revision of the southern rate structure was required by the amendments to the long and short haul clause contained in the Transportation Act, 1920, which provided that the rates to the more distant point must be reasonably compensatory and that no departures were to be permitted because of merely potential water competition. As a result of the passage of the Mann-Elkins Act and the Transportation Act, 1920, the unreasonable discrimination which characterized the southern rate structure in the days of the basing point system has disappeared.

Transcontinental rate structure. The transcontinental rates discussed at this point are those which apply on freight moving between the East and the Middle West on the one hand and the Pacific coast and interior western points on the other. It may be useful to point out in this connection that no single railroad spans the country from coast to coast, and all freight moving between the East and the West must be handled by at least two and frequently three or more different lines, the major inter-changes taking place at various points in the Mississippi Valley region.

Before the completion of the Pacific railroad in 1869 practically all freight moving between the two coasts was carried by water, and this water competition led to the establishment of two entirely different scales of rates on rail movements from the Atlantic to the Pacific. On goods which could not be handled by water, rates to the Pacific coast were based on the distance principle, being higher for shipments from New York to the Pacific than they were from Chicago and other intermediate points; but on goods which could move by water exactly the opposite situation prevailed. In the latter case, rates to the Pacific coast were lowest at eastern seaboard points and were scaled up in a westerly direction, the rate from Chicago to the Pacific coast being higher than the rate from New York to the Pacific coast. This was because rates from the Atlantic coast were made in competition with water carriers, and the eastern rail-roads did not wish to extend these low rates to interior points where water competition did not exist.

The adjustment of rates on water competitive traffic was not at all to the liking of the railroads running west from the Mississippi Valley region. Naturally they were interested in building up manufacturing and commercial centers in the Middle West which could supply the needs of the Pacific coast and the intervening area, but not much progress along these lines could be expected as long as freight rates to the Pacific were lower from New York than they were from the Middle West. Further-more, the existing arrangement was not particularly profitable to the western lines because they received only a portion of the low through rate from the east coast whereas they could retain for themselves the full amount of the rate charged on goods moving from the Middle West to the Pacific.

The diverse interests of the eastern and western railroads led inevitably to disagreements and rate wars, and the conflict was finally resolved by an agreement based on the *blanketing principle* of rate making. This principle involves the establishment of a single schedule of rates which applies to or from every point within a specified area. The rate charged for carrying first class mail is an extreme example of a blanket rate, a single rate per ounce applying to and from every point in the United States regardless of distance.

Application of blanketing principle. The transcontinental rates on water competitive traffic had given eastern points a rate advantage over mid-western points even though the latter were considerably closer to the Pacific, but if these rates were put on a distance basis and scaled down from the Atlantic coast, then the midwestern points would have a definite advantage over their long established rivals in the East. In order to avoid destructive competition it was necessary to work out a rate system which would enable the eastern railroads to compete with water carriers for a share of the transcontinental traffic and which would also be acceptable to the western railroads and midwestern industrial and commercial centers.

To this end the railroads agreed to blanket the entire area between the Atlantic coast and the Missouri River, and in some cases as far west as Denver and related points, on shipments to the Pacific coast. In other words, a single rate was quoted for shipments of a given commodity from any point in the blanketed area to the Pacific coast. If, for example, the rate from Kansas City to the Pacific coast was $1.00, this same rate of $1.00 applied to Pacific coast shipments from New York, Boston, Charleston, Chicago, Pittsburgh, and any other city in the blanket area. In some cases far eastern cities were as much as 2000 miles more distant from the Pacific than were some of the cities along the western edge of the blanket, but all shipped under identical rates.

Once the Interstate Commerce Commission obtained effective control over rates, it took steps to bring about a readjustment of this peculiar situation, although the fact of water competition at the Atlantic seaboard could not be ignored. Consequently the Commission substituted a series of much smaller blankets or groupings with a common rate for each city in the group. The rates applied to each group were, however, scaled up or down with distance so that the rates to and from the Chicago group and the Pacific coast, to use one example, were lower than those to and from the New York group and the Pacific coast.

Long and short haul violations. Another characteristic of the transcontinental rate structure was a general disregard of the long and short haul principle in fixing rates from eastern and midwestern points to Intermountain Territory, that part of the country between the Rocky Mountains and the Sierra Nevadas. Rates to cities and towns in this area were higher than they were to the Pacific coast terminals even though rail freight moved through intermountain points on its way to the Pacific coast. The railroads, of course, were unwilling to extend the low Pacific coast rates to inland points where water competition did not exist.

The Commission's first important act after the revitalization of the long and short haul clause was to establish a zoning system in connection with transcontinental rates. From the North Atlantic states, where water competition was active, the Commission permitted the establishment of commodity rates to intermediate points which were as much as 25 per cent higher than those charged to the Pacific coast. For points inland from the Atlantic coast this percentage grew progressively less as the distance from the Atlantic coast increased, however, until on shipments from St. Paul, Omaha, Kansas City and other similarly located cities, no departures from the long and short haul clause were permitted.

The opening of the Panama Canal made it possible for the water carriers to reduce their rates and improve their service, and in order to enable the railroads to meet this competition the Commission permitted them to cut the through rates on a substantial number of low grade commodities without making any changes in the intermediate rates. The shipping demands of the First World War soon necessitated a withdrawal of shipping from the transcontinental freight business, however, and in 1917 the Interstate Commerce Commission called for an elimination of long and short haul departures. The railroads thereupon raised the Pacific coast rates to the level of the intermediate rates, thus establishing a rate blanket which extended inland several hundred miles from the coast.

Since 1920 a number of applications have been made for departures from the long and short haul clause in connection with transcontinental traffic in order to meet renewed water competition, but such departures have been permitted only in an extremely limited number of cases. Business interests in the interior cities in the West and their spokesmen in Congress have fought continuously to prevent a return to the old system of lower rates to Pacific coast points and have urged elimination of all long and short haul departures. Furthermore, the Transportation Act, 1920, contained a statement of Congressional desire to encourage the development of water transportation, and it would be inconsistent with this policy to permit such departures.

Texas intrastate rates. The railroads serving Texas once made use of a *graded and maximum rate* principle whereby local rates were graded upward with distance for a certain number of miles, the distance varying with the nature of the commodity, with a single uniform rate prevailing beyond this point without regard to distance. The effect of this rate scheme was to give each commercial center in Texas an advantage in the territory naturally tributary to it while at the same time giving all such centers an equal opportunity in the over-all area. The system was worked out by the Texas Railroad Commission in the interest of an even development of the state rather than by the railroads in their own interest. As a result of the extension of Interstate Commerce Commission power over intrastate rates, Texas intrastate rates are now made on a somewhat more orthodox basis.

Mississippi and Missouri River adjustment. Through traffic from the East to important trading and manufacturing centers on the Missouri River can cross the Mississippi over the lines of any one of several railroads at numerous points between Dubuque and St. Louis known as

Mississippi River crossings. All of these Mississippi River crossings were accorded identical rates from the East under the Trunk Line rate structure previously discussed, the rate being computed at 125 per cent of the Chicago-New York rate.

West of the Mississippi and east of the Missouri the country is so crisscrossed with railroads that a practical route from the East to every one of the Missouri River centers exists by way of every one of the Mississippi River crossings, and this led to keen competition between the railroads serving the various Mississippi River crossings for a share in the through traffic from the East to the Missouri River. The result was the establishment of a single scale of class rates based on a first class rate of 60¢ per hundred pounds which was uniformly applied on shipments from any one of the Mississippi River crossings to almost all of the Missouri River points, even though some of the routes were several hundred miles longer than others. Later this equalization of rates was extended to include the railroads running west from Chicago by providing an 80¢ rate from Chicago to Missouri River points regardless of the route followed.

ACCEPTANCE OF MODERN DISTANCE PRINCIPLE OF RATE MAKING

Early disregard of distance. All of the early rate systems discussed previously, with the exception of the trunk line rate system, were notable for the way in which the length of haul was ignored in fixing rates between numerous points. It should be noted, however, that departures from the distance principle were usually confined to rates on the longer hauls where competition, either between carriers or commercial centers, was a factor which had to be taken into consideration. Local traffic all over the country commonly moved under rates which were graded upward with distance and which were usually quite high relative to through rates between important points. In the South the railroads claimed that high local rates were made necessary because of a dearth of local traffic, although in some cases it was debatable whether the high local rates were the result of light traffic or whether the light traffic was the result of high local rates. It seems reasonable to suppose, too, that the practice of fixing rates on the basis of what the traffic will bear influenced railroad managements to adopt high rates on noncompetitive traffic to make up in some degree for the lower rates that were necessary at competitive points.

Revision of rate structures to conform with distance. As a result of a series of adverse Supreme Court decisions, particularly those made in connection with the Maximum Freight Rate and Alabama Midland cases, the Interstate Commerce Commission was unable to do much to eliminate even the most obvious inequities and inconsistencies that had arisen out of the widespread disregard of distance in fixing rates on through hauls. After 1906, when it was given the power to fix maximum rates, and more especially after 1910, when the "under substantially similar circumstances and conditions" qualification was removed from the long and short haul clause, the Commission proceeded to examine one by one the various rate structures and in a few years time it ordered the elimination of numerous violations of the long and short haul clause in the southern and transcontinental rate systems.

The modifications of the long and short haul clause found in the Transportation Act, 1920, prohibiting departures from the long and short haul principle because of merely potential water competition and requiring that the rate to the more distant point be reasonably compensatory when a departure is permitted, together with the statement of Congressional policy encouraging water transportation, required a further examination and revision of the various rate structures. In all of its rate revision activities the Interstate Commerce Commission has shown a decided preference for the distance principle of rate making, and today rates in all parts of the country are based on distance with only minor exceptions to take care of unusual circumstances.

Justification of distance rates. For the most part rates based on distance are easier to justify than rates based on other criteria. Rates based on distance are inherently just in that they preserve for each community such natural advantages as it may enjoy by virtue of its location with reference to markets or to supplies of raw materials. Also, such rates promote the development of the nation along economically sound lines by preventing the growth of trade centers and industries at points which are economically not well suited to such activities and which might better develop along other lines. Furthermore, rates which disregard distance may cause a considerable economic waste by encouraging the hauling of commodities from far distant points when these same commodities can be supplied from points much closer to the sources of demand.

Distances are definite, specific, and not subject to change, and so rates based on distance are more stable than rates based on some other factors. Where rates have been based on what the traffic will bear they have often been unstable, causing a great deal of uncertainty in business activities. Finally, rates based on distance reflect differences in the cost of rendering the service, and rates which vary with cost are certainly easier to justify in the public mind than rates which appear to ignore differences in cost. Rates which are based on cost are easy to understand, but rates which seemingly are made without regard to cost are sure to bring objections from the public in general and particularly from those against whom such rates appear to discriminate.

Rate increases not proportionate with distance. Although railroad freight rates today are scaled upward with distance, they do not increase proportionately with distance. Other things being equal, the charge for a two-hundred mile haul will not be double the charge for a comparable one-hundred mile haul, and the charge for a four-hundred mile haul will not be double that made for the two-hundred mile haul. The total charge increases with distance but at a decreasing ratio so that if a given rate scale were plotted on a graph with rates on the vertical axis and distances on the horizontal axis, the result would not be a diagonal straight line but a curve which tapered off gradually as it moved to the right. There are several reasons for this so-called tapering principle, some arising out of the peculiar nature of railroad costs and some having to do with the demand for transportation service.

Influence of terminal cost. One of the principal reasons why railroad freight rates do not increase in exact proportion with distance is that the cost of handling and moving railroad freight does not increase proportionately with distance. This in turn is due to the fact that every railroad incurs certain expenses in connection with the handling of freight at points of origin and destination, and these terminal expenses are the same for all shipments of a given size and type irrespective of the length of haul involved. Since railroad terminal costs tend to be high relative to the cost per mile of moving goods over the line, they make for a relatively high rate on short hauls, but as the length of the haul increases their influence becomes progressively less important.

Suppose, by way of an illustration, that the terminal costs incurred in handling a thousand pound shipment of first class freight are estimated to be $3.00 and that the line haul costs come to approximately 10¢ for each five miles the freight is carried. On a shipment moving a total distance of five miles such a cost structure would justify a charge of $3.10, exclusive of profit and overhead, of which $3.00 would be for terminal costs and 10¢ for line haul costs. If, now, rates increased with distance on the basis of $3.10 for each five miles hauled, the charge for a ten mile haul would be $6.20; for a hundred mile haul, $62.00; and for a thousand mile haul, $620. Under such a scale of rates the charge made for shipping a thousand pounds of first class freight from New York to San Francisco would be in the neighborhood of $1,800! Actually, of course, no such rates are charged for the longer hauls, and one reason for this is the fact that it would be impossible to justify the multiplication many times over of terminal expenses incurred only once.

Because terminal costs do not increase with distance, the only increases in cost incurred on the longer hauls are those which result from the actual movement of the goods, plus any intermediate handling costs which may be incurred as the goods move into and out of various division and junction points. Thus for a ten mile haul of one thousand pounds of first class freight the railroad would charge $3.20 rather than $6.20, this charge being made up of the $3.00 terminal cost plus a line haul cost of 20¢, this last figure representing the cost of moving a thousand pounds of freight ten miles at the rate of 10¢ per thousand pounds for each five miles. No intermediate handling costs would be involved on a haul as short as this.

Similarly, the charge made for a one-hundred mile haul would be $5.00, this figure being made up of the $3.00 terminal cost plus $2.00 for the line haul at 10¢ per thousand pounds per five miles. In the case of a thousand mile haul some intermediate handling expenses probably would be incurred, but if another $3.00 were added to cover these expenses, the over-all charge would still be no more than $26.00 as compared with $620, the $26.00 representing a $3.00 terminal charge, a $3.00 intermediate handling charge, and a $20.00 line haul charge. In terms of cents per mile a charge of $26.00 for a thousand mile haul equals 2.6¢ per mile as compared with a charge per mile of 62¢ for a five mile haul at $3.10.

Influence of decreasing line haul costs. In the preceding illustration it was assumed that the line-haul cost per mile did not increase or decrease with distance but remained constant at 10¢ per thousand pounds for each five miles hauled, but there is some difference of opinion whether or not this is true. It has been pointed out that short haul traffic is carried by local freight trains, often pulled with older and less efficient motive power, and making frequent stops for loading and unloading during which a good deal of the crew's time is wasted. By way of contrast long haul traffic is likely to move in through freights employing the most modern equipment and sometimes operating almost on passenger train schedules. Furthermore, cars are likely to be loaded more nearly to capacity, and there are many more cars to the train. Thus it would seem reasonable to suppose that a crew of a given size can handle a great deal more freight on a long haul than on a short haul with an attendant reduction in cost per unit of freight per mile.

On the other hand, long hauls commonly involve anywhere from one to several intermediate handlings which not incurred on short hauls. Also, the time wasted by train crews in the frequent stops made by local freights is offset somewhat by the fact that train crews are paid on the basis of a certain number of hours worked or a certain number of miles run, whichever method is more favorable to the men. Thus at the same time that the crew of a local freight is being paid for idle time while their train is standing still, the crew of a through freight is being paid a similar wage for working a smaller number of hours.

Influence of demand. If rates increased in exact proportion with distance instead of in accordance with the tapering principle, many commodities would not be able to move more than a relatively short distance from their point of origin. Manufacturing would have to be carried on locally in small plants, and the people would lose the economies of large scale production. Nor could the people enjoy the economies and advantages of regional specialization, such as raising cattle on the grasslands of the West, grain in the grain belt, and cotton and tobacco in the South. While some products like cattle and grain can be produced with some facility in various parts of the country, in many sections such production would be at the expense of products for which these sections are especially adapted. Many people would be deprived altogether of such useful products as coal, iron and steel, cotton, and citrus fruits. Even if railroad costs did increase proportionately with distance, it might be necessary in the public interest to adjust rates to permit goods to move over relatively long distances.

Illustration of tapering principle. In 1930 the Interstate Commerce Commission ordered a revision of class rates in the East which resulted in the adoption of a scale of class rates which illustrates the use of rates based on distance in accordance with the tapering principle.[1] An initial first class rate of about 30¢ per hundred pounds was adopted, this figure reflecting the terminal charge, and on distances up to 75 miles the rates were to increase 3¢ for each 10 miles. From 75 to 150 miles rates increased 2¢ for each 10 miles; from 150 to 300 miles, 1½¢; from 300 to 700 miles, 1¼¢, and from 700 to 2000 miles, 1¢ for each 10 miles. These rates are no longer in effect but the principle itself has not been changed. Similar scales of rates based on the tapering principle were applied in other parts of the country as a result of the efforts of the Interstate Commerce Commission to put railroad freight rates on a more scientific basis.

REGIONAL DIFFERENCES IN COST

Costs not uniform in all parts of country. Although the nature of railroad costs is such that freight rates need not increase proportionately with distance, it does not follow from this that the charge made for a

---

[1] *Eastern Class Rate Investigation*, 164 I.C.C. 314.

haul of a specified length will be identical in all parts of the country. A railroad operating in a mountainous area will have higher operating costs mile for mile than one operating in plains country or along a river valley. Railroads in the northern part of the United States face severe winter operating conditions of a type unknown to southern railroads. Other railroads in other areas face other peculiar operating problems. Obviously differences in operating costs may justify different rates in different parts of the country for hauls of identical length.

Along somewhat different lines, railroads in light traffic areas may have to spread their costs over a relatively small volume of traffic, thus necessitating a higher charge for a haul of a given length than would need to be made by railroads operating in areas of high traffic density. Differences in operating conditions and traffic densities which justify different levels of rates for railroads in different parts of the country also may justify different levels of rates on different parts of a single railroad system or even on different segments of the same line.

Some illustrations of rate differentials. There are many illustrations of rate adjustments which have been made to allow for differences in operating costs and traffic densities. For example, for the purpose of computing class rates New England is divided into two zones, Zone A and Zone B. Zone A includes the relatively small manufacturing area in southern New England while Zone B comprises the much larger northern area which is lightly populated and produces for the most part agricultural products and raw materials. In the Eastern Class Rate Investigation referred to previously a scale of rates for Zone A 5 per cent higher than those specified elsewhere in the East was prescribed, and Zone B rates were made 10 per cent higher than those prescribed for Zone A. In some cases an adjustment is made by adding a certain number of cents per hundred pounds to the rates provided in some existing rate scale. The addition of such a flat amount, called an arbitrary, has been sanctioned in computing the rates which may be charged by certain weak or short line railroads which could not survive if required to charge the general level of rates established for the area in which they operate.

Cost differentials not always reflected in rates. It by no means follows that all differences in operating conditions or traffic densities are accepted by the Interstate Commerce Commission as justifying different levels of rates. Sometimes difficult operating conditions, which taken by themselves might justify a higher level of rates, are offset by high traffic densities, while light traffic densities sometimes coincide with easy operating conditions. Furthermore, slight differences in traffic density and operating conditions exist all over the United States, and to attempt to take all of these slight differences into consideration would unnecessarily complicate an already complex problem. In the interest of simplicity it is better to ignore small differences in cost where possible and limit the establishment of different levels of rates to those situations where such action appears to be essential. In this connection, too, it is worth noting that both the Interstate Commerce Commission and the courts have held for years that a railroad is not entitled to earn a profit on every segment of its line.[2] Thus operating conditions and traffic densities may vary considerably as between different parts of a railroad system, but this does not necessarily justify the application of different levels of rates.

OTHER LIMITATIONS ON DISTANCE PRINCIPLE

Intercarrier competition. Although rates in general are based on distance today, there are numerous exceptions to this rule, some applying to class rates as a whole and some applying to rates on specific commodities. Many of these departures from the distance principle have been necessitated by competition of one sort of another, for in spite of the increased power of the Interstate Commerce Commission, competition still remains an important factor in setting freight rates. Traffic moving between widely separated points such as Chicago and New York and Chicago and San Francisco may be carried over widely divergent routes, some of which are considerably longer than others, and if the long haul carriers wish to compete for the through traffic, they must adjust their rates accordingly.

When class rates are based on distance scales, the rate between any two points is computed on the distance via the shortest route over which carload traffic can move without transfer of lading, and this rate is applied via all of the standard rail lines competing for the business. This means, of course, that the through rate via the more circuitous routes will be less than would be the case if the distance scale were strictly applied to these lines. If the route involved happens to be quite circuitous, the carriers involved may not try to compete for the through traffic, but generally such carriers will seek their share of the traffic as long as the rate is sufficiently high to bring them anything over and above variable costs.

If the through rate via a circuitous route is less than it would be if a distance scale were strictly applied, the result may very well be a lower

---

[2] *St. Louis & San Francisco Ry. Co. v. Gill*, 156 U.S. 649 (1895); *Puget Sound Traction Co. v. Reynolds*, 244 U.S. 574 (1916); *Fort Smith Traction Co. v. Bourland*, 267 U.S. 330 (1925); 70 I.C.C. 251 (1921); 71 I.C.C. 225 (1921).

rate on the through haul than is charged to intermediate points, and this would constitute a direct violation of the long and short haul clause. Under such circumstances two adjustments are possible, both of which involve a departure from the distance principle. The carrier may be permitted to charge less for the through haul than for the shorter haul, or it may blanket the rates on either end of its line. Suppose, for example, that if a distance scale were applied, the through rate via the circuitous route would be $1.25, but the actual rate as determined by the short line route is $1.00. Under these circumstances rates via the circuitous route might be scaled upward with distance to the point where they equalled $1.00, and from this point to the competitive terminal point a single rate of $1.00 would apply.

Competition between carriers may take many and diverse forms. Instead of moving over one of the usual trunk line routes, traffic between Chicago and New York may move over one of the Canadian railroads in connection with a New England line. It may move partly via the Great Lakes with a rail haul at either end, or it may move via rail-lake-rail. From New England ports traffic may move by water to a connection with one of the trunk line railroads and thence west to Chicago and intermediate points. It may even move by rail from interior New England points to a New England port and then by water and rail to Chicago. Here, again, distance must be disregarded if traffic is to move via the less direct routes. Indeed, it has been necessary to establish lower rates via these so-called differential routes than are applied by way of the trunk line or standard rail routes in order to make up for the greater length of time in which the goods are in transit.

Water competition is still an important factor in the determination of rates on transcontinental traffic and has brought about blanketing transcontinental rates over considerable areas in the Far West in order to avoid violations of the long and short haul clause. The improvement of inland waterways in recent years has added a further competitive element to the rate structure. Motor truck competition is yet another factor which has necessitated numerous departures from the distance principle of rate making. In all of these cases, however, the departures are more often made with reference to particular commodities rather than traffic in general.

Some doubt may be expressed about the economic soundness of all of this roundabout hauling of freight, as well as much of the competition between rail, water, and motor carriers, but the Interstate Commerce Commission's jurisdiction over water and motor carriers is still limited in many respects, and congressional policy on the subject of intercarrier competition has not been expressed clearly. Hence at the present time all of these elements continue to play a part in fixing railroad rates which are not in strict conformity with the distance principle.

Market competition. It often happens that different producing or commercial points compete with one another for the business of a common market, and in some cases this competition may justify, or is said to justify, departures from the distance principle of rate making. If one producing or distributing point is more distant from the common market than is another, the more distant point may demand a through rate comparable with that in effect from the nearer point. Similar to market competition is the situation which exists when one producing or distributing point is more distant from a common source of supply of raw materials than is another and seeks rate equalization to offset this disadvantage.

The carriers serving the more distant points will find it advantageous to make the reductions if the resultant rates will more than cover variable costs, but they may not want to extend these low rates to intermediate points. Numerous examples of this sort of competition suggest themselves. Lumber is produced in widely separated areas but competes in common markets. Cotton cloth produced in the southeastern section of the United States competes with cloth produced in New England. Sugar, salt, shoes, granite, and oranges are a few of the other items of traffic that are produced in widely separated centers and sold in common markets.

It is a nice question to decide when market competition constitutes a valid reason for departing from the distance principle of rate making. As a general rule it is both just and economically sound to protect the natural advantage a producing area or commercial center may have by virtue of its nearness to a given market. Nor is it wise, other things being equal, to use special rate concessions to stimulate artificially the growth of certain industries at points that are not economically suited to those industries. Furthermore, market competition of a sort exists at innumerable points, and it is easy to use it as an excuse for making all sorts of demands for special rate concessions.

On the other hand, market competition is not always without merit and has influenced the decisions of the Interstate Commerce Commission on a number of occasions. While it seems reasonable to protect the advantage a commercial or industrial center may have by reason of its nearness to a given market, a certain amount of competition is not undesirable, and this may necessitate rate concessions which will open the market to competing concerns located at more distant points. Also, where industries have developed solely by virtue of rate concessions made in earlier times, economic disaster may follow upon any attempt to remove these concessions in the interest of the adoption of rates based on distance.

Tariff simplification. Minor departures from the distance principle arise out of the efforts of the railroads to simplify the publication of rates. Instead of publishing tariffs which quote rates to or from every point on a given line or in a given area, it is a common practice to establish rates to certain key points and then apply these same rates to nearby points. For example, a rate might be quoted from Chicago to Kansas City, with the tariff providing that the same rate will apply to shipments to other towns in the general region of Kansas City. Or the rate to the key point plus an additional charge which varies with distance may be applied to other towns in the area. This grouping or blanketing of rates around key points considerably simplifies tariff publication, although it does result in moderate departures from a straight distance scale.

Reverse hauls. One of the seeming inconsistencies of railroad freight rates is the fact that the rate between two points may vary with the direction of the haul. Thus the first class rate from A to B may be $1.00 while the rate from B to A over the same line is $1.10. Aside from the possibility of outright discrimination, two factors suggest themselves as being responsible for this seemingly odd departure from the distance principle. Perhaps the most obvious explanation is that operating costs are not necessarily identical in both directions. The haul in one direction may involve long heavy grades requiring considerable additional fuel, and possibly one or more helper locomotives. But by the same token the reverse haul is down grade, permitting higher speeds and a smaller fuel consumption, all of which function to reduce operating costs.

More important than terrain, however, is the influence of unbalanced traffic. If a railroad can depend upon handling about the same amount of traffic in each direction, it can make maximum use of its equipment, but it frequently happens that the general flow of traffic is persistently heavier in one direction than in the other, and this makes it necessary to back haul many empty cars at no little expense to the carrier. In order to make the best of this unprofitable situation a railroad is justified in establishing lower rates, either in general or on particular commodities, on the back haul if such lower rates will create sufficient business to fill some or all of the cars which otherwise would have to be returned empty. Unbalanced traffic is a recognized justification for lower rates in one direction than in the other if such rates are sufficiently high to cover something more than the variable costs incurred.

PRINCIPLES OF RATE MAKING

SUGGESTED READINGS

Bigham, Truman C., *Transportation, Principles and Problems.* New York: McGraw-Hill Book Company, Inc., 1946. Chapter 16.

Jones, Eliot, *Principles of Railway Transportation.* New York: The Macmillan Company, 1924. Chapter 9.

Locklin, D. Philip, *Economics of Transportation,* 3rd Ed. Chicago: Richard D. Irwin, Inc., 1947. Chapter 19.

Ripley, William Z., *Railroads, Rates and Regulation.* New York: Longmans, Green & Company, 1912. Outstanding description of early rate structures.

I3.

Regional
FREIGHT RATE STRUCTURES

INTRATERRITORIAL RATES

Regional differences in rates. Until quite recently the Interstate Commerce Commission had never attempted to set up a general level of class rates which would apply uniformly to the railroads in all parts of the country. Instead it set up one mileage scale to be used in computing class rates between points in Official Territory and another scale for use in Southern Territory. The vast region encompassed by Western Classification Territory was divided into three separate areas for rate-making purposes, Western Trunk Line Territory, Southwestern Territory, and Mountain-Pacific Territory; and in each of these areas, with the exception of Mountain-Pacific Territory, separate scales of class rates were established. The boundaries of the five major rate territories, together with certain subdivisions, are shown on the accompanying map. It should be emphasized that the rate scales under discussion were established for the purpose of computing class rates. Commodity rates do not follow any special territorial patterns since they are made to move important items of freight, which items vary as between different territories.

Reference will be made presently to a recent order of the Interstate Commerce Commission requiring the establishment of a single scale of class rates applicable to all parts of the country other than Mountain-Pacific Territory, and when this order goes into effect regional rate scales will disappear. Nevertheless, some consideration of these scales is desirable, partly because they illustrate the complexity of the rate-making process, partly because of their effect on the economic development of the country, and partly because it was their very existence which led to the demand for a single uniform rate scale.

Class rates in Official Territory. The basic class rate structure for Official Territory was established in 1930 by the Interstate Commerce Commission in the Eastern Class Rate Investigation.[1] In its original form it involved an initial first class rate of 30¢ per hundred pounds for movements of 5 miles or less, this figure including the terminal charge. For distances in excess of 5 miles the 30¢ rate was increased in

---

[1] 164 I.C.C. 314.

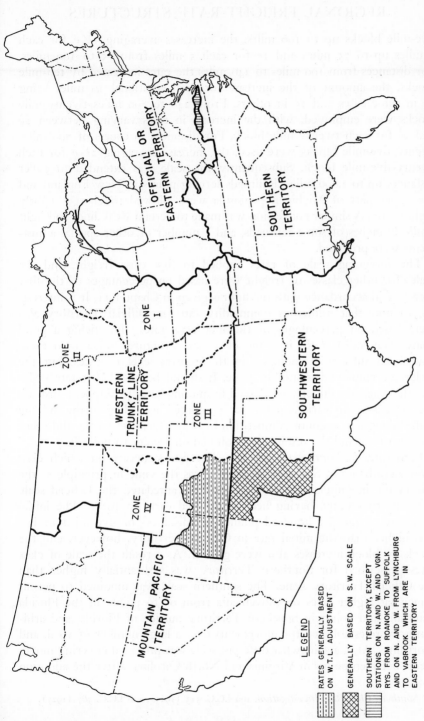

FIGURE 4. *Approximate Boundaries of Major Railroad Freight Rate Territories.* (Adapted from Board of Investigation and Research, *Report on Interterritorial Freight Rates*, House Document 303, 78th Congress, 1st session (1943), p. 1.

five-mile blocks up to 100 miles, the increases averaging 1½¢ for each 5 miles up to 75 miles and 1¢ for each 5 miles from 75 to 100 miles. For distances from 100 miles to 240 miles the rates increased by ten-mile blocks, the amount of the increase for each additional 10 miles being 2¢ in some cases and 1¢ in others. From 240 to 800 miles twenty-mile blocks were employed, with the increase in rates varying between 2¢ and 3¢ for each twenty-mile block. For distances in excess of 800 miles twenty-five-mile blocks were used, the increase averaging 2½¢ for each twenty-five-mile block. Subsequently the scale was extended to cover distances up to 2,000 miles. Railroads serving points in New England and the upper part of Michigan peninsula were allowed to charge slightly higher rates. A similar concession was made to certain weak lines and light traffic branches of some railroads, and a number of other special adjustments were provided.

The foregoing scale of rates applied to first class freight, and the scales for other classes of freight were based on percentages of the first class rate in accordance with the figures given in Chapter 11. It is interesting to note that numerous commodity rates in Official Territory also were based on percentages of the first class rates, thus tieing a good many commodity rates into the class rate structure. Since 1930 there have been substantial increases in the general level of rates, but the technique employed is still the same. It should be noted that rate scales like these are not directly employed in quoting rates to shippers. Instead, the rates between various points are computed according to the mileage scale, taking into account competition by way of shorter routes and other modifications, and the results are published on a point to point basis.

Class rates in Southern Territory. The rate structure on which class rates were based in Southern Territory was the same in principle as the one in use in Official Territory. Indeed, it antedated the Official scale by some two years, having been established early in 1928.[2] The initial class rate of 34¢ per hundred pounds for distances of five miles or less was higher than the initial rate in Official Territory, however, and the block by block increases also were greater. As a result the scale of class rates prescribed for Southern Territory was susbtantially higher than the Official Territory scale. The southern scale was modified to permit somewhat higher rates on movements from or to points in the Florida peninsula and points in Southern Territory outside of Florida, and arbitraries were established for movements over a large number of weak and short lines. Also, a somewhat different scale was provided covering movements between points in Virginia and North Carolina. After the adoption

---

[2] *Southern Class Rate Investigation,* 100 I.C.C. 513 (1925), 128 I.C.C. 567 (1927).

of the southern class rate scale, numerous adjustments were made in southern commodity rates, somewhat in accordance with the block and tapering principles used in determining class rates.

Class rates in Western Trunk Line Territory. Western Trunk Line Territory includes that part of Western Classification Territory which lies east of a line following the western boundaries of North and South Dakota, jogs slightly west and south into Wyoming to include Cheyenne, Wyoming, and then follows the line of the Rocky Mountains to the northern boundary of New Mexico; and north of a line drawn along the northeastern boundary of New Mexico and the southern boundary of Kansas to the Missouri State line, and then across Missouri to the Mississippi River. That part of Missouri which lies to the south of the indicated boundary occupies a somewhat indeterminate position, sometimes being treated as a part of Western Trunk Line Territory and sometimes as a part of the adjoining Southwestern Territory.

In 1930 the Interstate Commerce Commission prescribed a class rate structure for this area which was the subject of several subsequent modifications.[3] Like the rate structures employed in the East and South, a distance scale making use of the tapering principle was adopted, but there was a marked difference between the Western Trunk Line rate system and those previously described. In the East and South a single scale was applied to the whole territory, but Western Trunk Line Territory was divided into three zones, called Zones I, II, and III, Zone I being the most easterly, and a separate scale of rates was established for movements within each zone. In addition, a Zone IV to the west of the territory proper was established for the purpose of computing rates between points in that zone and points in the other three zones. The approximate boundaries of these zones are shown on the map on page 267.

The reason why the Commission found it desirable to break up Western Trunk Line Territory into separate rate-making zones is that susbtantial differences in transportation conditions exist in different parts of this large territory, particularly with reference to traffic densities. Conditions in the eastern part of Western Trunk Line Territory are similar in many ways to those existing in the western part of Official Territory, with perhaps somewhat lighter traffic and population densities. The relatively sparse population and lighter local traffic in Zone III, however, seemed to justify a higher scale of rates than needed to be applied to Zone I. The establishment of a rather narrow Zone II, with a scale of rates intermediate between those fixed for Zones I and III, prevented an un-

---

[3] *Rate Structure Investigation No. 17000*, Part 2, 164 I.C.C. 1. See also 173 I.C.C. 637 (1931); 178 I.C.C. 619 (1931); 196 I.C.C. 413 (1933); 204 I.C.C. 595 (1934); 226 I.C.C. 467 (1938).

desirably sharp break in rates between the eastern and western parts of the territory.

The basic first class rate for movements of five miles or less in Zone I was fixed at 32¢ per hundred pounds as compared with a 30¢ rate for movements of the same distance in Official Territory. For Zone II the basic first class rate was fixed at 34¢, and for Zone III it was fixed at 36¢. In each zone rates progressed upward with distance in accordance with a block system similar to that already described in connection with rates in Official Territory. These increases were somewhat greater per block in Zone III than in Zone II; greater in Zone II than in Zone I; and the increases per block in Zone I were somewhat greater than those employed in Official Territory. A few rates selected at random are given in Table VII to indicate the general relationships existing between the different zones.

Table VII

| Distances | | Rate Scales | | |
| | Official | Western Trunk Line | | |
		Zone I	Zone II	Zone III
5 miles and under	30	32	34	36
100 miles and over 95	56	66	75	82
300 miles and over 280	87	106	122	134
400 miles and over 380	99	124	142	156
500 miles and over 480	111	142	162	178

In order to determine the rate to be charged for a movement between points located in different zones the Interstate Commerce Commission ordered the adoption of a rate-making technique which came to be known as the Western Trunk Line or laminated formula. The scale of rates prescribed for use in the lowest rate zone involved was applied to the entire length of the haul, and to this was added a predetermined number of cents, called a differential, to cover that part of the haul which took place in the higher rate zone or zones. A few of these differentials are shown in Table VIII.

Table VIII

| Distances | Differentials | | | |
	Zone I [4]	Zone II	Zone III	Zone IV
5 miles and under	2	2	2	2
100 miles and over 95	9	9	7	12
200 miles and over 190	10	13	11	16
300 miles and over 280	13	16	12	19
400 miles and over 380	15	18	14	23
500 miles and over 480	17	20	16	27

[4] Zone I differentials were used in connection with the determination of rates between points in Western Trunk Line Territory and points in the western part of Official Territory. Their use is discussed presently in connection with the determination of interterritorial rates.

Suppose, for example, that a shipment between two points involved a haul of 200 miles in Zone I and 100 miles in Zone II. The first class rate would be calculated by taking the Zone I rate of 106¢ for the entire 300 miles hauled and adding to it the 9¢ Zone II differential for the 100 miles the shipment was carried in Zone II, giving a total charge of 115¢ for the 300 mile haul.

A similar system was adopted for calculating rates between points which were not located in adjacent zones. Take, for example, a shipment from a point in Zone I to a point in Zone III involving a haul of 100 miles in Zone I, 200 miles in Zone II, and 200 miles in Zone III. Using the scale of rates in effect in 1930, the first class rate between these two points would be computed by taking the Zone I rate of 142¢ for the entire 500 miles of the haul, then adding to this the Zone II differential of 18¢ for the entire 400 mile distance moved in Zone II and Zone III, and finally adding the Zone III differential of 11¢ for the 200 miles moved in Zone III, thus arriving at a final rate of 171¢ for the 500 mile haul. Rates between points in Zone I, II, and III, and points in Zone IV were computed in a similar fashion.

It is important to note that a very large volume of traffic moves under commodity rates and exception ratings in Western Trunk Line Territory. Some of the commodity rates are tied to the class rate structure but others are quite unrelated to it. Also, truck competition has necessitated the establishment of numerous special adjustments in this part of the country.

Class rates in the Southwest. Southwestern Territory includes the states of Texas, Oklahoma, Arkansas, and all of Louisiana except the relatively small area lying east of the Mississippi River. A very complicated rate structure had developed in this area prior to effective rate regulation, and as early as 1922 the Interstate Commerce Commission set to work to do something about it. Its first decision was handed down in 1927, but this was followed by numerous changes, and an extensive revision was ordered in 1934.[5]

Two zones, Zone III comprising the eastern two-thirds of the territory and Zone IV comprising the western one-third, were set up, and a separate scale of rates was provided for each zone. The initial first class rate for movements of 5 miles or less was fixed at 36¢ per hundred pounds for Zone III and 38¢ for Zone IV, and rates in each zone were scaled upward with distance as in the various rate scales already described. Rates between points in Zone III and points in Zone IV were computed by the addition of differentials in exactly the same way in which inter-

---

[5] *Consolidated Southwestern Cases,* 123 I.C.C. 203 (1927); 205 I.C.C. 601 (1934).

zone rates were fixed in Western Trunk Line Territory. The carriers of their own volition eliminated Zone IV in 1941, however, and Zone III rates were applied to the whole area. These Zone III rates were identical with Zone III rates in Western Trunk Line Territory.

Class rates in Mountain-Pacific Territory. The Interstate Commerce Commission has never put into effect a single basic class rate scale in Mountain-Pacific Territory, although it has established a number of class rate scales within and between different sections of this vast area and between points in Mountain-Pacific Territory and points in other rate territories. The class rate scales that have been established are in general conformity with the distance principle, but mile for mile there are large differences in the rates charged in different parts of this territory. Water competition has had a marked influence on railroad rates covering movements between the various Pacific coast ports, and water competition between east and west coast ports has long been a factor in fixing transcontinental rates, leading to the blanketing of rates over considerable areas as previously noted.

INTERTERRITORIAL RATES

Rates between territories. It will be observed from the preceding discussion that the Interstate Commerce Commission applied the same basic principles to the establishment of class rate scales in all rate-making territories with the exception of Mountain-Pacific Territory. First a basic rate was established which applied to all movements of five miles or less in length within a given territory, and this rate was increased gradually by blocks of increasing length, the net result being a scale of rates which increased with distance but not in exact proportion with distance. It will be observed, too, that while the technique employed was the same in each rate-making territory, the actual level of rates was different in each case, with the exception of rates in Southwestern Territory which were identical with those prescribed for Zone III in Western Trunk Line Territory. Because of the very large movement of goods between points in different rate-making territories, these interterritorial differences in rate levels presented rate making authorities with a very special problem.

Interterritorial rates based on sum of the locals. Until fairly recent times it was not uncommon to construct interterritorial rates by taking the intraterritorial rate for the distance a shipment moved in the territory in which it originated and combining this rate with the intraterritorial rate for the distance moved in destination territory. Assume, for example, a shipment moving from A in Territory X to C in Territory Y, the movement taking place through B, a border point intermediate between A and C. In such a case the through rate might be constructed by adding the Territory X rate from A to B to the Territory Y rate from B to C. This method of constructing interterritorial rates was simple, but did not conform with the modern tapered distance ,principle because the sum of the rates charged for two short hauls would be more than the rate charged for a single long haul of equal length. Consequently, interterritorial rates based on the sum of the locals, were higher than the rate charged for a movement of equal length within the lower rated territory. And unless the haul in the higher rated territory was relatively short, the through rate was likely to be higher even than the rate charged for a haul of equal length in the higher rated territory.

Furthermore, this scheme of rate making resulted in sharp breaks in rates at border points, giving those cities fortunate enough to be located on the border between rate-making territories an unfair advantage over nearby points on either side of the border. Thus rates might scale upward gradually in accordance with the tapering principle from a point of origin in one territory to a border point and then increase sharply to nearby points in an adjacent territory. Under these circumstances it is obvious that businessmen located at border points enjoyed a definite rate advantage over businessmen at nearby nonborder points who had to pay the combination rate. In order to make the distance principle work properly it became necessary to work out some scheme of blending the rates charged on interterritorial movements to avoid these sharp breaks at border points.

Interterritorial class rates between Official and Southern Territory. Early in 1928 the Interstate Commerce Commission put into effect the first of a series of rate adjustments applicable to the interterritorial movement of freight, this particular adjustment involving class rates between points in Official Territory and points in Southern Territory. Generally speaking, rates between points in the western part of Official Territory and points in Southern Territory were constructed by calculating the rate for the distance in Southern Territory in accordance with the basic class rate scale prescribed for that territory and adding to this amount a differential which increased with the length of the haul in Official Territory, and which also varied slightly with the length of the haul in Southern Territory.

Interterritorial rates between the eastern part of Official Territory and most points in Southern Territory were calculated for the most part on the so-called key point plan. This system provided for the division of Southern Territory into a number of groups, and specific first class rates were quoted between a limited number of key cities in the East and each of the southern groups. Other cities in the East not specifically singled out as key points were granted the same rates as those applying to nearby cities which had been designated as key points. The rates calculated in this way were relatively lower than those based on the Official Territory differentials described above. In this connection, too, it should be noted that the force of water competition has had some effect on interterritorial rates between eastern cities and the South.

According to a study made by the Board of Investigation and Research, the general level of class rates applying interterritorially between the South and Official Territory was higher in relation to distance than the level of class rates prevailing in Official Territory but was lower, generally speaking, than the level prevailing in Southern Territory. The interterritorial rates were closer, for the most part, to the level of rates prevailing in the South than they were to rates in Official Territory, and this was true even though more than one-half of the haul took place in Official Territory. It follows, as a matter of course, that the greater the proportion of the haul taking place in Southern Territory the more nearly the interterritorial rate approached the level of rates applying intraterritorially in the South.[6]

Interterritorial class rates between Official and Western Trunk Line Territories. Interterritorial class rates between points in Western Trunk Line Territory and points in Official Territory east of the Indiana-Ohio line and the southeastern corner of Michigan were based on key point rates of the type described in connection with interterritorial rates between the eastern part of Official Territory and Southern Territory. Between points west of the Ohio-Indiana line and points in Western Trunk Line Territory rates were figured for the entire distance in accordance with a prescribed basic distance scale which provided rates slightly lower than the Zone I rates in Western Trunk Line Territory, and to this basic rate was added one or more differentials covering that part of the haul taking place in Western Trunk Line Territory. These differentials were the same as those previously described in connection with the determination of interzone rates in Western Trunk Line Territory. To avoid excessive humps in rates to and from points in the eastern part of Zone I, the charge for the entire distance in such cases was calculated on the basis of the Official Territory scale, to which was added a scale of so-called "bridge arbitraries" for distances up to 170 miles west of border or gateway cities. The rates charged for moving freight interterritorially between points in Official and Western Trunk Line Terri-

---

[6] Board of Investigation and Research, *Report on Interterritorial Freight Rates*, pp. 165-166. House Document 303, 78th Congress 1st Session, 1934.

tory were higher than they were for intraterritorial movements of comparable distance in Official Territory, but they were not as high as those charged for comparable movements in Western Trunk Line Territory.

Other interterritorial rate adjustments. Class rates between points in Western Trunk Line Territory, including points in southern Missouri, and points in Southern Territory were made on the key point system. Key point rates also were used between various points in Southwestern Territory and specified points in Western Trunk Line, Official, and Southern territories. Where key point rates were not specified, distance rates making use of basic rate scales and zone differentials were employed. Interterritorial rates between points in Mountain-Pacific Territory and points in the other rate-making territories are based on the blanketing arrangement discussed in connection with the transcontinental rate structure and show the effect of water competition. Rates between interior points in Mountain-Pacific Territory and points in other territories are the same as or lower than the rates charged between points in other territories and the Pacific coast. In some cases the westbound rates are lower than rates eastbound.

EQUALIZATION OF CLASS RATES

No common level of rates. As previously noted, the various class rate structures prescribed by the Interstate Commerce Commission were all built on the same basic plan, but the actual rate scales adopted were not uniform for all territories, and it was not until 1945 that positive action was taken in the direction of achieving uniformity in scales as well as in method of construction. Table IX, showing first class rates for representative distances in each territory as they existed prior to 1945, reveals the wide differences in rate scales.[7]

Table IX

Distance		Territory				
	Offi- cial	South- ern	Western Trunk Line			South- western
			Zone I	Zone II	Zone III	
5 miles and under	33	40	35	37	40	40
10 miles and over 5	34	40	36	40	42	42
50 miles and over 45	47	57	53	61	65	65
100 miles and over 95	62	79	73	83	90	90
200 miles and over 190	80	112	97	111	123	123
500 miles and over 480	122	173	156	178	196	196
1000 miles and over 975	182	249	240	273	300	300
1500 miles and over 1475	237	315	315	359	394	394

[7] Rates in this table are higher than those shown in earlier parts of this chapter because of subsequent increases and adjustments. The full table is given in *Class Rate Investigation, 1939*, 262 I.C.C. 447, 744-746 (1945).

Interterritorial rates. In addition to differences in class rate levels within each territory, the various schemes adopted for fixing class rates between territories led to the establishment of interterritorial rate levels which differed from each other and from the various intraterritorial levels. Furthermore, in some cases interterritorial rates differed with the direction of the haul, although in general they tended to be the same in both directions. Directional differences in rates sometimes resulted from an intentional fixing of different rates for movements in opposite directions, as in the case of some of the transcontinental rates which were higher eastbound than westbound; and sometimes they resulted from the use of different classifications. If one classification applied to interterritorial movements in one direction while another classification applied to movements in the opposite direction, then differences in rates developed wherever classification ratings were different.

Historical basis for different rate levels. Although the rate structures described above were prescribed by the Interstate Commerce Commission, they did not reflect any calculated attempt on its part to create different levels of rates in different parts of the country. On the contrary, different rate levels existed in each rate-making territory long before the Commission undertook its general revision of rate structures in the twenties and thirties and these differences can be explained in some measure in historical terms. All of the nation's major railroad systems, with the exception of the Illinois Central, developed almost exclusively within the confines of one or the other of the three major classification territories. Naturally the railroads in each territory competed with one another, and they also found it necessary to cooperate with each other to solve various common problems; but they did not compete, directly at least, with railroads in other parts of the country nor were they immediately concerned with the transportation problems peculiar to territories other than their own.

In view of the way in which railroads developed regionally, it is not surprising that rate structures were developed in each territory to meet the special needs of carriers and shippers in that territory without much regard to the rate structures being developed elsewhere. Thus class rates in the South, to take one example, tended to be high relative to the commodity rates established for the movement of various basic raw materials, partly because manufactured goods, which more than other types of commodities tend to move under class rates, were not produced to any extent in the South and so did not constitute an important item of traffic. In the East, on the other hand, the railroads carried a much larger volume of manufactured goods, and this justified, in part at least, a somewhat lower level of class rates.

REGIONAL FREIGHT RATE STRUCTURES

When the Interstate Commerce Commission undertook its general revision of rate structures, it did so on a territorial basis, establishing a rate structure first for one part of the country and then for another, and these new rate structures naturally bore some relationship to the rates already being charged. Efforts were made to eliminate gross inequities in the rates charged for movements between different points in the particular rate-making territory under investigation, but no particular attempt was made to equalize rates within the territory under investigation with rates prevailing in other territories which were not involved in the immediate proceedings.

Equalization of rates between territories. In the 1930's a strong demand developed in the South for a scale of class rates which would be no greater in the South than in Official Territory. Various interests in the Southwest and West also were interested in uniformity, or at least a reduction in the spread between class rates in the Southwest and West and similar rates in Official Territory. The Tennessee Valley Authority, which desired to promote the industrial development of the South, published several studies which criticized existing differences in the levels of class rates. And in 1939 the Interstate Commerce Commission undertook an investigation of differences in classifications and in the level of class rates as between all of the major rate-making territories except Mountain-Pacific Territory. In the meantime the issue had gotten into politics and found its way into the Transportation Act of 1940 which provided, as mentioned previously, that there must be no unreasonable preference accorded to any *region, district, or territory*.

Although the nation was plunged into war late in 1941, the Commission continued the investigation of classifications and class rates instituted in 1939, and on May 15, 1945, it found that existing classifications were unlawful and that the varying levels of class rates violated the anti-discrimination provisions of the Interstate Commerce Act. As noted in Chapter 11 the railroads were ordered to establish a uniform classification, and acting under its power to prescribe just and reasonable rates, the Commission prescribed a new scale of maximum class rates to apply uniformly in and between Official, Southern, Southwestern, and Western Trunk Line territories. The rates prescribed were somewhat higher than existing rates in Official Territory but less than those prevailing elsewhere. The Commission found that the revenue needs of the eastern carriers were greater with respect to class rate traffic than was true of carriers in other parts of the country. At the same time any drastic reduction in rates in other parts of the country had to be avoided because of its effect on carrier revenues.

Interim adjustment. The new scale of class rates was prescribed to go into effect simultaneously with the adoption of a uniform classification, but the Commission recognized that working out a uniform classification which would be acceptable to carriers, shippers, and rate-making authorities, would take a considerable period of time. Consequently an interim adjustment which would reduce the spread between the different rate levels seemed to be in order, and to this end the Commission ordered a 10 per cent reduction in interstate class rates within and between Southern, Southwestern, and Western Trunk Line territories, and between these territories and Official Territory; and a 10 per cent increase in interstate class rates within Official Territory. The new uniform scale of class rates prescribed for ultimate adoption was to constitute a minimum below which no rate was to be reduced, and no changes in existing exception or column rates were contemplated. The Commission's order was challenged by nine northeastern states and most of the western railroads, but on May 12, 1947, it was upheld by the Supreme Court.[8] The interim adjustment, with a minor modification, went into effect on August 22, 1947.

Subsequent developments. The series of freight rate increases which followed the close of World War II rendered the uniform rate scale prescribed in 1945 obsolete, and subsequently the Interstate Commerce Commission proposed a new scale about 60 per cent higher than the original. Hearings were held on this proposal in December 1950, at which time the eastern and southern carriers offered certain amendments. Among other things, the eastern lines wanted the scale reduced on the shorter distances in order to help them meet highway competition, and the southern lines thought the scale should be higher for the longer distances. The western lines were of the opinion that the scale would result in a substantial reduction in their revenues and proposed a scale of their own. On July 26, 1951, the Commission established a new class rate scale which was somewhat more than 60 per cent higher than the original. The new scale was to be used in connection with the new uniform classification when adopted. Late in May 1952 the Commission ordered it into effect.

It will be recalled that the Commission's original orders requiring the establishment of a uniform classification and a uniform class rate scale did not apply to Mountain-Pacific Territory. A conflict of interests existed in this area between Pacific coast shippers and shippers in the interior, and many complex adjustments existed. In 1950 the Commission undertook an investigation of class rates in Mountain-Pacific Territory and class rates on Transcontinental traffic, and hearings were called for Salt Lake City in September of 1951. California interests argued that most markets in the West were far removed from sources of supply and that rates had to be made on a commodity basis to fit marketing needs rather than on a

---

[8] *State of New York* v. *United States*, 331 U.S. 284.

distance basis as would be the case if a class rate structure were adopted. They also were afraid that they would lose the benefit of special rates granted on quantity shipments intermediate between carload and less-than-carload lots. Wyoming interests, on the other hand, supported the substitution of a uniform scale for what they described as discriminatory rates resulting from a hodge podge system.

EFFECT OF FREIGHT RATES ON INDUSTRIALIZATION

Retardation of industry. Organized opposition to the class rate structure as it existed prior to the Commission's rate equalization order came principally from southern industrialists and political leaders, although substantial opposition also was expressed by similar interests in the Southwest and in Western Trunk Line Territory. The basic complaint raised was that the lower level of class rates in Official Territory, together with the various class rate scales prescribed by the Interstate Commerce Commission for application to interterritorial movements of freight, gave producers of manufactured goods in the East a selling advantage over manufacturers in other parts of the country since manufactured goods move under class rates to a greater extent than is true of other types of commodities. It was said that the industrial development of other parts of the country was being retarded as a result of this advantage. Southern interests were especially bitter in their attack on the existing class rate structures, and because their protests were expressed more vociferously and extensively than in other parts of the country, the following brief discussion centers around the effect of railroad class rates on the industrialization of the South.

The way in which different levels of intraterritorial and interterritorial class rates might react unfavorably on manufacturing in the South may be shown by a simple illustration. Under the various rate scales as they existed prior to 1938, the first class rate for a 700 mile haul in Official Territory was fixed at $1.35 per hundred pounds as compared with a rate of $1.87 for a haul of the same length in Southern Territory. At the same time the interterritorial rate for a haul of 700 miles, assuming for the purpose of illustration that half of the haul took place in each territory, would have been $1.80. Assume now the existence of two competing manufacturing establishments, one in the East and one in the South, both being 700 miles distant from a common market in Official Territory. On any commodity moving as first class freight, the rate from the eastern point of supply was $1.35 per hundred pounds according to the Official Territory scale, but the southern manufacturer had to pay the interterritorial rate which was $1.80. If the common market happened to be in

Southern Territory, the eastern manufacturer paid the interterritorial rate of $1.80, but the southern manufacturer had to pay the southern intraterritorial rate which was $1.87. Thus the eastern manufacturer had a definite rate advantage over his southern competitor whenever hauls of identical length were involved, and in numerous cases the differences in the rate levels were sufficient to give the eastern manufacturer the advantage even though his southern counterpart was actually closer to a given market.

Influence of variations in classification ratings. In the illustration used above no consideration was given to possible differences in classification ratings, it being assumed that the commodities involved were rated the same in both territories. But suppose that some of the items involved were rated first class in the Official Classification and third class in the Southern Classification. On a 700 mile haul to a common market located in Central Freight Association Territory the eastern shipper would pay the $1.35 first class rate provided by the Official Territory class rate scale. From the South, however, the shipment would move interterritorially as third class freight since the Southern Classification governed interterritorial movements between Southern Territory and Official Territory as pointed out in Chapter 11. This would mean that the southern manufacturer would pay a rate of only $1.26, the third class rate provided by the interterritorial scale, thus giving the southern manufacturer a rate advantage over his eastern rival. If the common market happened to be in the South, however, the eastern shipper again had the advantage. Both shipments would move as third class freight, but the eastern shipper would pay the interterritorial rate of $1.26, while the southern manufacturer paid $1.31, the third class rate under the southern scale.

The above illustration assumes a rather substantial difference in classification ratings. If the commodity happened to be one which was rated first class in Official Territory and second class in Southern Territory, the difference in ratings would be insufficient to offset the rate advantage enjoyed by the eastern manufacturer in either of the two cases described. Also there would be no reason to assume that where different ratings existed they favored the South. A detailed study of differences in classification ratings as they existed in 1942 was made by the Interstate Commerce Commission which showed that in the all important carload ratings approximately half were the same in all three territories. But where differences existed a large percentage of the ratings were higher in the South and West than they were in the East.[9] Such comparisons are misleading in that they give equal weight to all items in the Classification regardless of their transportation importance, but they do suggest that differences in

---

[9] *Class Rate Investigation, 1939,* 262 I.C.C. 447, 471 (1945).

ratings, if they did anything, increased rather than decreased the spread between eastern and southern rate levels.

Length of haul. Any analysis of the advantages shippers in one territory may have over shippers in another rate territory also must take into consideration the average lengths of the hauls involved. An examination of Table IX on page 275, showing the rates for hauls of various lengths in different territories as they stood prior to 1945, reveals that the spread between rates in different territories in terms of cents per hundred pounds was not great on short hauls, but this spread increased as the length of the haul increased. Thus, the Table shows a spread of only 2¢ between the Official Territory first class rate and the Western Trunk Line Zone I rate for hauls of five miles or less, but on a 100 mile haul this spread increases to 11¢, on a 500 mile haul to 34¢, and on a 1,500 mile haul to 78¢. Interterritorial rate scales in effect in 1945 showed a similar increase in the spread on longer hauls since the interterritorial scales were based on existing intraterritorial scales.

The significance of the foregoing characteristic of the then existing rate scales is found in the fact that a producer in a higher rate territory might have certain compensating advantages over a producer in a lower rate territory, which advantages would enable him to absorb the few cents difference in the rates on short hauls, but as the length of haul increased this would become more and more difficult to do. This fact was of no little significance to producers outside of Official Territory because in the nature of the case it was on the longer hauls that opportunities for competition existed.

Influence of exception, column, and commodity rates. While it is true that prior to the Interstate Commerce Commission's 1945 uniform rate order the class rates paid by southern and western shippers were substantially higher than those paid by eastern shippers, it is important to point out that the great bulk of freight did not then and does not now move under class rates. In its 1945 report the Commission estimated that only 4.1 per cent of the total number of carloads of freight moved under classification ratings, the balance moving under exception ratings and column and commodity rates. The Commission also pointed out that the exception ratings covered hundreds of articles on which there was an appreciable movement, that they were generally lower than the classifications provided, and that their use was more extensive in the South than elsewhere. This and other studies suggest that the spread between eastern and southern rates was not quite as great as the rate scales seemed to indicate. On the other hand, it should be noted that exception ratings and commodity rates apply only to specified items of traffic and are of no benefit to individuals seeking to establish or develop industries producing commodities which have not been accorded exception ratings or commodity rates.

Industrial development of the South. In its 1945 report the Interstate Commerce Commission noted the rapid growth of industry in the South and cited numerous figures to show that the position of southern manufacturing had improved relative to manufacturing in Official Territory. It is, of course, undeniable that the South has made substantial progress industrially in recent years, and this fact led some people to contend that the differences in class rate structures were unimportant. It is difficult to pass judgment on the extent to which the large differences in class rates existing prior to August 22, 1947, affected the development of southern industry because the level of class rates is only one of a number of factors which determine the location of industry. It seems reasonable to suppose that there are some industries which would never develop in the South regardless of the general level of class rates. On the other hand, those industries which have been developing in the South because of nearness to raw materials, cheap power, cheap labor, mild climate, or some other reason, might have developed even more with a more favorable rate structure. Finally, it must be clear that an indeterminate number of industries did not locate in the South because of the artificial barrier created by a level of class rates higher than those provided for manufacturers located in Official Territory. What has been said about conditions in the South can also be applied to the Southwest and to Western Trunk Line Territory.

Regional specialization. The growth of manufacturing in the northeastern part of the United States was an historical accident and not the result of differences in railroad freight rates. This area very early became the principal center of population which meant that it at once provided a market for manufactured goods and a source of labor supply for the production of such goods. The development of shipbuilding, the fame of the Yankee clippers, and the seafaring nature of many of the people may also have contributed to this growth. In addition, there was abundant water power in New England, the people were energetic, and the land was not as well suited to agriculture as other parts of the country. Availability of capital, an early problem in all parts of the country, also was somewhat less of a problem in the northeast. As pointed out in Chapter 2, population expanded westward into the Ohio Valley country following the successful conclusion of the Revolutionary War, and as a result the center of population gradually moved westward into Ohio, Indiana, and the other states in this area. And as the country became more settled manufacturing, too, gradually moved westward with the result that eventually the whole area north of the Ohio and east of the Mississippi became industrialized.

As the country east of the Mississippi and north of the Ohio gradually filled up, settlers continued to press westward. The huge expanse of the country west of the Mississippi naturally meant a thin and widely scattered population, a condition not conducive to the development of manufacturing. Furthermore, the abundance of fine agricultural and grazing land and the discovery of tremendously important mineral resources made this area an outstanding supplier of agricultural products and basic raw materials. In the South, however, an entirely different situation developed. The South was first settled by a landed aristocracy originating in England to whom manufacturing as a way of making a living was largely foreign, and this landed aristocracy soon developed an agricultural economy based on slave labor. With the land well adapted to the production of such important crops as cotton and tobacco, the South naturally progressed along agricultural lines, becoming a supplier of raw materials which were shipped elsewhere for processing.

It will be clear, then, that regional specialization in the United States developed quite independently of any regional differences in the level of freight rates, but many people came to believe that the early advantage of the North and East in manufacturing was being perpetuated by the artificial device of discriminatory freight rates. Indeed, some went so far as to imply that a sort of conspiracy existed to prevent the development of manufacturing in the South and West in order to protect the manufacturing interests of the North. In the North, however, it has been argued that freight rates reflect regional differences in economic conditions rather than cause or perpetuate such differences. If manufacturing industries provide an important source of traffic in a given region, the railroads of that region, according to this point of view, naturally will encourage their further development by as favorable rates as possible.

To some extent, too, if certain industries are widely developed in a given area, it has been pointed out that the operators of these industries can exert considerable influence on the railroads serving them to gain rate concessions. Similarly, in an agricultural or extractive industry area the railroads will favor shippers with rates designed to encourage and increase the flow of freight in the form of agricultural products and extracted materials. Hence it is argued that economic conditions determine rates rather than being determined by rates. As is so often the case where such diverse points of view are involved, there is probably truth in both statements.

Quite apart from the question of whether freight rates determine or are determined by economic conditions, some people believe that it is a mistake to force a realignment of economic activities at this late date. As long as manufacturing already is established in Official Territory where it has all the advantages derived from an early start, why not encourage its continued development there, and at the same time encourage the South and the West to continue to play their own specialized roles as suppliers of raw materials? If an extensive development of manufacturing takes place in the South and West, it may mean the destruction of a large amount of valuable capital now existing in present manufacturing areas and a disruption of economic life, with attendant losses to workingmen and tradespeople as well as a loss of capital. Furthermore, if decentralization of industry is encouraged by spreading it all over the country, it may result in the substitution of small-scale production for large scale production with an attendant over-all loss in total product available to the people.

On the other hand, if manufacturing is concentrated in the North and East solely because of the existence of discriminatory freight rates, it would seem to be wiser in the long run to remove such barriers and permit economic forces to take their course. Also, there are limits beyond which volume production cannot go without sacrificing efficiency, and it may be more economical to substitute several strategically located smaller plants for one huge plant.

Advantages of diversified economy. It is not difficult to appreciate the advantages that would accrue to the North and East from a continued concentration of manufacturing industry in that part of the country, but the people of the South and West have also put up a good case for the advantages that would accrue to them from a wider diversification of economic activity. Except for wartime prosperity, agriculture has long been a depressed industry and has been kept going only by large and continued subsidies. This has been true, too, of the livestock industry, and to a lesser extent of mining and other types of extractive industry. Under the circumstances it is not surprising that the average real income of the people in the South, the Southwest, and to a lesser extent the people in Western Trunk Line Territory, is substantially below the average income of those living in Official Territory.

Spokesmen for the South and West have contended that the people of their areas are engaged too largely in agriculture and in the extractive industries and that if manufacturing and various commercial activities are developed, a greater portion of the population will be drawn into these activities. Thus the incomes of those individuals remaining in the extractive industries should be improved by the removal of surplus workers, while at the same time the manufacturing and trade activities will create new sources of income. Furthermore, the development of manufacturing in the South and West should provide a new market for the raw materials of these areas, and producers of raw materials would no longer have the disadvantage of having to dispose of their products in a single market. This would eliminate the complaint frequently voiced that producers of raw materials in the South and West are at the mercy of the buyers of their products located in the North and East.

REGIONAL DIFFERENCES IN TRANSPORTATION COSTS

Importance of costs. The balance of the argument up to this point would seem to support the position of the Interstate Commerce Commission in ordering an equalization of class rates within and between the various rate territories involved in the equalization case. But all of the factors discussed above are related to the demand for transportation service, and before any conclusions can be reached with reference to the justice or injustice of rate equalization, consideration must be given to the supply or cost side of the price equation. Clearly, if the cost of rendering transportation service is greater in one part of the country than in another, it may be necessary to permit the railroads in the high cost areas to charge higher rates. To do otherwise would be to encourage poor transportation service, bankruptcy, or both. Among the various factors which may contribute to differences in costs within different territories the more important include the nature of the terrain over which the carriers must operate, the density of traffic, the composition of traffic, labor costs, taxes, and the like.

Nature of terrain. A casual examination of a relief map of the United States reveals that all four of the rate-making territories involved in the Commission's rate equalization order include both difficult and easy terrain. Official Territory and Southern Territory are roughly the same with reference to the amount of mountainous as compared with flat or rolling country. Western Trunk Line Territory, on the other hand, contains a large amount of relatively flat land and the same is true for the most part of Southwestern Territory. As far as terrain is concerned there are far greater differences in operating conditions within territories than between them, and if the same level of rates is applied to all railroads within a single territory without regard to the nature of the terrain over which they operate, it is hard to see how differences in terrain could be used to justify different rate scales as between different territories.

Density of traffic. While differences in terrain do not affect costs appreciably as between different territories, the same cannot be said of traffic densities. Attention has been called to the fact that the railroad business is one which operates under conditions of increasing returns, and from this it follows that the greater the volume of traffic the lower will be the per unit cost of handling that traffic. Since traffic densities are greater in Official Territory than in other parts of the country, this taken by itself would seem to justify a somewhat lower level of rates in Official Territory than elsewhere. Again, however, it may be noted that differences in traffic densities are often as great between railroads in the same territory as they are between the railroads of different territories, although in some cases adjustments have been made in the form of arbitraries for weak or light traffic lines.

Composition of traffic. To the extent that rates on individual commodities are based on what the traffic will bear the composition of the traffic carried by the railroads of a given section of the country may be a factor in determining the level of class rates. Thus if the railroads in one section of the country haul mostly low grade freight moving under low commodity rates, they may find it necessary to charge relatively high rates on higher grade traffic in order to cover their over-all costs. Since class rates apply primarily to high grade traffic, a higher level of class rates might seem to be justified in those areas where the volume of high grade traffic is small relative to the lower grades of traffic. Some such argument as this was used by the southern carriers to justify a higher level of class rates in the South than was applied in Official Territory. It also led a number of shippers' organizations in the South to oppose the movement to equalize class rates because they were afraid that the carriers would then find it necessary to raise the low commodity rates on which much traffic was then moving.

A study of the relative distribution of carload traffic in 1939 was made in connection with the Interstate Commerce Commission's 1945 rate equalization report, and the figures given in that study do not bear out the contention that substantial differences exist in the relative volume of high grade traffic moved in different territories. As a matter of fact the relative volume of goods in the Manufactures and Miscellaneous group, the group in which most high grade traffic would be found, was approximately the same in all three territories.[10] Furthermore, as in the case of differences in terrain and traffic densities, differences in traffic composition often are greater between individual railroads within a single territory than they are between territories. Again, it should be pointed out that a substantial volume of traffic moving under low commodity rates may be

---

[10] *Class Rate Investigation, 1939*, 262 I.C.C. 447, 612 (1945).

quite profitable of itself, especially if relatively long hauls are involved,[11] and a railroad hauling a large volume of low grade traffic may find it worth while to accept whatever other traffic it can get at rates not greatly in excess of variable costs. Finally, the possibility that lower class rates might encourage the development of trade and industry in the South and West and so lead to an increase in the volume of such traffic should not be overlooked.

Other costs. In connection with its study of regional costs the Interstate Commerce Commission concluded that the lighter trains and smaller loads of the South were compensated for in some degree by lower operating costs. It noted that the southern region had a lower compensation per employee per annum, a lower ratio of empty to loaded car miles, more miles actually run per hour per train and engine employee in freight service, and more transportation service car miles per employee. No similar statement was made with reference to costs in Southwestern and Western Trunk Line Territory.

Conclusions concerning costs. Elaborate studies of the relative cost of handling traffic in the different territories were made by Dr. Ford K. Edwards, the Commission's head cost analyst, and on the basis of these studies the Commission concluded that costs in the South were approximately the same or slightly lower than costs in Official Territory, excluding Pocahontas Territory; but costs ran from 5 to 10 per cent higher in the West. The West in this case included Western Trunk Line, Southwestern, and Mountain-Pacific territories, but differences in costs as between the West as a whole and the three separate territories were found to be relatively small. Variable costs in the South and West frequently were found to be as low as or lower than variable costs in Official Territory. The relatively low total costs of transportation in the South were attributed by the Commission principally to low terminal costs in that area, while the higher total costs in the West were due to a somewhat larger proportion of constant costs and to deficits incurred in the handling of passengers and less-than-carload freight. It is worth noting, however, that the subsequent abolition of land-grant rate reductions favors the western railroads in comparison with those in Official Territory.

Finally, in recent years the rate of return earned by the western and southern carriers has been improving in relation to the return earned by

---

[11] The railroads in Pocahontas Territory illustrate this point. Pocahontas Territory is a small strip stretching inland from the Atlantic Ocean where Southern Territory and Official Territory meet. The great bulk of traffic moved in Pocahontas Territory consists of coal, 87.4 per cent of the total in 1939, which is hauled under highly favorable operating conditions, and the railroads serving the area are among the most prosperous in the nation.

carriers in Official Territory. In connection with the judicial proceedings which followed upon its uniform rate order the Interstate Commerce Commission noted that there was a greater need for revenue by rail carriers in the eastern district as compared with rail carriers in the western district or in the southern region. It also noted that a much larger percentage of the total traffic in the eastern district moved on class rates than in the western district or in the southern region.

CONCLUSION

Effect of rate equalization uncertain. It is difficult to say just what effect the equalization of class rates will have on the industrialization of the South and West. Both the South and West experienced a notable expansion of industry during the Second World War, but whether or not the equalization of class rates will make it possible to maintain and increase this expansion is another question. New industries established in such areas as the Gulf coast are at least partly independent of railroad transportation and so, perhaps, not greatly affected by changes in railroad class rates; and some produce commodities which probably would not move under class rates anyway. In some cases the concentration of skilled labor and the advantage of a head start give eastern manufacturers an edge which the South and West may not be able to overcome even with equal rates. And as long as the center of population remains north of the Ohio and east of the Mississippi many manufacturers in that area will continue to enjoy an advantage if for no other reason than that they are closer to the market for their products.

Those industries which have been excluded from the South and West by a higher level of freight rates will now have an opportunity to develop and expand. But since, as was pointed out above, freight rates are only one of a number of factors determining the location of industry, there is no way of estimating satisfactorily the over-all effect of the Interstate Commerce Commission's equalization order. While it will unquestionably encourage some industrial development there is reason to doubt that the effect of class rate equalization will be as great as the people in the South and West have been led to believe. One very recent development, however, should be noted. The increasing development of atomic weapons, guided missiles, and long range bombing planes, is making the great industrial centers of the nation, and particularly those in the North and East, increasingly vulnerable to destructive attacks by air in the event of war. Hence a wide scattering of industry throughout the interior part of the nation has become significant, and this desire to decentralize industry, coupled with an equalization of freight rates, may contribute importantly to a growing industrialization in the South and West. Illustrative of this practice was the movement of the entire Chance Vought Division of United Aircraft Corporation 1,700 miles from Stratford, Connecticut, to Dallas, Texas, in 1948 and 1949.

SUGGESTED READINGS

Board of Investigation and Research, *Report on Interterritorial Freight Rates,* House Document No. 303, 78th Congress, 1st Session, 1943.

Interstate Commerce Commission, *Reports,* Volume 262, pp. 447-766, *Class Rate Investigation, 1939.*

Morton, Mignon, *The Complicated ABC's of Changes in Class Railroad Rates.* Lawrence, Kansas: University of Kansas Publications, 1948.

Wilson, G. Lloyd, *Railroad Freight Rate Structure.* Chicago: The Traffic Service Corporation, 1941.

A voluminous literature in the form of pamphlets issued by carriers, shippers' organizations, and other interested groups exists on the subject of regional rate discrimination.

14

Railroad Finance
and
FINANCIAL REGULATION

RAILROAD FINANCIAL STRUCTURE

Two broad types of securities. The railroad transportation industry has adopted the corporate form of organization, and over the years railroads have issued just about every kind of security known to the corporation. Railroad securities, like the securities of other corporations, fall into two broad groups, *capital stock* and *funded debt*. The stockholders of a corporation are its legal owners, and capital obtained through the sale of stock is sometimes spoken of as equity capital. While the owners of stock may sell their holdings to others, the stock itself represents a permanent investment, and corporations are under no obligation to return a stockholder's investment except in the case of dissolution, and then only if anything remains after satisfying creditors. Stockholders receive a return on their investment in the form of dividends, but only to the extent that funds are available or made available after all other obligations of the corporation are met. The holders of funded debt, unlike stockholders, are not owners. They are lenders, and the railroad is obligated to make interest payments to them periodically and to return the amount borrowed when due. Payment of interest and principal on funded debt is not contingent upon earnings, and these amounts must be paid as promised if the railroad expects to remain solvent.

Capital stock. There are two broad classes of capital stock, common and preferred, and as far as railroad finance is concerned the principal difference between the two is that the holders of preferred stock have first claim on any funds made available for dividends. No small amount of railroad preferred stock has resulted from the financial reorganization of bankrupt lines, bondholders sometimes being forced to exchange their bonds for preferred stock in order to reduce the fixed charges of the reorganized company.

Funded debt. Funded debt takes the form of bonds of one sort or another and equipment obligations, usually issued for fairly long periods of time. In addition, railroads borrow to meet temporary needs, and the sum total of railroad borrowing for periods not exceeding one year is called the *unfunded debt*. It is useful at times to make a distinction between *debt in default* and *unmatured funded debt*. Debt in default refers to funded debt on which the principal is due but unpaid. Unmatured funded debt refers to debt on which the principal is not yet due and payable.

Bonds. The commonest type of bond issued by railroads is the real estate bond which is protected by a mortgage of one sort or another. In some cases the mortgage covers the whole property and in other cases it covers some specified part or parts of the property. If a railroad fails to meet interest or principal payments when due, the bondholders may foreclose the mortgage and assume control of the property. Since a railroad usually cannot operate without the property involved, it will make every effort to meet its obligations on these bonds.

A second type of bond is the collateral trust bond, the holders of which are protected by the deposit of securities owned by the issuing corporation with an independent trustee, usually a bank or trust company, and should the company fail to meet interest or principal payments on such bonds, the trustee may dispose of the securities in the interest of the owners of the bonds. Collateral trust bonds were used extensively in the past in connection with the acquisition of one railroad by another. The management of a given railroad would buy enough of the stock of another line to gain control of it, and then use this stock as collateral against which to issue collateral trust bonds. In this way the securities of the controlled railroad were used to provide the funds necessary to obtain its control.

Other types of bonds include debenture bonds which are little more than unsecured promises to pay at some future date the amount stated on their face. No specific property is provided as security to protect the holders of debenture bonds in the event the corporation should fail to pay the principal amount when due. Obviously debenture bonds do not constitute an attractive investment. They have been issued largely in connection with railroad reorganizations rather than for direct sale to investors. The so-called income bond, while perhaps not a distinct type, should be mentioned briefly. Income bonds may be protected by some sort of claim on railroad property in the same way that real estate mortgage and collateral trust bonds are protected, but interest payments are made contingent on earnings. Thus the income bond occupies a position intermediate between a stock and the mortgage or collateral trust bond. Income bonds, like debentures, are not particularly attractive investments; usually they are issued in connection with railroad reorganization processes.

Equipment obligations. The equipment obligation is a type of security which has found considerable favor among investors in the securities of transportation companies. The railroads use it in connection with the purchase of locomotives, cars, and even complete train units. The most common form of equipment obligation vests ownership of the equipment in trustees acting for the holders of the obligations, and the railroad undertakes to pay for the equipment involved over a period of years on the installment plan. If the railroad fails to meet installments when due, the legal owners of the equipment may assume control of it. Since the equipment is readily movable, it usually can be sold to other railroads, and especially if the original purchaser has made a substantial down payment, there is little danger that the holders of equipment obligations will suffer any loss. Also, no railroad can operate without adequate equipment, and so a railroad will exhaust every resource before failing to pay installments on its equipment obligations. Because of their high degree of safety, equipment obligations can be issued at low rates of interest and are a favored form of railroad investment today.

Railroad financial structure. The amount of various types of railroad securities outstanding in a recent year is shown in Table X.

Table X

SECURITIES ACTUALLY OUTSTANDING, LINE-HAUL RAILROADS AND LESSOR SUBSIDIARIES
(December 31, 1949) [1]

Capital stock:		
Common	$7,234,153,002	
Preferred	1,988,168,820	
Total		$ 9,222,321,822
Unmatured funded debt:		
Mortgage bonds	7,183,601,502	
Collateral trust bonds	220,533,813	
Debenture bonds	345,214,330	
Miscellaneous obligations	34,561,706	
Total		7,783,911,351
Equipment Obligations		1,336,334,506
Total		$18,342,567,679
Debt in default		$ 208,209,745

INVESTMENT TRENDS

Bond issues as a source of permanent capital. Under ordinary circumstances a corporation issues bonds to finance the purchase or construction of plant or equipment, with the expectation that the new plant or equip-

---

[1] *Statistics of Railways in the United States, 1949*, pp. 137, 138. Securities "actually outstanding" are those issued to bona fide purchasers for a valuable consideration (including those issued in exchange for other securities or other property) and which the purchasers hold free of all control by the issuing carrier.

ment will earn enough each year to meet interest on the bonds and at the same time permit the setting aside of a reserve or sinking fund which will be sufficient to repay the principal when due. If the expectation is realized, the property eventually will be paid for out of earnings, and after the bonds have matured and been paid off, all the profits derived from its operation will accrue to the stockholder owners. Until very recent times, however, this pattern was not followed to any great extent in the field of railroad finance. Over the years the railroads obtained capital in large quantities through the sale of bonds, but little or no effort was made to set up reserves or sinking funds to pay off the bonds at maturity. Of course, every effort was made to meet interest payments as they came due, but when a given bond issue was about to mature, a new issue was floated, and the funds obtained in this way were used to pay off the holders of the maturing issue. As a result of this practice of re-funding rather than retiring debt, a substantial part of the permanent capital of the nation's railroads came to be provided by creditors rather than by owners.

Early reliance on bonds. The first railroads in the United States were financed by the sale of stock, but from about 1855 on, the sale of bonds played an increasingly important role in railroad finance. Up to the turn of the century the ratio of bonds to stocks showed a tendency to fluctuate considerably, the bond total sometimes being more and sometimes less than the outstanding stock. During periods of active construction, the bond ratio increased, but in the periods immediately following the various financial crises which characterized the latter half of the nineteenth century the story was different. Unable to meet interest payments on a heavy funded debt many railroads were forced into receivership, and in the ensuing reorganization the original stock was often wiped out and bondholders sometimes had to accept stock in the reorganized corporation in exchange for the bonds they had held in the old.

Many reasons have been cited for the extent to which railroad construction was financed by bond issues during the great era of railroad building in this country. Promoters engaged in rapidly expanding their lines into the sparsely populated western areas found it easier to borrow than to sell stock in their somewhat uncertain ventures. The characteristic shortage of capital in the United States made it necessary to seek funds from foreign investors, and European capitalists demanded the seeming protection of mortgages as a condition prerequisite to investing in American railroads. Numerous states, anxious for more railroads within their borders, encouraged the issuance of bonds by offering to subscribe to railroad bonds or to guarantee interest on such bonds, and in some cases states and municipalities agreed to exchange their own bonds for the bonds of railroads. After the Civil War some states, drawing upon their experience with banking corporations, passed laws prohibiting the issuance of railroad stock at less than par, and these laws had the effect of increasing the sale of bonds. In view of the highly speculative nature of investments in many of the railroad projects of the time it was often difficult to sell stock at par, but the law could be circumvented by marketing stocks and bonds in units at less than par, the discount being made in theory on the bonds rather than on the stocks.

Increase in debt ratio. At the turn of the century railroad securities were about equally divided between funded debt and stocks, but in succeeding years the ratio of funded debt actually outstanding to total railroad securities outstanding gradually increased, reaching a high of 57.1 per cent in 1924. The reasons for this increase in funded debt, which extended well into the third decade of the twentieth century, are worth noting briefly. For some years after 1900 railroad earnings were substantially in excess of the interest rate necessary to attract loan capital to the railroad business, and under these circumstances stockholder-owners found it more profitable to finance new projects through the sale of bonds than through the sale of additional amounts of capital stock. If, for example, loan capital could be obtained at a 4 per cent rate of interest and could be made to earn a return of 8 per cent, stockholders found it immediately advantageous to obtain capital by borrowing because the difference between what the money earned and the rate of interest actually paid contributed to the profits of the corporation. Similarly, because bondholders had no voice in the affairs of the corporation, it was easier for existing stockholders to retain active control of a given property by obtaining needed capital through the sale of bonds rather than through the sale of voting stock. Again, the sale of bonds made it possible to tap the huge investment resources of insurance companies and savings banks, which institutions often were permitted by law to invest their reserves in properly secured railroad bonds. Attention should also be called to the role played by the collateral trust bond in connection with the consolidation movement. Great railroad systems were built up by the process of one railroad buying up the stock of other railroads and then using these stocks as security for the issuance of collateral trust bonds.

Consequences of reliance on funded debt. It is easy to explain the reliance placed on funded debt as a means of obtaining new capital and the advantages which might accrue therefrom to existing stockholders, but there are dangers inherent in such a policy which must not be overlooked. Interest payments constitute a fixed charge, and the greater the reliance upon funded debt the more difficult it becomes for a carrier to avoid bankruptcy during periods of slack business. Furthermore, the practice of refunding rather than retiring debt when due is fraught with danger. It is quite possible to have a bond issue mature at a time when market conditions are such that a refunding issue can be floated only at excessive cost if, indeed, it can be floated at all. If a carrier has made no provision for paying off a given issue when due and finds it impossible to refund the issue, bankruptcy and reorganization must follow. In these periodic reorganizations stockholders generally have been wiped out, and sometimes junior bondholders have suffered a similar fate. Some bondholders may become stockholders while other bondholders find that they must exchange what they thought were well secured bonds for junior liens or securities on which interest payments are contingent upon earnings. Such periodic losses made it increasingly difficult for railroads in general and certain railroads in particular to find a market for their securities.

Recent trends. As noted above, the ratio of unmatured funded debt actually outstanding, including equipment obligations, to total securities outstanding reached a high point of 57.1 per cent in 1924. In that year line-haul railroads and their lessor subsidiaries had outstanding $9,300,053,287 in capital stock as compared with an outstanding unmatured funded debt, including equipment obligations, of $12,380,730,224. Capital stock and funded debt increased in total amount after 1924, capital stock reaching a maximum of $10,042,761,815 in 1932 and unmatured funded debt a maximum of $12,788,784,664 in the same year. Since, however, capital stock issues increased at a more rapid rate than funded debt, the ratio of unmatured debt to total securities outstanding declined to 56.0 per cent. This ratio continued to decline after 1932, the decline being particularly marked after 1941. At the close of 1945 the ratio of unmatured debt, including equipment obligations, to total securities stood at 49.6 per cent, the first time in many years that outstanding stock exceeded in amount the unmatured funded debt actually outstanding. At the end of 1949 the ratio was 49.7 per cent.[2]

The reduction in funded debt which has taken place since 1932, and particularly since 1941, is traceable partly to involuntary debt reduction resulting from the reorganization of insolvent properties and partly to the energetic efforts of solvent railroads to reduce debt and so reduce fixed charges. Voluntary debt reduction has been accomplished in various ways. In some cases maturing bond issues have been retired without recourse to the earlier practice of refunding. Some bonds with "callable" provisions which permitted the issuing corporation to pay off the principal before maturity have been retired. And in some cases railroads have gone

---

[2] All of the above figures are from *Statistics of Railways in the United States* for the years 1924, 1932, 1946, and 1949.

into the open market and purchased certain of their unmatured obligations which happened to be offered for sale. These operations were made possible partly through the use of money in sinking fund reserves and partly through the use of earnings resulting from the record volume of wartime traffic. In other words, profits which in earlier years might have been distributed to stockholders were now being utilized in part for debt redemption. The Association of American Railroads has estimated that in the years 1941 to 1945 inclusive, a period in which over 53 per cent of the 1932-1946 debt reduction was effected, nearly two-thirds of the reduction resulted from the voluntary efforts of solvent carriers as contrasted with involuntary reductions resulting from railroad reorganization.[3] Regardless of the cause of debt reduction the result has been an improvement in the over-all financial position of the railroads as a whole. Interest accruals of all railroads, a figure which includes interest obligations of all sorts, came to $647,224,000 in 1932 as compared with $396,938,000 in 1949.

Railroads as a whole not overcapitalized. At one time it was common to blame high rates and railroad financial difficulties on general railroad overcapitalization, and this contention is still heard occasionally. While there is no denying the fact that overcapitalization was all too common in the earlier years of railroad transportation, the railroad system as a whole is not overcapitalized today and has not been for a good many years. Thus the $18,342,568,000 of railroad securities actually outstanding at the end of 1949 represented an investment in road and equipment of $29,519,832,000. Reduction in capitalization has been achieved partly through reorganization, partly through the reduction in funded debt already discussed, and partly through the reinvestment of earnings which in earlier years probably would have been passed on to stockholders.

NEED FOR REGULATION OF SECURITY ISSUES

Overcapitalization. Historically the demand for security regulation is closely related to public concern over the evils arising out of overcapitalization, a phenomenon which was all too prevalent during the period of the great expansion of the railroad network. Railroad construction itself contributed in various ways to overcapitalization. The use of the construction company device previously described is a case in point. Again, where risks were great, securities had to be sold at a discount, and in several cases promoters actually gave away common stock as an induce-

---

[3] Subcommittee on Finance, Railroad Committee for the study of Transportation, *Railroad Finance*, Washington: Association of American Railroads, 1947, p. 24.

ment for investors to buy bonds. In other cases promoters sought to finance construction by selling bonds, retaining the common stock as payment for services either real or imaginary. In still other cases insiders purchased land and other properties in advance of construction and then sold these properties to the railroad corporation at inflated prices, thus further contributing to the issuance of excessive amounts of securities.

But overcapitalization did not result from railroad construction activities alone. It resulted at times from the capitalization of such day-by-day expenses as maintenance of way and equipment. Failure to provide for depreciation led to overcapitalization, since the property involved wore out and became valueless without a corresponding decline in amount of outstanding securities. Overcapitalization also resulted from the practice of issuing stock dividends without the corporation having a capitalizable surplus on which to base such dividends. In numerous cases, too, overcapitalization resulted from the railroad combination movement described in Chapter 4 and which sometimes involved the exchange of an excessive amount of the securities of the controlling corporation for the securities of the railroads being purchased. Finally, overcapitalization at times accompanied the reorganization of bankrupt properties. In more than one reorganization the holders of underlying first mortgage bonds were induced to forego their favored position by an offer to exchange a larger face value of less favorable securities for their original holdings, and this naturally led to an increase in capitalization.

Protection of investors. The most obvious reason for regulating the issuance of securities is to protect innocent investors from the consequences of overcapitalization. The Union Pacific had $110,966,812 in securities outstanding at the time of its completion, although the railroad actually cost only $60,467,641 to build. The owners of Union Pacific stock, amounting to $36,762,300, had no real equity in the railroad, and even the bondholders were not fully protected insofar as tangible assets were concerned. When a railroad with a capital structure like this, and there were many of them, found itself unable to meet the claims of its creditors, the inevitable bankruptcy wiped out the common stockholders, and bondholders often found the value of their investments greatly reduced. A classic example of overcapitalization and disregard of the public interest is found in the history of the Erie during the days of its control by Jay Gould and Jim Fiske.[4]

Effect of overcapitalization on rates. The desire to protect investors from the consequences of the activities of irresponsible or fraudulent

---

[4] The amazing story of the financial history of the Erie Railroad has been well told by Charles Francis Adams in his classic *Chapters of Erie*. New York: Henry Holt and Company, 1886.

railroad management is obvious, but it does not of itself explain the demand for the regulation of security issues. Practices similar to those described above were common in other industries, but no large scale protection of investors in general was undertaken until the New Deal legislation of the early 1930's. In some measure the early demand for security regulation arose out of the belief that overcapitalization led to high rates, the idea being that the management of an overcapitalized railroad would seek to maintain solvency by charging rates sufficiently high to pay interest and dividends on its inflated capitalization. The extent to which this was true in the days prior to effective rate regulation is debatable. It has been pointed out that where competition existed rates had to be made to meet this competition, and where monopoly existed railroad management would tend to fix rates in such a way as to yield maximum returns whether a line was overcapitalized or not. In this latter case, however, there was always the temptation for the management of a railroad in desperate financial shape to charge rates which in the long run would be disastrous to it and shippers alike, and no doubt this did happen at times.

The development of the fair return on fair value doctrine, more or less divorced rate making from capitalization. But the 1933 rule of rate making and the opinions of the Supreme Court in the Hope Natural Gas and Natural Gas Pipe Line cases, suggesting a return to utility investors similar to that received by investors in other fields and sufficient to maintain the credit of the regulated enterprise, give capitalization some meaning in connection with rate making. And various writers have pointed out that commissions at times have been influenced in their rate-making activities by the needs of overcapitalized lines even though not legally required to do so.[5]

Effect of overcapitalization on service. While some uncertainty may exist about the effect of overcapitalization on rates, there can be little doubt about its effect on service. In case after case overcapitalized railroads sought to avoid bankruptcy in part by reducing expenses, and this could be done to some extent by giving poorer service on noncompetitive traffic. There also was a tendency to cut costs by skimping on maintenance of equipment and right of way. But undermaintenance only puts off the evil day because eventually the condition of the property becomes such that a costly rehabilitation is necessary if the line is to continue to operate at all. If security regulation can prevent overcapitalization, it is worth while from the service angle alone.

---

[5] See Eliot Jones, *Principles of Railway Transportation.* New York: The Macmillan Company, 1927, pp. 315-317. See also D. Philip Locklin, *Economics of Transportation,* 3rd Ed. Chicago: Richard D. Irwin, Inc., 1947, pp. 576-578.

FINANCE AND FINANCIAL REGULATION

Effect of overcapitalization on new investment. To the extent that overcapitalization brought disaster to early investors, it tended to deter other investors from putting their savings into new railroad securities. Thus by preventing overcapitalization security regulation could improve the market for railroad securities and so promote the future improvement of the industry. The difficulties encountered by railroads in financing improvements in modern times, while not primarily due to overcapitalization, indicate clearly what happens when investors lose faith in the quality of railroad securities.

Stock and bond ratio. As previously mentioned, a substantial part of railroad financing has taken the form of bonds and other types of securities carrying a fixed rate of interest. This has been due in part to the greater ease with which bonds could be sold, in part to the fact that low interest rates made possible larger returns to stockholders, and in part to the desires of promoters to retain control of their railroads with little or no investment of their own funds. But the necessity of meeting large interest payments injects a continuous element of uncertainty into the life of a railroad because of the ease with which it can be thrown into bankruptcy when competition or hard times appear. This may suggest the desirability of security regulation to force the issuance of stocks instead of bonds. Such a proposition is highly academic, however, for as will be brought out presently, no market for railroad stocks exists today.

HISTORICAL DEVELOPMENT

State regulation. As might be expected the regulation of railroad security issues was first undertaken by the states, Massachusetts entering the field in the 1850's with an eye to the welfare of investors. But the real beginning of security regulation dates from the Texas Stock and Bond Law of 1893 which was designed to prevent Texas railroads from charging rates sufficiently high to pay interest and dividends on excessive issues of stocks and bonds. Other states soon followed the lead of Texas, and by the time Congress entered the field in 1920, about half of the states had provided for some form of regulation of railroad security issues. State regulation was far from satisfactory, however, because many states had no laws at all, and those which did differed greatly in the nature and scope of their activities. As far as railroads serving more than one state were concerned the result was wholly unsatisfactory since it was well-nigh impossible to issue securities which would comply with all of the varied requirements of the different states in which they operated.

Demand for federal regulation. There does not seem to have been any great demand for federal regulation of security issues until about 1907. In that year the Interstate Commerce Commission recommended such regulation as a result of its investigations into the financial activities of the Harriman railroad empire, and security regulation entered into the political campaign of 1908. President Taft recommended to Congress the regulation of railroad stock and bond issues in accordance with his party's platform, but the proposal met with almost unanimous opposition in the Senate. The Senate did, however, approve the appointment of a special Railroad Securities Commission to investigate the matter. The President appointed what has been described as an able but distinctly conservative commission, and this commission, under the chairmanship of President Hadley of Yale University, reported late in 1911, recommending publicity as a corrective for financial abuses rather than federal regulation. The Interstate Commerce Commission continued to recommend legislation, and by 1920 the demand for security regulation had become so widespread, and the difficulties of state regulation had become so obvious, that little opposition was voiced to its inclusion in the Transportation Act, 1920.

Powers of Interstate Commerce Commission. As previously noted, the Transportation Act, 1920, makes it unlawful for any railroad to issue its own securities or to assume liabilities with respect to the securities of any other person or corporation without the approval of the Interstate Commerce Commission. Permission to issue securities or to assume obligations is required even though such action is permitted by the laws of the state in which a railroad happens to be incorporated. An exception is made for short term notes of two years duration or less, providing such notes do not in the aggregate exceed 5 per cent of the par value of the securities of the carrier outstanding at the time of issue. The law also provides that the Commission's authority does not extend to street, suburban, or interurban electric railroads not operated as part of a general steam railroad system of transportation.

POLICY OF INTERSTATE COMMERCE COMMISSION

General policy. The law vests the Interstate Commerce Commission with considerable discretionary power in connection with the regulation of security issues. Professor Sharfman, writing in 1935, stated that the Commission had not sought to interfere extensively with the freedom of the carriers in the issuance of securities but had approved the vast bulk of the applications in a more or less routine fashion.[6] Of course,

---

[6] I. L. Sharfman, *The Interstate Commerce Commission*, Part III, Vol. A. New York: The Commonwealth Fund, 1935, p. 506.

the mere fact that the Commission possesses broad powers over security issues operates in itself as a deterrent to unwise activities in the field of finance. It is not to be supposed, however, that the Interstate Commerce Commission approves all applications as a matter of course. In a number of cases it has denied applications, and in others it has imposed certain conditions as a prerequisite to approval of an issue. From its reports on these cases some general observations may be drawn with reference to its policy.

Overcapitalization. The Interstate Commerce Commission generally has followed the policy of limiting the amount of a new issue of securities to the reasonable cost of the improvements to be made or the property to be purchased with the proceeds. Not only does it consider the face value of the proposed issue, but it also concerns itself with the price at which the securities are to be sold and the compensation paid to banking houses for selling them. The Commission also seeks to prevent excessive capital issues in connection with acquisitions of control and conversion or refunding operations.

One of the earliest problems it had to face related to requests to issue securities coming from already overcapitalized railroad corporations. At first thought it might seem wise to require an overcapitalized railroad to take steps to reduce its existing overcapitalization before permitting it to add to its financial obligations, but there have been times when a new capital issue appeared to be necessary to improve service or even to maintain existing service. Indeed, it is possible that contemplated improvements in the property of an overcapitalized railroad might increase its earnings and enable it ultimately to reduce or even eliminate the objectionable overcapitalization. Thus the Commission found on various occasions that if a proposed issue did not in itself produce overcapitalization, there might be good reason for permitting its sale.

Capitalizable v. noncapitalizable assets. A capitalizable asset may be defined as one which has been provided for or is intended to be used in connection with the rendering of transportation service. Conversely, noncapitalizable assets are those assets which are not used in rendering transportation service. In general the Commission has followed a policy of permitting the issuance of securities only where capitalizable assets are concerned. This will not prevent a railroad from investing surplus funds in noncarrier properties or in government obligations, but the Commission does not look with favor upon the issuance of carrier securities to cover such purchases. Obviously the operation of noncarrier properties is beyond the control of the Interstate Commerce Commission, and if carriers were permitted to issue securities based on such investments and the investments did not pay off, it might be difficult for them to meet their obligations in connection with investments made directly in transportation property. In the light of the present rule of rate making and the decisions of the Supreme Court in the Natural Gas Pipe Line and Hope Natural Gas cases such investments could have an effect on rates, too, since the implications of the rule and the judicial decisions is that rates should be sufficient to maintain carrier credit.

The Commission has been called upon from time to time to indicate just when a given investment is or is not capitalizable. It has held that holdings of the capital stock of advertising, mining, timber, and land companies are not capitalizable; and it has held the same with reference to steel company bonds, and federal and municipal obligations. On the other hand, it has stated that ordinarily a carrier which owns stock in another railroad corporation may capitalize such stock if its holdings are necessary and sufficient to give it control of the issuing corporation and if it appears that such control probably will be permanent. Some nice problems have arisen where carriers have purchased the stock of leased lines. Where a line has been leased in perpetuity, the purchase of its stock would not seem to be essential to control, and such stock ordinarily would not be considered a capitalizable asset. Other difficult problems arise when an operating carrier seeks to capitalize permanent improvements it has made on the property of a leased line.

Control of indebtedness. The Interstate Commerce Commission has the power to require the issuance of stocks instead of bonds where either may be used, and in some early cases it made such a requirement. It must be kept in mind, however, that the choice between bonds and stocks is seldom one which carriers have been free to make in recent years. Even in the case of carriers which have been fortunate enough to be able to sell either stocks or bonds opinion has been divided over the extent to which the Commission is justified in interfering with managerial freedom by requiring stocks if management prefers bonds. In view of the fact that the choice between stocks and bonds seldom has existed, in recent years Commission action more commonly has taken the form of cutting down the amount of a proposed bond issue, ordering a reduction in interest rates, or in some other way trying to keep fixed charges in line with anticipated earnings.

Stock dividends. Sometimes a corporation issues additional shares of stock and gives them to its existing stockholders as a dividend. Many corporations finance improvements by using profits which ordinarily would be expected to go to stockholders in the form of cash dividends, and then later on issue additional shares of stock to cover the resultant increase in the value of the property. If a corporation is unusually profitable, it may issue a stock dividend, and then by distributing profits over a large number of shares, its dividends per share will not be so large. In this way its earnings may not appear to be excessive. Where a corporation has a surplus, that surplus is the property of the stockholders, and if the surplus is substantial, the corporation's stock will sell above par on the market. It is said that stocks sell more easily and more nearly at their true value when they sell at or below par, and a stock dividend may be issued to reduce the surplus and so reduce the market value of the stock.

There are various special reasons why railroads at times have wished to issue stock dividends. Certain financial institutions, such as insurance companies and savings banks, are commonly prohibited by law from investing their reserves in the bonds of any railroad which has an excessive proportion of its outstanding securities in the form of funded debt; and in the past railroads sometimes sought to evade such laws by issuing stock dividends in order to increase the ratio of stocks to bonds and so make their bonds eligible for purchase by financial institutions. Stock dividends also have been proposed in connection with consolidation proceedings in which the stocks of the lines to be consolidated were to be exchanged for stock in a new corporation. If the stock of one railroad corporation was selling at par and the other at more than par, it might be in the interest of the holders of the stock of the latter to issue a stock dividend which would bring the market price down to par. In this way the stocks of both corporations could be exchanged on a par-for-par basis, with the owners of the stronger line benefiting.

The late Joseph B. Eastman, long-time member of the Interstate Commerce Commission, was a persistent opponent of the issuance of stock dividends by railroad corporations subject to Interstate Commerce Commission jurisdiction. He dismissed the various arguments offered in favor of stock dividends as either superficial or as designed to benefit stockholders without reference to the broad public interest. He pointed out that a substantial reserve strengthens the financial position of a carrier and enables it to issue additional securities under favorable terms if it should become desirable to do so at some later time. In general it may be said that the Interstate Commerce Commission has recognized that the issuance of stock dividends is an accepted practice in the field of corporate finance and has sought to avoid interference with managerial discretion in this respect. The Commission has insisted that if a surplus is to be capitalized, however, it must be a real surplus and not the result of questionable accounting practices. Furthermore, the surplus to be capitalized must represent capitalizable as distinguished from noncapitalizable assets. And finally, it has held that a substantial surplus must remain on the books after the stock distribution has been made.

Reorganizations. If a railroad corporation is unable to meet the claims of its creditors as they come due, it may be declared bankrupt and a financial reorganization effected. Such a reorganization will involve the substitution of new securities for some or all of the old securities, and these new securities must be approved by the Interstate Commerce Commission. This procedure would seem to offer the Commission an opportunity to remove any existing overcapitalization and to insist that fixed charges be within the range of probable future earnings. Before 1933, however, the Interstate Commerce Commission had no voice in the reorganization of bankrupt railroads, and this proved to be a serious handicap to it in connection with its approval or disapproval of the securities proposed to be issued. Since 1933 this difficulty has been removed, and the Commission is now in a much better position to direct the financial reorganization of railroads than was formerly the case. Its policies in this connection can be discussed more intelligently, however, in connection with the whole problem of railroad receivership and reorganization discussed in the next chapter.

Competitive bidding. Large corporations like railroads find it desirable as a rule to sell new issues of securities through investment banking concerns rather than directly to the public. Since the typical corporation issues and sells securities only at infrequent intervals, it would be difficult and impractical for it to establish and maintain contacts with individual investors throughout the country. Furthermore, a corporation sometimes needs money in a hurry, and it might require a considerable period of time for it to contact enough potential investors to dispose of a given issue, particularly if it were a rather sizable one. Investment banking concerns, however, make it their business to keep in contact with buyers of corporate securities. They maintain offices in large cities and have contacts with local investment dealers and banks, which in turn have regular lists of customers. While the issuing corporation must pay the investment banker a commission for his services, the net return to the corporation easily may be greater than if it attempted to sell its securities directly to the public. Furthermore, investment bankers may advance the money required by the corporation or agree to sell the securities within a specified period of time, thus assuring prompt provision of the necessary funds.

There are a number of large investment banking concerns in the United States, and these concerns naturally compete with one another in offering their services to corporations desirous of disposing of new issues of securities. Several banks may be asked to bid on a given issue, the idea being that the one offering to pay the highest price for the securities, or to undertake to sell them for the smallest commission, will get the business. Until recently, however, this competition between investment banking concerns did not exist as far as the disposal of railroad securities was concerned. As a general rule each carrier associated itself with a single banking firm and came to depend upon this firm regularly and uniformly for financial advice and for the sale of its securities. Two firms, Morgan Stanley and Co. and Kuhn, Loeb, and Co., handled the great bulk of railroad financing, each serving a separate group of railroads. This practice was defended on the ground that expert advice is necessary in the marketing of railroad securities, and to give such advice requires an intimate knowledge of a given railroad's financial structure as well as the likes and dislikes of investors. Presumably all of this would require a continued and close association between a given railroad and its banking firm. The practice was also said to be necessary because competitive bidding takes time and to depend upon it might involve a hazardous delay in obtaining funds.

A number of years ago a vigorous attack on the lack of competition in the sale of railroad securities developed. Proponents of competitive bidding, including the Chesapeake & Ohio Railroad and the banking firm of Halsey, Stuart, and Co., argued that railroads could increase the yield from the sale of their securities if they were offered to banking houses on the basis of competitive bidding. It was also alleged that the railroads failed to obtain competitive bids because of a monopoly of railroad financing exercised by the two dominant banking concerns in this field, which monopoly was maintained and perpetuated by banker domination of railroad financing.

Taking cognizance of these complaints, the Interstate Commerce Commission undertook an investigation of the matter of disposing of new railroad securities, and in 1944 issued a report and order covering this matter.[7] The Commission failed to find persuasive evidence of the existence of a conspiracy on the part of the big bankers to eliminate competition in the sale of railroad securities, but neither did it find that a railroad's need for financial advice necessitated a more or less permanent association with a single banking concern. The Commission concluded that probably a net financial gain would accrue to the railroads if competitive bidding were required in connection with the choice of a banking house to dispose of a given issue of securities. Consequently an order was issued requiring competitive bidding in the marketing of railroad securities with certain exceptions. Among the more important exceptions are common and preferred stocks, short term securities with a maturity not exceeding three years, issues not in excess of $1,000,000, certain intercarrier sales

---

[7] *In Re Competitive Bidding in Sale of Securities*, 257 I.C.C. 129.

FINANCE AND FINANCIAL REGULATION

and exchanges, and any issue where the Commission deems competitive bidding unnecessary or unsatisfactory.

SUGGESTED READINGS

Bigham, Truman C., *Transportation, Principles and Problems*. New York: McGraw-Hill Book Company, Inc., 1946. Chapter 19.

Jones, Eliot, *Principles of Railway Transportation*. New York: The Macmillan Company, 1924. Chapter XVI.

Locklin, D. Philip, *Economics of Transportation*, 3rd Ed. Chicago: Richard D. Irwin, Inc., 1947. Chapter XXIV.

Railroad Committee for the Study of Transportation, *Railroad Finance*. Washington: Association of American Railroads, 1947.

Sharfman, I. L., *The Interstate Commerce Commission*, Part III, Vol. A. New York: The Commonwealth Fund, 1935.

15

Receivership
and
REORGANIZATION OF RAILROADS

EXTENT AND CAUSES OF RAILROAD FAILURES

Extent of railroad failures. Statistics on the total number of railroad failures in the United States are not available for the earlier years, but since 1872 there have been well over a thousand such failures.[1] As might be expected the number of railroad failures follows closely the line of the business cycle, rising during years of depression and falling in times of prosperity. In the single year of 1893 there were 119 failures involving more than 15 per cent of the total railroad mileage, and the effect of the 1929 depression on railroad failures has been pointed out in an earlier chapter. While the number of receiverships occurring in any one year has not been large in modern times, the mileage involved has been great. On July 31, 1939, there were 108 companies operating 76,703 miles of railroads in the hands of the courts. This represented 31 per cent of the total railroad mileage of the country, an all time high.[2] Not many railroads can boast that they have never had a financial failure, and some have failed two and three and even more times.

Early causes of failure. Earlier writers have listed the principal causes of railroad failures as overexpansion, excessive competition, overcapitalization, and such things as speculation, mismanagement, and fraud. Overexpansion, of course, hardly can be listed as a cause of railroad failure today. Effective regulation has eliminated excessive competition between railroads so that this, too, is no longer a major cause of railroad failures. While individual railroads may still suffer from overcapitalization, the railroads as a whole are not now overcapitalized. The Interstate Commerce Commission can function in various ways to restrict speculation and fraud and, to some extent, mismanagement. Thus the early causes of railroad failures either have been eliminated or brought under control and are

---

[1] For data on failures see Henry M. Swain, "Economic Aspects of Railroad Receiverships," *American Economic Association Studies,* Vol. 3, No. 2 (1898); Stuart Daggett, "Recent Railroad Failures and Reorganizations," *Quarterly Journal of Economics,* Vol. 32, p. 446 (1918); and Interstate Commerce Commission, *Annual Report,* various years.

[2] Interstate Commerce Commission, *Annual Report,* 1940, p. 20.

not of major concern today, except to the extent that the financial structures of certain railroads still may show the effects of some of these early
difficulties.

Modern causes of railroad failures. The causes of railroad failures in
recent years are not too difficult to analyze. In some measure, as suggested above, they reflect the influence of policies adopted and obligations
assumed in the days before the Interstate Commerce Commission was
given the power to regulate railroad finance. The Erie, for example,
continued to suffer the consequences of its financial mismanagement by
Jay Gould and Jim Fiske long after those two gentlemen had passed out
of the picture. The same may be said for the Missouri Pacific, the Rock
Island, the New Haven, and other splendid modern railroad systems which
have had to fight an uphill battle to overcome the consequences of early
financial mismanagement and even fraud.

The agricultural situation of the 1920's and the general drying up of
traffic following the stock market collapse of 1929 often are cited as
the cause of the extensive failures which took place during the 1930's.
Situations like these, of course, reflect the vulnerability of any business
characterized by substantial elements of fixed cost to business depressions.
By the same token, however, such businesses should be quite profitable
during periods of good times and if managed properly, should be able
to set aside susbtantial reserves to provide for hard times. The ability of
the railroads to follow such a policy was limited during the 1920's, however, by the rule of rate making which provided for the recapture of
half of any earnings in excess of a fair return on fair value, and by the
policy of the Interstate Commerce Commission in keeping rates down to
the point where in only one year did earnings even approximate the fair
return on fair value provided for in the Transportation Act, 1920.

Since 1929 the threat of competition from motor, water, and air carriers
has been added to the threat of depression as a cause of railroad failures.
It is true that these agencies of transportation have been subjected to
regulation to a greater or lesser extent, and the Interstate Commerce
Commission and the Civil Aeronautics Board have sought to prevent
excessive competition from developing among each of the newer agencies.
But the fact remains that there has been a substantial increase in the
total amount of transportation service available, and the country now has
a greater supply of transportation service than it probably can support
under normal circumstances. On top of this there has been a rapid rise
in recent years in private transportation as more and more industries are
finding it economical to acquire their own equipment and haul their
own goods over the public highways and waterways. Unless Congress
does something to reduce or eliminate uneconomic interagency competi-

tion and bring the supply of transportation facilities into some sort of balance with the need for such facilities, continued failures are inevitable.

EQUITY RECEIVERSHIPS

Procedure. When a business finds itself in financial difficulties its creditors may appear before a court of law alleging that the business is unable to meet its obligations and ask the court to appoint a receiver to safeguard their interests. If such a receiver is appointed, he assumes control of the property, which he may continue to operate as a going concern or which he may close down pending a final decision on what disposition is to be made of it. Ultimately the court will offer the assets of the business for sale, usually to the highest bidder, either piecemeal or as a unit, and the proceeds of this sale will then be distributed among the creditors. If the proceeds are insufficient to meet their claims in full, they will have to be satisfied with pro rata shares, while if the proceeds are more than enough to meet these claims, the balance will be distributed among the original owners. If the property is purchased as a unit, the new owners may decide to continue operation of the business, or they may dispose of the property as they see fit. This whole procedure is known as an equity receivership.

Before 1933, at which time some major changes were made in the law, railroads were reorganized under equity receiverships, but the procedure was not quite the same as outlined above because of the need to provide for uninterrupted operation. The public interest requires that a railroad operate continuously, and since 1920 the abandonment of operations in interstate commerce has not been permitted without the approval of the Interstate Commerce Commission. Furthermore, a railroad property deteriorates rapidly when not in use, shippers must turn to other railroads or other means of transportation, and as a result a shutdown may be disastrous to possible future operations. Consequently when a railroad found itself in financial difficulties with a default of interest or principal on its funded debt in prospect, its directors got a friendly creditor to appear before a court and allege that the railroad owed him money which it could not pay. Having admitted this, the railroad management asked for the appointment of a receiver to take over the property. Otherwise, holders of various mortgage bonds might choose to foreclose on their mortgages, and without the property covered by these mortgages, the railroad might not be able to continue to operate.

If the court found the allegations to be correct, it appointed one or more receivers to operate the property for it, thus assuring continued operation. If the receiver or receivers found the property in a run-down condition they had to take steps to raise funds for at least a minimum of rehabilitation. To some extent such funds could be obtained by withholding interest on the bankrupt railroad's bonds, but principal reliance was placed on the sale of receivers' certificates. Naturally such securities had to be given some preference over other claims, since it would be difficult to sell them without some such protection. While rehabilitation was going forward under the guidance of the receivers, the bankrupt railroad's security holders organized committees to look after their interests, and representatives of these various committees combined to form an over-all reorganization committee.

Since the railroad usually was in financial difficulties because of an inability to meet fixed charges, one of the major functions of any reorganization committee was to reduce excessive fixed charges. As a rule this meant an exchange of some or all of the outstanding bonds for new bonds bearing a lower face value, a lower rate of interest, or both. If the value of the property was equal to or greater than the amount of the mortgages underlying the first mortgage bonds, the holders of these bonds might be able to hold out for full protection of their interests, but holders of junior issues invariably had to make sacrifices. To compensate junior bondholders for this sacrifice it was not uncommon to give them a certain number of shares of common or preferred stock or even fixed obligations of the income bond type on which interest was payable only if earned. By making such sacrifices junior bondholders were able to protect at least a part of their investment whereas they might stand to lose everything if the holders of the first mortgage bonds insisted on eventual foreclosure.

In addition to taking steps to reduce fixed charges the reorganization committee had to work out some means of obtaining funds to settle claims for unpaid wages, invoices for supplies and equipment, bank loans, and other similar debts existing at the time of foreclosure. Also, funds had to be raised to pay off the receivers' certificates after the line had been reorganized, to provide the new corporation with working capital, to pay for the expenses of reorganization, and to pay off any claims of security holders who did not wish to participate in the reorganization. The most practical means of raising such funds was by the assessment of security holders, and insofar as possible assessments were levied against the stockholders. Stockholders were not required by law to pay assessments, however, and in many cases they no doubt found it preferable to simply write off their claims as a total loss rather than to pay anything more than a small assessment. If not enough money could be obtained in this way from the stockholders, then the junior bondholders might be assessed. Seldom, however, were the holders of first mortgage bonds expected to pay an assessment since they could usually satisfy the full amount of their claims by eventually foreclosing on their mortgages.

When a majority of the various security holders' agreed upon a reorganization plan, the court set a minimum or "upset" price on the property and offered it for sale to the highest bidder. Almost invariably the only bidder was the reorganization committee, since the court required payment in cash or in the railroad's bonds, and the reorganization committee controlled the majority of such bonds. Any bondholder or other creditor who did not approve of the reorganization plan was paid his pro rata share of the purchase price, and the property then passed into the hands of the reorganization committee. This committee then conveyed the property to a new corporation organized for the purpose, the old security holders exchanged their holdings for securities in the new corporation, and the new corporation assumed control of the property. If anything remained after providing for the interests of creditors and bondholders, it would be used to protect the interests of the stockholders of the original corporation. Often, however, there was nothing left, and the original stockholders lost out completely unless they had acquired some claims as a result of paying the assessments mentioned above.

OBJECTIONS TO EQUITY RECEIVERSHIPS

Delay in reorganization. The equity receivership was used in railroad reorganizations for a hundred years, during which time various abuses and inequities developed and led eventually to a change in the law. One of the minor criticisms made of the procedure was the time that it took to effect a reorganization. The larger railroads, and particularly those which had been built up through the purchase of units already mortgaged at the time of their acquisition, had extremely complex financial structures, with securities involving all sorts of overlapping claims which were difficult to resolve. Extended litigation developed at times between different groups of security owners, each trying to protect its own interests. Small minorities sometimes contributed to delay by refusing to accept what appeared to be a satisfactory reorganization plan, hoping by this obstructionism to gain some special advantage for themselves. In the early 1920's railroad receiverships were said to average three years in duration, but there were many cases involving much longer periods. These extended receiverships were unfair to security holders who were deprived of any return on their investment during the period of receivership.

Expense. A second criticism of equity receiverships was the inordinately heavy cost of some of the proceedings, which cost was levied against security holders or charged against the property of the bankrupt railroad. The receivers appointed by the courts received a substantial remuneration. Reorganization managers, usually banking concerns, were employed at considerable expense to arrange the reorganization. Counsel for the receivers, for the reorganization managers, and for the various security holders' protective committees also received large fees, all chargeable against the property or the security holders. Litigation between various claimants, sometimes involved and expensive, usually was chargeable against the property. In some cases the participants appear to have had a financial stake in prolonging the receivership as long as possible. Thus the very procedure designed to conserve the assets of a bankrupt corporation was used at times to the detriment of the individuals whose interests the proceedings were supposed to protect.

Conflicting jurisdictions. An application for the appointment of a receiver was made in either a state or a federal court, more commonly in a federal court. If a railroad operated in or had property located in states or federal judicial districts other than the one in which the application was made, as would be the case with all large railroad systems, auxiliary suits had to be entered in each of these other states or judicial districts. Receivers were appointed by each of the various courts involved, although customarily the receiver or receivers selected by the court in the original action also were appointed to handle these auxiliary receiverships. Conflicting interests sometimes developed, however, which unduly complicated the process of reorganization.

Inequitable reorganization plans. The individuals who took the initiative in organizing committees to protect various classes of security holders sometimes had special interests of their own which ran counter to the interests of the security holders they were supposed to represent. Usually the individual security holder had to accept the plan set up by the dominant reorganization committee or take his share in the upset price. But often the upset price was so low as not really to constitute an alternative. In the Milwaukee receivership the reorganization was effected by the insolvent line's former bankers and actually resulted in the stockholders being favored at the expense of bondholders. In this case the reorganization plan left the original stockholders in control of the railroad even though its difficulties had been due in part to faulty management, for which these same stockholders were responsible.[3]

Protection of majorities and minorities. Sharply divergent views existed as to the extent to which the interests of majorities and minorities were protected in equity receiverships. Some argued that if the holders of the majority of a given type of security agreed upon a plan of reorganization,

---

[3] *Chicago, Milwaukee & St. Paul Reorganization,* 131 I.C.C. 673 (1928).

their decision should bind all holders of that particular security. In other words, it was contended that a minority should not be permitted to obstruct a plan acceptable to the majority. On the other hand, minority interests sometimes claimed that they were compelled to accept a re-organization plan whether it was in their interest or not because their only other alternative was to accept their share of the low upset price.

Inadequate jurisdiction by the Interstate Commerce Commission. One of the chief criticisms of equity receiverships was the fact that the Inter-state Commerce Commission had no direct voice in the reorganization proceedings. Equity receiverships were initiated in the courts. Reorgan-ization plans were worked out by committees supposedly representing the interests of the various security holders, and these plans were subject only to approval by the courts. Once this approval was obtained the plan went into effect and the new railroad corporation assumed control, except that after 1920 approval of the Interstate Commerce Commission had to be obtained before the new corporation could issue the securities agreed upon by the reorganization committees and the courts.

The task of the Commission in deciding whether or not to approve the securities which the new corporation proposed to issue was a peculiarly difficult one. In reorganization proceedings the courts were concerned primarily with the protection of the rights of various security holders, as were the various committees which had a hand in planning a reorgan-ization. The Commission, on the other hand, was concerned primarily with the public interest in the maintenance of a sound and adequate transportation service, and there was no necessary immediate relationship between protecting the public interest and protecting the equities of certain groups of security holders. Consequently the Interstate Commerce Commission was sometimes called upon to pass on proposed security issues which, while they might be of such a nature as to protect existing equities, were highly questionable from the point of view of sound transportation. While the Commission could refuse to approve a proposed issue of securities, it was reluctant to do so because refusal would have meant further extended and costly delay as the interested parties did their work all over again. Obviously what was needed was some arrangement whereby the Commission could pass on reorganization plans before they were finally completed and presented to the courts for approval.

SECTION 77

Background. For a few years following the stock market crash of 1929 a number of railroads were able to maintain an appearance of solvency by borrowing from the Reconstruction Finance Corporation and the

Railroad Credit Corporation, but it is perfectly obvious that a railroad in financial difficulties cannot borrow its way out of trouble during a period of declining traffic. Widespread recognition of the serious plight of many railroads brought to a head the criticisms of equity receiverships and led to the adoption of a new law in 1933. A new Section 77 was added to the Federal Bankruptcy Act of 1898, and it is common to speak of the proceedings under the 1933 law as Section 77 proceedings. The 1933 law was amended in 1935 and again in 1936, but it is not important to make a distinction between these various amendments. Section 77 did not repeal the earlier procedure and it was still possible for a creditor to apply to the courts to initiate a reorganization in the form of an equity receivership, but if this was done, the railroad or another creditor could act to have the case handled under Section 77. Between 1933 and 1948 the majority of reorganization proceedings were handled in accordance with the provisions in Section 77. In 1948 an entirely new law was enacted, as will be pointed out presently, but reorganizations can still be effected under the provisions of Section 77.

Initial procedure. Under Section 77 a railroad in financial difficulties may file a petition in court asking for a reorganization. Such a petition must state that the railroad corporation is insolvent or that it is unable to meet its debt as it matures. Creditors of the railroad also have the privilege of filing a petition, providing they have claims totaling 5 per cent or more of the corporation's indebtedness. In either case the petition is filed in the federal court in whose jurisdiction the principal executive or operating office of the railroad has been located for the greater part of the preceding six months, and a copy of the petition must be filed with the Interstate Commerce Commission at the same time. The court then holds a hearing and if the petition is approved, it assumes control over the entire railroad and appoints one or more trustees to administer the property and operate the line. If a trustee is appointed who has been connected with the insolvent railroad, as is often the case, an additional trustee or trustees must be appointed who have had no such connection. All such appointments must be approved by the Interstate Commerce Commission which also fixes the maximum compensation of the trustees.

Reorganization procedure. After approval of the reorganization petition by the court, the railroad is given six months in which to file a plan of reorganization with the court, and plans also may be filed by trustees, creditors, and stockholders. Copies of all plans are sent to the Interstate Commerce Commission, and hearings are then held by the Commission. After these hearings are concluded, the Commission may approve of one of the plans or it may approve of a plan in a modified form, or if none of the plans seem to be satisfactory, it may propose a plan of its own. Before giving its approval to any plan the Commission must find that it is equitable to the various classes of creditors and stockholders and also is in the public interest. Contemplated fixed charges must be within the probable earning capacity of the company, and various other requirements are provided. Once a plan is approved the Commission certifies it to the court having jurisdiction over the proceedings. If the court is not satisfied with the plan as proposed by the Commission, it is returned to the Commission for further consideration and modification.

If the court accepts the Commission's plan, it is submitted to the corporation's creditors and stockholders for their approval, and approval by the holders of two-thirds of the total amount of any security is sufficient to bind any who do not vote. In this connection, however, if the Commission has found that the interests of any group of creditors, or of the stockholders, have no value, their approval is not required. Nor is the approval of any group required if the Commission has found that the interests of that group, possibly the holders of first mortgage bonds, are fully protected by the plan approved.

Once approval has been obtained from the holders of two-thirds of each group of securities having an interest in the reorganization, the court approves of the plan. If the plan happens not to receive approval of all parties at interest, the court may still approve the plan if the judge finds that it provides fair and equitable treatment of the various parties involved. Final confirmation of the plan by the court is binding on all creditors and stockholders, even on minorities who have withheld their approval. There is no fixing of an upset price followed by a sale at foreclosure to a new corporation as was true under the old equity receiverships. The plan is simply put into effect by order of the court, the trustees dismissed, and the corporation resumes control of its property. Fees of trustees and counsel and all other expense of reorganization must be paid by the railroad corporation, but the Interstate Commerce Commission fixes maximum reasonable limits for these expenses.

Advantages of Section 77 proceedings. The various ways in which the new law was designed to overcome the objections to equity receiverships are more or less self-evident from the provisions of the law itself. The problem of divided and conflicting jurisdictions was eliminated by making a single court responsible for the entire proceedings regardless of the fact that a railroad may be located in more than one state or judicial district. Any tendency to milk bankrupt properties by charging excessive reorganization fees was restricted by empowering the Interstate Commerce Commission to fix maximum limits on reorganization expenses. By making approval of the Commission a prerequisite to the approval of any plan of reorganization, some assurance was given that the public interest would be protected along with the interests of security holders. This same approval made it much more difficult for special interests to dominate reorganization proceedings and so, in effect, force security holders to accept proposals which were not in their own interest. And perhaps as important as anything, the Commission was able to insist upon a sound financial structure for the reorganized company. No longer was it in the unenviable position of having to pass upon a financial structure after the reorganization plan had been effected and approved by the courts. There was also some hope that railroad reorganizations would be speeded up and that a greater opportunity might exist for stockholders to retain an interest in the business.

EXPERIENCE WITH SECTION 77

Policy of Interstate Commerce Commission. In its annual report for the year ending November 1, 1948, the Interstate Commerce Commission stated that fifty-six proceedings had been instituted under the provisions of Section 77 since its enactment, and that reorganization had been completed in twenty-seven cases and proceedings discontinued in fourteen cases, leaving fifteen cases in process of settlement at the end of 1948.[4]

The plans which were approved reveal certain significant facts with regard to Commission policy under the increased powers accorded it by the new law. A study made of the twenty-nine Section 77 plans approved (but not necessarily put into effect) at the end of 1944 showed a reduction of 45 per cent in funded debt and a 78 per cent reduction in fixed charges. Practically all of the first mortgage bonds provided for in the approved plans carried a fixed rate of interest, but second mortgage bonds were of the income type on which interest is paid only if earned. In practically all cases the terms of issue permitted the corporation to redeem its bonds before their maturity date in the event that earnings permitted such redemption. In a good many cases, too, provision was made for the establishment of sinking funds to be used to redeem bonds at maturity, thus avoiding the old practice of refunding rather than retiring debt at maturity.[5]

In principle, the Commission's insistence on substantial reductions in funded debt and fixed charges was commendable, since it should enable the reorganized corporation to weather future declines in traffic in a somewhat better fashion than was true during the years following the

---

[4] Interstate Commerce Commission, *Annual Report*, 1948, p. 27.

[5] *National Transportation Inquiry*, Report of the Special Subcommittee on Transportation of the Committee on Interstate and Foreign Commerce, Part 2, 79th Congress, 2nd Session, House Report No. 2735, p. 327.

1929 collapse. In certain other respects, however, Section 77 and the Commission's application of its provisions was subject to rather severe criticism.

Delay. A striking feature of the practical application of Section 77 has been the length of time required to effect reorganizations under its provisions. As already mentioned, there had been some hope that its use might have some effect in speeding up the reorganization of bankrupt railroads, but in actual practice the reverse proved to be the case. Most of the proceedings under Section 77 were initiated in the early 1930's, but it was not until the years immediately after World War II that any substantial number of important reorganizations were effected. The Rock Island reorganization required over fourteen years, the St. Louis-San Francisco a similar period, and others an even longer time. These long periods of delay have been criticized on the ground that security holders still having a financial stake in the operation of the railroad were being deprived of any return on their investment for an unreasonable length of time.

It should be pointed out, however, that responsibility for these extended delays does not rest altogether on the shoulders of the Interstate Commerce Commission. The necessity of "passing the ball" back and forth between the courts and the Commission is understandably time consuming. It also has been pointed out that the procedure required the parties at interest to deal with each other at arm's length and that there was no opportunity for them to negotiate with each other and agree on a compromise such as could be done under equity receivership proceedings. Furthermore, it must be kept in mind that many of these reorganizations involved large railroad systems with complex capital structures and overlapping claims, and the working out of an equitable arrangement under such conditions is bound to be time consuming. Finally, most of these proceedings were initiated in the early years of a long drawn out depression. It stands to reason that if a reorganized railroad is to have any chance at success, there must be some reasonable prospect that it will be able to meet its fixed charges in the foreseeable future, but with so much uncertainty about what traffic might be in prospect it was extremely difficult to forecast future earnings.

Excessive reductions in capitalization. The difficulties inherent in forecasting traffic trends did not, of course, relieve the Commission of the necessity of making such forecasts. In practice the Commission sought to relate the capitalization and the capital structure of a railroad in process of reorganization to reasonably prospective future earnings and refused to permit capitalizations and capital structures which in its opinion could not be supported by prospective earnings in the foreseeable future. Since the Commission's estimates tended to be somewhat on the pessimistic side, the result was in most cases a very substantial reduction in total capitalization, a reduction in total interest payments, and the substitution of contingent interest payments for fixed payments where practical. Reductions in capitalization were effected in most cases by completely wiping out the original common stock and to a considerable extent the preferred stock as well. In addition, some reductions were made in the face value of the old funded debt, replacing it partly with common and preferred stock and partly with income bonds or other types of securities inferior to those originally issued.

Railroad spokesmen and others have contended that the reductions in capitalization were unnecessarily drastic and threatened the ability of the railroads to obtain adequate financing in the future. It is easy to see how reductions in capitalization and fixed charges which are effected by wiping out the original stockholders and substantially scaling down creditor interests might operate to destroy the confidence of investors in railroad securities and so make the acquisition of needed additional capital from private sources increasingly difficult. On the other hand, it is just possible that smaller capitalizations and reduced fixed charges might make investments in reorganized railroad corporations rather more attractive, provided the lines themselves had reasonably sound traffic potentialities. While it is true that rail securities have not been in favor with investors for some time, this is due as much to relatively low earnings, and, to governmental policy encouraging the development of other forms of transportation, as it is to dissatisfaction with sharp reductions in capitalization and fixed charges following upon railroad reorganizations.

Destruction of stockholders' equities. It was hoped that reorganization effected under Section 77 would enable the original stockholder owners to retain some interest in the reorganized property instead of being eliminated as had often happened under equity receivership proceedings. As pointed out, however, the sharp reductions in capitalization insisted upon by the Interstate Commerce Commission generally resulted in wiping out stockholders' equities, and certain possible consequences of this policy are worth noting.

If stockholder equities are completely wiped out in reorganization proceedings, railroads are going to find it exceedingly difficult to sell further issues of capital stock, and in fact very little such stock has been sold for a good many years. This means that necessary improvements in railroad plant and equipment can be obtained only by reinvesting earnings or increasing the funded debt. But over the years earnings have not been sufficient to support any substantial improvement program, and in any event the reinvestment of earnings must be in some degree at the expense of stockholders, thus making sales of stock even less attractive as an immediate source of new capital. Any increase in funded debt means an increase in fixed charges, but heavy fixed charges are productive of trouble in times of financial stress. Sound financing requires that more emphasis be placed on the sale of stock and less emphasis on the sale of securities which tend to increase fixed charges, but it is hard to see how such financing can be achieved in the face of the repeated wiping out of stockholders' equities in reorganization proceedings.

One very interesting consequence of wiping stockholder interests has been a shift of the ownership and management function to individuals whose former interest in the railroads was simply that of a creditor. As mentioned previously, reductions in capitalization have been effected in part by reductions in the face value of the funded debt, and reductions in fixed charges have been effected by reduced interest rates and the substitution of contingent for fixed interest payments, and to offset these reductions in creditor claims it has been common to give the bondholders varying numbers of shares of common and preferred stock. Thus the ownership of a number of railroads has passed into the hands of individuals who presumably are not interested in assuming the responsibility of running a railroad. What effect this will have on management is somewhat uncertain.

Wartime earnings. Unquestionably a great deal of the criticism which developed with regard to reductions in capitalization and fixed charges was the result of the improved financial status of the railroads during World War II. As already mentioned, most of the proceedings under Section 77 were initiated during the early years of the depression, and many reorganization plans were worked out and approved by the Commission at a time when considerable uncertainty existed about the prospective earnings of the reorganized properties. In some cases financial plans worked out in the thirties were put into effect in spite of the greatly improved earnings of the war period. Of course, one reason for this was the belief that the heavy war traffic was of a temporary nature and that reorganizations should be effected in such a way as to assure some reasonable prospect of successful operation in the postwar period.

It has seemed to many people that in recent years the earnings of some railroads in process of reorganization have been sufficiently high to provide for a composition of debts without sacrificing original stockholders. The Cotton Belt, for example, faced with a maturing debt of $24 million, requested reorganization at the end of 1935, and subsequently the Interstate Commerce Commission approved of a capital reduction which would have wiped out all the line's common and preferred stock. Yet by the middle of 1947 the Cotton Belt had piled up such substantial earnings that it was able to pay off all back interest and $12 million on the principal of its funded debt. Its stock has been preserved intact, and if it can continue to reduce its funded debt out of earnings, it should be in good shape to weather future storms.

SUBSEQUENT DEVELOPMENTS

Chandler Act. In 1939 the Federal Bankruptcy Act was amended to provide for the adjustment of financial difficulties of a seemingly temporary nature without resort to an equity receivership or to a reorganization under Section 77. It sometimes happens that a railroad is unable to meet certain obligations, such as a maturing bond issue, although it would appear that if given time, the obligation could be met. The Chandler Act provided that if a carrier was not in need of major reorganization and the holders of two-thirds of the claims affected approved, a modification of its debts could be effected without its being declared bankrupt. The proposed plan had to meet with the approval of the Interstate Commerce Commission and the courts and had to be accepted by creditors holding more than three-fourths of the claims involved before it could be put into operation. The act provided that all such plans must be initiated by the end of July 1940, but it was reenacted in 1942 to run to November 1, 1945, at the end of which time it expired.

Hobbs Bill. Dissatisfaction with the way in which the Interstate Commerce Commission pared down capitalizations in reorganization proceedings, largely at the expense of stockholders, led to the introduction in the 79th Congress of the Hobbs Bill. This bill specified that the capitalization of any railroad reorganized under the provisions of Section 77 must not be less than the capitalization at the time reorganization proceedings were initiated. Furthermore, it provided that the court in which the case was brought in the first instance could make an independent review of the reorganization plan approved by the Interstate Commerce Commission. While the desire to protect stockholders from any unnecessary destruction of their equities is understandable, it may be doubted that such a rigid tying of the hands of the Commission is desirable. The Hobbs Bill was passed by the House, but it was opposed by Senator Wheeler of the Senate Interstate Commerce Committee and was never approved by the latter body.

Public Law 478. Quite apart from any dissatisfaction with the Interstate Commerce Commission's administration of Section 77, it had come to be recognized that railroad reorganization through the established judicial processes of receivership or trusteeship was not the solution to the financial problems of many railroads. It was recognized that the existing procedures provided about the only solution for individual railroads faced with a permanent loss of traffic or suffering from a burdensome financial structure. On the other hand, in the words of the Commission

... the approach of financial hardship may be anticipated by the management in many instances well in advance of the time when litigation becomes necessary. In such circumstances sound policy calls for procedure that will afford opportunity for free negotiation between railroads and their security holders with a view to avoiding insolvency.[6]

The movement for a new and simplified reorganization procedure ultimately led to the adoption in 1948 of Public Law 478 which added a Section 20b to the Interstate Commerce Act. Section 20b makes it lawful for a railroad, with the approval and authorization of the Interstate Commerce Commission, to alter or modify any provision of any class or classes of its securities or of any mortgage, indenture, deed of trust, corporate charter, or other instrument pursuant to which any class of its obligations is secured. The alteration of equipment obligations, alone, is not permitted.

Proceedings of this type are instituted by the carrier filing an application directly with the Interstate Commerce Commission, and if the Commission, after a hearing, finds that the proposal is in the public interest, the carrier's interest, in the interests of each class of stockholders and other security holders involved, and will not harm the interests of creditors not affected, it may cause the carrier to submit the proposal to the holders of the affected classes of securities for acceptance or rejection. If the holders of at least three-fourths of the total principal amount or number of shares outstanding of each of the affected classes of securities approve the proposal, the Commission is required to issue an order authorizing the changes.

The law further provides that the Commission may approve an application from carriers which were in equity receivership or in the process of reorganization under Section 77 on the date of enactment of the law if permission for such application is granted by the court before which the proceedings are pending. This part of the law, however, does not apply to carriers which have reached the final stages of reorganization under equity receivership or under the provisions of Section 77. If permission to file an application under the new procedure is granted, the earlier proceedings are suspended, and if a new plan is approved, the court is to take steps to dismiss the original proceedings. If the proposal is withdrawn or if the Commission fails to approve of the proposal within one year, the

---

[6] Interstate Commerce Commission, *Annual Report*, 1947, p. 26.

equity receivership or reorganization proceedings under Section 77 are to be resumed.

It will be noted that Public Law 478 is similar in some respects to the Chandler Act previously described, but it differs from that act in certain vital respects. The Chandler Act was limited to railroads which were solvent at the time of application, had been solvent for at least ten years previous to the application, and which were not about to be declared insolvent. Furthermore, the applicant had to show that his difficulties were of a temporary nature. All of these restrictions are eliminated in Public Law 478, which may be applied even to railroads already in the hands of the courts. A second major difference between Public Law 478 and the Chandler Act is the fact that Public Law 478 eliminates the previous concurrent jurisdiction of both the courts and the Commission, placing the entire procedure with the Commission. This characteristic of the new law should function to speed up the reorganization process by eliminating the necessity of two different jurisdictions passing on the same plan. Finally, the Chandler Act was a temporary measure, but no time limit is placed on the railroads in taking advantage of the provisions of Public Law 478. Since the adoption of the latter law, a number of carriers have sought to take advantage of its provisions.

Reopening of Section 77 proceedings. Section 3 of Public Law 478 contains some interesting provisions dealing with reorganization plans approved by the Commission under Section 77 but still in the hands of the courts on April 9, 1948. Upon the petition of any party the Commission is required to report to the court any changes or developments since December 31, 1939, not provided for in the approved plan, which make it desirable to reexamine the plan in order to make it equitable. Upon filing such a report the court must return the plan to the Commission, and a further hearing is had in which the Commission is required by law to take into consideration a number of specifically stated factors before deciding upon the old plan or a new one. A somewhat similar provision applies to reorganization plans approved after April 9, 1948. Obviously, these provisions are designed to take care of the objection previously mentioned that changed economic conditions justify a reconsideration of plans previously approved on the basis of the earnings prospects of depression years.

SUGGESTED READINGS

Bigham, Truman C., *Transportation, Principles and Problems*. New York: McGraw-Hill Book Company, Inc., 1946. Chapter 19.

Jones, Eliot, *Principles of Railway Transportation*. New York: The Macmillan Company, 1924. Chapter XVIII gives a good discussion of equity receiverships.

Interstate Commerce Commission, *Annual Reports.*

Locklin, D. Philip, *Economics of Transportation*, 3rd Ed. Chicago: Richard D. Irwin, Inc., 1947. Chapter XXIV.

Moulton, Harold G., and associates, *The American Transportation Problem.* Washington: The Brookings Institution, 1933. Part III.

Railroad Committee for the Study of Transportation, *Railroad Finance.* Washington: Association of American Railroads, 1947.

Railway Age.

Traffic World.

16.

Railroad Service
and
SERVICE REGULATION

DEVELOPMENT OF SERVICE REGULATION

Common law duty of service. Under the common law a common carrier of goods must accept all goods offered to it of the type it professes to carry, and a common carrier of passengers must transport all passengers who present themselves. In either case, a common carrier must serve all similarly circumstanced users without discrimination. The duty to serve is not without limitation. A carrier has the right to establish reasonable rules and regulations and to refuse service to those who do not comply or conform with these rules and regulations. Furthermore, a carrier need not hold itself out to carry anything and everything which is offered to it. Thus railroads refuse to carry money, legal papers, precious metals and jewels, and the like in freight services, and there are a good many short lines which do not carry passengers.

Early lack of service regulation. Railroad regulation under statute law owed its origin in this country to complaints against high and discriminatory freight rates, and commissions and legislatures at first concerned themselves primarily with these two aspects of regulation. Such other regulatory activities as were undertaken, especially those having to do with the prohibition of pooling and the encouragement of competition, were closely related to the rate problem. Except for some fairly early laws designed to promote safety, little thought appears to have been given to the regulation of railroad service, and the consequences of this neglect were not inconsiderable.

Encouragement of competition was of some value in promoting good service at competitive points, but it meant little to the thousands of communities dependent upon a single railroad. Furthermore, at competitive points keen competition between rival carriers led to the rendering of special services to certain favored shippers, either free or at reduced charges, and such discrimination was just as objectionable as direct discrimination in rates. Special mention also should be made of the periodic car shortages which plagued the country for many years. These shortages brought hardships to many and opened the door for further discriminatory practices.

Development of service regulation. In 1893 Congress passed the Safety Appliance Act which was the first of a long series of acts designed to protect railroad employees, the traveling public, and shippers in general. The Hepburn Act gave the Interstate Commerce Commission jurisdiction over a variety of railroad services in an attempt to wipe out personal discrimination. The Mann-Elkins Act gave shippers the right to select the routes over which their goods would move where a through movement involved the use of two or more railroads. The war-induced need for speed led in 1917 to the adoption of the Esch-Pomerene Act which specifically vested the Commission with authority to regulate car service and to suspend car service rules and regulations in the event of an emergency.

Before 1920 service regulation seems to have been largely incidental to the prevention of discrimination or the prosecution of war, but the Transportation Act, 1920, made the regulation of service a direct and major aspect of the work of the Interstate Commerce Commission. The Commission now has comprehensive control over the use, movement, distribution, and supply of cars, locomotives, other vehicles, and trains. Every railroad now is obligated to furnish a safe and adequate car service, and the Commission may compel the carriers to provide such service. It also may require carriers to provide various safety devices in connection with the operation of trains. Along entirely different lines, Interstate Commerce Commission approval is required for the construction or abandonment of a line of railroad. Furthermore, with appropriate safeguards for the rights of the owning carrier, the Commission may compel one carrier to permit another to use its terminal facilities to the extent that such facilities can accommodate an additional carrier. In the event of an emergency the Commission is given sweeping powers to suspend all rules and regulations dealing with car service, to direct the distribution of cars and locomotives without regard to ownership, to require joint use of terminals, to establish embargoes, and the like.

CAR SERVICE

Carriers' duty to supply cars. The law specifies that it shall be the duty of every carrier by railroad subject to the Interstate Commerce Act to furnish safe and adequate car service. This duty, however, is not absolute. A carrier is not liable if a failure to furnish cars is the result of a sudden and great demand which it had no reason to foresee.[1] There are some

---

[1] *Pennsylvania Railroad Company* v. *Puritan Coal Mining Company*, 237 U.S. 121 (1915).

limitations, too, on the provision of certain highly specialized types of equipment, especially where the demand for such equipment is quite limited.[2] Carriers, of course, are expected to provide the more commonly used types of equipment, but their obligation to supply more specialized equipment does not carry with it the necessity of owning such equipment. Many short line railroads own very few cars and most of the nation's tank cars and refrigerator cars are owned by private companies and are used by railroads or shippers on a sort of rental basis. Provision of adequate passenger carrying equipment is not covered by the federal law but may be required by state law.

Car shortages. For years before the 1920's the country was plagued with periodic car shortages which frequently reacted unfavorably upon the whole economy. Factories had to be closed down for lack of raw materials or for lack of cars to transport finished products to market, and substantial quantities of perishables spoiled while waiting transportation. Severe losses were suffered by businessmen, men were thrown out of work, and the public suffered from a shortage of goods. These damaging car shortages have been traced to the failure of railroad management to anticipate needs, inadequate earnings resulting from low rates, failure of shippers to load and unload cars promptly, the practice of reconsignment discussed presently, inadequate terminal facilities, and various other reasons.

In some cases car shortages were regional rather than national, with a shortage in one part of the country and a surplus in another. Such regional shortages sometimes developed during the wheat harvesting season. Shortages of particular types of equipment also developed, being especially serious in the case of open top cars required for the movement of coal. If a winter happened to be particularly severe, and if at the same time the industrial demand for coal was heavy, a shortage of cars promptly developed. The prolonged strikes which have continuously plagued this industry have been another factor contributing to shortages of coal carrying equipment.

Demurrage. An early attempt to improve the utilization of cars took the form of the assessment of a charge called demurrage against shippers and receivers of carload freight who took an undue amount of time to load and unload their shipments, a practice which still exists. Today, as a general rule, carriers allow forty-eight hours for loading or unloading a car before demurrage charges are assessed, although there are numerous exceptions to cover special situations. Demurrage charges may be increased

---

[2] *In the Matter of Private Cars,* 50 I.C.C. 652 (1918). *National Supply Company, Midwest,* v. *Cleveland, Cincinnati, Chicago, & St. Louis Railway Company,* 140 I.C.C. 66 (1928).

during periods of car shortage in an effort to induce the speedier release of cars. Earlier in the century some states enacted reciprocal demurrage laws which penalized carriers for failing to provide shippers with cars or to move cars within a reasonable period. Since a carrier could not be expected to maintain a supply of cars sufficient to meet all emergencies, the effect of these laws was to concentrate car supplies in reciprocal demurrage states in times of shortage. The Supreme Court has rejected reciprocal demurrage regulations insofar as interstate commerce is concerned.[3]

Shipper-carrier cooperation. There is little doubt that much could have been done to prevent car shortages if the carriers could have subordinated immediate individual self-interest to the general welfare. Car shortages were in part responsible for federal control during the First World War, and the brief experience with government operation no doubt convinced the carriers of the need for greater cooperation. In any event the railroads got together after the war and placed responsibility for cooperation in the elimination of car shortages in the hands of the Car Service Division of the American Railway Association (now the Association of American Railroads). So successful has been the work of the Car Service Division that the Interstate Commerce Commission has had little need to exercise its powers over car service except in times of emergency.

In 1923 the Car Service Division sponsored the organization of thirteen Shippers' Regional Advisory Boards located in various parts of the country. These boards are made up of representatives of various users of railroad transportation service in a specified area, and each board meets once every three months with representatives of the various railroads interested in that area. At these meetings shippers estimate their needs for various types of equipment for the coming three months' period, and these estimates are invaluable to the Car Service Division in arranging with the railroads of the country for the movement of equipment to points of need in time to prevent the development of regional car shortages. The railroads have agreed among themselves to carry out the orders of the Car Service Division for the concentration of cars at these points or in those areas where they are most needed. To do otherwise would be to invite general public hostility and the distribution of cars by law. Furthermore, if a carrier with a surplus of cars sought to hoard them it could not expect any help from other carriers when it was in need of more cars.

Car pools. In order that carload shipments of freight can move between points located on two different railroads arrangements must be made which will permit the cars of one railroad to move freely over the lines

---

[3] *Chicago, Rock Island & Pacific Railway Company* v. *Hardwick Farmers Elevator Company*, 226 U.S. 426 (1913). See also 227 U.S. 1 (1913) and 227 U.S. 265 (1913).

of all other railroads. In order to assure the owners of such interchanged equipment that their cars will be returned to them promptly and not retained for long periods on lines of distant railroads, the interchange of freight cars is governed by a code to which all carriers subscribe. Among other things this code requires the using carrier to pay the owning carriers a charge of so much per day for each "foreign" car on its line. It also functions to encourage the return of cars under load if possible.

Before 1920 there was considerable discussion of the possibility of establishing car pools, and this proposal still comes up from time to time. If a nationwide car pool were established, all freight cars would be owned or controlled by a central agency, and these cars would move freely from line to line, each railroad paying the central agency some sort of a rental for their use. The central agency would have power to distribute cars where they were needed, a considerable amount of car accounting would be eliminated, and it has been said that the scheme would reduce the expensive and uneconomic movement of empty cars to their owners. More recently it has been suggested that the Government build a reserve supply of cars which could be rented or leased to carriers.

The larger and more important railroads generally have opposed the idea of car pooling. It has been pointed out that an efficiently operated railroad endeavors to maintain an adequate supply of cars for its customers and that a car pool would deprive it of this competitive advantage. Furthermore, some railroads have a greater need for certain types of special equipment than do others, and they have greater assurance of maintaining an adequate supply of such equipment if they provide it themselves. It also has been contended that cars would be kept in better mechanical condition if they were individually owned than if they were owned by a central agency. System pools have been established governing the supply of cars moving over the lines of individual railroad systems, and what amounted to a nationwide pool existed during the period of federal control. In the absence of any experience with nationwide car pooling under normal conditions it is difficult to evaluate the pros and cons of the proposal.

Distribution of cars in times of car shortage. No legislation can prevent car shortages from developing because railroads do not have the resources to maintain a reserve sufficient to meet sudden needs resulting from unusual circumstances. Nor can they be expected to meet such an abnormal situation as existed during and after the Second World War. Normal car replacements were impossible during that war because of the allocation of labor and steel to war production, and existing equipment deteriorated rapidly under the excessive load of wartime traffic. Of course, in time of war government agencies like the Office of Defense Transportation as-

sume responsibility for the allocation of cars, but when peacetime shortages occur, great care is necessary to distribute the available supply fairly
and in such a way as to avoid any suspicion of discrimination. The Interstate Commerce Commission insists on an equitable allocation, but it
recognizes that conditions differ in different industries and from day to
day, and so it has not attempted to set up specific rules and regulations
governing this matter. Individual carriers find it necessary, however, to
establish regulations for the guidance of their agents in order to assure a
fair distribution of cars among shippers.

OTHER SERVICE PROBLEMS

Joint use of terminal facilities. At some points certain railroads have
fine terminal facilities which are more than adequate for their own needs,
and the Commission may require that they share these facilities with other
carriers if it is in the public interest to do so and it will not substantially
interfere with the owning carrier's ability to handle its own business.
The Commission has ordered such joint use in only a few cases. Possession
of superior facilities for handling cars at terminal points gives the owning
carrier a competitive advantage over other carriers in the areas, and there
is something to be said for the protection of the owning carrier in such a
situation.

Switching service. Shippers and receivers of freight are expected to
load and unload goods moving in carload lots, and to this end carriers
provide tracks on their own premises, known as public team tracks, where
cars are placed for loading and unloading. Most business concerns which
do any amount of shipping and receiving of freight, however, find it
more economical and convenient to have a siding at their plants, and these
sidings are connected by means of switches with some line of railroad.
While the advantage to a railroad of having industries connected with
its tracks is clear, especially at competitive points, railroads have sought at
times to favor certain shippers by finding some excuse for not making
switch connections with competing plants. The Hepburn Act and the
Mann-Elkins Act required common carriers to construct, maintain, and
operate upon reasonable terms switch connections with industrial sidings
provided that the connection was reasonably practicable, that it could be
put in with safety, and that it would furnish sufficient business to justify
the cost.

Numerous controversies have arisen whether or not a carrier should
be permitted to make a charge over and above the regular line haul rate
for switching cars to and from industrial sidings. If the receipt or delivery

of carload freight on a private siding constitutes nothing more than a substitute for a similar service performed at a public team track, no additional charge may be made for the service, but if anything more than this is required an additional charge is justified. In any event there must be no discrimination in charges or service as between similarly circumstanced owners of private sidings.[4]

In delivering a car to a private siding it is a common practice for the carrier to "spot" or place the car at whatever platform or warehouse door the shipper specifies. The Commission has found it necessary to make a sharp distinction between spotting cars on an ordinary private siding and placing cars at specified points within the premises of a large industrial establishment with an extensive and complicated network of private tracks. The Commission has held that when cars are placed on a track within the plant inclosure, delivery has been effected as far as the carrier is concerned, and any subsequent switching of cars within the plant inclosure constitutes an additional service for which an additional charge must be made.[5]

Interchange tracks. To make possible the through movement of freight in carload lots without transfer of lading it is necessary to establish track connections between railroads at junction points, but in times past carriers were not always willing to make these connections. Under certain circumstances such a connection might lead to a loss of traffic by one of the railroads involved, or the amount of interchange traffic might be insufficient to justify the expense of construction and maintenance. In some cases, however, discrimination between carriers was involved, with one railroad connecting with a second line but refusing to connect with a third. At common law the courts were without power to compel track connections,[6] and it was not until 1920 that the Interstate Commerce Commission was clothed with authority to require carriers to afford all reasonable, proper, and equal facilities for the interchange of traffic between their respective lines. In administering this phase of the law the Commission has held, among other things, that a carrier is not required to establish a switch connection when there is no showing that a substantial amount of traffic would move over the connection.[7] It also has held that carriers may effect necessary interchanges through the medium

---

[4] The leading case in connection with switch connections is *The Los Angeles Switching Case*, 234 U.S. 294 (1914), sustaining an order of the Interstate Commerce Commission in *Associated Jobbers of Los Angeles v. Atchison, Topeka and Santa Fe Ry. Co.*, 18 I.C.C. 310 (1910).

[5] *Marting Iron & Steel Co.*, 48 I.C.C. 620 (1918).

[6] *Wisconsin, Minnesota and Pacific Railroad v. Jacobson*, 179 U.S. 287 (1900).

[7] *Pittsburgh & West Virginia Railway Company v. Lake Erie, Alliance & Wheeling Railroad*, 81 I.C.C. 333 (1923).

of a switching railroad rather than through the construction of actual track connections.[8]

Through movement of freight. It is the duty of the railroads to establish through routes and joint rates with each other and to assume the responsibility for the interchange of freight at junction points. Furthermore, the Commission has the power to require the establishment of such routes and rates when the carrier or carriers involved refuse to do so. This power is limited in some measure by a provision originally included in the Mann-Elkins Act and subsequently modified by later legislation to the effect that a carrier cannot be compelled to short haul itself. Suppose, for example, that Railroad X operates between A and C, and that it connects at an intermediate point, B, with Railroad Y which also runs to C. Under this provision of the law X cannot be compelled against its will to establish a through route which would require it to haul traffic from A to B and turn it over to Railroad Y at B for the final movement to C. Certain limitations are placed on this general principle. If in the above situation Y had a direct line from B to C while X's line between these two points was extremely roundabout, the Commission might order the establishment of a through route employing the lines of both X and Y. It is also specified that the Commission may establish a route which short hauls a carrier if such a route is needed to provide adequate and more efficient or more economical transportation service, and it may establish temporary through routes which short haul a carrier in the event of an emergency.

Shipper's right to route freight. The right of the shipper to designate the connecting line or lines to be used when a shipment moves over two or more railroads has been a matter of considerable controversy in the past. Where the originating carrier insisted upon determining the routing, it was in a position to discriminate against certain lines. Furthermore, it could discriminate against shippers by selecting slow or high rate routes for some and fast or low rate routes for others. These difficulties were recognized by Congress, and in the Mann-Elkins Act shippers were given the right to designate the routing of shipments where two or more through routes and rates had been established. The carriers have the right under certain circumstances to establish embargoes at specified points or over certain lines, however, and under these circumstances it may be impossible for the initial or intermediate carriers to comply with routing instructions. Also, the Commission has the right to establish such reasonable exceptions and regulations as may be necessary and to reroute freight if a given carrier is unable to transport the traffic to serve the public properly.

---

[8] *Intermediate Switching Charges at Peoria, Ill.,* 77 I.C.C. 43 (1922).

If the shipper does not designate the route to be followed, the routing is done by the originating carrier. The carriers, however, are directed not to prejudice unduly any connecting line in the distribution of this unrouted traffic. While the law gives the Interstate Commerce Commission authority to route unrouted freight, it acts only to prevent undue prejudice and to protect shippers from being victimized by the carriers in any way. In a long list of cases the Commission has held that ordinarily it is the duty of the carrier, in the absence of routing instructions from the shipper, to route freight by the cheapest reasonable available route.

CONSTRUCTION OF RAILROADS

Early policy of Commission. Between 1920 and 1929 the Commission made extensive use of its power to control railroad construction. As a rule it raised no objections to the construction by existing railroads of cutoffs, connecting lines, line relocations, and similar projects when undertaken for purposes of railroad convenience and economy. Proposals involving extensions or the construction of new railroads, however, were given more careful consideration. In these cases the Commission inquired into the need of the area proposed to be served for railroad service, the prospects for traffic sufficient to make the line pay, and the ability of the applicant to finance construction if permitted to go ahead. The Commission also felt that existing railroads should be protected from unnecessary competition, especially in light traffic areas. It commonly refused to sanction projects which would draw any substantial amount of traffic from existing lines, although in a very few cases it permitted construction on the ground that a little competition would be wholesome.[9]

Policy since 1930. Since the 1929 depression and the rapid rise of motor vehicle transportation the Commission has had little occasion to exercise its powers over railroad construction. The problem facing railroads since 1929 has been one of finding additional traffic for existing lines rather than building new ones. The limited amount of construction which has taken place since 1930 has been to relocate lines and similar activities designed to improve existing systems rather than to extend the scope of railroad service.

Compulsory extension of lines. The Interstate Commerce Act authorizes the Interstate Commerce Commission to require a carrier to extend its line or lines provided that such an extension is reasonably required and that the expense involved will not impair the ability of the carrier to perform its

---

[9] *Construction of Railroad Lines in Eastern Oregon,* 111 I.C.C. 3 (1926). See also 111 I.C.C. 137 (1926).

duty to the public. In 1929 the Commission ordered a subsidiary of the Union Pacific to extend a relatively short branch in eastern Oregon some 185 miles westward across the semiarid central part of that state. The carrier contended that this was not an extension as contemplated by the law but an entirely new line of railroad, and the Supreme Court agreed with the carrier.[10] No other cases involving compulsory extension have arisen, and in view of the availability of motor transportation for offering service to points remote from railroads there seems little likelihood that this provision of the law will be invoked in the future.

RAILROAD ABANDONMENTS

Trends. Between 1920 and November 1, 1951, the Interstate Commerce Commission authorized the abandonment of 36,254 miles of line as compared with 7,818 miles of line actually built under its jurisdiction during that period. Most of the new construction took place before the early 1930's, but the great bulk of abandonments has taken place since that time.

Policy of Commission where little public need shown for line. In a great many cases there is no longer any appreciable public need for the line proposed to be abandoned. Many a line has been built in the past to serve a forest or mining area or a particular industrial establishment or establishments, and when the forest is logged off, the mines exhausted, or the industrial establishments closed down or moved away, there is no longer any need for the line involved. Also, the development of highway transportation has played an important part in rendering the further operation of much railroad mileage unnecessary. In some cases applications have come from short line railroads which have found it financially impossible to continue operations, and in such cases the Commission has had no choice but to permit abandonment regardless of public need, although seldom could much public need be shown for a line in such a condition. Similarly, with the deepening of the depression, the Commission became increasingly inclined to permit the abandonment of flood damaged branch lines of larger railroads when the traffic available did not seem to justify the heavy expense of reconstruction.

Contested cases. Where little or no public need is shown for a line proposed to be abandoned, permission to abandon has followed as a matter of course. Where a real public need is shown for a railroad or one of its

---

[10] *Interstate Commerce Commission* v. *Oregon-Washington Railroad and Navigation Company,* 288 U.S. 14 (1933).

branches and at the same time it is shown that operation of the line is working a financial hardship on its owners, the Commission must balance the public need for the line against the effect of continued operation on the carrier. Essentially each of these cases must be settled on its own merits, but it is possible to distinguish certain general principles and policies followed by the Interstate Commerce Commission in deciding whether or not to permit abandonment.

If reasonably adequate facilities can and will be provided for dependent communities by other railroads or by motor carriers, the Commission often has permited the abandonment of an unprofitable line. Where the opponents of a proposed abandonment argue that business will improve in the future and so enable the carrier to operate successfully, their case must rest on something more than mere wishful thinking if it is to impress the Commission. Where prospects for the future appear to be uncertain but at the same time a definite public need is shown for a given line, the Commission may order continued operation for a test period, thus leaving it squarely up to the communities and shippers involved to show whether or not they can support the line. In some cases the Commission has suggested that local protestants of a given abandonment take over the line in question and operate it themselves. Owners of unprofitable lines usually are willing to sell out for the scrap value of their property, but only in rare instances have protestants shown any willingness to shoulder the risk of continued operation.

Objections sometimes have been raised to a given abandonment on the ground that it would result in a decline in property values. In these cases the Interstate Commerce Commission has held repeatedly that the owners of a railroad cannot be expected to operate it at a loss in order to maintain the property values of others. Protestants occasionally have pointed out that they were solicited for contributions at the time the line was constructed, with the understanding that they were to be given permanent railroad service, but the Commission has held that its sole responsibility is to determine whether or not present public convenience and necessity requires continued operation and that such understandings can have no bearing on its decisions. This is true even when a contractual obligation to continue operations exists or when abandonment would violate some provision of the carrier's charter. The Commission has said that any contractual violations resulting from the act of abandonment are matters to be decided by the courts rather than by it.[11]

---

[11] See, for example, *Central Pacific Railway Company Abandonment*, 224 I.C.C. 291 (1937). This abandonment involved an agreement dating back to 1882 between the railroad and the Piaute tribe of Indians.

Effect of abandonment on carrier as a whole. One of the most important doctrines developed by the Interstate Commerce Commission in connection with railroad abandonments is the necessity of giving consideration to the effect of a proposed abandonment on the financial condition of the carrier as a whole. Where a public need is shown for a branch of a financially weak carrier, yet continued operation of the branch at a loss may wreck the whole line financially or result in a serious deterioration of its service, the larger public interest may require abandonment of the branch.

Where a public need is shown for the continued operation of a non-paying branch of a substantial railroad system, however, the situation may be somewhat different. Many years ago the Supreme Court held that a railroad could not claim the right to earn a net profit from every section or division of its line.[12] And in 1925, after the passage of the Transportation Act, 1920, the Court held that a railroad might be compelled to continue the service of a branch or a part of a line even though the operation involved a loss and even though the system as a whole was not earning a fair return upon the value of its property.[13]

The Interstate Commerce Commission has not followed any hard and fast policy in regard to the abandonment of nonpaying branches of strong lines where some public need has been shown for continued operation. It recognizes that there is a point at which lack of earning power will justify the abandonment of a portion of a system regardless of the prosperity of the system as a whole, but the determination of this point is a matter of sound judgment to be determined by the circumstances of each case.[14]

Obligation of the public. When the Interstate Commerce Commission finds that public convenience and necessity does not permit the abandonment of a given line or branch, even though future prospects of profit are not bright, it has pointed out in no uncertain terms the obligation to shippers to do all that they can to provide traffic for the railroad. In this connection the Commission has said, in effect, that if a community can support both rail and motor transportation, it is entitled to both, but if a community can support only one, it cannot insist upon the retention of both if the patronage accorded to the least favored one is not sufficient to enable it to live.[15]

---

[12] *St. Louis and San Francisco Railway Company v. Gill*, 156 U.S. 649 (1895).

[13] *Fort Smith Light & Traction Company v. Bourland*, 267 U.S. 330.

[14] *Abandonment of Morristown-Corryton Line by Southern Railway*, 105 I.C.C. 228 (1925).

[15] *Sumpter Valley Railway Company Abandonment*, 175 I.C.C. 13 (1931); 184 I.C.C. 253 (1932).

SERVICE AND SERVICE REGULATION

TRAIN SERVICE

Supply of trains. The Interstate Commerce Commission has ample authority under the car service provisions of the law to regulate the supply of trains for the transportation of property. In addition, the construction and abandonment provisions of the Interstate Commerce Act give the Commission authority to grant or deny a carrier permission to abandon operations on a given line, although here the courts have ruled that its authority is limited to abandonment of operations in interstate commerce where complete abandonment of a line located wholly within a single state is concerned. The law gives the Commission no direct power to regulate railroad passenger service, although it has exercised some jurisdiction over passenger service under its emergency powers.[16]

SPECIAL RAILROAD SERVICES

Importance of freight service. The typical "man on the street" is apt to think of railroad transportation in terms of passenger service, and the success or failure of a railroad often is judged in terms of the quality of its passenger service and the extent to which that service is patronized. In point of fact, however, passenger traffic accounts for only a small portion of total railroad revenue, slightly more than 10 per cent in 1949. The service has proved to be quite costly, and while some railroads operate high quality passenger service partly for its advertising value, there are no doubt many lines which would be glad to get out of the business altogether were it not for state laws requiring a certain minimum of service. Only in the case of a few relatively short railroads operating in densely populated areas does passenger service account for a substantial amount of revenue. It is to freight service that railroads look for their revenues.

Protection of perishables. The principal function of the railroad is the movement of raw materials to factories or processing plants, and the movement of finished products and produce to markets. Railroad service as it has developed over the years, however, involves a variety of activities which extend far beyond the mere movement of loaded cars of freight from one shipping point to another. One of the earliest and best known of these special services to develop was the handling of perishable products such as meats and fresh fruits and vegetables. While the refrigerator cars required to protect many perishables usually are owned by shippers or private car companies, the carriers have had to establish icing stations at

---

[16] *Traffic World,* September 2, 1950, p. 26.

various points for the icing and reicing of cars en route. In some sections at certain times of the year heater service is provided to protect commodities like potatoes from freezing, this service commonly being provided by equipping some sort of an insulated car with a charcoal stove.

Livestock. Livestock constitutes a special kind of perishable product, and the slatted stock car is a familiar sight in many parts of the country. Loading facilities are provided at various points, and the carriers are required to load and unload livestock without extra charge at public stockyards. Facilities also must be provided for unloading and loading cattle en route because federal law prohibits the movement of stock for periods exceeding twenty-eight hours without being unloaded for rest, feed, and water. The provision of bedding for stock is another service provided by the carrier, but the shipper must pay the additional cost of any special bedding he may require. Carriers are expected to provide shippers with clean cars, but if special cleaning or disinfecting is requested by the shipper or required by law as a result of quarantine restrictions, an extra charge may be made for the service.

Store-door pickup and delivery service. For many years railroad less-than-carload freight was handled on a station-to-station basis only. This practice was far from satisfactory as far as the users of railroad freight service were concerned because of the cost of hauling shipments to and from freight stations. It was not entirely satisfactory from the railroad point of view either because shippers tended to accumulate their outbound shipments during the day and deliver them to the carriers all at once in the late afternoon. As a result it was necessary to provide crews of freight handlers not otherwise needed and much congestion existed. With the development of motor freight transportation a change took place in this method of handling less-than-carload freight. The truckers picked up and delivered freight right at the factory or store door, and the railroads of necessity had to provide a similar service in order to meet this competition. Store-door pickup and delivery of railroad less-than-carload freight is a common practice today, some railroads making use of their own trucks and others contracting with local trucking concerns for the service.

Expedited freight service. The movement of railroad freight always has been a rather slow process. It takes time to move a loaded car from a private siding or a public team track to the local freight yard, to get it lined up with other cars destined for specified points, and to get the train on its way. Local freights make numerous lengthy stops to take on and drop off cars. At division or junction points trains are broken up and cars reclassified for movement in other trains, causing further delay. In addition to these delays, the trains themselves often cannot move at high speeds over the line because of the heavy tonnage carried. Moreover, freight trains are required to shift to passing tracks to permit passenger trains and other trains having priority of movement to pass them. Because of these various delays the over-all average speed of a freight train was only about twelve miles per hour at the end of World War I.

More recently terminal delay has been reduced somewhat by improved methods of switching, the operating speeds of freight trains have been increased, and better operating methods and better scheduling have made possible a reduction in passing track delay. As a result the average speed of freight trains had increased to sixteen miles per hour in the years following the end of the Second World War. Percentagewise this represents a substantial improvement in freight train speeds, but an average speed of sixteen miles per hour seems almost pathetic in a day and age when passenger trains average a mile a minute and an airplane can fly coast to coast in a few hours. On the other hand, high speeds go hand in hand with high costs. While the typical freight train does not move goods at high average rates of speed, it is capable of hauling enormous tonnages, and this means that it provides transportation at a very low unit cost. Fortunately there is a large volume of freight tonnage which does not require rapid transportation, and for such tonnage slow speeds are more than offset by low freight charges.

For goods which require a more rapid movement between points of origin and destination the railroads have been developing and perfecting an expedited freight service. The larger railroads now operate through freight trains between important points, many of which leave each day at a specified time and operate at high speeds on regular schedules in much the same way as a passenger train. If any intermediate stops are made to set off or pick up cars, they are few in number and are made with a minimum of delay. Originally these expedited freight services were established to handle livestock and perishables, but gradually the service has been extended to include nonperishables between points where competition or the needs of shippers require rapid delivery.

In the ordinary course of events the movement of less-than-carload freight is even slower than the movement of freight in carloads because of the additional handling necessary at freight houses. Individual shipments are accumulated during the day and loaded into cars in accordance with destination. When these cars have been loaded they are pulled out to the yards and handled in the same way as carload freight. At destination, of course, they are placed at freight houses, the freight unloaded, classified, and sent on its way to the consignee. In order to avoid an uneconomic light loading of cars it also is sometimes necessary to unload less-than-carload freight at division or junction points and reload it in other cars, all of which further contributes to delay.

The development of motor freight transportation has brought about some changes in this procedure. Between points where there is a substantial movement of small shipments, many railroads have established what is known as merchandise or package car service. At certain specified points carriers undertake to move out a car of package freight to certain other specified points at a given time each day or on given days of the week. These cars are placed in fast freights where available, most often in connection with trains providing overnight service between important points. In cases where a considerable volume of less-than-carload freight is available separate fast freight trains have been established to handle nothing but such shipments.

Reconsignment. After a car has been turned over to the carrier and is en route to its billed destination, the shipper may request the carrier to deliver it to another consignee in the same city or to a consignee in a different city. If certain regulations are complied with, the carrier will attempt to locate the car en route or before it is turned over to the original consignee and make the changes requested. Such reconsignments are useful when the original consignee cancels his order after the goods have been shipped and the shipper is able to sell the goods to someone else at the original destination or at some other point. If the car had to be returned to the point of origin and then reshipped to another customer, it would put shippers to considerable expense in the form of additional freight charges and result in the goods themselves being in transit for unreasonably long periods of time.

The practice of reconsignment has been of tremendous value in the movement of fresh fruits and vegetables. When fresh fruits and vegetables are ready for the market, they either must be placed in expensive storage or shipped out promptly in order to prevent deterioration. In many cases, also, packing and storage facilities are adequate only for the handling of daily receipts. Shippers naturally want to sell their produce in the best market, but market conditions vary from day to day, and shippers frequently do not know where or to whom to send their produce when it is ready to move out. This problem has been solved through the use of the reconsignment privilege. Oranges, for example, are shipped east from the Pacific coast in large quantities consigned to various points. While they are en route, agents of the orange growers seek information on the best markets, and one by one the cars are reconsigned to those markets where the best prices prevail. Other commodities which are subject to reconsignment include coal, grain, cotton, hay, lumber, and the like.

Transit privileges. A transit privilege allows for the stoppage of certain commodities at a point intermediate between origin and final destination for some sort of processing or handling, the railroad charging the through rate from origin to destination plus a small charge for the additional expenses involved at the transit point. The best known use of transit privileges is found in connection with the milling of wheat into flour. Many years ago flour milling centers grew up in the East, and in these centers the grain produced in nearby areas was milled into flour for consumption in various eastern markets. With the growing industrialization of the East and the westward movement of the population, the grain-growing areas were pushed farther west, and new flour milling centers developed near the new areas of production. Western flour mills, securing their wheat from local sources, milled it into flour and shipped the flour to the eastern centers of population under one through rate. The eastern mills, on the other hand, had to pay the local rate on wheat from the producing areas to their mills, and then pay the local rate on flour from the mill to centers of consumption.

As pointed out in Chapter 12, freight rates increase with distance but not in proportion with distance, and because of this the sum of two local rates will be higher than a through rate covering the same distance. For example, the original class rate scale laid down by the Commission in 1930 for Eastern Territory, provided a basic first class rate of 99¢ for movements of 400 miles while the basic first class rate for an 800 mile movement was fixed at $1.45. Thus the basic charge for two 400 mile hauls was $1.98 as compared with a rate of $1.45 for a single 800 mile haul. In order to reduce the competitive disadvantage of the eastern mills, the railroads permitted them to ship wheat from the producing areas to their mills, mill it into flour, and ship the flour to consuming points, all under one through rate plus a modest charge for the extra service performed in switching cars to and from the mills.

Transit privileges have been extended to cover many products other than wheat and many intermediate services other than milling. All kinds of grain are now shipped under transit privileges which permit a variety of processing activities. Soybeans, cotton seed, and other oil bearing vegetable products are converted into oils and meal under transit arrangements. Lumber is stopped in transit for processing of one sort or another, steel for fabrication, coffee for roasting, ore for smelting, cement for storage, cattle for dipping, and many other products for many other processes.

In some cases the through rate applied is the rate on the original commodity and in other cases the rate is that charged for the processed product. Obviously transit arrangements work best when the rates on the raw material and the processed product are the same or about the same, for if the rate on the processed product is high relative to the rate on the raw material, and the processor must pay the through rate on the finished product, the value of a transit privilege is greatly reduced. Transit privileges involve many complex problems arising out of shrinkage in processing, disposition of by-products, and the like, all of which necessitate the publication of elaborate tariffs and detailed rules and regulations; but they are of tremendous benefit to those processors who are in a position to use them.

Other services. The railroads offer shippers a large number of other special services. It is necessary at times to repack shipments en route to avoid damage. Sometimes it is necessary to level coal and other heavy bulk commodities in order to prevent loss of lading. Numerous important services are provided at port areas in connection with the transshipment of freight from cars to ocean vessels and vice versa. Some of these special services are included as a part of the service covered by the line-haul rate, but in other cases charges are assessed in accordance with special tariffs published to govern the service. If the service is of such a nature that it is used by large numbers of shippers, it is easier to include the extra expense in the line-haul rate. If, however, the service is one which is not common to large numbers of shippers, it is better to separate the extra charge from the line haul rate in order to eliminate possible discrimination and treat all shippers fairly.

SUGGESTED READINGS

Bigham, Truman C., *Transportation, Principles and Problems.* New York: McGraw-Hill Book Company, Inc., 1946. Chapter 18.

Daggett, Stuart, *Principles of Inland Transportation,* 3rd Ed. New York: Harper and Brothers, 1941. Chapter XII.

Huebner, Grover G. and Emory R. Johnson, *The Railroad Freight Service.* New York: D. Appleton and Company, 1926. Part I.

Interstate Commerce Acts, Annotated. Washington: Government Printing Office. First published in 1930 in five volumes, this annotation of the Interstate Commerce Act is kept up to date by periodic supplementary volumes. It is an invaluable source of information on the law and its interpretation by the Interstate Commerce Commission and the courts, not only with regard to service but also in connection with other regulatory activities.

Jones, Eliot, *Principles of Railway Transportation.* New York: The Macmillan Company, 1924. Chapter XIX.

LaSalle Extension University, *Traffic Management Training Service.* Chicago: LaSalle Extension University, various dates. Several of the manuals in this series contain useful information with regard to service matters presented in a concise and easy to read form.

SERVICE AND SERVICE REGULATION

Locklin, D. Philip, *Economics of Transportation*, 3rd Ed. Chicago: Richard D. Irwin, Inc., 1947. Chapter XXV.

Moulton, H. G., and associates, *The American Transportation Problem*. Washington: The Brookings Institution, 1933. Chapter VIII.

Railway Age and *Traffic World*, publish current information on service matters.

Sharfman, I. L., *The Interstate Commerce Commission*, Vol. 1, 1931; Vol. 3A, 1936; and Vol. 3B, 1936; New York: The Commonwealth Fund.

17

Railroad Labor
and
LABOR PROBLEMS

NATURE OF RAILROAD WORK

Train and engine service. The men who operate trains are called train and engine service employees. The locomotive is operated by an engineman, usually an employee with many years of service, a great deal of experience, and of sound judgment and dependability. Particularly is this true of enginemen in line-haul service. On a steam locomotive a fireman keeps the fire going and steam pressure up. On a diesel the fireman or helper functions as a sort of assistant engineer. The presence of a second man in a locomotive cab, even when there is no coal to shovel or steam to regulate, is an important safety measure since he checks signal positions and train orders with the engineman and can operate the locomotive in an emergency.

The conductor is the man in charge of a train. On passenger runs he is responsible for collecting tickets and seeing to the safety and comfort of passengers. On a freight train the conductor is responsible for the paperwork necessary in handling freight and for properly setting off and picking up cars at stations along the way. Every train crew includes at least two other employees called brakemen. When it is necessary to stop a train between stations one brakeman walks back along the track and another walks ahead to "protect" the train by signalling any approaching train to stop. In passenger service the brakemen assist the conductor, and on freight trains they help in switching cars, watch for hotboxes, and the like. On important passenger trains today a crew of porters is provided to assist passengers.

Maintenance of way. The maintenance-of-way men are responsible for keeping the track in safe operating condition. Section gangs are directly responsible for the maintenance of a definite stretch of track. In addition, other gangs do work which is too heavy or too specialized for the section gang. These include the bridge and building men, the water-service men, and the signal-maintenance men. Many railroads are now using weed burners, mechanical tie tampers, ballast cleaners, and other specialized machinery for maintenance work.

Train dispatching. The train dispatcher is located at some strategic point and is responsible for the movement of trains over a given division or section of line. Through constant telegraphic or telephonic communication with stations along the line, he knows at all times the approximate location of every train on his part of the railroad, and he knows when to direct one train onto a passing track in order to let another go by. Some railroads have installed centralized traffic control on sections of their lines where traffic is unusually heavy. In this type of control an operator sits at a board on which the section of line is shown in miniature. He follows the movement of each train and from this board he can move signals and throw switches so that the movement of each train onto and off of passing tracks is controlled automatically.

Station and terminal employees. Every railroad maintains a local agent in each community it serves, and this agent is the responsible representative of the railroad in that community. In a small country station he sells tickets, solicits and handles freight, and maintains telegraphic or telephonic communication with the train dispatcher. In larger communities there are separate local passenger and freight agents. In a large passenger station there will be a corps of ticket sellers, baggagemen, telegraphers, train callers, information clerks, redcaps, janitors, maintenance men, restaurant employees, car inspectors, and employees of concessionaires. A large freight station will employ numerous freight handlers, rate clerks, cashiers, claim agents, and other employees. In the yards there will be yardmen, switchmen, engine hostlers, and others.

Maintenance of equipment. The largest single group of employees engaged in railroad work is the group responsible for the maintenance of equipment. This work is divided into light repairs and heavy repairs, and railroad shops employ a wide variety of skilled workmen, including mechanics, machinists, electricians, plumbers, carpenters, steam fitters, storekeepers, and countless others. The increasing use of diesel locomotives has necessitated the construction of diesel shops and the employment of specialists to adjust and repair their intricate mechanisms. It is the responsibility of these men to see that motive power and rolling stock is maintained in tiptop operating condition.

Other employees. A large number of employees is required to handle accounting records, the billing of freight, and the handling of records involving relationships between railroads. The traffic department employs a large number of men and women to solicit and develop freight traffic and to handle matters relating to rates. The men in the purchasing and stores department are responsible for the purchase of the numerous supplies required to operate a railroad. Other employees are found in the claim department, the legal department, and the like.

LABOR AND LABOR PROBLEMS

RAILROAD LABOR ORGANIZATION

Operating unions. During the formative period of railroad transportation, relationships between workers and owners were on an individual basis, but as large systems developed the groundwork was laid for the organization of unions. In 1855 the National Protective Association of Locomotive Engineers of the United States was organized, and it had a life as short as its name was long. In the 1860's railroad managements introduced the policy of paying engineers so much per run rather than on an hourly basis, a pretty unsatisfactory arrangement from the workers' point of view because of the uncertainties and delays of railroad operation at the time. This method of wage payment, together with other grievances, led the engineers to organize the Brotherhood of the Footboard in 1863 which in the following year became the Brotherhood of Locomotive Engineers.

The organization of the Brotherhood of Locomotive Engineers was followed by the organization of the Order of Railway Conductors in 1869, the Brotherhood of Locomotive Firemen and Enginemen in 1873, the Brotherhood of Railway Trainmen in 1883, and the Switchmen's Union of North America in 1894; and these five unions now represent practically all of the employees engaged in the actual operation of trains. There is some overlapping of membership, but it does not seem to have caused serious trouble. The Switchmen's Union of North America is affiliated with the American Federation of Labor, but the other operating brotherhoods are independent bodies.

Nonoperating unions. Nonoperating employees are represented by some sixteen or seventeen nationwide organizations, not all of which are made up exclusively of railroad workers. A number of these so-called "nonops," including the bulk of nonoperating employees, are affiliated with the American Federation of Labor. In addition, there are a number of other unions which are local or systemwide in nature.

Union cooperation. In 1893 Eugene Debs organized the American Railway Union which was intended to bring all railroad workers together in one big union. The American Railway Union made considerable progress and in 1894 essayed a great strike which centered in Chicago. The arrival of United States troops was followed by the collapse of the strike and the end of the union. The American Railway Union was the only serious effort made to combine railroad workers into a single organization, but the leaders of the various unions in the railroad field are not unaware of the value of cooperation. It is not uncommon for two or three or even all of the operating brotherhoods to cooperate in their bargaining activities, making common cause in an effort to gain higher wages or better working conditions. As mentioned previously, most of the nonops are members of the American Federation of Labor, and in recent years they have followed a policy of bargaining more or less as a unit with railroad management. In addition, all have an organ of cooperation in the form of a Railway Labor Executives' Association.

Strength of railroad labor. The early railroad unions were more in the nature of fraternal organizations than trade unions in the modern sense, and only rarely did they attempt to use the economic sanction of the strike in an effort to improve wages or working conditions. Railroad workers had a number of legitimate grievances, however, and in the course of time their organizations came under the control of men who realized the economic power inherent in collective action. By the turn of the century the operating brotherhoods had achieved recognition of their unions as collective bargaining agencies and had won various improvements in wages and working conditions.

In the early years of the twentieth century the strength of the operating brotherhoods continued to grow and was augmented by the adoption of a policy of making regional agreements covering all of the railroads in a given area rather than making individual bargains with individual railroads. Success in regional bargaining was followed by bargaining on a national scale which was achieved in 1916, although not without a bitter struggle.[1] Much of the strength of the operating brotherhoods is derived from the strategic position they occupy in railroad transportation. The operation of trains is a highly specialized occupation requiring a thorough knowledge of numerous rules and operating practices which is achieved only by long experience, and since practically all operating employees belong to one or the other of the operating unions, any concerted work stoppage on their part will bring the movement of freight and passenger trains to an immediate halt. This is particularly true when two or more unions act as a unit.

For the most part the nonoperating unions do not possess the strategic advantage enjoyed by the operating brotherhoods, and for many years they lagged behind the operating unions in bargaining power. During World War I, however, the United States Railroad Administration found it much more convenient to deal with labor on a collective rather than on an individual basis, and this policy contributed importantly to the growth of trade unionism in all branches of the railroad industry. After the return to private operation some sharp skirmishes took place, but on the whole the nonops maintained and improved their position. In more

---

[1] For an account of this struggle see Eliot Jones, *Principles of Railway Transportation*, pp. 428-431.

recent years they have drawn a page from the experience of the operating brotherhoods and have sought to bargain as a unit rather than by individual unions. The advantages of such a concentration of strength are obvious.

SETTLEMENT OF LABOR DISPUTES

Early legislation. The public interest requires that railroad service be continuous, and it was recognized many years ago that steps should be taken to prevent labor disputes from disrupting continuity of service. A law providing for voluntary arbitration and investigation of labor disputes was enacted in 1888 but used only once during its ten year life. The Erdman Act, adopted in 1898, provided that either party to a controversy between a carrier and its train service employees could request the Chairman of the Interstate Commerce Commission and the Commissioner of Labor to try to bring the two parties together to effect a settlement. If this technique failed, the two public officials were to attempt to get the parties to arbitrate the dispute. During the arbitration period no change was to take place in the status quo, and the award was to be binding for one year.

The Erdman Act procedure was invoked successfully on a number of occasions, but practical experience revealed the need for some changes which were incorporated in the Newlands Act in 1913. This act created a permanent United States Board of Mediation and Conciliation which could offer its services to the parties without being requested to do so. Although differing in details, the general procedure followed was much the same as that provided in the Erdman Act. A number of disputes were settled under the provisions of the Newlands Act, but it failed completely to settle a nationwide dispute between the railroads and their operating employees in 1916. During the period of wartime control, the Government dealt directly with the unions.

Railroad Labor Board. The Transportation Act, 1920, contained detailed provisions covering the settlement of labor disputes. The law declared it to be the duty of both management and employees to exhaust all efforts to get together to prevent a dispute from interrupting service. To handle the numerous minor disputes arising out of grievances, working conditions, and interpretation of rules, the railroads and their employees were authorized to establish Railroad Boards of Labor Adjustment. The law further provided for the creation of a permanent Railroad Labor Board composed of nine members appointed by the President, three selected from a list presented by the railroads, three from a list presented by the workers, and three selected directly by the President to represent the public. The purpose of the Railroad Labor Board was to hear and decide disputes involving grievances, rules, and working conditions in the event the parties at interest could not agree on the establishment of a Board of Labor Adjustment; to hear and decide disputes which a Board of Labor Adjustment could not decide in a reasonable length of time; and to hear and decide disputes regarding wages which could not be decided directly by management and men. The Railroad Labor Board was given no power to enforce its decisions, and no penalties were provided for the failure of either the carriers or labor to abide by its orders.

These provisions of the Transportation Act, 1920, had an unhappy history almost from the beginning. For one thing, the railroads wanted the adjustment boards established on a regional basis whereas most of the unions wanted national boards, and as a result not many adjustment boards were established. A consequence of the failure to establish these boards was to swamp the Railroad Labor Board with a mass of individual minor grievances which hampered its more significant activities.

The tripartite nature of the Railroad Labor Board also proved to be a major difficulty. Although all nine members were officially employed by the United States Government, six of them represented parties who had a direct interest in the outcome of the Board's deliberations and were often at swords points. Furthermore, the Board's difficulties were augmented by an unfortunate selection of its personnel. Two of the three labor members appointed by President Harding had neither the confidence nor the support of organized labor, and labor had no confidence at all in the impartiality of the chairman. Added to these difficulties was the fact that when the Board sought to protect the rights of labor in a dispute with the Pennsylvania Railroad the railroad simply refused to obey the Board's order, and the courts held that the decisions of the Board were unenforceable at law.

Railway Labor Act. The Railway Labor Act of 1926 abolished the Railroad Labor Board and set up a new procedure worked out by the carriers and the unions themselves. This act, as amended in 1934 and 1936, constitutes the present legal basis for the settlement of railroad labor disputes and also applies in part to airline labor. The law makes a sharp distinction between those disputes which involve changes in wages, rules, or working conditions, and those disputes which relate to individual grievances and to the application or interpretation of existing agreements. Separate machinery has been set up to handle each type of dispute.

Whenever a change in wages, rules, or working conditions is proposed, the two parties at interest are expected to get together and attempt to settle any differences in conference. In order to take care of situations arising out of a failure of the parties to reach an agreement in this way a National Mediation Board, made up of three members appointed by the

President with the advice and consent of the Senate, has been established, and its services may be invoked by either party to the dispute or it may offer its services on its own account. Unlike the old Railroad Labor Board the new Board is supposed to be made up of impartial public officials who do not represent the interests of either management or labor.

The National Mediation Board has no authority to hear disputes and render decisions. When it enters a dispute, it first tries to use whatever means are available to get the parties to reach an agreement. If it fails to do this, it next urges them to submit their dispute to arbitration, and if this fails and it appears that the dispute threatens an important interruption of interstate commerce, the Board so reports to the President. The President himself may then appoint a special emergency board to investigate and report on the dispute. A separate emergency board is appointed for each dispute, and it has thirty days in which to make its investigation. During the period of investigation and for thirty days after the Board makes its report to the President, no change, except by agreement, may be made by either party in the conditions out of which the dispute arose. In practice, emergency boards make a recommended award in their reports, but these recommendations are not binding. Since the members of emergency boards represent neither party and are presumed to be impartial in their attitude toward the disputes they are investigating, it was expected that the weight of public opinion would induce acceptance of their recommendations.

National Railroad Adjustment Board. To handle the numerous minor disputes involving grievances and the application and interpretation of trade agreements to specific situations, the law has created a National Railroad Adjustment Board. This Board is made up of thirty-six members, eighteen selected by management and eighteen by labor, and is broken up into four divisions, each division having jurisdiction over specified classes of employees. Any dispute of the type in question which cannot be settled between the parties themselves goes to the appropriate division of the National Railroad Adjustment Board. Since membership on the Board and on its four divisions is divided equally between management and labor, there is always the possibility of a deadlock, and so the law provides for the appointment of a neutral referee when necessary. If the members of a division cannot agree on a neutral referee, the appointment is made by the National Mediation Board. Decisions of the National Railroad Adjustment Board are final and binding on both parties. The idea of handling the multitude of minor disputes through a separate board with the power to make binding decisions is sound in that it leaves the machinery for the settlement of wages, rules, and working conditions free to handle major issues which may constitute a threat to interstate commerce.

LABOR AND LABOR PROBLEMS

SETTLEMENT OF DISPUTES UNDER RAILWAY LABOR ACT

Early success of act. The new machinery for the settlement of labor disputes functioned successfully for a number of years. Many issues were settled directly in conference, and numerous others were settled as a result of the activities of the National Mediation Board. A relatively small number of cases went to arbitration, and in only a few cases did disputes reach the point where the establishment of an emergency board was necessary. Furthermore, until late in 1941 the recommendations of emergency boards, although unenforceable at law, were accepted as final by both parties. Acceptance of emergency board recommendations may be attributed in part to the force of public opinion and in part to the desire of both parties to avoid any action which might destroy the procedure. Also, it is perhaps not without significance that emergency board recommendations tended to be more favorable to labor than to the railroads.

Recent developments. In 1941 a dispute developed between the carriers and the operating and fourteen of the nonoperating unions involving, among other things, a substantial increase in pay. Ultimately the dispute went to an emergency board which made a recommendation satisfactory to neither side. The carriers stated that they would accept the recommendation, but the workers rejected it and the operating brotherhoods announced a strike for December 7, 1941. In an effort to prevent a crippling strike at a critical period President Roosevelt conferred with both parties without result, after which he reconvened the emergency board and asked it to rehear the case or act as a mediatory body. Thereafter an agreement was reached which resulted in a somewhat larger wage increase than the Board had recommended originally. It should be noted that there was nothing unlawful about these maneuvers since the law made no provision for further procedure in the event that the recommendation of an emergency board was rejected, but a significant precedent had been established. Labor had discovered that it was worth while to reject the recommendations of an emergency board which did not please it.

Space does not permit a detailed account of the numerous disputes which went before emergency boards during and following the close of World War II, but in general they followed the pattern established by the operating brotherhoods in the 1941 dispute. Case after case went before an emergency board which, while making some concessions, failed to recommend all that the unions had demanded. And in case after case the operating brotherhoods refused to accept the recommendations and then went on to achieve better results through subsequent negotiations, utilizing whatever opportunistic device of persuasion the Government was able to produce. Since the close of World War II the carriers have become increasingly reluctant to agree to further concessions following a union rejection of the decision of an emergency board, and in a few cases the Government has had to resort to injunctions or government seizure to keep the railroads operating. But at best these are temporary expedients which satisfy nobody and solve nothing. Without attempting to pass judgment on the merits of any dispute or on the wisdom of any particular emergency board recommendation, it is clear that during this period the machinery set up in the Railway Labor Act to settle major disputes had failed to accomplish its purpose.

National Railroad Adjustment Board. The National Railroad Adjustment Board, created to settle the numerous day-to-day disputes arising out of grievances and the application and interpretation of existing agreements to specific individual situations, has functioned actively since its inception in 1934. There is much to be said for the use of a bipartisan board in settling disputes of this sort, providing the members can resolve their differences in a spirit of give and take. In practice, however, they have been unable to do this, and it has been necessary to make use of neutral referees as provided for in the law. The neutral referee has assumed the role of judge and jury, handing down binding decisions in accordance with his particular ideas of justice, and the advantage of decisions reached by mutual agreement has been lost.

The carriers have been dissatisfied with the functioning of the National Railroad Adjustment Board almost from its inception, and they have contended that interpretations made of the provisions of trade agreements have become progressively more onerous and oppressive to the carriers. Spokesmen for the railroads also have criticized what they refer to as the "capricious" nature of some of the decisions of the neutral referees. For example, one case involved an engineer who had reported for duty under the influence of alcohol and was discharged in accordance with the provisions of "Rule G.". This rule, which has been in effect on the railroads of the country for many years, prescribes discharge as the penalty for even the slightest violation of the long-time ban on the use of alcoholic beverages by employees whose duties involve the safety of train operations. The Brotherhood of Locomotive Engineers intervened in behalf of the discharged employee, and two years later a neutral referee ruled that the engineer should be reinstated and given half pay for the two years he had not worked on the grounds that only a mild infraction of the rule was involved. This decision was widely exploited as the "half drunk-half pay" ruling. It should not be inferred, of course, that this is a typical case, but it is not an isolated one.

LABOR AND LABOR PROBLEMS

OBSERVATIONS ON PRESENT SETTLEMENT OF RAILROAD
LABOR DISPUTES

Public interest in continuous service. The public has an interest in the peaceful settlement of any labor dispute which threatens a work stoppage, but in many industries the public interest is not so immediate that it should take precedence over the right of workers and employers to protect their own individual interests. In the case of a few industries, however, of which railroad transportation is one, a work stoppage may have such far reaching economic and social consequences that the public interest in preventing a work stoppage is at least equal to the individual rights of workers and employers. This is more particularly true when bargaining in these industries is conducted on a nationwide basis, for in this case even a brief work stoppage may do great damage to the economic life of the nation. This fact was brought home to the people of the United States in a most dramatic fashion during a two day strike of enginemen and trainmen in 1946. Travelers were stranded, industrial operations slowed down, and large numbers of workers were laid off through no fault of their own. Had this strike continued for a few more days a large part of the economy would have been shut down for lack of raw materials and means of transporting finished goods to markets, and large quantities of perishable food products would have spoiled in the agricultural areas.

Responsibility of carriers. The carriers can do their part toward preventing transportation tieups resulting from work stoppages by paying fair wages and providing satisfactory working conditions, although it will have to be admitted at once that the fair wage concept is one which very nearly defies definition. Nineteenth century railroad workers had much to complain about on the score of wage cutting, long hours of work, and dangerous working conditions; but the likelihood of these practices leading to a nationwide tieup of railroad service, and the economic consequences of such a tieup, was not as great then as now. Unions were not strong in those days and strikebreakers could be and were obtained to keep trains running. Furthermore, work stoppages tended to be localized on single railroads or even a part of a railroad, and so did not have the widespread effect that characterized the strike of engineers and trainmen in 1946. This is not to condone the labor policies of early railroad management, but it does suggest that the public interest in railroad labor disputes, insofar as continuous operation is concerned, is greater now than was formerly the case.

Responsibility of labor. Where disputes are presented before impartial boards the public has a right to expect both parties to give serious consideration to the findings of such boards regardless of whether their decisions are legally binding or not. In a book published by the Bureau of Information of the Eastern Railways, blame for the failure of the various legislative measures adopted at one time or another for the peaceful settlement of railroad labor disputes is placed on the shoulders of labor, and the statement is made that "any legal provision for the settlement of controversies is effective and workable only so long as it serves to achieve for labor the minimum that it is willing to accept." [2] While this statement of the position of the railroads will not come as a surprise to anyone, nevertheless it does seem to be in general accord with the observed history of labor controversies. In some recent cases labor leaders have stated in advance that they would not accept the recommendation of a given emergency board if it did not give them what they were asking. If such an attitude becomes general, the emergency board procedure might just as well be abandoned, for no board can function effectively if it is told in advance what decision it must reach in order to prevent a strike.

Basic weakness of machinery for preventing work stoppages. The obvious weakness of all the various legislative devices enacted to prevent work stoppages on the railroads is the complete absence of any form of compulsion. In the last analysis all of these measures have depended upon the force of public opinion to bring about compliance with the recommendations of some public body. But during World War II public opinion failed completely to bring about such compliance, labor having discovered that it was profitable to reject the recommendations of emergency boards and capitalize on the fear of a nationwide strike. The railroads have not as yet refused to comply with the recommendations of an emergency board, and during the war years even yielded to the urging of the President to make concessions which went beyond emergency board recommendations. This position probably reflects in part a greater respect for the force of public opinion, in part the effect of wartime excess profits' taxes which made possible higher wages without too great a reduction in net profits, and in the postwar years the hope of offsetting higher wages with higher rates.

Future of Railway Labor Act. The competitive situation in transportation has created a situation in which the railroads no longer can depend upon rate increases as an effective device for meeting higher labor costs. Every rate increase tends to divert some traffic to other carriers, and this process cannot continue indefinitely if the railroads expect to survive as private enterprises. Furthermore some shippers have been objecting

---

[2] Harry E. Jones, ed., *Railroad Wages and Labor Relations, 1900-1946.* Bureau of Information of the Eastern Railways, 1947, p. 134.

strenuously to the merry-go-round of higher wages and higher rates which shifts a large part of the burden of increased labor costs onto their shoulders. This has been particularly true among shippers who cannot make effective use of motor and water transportation because railroad rate increases tend to fall more heavily on them.

Although the railroads have continued to press their applications for increased rates, it is not without significance that they have carried on aggressive campaigns to enlist public support in connection with some labor controversies in recent years, something which they had not bothered to do in earlier disputes. Numerous advertisements have been published in newspapers both large and small all over the United States, these advertisements emphasizing those demands of labor which appeared to be the least justifiable. Without attempting to analyze the validity of the arguments presented, it is difficult to deny the effectiveness of the advertisements, and the issues raised have been resolved in favor of the railroads in emergency board recommendations.

The present attitude of railroad labor with regard to a continuation of the existing machinery for the peaceful settlement of disputes is not entirely clear. The 1946 strike was stopped by vigorous government action and did not achieve for labor the benefits derived from the adoption of similar tactics in 1941 and 1943. The threat of a strike in 1948 was overcome by an injunction, and this step cast some doubt on the future ability of labor to ignore the general public interest by threatening nationwide strikes. Furthermore, widespread antagonism was generated both in and out of Congress by the 1946 strike, and a repetition of such a strike might well mean the scrapping of the present procedure in favor of some form of compulsory arbitration. Nobody wants such a law for it is contrary to the broad concepts of freedom on which this nation has operated, and it could lead to widespread violence and engender lasting bitterness. But neither does anyone want a continuation of the uncertainty generated by repeated strike threats, government seizure, and the use of the injunction.

Labor, perhaps realizing the dangers inherent in the existing situation, suggested another alternative. On May 25, 1948, following seizure of the railroads by the Government in an effort to head off the threat of a nationwide tieup of railroad service, the Railway Labor Executives' Association, representing twenty-one railroad brotherhoods, advocated government ownership of the railroads as their solution to the labor problem. Such a proposal immediately raises the question of the right to strike against the Government, but the union leaders took the position that the right of workers on nationalized railroads to strike is protected by the International Labor Organization of the United Nations, of which the

United States is a member. The union leaders also declared that they would rather have Congress handle their wage grievances than continue to rely on the existing emergency board procedure.

Little or nothing has been heard of this proposal since it was first made, and it is difficult to say whether the union leaders were serious in making it or whether it was the result of irritation over the immediate situation. Quite apart from the whole question of the general desirability or undesirability of government ownership, it is not at all clear that railroad labor would improve its position by working for the Government. It is true that railroad labor has many friends in Congress, but there are strong counterforces at work there, too, as was evidenced by the failure of a friendly administration to secure repeal or major modification of the Taft-Hartley Act in 1949. As far as the right to strike is concerned it may be doubted that public opinion would countenance a nationwide railroad strike of any duration, regardless of who happened to own the railroads. And in spite of any protection which might be afforded by the International Labor Organization, the Government could hardly afford to back down in the face of a strike of its employees, for to do so would be to make railroad labor superior to the Government itself. It is true, of course, that the Government could avoid such a turn of affairs by simply acquiescing in any demands made by railroad workers, but if the result of such action would be higher rates or substantial losses, shippers and large taxpayers might be able to bring pressure of their own to bear on Congress.

National Railroad Adjustment Board. In conclusion some reference should be made to the separate problem presented by the National Railroad Adjustment Board. The intervention of the brotherhoods in cases where obvious and sometimes flagrant violations of the rules have been involved has been criticized as destructive of railroad discipline, and the decisions of neutral referees in some of these cases are open to the same criticism. The reinstatement of train-service men found guilty of violating the long-standing rule against the use of intoxicating liquor is a matter of genuine public concern because such reinstatements tend to encourage violations, and the public has too much at stake in the safety of lives and property to permit such violations. It would be most unfortunate if nothing were done about such decisions until some tragedy calls public attention to them.

Labor has objected strongly to the extended delay which has characterized the handling of grievances by that division of the National Railroad Adjustment Board responsible for settling individual disputes between the carriers on the one hand and train- and engine-service employees on the other. This division has labored for a long time under a large backlog of unsettled cases, and labor places the blame for this condition on the carriers. Labor's position has been that the carriers have swamped the division by insisting that each individual grievance be considered and decided as a separate case. As labor sees it, if the past decisions of neutral referees were accepted as precedents to be applied more or less automatically to all subsequent like cases, a great deal of unnecessary delay would be eliminated. It may be true as labor says that the carriers have adopted a stalling technique, but at the same time the carriers hardly can be blamed for refusing to accept some of the apparently capricious decisions of neutral referees as precedents to apply to future cases.

The basic difficulty with the National Railroad Adjustment Board procedure appears to involve the functioning of the neutral referees, who play a far greater role in the adjustment of disputes than probably was intended originally. In holding hearings and rendering decisions they are not bound by established judicial practices and can adopt whatever principles and procedures they see fit, with no appeal from their rulings possible. The carriers have suggested that provision be made for the appointment of permanent referees, men who can acquire in the course of time knowledge in the highly technical field of working rules and so be able to adjudicate deadlocked disputes in a way which is in full accord with existing regulations. They also have proposed that dissatisfied parties be permitted to appeal board decisions to the courts. As labor sees it, however, such a procedure would simply add to the existing delay in the settlement of disputes.

SECURITY

Retirement pay. For many years the seniority principle has applied in connection with railroad labor. Promotion in most jobs is based on years of service, and when declining traffic necessitates a reduction in the labor force the most recently employed are laid off first. Partly because of this and partly because many railroad jobs require maturity of judgment rather than physical strength, railroad workers hold positions of responsibility to a somewhat more advanced age than is true of industry in general. Consequently when a man is no longer able to work on the railroad he is not likely to be able to work anywhere else. Furthermore, a retired railroad man may not have the ability to do other types of work even if he is in good physical condition. Because of these things the problem of old age dependency has long been a matter of real concern to railroad workers. A number of railroads recognized this situation and voluntarily undertook to provide retirement pay for men who could no longer perform their jobs.

The private pension plan was never a completely satisfactory solution to the problem of old age dependency. By no means all railroads provided such pensions, eligibility requirements limited the scope of their application, the payments themselves were small, and the railroads providing them were under no compulsion to continue to do so. Congress became interested in this matter in the 1930's and has passed a number of laws relating to annuities for railroad workers. The present law, which was enacted in 1937 and amended in 1946, 1948, and 1951 applies to railroad employees, officers of railroad labor unions, and employees of traffic associations and other joint carrier bodies. It provides annuity payments to individuals sixty-five years of age or over, to individuals of sixty years of age or over who have had thirty years service, to their spouses, to survivors of railroad employees, and under certain circumstances to individuals who have become totally and permanently incapacitated. Equal contributions are made by the carriers and the employees. In 1948 the amount of the contribution from each party was fixed at 5¾ per cent on individual wage payments up to $300 per month, this amount to increase to 6¼ per cent by January 1, 1952. Under the 1951 amendments the average payment to a retired man and wife, aged 65 or over, was estimated at $135 per month.[3] Administration of the law is in the hands of a Railroad Retirement Board. Persons with less than ten years service are credited for this service under the general old age insurance system.

Unemployment compensation. It is possible to recognize three kinds of unemployment in railroad work. First is the permanent dismissal of workers resulting from technological changes, unifications, abandonments, and more or less permanent declines in traffic. About all that can be done in these cases is the payment of a dismissal wage, and some arrangements have been made between the carriers and the unions relative to such payments. A second kind of unemployment results from seasonal and cyclical variations in traffic. And a third type of unemployment results from the irregularity of certain kinds of work which is of such a nature that the individual cannot find or accept other employment.

To provide some help for workers in the last two categories Congress adopted an Unemployment Insurance Act applicable to railroad workers in 1938, and in 1946 this act was amended in various respects to liberalize its provisions. The program as presently constituted is supported by a tax on the carriers of from ½ per cent to 3 per cent of the wages of any employee not in excess of $300 per month. A waiting period is provided during which no benefits are paid and annual payments are limited to a maximum of twenty-six weeks per year. Maximum benefits are fixed at $25.00 per week. The 1946 amendments expanded the coverage to include

---

[3] *Traffic World*, November 3, 1951, p. 69.

unemployment due to sickness and maternity. In order to eliminate the need for paying unemployment compensation to very casual labor the law excludes individuals receiving less than $150 during the preceding year. Administration of the act is in the hands of the Railroad Retirement Board.

Since the Social Security Act makes general provisions for unemployment insurance for workers in private employment, it is legitimate to ask why railroad workers are singled out for separate treatment. Unemployment insurance laws are state laws, with the Social Security Act providing financial assistance in their administration, and there is a considerable variation from state to state in the nature of these laws. But railroads by their very nature cannot take much cognizance of state boundaries in their operations. The same employee may work in more than one state, and it is necessary from time to time to shift employees from one state to another. Under such circumstances it is not always easy to apply state unemployment insurance laws without doing injustice to the individuals involved. A national law solves this problem in the interest of the workers and is beneficial to the railroads as well, since it makes it unnecessary for them to maintain separate records and contribute to as many unemployment insurance funds as states in which they operate.

SOME RAILROAD LABOR PROBLEMS

Seniority. Brief mention has been made of the seniority principle which involves the assignment of individual employees to specific jobs on the basis of years of service. This means that the best jobs, best in the sense of desirable hours or high earnings or some other factor, are held by individuals with the longest service. If one of these jobs is opened up by reason of death, retirement, incapacity, or otherwise, it is "advertised," and any workers in that category and within the area involved can "bid" on the job. The bidding is in terms of years of service, and the bidder with the most years, or the "longest whiskers," gets the job. Also if a worker in a given category desires a particular job held by another worker in that category but with fewer years of service, the first man can "bump" the second man off of his job. Up to a certain point promotions are handled in the same way, the only requirement being that the individual be capable of doing the work involved.

The seniority principle has merit in that it assures the individual worker of stability of employment after he has been with the railroad a certain period of time. It is true that during periods of slack business he may have to accept demotion to an inferior job as he is bumped down by men of longer service, but he will not be dismissed unless he happens to be at or near the bottom in years of service. On the other hand, the seniority plan has a grave disadvantage in that it discourages able young men from entering the railroad business. The fact that capable young men have been discouraged from entering the railroad business is becoming a matter of major concern to some railroad managements today because as men in key positions approach the age of retirement, there is a notable lack of younger men capable of taking their places. This has been more particularly true in the engineering departments, but it is also true elsewhere, and a few railroads now are making some effort to attract college graduates.

Wages and hours. It is not difficult to make comparisons of hourly rates of pay as between different occupations or for the same occupation in different years, but from the point of view of labor such comparisons are of relatively little significance because of wide variations in the regularity of employment in different types of work and in different industries. Generally speaking it is the annual wage income which is important to the worker, although the number of hours it is necessary to work to obtain a given annual wage is becoming a matter of increasing interest to labor. Among certain classes of railroad workers, and particularly among those employed in train and engine service, the annual wage is a matter of major concern because many such employees are prevented by traffic variations or union regulations from working regularly throughout the month or year.

From the point of view of railroad management hourly rates of pay are significant only to the extent that they affect the labor cost per hour actually worked, and for various reasons there may be a wide gap between rates of pay per hour and the cost of an hour's labor. In the first place, consideration must be given to the peculiar way in which train- and engine-service employees are paid. In freight service these employees receive a day's pay for 8 hours work or 100 miles run, whichever comes first. In regular passenger service 5 hours or 100 miles constitutes a day's work for enginemen and firemen, and 7½ hours or 150 miles a day's work for conductors and brakemen. A second factor which makes the hourly rate of pay meaningless is the payment of penalty overtime. It is not always possible or practical, for example, to have a freight train crew quit at the end of 8 hours, nor is it practical to divide runs into lengths of exactly 100 miles, and time and one half must be paid for work in excess of 8 hours or 100 miles run. Finally, it may be noted that union rules sometimes necessitate payment for work not actually performed or payments which have no relationship to the time actually required to do the work. For example, union regulations sharply delimit the kinds of work which may be performed by different categories of workers, and if it becomes necessary for a man in one category to perform some incidental function which belongs to another category, the carrier may have to pay him extra for this work and at the same pay scale that would be paid a man in the proper category who was not called upon to do the work.

Featherbedding. The term "featherbedding" is used with reference to union rules which result in payments made for work which is not performed or payments which are excessive considering the actual work done. For example, the present provisions of the miles-run or hours-worked rule were developed in the more leisurely days of railroading. They still make sense in some types of runs, but on numerous high speed diesel powered runs they result in the crew's performing a day's work and receiving a day's pay for three or four hours of running time. Union rules narrowly limit the kinds of work which may be performed by different categories of workers. This is in line with union practices in the building trades and some other fields, but in railroad transportation it sometimes is impractical or even impossible to observe these narrow limitations. But when a man performs a task out of his field he must be paid extra, and a man in the category to which that particular task is assigned also may have to be paid for not doing the work. In what was perhaps an extreme case a local freight crew was required to do some switching and move some cars standing on a siding at an intermediate point where no switch engine crew happened to be on duty. For this work the conductor and crew of the local freight train received, in addition to their regular pay, a day's pay for work at yard rates, and an extra yard conductor and brakeman who were not on duty were given a day's pay because they were not called to do this work. The entire job took about fifteen minutes.[4] While the desires of workers to spread the work around are understandable, such practices are indefensible economically speaking.

Ever since the introduction of diesel locomotives in line haul service labor has contended for additional men to operate them. The engineers wanted one engineman in the cab and another engineer to supervise engine room work. The firemen wanted one man in the cab and another fireman to work in the engine room. The shop craft unions, while not filing any formal complaints, have contended that if an extra man is put on diesels for maintenance work, he must be a member of their union. At first these demands were based on claims that safety and protection of the engines required an extra man, but these claims have been so thoroughly disproved that they are seldom heard anymore. The height of absurdity in the diesel cases was reached in 1947 when labor demanded the employment of one

---

[4] This and various other cases are cited by Harry E. Jones, ed., *Railroad Wages and Labor Relations, 1900-1946.*

full train and engine crew for every diesel power unit employed in pulling a train. A diesel locomotive consists of a control unit to which may be added one or more power units, the number employed depending upon the weight of the train and the nature of the terrain. Since as many as four units, all controlled by a single crew from a single cab, are used on some freight trains, this demand would have required as many as four complete train crews to operate a single train. So far labor has been unsuccessful in achieving any of these demands.

Numerous other examples of rules which lead to featherbedding could be cited, but the above are sufficient to illustrate the practice.[5] It is easy, of course, to blame labor for the establishment and maintenance of featherbed rules, but it should be pointed out that some of these rules are the outgrowth of earlier carrier policies which attempted to take advantage of railroad labor. The railroads themselves introduced the practice of paying engine and train crews on the basis of so much per run rather than so much per hour or day, and because of the uncertainties and delays of train operations in earlier days, the brotherhoods were justified in demanding the dual basis of pay. It seems probable, too, that as the speeds of passenger trains increase, the added strain on the engineman justifies a reduction of working hours. Furthermore, engine and train crews in line haul service are put to some expense and loss of time due to the fact that when they finish a run they are at some distance from their home station and must wait over to work a train back or "deadhead" it back on the next passenger train. Also, the various categories of workers ought to be protected within limits so that they need not sit idle while others do the work they are employed to do.

Technological unemployment. The trouble with some of the working rules is that they have extended beyond the bounds of their original purpose and have become "make work" rather than protective rules. It is difficult, for example, to justify the mileage limitations in high speed freight and passenger service today. It ought to be possible to arrange schedules so that a train crew could work a train for a hundred miles more or less and then pick up and work another train back to the crew's original starting point, and do it all within the confines of a reasonable working day, and for a day's pay. But to do so would eliminate the need for one whole crew.

As locomotives have become more powerful and capable of handling heavier loads the brotherhoods have demanded limitations on the number of freight or passenger cars carried on a single train. While these demands

---

[5] The book by Harry E. Jones, cited previously, gives a number of examples. See also, Charles E. Landon, *Transportation.* New York: William Sloane Associates, Inc., 1951, pp. 550-553.

are made on the score of safety, the relationship of train length rules to employment is obvious. This same fear of technological unemployment lies at the roots of the demands made for additional men in the engine rooms of diesel locomotives, and it existed in an undisguised form in the 1947 demand for a full train and engine crew for every diesel power unit employed. It is also found in rules which the unions have set up restricting the number of hours a member can work in a given period of time.

Conclusion. Although railroad wages did not increase as rapidly as wages in other types of employment during World War II and the years following, they still are among the highest in the country today, both in terms of annual return to the workers and in terms of labor cost per hour worked to the railroads. When any industry experiences an increase in labor costs such as this, one or more of several things will happen. If the industry does nothing to offset these higher costs its profits will decline, and unless it happens to be earning excessive profits at the time, investors will seek opportunities for their savings in other fields. Under such conditions further growth of the industry may be halted and a gradual deterioration set in. The labor force itself will not be expanded and may gradually decline. And if profits in the industry are low or even nonexistant, any substantial increase in labor cost will mean bankruptcy for individual units within the industry and an absolute decline in employment.

Usually, however, an industry faced with increased labor costs will attempt in one way or another to do whatever it can to offset these higher costs. It may seek to shift them forward in the form of higher prices for its product, but unless the demand for its product is highly inelastic, it will find that the higher prices are accompanied by a decrease in demand, and this in turn will be translated into a reduction in employment. There is always a strong tendency, too, for industry to attempt to offset high labor costs by making more efficient use of its labor supply, either by improved methods or by the substitution of machinery for labor, and this again means a reduction in employment.

All of the tendencies noted above are observable in the field of railroad transportation. Railroad earnings have fallen to the point where there is no longer a market for railroad stocks and very little market for other types of securities with the exception of equipment obligations. It is not intended to imply that high labor costs are responsible for this situation; the low estate of railroad securities is the result of a variety of factors. Few would deny that the development of new forms of transportation has been a major consideration influencing railroad earnings, however, and it seems reasonable to suppose that relatively high labor costs have had some effect on the ability of the railroads to meet this new competition. Many small railroads, unable to operate at a profit, have been abandoned, and partial abandonments by larger lines have been extensive. Here again the competition of newer agencies of transportation has been a major factor, and it would be difficult to determine to what extent, if any, high labor costs played a part in these abandonments.

In recent years the railroads have sought to meet increased costs with higher rates, and in some of these rate cases the Interstate Commerce Commission has recognized a direct relationship between the need for higher rates and increased labor costs. But each of these rate increases has been followed by some diversion of traffic, and it appears that this solution to the higher labor cost problem is no longer to be relied upon. Finally, in the last twenty-five years the railroad industry has sought in numerous ways to increase the efficiency of its labor force. Since union rules operate to retard rather than promote more efficient use of labor, efforts along this line have taken the form of an ever greater application of machinery to work formerly done by hand with an attendant decline in employment.

Labor has variously contended that railroad profits are adequate to pay higher wages and that the profit position of the railroads could be improved by more efficient management. But a study of available data shows pretty conclusively that railroad profits are not large by any standard, and this is substantiated in some measure by the lack of interest in railroad securities on the part of the investing public. The charge that railroad management could be more efficient is difficult to evaluate. In the past railroad management has exhibited more than a degree of inertia, but this has not been true in recent years. And management itself insists that efficient management is handicapped by numerous union rules limiting the amount of work a man can do and requiring the payment of substantial sums of money for work that is not actually performed. In any event, as wages have gone up employment on the railroads has declined. Thus while the position of those workers still in the railroad business has improved substantially, and to the point where they are among the highest paid workers in the country, a large number of the railroad workers have been displaced, and if present trends continue, the number of displaced will increase rather than diminish.

SUGGESTED READINGS

Britton, Lewis W., *Transportation in 1948* and *Transportation in 1949*. Washington: The Traffic Service Corporation, 1949 and 1950. A review of transportation in 1948 and 1949 as reported by the editorial staff of *Traffic World*.

Daggett, Stuart, *Principles of Inland Transportation.* New York: Harper and Brothers, 1941. Chapter 27.

Healy, Kent T., *The Economics of Transportation in America.* New York: The Ronald Press Company, 1940. Chapters 16 and 17.

Jones, Eliot, *Principles of Railway Transportation.* New York: The Macmillan Company, 1924. Chapter 20 contains an excellent brief account of legislation and major disputes up to the time of publication.

Jones, Harry E., ed., *Railroad Wages and Labor Relations, 1900-1946.* Bureau of Information of the Eastern Railways, 1947. Although a railroad publication, this book contains a useful chronological survey of labor legislation and labor disputes and a large amount of statistical data based on Interstate Commerce Commission reports.

King, Ernest L. and Robert E. Mahaffay, *Main Line.* Garden City, New York: Doubleday & Company, Inc., 1948. An account of Mr. King's fifty years as employee and official of the Southern Pacific Lines. Chapter 13 contains an interesting first hand account of labor problems and working rules.

Locklin, D. Philip, *Railroad Regulation Since 1920.* New York: McGraw-Hill Book Company, Inc., 1928. Chapter 9.

Parmalee, Julius H., *The Modern Railway.* New York: Longmans, Green & Company, 1940. Chapters 21-24.

Railway Age.

Traffic World.

Vanderblue, H. B., and K. F. Burgess, *Railroads, Rates—Service—Management.* New York: The Macmillan Company, 1924. Chapter 25.

Part Three

HIGHWAY TRANSPORTATION

18.

Development
of
HIGHWAY TRANSPORTATION

HIGHWAY DEVELOPMENT

Nineteenth century road building. With the development of canal and railroad transportation, both the Federal Government and the states lost their early interest in road building, turnpike companies were forced out of business, and responsibility for road building and maintenance was vested in local governmental units, particularly the township. Much of the work was done by the local citizenry under the supervision of elected overseers who might or might not know anything about road construction and maintenance, and rural roads in the United States were in a most unsatisfactory condition throughout most of the nineteenth century.

Demand for better roads. In the latter part of the nineteenth century people all over the United States began to display a growing interest in better roads. The rapid expansion of the railroad network had promoted the growth of trade and industry in urban areas, which in turn was improving the status of urban population, but the benefits of improved transportation did not extend to the same degree to rural areas still bogged down in the mud of nineteenth century highway policies. It has been said that the fundamental basis of the road reform movement lay in the effort to remove some of the disparities that existed between rural and urban life.[1] The rural free delivery system, started in a small way in 1896, was a reflection of the desire to extend the benefits of urban life to rural areas, and its expansion necessitated better roads. Bicycle riding which had become a national craze also contributed to the demand for improved roads. But regardless of the origins of the demand, it was the low priced mass-produced automobile that really brought about the development of the modern highway system.

County and state highway administration. Better roads made necessary the employment of trained engineers and regular crews of skilled workers equipped with proper tools and machinery. Also, the greater distances

---

[1] Charles L. Dearing, *American Highway Policy*. Washington: The Brookings Institution, 1941, pp. 45-47.

covered by the automobile required that standards of construction and maintenance be uniform over fairly long stretches of road. All of this meant the abandonment of the old township road district method of highway administration and the substitution of a larger unit. At first the county was used for this purpose, but as the use of the automobile expanded state control was substituted, and one after the other the states established highway departments and assumed direct responsibility for the construction and maintenance of designated systems of state highways.

Federal Aid Road Act of 1916. With the continued growth of automobile ownership, both motorists and manufacturers urged the establishment of an integrated system of highways on a national basis to promote interstate highway travel, and agricultural interests called for federal participation in the construction of farm to market roads. Active participation of the Federal Government was initiated by the Federal Aid Road Act of 1916 which provided an appropriation of $75 million to be used during the next five years under the supervision of the Secretary of Agriculture to aid the states in improving rural post roads. For every dollar contributed by the Federal Government the states were to contribute an equal amount, and the states or subdivisions thereof were to be responsible for maintenance. Federal participation was limited to a maximum of $10,000 per mile exclusive of the cost of bridges more than twenty feet long. An important provision of this act was the requirement that a state must create a highway department with adequate equipment and authority to cooperate with the Government and supervise actual construction. Those states which did not have such departments created them promptly in order to be eligible for federal aid.

Federal Highway Act of 1921. The Federal Highway Act of 1921 made certain important changes in the 1916 law. Federal aid was limited to a system of highways designated by the state, not to exceed 7 per cent of its existing mileage. The Secretary of Agriculture was to give preference to projects which would expedite the completion of an interconnected system of state highways, but not all aid was to be confined to such roads. And under certain circumstances federal contribution could be increased to a maximum of $25,000 per mile.

Federal aid during the 1930's. Throughout the 1920's federal aid functioned to encourage the steady and orderly development of a system of interconnected highways, with funds about equally divided between main or primary roads and secondary roads serving local needs. This program of orderly development was cast aside during the 1930's, however, in favor of road building for relief and recovery purposes. Special appropriations were made to help the states match federal funds, and large sums were made available for feeder roads without matching aid. In 1934 the limitation on the amount of money the Federal Government could contribute per mile of road was removed, and in 1936 federal aid was extended on a matching basis for rural roads not in the designated federal aid system. In order to discourage states from diverting motor vehicle tax revenues to nonhighway use, a strong temptation during the depression, it was provided that such action would bring about a reduction in federal aid funds.

Federal Aid Highway Act of 1944. For some years interest had been shown in the development by the Federal Government of a key system of highways designed to promote the national defense. In 1944 Congress passed the Federal Aid Highway Act which provided, among other things, for the designation of a national system of interstate highways not to exceed 40,000 miles which would connect as directly as practicable the principal metropolitan areas, cities, and industrial areas; suitable border points in Canada and Mexico; and serve the national defense. This law provided that if the construction of any additional mileage was found necessary, such construction was to be added to the federal aid highway system without regard to any existing mileage limitations.

Federal aid v. federal ownership. Although the Federal Government has contributed large sums of money for highway improvements, it has preferred to leave actual construction, maintenance, and supervision to the states; and the completed highways belong to the states in which they are located. Decisions of the Supreme Court previously discussed suggest that Congress has power to establish a system of federally-owned interstate highways, but there are advantages to the policy of public aid which has been adopted. In the first place, most of the highway mileage has been built to handle and does handle intrastate traffic. This mileage, of course, must be administered by the states and a substantial saving is effected by making the states also responsible for the relatively small mileage of primarily interstate highways. Second, it would lead to confusion if separate federal and state highway systems were set up because of the inevitable intermingling of interstate and intrastate traffic which would occur on both systems. Finally, the requirement that state authorities must establish adequate highway departments and conform with high standards in order to obtain federal funds contributes to a general improvement in the quality of all road building.

Present highway system. Responsibility for administering the federal aid program now rests with the Bureau of Public Roads of the Department of Commerce. From 1916 through fiscal 1948, federal funds authorized for highways totaled $5,989,332,124,[2] and the Board of Investigation and

---

[2] Public Roads Administration, *Highway Statistics, Summary to 1945*, p. 57.

DEVELOPMENT OF HIGHWAY TRANSPORTATION

Research fixed total expenditures of all governmental units for streets, roads, and highways at $41,332,004,000 for the period 1921-40.[3] Table XI shows the makeup of the highway system as of the end of 1948.

Table XI

RURAL ROAD MILEAGE, 1949 [4]

(*in thousands of miles*)

System	Total	Nonsurfaced Mileage			Surfaced		
		Unimproved	*Graded and Drained*	*Total*	*Other than High Type*	*High Type*	*Total*
Under State Control:							
State primary systems	358	5	9	14	207	137	344
State secondary systems	85	10	6	16	58	11	69
County roads under state control	121	21	23	44	75	2	77
Roads in state parks, forests, etc.	8	1	4	5	2	1	3
Total under state control	572	37	42	79	342	151	493
Under Local Control:	2,361	682	570	1,252	1,059	50	1,109
Under Federal Control: Roads in national parks, forests, etc., not part state or local systems.	70	29	26	55	14	1	15
Total rural roads	3,003	748	638	1,386	1,415	202	1,617

DEVELOPMENT OF MOTOR TRUCK TRANSPORTATION

Development of motor truck. The growth of motor truck registrations is shown in Table XII. Originally the automobile was designed as a pleasure vehicle, and it was not until the period of the First World War that any significant use was made of motor vehicles for commercial purposes. The growth in registrations at this time probably reflects the development of more dependable trucks and an attendant realization of the advantages of the truck over horse drawn vehicles. Growth since 1920 reflects continued mechanical improvements, construction of better roads

---

[3] *Public Aids to Domestic Transportation*, p. 213.

[4] Bureau of Public Roads, *Highway Statistics, 1950*, Washington, 1952. High type surfaces include brick and block, Portland cement concrete, bituminous concrete, bituminous penetration, and sheet asphalt. Other surfaces include slag, stabilized soil, gravel or stone, bituminous treated, and mixed bituminous. Low type surfaces include bituminous macadam, bituminous mix, water bound macadam, gravel, and sand-clay.

and streets, the substitution of trucks for horses by farmers, the growth of intercity transportation for hire, and the increased use of trucks by private industries as a substitute for commercial transportation.

Table XII

MOTOR TRUCK REGISTRATIONS IN THE UNITED STATES [5]

1905	1,400		1925	2,483,215		1945	4,834,742
1910	10,123		1930	3,518,747		1950	8,604,448
1915	158,506		1935	3,675,865			
1920	1,107,639		1940	4,590,386			

Development of highway transportation. Prior to about 1920 it seems reasonable to suppose that practically all use of the motor truck was within urban areas, but after 1920 the continued improvement of both trucks and highways, plus the speed and flexibility of transportation by truck, led to an enormous increase in the number of trucks in use. No reliable statistical information is available on the volume of intercity truck traffic prior to 1937, but in that year the Interstate Commerce Commission began publishing an annual estimate of this traffic, including tonnage moved by private trucks as well as by carriers for hire. These figures, given in detail on page 21, show an increase from 44 billion ton miles in 1937 to 126 billion ton miles in 1950.

Types of highway carriers. Over-the-road trucking may be classified according to its availability for use by the public. Common carriers by motor vehicle have the same duties and obligations as common carriers by railroad, although usually the service they render is somewhat restricted in scope. Contract carriers by motor vehicle differ from common carriers in that they do not hold themselves out to serve the general public but provide transportation service for specific users with whom they make special contractual arrangements. A third group consists of the private carriers, which are not carriers at all in the sense that they offer their services to others. This group includes all of the owners or lessees of vehicles who use these vehicles exclusively in connection with their own private business activities.

Some idea of the relative importance of different types of truck ownership and use may be gleaned from the detailed breakdown of truck ownership and use shown in Table XIII. It will be observed that truck ownership is overwhelmingly concentrated in the hands of private carriers, including government agencies, and that most trucks still are used for local hauling. In over-the-road service, however, common and contract carriers, including tank trucks for hire, accounted for about 43 per cent

---

[5] Public Roads Administration, *Highway Statistics, Summary to 1945*, p. 18. Bureau of Public Roads, *Highway Statistics, 1950*, p. 15.

Table XIII

BREAKDOWN OF TRUCK FLEET BY VOCATIONAL USES [6]

(as of about the end of 1943)

Agency	Local	Over the Road	Total	% in Over-the-Road Service
Governmental Agencies	211,117	18,175	229,292	7.9
Agricultural Agencies	1,552,321	41,503	1,593,824	2.6
Extractive Industries	71,151	15,087	86,238	17.5
Construction Industries	395,234	26,047	421,281	6.2
Manufacturing Industries	136,761	38,569	175,330	22.0
Wholesale Distribution	256,414	97,036	353,450	27.5
Consumer Distribution	638,820	46,907	685,727	6.8
Public Utilities:				
Contract Carriers (except tank trucks)	260,800	69,511	330,311	21.0
Common Carriers (except tank trucks)	119,915	169,255	289,170	58.5
Other Public Utilities	76,825	7,153	83,978	8.5
Total All Public Utilities (except tank trucks)	457,540	245,919	703,459	35.0
Tank power units:				
Wholesale Distribution	28,845	11,508	40,353	28.5
Consumer Distribution	40,485	3,945	44,430	8.9
For Hire	5,002	9,627	14,629	65.8
Miscellaneous—All Other	2,796	1,523	4,319	35.3
Total All Tank Trucks	77,128	26,603	103,731	25.6
Business, Professional and Personal Service Agencies	116,811	13,201	130,012	10.2
Institutional Agencies	19,296	916	20,212	4.5
Personal Transportation	149,524	5,135	154,659	3.3
Not Classified	2,009	61	3,070	2.9
Total Property Carriers	4,084,126	575,159	4,659,285	12.3

of all trucks used in this way in 1943. It should be noted, too, that carriers for hire use their equipment much more intensively than do other agencies.[7]

The Interstate Commerce Commission also classifies motor carriers according to the type of service in which they are engaged as follows: (1) Regular route, scheduled service, (2) Regular route, nonscheduled service, (3) Irregular route, radial service, (4) Irregular route, nonradial service, (5) Local cartage service. The first type of carrier undertakes to provide a regularly scheduled service to and from specified terminals and at intermediate points. The second type serves specified points but does not hold itself out to provide service at regularly scheduled times. The third type does not confine itself to any particular route but operates to

[6] From a study made by the Office of Defense Transportation. See Department of Commerce, *Industry Report, Domestic Transportation*, May-August, 1948, p. 23.

[7] See, for example, figures given in *America's Truck Fleet*, American Trucking Associations, 1945, p. 5.

and from various points in a specified area. The fourth type confines itself neither to a specified route nor to a specified area. The fifth type is self-explanatory.

Finally, the Interstate Commerce Commission classifies motor carriers according to the types of commodities they hold themselves out to transport. These are (1) general freight, (2) household goods, (3) heavy machinery, (4) liquid petroleum products, (5) refrigerated liquid products, (6) refrigerated solid products, (7) dump trucking, (8) agricultural commodities, (9) motor vehicles, (10) armored truck service, (11) building materials, (12) films and associated commodities, (13) forest products, (14) mine ore, not including coal, (15) retail store delivery service, (16) explosives or dangerous articles, (17) specific commodities not subgrouped.

DEVELOPMENT OF INTERCITY MOTOR FREIGHT TRANSPORTATION
FOR HIRE

Reasons for development. Numerous factors have contributed to the growth of intercity trucking for hire. The slowness of railroad less-than-carload freight service made it necessary for small town merchants to tie up capital in large inventories, with an attendant danger of loss through deterioration or changes in demand. But with the development of over-the-road trucking these merchants were able to get fast and frequent service on small shipments from nearby urban centers. Furthermore, the truckers offered a door to door service which eliminated the expense of hauling shipments to and from the railroad freight houses. The first motor carrier rates tended to be higher than railroad rates, but competition forced them down. Another factor which contributed to the development of intercity trucking was the ease with which an individual could get into the business. Only a small investment was required, and early freedom from regulation left the interstate field, at least, open to all comers. The railroads did not appear to appreciate the possibilities of the motor truck, and at first they did little to use it themselves or to meet the competition of independent operators. Under the circumstances it is not surprising that intercity trucking appeared and grew like Topsy.

Fly-by-night operations. A near chaotic element was brought into the trucking industry in the early years of the 1929 depression by unemployed truck drivers who purchased trucks on credit and went into the intercity trucking business. Usually these operators knew little and cared less about the intricacies of depreciation, depreciation reserves, and other sound business practices; striving only for sufficient revenues to pay for gas and oil, make the payments on their trucks, and have enough left over to live on. A major repair bill or a major loss or damage claim might force them out of business, but others came along to take their places. This sort of operation was hard on the railroads and on established trucking concerns, and the irresponsible and uncertain services of these fly-by-night operators gave the intercity motor transport industry a black eye among shippers. Fortunately, the extension of state and federal regulation brought this sort of activity to an end and made possible the development of the industry on a solid and responsible basis.

Size of individual carriers. As might be expected, there has been a tendency in recent years for large intercity trucking concerns to develop, partly through the unification of smaller concerns and partly through the extension of the operations of existing companies. Nevertheless, the industry still remains one of predominantly small units. In 1948, Mr. E. M. Welliver, an official of the American Trucking Associations, estimated that there were 30,000 for-hire companies in existence, most of them small operators. Of carriers subject to the jurisdiction of the Interstate Commerce Commission 26 per cent operated one truck, 44 per cent one or two trucks, 56 per cent one to three trucks, and 92 per cent fewer than ten trucks. Companies having average gross operating revenues of $100,000 or more per year made up only 7 per cent of the motor carriers subject to the Commission's jurisdiction at that time, and even these carriers operated an average of only twenty-nine vehicles per company.[8]

Average length of haul. Intercity motor freight transportation is especially adapted to short haul movements. Motor carrier terminal costs are low relative to railroad terminal costs, but over-the-road costs are relatively high per ton mile because of the limited carrying capacity of the truck. On short hauls the lower motor carrier terminal costs more than offset the higher over-the-road costs, thus giving the motor carrier a clear cost advantage on the short haul. But as the length of the haul increases the lower railroad line-haul costs more than offset the higher terminal costs, and the cost advantage shifts to the railroad. Thus as the length of haul increases the motor carrier finds it increasingly difficult to compete with the railroad. Also, although this is of lesser importance, the service disadvantage of the railroad diminishes somewhat as the length of haul increases. In 1949 the average length of haul per ton of freight carried by motor carriers subject to the Interstate Commerce Commission and having average annual gross operating revenues of $100,000 or more was 218 miles for common carriers and 129 miles for contract carriers.[9] By con-

---

[8] Department of Commerce, *Industry Report, Domestic Transportation,* May-August, 1948, p. 58.
[9] Interstate Commerce Commission, *Statistics of Class I Motor Carriers,* 1949, pp. 39, 40.

fining itself to high grade freight moving under high rates, however, a motor carrier can compete for traffic over considerable distances.

MOTOR FREIGHT V. RAILROAD FREIGHT TRANSPORTATION

Advantages of motor freight. Although there is not a great deal of difference between railroad and motor freight rates, many shippers have found motor transportation the more economical. Goods need not be packed so carefully, and in some cases they need not be packed at all. Thus there results a saving in the cost of containers and packing and a saving in the weight on which the total charge is computed. Some shippers find, too, that damage is less when goods are shipped by truck. Because of the smaller capacity of the truck, motor carriers can offer a rate on truckload lots intermediate between the railroad carload and less-than-carload rates, and this is an advantage in the case of shipments which, while fairly large, are not large enough to justify a carload rate. Shippers and receivers of carload freight are expected to load and unload their freight, but on truckload shipments this work is done by the carrier. And if a business concern has no railroad siding, it must transport carload freight to or from a public team track, an expense which is not incurred when motor carrier service is used.

Another advantage of motor freight transportation is an inherent flexibility which makes it adaptable to changing conditions and needs. Furthermore, railroad transportation service is restricted to communities located on railroad tracks, but the motor carrier can reach practically any point in the United States. A note of caution, however, is in order here. The impression is sometimes given that motor carriers for hire provide service to every community in the country, but it does not follow that ability to serve is identical with an actual provision of service. Regular route carriers will serve only those communities along the route they have selected, and routes are not likely to be established to communities which will not generate enough traffic to make service worth while. Similarly, the services of irregular carriers will be confined to points where traffic is available. This is not intended to belittle motor freight transportation, for it provides service to a large number of communities which would not otherwise have commercial transportation available.

Elimination of terminal delay, among other things, makes motor freight service faster than railroad freight. Furthermore, since the motor truck is a much smaller unit than a railroad freight train, motor carriers are in a position to offer more frequent service wherever they generate enough traffic to make such service possible. For this same reason railroad freight service must be adapted to meet the needs of shippers in general and the exigencies of efficient railroad operation, while motor freight service is more readily adaptable to the needs of individual shippers. Motor truck transportation also has demonstrated special advantages in connection with the movement of certain kinds of freight. Perishables can be handled rapidly, and sometimes over fairly long distances, without the necessity of refrigeration or expensive packing. Liquid petroleum products are delivered at small communities without the need for railroad sidings, tank car unloading devices, and large above ground storage facilities. Farmers can move cattle to market in small lots to take advantage of favorable price conditions and with a smaller degree of loss from shrinkage. And in various other ways motor transportation is being adapted to special uses.

Advantages of railroad freight transportation. The demonstrated advantages of railroad freight transportation are two in number. In the first place, railroads are organized in such a way as to provide low cost mass transportation. Where volume shipments are concerned, motor carriers simply cannot compete. For example, on the basis of average loads carried it will take more than four large tractor and trailer combinations to handle the freight moved in a single freight car.[10] Thus a locomotive hauling a train of fifty cars with a crew of perhaps five men can pull as much freight as 200 large highway vehicles driven by 200 men, and burning fuel in 200 separate engines. The second big advantage of the railroad lies in its ability to handle practically every kind of freight. Although it is said that trucks can haul anything, anytime, and anywhere, truck transportation is very definitely limited by costs and highway restrictions.

Since each type of carrier has special advantages in certain types of movements, it would seem that shippers would benefit by making use of motor freight transportation for relatively short hauls of specified commodities and using the railroad to handle volume freight and such goods as the motor carriers cannot handle either because of physical or cost limitations. Obviously such a procedure would be advantageous to shippers, but it is possible only to the extent that shippers at any given point can provide sufficient traffic to enable such a division of business to be made. As pointed out in Chapter 16, the Interstate Commerce Commission has said that shippers are entitled to such transportation service as they can support, but they cannot have more than they can support.

Private carriers. The figures on truck ownership given on page 372 indicate that a substantial volume of intercity freight is moved by commercial and industrial concerns in their own vehicles. Two principal

---

[10] In 1949 the average load carried by tractor-trailer combinations was 10.19 tons. See Bureau of Public Roads, *Highway Statistics, 1949,* p. 32. Rail carloads averaged 46.13 tons. See Interstate Commerce Commission, *Statistics of Railways in the United States,* 1949, p. 44.

advantages accrue from private ownership of transportation facilities. In the first place, for a relatively small investment a manufacturing or distributing concern can provide a transportation service which is directly keyed to the needs of its business, thus obtaining maximum flexibility of service. And in the second place, if a relatively steady volume of traffic is available, substantial economies may result from industry ownership. Substantial increases in railroad and motor carrier freight rates have provided a further incentive to the growth of private transportation. It should be noted, however, that many concerns do not have sufficient volume or a sufficiently steady volume of traffic to enable them to provide their own transportation facilities. Furthermore, in many cases private carriers have to move empty in one direction, and this increases costs.

Rail and motor traffic trends. Some idea of the effect of highway transportation, private as well as for hire, on railroad traffic can be gleaned from the figures shown on page 21. Before the Second World War there was a slow but steady increase percentagewise in the volume of highway traffic as compared with rail traffic. During the war there was both a relative and an absolute decline in highway transportation, but as soon as the wartime disabilities on truck transportation were removed, shippers began to turn again to the motor carriers. The shift to trucks covers a wide variety of products, particularly in the higher grades of freight. Perhaps one of the most marked shifts has occurred in connection with the movement of livestock, long a major item of traffic for many railroads, to the trucks.

MOTOR PASSENGER TRANSPORTATION

Motor bus transportation. The motor bus as a distinct type of vehicle appeared about 1922, and for a number of years it was little more than an elongated passenger automobile. In due course, however, manufacturers began to produce specialized vehicles for different uses, and many of today's buses bear little resemblance to their prototypes of the early 1920's. Probably the first major use of the motor bus was by urban traction companies who used it for line extensions and as a substitute for street cars on light traffic runs. Today, as a result of the greater economy of operation, bus service has largely replaced street railway service in all except the larger cities. The bus also has found a very important use in the transportation of school children in rural areas, and it has made possible the development of consolidated schools with superior educational facilities. Buses are used extensively for sight-seeing purposes and to transport athletic teams, orchestras, and other organized groups. And, of course, there has been an extensive development of intercity common carrier bus transportation.

The figures in Table XIV give some idea of the relative importance of different types of bus use.

Table XIV

BUS OWNERSHIP CLASSIFIED AS TO BUS USE, DECEMBER 31, 1947 [11]

Nature of Use	Number of Buses Owned
Common carriers:	
Intercity operations	31,900
City operations	34,250
City-suburban operations	19,850
Charter hire and sightseeing operations	3,000
School bus operations	85,900

Common carrier intercity bus service. The tremendous growth in the popularity of the private passenger automobile in the 1920's, together with the expansion of hard surfaced highways, brought about a serious decline in electric interurban and local steam railroad traffic, and in time this decline spread to longer distance movements as well. Frequency of service was reduced to conform with the reduced volume of traffic as nearly as state laws and regulatory commissions would permit, and little or nothing was done to improve the quality of railroad passenger service, particularly on local runs.

The deterioration of railroad passenger service provided a ready made opportunity for motor bus operations in intercity service. The motor bus provided a transportation unit which was much more in keeping with the available volume of intercity traffic, and it could be operated at a mere fraction of the cost of operating a railroad passenger train. Under the circumstances motor bus operators were able to offer service at rates substantially below those charged by the rail lines. Also, the small carrying capacity of the bus made possible more frequent service where volume of traffic permitted. Except in congested areas a faster service could be offered, and the bus trip was infinitely cleaner and more pleasant than local railroad service. Also contributing to the growth of motor bus service was the early absence of regulation and the fact that the purchase of a bus required only a relatively small investment, a down payment of 25 per cent with the balance paid off over a period of three years being all that was necessary. These factors proved to be an inducement for large numbers of small operators to go into the business.

Offsetting in some degree the advantages of early bus travel was the unreliability and the financial irresponsibility of some early operators, but with the development of larger and more responsible bus companies, and

---

[11] National Association of Motor Bus Operators, *Bus Facts*, 18th ed., Washington, 1948, pp. 30-31.

the enactment of state and federal laws requiring safety devices, operating rules, maximum hours of service for drivers, and liability insurance of one sort or another, this feature of early bus operations has been largely eliminated. Another factor which tended to retard the development of intercity motor bus transportation was the unsatisfactory nature of the buses used. Their riding qualities left much to be desired, and they grew worse as a bus grew older. Heating devices using exhaust gases from the motor were hazardous and hard to control, lighting was inadequate, and seats were uncomfortable. Continuous improvement, however, eliminated these difficulties to a large extent. Improved tire equipment, low hung bodies, shock absorbers, smooth running power plants, and careful attention to maintenance have worked a revolution in the riding qualities of modern buses. Hot water heating, air conditioning, improved lighting, and better seats all have contributed to the comfort of bus passengers.

Volume of traffic. Statistics on the volume of intercity bus traffic are shown on page 22. During World War II bus travel increased substantially but declined relative to railroad passenger traffic. Since the end of the war there has been a steady decline in bus travel, but the decline is not nearly as marked as the decline in rail passenger traffic.

Length of haul. Bus trip lengths vary widely with operating conditions and other factors, but it is agreed that the average distance traveled by the typical bus patron is short. A survey conducted during the first two weeks of December 1942, and shown in Table XV, reveals this fact clearly.

Table XV

DISTANCES TRAVELED BY PASSENGERS ON INTERCITY BUSES AND MILES IN EACH DISTANCE GROUP
in percentages of total [12]

Distances Traveled	% of Total Number of Passengers	% of Total Passenger Miles
Under 25 miles	56.8	14.2
26 to 50 miles	19.3	14.1
51 to 75 miles	7.3	8.9
76 to 100 miles	4.6	7.7
101 to 150 miles	4.8	11.7
151 to 200 miles	2.2	7.4
201 to 250 miles	1.6	6.7
Over 250 miles	3.4	29.2

The fact that more than three-fourths of all bus passengers traveled fifty miles or less establishes a pattern for the function of the intercity motor

---

[12] National Association of Bus Operators, *The Intercity Bus Industry at War.* Washington: 1943, p. 35. Figures based on operations of companies having average gross operating revenues of $100,000 or more per year.

bus, but the fact that almost 30 per cent of the total passenger miles was generated by individuals traveling in excess of 250 miles indicates the importance of the longer haul traffic to the bus companies themselves.

Size of companies. Unlike the motor freight business which is characterized by many small operators, the motor bus industry has shown strong tendencies toward integration. Many of the numerous small operators of the 1920's were unable to survive. Irregular service, poor maintenance, failure to keep schedules, and general irresponsibility made it clear that the motor passenger carrier industry would have to be put on a sound business basis if it were to survive. Larger companies could afford to employ specialists in the various phases of motor bus operations, provide adequate maintenance facilities and standby equipment, and in various other ways achieve economies and improve service in ways not open to the small operator.

Other factors contributed to the movement toward integration. Since railroad passenger fares are based on a flat charge per mile, motor bus operators can compete with the railroads on a price basis for longer haul traffic in a way not open to motor freight carriers. But to do this meant that schedules had to be integrated and service established by the most direct practical routes between distant points. To attempt to establish interline arrangements involving a large number of companies operating over short distances with uncertain and unreliable schedules was obviously impossible. Finally, the necessity of providing new and costly equipment to meet the challenge of the railroads, at last undertaking a competitive struggle to regain some of the traffic lost to the bus and private automobile, required capital outlays far beyond the abilities of small operators. The number of common carrier bus companies declined from a peak of 23,301 in 1928 to about 2,700 in 1948.

The first nationwide service was established in 1929 with the consolidation of a number of companies into the Greyhound system. Another nationwide service is offered by the National Trailways System, but this is made up of separate companies which cooperate in the handling of through traffic. Motor bus companies having gross annual operating revenues of $100,000 or more numbered only about 280 in 1948, but these companies performed an estimated 91 per cent of the service rendered by motor bus companies.[13]

Bus v. rail travel—local service. The bus still holds a commanding advantage over the railroad train in local service. Perhaps its outstanding advantage is the greater frequency of service made possible by the smaller

---

[13] National Association of Motor Bus Operators, *Bus Facts*, 19th ed., Washington, 1949, p. 5.

size of the bus unit. It is difficult to generalize on the subject of speed as between local rail and bus service, but differences in elapsed time between stations on short hauls are not likely to be sufficient to be of any significance. The quality of the accommodations provided on local passenger trains has improved considerably on many runs, but as a general rule the bus offers a cleaner and more pleasant trip. Local bus fares today do not depart greatly from railroad fares although they are still somewhat below the railroad level. In view of the great service advantages enjoyed by the bus in local transportation service there is no particular reason why short haul bus fares need be lower than rail fares for similar hauls.

Bus v. rail travel—long haul. On longer hauls the service advantages of the bus disappear rapidly. Modern through passenger trains operate in rural areas at speeds far in excess of those which the law and prudent driving permit on the highways. And in congested urban areas railroad trains operating over a private right of way maintain even greater relative speeds than buses complying with city speed laws and slowed down by traffic lights and congestion. Through passenger trains make few stops, while except on a relatively small number of express runs, buses stop frequently to provide local short haul service. Furthermore, rest stops and meal stops are unnecessary on through railroad passenger trains, providing a further saving in time. All of this adds up to the fact that railroad passenger service is much faster, generally speaking, than even through bus service on the longer hauls.

Other advantages accrue to the railroad on long hauls. The greater space available in railroad cars makes it possible to provide more comfortable accommodations. Dining car meals, while more expensive than the bus station variety, usually may be eaten at leisure and in comfort as compared with the hurried bolting of food while sitting on lunch counter stools. Finally, where overnight travel is necessary the traveler may have a choice of a variety of reasonably comfortable bed arrangements. Even the railroad coach traveler who prefers to sleep in his seat has an advantage over the bus traveler because of the wider seats and greater leg room provided.

Long haul traffic is of some importance to motor passenger transport companies because of the substantial volume of passenger miles which such traffic generates, because of the possibility of increasing the load factors of buses operating in essentially local service, and possibly because it may have some advertising value. In order to offset the speed and service advantages of through railroad travel the bus lines have had to resort to reduced fares to get a share of the long distance travel, and these lower fares constitute the principal incentive today for long distance bus travel.

Railroad operation of bus service. The superior advantage of the bus in short haul service, together with the way in which bus operators were cutting into railroad passenger traffic, led the railroads themselves to inaugurate bus service as far back as 1924, and today bus service is offered by railroads in all parts of the United States. While some railroad bus operations are directly competitive with independent bus companies, the railroads have found the bus useful as a substitute for branch line passenger service. Buses may be used to provide service at poorly patronized points on main lines, thus reducing the number of train stops which in turn reduces operating costs and speeds the time of train service. And in various other ways buses are used to supplement railroad service.

SUBSIDY PROBLEM

Problem stated. For a good many years the railroads complained that highway transportation was unfairly subsidized because motor carriers made inadequate payments for the use of the highways. At first the motor carriers ignored these complaints, but as highway user taxes mounted, they began to talk back, and more recently they have taken the position that motor transportation pays its full share and more of all highway costs. Before World War II the public did not seem to concern itself greatly over this controversy. Indeed, some were inclined to believe that it was just a matter of the big railroads trying to squeeze their little motor carrier competitors out of business. Highway deterioration in the postwar years, however, coupled with rising costs of construction and maintenance, has completely altered this picture; and motor carrier use of the highways has become a matter of very definite public concern. This concern has given rise to two important questions. Are present weight restrictions adequate to protect the highways, and are motor carrier user charges adequate to cover the motor carriers' share of construction and maintenance costs? While these two problems are closely interrelated, it is with the second that the present discussion is concerned.

Difficulties encountered. In attempting to determine whether or not motor carriers are paying their share of highway costs, the student must recognize that motor carriers are not the only beneficiaries of highway improvements. It is recognized that a part of the cost of highway construction and maintenance is chargeable to the general public because of the broad economic and social benefits derived from this expansion of the nation's transportation facilities. A part of the cost also is chargeable to special local beneficiaries, such as property owners who find the value of their property enhanced as a result of highway improvements. And, of course, a part is chargeable to highway users as a group, including motor carriers. Hence the first step in determining whether or not motor carriers pay their way is to determine what portion of highway costs is chargeable to highway users as a class. Actually no completely logical basis exists for making this allocation, although obviously the method used will have a profound effect on the final result. Differences of opinion on this point alone may lead competent and unbiased students to reach entirely different conclusions, and it provides an opportunity for the special pleader to reach any conclusion he wishes.

Once determined, the highway users' share must be divided between the operators of light vehicles and the operators of heavy buses, trucks, and trucking combinations. Here, again, the possibility of wide variations in estimates exists. It is claimed by some that vehicle sizes and weights affect highway costs only to a minor extent, but others maintain that heavy buses and trucks require wider and thicker road surfaces than are necessary for passenger car and light truck operations. Finally a division of costs must be made between different kinds of users. It would seem reasonable to suppose that operators who make regular and frequent use of the main rural highways should pay more for their use than operators who rarely leave the city streets or the operators of farm vehicles which move extensively over country roads. But whether such cost allocations should be made on the basis of vehicle miles traveled, ton miles carried, or some other measure of frequency of use is a problem on which there are sharp differences of opinion.

Having arrived at some figure which purports to show the highway carriers' share of total highway costs, this figure must be compared with the user payments made by intercity motor carriers. Sometimes total tax payments made by all bus and truck operators are cited as if they represented the highway carriers' contribution to highway costs, but taxes paid on urban vehicles and on farm vehicles operated in part on country roads should not be included as a part of the highway carriers' contribution. Nor do all highway carrier tax payments represent payments for the use of the highways. Highway carriers, like other business concerns, are expected to pay taxes for the general support of government, and such taxes should be sharply distinguished from highway user charges. This distinction is of some importance in comparing the relative burden of rail and motor carrier taxation.

Hypothetical taxes. If motor carriers were required to provide their own highways, these highways would be subject to property taxation in the same way that railroad rights of way are taxed today. Since, however, motor carriers operate over publicly owned roads, they are relieved of this particular tax burden and the Government is deprived of a source of tax revenue. It should be pointed out that the problem involved here has nothing to do with taxes paid for the use of the highways but relates rather to taxes levied for the general support of government. It is possible to estimate the amount of property tax the motor carriers would have to pay if they owned their own roads and to consider their freedom from these hypothetical taxes as an element of subsidy. Such a procedure, however, is questionable because it is the total burden of all taxes levied for the support of government that is important, not the burden of any one tax.

The Board of Investigation and Research made a study of relative tax burdens as of 1940 but was unable to find any completely satisfactory base for measuring these burdens. Using the ratio of all taxes paid, exclusive of highway user and old age insurance taxes, to operating revenues, the Board found that the tax burden constituted the following percentages of operating revenues:

Pipe lines	20.1%	Water carriers	5.5%
Railroads	8.2	Air lines	5.2
Bus lines	7.4	Truck lines	4.1

Using national income contributions as a base, bus lines displaced railroads in second place, but otherwise the rankings remained unchanged.[14] These figures suggest that as of 1940 there was little difference in the burden of railroad and bus line taxes but that the lower truck line tax burden created an artificial advantage in favor of motor freight carriers.

Report of Federal Coordinator of Transportation. A study of public aid to highway transportation was made by the staff of the Federal Coordinator of Transportation during the 1930's.[15] The Coordinator's staff first calculated the cost and expected life of street and highway improvements made during the period 1921-37, and from this information derived the annual cost of the improvements. An annual interest charge on the capital outlay and an annual charge covering maintenance and other expenses were added, thus giving the total annual cost of providing streets and roads.[16] Next, the amount of the annual cost chargeable to motor vehicle users as a class was estimated, and this amount was divided among different vehicle groups on the basis of conditions existing in 1932. The conclusion reached by the Coordinator's staff was that school buses, farm trucks, and certain sizes of private trucks failed to pay their share of highway costs; that passenger automobiles paid slightly more than their share; and that vehicles operated for hire, except five ton trucks and trucks of 1½ tons capacity or less, paid more than their share, in some cases by very substantial amounts.

The methods employed in reaching the above conclusion were too de-

---

[14] *Carrier Taxation,* 79th Congress, 1st Session, House Document No. 160, p. 49.
[15] *Public Aids to Transportation,* Vol. IV. A convenient summary is given in Vol. I, pp. 25-30.
[16] This procedure is described in greater detail in Chapter 22.

tailed and technical to warrant discussion here, but they did not go un-challenged.[17] The Coordinator's staff used seven different methods of cost allocation, each of which, with the exception of the one adopted, showed that for-hire trucks failed to pay their way, sometimes by very substantial amounts. Also, some question was raised about the propriety of ignoring all street and road improvements made before 1921, but this is proper since these earlier improvements conferred little benefit on highway transportation in its modern form. The point would not be worth mentioning if the Coordinator's staff had followed a similar procedure in calculating public aid to railroads. As pointed out in Chapter 3, the Coordinator's study included every sort of public aid to railroads from the beginning of railroad history even though a number of these aids were of no conceivable benefit to present-day railroads. As far as the present value of the study is concerned it is pertinent to point out that conclusions based on 1932 conditions are meaningless in the light of the increased carrying capacity of the typical freight vehicle and the enormous increase in intercity trucking which has taken place since 1932.

Report of Board of Investigation and Research. The Board of Investigation and Research made a study of public aid to highway transportation as of 1940, using the same general procedure employed by the Coordinator's staff.[18] Its conclusions, however, were quite different. In allocating the highway users' share of total annual costs among different vehicle types the Board's staff concluded that passenger cars, light delivery trucks used locally, and miscellaneous bus types more than paid their way, while payments were approximately equal to costs for smaller intercity buses. Large intercity buses failed to pay their share by 30 per cent, farm trucks by 24 per cent, nonfarm single unit trucks by from 13 per cent to 28 per cent depending upon size, and trucking combinations by 39 per cent. Thus it would appear from the Board's study that vehicles of the type used by highway carriers failed to pay their share of highways costs by rather substantial amounts.

The Board's study also has been subject to criticism. Motor carriers objected particularly to the fact that the highway users' share of total costs was allocated among different types of vehicles on the basis of gross ton miles moved. This technique throws a heavy burden of cost onto highway carriers since they use the largest vehicles and use them more intensively than do other operators. The procedure has the effect of charging as much cost to one 15 ton truck as is charged to ten 1½ ton passenger cars, and it is said that it takes more road investment and main-

---

[17] See Association of American Railroads, *What is Public Aid to Transportation?* Washington, 1940.

[18] *Public Aids to Domestic Transportation,* Chapter IV.

tenance to provide for ten passenger cars than one large vehicle. Furthermore, the technique ignores the fact that on large vehicles the load is distributed over several axles and wheels, and it is generally agreed that wheel and axle loads are more significant than gross weights in measuring wear of highways. Finally, there are some highway costs which have no relationship at all to the weight of the vehicle.

Significance of reports. It is clear that the conclusions reached by the Board's staff cannot be accepted as proof that motor carriers are being subsidized. But neither can it be said that the Coordinator's report presents satisfactory evidence that they are not being subsidized. The reports, however, are not without a certain significance. This is because they have enabled both the proponents and the opponents of the highway carriers to cite the work of presumably impartial and publicly sponsored agencies as proving their respective points of view. The student of transportation should, therefore, have some familiarity with the shortcomings of these two studies and should question any conclusion which may be drawn from them.

Postwar deterioration of highways. Since the end of World War II there has been a noticeable deterioration of highway surfaces all over the United States, and this fact, coupled with increased costs of highway construction and maintenance, has caused considerable alarm. The railroads have not hesitated to exploit this highway deterioration, blaming it on the "box cars of the highways," and pointing out that railroads build and maintain their own rights of way without cost to the taxpayer. Motor carriers have taken the position that they are the victims of a "well heeled" railroad propaganda machine designed to drive motor carriers out of business and deprive shippers of the advantage of highway transportation. They also have maintained that such highway deterioration as existed was the result of deferred maintenance and lack of new construction during the war years. Nevertheless, there is a growing popular belief that the nation's highways are being worn out by heavy commercial vehicles faster than they can be replaced, and legislatures are considering and adopting more stringent regulations of highway use and increased taxation of motor carriers.

To some extent highway officials and engineers blame highway deterioration on the *overloaded* vehicle rather than on the heavy vehicle as such. About two-thirds of the states prohibit axle loads in excess of 18,000 pounds, and it is said that most main roads were built to sustain such loads, but some truckers do not hesitate to violate load limits wherever they can. Commissioner MacDonald of the Bureau of Public Roads has testified that no more than 8 axles per 1,000 trucks were overloaded in 1931 but that in 1950 there were 86 overloaded axles per 1,000 trucks.

DEVELOPMENT OF HIGHWAY TRANSPORTATION

Taking into consideration a three-fold increase in truck traffic, Mr. Mac-Donald reached the conclusion that there has been a thirty-fold increase in overloading since 1931.[19] If this is correct, then it would appear that the public and the law abiding majority of highway carriers are suffering from the sins of an irresponsible minority of truckers.

La Plata road tests. Until recently there has been a dearth of objective evidence on the effect of heavy vehicle loads on highway surfaces. In 1950, however, several states, in cooperation with the Bureau of Public Roads, initiated tests under conditions of actual use. A 1.1 mile strip of concrete pavement south of La Plata, Maryland, was divided into four separate one-half mile lanes, and over each lane a different vehicle moved back and forth continuously over a period of several months. On two lanes weights of 18,000 pounds and 22,400 pounds were carried on single axles, and on the other two lanes weights of 32,000 pounds and 44,800 pounds were carried on tandem axles.[20] At the end of the test period observations revealed that 26 per cent of the slabs under 18,000 pound single axle loads showed cracks which were attributed to the application of the test axle load, while 58 per cent of the slabs under 22,400 pound single axle loads showed similar failures. Twenty-seven per cent of the slabs under 32,000 pound tandem axle loads showed failures, and 96 per cent of the slabs under 44,800 pound loads showed cracks attributed to the vehicle load. The 44,800 pound loads were discontinued before the end of the test period because of the rapid rate of cracking of the pavement. The quality of the concrete used in the road and the nature of the subsoil were similar to much other pavement. The figures would seem to suggest a definite relationship between axle loads and highway deterioration. Other tests are being made on different types of highway surfaces, and these tests should prove extremely valuable in determining whether or not present load limits and user payments are adequate.

SUGGESTED READINGS

American Trucking Associations, Inc., *America's Truck Fleet* and other pamphlets in the series *American Trucking*, Washington, various dates.

Association of American Railroads, *Highway Motor Transportation*, 1945. One of a series of publications dealing with transportation problems. A worthwhile source of information on bus and truck operations containing a substantial amount of objective material.

Board of Investigation and Research, *Public Aids to Domestic Transportation*, 79th Congress, 1st Session, House Document No. 159. Chapter IV contains useful data on highway use.

[19] *Traffic World*, July 8, 1950, pp. 41-43

[20] Tandem axles consist of two axles and two sets of wheels, one directly in front of the other.

Daggett, Stuart, *Principles of Inland Transportation*, 3rd Ed. New York: Harper and Brothers, 1941. Chapter V contains a summary of the development of highway vehicles.

Dearing, Charles L., *American Highway Policy*. Washington: The Brookings Institution, 1941. A substantial study of highway policy.

Department of Commerce, *Industry Report, Domestic Transportation*, October-November, 1945; February-March, 1946; May-August, 1948. The first and third deal with motor freight transportation, the second with rail and bus passenger transportation.

Federal Coordinator of Transportation, *Public Aids to Transportation*, Vol. IV. Public aids to motor vehicle transportation.

Johnson, Emory R., Grover G. Huebner, and G. Lloyd Wilson, *Transportation*. New York: D. Appleton-Century Company, 1940. Part VI.

Locklin, D. Philip, *Economics of Transportation*, 3rd Ed. Chicago: Richard D. Irwin, Inc., 1947. Chapter XXVIII.

Moulton, Harold G., and associates, *The American Transportation Problem*. Washington: The Brookings Institution, 1933. Part VI.

National Association of Motor Bus Operators, *Bus Facts*. Washington: various dates. These annual publications contain a large amount of useful statistical data relative to the motor bus industry.

19.

Regulation
of
HIGHWAY TRANSPORTATION

NATURE OF STATE REGULATION

General. Regulation of intercity highway transportation was undertaken first by the states. As more and more buses and trucks appeared on the highways, some sort of restriction on their use for commercial transportation became necessary in the interest of highway conservation and public safety. Furthermore, some early bus and truck services were operated on a shoestring, often by individuals with little knowledge of sound business procedures, and the financial irresponsibility of some of these early operators made it desirable to enact legislation to protect shippers and the public generally. No doubt, too, the complaints of the railroads about the unfairness of unregulated competition contributed to the development of motor carrier regulation. As might be expected state laws vary widely in scope and specific detail, and for that reason it is not possible to discuss state regulation in a book like this except in rather general terms.

Legal bases for regulation. The police power provides the states with a clear basis for regulating motor common carriers, and at least a partial basis for regulating the activities of contract and private carriers.[1] In addition to the police power, the states have another clear right to regulate all types of highway carriers through the exercise of what may be called the proprietary power. As the owners of the highways the states have an indisputable right to regulate the conditions of their use in the interest of conservation and to protect the rights of all users. It should be noted, too, that the rights of the states to regulate intrastate highway transportation have not been subordinated to Interstate Commerce Commission control as has happened in connection with the regulation of intrastate railroad transportation. State regulation of highway transportation is real.

Regulation of highway use. All states have found it necessary to specify the physical characteristics of the vehicles which are permitted to operate on their highways. Limitations are placed on the width, height,

---

[1] For a discussion of the police power see p. 99.

length, and weight of highway vehicles, with maximum lengths and weights varying with the type of vehicle and the number of axles and wheels supporting its weight. In addition, lighting and brake equipment must conform with certain standards. Other highway use regulations include speed limits, limitations on the number of hours a driver may work, minimum age of drivers, and the like. All such regulations clearly are within the scope of the police and proprietary powers of the states.

Regulation of common carriers. The right of the states to regulate common carriers had become so well established that laws enacted for the purpose of regulating motor common carriers were not challenged. There are, of course, wide variations in state laws, but intrastate motor common carriers are quite generally subject to the following requirements. A certificate must be obtained from the proper state authority as a prerequisite to operation, and in almost all states the applicant must prove that public convenience and necessity require the issuance of such a certificate. This requirement makes it possible for regulatory bodies to exercise some control over competition without eliminating it altogether. In general, the authority of state regulatory bodies over intrastate common carriers by highway is similar to that exercised by the Interstate Commerce Commission over railroads. It includes, in most states, the regulation of rates, fares, and charges; the usual provisions with reference to the filing and publishing of tariffs and abiding by them; suspension of proposed rate changes; prohibition of discrimination; regulation of service; control over accounts; requirement of periodic reports; and, in a number of cases, control over security issues and intercorporate relationships. The reasons for these various provisions have been discussed in connection with the development of railroad regulation and need not be repeated here.

Regulation of contract carriers. While the right of the states to regulate common carriers had been recognized by the courts for many years, no similar judicial sanction existed for the regulation of contract carriers. Indeed, since contract carriers did not hold themselves out to serve the public at large, there appeared to be a sound basis for believing that their's was not a business affected with the public interest in the same sense as was the business of common carriage. Nevertheless, the states sought from the beginning to regulate motor contract carriers in much the same way as motor common carriers.

There were sound reasons why the states believed it to be necessary to regulate contract carriers. Common carriers were required to accept all goods offered to them of the type they professed to carry. They accepted small shipments as well as large, and they handled some unprofitable business along with the profitable. Contract carriers, on the other hand, assumed no obligation to handle small and unprofitable ship-ments, and this made it possible for them to undercut common carrier rates on the more desirable traffic. But obviously the common carriers could not be expected to render a general transportation service unless they could get a reasonable share of profitable business to go along with the unprofitable. If no control were exercised over contract carriers, it might be necessary to relax the restrictions on common carriers or per-haps see them forced out of business. Experience had demonstrated that a relaxation of regulation was out of the question, yet abandonment of operations would work a real hardship on numerous shippers whose business was too small to be of interest to contract carriers.

Furthermore, failure to regulate contract carriers would open the door to widespread evasion of laws enacted to regulate common carriers. For example, a contract carrier by providing itself with the necessary equipment could put itself in a position to serve such a large part of the public that to all intents and purposes it would be operating as a com-mon carrier. Yet as long as it went through the formality of making a separate contract with each shipper it remained legally a contract carrier. Finally, if no limitations were placed on their operations, con-tract carriers might become so numerous as to damage the highways and constitute a nuisance and a hazard to other highway users.

In 1923 Michigan sought to regulate contract carriage by declaring that any person transporting goods for hire on the public highways was a common carrier, but in 1925 the Supreme Court held that a state could not make a common carrier out of a contract carrier by legislative fiat.[2] A year later the Court threw out a California law for the same reason.[3] In 1931 Texas tried a different approach. In that year legislation was enacted requiring contract carriers to obtain a permit before they could operate. At the same time the railroad commission of the state was given broad powers to control the operation of contract carriers, including the right to fix minimum rates. The law was based largely on the right of the state to protect its highways and to minimize highway congestion in the interest of public safety and in the interest of other highway users. The Supreme Court upheld the Texas law, stating its opinion that the permit requirement was valid as a means of preventing the overtaxing of certain highways. Similarly, control over minimum rates was upheld on the ground that it would

---

[2] *Michigan Public Utilities Commission* v. *Duke*, 266 U.S. 570. In this early case the Court used the terms "public carrier" and "private carrier for hire" instead of those used above.

[3] *Frost & Frost Trucking Co.* v. *Railroad Commission of California*, 271 U.S. 583. See also *Smith* v. *Cahoon*, 283 U.S. 553 (1931).

prevent contract carriers from undercutting railroad rates and thus diverting an excessive amount of traffic to the highways.[4]

Thus Texas found in the proprietary power a broad basis for the regulation of contract carriers, and the other states were not slow in enacting legislation based on the same principle. There is, however, even more variation in the extent and nature of state regulation of contract carriers than is true of state regulation of common carriers.

Regulation of private carriers. In recent years an increasing amount of traffic has been moving over the highways in vehicles owned or leased by industrial and commercial concerns for the transportation of their own goods. The effect of the private carrier on the carrier for hire is similar in some respects to the effect of contract carriers on common carriers, and any large-scale expansion of private transportation could lead to the overcrowding and overloading of certain highways. The regulation of private carriers, however, involves real constitutional difficulties. A state might require private carriers to obtain a permit of some sort, but it is hard to see how a state could grant permits to some and not to others. Only a few states have attempted any regulation of private carriers, and where such regulation has been attempted it usually is limited to requiring a permit, restricting the hours of service of drivers and helpers, or the filing of a liability insurance policy or bond. Of course, private carriers are subject to the laws of road use applicable to all vehicle operators.

STATE REGULATION OF INTERSTATE COMMERCE BY HIGHWAY

Right of interstate carriers to use highways. The fact that interstate carriers operate on state-owned highways gives the states a somewhat greater jurisdiction over interstate commerce by motor vehicle than is true of interstate commerce by railroad. In has been held, for example, that it is a valid exercise of the police power for a state to require interstate carriers to obtain a certificate or permit as a condition prerequisite to the use of its highways.[5] But a state may not refuse such a certificate or permit to an interstate carrier doing an interstate business solely on the ground that the route involved already is adequately served.[6] The state may, of course, refuse to grant an interstate carrier the right to do an intrastate business within its borders. A somewhat different situation exists when an interstate carrier wishes to operate over a state highway which is carrying capacity traffic and additional

---

[4] *Stephenson* v. *Binford,* 287 U.S. 251 (1932).
[5] *Clark* v. *Poor,* 274 U.S. 554 (1927).
[6] *Buck* v. *Kuykendall,* 267 U.S. 307 (1925); *Bush* v. *Maloy,* 267 U.S. 317 (1925).

use will endanger the highway or the public safety. Under these circumstances a state is within its rights in refusing an interstate carrier permission to use the highway in question.[7]

Compliance with traffic rules, size and weight limits, etc. It stands to reason that interstate carriers must conform with the speed limits and other ordinary rules of road use as established by the various states. Such regulations are well within the police power of the states, and a dangerous situation would result if intrastate traffic were subject to one set of rules and interstate traffic to another, or to no rules at all. The application of state size and weight limit laws to vehicles operating in interstate commerce has been challenged, but in an early case the Supreme Court held that the states could regulate the size of interstate vehicles in the absence of federal regulation.[8] Obviously the states have some rights in this matter because of their interest in conserving the highways and protecting highway users in general. Whether or not these rights are superior to the right of the Federal Government to regulate interstate commerce is a matter of some uncertainty since Congress has been reluctant to invade this field.

Power to tax interstate carriers. The right of a state to tax interstate carriers using its highways has been the subject of litigation extending back over many years.[9] Inasmuch as interstate carriers, along with intrastate carriers, make use of state highways for purposes of financial gain and at the same time contribute to the wear and tear on such highways, it is reasonable that they should pay a fair sum for their use, and this they are required to do. The courts have rejected the contention that a state tax on motor carriers is invalid as applied to interstate carriers,[10] but it is necessary to make a sharp distinction between taxes levied for the use of the highways and taxes levied on the business of carrying on interstate commerce as such. State taxes of the latter sort have been held unconstitutional.[11]

DEMAND FOR FEDERAL REGULATION

Attitude of states. Since early trucking movements accounted for only an insignificant volume of traffic and most of this was intrastate in nature, there was no initial public demand for federal regulation. As already

---

[7] *Bradley* v. *Public Utilities Commission of Ohio,* 289 U.S. 92 (1933).

[8] *Buck* v. *Kuykendall,* 267 U.S. 307 (1925). See also, *Morris* v. *Duby,* 274 U.S. 135 (1927); *Sproles* v. *Binford,* 286 U.S. 374 (1932).

[9] *Hendrick* v. *State of Maryland,* 235 U.S. 610 (1915); *Kane* v. *State of New Jersey,* 242 U.S. 160 (1916).

[10] *Clark* v. *Poor,* 274 U.S. 554 (1927).

[11] *Interstate Transit, Incorporated* v. *Lindsay,* 283 U.S. 183 (1931).

mentioned, as intercity trucking developed the states sought to control it, but when they tried to limit the use of their highways by carriers operating in interstate commerce they were rebuffed by the Supreme Court. If, then, any limitations were to be placed on the use of the highways by vehicles operating in interstate commerce, Congress would have to act. Hence, soon after the decisions of the Supreme Court in *Buck v. Kuykendall* and *Bush v. Maloy* the National Association of Railroad and Utilities Commissioners selected a committee to draft a federal regulatory proposal. Congress, however, failed to take action on the committee's proposal.

Attitude of railroads. As noted in the last chapter, the railroads did not at first appreciate the potentialities of highway transportation and paid little attention to it. In the course of time, however, highway transportation developed to the point where it became a genuine threat to railroad revenues, and its effect was the more noticeable because of the progress made after 1929, at a time when the railroads were staggering under the effects of a depression-born decline in traffic. Depression-harassed railroad officials were in the vanguard of those urging Congress to assume jurisdiction over the interstate operation of motor carriers.

Attitude of motor transport industry. The motor freight carriers quite generally were opposed to federal regulation. Contract carriers in particular opposed regulation because they feared that it would reduce the advantages they enjoyed over common carrier operators, and both common and contract carriers expressed fear that federal regulation would promote the growth of an unregulated movement of freight by private carriers. In the later stages of the development of the demand for federal regulation, however, some support was received from the larger and more established trucking concerns, the operators of which realized that only disorganization and confusion could result from the continued activities of large numbers of small truckers whose rates and services were subject to no control.

The motor bus industry, unlike the trucking industry, generally favored the adoption of federal regulation. Motor passenger transportation generally was conducted on a much larger scale than was true of motor freight transportation, and because of the necessity of earning a return on a fairly substantial investment, motor bus operators were not unaware of the dangers of duplication of service and unexpected rate wars. They also were harassed at certain points and at certain times of the year by small operators whose sometimes irregular and unpredictable activities constituted a threat to companies seeking to provide regular and dependable service.

Attitude of shippers. Shippers, like motor freight carriers, were divided in their attitude toward federal regulation. Some shippers, concerned only with their immediate self-interest, were afraid that federal regulation would result in higher freight rates, little realizing that the motor transport industry could not survive except on the basis of adequate rates and sound business procedures. Others feared that flexibility of service would suffer if regulation were established. Some shippers, however, saw in regulation a means of ending the uncertainty resulting from unstable rates and unsatisfactory service. Also, small shippers stood to gain because regulation would prevent large shippers from forcing concessions from needy motor carriers.

Other interests. The Joint Committee of Railroads and Highway Users, including delegates from the National Automobile Chamber of Commerce, the National Association of Motor Bus Operators, the American Petroleum Institute, the American Automobile Association, the National Chain Stores Association, and the National Grange, recommended legislation but did not agree on its extent. A large majority of the members of the United States Chamber of Commerce favored comprehensive regulation, but the National Industrial Traffic League, representing shippers, was opposed to more than a minimum of regulation. The Interstate Commerce Commission made two extensive investigations of motor transportation and in 1934 supported a comprehensive regulatory measure. The Federal Coordinator of Transportation also supported comprehensive regulation.

Separate mention may be made of certain elements in the truck marketing field, including sellers of both new and second hand or repossessed trucks. There had been a considerable amount of high-pressure selling of trucks on the installment plan, often to ignorant individuals of little means, on the basis of reckless representations about the profits to be made in trucking; and it may be taken for granted that this enterprising gentry did not look with favor on federal regulation.

Motor Carrier Act, 1935. The Motor Carrier Act, 1935, was the culmination of several years of debate and discussion. The new law, the provisions of which were set up as Part II of the Interstate Commerce Act, applied to the transportation of passengers or property by motor carrier in interstate commerce, to brokers involved in such transportation, and to a limited extent, to private carriers. Actual administration of the law was placed in the hands of the Interstate Commerce Commission. Certain amendments were adopted in 1938, in the Transportation Act of 1940, and during World War II, but it is not necessary to detail these changes here. The discussion which follows is based on the provisions of the law as they existed in early 1952.

REGULATION OF HIGHWAY TRANSPORTATION

GENERAL PROVISIONS

Rights of states. Congress has made it clear that it does not wish to extend its jurisdiction into the field of intrastate commerce by motor vehicle. The law states quite specifically that nothing in its provisions is to be construed to affect the tax powers of the states and that the fact that the Interstate Commerce Commission has permitted a common carrier to operate in interstate commerce does not give that carrier any proprietary or property rights in using the highways of any state. Furthermore, permission to operate in interstate commerce does not carry with it the right to do an intrastate business, nor is there to be any interference with the exclusive right of the states to regulate intrastate commerce by motor carrier. The law even goes so far as to permit common carriers operating wholly within a single state to carry goods and passengers moving in interstate commerce between points within the state without obtaining the permission of the Interstate Commerce Commission, providing that the carrier is lawfully operating under the jurisdiction of a state regulatory authority. In other respects, however, such transportation is subject to the jurisdiction of the Interstate Commerce Commission.

Joint boards. The Commission must, when the operations of a common or contract carrier or of a broker do not involve more than three states, refer to a joint board made up of one representative from each state involved for appropriate proceedings thereon, any of the following matters on which a hearing is required or is deemed desirable by the Commission: (a) applications for rights to operate, including the suspension, modification, or revocation of such rights, (b) applications involving unifications of one sort or another, (c) complaints with regard to rates, and (d) complaints with regard to service, employees' hours of work, requests of intrastate carriers performing an incidental interstate service to be exempted from the law, and certain other miscellaneous matters. The Commission may refer such matters to joint boards where more than three states are involved, and it may refer other matters to these boards. Joint boards hold hearings and report to the Commission, either with or without recommended orders, and these reports and recommended orders are treated in the same way as are the reports and recommended orders of individual Commissioners and examiners in connection with railroad matters.

Size and weight limitations. Motor carriers have complained frequently about the wide variations in the requirements of the various states with reference to size and weights of motor vehicles because these variations unduly complicate their interstate operations. The law does not authorize

REGULATION OF HIGHWAY TRANSPORTATION

the Interstate Commerce Commission to establish size and weight limits for interstate carriers, but it does authorize the Commission to investigate and report on the need for federal regulation in this area.

COMMON CARRIERS

General duties and powers of the Commission. The Commission is charged with the regulation of common carriers by motor vehicle in interstate commerce, and to that end it may establish reasonable requirements with respect to continuous and adequate service, uniform systems of accounts, and so forth, qualifications and maximum hours of service of employees, and safety of operation and equipment.

Certificates of public convenience and necessity. The right to operate as a common carrier is conditioned upon the issuance of a certificate of public convenience and necessity by the Interstate Commerce Commission, and before such a certificate may be issued, the Commission must find that the applicant is fit, willing, and able to perform the service in question and that its proposed service is required by the present or future public convenience and necessity. The certificate, if issued, must indicate the service to be rendered and the route or area to be covered. The law further provides that any certificate may, upon application by the holder and at the discretion of the Commission, be amended or revoked; or it may be suspended, changed, or revoked in the event of a willful failure to comply with the law, Commission regulations, or the terms of the certificate. Certificates are transferable, subject to such rules and regulations as the Commission may prescribe, and subject to the consolidation provisions of the law noted below. As previously noted, carriers operating solely within a single state under the authority of a state regulatory agency need not obtain a certificate to carry interstate property and passengers between points within the state. The Commission may grant temporary operating authority under certain conditions, and many temporary authorizations were issued during World War II.

Grandfather clause. The law contains what is known as a "grandfather clause" which entitles common carriers in bona fide operation on June 1, 1935, to a certificate solely by virtue of that fact. This part of the law is, of course, no longer of any significance.

Dual operation. A single concern may not operate both as a common and as a contract carrier of property over the same route or within the same territory unless the Commission finds that such operation is consistent with the public interest and with the declared policy of Congress. Experience under state regulation had shown that opportunities for mischief existed where carriers enjoyed both a common and a contract status. For example, such a carrier might discriminate between shippers by carrying the goods of a favored shipper under its contract carrier status at a lower charge than was paid by other shippers who were offered only a common carrier service. Congress recognized the possibility of a situation arising in which there might be a legitimate need for dual operation, however, and so it left the final decision up to the Commission.

Issuance of securities. Common carriers and corporations authorized to control such carriers are subject to the same security regulation provisions as apply to railroads, with certain exceptions. Carriers whose total securities do not or will not exceed a par value of $500,000 are exempt from security regulation. Also, notes with a maturity of two years or less may be issued without regard to the percentage relationship of all such notes to the total amount of outstanding securities if such notes in the aggregate do not or will not exceed $100,000. These exceptions take into account the large number of small scale operators carrying goods in interstate commerce by motor vehicle. To require each of them to make formal application for permission to issue securities would swamp the Commission and place an undue financial burden on the carriers themselves. In any event, there is no great public need for controlling the financial practices of the small carrier.

Security for protection of public. Carriers are expected to purchase insurance policies or provide other evidence of responsibility, in such amounts as the Commission may require; and to satisfy judgments arising out of bodily injury, death, or property damage resulting from the operation of their vehicles. Thus a motor carrier is required to do what any responsible motor vehicle operator is expected to do. The Commission also may require common carriers to provide similar protection to meet the valid claims of shippers and consignees arising out of loss or damage to freight. This latter provision reflects the lesser degree of financial responsibility of the typical motor carrier as compared with the typical railroad. Also, the large volume of traffic handled by the railroads makes it possible for them to estimate in advance the extent of their annual liability and make reasonable provision for it.

Rates, fares, and charges. Common carriers of passengers by motor vehicle are required to provide safe and adequate service, equipment, and facilities; just and reasonable rates; and just and reasonable regulations and practices relating thereto. They must also establish reasonable through routes and joint rates with each other, and they may establish such routes and rates with common carriers by rail or water. Wherever joint rates are established the carriers involved are expected to divide them equitably. If the Commission finds after a hearing that an individual or joint rate, or the regulations and practices relating thereto, is unjust or unreasonable or discriminatory, it may fix the rate to be charged, the maximum or the minimum rate, or the maximum and minimum rates, and it may establish lawful regulations and practices related thereto. It is authorized, after a hearing, to require the establishment of through routes and joint rates between motor passenger carriers, and in all cases where joint rates have been established it has the authority to determine an equitable division of such rates.

Common carriers of property by motor vehicle must provide safe and adequate service, equipment, and facilities; establish just and reasonable rates, charges, and classifications; and just and reasonable regulations and practices relating thereto. Common carriers of property by motor vehicle are not required to establish through routes and joint rates, but they may do so, either with other common carriers by motor vehicle or with common carriers by railroad, express, or water. If the Commission finds after a hearing that an individual or joint rate, or a classification, regulation, or practice affecting rates is unjust, unreasonable, or discriminatory, it may fix the lawful rate, the maximum or minimum, or the maximum and minimum, and it may establish lawful classifications, regulations, and practices. Where joint rates have been established it has the authority to determine equitable divisions of such rates.

Various reasons may be cited for the failure of Congress to require motor carriers of property to establish through routes and joint rates. Establishment of a through route may necessitate the participation of a large number of carriers because of the limited range of operation of the typical motor carrier, and this makes it difficult to work out satisfactory arrangements covering liability, equitable divisions of rates, and the like. Furthermore, it may be difficult to coordinate schedules to eliminate delays on through movements, and it is difficult for originating carriers to keep track of changed conditions at numerous distant points. Also, some carriers may be unwilling to accept part hauls of through freight because the rates that would have to be charged in competition with the lower railroad rates for long hauls are not commensurate with the cost of rendering the service. Some through routes and joint rates may be profitable and desirable, however, particularly those involving relatively short movements or where connecting carriers have unused capacity in their trucks, and so the law wisely permits the establishment of such routes and rates at the discretion of the carriers.

Rate-making directives. In determining the justness or reasonableness of motor carrier rates the Commission may not include in property value either good will, earning power, or the value of the certificate under which a carrier is operating. This is followed by a rule of rate making which directs the Commission, in the exercise of its power to prescribe just and reasonable rates, to give due consideration, among other factors, to the inherent advantages of transportation by motor carriers; to the effect of rates upon the movement of traffic by the carrier or carriers for which the rates are prescribed; to the need, in the public interest, of adequate and efficient transportation service by such carriers at the lowest cost consistent with the furnishing of such service; and to the need of revenues sufficient to enable such carriers, under honest, economical and efficient management, to provide such service. This is identical with the railroad rule of rate making except for the consideration to be given to the inherent advantages of motor transportation.

Discrimination. Every unjust and unreasonable charge is prohibited, and it is unlawful for any common carrier to make, give, or cause any undue or unreasonable preference or advantage to any particular person, port, gateway, locality, region, district, territory, or description of traffic. Personal discrimination also is outlawed, with rebates of all sorts prohibited, and the provisions of Part I relative to the granting of passes, free transportation, and transportation at reduced rates are made applicable to motor common carriers. There is no long and short haul clause, but the Commission has adequate authority to prevent place discrimination of this sort.

Tariff regulations and rate suspension powers of Commission. Common carriers are required to file their tariffs, print them, and keep them open for public inspection. Thirty days' notice is required for any change in rates or classifications or in any regulation or practice which will affect the charges made for service, but the Commission may permit such changes to go into effect on shorter notice for good cause shown. The Commission may suspend the effective date of any of the above changes for a maximum of seven months beyond the time when it would otherwise go into effect. If the matter has not been decided at the end of the suspension period, the change goes into effect, but nothing is said about requiring the carriers to keep records for possible refunds.

Intercorporate relationships. Motor common carrier intercorporate relationships are governed in part by the provisions of Part I of the Interstate Commerce Act, including Interstate Commerce Commission control of pooling, acquisitions of control, and consolidation. In addition to the provisions of the law already discussed in connection with railroad regulation,[12] there are two or three provisions which relate specifically to motor carriers. Part I states that applications involving inter-

---

[12] See pp. 142-143.

corporate relationships shall be approved by the Commission upon a finding that they are consistent with the public interest, but if a railroad is seeking to control a motor carrier, the Commission also must find that the proposal will enable the railroad to use motor vehicle service to public advantage in its operations and that it will not unduly restrain competition. In all cases involving intercorporate transactions the Commission is to consider the interests of carrier employees, but the detailed provisions relating to the protection of railroad employees do not apply in motor carrier combinations. The provisions of this part of the law do not apply where the only parties to a transaction are motor carriers and the aggregate number of motor vehicles involved does not exceed twenty. Finally, the Commission may grant temporary approval of combined operations pending final determination of an application. In addition to the provisions found in Part I, Part II permits the transfer of operating rights subject to the approval of the Interstate Commerce Commission.

Unlawful operation. Knowing or willful violations of the law relative to personal discrimination, whether by giver or receiver, are subject to a fine of not more than $500 for the first offense and not more than $2,000 for any subsequent offense. Carriers who willfully fail to make reports as required, to keep accounts and records as prescribed, or falsify reports or accounts, are subject to a maximum fine of $5,000 for each offense. Willful violations of other provisions of the law are subject to a fine of not more than $100 for the first offense and $500 for subsequent offenses, with each day of violation constituting a separate offense. In all cases a conviction must be obtained through the usual judicial channels. It is also declared to be unlawful for a carrier or its agents to divulge information with regard to a shipper or consignee's business which may be used to his detriment or which may improperly disclose his business transactions to a competitor.

CONTRACT CARRIERS

General duties and powers of Commission. The Commission is directed to regulate contract carriers by motor vehicle in interstate commerce, and to that end it may establish reasonable requirements with respect to uniform systems of accounts, records, and reports, preservation of records, qualifications and maximum hours of service of employees, and safety of operation and equipment.

Permits. The right to operate as a contract carrier is conditioned upon the issuance of a permit, and before such a permit may be issued the Commission must find that the applicant is fit, willing, and able to perform service as a contract carrier, and that the proposed operation is consistent with the public interest and the national transportation policy. The permit, if issued, must specify the business covered thereby, and such conditions as the Commission may deem it necessary to attach. Permits may be amended, revoked, suspended, or transferred in the same way and under the same conditions as certificates of public convenience and necessity, and there is a "grandfather clause" applying to carriers in business on July 1, 1935.

Rates and schedules. Contract carriers must establish and observe reasonable minimum charges and regulations applicable thereto, and such schedules of charges must be filed with the Commission, published, and kept open for public inspection. Thirty days' notice of a reduction in minimum charges is required, but reductions may be allowed to go into effect sooner for good cause shown. If after a hearing the Commission finds that a minimum charge or a regulation affecting the value of the service is unlawful, it may prescribe the charge or regulation to apply. Such charge or regulation is not to give any advantage to contract carriers over common carriers which will be inconsistent with the public interest and the national transportation policy. In determining rates the Commission is to give due consideration to the cost of the service rendered and to the effect of the rates prescribed on the movement of traffic by contract carriers. The Commission is authorized to hold hearings on rate applications and to suspend the effective date of such an application for a maximum of seven months beyond the time it would otherwise go into effect. If at the end of that time a decision has not been reached, the new charge or regulation goes into effect, but no provision is made for possible refunds.

Other provisions. Contract carriers are subject to the same provisions as common carriers with reference to dual operation, temporary operating authority, issues of securities, intercorporate relationships, and unlawful operations. They are required to provide the same protection for the security of the public from death, accident, or loss or damage to property resulting from the operation of motor vehicles, but since they do not have the status of common carriers, they are not required to provide security for the protection of goods entrusted to their care. They are subject to the same provisions as common carriers with reference to accounts, records, reports, and the like, with the provision that the Commission must not make public any contracts between carriers and shippers except as a part of the record in a formal proceeding where it considers such action consistent with the public interest.

The laws relating to discrimination do not apply to contract carriers.

REGULATION OF HIGHWAY TRANSPORTATION

The amount a contract carrier charges any given shipper will vary with the volume of traffic the shipper can offer, the regularity of the traffic, the possibility of obtaining a back haul for trucks which would otherwise have to return to their point of origin without a pay load, the cost and practicability of a shipper providing his own motor transport facilities, and possibly other factors which vary from shipper to shipper. To attempt to establish a uniform schedule of rates under such conditions would destroy the peculiar advantages of this type of transportation. Hence the law does not prohibit discrimination in rates and charges as long as the carrier does not, by one means or another, transport property or passengers for less than the minimum charges filed with the Commission and published for the information of patrons.

BROKERS AND PRIVATE CARRIERS

Brokers. A broker is a person who is not a carrier or a carrier's agent but who sells or arranges for transportation by motor vehicle. Brokers must obtain licenses from the Interstate Commerce Commission to do business in interstate transportation, and such licenses may be suspended, changed, or revoked, but no provision is made for their transfer. Brokers may utilize only the facilities of common and contract carriers operating under the jurisdiction of the Interstate Commerce Commission, and the Commission is required to prescribe reasonable rules and regulations for the protection of travelers or shippers doing business with brokers. A bond or other security is required to insure financial responsibility and the supplying of transportation in accordance with arrangements made therefor. Brokers are subject to the same provisions relative to accounts and reports and unlawful operations as are common and contract carriers. A broker in business at the time the law was passed was entitled to apply for and receive a license and continue operations until otherwise ordered by the Commission.

Private carriers. The law with reference to private carriers is quite limited in nature. It states that the Commission is to establish for private carriers of property, *if need therefor is found*, reasonable requirements to promote safety of operation, and to that end prescribe standards for equipment and qualifications and maximum hours of service for employees. If such requirements are established, the carriers are subject to certain administrative procedures, including the hearings before joint boards, and to the provisions of the law relative to accounts and reports, unlawful actions to the extent applicable to private carriers, and the marking of interstate vehicles.

REGULATION OF HIGHWAY TRANSPORTATION

Unconditional exemptions. The following vehicles are exempted from the provisions of the Interstate Commerce Act, except for those provisions authorizing the Commission to establish qualifications and maximum hours of service of employees and safety of operation or standards of equipment: (1) school buses, (2) taxicabs with a capacity of no more than six and not operated over a regular route or between fixed termini, (3) hotel buses used to transfer patrons between hotel and common carrier stations, (4) vehicles under the control of the Secretary of the Interior used to transport persons in and about national parks and monuments, (5) farmer-owned vehicles used for farm business, (6) vehicles controlled and operated by cooperatives as defined in the Agricultural Marketing Act of 1929, as amended, (7) trolley buses operated in urban service, (8) vehicles used in carrying livestock, fish, or agricultural commodities, (9) vehicles used exclusively in the distribution of newspapers, and (10) vehicles used in the transportation of persons or property incidental to transportation by air.

The reasons for some of these exemptions are obvious. No good purpose would be served by regulating school buses, nor would there be any good reason for prohibiting taxicabs, which are instruments of local transportation, from making an occasional trip outside their customary area of operations. The same may be said for hotel vehicles, and it is better to have park vehicles regulated as a part of the park service. Farm vehicles and the vehicles of agricultural cooperatives are used to haul the property of their owners and are not public carriers. In any event, control of the interstate movements of such vehicles would involve enormous administrative and enforcement problems. The trolley bus is neither flesh nor fowl, having some of the characteristics of a motor bus and some of the characteristics of an electric street railway. Presumably the regulation of this type of vehicle is to be left in the hands of state and local authorities. Motor carriers used in connection with air transportation constitute an adjunct of the latter.

The exemption of vehicles used in the transportation of livestock, fish, agricultural commodities, and newspapers is not so easy to justify from a transportation point of view. The first three may reflect the influence of agricultural interests in Congress while the latter may by a stretch of the imagination have something to do with freedom of the press.

Conditional exemptions. In addition to the foregoing exemptions the law exempts two other types of movements until or unless the Commission may find it necessary to bring them under regulatory control. One of these involves the transportation of passengers or property in interstate or foreign commerce within the limits of a municipality, adjacent municipalities, or in a so-called metropolitan area. There are a number of urban centers in the United States which lie partly in one state and partly in another, Kansas City, Missouri, and Kansas City, Kansas, for example. Transportation in these areas is interstate whenever a state line is crossed, but it is essentially local in nature and best regulated by local authorities. If, however, such transportation is under a common control, management, or arrangement for a continuous movement to or from a point outside the defined area, it is not exempted. One other conditional exemption is provided to permit the casual, occasional, or reciprocal transportation of passengers or property in interstate and foreign commerce for compensation by any person not engaged in transportation by motor vehicle as a regular business.

Other exemptions. The use of motor vehicles in terminal areas by or for a rail or water carrier subject to the Interstate Commerce Act is subject to regulation under the rail and water carrier sections of the act. The Commission also is authorized to exempt carriers lawfully engaged in operation solely within a single state from the provisions of the law if it finds that the transportation in interstate and foreign commerce performed by such carriers is of such a nature, character, or quantity as not to affect substantially uniform regulation of interstate and foreign commerce.

ACCOMPLISHMENTS

Administrative procedures of Interstate Commerce Commission. In order to handle the administrative details of motor carrier regulation the Commission established within its organization a Bureau of Motor Carriers divided into sections of Accounts, Certificates, Insurance, Law Enforcement, and Safety. Because of the small scale and localized nature of the activities of the typical interstate motor carrier, it is impractical and it would be unduly expensive to the carriers to attempt to handle all regulatory activities in Washington, and a large majority of the matters relating to regulation is handled at some stage by a field force scattered over the country. In view of the large number of carriers involved and the wide and varied extent of their operations, this has proved to be a job of considerable magnitude, and the Commission has complained regularly that its staff is inadequate to obtain the results which should be obtained, especially with respect to safety of operations.

Usually when hearings are necessary they are held by examiners who report and make recommendations to the Commission. Only rarely does the Commission itself hold such hearings.

Nature and disposition of applications received. Table XVI gives a picture in summary form of the extent and nature of the Commission's work with reference to applications made to it under various provisions of the law.

Table XVI

INTERSTATE MOTOR CARRIER APPLICATIONS, CUMULATIVE TO OCTOBER 31, 1951 [13]

Nature of Application	*Number of Applications*
"Grandfather" applications	89,574
Applications to institute new operations	41,889
Broker applications	1,526
Statements of carriers operating in interstate or foreign commerce solely within a single state	7,693
Applications for temporary operating authority	39,342
Applications claiming exemption from regulation which will not substantially impair uniform regulation	135
Extension of temporary authority granted	13,543
Applications involving intercorporate relationships	33,455
Applications for temporary authority to unify pending determination of applications received	1,523
Other	122
Total applications received	228,802
Applications granted	105,904
Applications denied, dismissed, withdrawn, or revoked	118,873
Applications pending	4,025
Total	228,802

Table XVII shows the number of carriers and brokers engaged in motor transportation activities under the Commission's jurisdiction. These figures do not include carriers operating exclusively under temporary authority.

Safety regulations. On December 23, 1936, in its very first report issued under the provisions of the Motor Carrier Act, 1935, the Commission prescribed safety regulations applicable to common and contract carriers, and additional regulations have been issued from time to time since then. On May 1, 1940, safety regulations were prescribed for private carriers as permitted by the law. These regulations cover qualifications and maximum hours of service for drivers and numerous details relative to the equipment and operation of vehicles. In addition, accident reports on forms prescribed are required of common and contract car-

---

[13] Interstate Commerce Commission, *Annual Report,* 1951, p. 101.

riers. During and since World War II there have been numerous violations of the safety regulations, partly due to the inadequacy of the Commission's field force to carry on inspection and investigative work. The Commission is doing what it can to bring about better compliance with safety regulations and has secured the cooperation of the top executives of some companies, the states, educational institutions, and carrier associations. Some insurance companies are refusing to cover the operations of drivers with bad safety records, and the unions and the drivers themselves are taking an interest in driving safety.

Table XVII

MOTOR CARRIERS OPERATING UNDER PERMANENT AUTHORITY, CUMULATIVE TO OCTOBER 31, 1951 [14]

Type of Activity	Number of Operators	
Property carriers:		
Common, operating under certificiate	14,579	
Common, no certificate required (intrastate)	1,966	16,545
Contract		2,833
"Grandfather," operating pending final decision on application		2
Total property carriers		19,380
Passenger carriers:		
Common, operating under certificate	1,410	
Common, no certificate required	132	1,542
Contract		18
"Grandfather," final authority not issued		1
Total passenger carriers		1,561
Brokers:		
Property		88
Passenger		97
Total brokers		185

Insurance. The Commission has prescribed rules and regulations governing the filing of insurance policies, surety bonds, other securities and agreements as required by law, and qualifications as self-insurers. In the overwhelming majority of cases the protection provided has taken the form of insurance. The actual policy itself is not filed with the Commission, but it receives a certificate of insurance giving the data necessary for its approval of the policy. In a number of cases the Commission has approved self-insurance applications from motor carrier subsidiaries

---

[14] Interstate Commerce Commission, *Annual Report*, 1951, p. 102.

of railroads and from other established and financially responsible concerns, but otherwise it has been most circumspect in its approval of carriers as self-insurers.

Some carriers, and particularly some of the smaller carriers, have experienced difficulty in obtaining insurance as required by law because of experience factors which make it difficult to calculate premiums to cover the risk involved or because they are considered to be bad risks. The trucking industry and the insurance companies are cooperating in an effort to provide worthy carriers with adequate insurance, and some of the states have worked out cooperative arrangements with insurance companies. Insurance companies doing business in Arkansas, for example, have agreed jointly to assume responsibility for the coverage of worthy applicants who have been refused insurance by three different companies. The plan applies to vehicles registered in the state, but coverage is not extended to known bad risks or where vehicle operators have major disabilities.

Other activities. The Interstate Commerce Commission has established a classification of carriers according to type of service, area of service, nature of service, and kinds of goods carried, as described in Chapter 18. It has made a further grouping of carriers according to size of operations into the following classes: Class I, carriers with average gross operating revenues of $200,000 a year or more from motor carrier operations ($100,000 or more prior to 1950); Class II, carriers with revenues of $50,000 or more but under $200,000 ($25,000-$100,000 prior to 1950); and Class III, carriers with revenues of less than $50,000 annually (less than $25,000 prior to 1950). A uniform system of accounts has been established for Class I carriers but not for the smaller carriers, and Class I carriers are required to submit quarterly and annual reports. In addition, Class I carriers of passengers are required to submit monthly reports. Carriers are required to display their name or trade mark and an I.C.C. docket number on both sides of each power unit operated.

SUGGESTED READINGS

Association of American Railroads, *Highway Motor Transportation*, 1945. This publication contains some useful compilations of state laws relative to size and weight limits of various dates.

Federal Coordinator of Transportation, *Regulation of Transportation Agencies*, 73d Congress, 2nd Session, Senate Document 152, 1944. Contains detailed summaries of state laws prior to federal regulation.

Interstate Commerce Commission, *Annual Reports*, 1937 to date.

Interstate Commerce Commission, *Interstate Commerce Acts, Annotated*, Vols. 9-14. This is the principal source of material relative to federal regulation.

REGULATION OF HIGHWAY TRANSPORTATION

Interstate Commerce Commission, *Motor Carrier Reports.*

McCollester, Parker, and Frank J. Clark, *Federal Motor Carrier Regulation,* New York: The Traffic Publishing Company, 1935. A useful source of information on early state regulation, and an analysis of the Motor Carrier Act, 1935.

National Association of Motor Bus Operators, *Bus Facts.* Washington: various years.

The Motor Truck Red Book. New York: Traffic Publishing Company, 1937.

20

Some Problems and Policies
of
HIGHWAY TRANSPORTATION (I)

GRANDFATHER OPERATIONS

Bona fide operations. At the time the Motor Carrier Act, 1935, was under discussion numerous common and contract carriers were operating over the highways transporting goods and passengers in interstate commerce, and it was recognized that these carriers were entitled to continue the operations in which they were already engaged. Hence the Interstate Commerce Commission was directed to issue certificates to common carriers in bona fide operation on June 1, 1935, and to contract carriers in bona fide operation on July 1, 1935, without requiring them to prove that their operations were required by or consistent with the public convenience and necessity. Since operating rights possess a distinct monetary value, the Commission received a good many applications of doubtful validity. In this connection it has held that a mere intention to operate or an attempt to commence to operate, or a holding or an offer to operate, did not constitute bona fide operation, guiding itself by the obvious intent of the law.[1]

Service limitations. The law limited applicants for grandfather rights to the route or territory over which or in which they had been operating. In addition, it was specified that a company which had been operating both as a common and as a contract carrier could not continue both operations without the approval of the Interstate Commerce Commission. The law was silent on other matters relating to service, but the Commission took the position that grandfather rights should be limited to the service actually rendered on the critical dates mentioned above. Thus a carrier which showed service to only one intermediate point on a long route was not authorized to serve all intermediate points on its route,[2] but where a carrier had rendered service to a number of intermediate points, the Commission authorized or ordered service to all inter-

---

[1] *Benjamin Franklin Line, Incorporated,* 1 M.C.C. 97 (1936); *Crescent Transportation Company,* 2 M.C.C. 313 (1937).
[2] *Transamerican Freight Lines, Inc.,* 28 M.C.C. 493 (1941).

mediate points.[3] A carrier which held itself out to handle goods in truckload lots did not acquire, according to the Commission, grandfather rights to haul goods in less-truckload quantities.[4] It also held that grandfather rights were limited to the specific commodities or types of commodities an applicant held himself out to handle on the critical date.[5] In the case of contract carriers the Commission did not attempt to limit service to shippers actually served on or before the critical date, but it did at times limit a contract carrier to serving the class of shippers it had been serving.[6]

As might be expected a large number of carriers filed applications covering operations considerably more extensive than those they had actually conducted, and this necessitated an enormous amount of checking with state authorities and others. Irregular route carriers presented a particularly difficult problem in this connection, and each individual case had to be decided on its merits.[7] Those carriers who professed to haul commodities in general also presented a problem, since some of them actually had been hauling only a narrow range of commodities.

The Commission very early concluded that regular route common carriers maintaining regular service at various points and accepting freight in whatever quantities were offered needed some protection from irregular route carriers seeking to invade common carrier routes for the purpose of handling the cream of the traffic thereon. The Commission may not, however, apply a different or stricter test about what may be carried by an irregular carrier than it applies to regular route carriers.[8]

Some observations. The various restrictions placed on grandfather rights functioned to protect existing carriers from excessive competition, but they also functioned in some degree to hamper a sound economic development of the motor transport industry. Interstate motor carrier transportation was a relatively new and developing industry in 1935, and it seems highly unlikely that the nature and scale of operations of any appreciable number of carriers had reached the point of maximum efficiency or profitability at that time. Yet under the law, whatever

---

[3] *Richards*, 27 M.C.C. 489 (1941).

[4] *Slagle*, 2 M.C.C. 127 (1937); *Jones*, 33 M.C.C. 319 (1942).

[5] *Sasser*, 4 M.C.C. 381 (1938).

[6] In *Keystone Transportation Company*, 19 M.C.C. 475 (1939), the carrier was authorized to serve chain stores. *Brashear Freight Lines, Inc.*, 33 M.C.C. 279 (1942), authorized service to manufacturers of boots and shoes.

[7] See, for example, *Eli E. Wagner, Jr.*, 27 M.C.C. 517 (1941); *Dixie Truck Line*, 29 M.C.C. 303 (1941); *Centre Trucking Co., Inc.*, 32 M.C.C. 313 (1942); *Bekins Van & Storage Company*, 43 M.C.C. 401 (1944).

[8] *United States* v. *Carolina Freight Carriers Corp.*, 315 U.S. 475 (1942); *Howard Hall Co.*, v. *United States*, 315 U.S. 495 (1942).

service an applicant held himself out to offer on June 1 or July 1, 1935, marked the practical limit on what he could do thereafter as a matter of right. In other words, the law tended to freeze motor carrier operations as of the critical dates without regard to the need for an efficient and economical development of the industry.

It is true, of course, that any carrier operating under grandfather rights is free to apply for additional operating authority. If the Commission finds that the applicant is fit, willing, and able to perform the proposed service, and if it finds that the service is required by or consistent with the public convenience and necessity, the authority requested will be granted. In numerous cases such authority has been granted, but in numerous other cases it has been denied in whole or in part because the proposed operations would conflict with the grandfather rights of other carriers. It is true, too, that the operating rights of two or more carriers may be combined, and this has been done in a good many cases. But such combinations are not always easy to achieve as will be discussed presently.

Some idea of the extent to which motor carrier operations have been restricted may be gained from a brief summary of the more important service limitations. A number of regular route motor carriers offer through service but are not permitted to serve intermediate points along their routes. Others may serve certain intermediate points, and still others may serve intermediate points but may not offer a through service. There are cases where full service is permitted at some points but only limited service at others, and there are cases where a carrier may serve points along a specified route but may not provide service at points close to but not actually on its route. Because of existing route restrictions some regular route carriers have to operate over circuitous routes to reach certain points, and some irregular route carriers may have to traverse large areas, sometimes several states, in order to serve authorized points, without being able to provide service within the intermediate areas. A great many motor carriers are authorized to carry only one or a limited number of commodities or classes of commodities. Some are permitted to haul a wide variety of products in one direction but only a limited number in the other, and some may not be permitted to carry anything at all on the return trip.

In some cases service limitations are in the very nature of the business. For example, a carrier of petroleum products in tank trucks cannot expect a haul in both directions. Nor would any particular harm be done by refusing to permit such a carrier to transport goods requiring the use of other kinds of vehicles. Then there are various situations in which the carrier wishes to restrict its activities. Thus a carrier may seek to limit its service to certain types of goods or to certain points in order to avoid unprofitable traffic. On the other hand, some motor transport concerns find restrictions on their operating rights exceedingly onerous, and there are a great many which find them irritating to a greater or lesser extent. They result in an uneconomic utilization of truck space and unnecessarily long and expensive truck hauls by roundabout routes when more direct routes are in existence. Such restrictions reduce the profits of operators unduly and reduce the quality of the service rendered to the public.

COMPETITION

Motor carrier v. motor carrier. It should not be inferred from what has been said above that it is the policy of the Interstate Commerce Commission to foster monopoly in highway transportation. If no legal restrictions existed, highway transportation would be highly competitive, and there is no reason why the public should not be permitted to enjoy the benefits of some competition in this field. The Commission, recognizing both the good and bad features of competition, has sought to control rather than eliminate it. In numerous cases competitive services have been authorized on the ground that competition would be beneficial to shippers.[9] The Commission also has taken the position, however, that sound economic conditions in the industry require that existing carriers should normally have the right to transport all traffic they can handle adequately, efficiently, and economically,[10] and it has often denied authority for new operations which would adversely affect existing carriers without a commensurate benefit to the public.[11]

Motor v. railroad and water competition. One of the earliest problems the Commission had to face was that of deciding what consideration, if any, should be given to the availability of railroad transportation in deciding whether or not to authorize service by motor vehicle. In this connection it has held repeatedly that the fact that a particular point has adequate railroad service or the fact that railroads might be adversely affected by motor transport competition is not a sufficient reason for denying operating authority.[12] Its position on this point has been that shippers and consignees are entitled to adequate service by motor vehicle as well as by railroad.[13] As already mentioned, if a community cannot

---

[9] For example, *Santa Fe Trail Stages, Inc.*, 21 M.C.C. 725 (1940).
[10] *Justice*, 2 M.C.C. 699 (1937); *Brundage*, 11 M.C.C. 187 (1939).
[11] *Public Service Interstate Transportation Company*, 43 M.C.C. 599 (1944).
[12] *Bowles*, 1 M.C.C. 589 (1937); *Tri-State Transit Company of Louisiana, Inc.*, 29 M.C.C. 381 (1941); and many others.
[13] *Petroleum Transit Corporation*, 11 M.C.C. 164 (1939).

support both types of transportation, the Commission has said that it is up to the community to decide which one it wants. What has been said about railroad carriers applies also to water transport concerns.[14]

Until recently, cases involving the effect of motor carriers on railroad transportation have been confined to specific local situations, but in 1950 the problem appeared on a much broader scale. The Pacific Intermountain Express, a motor carrier providing service between the Pacific coast and Chicago, applied to the Commission for permission to purchase the properties of Keeshin Freight Lines, operating north of the Ohio River, between the Mississippi Valley region and the Atlantic coast. Approval of this application would have resulted in the establishment of a coast-to-coast motor freight service, but the Commission did not approve the application, and it based its action in part on a belief that services of this sort would have an adverse effect on the railroads and those who were dependent upon railroad transportation.[15] This constitutes one of the most significant decisions to come from the Commission in recent years.

Common v. contract carrier competition. In numerous cases the Commission has found it desirable to restrict competition between common and contract carriers. It has said that common carriers, since they undertake to serve the general public, should be protected against contract carriers who take the cream of the traffic and thus make it difficult for common carriers to continue their broader operations.[16] If a contract carrier is able to move certain types of traffic at rates substantially below those charged by common carriers, however, a legitimate question may be raised over the extent to which shippers able to use contract carrier service should be required to subsidize smaller shippers by using a more costly common carrier service. Furthermore, any limitation on a more economical contract carrier service is likely to lead to the increased use of private transportation.

COMBINATION

Reasons for combined operations. As of October 31, 1951, the Interstate Commerce Commission had received 33,455 applications having to do with intercorporate relationships, most of them involving the transfer

---

[14] *Clark*, 16 M.C.C. 535 (1939).

[15] *Traffic World*, November 18, 1950, pp. 37-39; November 25, 1950, pp. 36-37; January 6, 1951, pp. 34-36; April 14, 1951, pp. 32-34. See, also, denial of application in MC 112737, reported in *Traffic World*, March 8, 1952, pp. 24-25.

[16] *Gollock*, 1 M.C.C. 161 (1936); *Keystone Transportation Company*, 19 M.C.C. 475 (1939).

or lease of operating rights, and in the great majority of cases it has approved the applications. There can be little doubt that a major factor behind this large number of applications has been the desire of carriers to free themselves of onerous restrictions included in their certificates or permits. Obviously much can be done to improve efficiency of operations through the combination of complementary rights. Indeed, in many cases such a combination appears to be about the only means available for achieving an efficient and economical transportation service without destroying existing grandfather rights. Other advantages accruing from combinations include the ability to offer service over a wider area or over longer routes, elimination of interchanges of traffic between carriers, more efficient use of equipment and terminal facilities, reduction or elimination of competition, and the opportunities inherent in larger scale operations for specialization in traffic solicitation, maintenance work, and the like.

Difficulties encountered in obtaining operating rights. While a number of fairly large motor transport concerns have been established under the provisions of Part I of the Interstate Commerce Act,[17] the more common procedure is for an existing carrier to extend its service or to eliminate operating restrictions through the purchase or lease of the operating rights of other carriers. This procedure is not always as easy as it sounds, for it may not be a simple matter to locate and acquire operating rights which are fully complementary with those already possessed. It may be necessary to secure rights from a number of different companies, and the more companies involved the more difficult it becomes to consummate the transaction. Also, the acquisition of the desired rights may become unduly expensive. A small carrier may possess certain rights which are not particularly productive of revenue, but if a larger carrier, interested in maximum utilization of its equipment or in rounding out its system, needs these rights, it may find the asking price pretty high.

Splitting. A good many cases coming before the Commission involve the transfer of only a part of a carrier's rights. It is easy to see how this "splitting" of rights may be in the public interest, since such a reshuffling of rights can make more efficient and economical operations possible for all concerned, and the Commission has approved the sale of split rights in numerous cases.[18] The Commission has not looked with favor, however, on the splitting of rights in such a way that the

---

[17] See, for example, *Associated Transport, Inc.,* 38 M.C.C. 137 (1942); *Consolidated Freightways, Inc.,* 38 M.C.C. 577 (1942).

[18] For example, *Lecrone-Benedict Ways, Inc.–Purchase–Great Central,* 39 M.C.C. 591 (1944).

seller remains in a position to duplicate the service to be offered by the buyer.[19] Such splits result in the provision of an added service, and the Commission feels that they should be handled in the same way as if an application were being made for new operating authority.

Tacking. Tacking is a problem peculiar to the contract carrier type of operation. Suppose that a contract carrier is authorized to provide service between A and B and that it wishes to obtain the operating rights of another carrier which operates between B and C. There is nothing fundamentally wrong with such a transaction, but the Commission will not authorize the applicant to "tack" the acquired rights onto its existing rights in such a way as to enable it to offer a through service between A and C. This is because the law does not authorize contract carriers to participate in through routes and joint rates, and the tacking of the two rights would result in a new through service. In a case like this the carrier would have to make a separate application for authority if it wished to operate between A and C.[20]

Gateway rule. One policy adopted by the Commission which has evoked considerable criticism is the so-called gateway rule, first imposed in 1940.[21] Briefly stated this rule requires that when combined operations involving two or more carriers serving different routes or territories are undertaken, shipments between points in the formerly separate routes or territories must be routed via common points or gateways served by both carriers prior to the combination of operations. The basic criticism of this type of restriction is that it contributes to circuitous and uneconomical transportation, a fact which may be shown by a simple illustration. Suppose that Carrier X operates over the route A-D-B and Y over the route B-E-C, their only common point being B. Assuming that X purchases Y's operating rights and the gateway restriction is attached, X cannot haul goods directly from A to C through D but will have to haul them to B and then back through E to C.

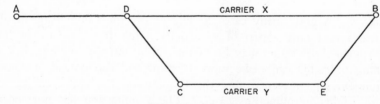

FIGURE 5. *Illustration of Gateway Rule.*

[19] *Carolina Coach Co. of Va.—Purchase—Richmond-Greyhound,* 38 M.C.C. 347 (1942).

[20] *Clare M. Marshall, Inc.—Purchase—Cunningham,* 36 M.C.C. 507 (1941).

[21] *Carolina Freight Carriers Corporation—Purchase—Edmunds,* 36 M.C.C. 259 (1940).

The reasoning behind the gateway rule seems to be that when the carriers involved were operating independently, they could interchange traffic only at common points, and the location of these common points determined the extent to which it was practical for them to engage in joint hauls. Thus in the above illustration it is quite possible that X and Y as independent operators would not interchange traffic moving between A and C, and such traffic no doubt would move via some carrier directly serving A and C or by X to D for interchange with another carrier. Under these circumstances to permit X to haul directly from A to C, once it had acquired Y's operating rights, would be tantamount to extending X's operating authority. Where extreme circuity prior to unification made a joint route impractical, there may be some basis for protecting the rights of other carriers by requiring an application for authority to operate directly between A and C. If, however, the circuity is not so great that the carrier can compete in spite of the circuity, then the value of the gateway rule is not so clear. For example, if a substantial volume of traffic existed between A and E, X might find it worth while to compete for this traffic by way of the gateway at B, giving almost as good service as a carrier operating more directly. But obviously it would be more economical to provide a direct service.

Effect on competition. Where a strong carrier seeks to obtain control of operating rights in order to extend its service, other carriers serving the area or route involved may object on the ground that the greater resources of the strong carrier will result in undue intensification of competition. Here the Commission must balance the benefits of improved service to the public against possible adverse effects on existing carriers, and its decision will vary with circumstances.[22] In some cases combinations have been opposed on the ground that they would reduce or eliminate rather than increase competition. The Commission has approved some such applications on a showing that there was insufficient traffic to support two competing lines which it was proposed to consolidate[23] and approved others on the ground that better service would result.[24] On the other hand, it has not always approved of the elimination of competition, particularly where duplicate operations would be carried on by separate motor carriers under common control.[25]

---

[22] For example *Mason & Dixon Lines, Incorporated—Purchase—Coggin and Cox,* 36 M.C.C. 475 (1941), granting authority, and *Nevada Consolidated Fast Freight—Control—Fleetlines, Inc.,* 40 M.C.C. 499 (1946), denying authority.

[23] *Southwestern Greyhound Lines, Inc.—Purchase—Lee,* 36 M.C.C. 753 (1941).

[24] *Richmond-Greyhound Lines, Incorporated—Control—Peninsula Transit Corporation,* 36 M.C.C. 747 (1941).

[25] *Textile Transportation, Incorporated—Purchase—Textile Transportation Corporation,* 38 M.C.C. 256 (1942).

The Commission is not concerned over the possibility of monopoly developing in the motor transport business. Taking into consideration the great number of motor carriers, the small amount of capital required, and the advantages which smaller motor carriers have over larger ones through their more intimate relations with shippers and their ability to render a more personalized service, it concluded in a 1942 report that monopoly was little to be feared at that stage of the development of the trucking industry.[26] The motor bus business presents a somewhat different picture, but as Commissioner Eastman once pointed out, if a monopoly should develop on any route, the Commission has the power to authorize additional operations.[27]

Capitalization of operating rights. Operating rights issued by the Interstate Commerce Commission possess a distinct monetary value since they are not issued freely to all comers. Hence when one carrier purchases operating rights from another carrier, it looks upon them as a part of the worth of its business. Furthermore, if the competitive situation permits, a carrier will desire to fix its general level of rates sufficiently high to earn a return on the amount invested in purchased operating rights. But since the right to do business free of competition, or with competition restricted, is a privilege which has been bestowed upon the carriers by the people, whatever value an operating right possesses has been created by the people, and the people should not be required to pay rates which will bring the carrier a return on a value which they themselves have created. To this end the law provides, as noted in Chapter 19, that good will, earning power, or the claimed value attached to a certificate under which a carrier is operating, may not be taken into consideration by the Commission in any rate-making procedure. In November 1939, the Commission inaugurated a policy of requiring the amortization of amounts paid for operating rights, good will, and the like, by charges to income over a specified period of years, or by writing such payments off immediately if there is a surplus sufficient to make this possible.

RAIL-MOTOR SERVICE

Railroad use of motor vehicles. Railroads today make extensive use of motor vehicles in terminal areas for pick up and delivery and other purposes, such uses being subject to regulation under the provisions of Part I of the Interstate Commerce Act. Railroads also make extensive

---

[26] *Associated Transport, Inc.—Control and Consolidation—Arrow Carrier Corporation,* 38 M.C.C. 137.

[27] *Transport Company—Control—Arrow Carrier Corporation,* 36 M.C.C. 61 (1940).

use of motor vehicles in rendering a common carrier over-the-road service, either directly or through affiliated companies, and such transportation is subject to the provisions of Part II of the Interstate Commerce Act. Some over-the-road operations are carried on under grandfather rights, some through the acquisition of independent motor carriers or motor carrier rights, and some through direct application to the Commission for new rights or the extension of existing rights. In some cases highway transportation has been substituted for railroad service, and in some cases it is provided in addition to railroad service.

Limitations on railroad acquisition of motor carriers. As previously noted, combined operations in the motor transport field are permitted on a showing that the proposed operation will be consistent with the public interest, but if a railroad is involved in the proposal, there must be an additional showing that the rail carrier can use motor vehicle service to public advantage and that competition will not be restrained unduly. The Commission has followed a rather restrictive policy with regard to the acquisition of motor freight lines by railroads, apparently fearful that the railroads might suppress highway transportation if given an opportunity to do so. In 1936 the Commission stated that it was the intent of the Motor Carrier Act, 1935, to surround the acquisition of motor carriers by carriers engaged in other forms of transportation with special safeguards.[28] In the following year it stated that it would approve the acquisition of motor carriers by railroads when the resultant operations by motor carrier would be auxiliary or supplementary to railroad service; but it would not approve operations which would compete with the railroad itself by duplicating existing service, which would compete with another established motor carrier, or which would invade to a substantial degree a territory already adequately served by another rail carrier.[29] Insofar as freight service is concerned the Commission has continued to follow this policy.

Key point plan. The law does not establish any special restrictions on railroads or their motor carrier affiliates in making applications for new operating rights or the extension of existing rights. In these cases, however, the Interstate Commerce Commission has followed much the same policy as outlined above in connection with railroad acquisitions of existing motor carriers. In 1938 it permitted the Kansas City Southern Railway to utilize a motor carrier affiliate in providing a coordinated rail and motor freight service to and from points on its lines, but the

---

[28] *Pennsylvania Truck Lines, Incorporated, Acquisition of Control of Barker Motor Freight, Incorporated,* 1 M.C.C. 101.

[29] *Ibid.,* 5 M.C.C. 9.

motor carrier was allowed to handle only such traffic as had received or would receive a haul by railroad, thus making the motor service completely auxiliary to the rail service.[30]

The foregoing arrangement was useful in that it permitted the railroad to substitute highway transportation for the costly operation of lightly loaded local freight trains in serving small communities located on its lines. This was accomplished by using motor trucks to pick up small shipments and haul them to larger stations on the line for consolidation with other freight, and to pick up freight at the larger stations for delivery to small communities. Since, however, the trucks could carry only such freight as had received or would receive a rail haul, railroad service was still necessary to move local freight to and from small stations which were between larger stations. To eliminate this difficulty the Commission designated certain of the larger communities on the Kansas City Southern as "key points." The movement of traffic by truck from local points to key points and from key points to local points was continued as before and such traffic was restricted to freight which had received or would receive a rail haul, but direct motor truck hauls were permitted between points other than key points without the rail haul restriction.[31]

The key point plan adopted in the Kansas City Southern cases has been applied, almost without exception, to subsequent grants of operating authority of any significance where a railroad or railroad affiliate was involved. The railroads have objected to the differentiation which the Commission has made between applications made by railroad affiliates and those made by motor carriers generally, particularly because no such differentiation is specifically required by law, but the Commission has said that a railroad applicant has a special burden to prove public convenience and necessity simply because it is a railroad.[32] It should be pointed out, perhaps, that the restrictions placed on railroad operation of motor trucks do not apply to operations carried on under grandfather rights.[33]

Railroad operation of motor bus service is not as severely restricted as is true of railroad truck operations. Railroads were using buses as far back as 1924, and sixty-two railroads were offering bus service at the time the Motor Carrier Act, 1935, was adopted. Thus for better or for

---

[30] *Kansas City Southern Transport Company, Incorporated*, 10 M.C.C. 221.

[31] *Kansas City Southern Transport Company, Incorporated, Common Carrier Application*, 28 M.C.C. 5 (1941).

[32] *Rock Island Motor Transit Company—Purchase—White Line Motor Freight Company, Incorporated*, 40 M.C.C. 457 (1946).

[33] *Pacific Motor Trucking Company*, 34 M.C.C. 249 (1942).

worse numerous railroads possess grandfather rights in the bus field which cannot be ignored. In a good many cases railroads have sought authority to operate motor buses as a substitute for local or branch line passenger service, which is costly and unsatisfactory, and the Commission has approved a number of such applications.[34] In addition, a good many railroad-controlled bus lines provide an alternative service closely paralleling the tracks of the railroad. The key point system would be quite unsatisfactory as far as passenger service is concerned and its use has not been required.

Through routes and joint rates. The law permits but does not require railroad and motor common carriers to establish through routes and joint rates but as might be expected the railroads have been considerably less than enthusiastic about cooperating with motor carriers in establishing such routes and rates. The Commission once said that it would be impossible to coordinate rail-truck service on a sound basis unless the same management controlled both means of transportation,[35] but since the Commission has rigidly limited railroad use of motor trucks, the possibilities of developing a coordinated rail-motor service have scarcely been scratched. This matter will be given further consideration in the concluding chapter of this book. In 1950 the Commission approved tariff schedules permitting the movement of loaded truck trailers on railroad flat cars between Chicago and Kansas City and Chicago and St. Joseph, Missouri. The motor carrier solicited the traffic and handled the goods at both ends, simply substituting a rail haul for an over-the-road haul.[36] The Commission has held, however, that it cannot require a railroad to establish a special rate for such service, since this would amount to a through joint service which is not required by the Interstate Commerce Act.[37]

COMMON CARRIAGE AND CONTRACT CARRIAGE

Common v. contract carriage. The Interstate Commerce Commission, like the various state commissions before it, has had to cope with the problem of what constitutes a practical and workable distinction between common and contract carriage. In an early case it held that the fundamental distinction between the two was the presence or absence of a

---

[34] For example, *Rock Island Motor Transit Company*, 30 M.C.C. 224 (1941). Of course, state approval is necessary for abandonment of intrastate passenger train service.

[35] *Gulf, Mobile & Northern Railroad Company*, 18 M.C.C. 721 (1939); *Rock Island Motor Transit Company*, 21 M.C.C. 513 (1940).

[36] *Traffic World*, September 23, 1950, p. 25.

[37] *Ringsby Truck Lines, Inc.* v. *Atchison, Topeka & Santa Fe Railway Company*, 263 I.C.C. 139 (1945).

holding out to serve the general public,[38] but since the law permits contract carriers to add to their contracts, the Commission has recognized that the number of shippers served by a contract carrier may increase to the point where a general holding out to serve the public becomes apparent, in which event the operation approaches that of common carriage. But it is impractical to lay down any rule on the maximum number of shippers who may be served without losing contract carrier status, and each case must be decided on its merits.[39] In a number of cases the Commission has held that contract carriers must, in addition to serving under individual contracts, provide a definitely special service designed to meet the peculiar needs of a particular shipper or a limited number of shippers as distinguished from the common needs of shippers generally.[40] On the other hand, where the number of shippers actually served was not large it has authorized contract carrier status even though the physical nature of the service rendered hardly could be called specialized.[41]

Because common and contract carriers are essentially different in character and in their relations with shippers, they are not permitted to join in establishing through routes and joint rates. A shipper may, however, employ a contract carrier to act as his agent in arranging for transportation with a common carrier beyond the points reached by the contract carrier.[42]

Dual operations. The Commission has consistently refused to sanction dual operations where the two types of service will be in any way competitive. In one case it refused to permit a carrier to move linoleum as a contract carrier while transporting general commodities as a common carrier because linoleum would be included in the list of the general commodities it carried.[43] The Commission has permitted operation as a common carrier over one route or in one area and as a contract carrier over another route or in another area. Similarly, it has permitted one company to operate both as a common and as a contract carrier if the commodities moved in the two types of service are entirely different. And it has held that slight duplications resulting from dual operations may not be inconsistent with the public interest.[44] The law does

---

[38] *Slagle,* 2 M.C.C. 127 (1937).
[39] *Craig,* 28 M.C.C. 629 (1941).
[40] *Ibid.* See also *Hunter Motor Freight, Inc.,* 27 M.C.C. 51 (1940).
[41] *Zimmerman Trucking Service, Inc.,* 43 M.C.C. 33 (1943).
[42] *Holmes,* 8 M.C.C. 391 (1938); *Motor Haulaway Company,* 27 M.C.C. 19 (1940).
[43] *C. Louis Lavine, Incorporated,* 14 M.C.C. 555 (1939).
[44] *Decatur Warehouse Company, Inc.,* 41 M.C.C. 259 (1942).

not apply to operation as a common carrier in intrastate commerce over a route also served as a contract carrier in interstate commerce,[45] nor to dual operations where one operation falls within one of the exempt classifications.[46] Where the same concern possessed grandfather rights to provide both services, and the combined operation would otherwise be unlawful, the Commission required the carrier to choose one and withdraw from the other.[47]

PRIVATE CARRIAGE AND CARRIAGE FOR HIRE

Primary business test. The Commission has defined a private carrier as one whose transportation is performed as an incident of some other bona fide undertaking and not with a purpose to profit from any transportation charge which might be made.[48] In other words, the owner's source of profit is some industrial or commercial undertaking and not transportation as such. It is possible, however, to engage in some industrial or commercial undertaking primarily as a source of traffic from which to derive a transportation profit. Here the Commission has said that persons engaged primarily in supplying transportation for compensation and with a purpose to profit therefrom are carriers for hire, notwithstanding that each may be the owner of the goods transported and transports them for the purpose of sale, and also may have some other characteristics of a merchandiser.[49]

In applying the primary business test the Commission must make a careful analysis of the business activities involved, for outwardly similar circumstances may yield surprisingly different results upon analysis. For example, in one case the applicant bought, cut, and hauled timber, the timber remaining his property until delivered to the purchaser. In this case it was held that the applicant's principal business was that of buying and cutting timber and that his hauling activities were those of a private carrier.[50] In what appeared to be an almost identical case the applicant cut, peeled, and hauled logs, and was paid a single sum for the entire operation. But in this case the Commission determined that a substantial portion of the price paid for the operation was for hauling the logs, and so it held that the transportation was not a mere incident to the

---

[45] *Cook and Fulmer*, 27 M.C.C. 759 (1941).
[46] *D. S. Woodberry Company*, 33 M.C.C. 199 (1942).
[47] *Centre Trucking Co., Inc.*, 32 M.C.C. 313 (1942).
[48] *Ulrich Oil Company*, 34 M.C.C. 147 (1942).
[49] *Woitishek*, 42 M.C.C. 193 (1943).
[50] *Higgins*, 7 M.C.C. 677 (1938).

cutting and peeling but was transportation for hire.[51] Such decisions must be difficult to make at times, but this is unavoidable where the primary business test is used.

Compensation test. In a major decision the Commission held that the element of compensation found in the definition of both common and contract carriers is the principal feature distinguishing common and contract carriers from private carriers.[52] Nevertheless, it is obvious that a private carrier must be compensated in some way for the expenses incident to the performance of a transportation service, whether that compensation be contained in the selling price of the product transported or is in addition to the price at the point of origin. With this in mind the Commission has defined transportation for compensation as that which is supplied with a *purpose to profit from the effort* as distinguished from that which is supplied as an incident to some other primary business, even though in the latter case the cost is recouped by a charge which may or may not be identifiable as compensation for transportation as such.[53] It has gone so far as to say that a private carrier may collect compensation for transportation either indirectly *or in the form of a direct charge,* and such compensation may even include an incidental element of profit, so long as the *purpose* of the transportation is not to yield a profit as a carrier.[54] For-hire carriers, not unmindful of the inroads made on their business by private carrier operations, would like to have compensation made the sole test of whether a particular operation is private or for hire, but this view has not been accepted by the Commission.

Combined operations. In a number of cases industrial and commercial concerns delivering their own products in their own trucks have sought to secure permission to carry traffic on a for-hire basis on the return trip in order to avoid the expense of empty truck movements. Such an operation is economically sound from the point of view of the private carrier, and it could result in very economical transportation for those shippers who could use the service, since the carrier would find it worth while to haul freight for anything at all over and above the actual cost of handling the freight. The Commission, however, has been unwilling to sanction such combined operations because they divert traffic from existing common and contract carriers and in the long run would

---

[51] *Roberts,* 28 M.C.C. 238 (1941).

[52] *Woitishek,* 42 M.C.C. 193 (1943).

[53] *Williams Brothers Corporation,* 44 M.C.C. 557 (1945).

[54] *Schenley Distillers Corporation Contract Carrier Application,* 48 M.C.C. 405 (1948).

be detrimental to the general public dependent upon the services rendered by such carriers.[55]

EXEMPT CARRIERS

Vehicles transporting farm products and seafoods. As pointed out in Chapter 19, the law provides for numerous exemptions from regulation, other than safety regulation, and with one exception these exemptions have caused little trouble. The exception relates to the exemption of vehicles transporting fish, livestock, or agricultural products, but not including the manufactured products thereof, when such vehicles are not used for moving other traffic for compensation. This exemption has given rise to two closely related problems, one having to do with the definition of a manufactured product and the other having to do with the extent and scope of exempt operations.

Nature of unmanufactured products. Initially the Commission took the position that the fish exemption applied only to fish as taken from the water,[56] but this definition had to be enlarged very considerably because of a court decision holding that shrimp which had been beheaded, cleaned, and frozen came within the exemption.[57] This same problem of definition occurred in connection with the movement of farm products, and a bitter controversy developed when one of the divisions of the Commission ruled that a carrier transporting spinach which had been washed, cleaned, and packaged ready for consumer use was not entitled to an exemption under the law.[58] This ruling was protested by agricultural interests on the ground that an agricultural commodity did not become a manufactured product until it had been processed in such a way that a new and different article resulted. Furthermore, they contended that the perishable nature of agricultural commodities necessitated the use of all available vehicles to move a crop when its marketing season arrived and that the order would place an intolerable burden on producers.

In April 1951, the full Commission defined an unmanufactured farm product in such a way as to include all farm products other than those which, as a result of some treatment, have been so changed as to possess

---

[55] *Geraci,* 7 M.C.C. 369 (1938); *L. W. Hardman Contract Carrier Application,* MC-109311 (1948), in Lewis W. Britton, ed., *Transportation in 1948.* Washington: The Traffic Service Corporation, 1949, p. 99.

[56] *Monark Egg Corporation Contract Carrier Application,* 44 M.C.C. 15 (1944).

[57] *Interstate Commerce Commission v. Love,* 172 F. 2nd 224.

[58] *Norman E. Harwood, Contract Carrier Application,* 47 M.C.C. 597 (1948).

new forms, qualities, or properties, or result in combinations. Presumably this definition exempts the movement of washed and packaged raw spinach but not spinach which has been chopped up, canned, or frozen. The report included a long but incomplete list of commodities and the condition in which they must be in order for their movement to be exempted from regulation. Seafoods which have been hermetically sealed or preserved in some way other than by freezing are not subject to movement in exempt transportation.[59]

Extent and scope of movement. Although it was believed by some that the intent of the foregoing exemption was to help farmers and fishermen by permitting the unregulated movement of farm products and seafoods in their natural state to nearby primary markets or processing plants, others took a different view, and exempt carriers began to move farm products and seafoods out of the growing and processing areas to distant markets. Regulated carriers have taken the position that the exemption was intended to cover only the movement to primary market or processing plant, and that after the product enters the ordinary channels of commerce its movement is subject to regulation. The Commission, however, has held that there is nothing in the law placing any such limits on the points to and from which the products may be transported.[60]

Effect on regulated carriers. The foregoing interpretation of the law by the Interstate Commerce Commission and the courts has created a difficult situation for regulated carriers because it has resulted in the growth of long distance exempt transportation to startling proportions. Commissioner Rogers estimated that, as of February 1, 1950, there were 40,000 carriers using 150,000 power units transporting exempt commodities, principally farm products and fish, as compared with 20,042 carriers using 250,000 power units operating under the authority of the Interstate Commerce Commission.[61] Some of these exempt operations have been and are being conducted on a scale and in a way similar to those of regulated carriers, but the absence of regulation gives the exempt carrier a distinct competitive advantage. In addition, a good deal of this traffic has been handled by individual owner-operators ready to cut their charges to the bone in order to get business. Such an extensive exemption of carriers performing a transportation service which differs in no essential respect from the transportation services performed by regulated carriers is a little hard to justify.

---

[59] *Traffic World*, April 28, 1951, pp. 36-37.
[60] *Ibid.*
[61] *Ibid.*, March 11, 1950, pp. 42-43.

SOME PROBLEMS AND POLICIES

Trip leasing. For a good many years numerous itinerant or "gypsy" truckers have engaged in transportation all over the United States. The gypsy trucker follows the practice of leasing his truck to some regulated carrier to haul a load to a point covered by the latter's operating authority. Arriving at destination, the trucker may then seek to lease his equipment to another regulated carrier for a movement to some other point. A similar practice has been followed by carriers engaged in exempt transportation in order to obtain a load back in the direction of the home base. In some instances loads have been directly solicited from shippers, and if a load was obtained in this way, the exempt carrier would seek out a regulated carrier having the proper authority and lease his equipment to that carrier for the return haul.

The gypsy operator has been a cause of considerable concern because of the frequency with which he has cut corners on safety, failed to provide insurance, and otherwise violated the law. Also, some regulated carriers have argued that they were forced to use itinerant truckers whether they wanted to or not because competing concerns employing gypsies were able to engage in transportation at lower rates than would otherwise be the case. The Interstate Commerce Commission became convinced that the trip lease was undesirable and trip leasing was prohibited after August 1, 1951. However, the validity of this action was attacked in the courts, and the Commission postponed the effective date of its order pending a judicial opinion on the matter. It should be noted, too, that private carriers are opposed to any regulations which may prevent them from engaging in leasing operations.

SUGGESTED READINGS

See references for Chapter 21.

21

Some Problems and Policies
of
HIGHWAY TRANSPORTATION (II)

Nature of problem. Up to this point the discussion of highway transportation problems has revolved around the conflicting interests of different types of carriers, but some attention should be given at this point to one or two problems of common concern to highway carriers in general. One of the most significant of these problems arises out of the diversity of state laws relative to highway use, particularly with reference to maximum size and weight limits for trucks and buses. While the situation today is somewhat better than it was prior to World War II, there are still some rather wide differences between the states in these regulations. Vehicle width limitations present no particular problem because of the almost universal adoption of a 96 inch maximum, and there is a sufficient degree of uniformity in height limits to make this a minor problem. The big problem comes in connection with maximum legal weight and length limits, and differences here have become a matter of major concern to interstate highway carriers.

Reasons for variations. Differences in state laws relative to highway use reflect, in part, differences in the highways themselves. As every motorist knows, standards of highway construction vary from state to state, being better in the more populous and wealthy states than in the less populous and poorer or economically undeveloped states. In planning its highway system each state must take into consideration the needs of its people and their ability to meet the cost of different types of highway construction. If the financial resources of a state are not great and no great use is made of heavy vehicles by its citizens, the state will get more for its highway dollars by building low type flexible pavements, and it may find it necessary to protect these highways by establishing lower maximum weight limits than are permitted by another state.

The type of highway surface, however, is by no means the only factor which enters into the determination of weight limits. For example, the Interstate Commerce Commission found that eleven western states, with thousands of miles of low type paving, allowed wheel loads which were exceeded by only seven other states. The ability of these roads to hold up under heavy loads was attributed to the large number of wheels and large tires used on the big equipment employed in this area, to generally good subgrade conditions, to the relatively infrequent passage of the heaviest vehicles, and to a generally light total volume of traffic.[1] Thus the financial ability of the state, the type of equipment commonly used, the nature of subgrade, and the volume of traffic are all factors to be taken into consideration in determining reasonable size and weight limits.

Motor carrier interests have urged that vehicle sizes and weights are not responsible for highway wear and tear. They tend to attribute highway deterioration to such things as faulty subgrades, weather, and frequency of use. The answer, then, would seem to lie in better construction rather than in restrictive size and weight limits. To no small extent, also, motor carrier interests have been inclined to view severe size and weight restrictions as due in part to railroad influence, although probably not so much now as formerly.[2] It has been argued, too, that state legislatures have failed to liberalize size and weight limitations to keep pace with improvements in highway construction and in highway vehicles.

Effect on interstate commerce. Regardless of the reason for wide differences in state size and weight limits, their effect on interstate commerce by motor vehicle is scarcely open to question, nor is there any doubt about their effect on the motor carrier industry. In order to carry on operations in states having diverse size and weight limits, interstate carriers may do one or more of several things. First, they may purchase equipment and load their trucks to conform with the lowest maximum provided on each requirement in any state in which they operate. Naturally they do not want to restrict their operations in this way. Second, they may be able to bypass states with severe size and weight limitations, but this is undesirable, too, because it may mean following a circuitous route when a much more direct route exists. Third, they may transfer ladings at state lines to trucks conforming with the laws of the state they are entering. This, again, is objectionable since it involves the purchase of extra equipment, and the interchanges increase the cost of operation. Finally, some have chosen simply to conduct operations in violation of the law. In states where enforcement has been lax, evasion is easy, and in some cases it has proved to be cheaper to pay the fines assessed if caught than to obey the law.

---

[1] Interstate Commerce Commission, *Federal Regulation of the Sizes and Weight of Motor Vehicles*, 77th Congress, 1st Session, House Document 354, 1941, p. 23.

[2] In this connection, however, it should be noted that motor carrier interests have not been without influence in legislative matters.

Demand for federal regulation. For some years there has been a demand that the Federal Government establish size and weight limits for motor vehicles engaged in interstate commerce. At various times in the past such regulation has been supported by the interstate motor truck and bus operators, with some support from shippers. Federal regulation also has been supported by the Bureau of Public Roads and the Department of Agriculture. In addition, there is a substantial body of public opinion which desires uniformity but is not wedded to federal regulation. Some advocate the acceptance by the states of a uniform code of regulations, with federal regulation acceptable only as a last resort. The Interstate Commerce Commission recommended that it be given authority to fix size and weight limits to the extent necessary to eliminate unwarranted restrictions on interstate commerce. It did not, however, recommend national uniformity of standards, holding that it should take action only on complaints filed by responsible parties against a state or one of its political subdivisions and only after a proper hearing.[3] Opposition to federal regulation has come principally from the railroads and from the states themselves.

Constitutionality of federal jurisdiction. The possibility of having the Interstate Commerce Commission fix size and weight limits for vehicles operating in interstate commerce raises an interesting constitutional question. Nobody, of course, will question the right of Congress to regulate interstate commerce. On the other hand, the states own the highways, and it would seem that they have a clear cut right to protect them from undue wear and to regulate their use in the interest of public safety and the general welfare. The Commission studied this matter carefully and concluded that Congress had the power to remove state regulations which constituted unreasonable obstructions to interstate commerce.[4] This would seem to be a valid conclusion, but the determination of just what constitutes an unreasonable obstruction to interstate commerce is no easy matter. It has been suggested that the Bureau of Public Roads attach reasonable size and weight limits to future grants of federal aid, with these limits applicable on the roads to which these funds are applied. There can be little doubt that such a policy would be constitutional, but it would be most unsatisfactory unless the states were willing to make their own road use regulations conform with the federal standards.

Reciprocity. There has been considerable complaint about the pyramiding of state taxes on interstate motor carriers, and reciprocity agreements

---

[3] Interstate Commerce Commission, *Federal Regulation of the Sizes and Weight of Motor Vehicles,* 77th Congress, 1st Session, House Document 354, 1941, p. 26.

[4] *Ibid.,* pp. 24-25.

have been urged and to some extent adopted. Under reciprocity agreements if a motor carrier pays a tax in its home state, it is not required to pay the same tax in other states which have entered into the agreement. Duplication of taxes levied on carriers could become a genuine burden on interstate commerce, but to the extent that the taxes assessed represent a fair payment for the use of a state's highways it is difficult to see why payment for the use of the highways in its home state should excuse a carrier from paying for the use of highways in the other states in which it operates. It is possible, too, that under a system of reciprocity, needy or greedy states would attract motor carrier concerns by reducing the level of taxes, in which case the states might enter into a competitive battle of tax reductions.

Conclusion. There is not complete agreement on the effect of motor vehicle operation on highways of various types, and if the experts disagree, it seems hopeless to attempt to draw any conclusions whether different state regulations with reference to size and weight limits are necessary or whether they constitute an unnecessary burden on interstate commerce. It may be that some limitations are unduly severe and do constitute an unnecessary burden on interstate commerce. On the other hand, it does not follow that any restriction which is below the maximum provided by the most liberal state constitutes such a burden. The various states may be expected to offer considerable resistance to any attempt by Congress to regulate size and weight limits of motor vehicles engaged in interstate commerce, and they could and no doubt would exert considerable pressure on their congressmen to oppose such legislation.

LABOR

Organized labor. Motor transport workers are well organized, but they probably do not possess quite the same degree of strength as do the railroad brotherhoods. For one thing, the industry type union characteristic of railroad labor organizations has not developed in the motor carrier field. Instead, union labor has been absorbed mostly into existing A. F. of L. and C.I.O. unions, principally the A. F. of L. Teamsters' Union. Nor have the unions of motor carrier employees developed the unity of action which has made it possible for railroad workers to present a common front in pressing their demands on the railroads. Another factor which must be taken into consideration is the existence of a substantial number of owner-operated trucking concerns which compete with the larger companies dependent upon hired labor. Also, operating employees are not required to have the high degree of specialized training required for many types of railroad work. While driving a truck is by no means an unskilled operation, the general familiarity of millions of Americans with the motor vehicle makes for a potentially large supply of motor carrier labor. Finally, negotiations between the unions and the carriers are not conducted on a nationwide basis. Some agreements are local, although there is a definite tendency toward the effectuation of regional contracts, and nationwide bargaining may come in time.

Labor relations. A number of motor carrier employers' associations have sprung up on a regional basis to deal with labor matters. Although the Government once found it necessary to take over a number of motor carrier concerns in order to prevent a work stoppage, labor-management relations appear to be reasonably satisfactory. Certainly there is a conspicuous absence of the almost constant warfare which seems to have characterized labor-management relations on the railroads since 1941.

Wages and hours. Because of the small scale of operations and lack of regulatory control, little information on working conditions in the motor transport industry is available for the earlier years of its development, but it is conceded that hours were long and wages low. The National Labor Relations Act, the Fair Labor Standards Act, and the growth of organized labor in the industry, however, have led to a considerable improvement in the position of motor transport employees, particularly since 1940. The existence of numerous small operators who are not required to make detailed reports on their operations and the negotiation of contracts on a local or regional basis make it impossible to present an over-all picture of the present status of motor transport workers. From such information as is available it would appear that wages at least have kept pace pretty well with wages in other industries.

Social security. Some of the agreements entered into between unions and motor transport concerns provide for seniority arrangements which protect employees of long standing from unemployment, these agreements being similar to those used on the railroads and having similar advantages and disadvantages. Motor transport workers are subject to the same provisions dealing with unemployment insurance, old age benefits, and the like, as are applicable to workers in industry generally. Hence they do not receive social security benefits which are as large as those received by railroad workers, and railroad spokesmen have complained that the heavier burden of financing railroad social security payments places the railroads at a competitive disadvantage in their struggle for traffic. In recent years, however, some motor transport concerns have negotiated agreements with their employees which include social security benefits.

I.C.C. regulations. The Interstate Commerce Act authorizes the Interstate Commerce Commission to establish qualifications and maximum hours of service for employees of common, contract, and private carriers, and of the employees of carriers otherwise exempt from the provisions of the law. Both the Supreme Court and the Interstate Commerce Commission are in agreement that the Commission's jurisdiction is limited to those employees whose activities affect safety of operations and not to employees in general.[5] The Commission has acted to assume jurisdiction over the hours of work of drivers, drivers' helpers, loaders, and mechanics as being employees whose activities affect safety of operations.[6] In addition to Interstate Commerce Commission regulations applying to interstate operations, there are numerous state laws regulating the hours of service of employees engaged in intrastate operations.

The Commission has promulgated detailed regulations relative to the qualifications and hours of work of employees subject to its jurisdiction. It recognizes that long hours on active duty are incompatible with safety of operations, but delays caused by shippers, and by weather, road, and traffic conditions make rigid restrictions on hours of work impractical. It also has recognized that drivers often prefer to work somewhat longer hours and make a round trip from and to their home town rather than to work shorter periods and have to lay over away from home.

After a driver has driven an aggregate of ten hours, he must be off duty for eight hours, with an exception made when safety makes a longer period necessary. A somewhat longer daily working period is permitted to cover time "on duty," or time working at tasks other than actual driving, but the maximum in any week is fixed at sixty hours. The various maxima provided for motor transport employees are substantially in excess of those recognized by society as desirable for workers in general, but in the trucking branch of the motor transport industry, operations cannot be fitted into the neat patterns possible where workers are employed within the confines of a single city or metropolitan area. Some of the larger concerns can employ drivers in relays, but this is not the case with many small operators. In the motor bus industry, on the other hand, long hours of service for bus drivers are neither necessary nor desirable.

RATES, RATE MAKING, AND MOTOR CARRIER COSTS

Relative unimportance of constant costs. Before undertaking a consideration of motor carrier rates and rate making, it is necessary to point out certain fundamental differences between motor carrier costs

---

[5] *United States* v. *American Trucking Associations, Inc.*, 310 U.S. 534 (1940).

[6] *In the Matter of Maximum Hours of Service of Motor Carrier Employees*, 28 M.C.C. 125 (1941).

and railroad costs. In the first place, the high ratio of constant costs to variable costs which is characteristic of the business of railroad transportation is reversed in the motor transport field, where constant costs are small relative to variable costs, being estimated roughly to be no more than 10 per cent of total costs. This is due principally to the fact that capital requirements in the motor transport industry are small as compared with the amount of capital necessary to construct and operate a railroad. A railroad must invest a substantial sum in an expensive right of way, but no such investment is required of motor carriers. The first cost of trucks and, to a lesser extent, buses is quite modest as compared with the cost of railroad equipment, and the same may be said for terminal facilities. Trucking concerns perform much of their terminal service at the loading docks of shippers and consignees and require only minor facilities in the way of freight houses and repair facilities. In thousands of small communities the bus terminal is a hotel, eating house, or drug store, while in larger communities union bus depots are operated at a saving in cost to the various users. All of these factors mean that interest on investment, a major contributing factor to heavy railroad constant costs, is of minor importance in the motor transport field.

It also appears to be true that motor carrier operating costs are somewhat more responsive to variations in volume of traffic than is true of railroad operating costs. Attention should be called to the smaller carrying capacity of the motor vehicle which makes it more adaptable to variations in the volume of traffic than is true of a railroad train. The principal motor carrier operating costs, including motor fuel and oil, labor, depreciation, and maintenance, all vary pretty directly with the number of vehicles operated. It is interesting to note that motor fuel taxes, which are analogous in a sense to the interest and maintenance costs incurred by a railroad in providing its own right of way, vary with the number of vehicles and somewhat with the weight of the load hauled, and so are largely variable in nature, whereas railroad right-of-way costs are largely constant.

Terminal and line-haul costs. Motor carrier terminal costs are small relative to over-the-road costs, again reversing the railroad cost situation. The large investment which the railroad must make in land, track, and buildings for the purpose of making up and breaking up trains is avoided by the motor carrier, and the labor costs incurred in handling small shipments are less for motor carriers than for railroads. Once a train has been made up and is on its way, however, the advantages and economies of mass transportation immediately become apparent. The cost of operating the train as a whole is, of course, substantial, but the cost of moving a ton mile of freight is very low. Furthermore, up to a certain point additional freight can be handled at only an insignificant increase in cost, and this contributes to ever lower ton-mile costs as traffic increases. Motor carriers, on the other hand, because of the small carrying capacity of the motor vehicle, are not in a position to enjoy the line-haul economies characteristic of mass transportation, and as a result their over-the-road costs are high relative to railroad line-haul costs, and costs per unit of traffic handled are affected only to a minor extent by increased volume of traffic.

GENERAL LEVEL OF RATES

Rule of rate making. In prescribing just and reasonable motor carrier rates the Commission is to consider, among other things, the inherent advantages of motor transportation, the effect of rates on the movement of traffic, the need for adequate and efficient service at the lowest cost consistent with providing such service, and the need of revenues sufficient to enable the carriers under honest, economical, and efficient management, to provide the required service. This rule is identical with the railroad rule of rate making except for the additional requirement that the Commission is to give consideration to the inherent advantages of motor carriers in fixing motor carrier rates. The national transportation policy adopted in 1940, however, declares that it is the intention of Congress to have regulation administered in such a way as to recognize and preserve the inherent advantages of each form of transportation subject to the Interstate Commerce Act, and the Commission has held that it must recognize and preserve the inherent advantages of each type of carrier rather than just the inherent advantages of motor carrier transportation.[7] Hence this difference between the railroad rule and the motor carrier rule is of no practical significance.

Effect of rates on the movement of traffic. The original Motor Carrier Act, 1935, specified that the Commission, in the exercise of its power to prescribe just and reasonable rates for motor carriers, was to give due consideration to the effect of rates upon the movement of traffic by such carriers. This statement was somewhat ambiguous and in some cases it led motor carriers to argue that certain railroad rates should be raised to permit motor carriers to obtain some of the traffic at a reasonable profit. In the Transportation Act of 1940 this provision was reworded to direct the Commission to give consideration to the effect

---

[7] *Tires between Points in the South*, 243 I.C.C. 767 (1941); *Petroleum and Petroleum Products from California to Arizona*, 241 I.C.C. 21 (1940).

of rates on the movement of traffic by the carrier or carriers *for which the rates are prescribed.* The Commission has held that to direct a low cost agency to increase its rates in order that a high cost agency may participate in the traffic and earn a profit is to disregard the interests of shippers and consumers, and that no carrier should be required to maintain rates which would be unreasonable, judged by other standards, for the purpose of protecting the traffic of a competitor.[8]

Honest, economical, and efficient management. In some cases involving applications for general increases in freight rates, shippers have urged that the carriers' difficulties are the result of a lack of honest, economical, and efficient management and that if management were more efficient, the proposed increases would not be necessary.[9] In this connection attention is sometimes called to the fact that some carriers operate at a loss while others operate at a profit. The Commission, however, has not accepted the mere fact that some carriers operate at a loss while others operate at a profit as adequate evidence of inefficient management because conditions differ widely in the different sections of the country and even between different carriers in the same section. For example, carriers serving only large communities may show more profitable operations under a given scale of rates than carriers which also serve a number of small intermediate points. Under such circumstances differences in profits do not necessarily reflect differences in managerial efficiency.[10]

Adequate rate of return. In determining the general level of railroad rates the Commission must, whether it is required to do so by law or not, take into consideration the rate of return which a given level of rates will yield on the carriers' investment, for unless railroads are permitted to earn a reasonable return on investment, new capital will not be attracted to the field, and existing investors will be at a disadvantage as compared with investors in unregulated enterprises. Motor carriers, however, have urged that the return on investment test of the reasonableness of rates is not applicable to the motor transport industry because of their relatively small investment in tangible property. The Commission has recognized that this is a factor to be considered,[11] and in rate-level cases it has placed principal emphasis on carrier costs as a criterion of the need for rate increases.[12] Rates should be sufficiently

---

[8] *Petroleum and Petroleum Products from California to Arizona,* 241 I.C.C. 21 (1940).

[9] See, for example, *Trunk Line Territory Motor Carrier Rates,* 24 M.C.C. 501 (1940).

[10] *New England Motor Carrier Rates,* 28 M.C.C. 31 (1941).

[11] *Union Bus Lines, Incorporated—Purchase—Amberson,* 5 M.C.C. 201 (1937).

[12] *Middle West General Increases,* 48 M.C.C. 541 (1948).

high to permit a safe margin of operating revenues over expenses,[13] although the spread between net operating revenue and net income before income taxes need not be as large for motor carriers as for railroads. This is because net operating revenues in any case must be sufficient to cover fixed charges, and fixed charges are relatively very much greater in the case of the railroads than in the case of motor carriers.[14]

In attempting to establish an adequate level of rates for motor freight carriers the Commission has had to face the fact that a scale of rates which will yield a satisfactory return to some carriers will bring more or less than an adequate return to others. Yet to the extent that these carriers are in competition with one another their rates must be the same. This situation will be recognized as similar to that which exists in the railroad field in connection with the rates and earnings of competing strong and weak lines. The Commission has held that the general level of rates should not be adjusted upwards sufficiently high to enable all carriers to conduct profitable operations, for if this were done, most of the carriers would earn excessive profits, assuming that railroad competition was not of such a nature as to forestall an upward adjustment of rates. Carriers with operating ratios substantially higher than the average have the right, however, according to the Commission, to propose rates which will provide them an opportunity to earn a satisfactory profit, again assuming that the competitive situation will permit higher rates.[15]

Trends. When the first motor carrier freight rates were filed with the Interstate Commerce Commission in 1936, they were based for the most part on railroad freight rates, and in the years which followed motor freight rates have tended to follow the trend of railroad freight rates. Numerous rate increases were granted by the Commission during and after World War II, following somewhat the pattern of railroad rate increases. It is interesting to note, however, that while the railroads usually band together and apply for uniform increases on a nationwide basis, this is not true of the motor carriers. Proposals for general increases are initiated independently by groups of carriers affiliated with the various motor carrier rate bureaus or conferences scattered over the country. For this reason it is impossible to make a comparison between the over-all increase in motor freight rates and the over-all increase in railroad freight rates. The increases, however, have been substantial.

---

13 *Increased Common Carrier Truck Rates in the East*, 42 M.C.C. 633 (1943).
14 *Ibid.*
15 *Ibid.*

RATES ON PARTICULAR COMMODITIES

Motor freight classification. The Motor Carrier Act, 1935, required interstate motor carriers to prepare and file with the Interstate Commerce Commission just and reasonable classifications of freight. To this end representatives of the trucking industry held numerous conferences in Washington, but sharply divergent views made the adoption of a classification acceptable to all carriers impossible. The New England carriers wanted to establish a classification grouping all articles into five classes in accordance with a formula based on weight and space occupied. They also advocated the establishment of class rates based on operating costs and on conditions peculiar to the motor transport industry. For the most part, however, representatives of the industry favored a classification based on the Consolidated Freight Classification and the establishment of class rates directly competitive with railroad class rates. This plan had the advantage that it would make possible the adoption of a uniform classification with a minimum of delay, a matter of considerable importance in view of the general lack of knowledge of rate-making procedures and the relatively short time the carriers had to prepare and file classifications. It was recognized that experience probably would demonstrate the need for changes, but such changes could be made later as found to be necessary or desirable.

Most of the New England carriers joined one or the other of two New England groups, each of which had its own classification based on the New England plan of independent classifications and rates. The bulk of the carriers outside of New England and a few of those operating in New England, adopted a National Motor Freight Classification patterned after the Consolidated Freight Classification. Some carriers chose to become parties to the Consolidated Freight Classification itself, and some adopted individual classifications.

In 1938 the Interstate Commerce Commission ordered the New England carriers to conform with a single New England classification and took the occasion to make some observations with reference to differences in motor carrier classifications. From the standpoint of abstract reason, it said, there was little doubt that the theory followed by the New England carriers of fixing motor carrier rates on the basis of motor carrier costs was sound, but in practice it was weak in its disregard of practical competitive conditions. The Commission pointed out that if motor carrier rates were based on cost, the motor carriers could not meet railroad competition in situations where the railroads had a cost advantage, but unless the same principle were applied to the fixing of railroad rates, there was nothing to prevent the railroads from meeting motor carrier rates where motor carriers had a cost advantage, thus placing motor carriers at a distinct disadvantage. The Commission felt, however, that further experimentation with both types of classifications and rate systems was desirable and acquiesced in the continuation of both the New England and the National Motor Freight classifications.[16]

National Motor Freight Classification. The National Motor Freight Classification is quite similar in structure and content to the Consolidated Freight Classification described in Chapter 11. It contains a section of rules and regulations similar to those applicable to railroad shipments and an extensive listing of items, together with the applicable ratings. There are three classification territories which are designated East, West, and South, these territories being roughly the same as Official, Western, and Southern Classification territories. If a given item is rated the same in each classification territory, only one rating is shown, but in numerous cases separate ratings are given for each territory. Ratings are provided for less-than-truckload quantities, and volume ratings applying on minimum weights about the same as carload minimum weights also are given. In addition, provision is made for the movement of goods in truckload lots. The letters "N.O.I." indicate a rating which is to be used in the absence of some more specific designation. The filing of a uniform classification by the railroads was followed by the preparation of a uniform motor freight classification.

Determinants of classification. For the most part the ratings assigned to specific commodities in the National Motor Freight Classification are identical with those provided for railroad freight shipments. Hence it would appear that the principal determinant of motor classification ratings is railroad competition, which means that the motor ratings are based only indirectly on the various cost and demand factors discussed in Chapter 11. To the extent that motor freight ratings are made independently of railroad ratings they will more nearly reflect average total cost than is true of railroad ratings. The typical motor freight carrier does not handle the volume and variety of traffic handled by the railroads, and so the motor carrier finds it more difficult to make up for low ratings on some commodities by means of higher ratings on others. Also, it will be recalled that motor carrier costs are largely variable, and since any carrier must charge rates which will at least cover the variable or out-of-pocket cost involved, this means that a rate which covers out-of-pocket cost for a motor carrier will more nearly cover total costs than is true in the case of the railroads. Motor carriers with

---

[16] *New England Motor Carrier Rates,* 8 M.C.C. 287 (1938). See, also, *Motor Carrier Rates in New England,* 47 M.C.C. 657 (1948).

operating authority to handle only one or a very few types of commodities are particularly limited in the extent to which they can ignore average total cost in bidding for any particular item of traffic.

Exception ratings and commodity rates. Motor carriers publish exception ratings and commodity rates of the same type and for the same reasons that such ratings and rates are published by rail carriers. Hence little need be added at this point to the discussion of exception ratings and commodity rates found in Chapter 11. Competition has been a vital factor in fixing motor carrier exception ratings and commodity rates, this competition including market competition, commodity competition, and intercarrier competition. Motor common carriers, for example, compete with railroads, contract carriers, private carriers, and other motor common carriers for certain types of traffic. Because of the relatively greater importance of short haul small shipments a larger proportion of motor truck traffic moves under class rates than is true of railroad traffic, but there is a substantial volume of motor freight traffic moving under exception ratings and commodity rates.[17]

Truckload minimum weights. Motor carriers provide lower rates on most commodities when they move in truckload lots than they do when they move in less-than-truckload lots because of the saving in handling and billing costs and because of the assurance of a full utilization of equipment. Reduced rates on truckload shipments have given motor carriers an advantage over the railroads in connection with a certain type of traffic because truckload minimum weights are less than carload minimum weights. Many shippers who find it impractical or impossible to ship in carload-lot quantities are able to ship in truckload lots at rates which are lower than the less-than-carload or less-than-truckload rates.

Because of widely different carrying capacities of vehicles used in moving intercity traffic, a problem arises over what constitutes a truckload minimum weight. If the Commission were to approve truckload minimum weights which varied with the carrying capacity of the individual vehicles employed, carriers operating large vehicles would be at a disadvantage since shippers would be able to ship smaller quantities at the truckload rate by making use of the services of carriers employing smaller vehicles.[18] Hence the Commission has said that a normal truck-

---

[17] Professor Locklin cites a 1945 study made by the Office of Defense Transportation of motor truck traffic in the Middle West, showing about 28 per cent of motor carrier tonnage moving under exception ratings and 28 per cent under commodity rates. D. Philip Locklin, *Economics of Transportation*, 3rd Ed. Chicago: Richard D. Irwin, Inc., 1947, p. 688.

[18] *Trunk Line Territory Motor Carrier Rates*, 24 M.C.C. 501 (1940).

load minimum on any given traffic is generally considered to be a minimum that conforms with the average capacity of the motor vehicles employed in the transportation of such traffic.[19]

Multi-minimum rates. An interesting feature of motor freight rate making has been the introduction by many carriers of graduated scales of rates on less-than-truckload shipments of different minimum weights. Thus a carrier might establish a scale of rates on shipments under 6,000 pounds in weight, a somewhat lower scale on shipments between 6,000 and 12,000 pounds, and still lower rates on shipments of 12,000 pounds or more. It has been found that the cost of handling less-than-truckload shipments decreases per one-hundred pounds as the size of the shipment increases, largely because the cost of the pickup and delivery service is about the same regardless of the size of the shipment.

Volume minimum weights. In order to compete with the railroads for traffic moving in carload lots the motor freight industry has established volume ratings and rates based on volume minimum weights identical with railroad carload minimum weights, even though the minima established may exceed the carrying capacity of the largest vehicle available and thus require the use of two or more vehicles. Such ratings and rates cannot be justified to any extent on the basis of lower costs because the cost of handling and moving a shipment requiring two trucks will, except under unusual circumstances, be very nearly double the cost of handling a single truckload shipment of the same commodity.

This was the view taken by the Commission, which held that reduced rates subject to minimum weights greater than could be loaded in a single vehicle were unlawful unless it could be shown that the cost per hundred pounds was less for a multiple unit shipment than for a shipment moved in a single vehicle.[20] The Supreme Court, however, did not hold with this view. It recognized the right of the Commission to relate volume rates to the savings in operating costs which might or might not result from large shipments, but it went on to say, in effect, that to tie rate differentials exclusively to minimum weights based on the size of a single vehicle ignored the factor of competition between rail and motor carriers.[21] Thus competition as well as cost must be taken into consideration in determining the lawfulness of ratings and rates based on volume minimum weights.

---

[19] *Activated Carbon, etc., from Texas to Kansas City,* 31 M.C.C. 597 (1942).

[20] *Rugs and Matting from the East to Western Trunk Line Territory,* 34 M.C.C. 641 (1942); *Cigarettes and Tobacco Between North Carolina Points and Philadelphia,* 42 M.C.C. 1 (1943); *Minimum Weight on Trisodium Phosphate,* 42 M.C.C. 407 (1943).

[21] *Eastern-Central Motor Carriers Association* v. *United States,* 321 U.S. 194 (1944).

RATES ON PARTICULAR HAULS

No uniform scale of class rates. As pointed out in Chapter 13, the Interstate Commerce Commission worked out and put into effect basic scales of class rates applicable, with exceptions, to every railroad operating within the territory for which the rates were prescribed. Although operating and traffic conditions vary considerably in different parts of a given territory, the same scale of rates was applied, partly because of the widespread scope of operations of the more important railroads and partly because in some cases favorable conditions tend to offset unfavorable ones. In the case of motor carriers it is not practical to establish general basic scales of class rates applicable over wide areas. The typical motor carrier operates in a restricted area, and if motor carriers are to survive, consideration must be given to the conditions existing in the areas in which they operate. In addition, motor carriers, even within a restricted area, differ in the profitableness of their operations due in some degree to conditions beyond their control, and this further limits the opportunities for the establishment of over-all rate scales. Some of the factors which enter into the determination of the rates charged by various motor carriers are discussed briefly in the following paragraphs.

Distance. Motor carrier rates, like railroad rates, reflect the influence of the distance principle. The Commission has observed that distance is always an element in determining the reasonableness of a rate and that rates should bear some reasonable relation to distances over the route of movement.[22] Distances, however, should be based on the short line highway distance over routes customarily used in the movement of traffic.[23] Although Part II of the Interstate Commerce Act contains no long and short haul clause, the Commission has condemned proposals which would result in lower rates to more distant points than would be charged to intermediate points unless there is some compelling reason for establishing such rates.[24]

Operating conditions. Variations in operating conditions may justify higher rates between certain points than between others, even though the distances involved are substantially equal.[25] Higher operating costs justify

---

[22] *Central Territory Motor Carrier Rates*, 30 M.C.C. 164 (1941); *Delaware and Maryland to Trunk Line Territory, Increased Rates*, 44 M.C.C. 355 (1945).

[23] *Clay, Concrete, and Shale Products in the South*, 28 M.C.C. 713 (1941).

[24] *Fifth Class Rates Between Boston, Mass., and Providence, R. I.*, 2 M.C.C. 530 (1937); *Commodities from Kansas to Illinois, Missouri, and Oklahoma*, 44 M.C.C. 90 (1944).

[25] *M. H. Winn Trucking Company, Commodities in New England*, 28 M.C.C. 228 (1941).

higher rates mile for mile in mountainous country than are necessary in level country.[26] Similarly, carriers serving highly congested areas encounter increased costs because of the slower speeds necessary in such areas, and this may be reflected in the rates charged. Unbalanced traffic causes motor carriers to seek to establish lower rates in one direction than in the other in order to attract a pay load for lightly loaded or empty trucks. Such rates, of course, must be sufficiently high to yield something more than the out-of-pocket costs incurred in moving the traffic.[27] Also care must be taken to avoid the possible disruption of existing rate relationships and to protect the rights of other carriers.

Railroad competition. While distance and operating conditions are both elements to be considered, motor carrier rates commonly are made to meet or beat railroad rates. Generally speaking, however, carriers are able to operate profitably on the basis of railroad rate scales only for comparatively short distances. Railroad terminal costs, it will be recalled, are high, but line-haul costs are low. Hence railroad costs and railroad rates do not increase proportionately with distance, following the tapering principle discussed in Chapter 12. Motor carriers, on the other hand, have low terminal costs and relatively high over-the-road costs, and so their costs tend to increase somewhat in proportion with distance. Thus motor carrier costs, at first lower per unit of traffic than railroad costs, approach the railroad cost curve as the length of haul increases, and in due course they equal and then exceed railroad costs, after which motor carriers find it increasingly unprofitable to compete on the basis of railroad rates.

One student of motor freight transportation has stated that motor carriers generally are safe in charging railroad class rates for hauls up to about 200 miles, assuming that the applicable railroad rates have not been depressed below a normal level.[28] The exact point at which it becomes unprofitable for a motor carrier to compete on the basis of railroad rates depends in part on the circumstances surrounding each individual run. In mountainous areas there are sometimes wide differences in railroad and highway distances between two points, sometimes favoring one carrier and sometimes the other. But far more important is the general nature of the traffic handled. A motor carrier handling mostly high grade freight can compete with railroads over greater distances than can a motor carrier handling lower grades of freight because of

---

[26] Specific examples of the effect of terrain on rates are given in H. E. Stocker, *Motor Traffic Management*. New York: Prentice-Hall, Inc., 1942, pp. 166-169.

[27] *D. & H. Motor Freight Company, Commodities in New Jersey, New York, and Pennsylvania*, 22 M.C.C. 389 (1940).

[28] H. E. Stocker, *Motor Traffic Management*. p. 173.

the greater total revenue derived from the high grade freight. Motor carriers can compete with railroads for unusually long distances if they can confine their service to high grade freight.

Class-rate stops. The practice of basing motor carrier rates on railroad rates poses a problem for motor carriers in connection with the transportation of commodities which will not move except under very low ratings or rates. Because of the limited carrying capacity of trucks and their relatively high operating costs per unit of freight handled, a motor carrier finds it quite unprofitable to handle the lower grades of freight at rail-competitive rates, and in an effort to avoid the movement of traffic at unremunerative rates motor carriers have adopted what are known as minimum class-rate stops. The effect of the use of class-rate stops is to establish the rate on a specified class of freight, say the fifth class rate, as the minimum rate which will apply on any commodity even though a lower rating may be shown in the National Motor Freight Classification. Class-rate stops are not uniform for all distances. Because of high terminal costs, railroad freight rates are high for shorter hauls, and this makes it possible for motor carriers to handle some fairly low rated commodities for short distances at rail competitive rates. Hence a given item may be moved for a short distance at the rating specified in the classification, but where long hauls are involved rate stops are applied, and the longer the haul the higher the rate stop.[29]

Many shippers have contended that rate stops are used deliberately to discourage the movement of unwanted traffic, but this has been denied by motor carriers.[30] It is confusing and certainly misleading, however, to publish low ratings on various commodities in the National Motor Freight Classification, which ratings are made quite meaningless by the application of rate stops. Another criticism of the use of class-rate stops has been that they have the effect of lumping all commodities rated lower than the specified minimum into a single group, thus depriving these commodities of the benefit of any more favorable transportation characteristics they may have as compared with commodities rated the same or higher than the minimum.[31]

The Interstate Commerce Commission has approved the use of class-rate stops on various occasions,[32] but it also has said that if the general bases of class rates are too low on the lower rated traffic, the situation

---

[29] *Victory Granite Company* v. *Central Truck Lines, Inc.*, 44 M.C.C. 320 (1945).

[30] Department of Commerce, *Industry Report, Domestic Transportation,* May-August, 1948. p. 104.

[31] *Minimum Class Rate Restrictions, Central and Eastern States,* 44 M.C.C. 367 (1945).

[32] For example, *Trunk Line Territory Motor Carrier Rates,* 24 M.C.C. 501 (1940).

should be corrected by revising the classification and the class rates rather than by establishing general bases of minimum class rates.[33] The Commission has stated on various occasions that minimum class rates should be related to the first class rates and that the percentage relationship should not be as high for short hauls as for long hauls.[34] Furthermore, the Commission has criticized lack of uniformity in the use of class-rate stops. Thus it has said that different stops should not be prescribed for some carriers than for others, nor should a different relationship to the first class rates be maintained between some areas than for application generally.[35] And any difference in class-rate stops between single line hauls and multiple line hauls between the same points should be no greater than the difference in the cost of transporting single line traffic and the cost of transporting joint line traffic.[36]

Other competition. In addition to the consideration given to railroad competition motor common carriers also must give consideration to the rates charged by other motor common carriers and by contract carriers, both interstate and intrastate. And both common and contract carriers must always keep in mind in their rate-making activities the ever-present threat of competition from private carriers. The Interstate Commerce Commission can, of course, act to prevent undue rate cutting as between interstate common carriers, and it has sought to protect common carriers in some measure from the competition of interstate contract carriers, but there is little or nothing it can do to protect common and contract carriers from the activities of private carriers, other than refuse to permit the latter to perform a for-hire service on back hauls. Motor carrier rates on a given commodity can never rise above the point where important shippers or users of that commodity will find it more economical to move it in their own or in leased trucks.

CONCLUSION

Inherent advantage and rate making. The Interstate Commerce Commission has declared that it is its duty under the law to fix general levels of rates for the different types of carriers subject to the Interstate Commerce Act in such a way as to recognize and preserve the inherent advantages of each. The Commission's interpretation of the law on this

---

[33] *Minimum Rate Restrictions to, from, and within the Southwest,* 43 M.C.C. 161 (1944).

[34] *Minimum Class Rate Restrictions, Central and Eastern States,* 44 M.C.C. 367 (1945); *Commodities from and to the Southwest,* 47 M.C.C. 155 (1947).

[35] *Minimum Class Rate Restrictions, Central and Eastern States,* 44 M.C.C. 367 (1945).

[36] *Transamerican Freight Lines, Classes in Central Territory,* 43 M.C.C. 189 (1944).

point carries with it certain rather interesting implications. The Commission, for example, has called attention to various natural advantages of motor transportation, particularly in the short haul field, but at the same time it has said that it must recognize the natural advantage possessed by the railroads in providing a low cost mass transportation service.[37] And it also has stated that attempts of motor carriers to meet the class rates of rail carriers on low rated long haul traffic generally result in unprofitable operations.[38] This suggests that the railroads should get out of the short haul less-than-carload business and that motor carriers should keep out of the long haul business, especially in connection with the movement of lower rated traffic. The decision of the Interstate Commerce Commission in the Pacific Intermountain-Keeshin case discussed in Chapter 20, suggests an effort on its part to protect in some degree what it considers to be a natural advantage of the railroad on the long haul.

Motor carrier interests have contended from time to time that railroad less-than-carload freight rates do not cover the cost of rendering the service, the railroads depending upon the profits made out of the movement of carload freight to cover the losses incurred in handling less-than-carload freight. This is unfair, according to the motor carriers, because they do not have any large volume of profitable carload freight against which they can offset possible losses or low profits resulting from railroad competition for short haul less-than-carload freight. It also has been pointed out that the system is unfair to the shippers of carload freight who must bear the burden of losses incurred by the railroads on less-than-carload traffic. The extent to which railroad costs are constant and the extent to which common costs are encountered makes it difficult to determine the extent to which any given rate or group of rates does or does not cover cost, but the consensus of opinion is that the railroad less-than-carload freight business is not, generally speaking, profitable.

Motor carrier rates and motor carrier costs. The extent to which motor carrier rates have been based on railroad rates gives rise to a problem which is of significance not only to motor carriers but also to the whole transportation system. The prices charged by any business or industry should reflect the costs incurred in that business or industry in producing the goods or services it offers for sale, and they should not be based on the costs incurred by some other business or industry. In the long run this must be true if the business or industry involved is to survive. As noted previously, the motor carrier cost structure differs markedly from the cost structure of the railroad industry, and when motor carriers charge railroad rates for the services they render, they are tying their

[37] *Commodities from California to Arizona and New Mexico,* 245 I.C.C. 545 (1941).
[38] *Trunk Line Territory Motor Carrier Rates,* 24 M.C.C. 501 (1940).

rates to the costs and operating conditions characteristic of an entirely different type of transportation rather than to their own costs and to the conditions peculiar to motor transportation. On its face such a system of rate making is neither logical nor economically sound. Yet as the Interstate Commerce Commission pointed out in connection with its discussion of New England motor carrier rates, the motor carrier industry would be placed at a severe disadvantage if it based rates entirely on costs unless the same principle were applied to railroad rates as well.

Certain possible solutions to the above difficulty suggest themselves. In the first place, the railroads should, perhaps, be permitted to get out of the less-than-carload freight business altogether. If this were done, it would be more nearly possible to base motor freight rates on motor freight costs. And in the second place, motor carrier rates and classifications should be studied carefully to determine the extent to which they conform with motor carrier costs. It is a common observation that numerous small motor freight operators have neither the facilities nor the know how to figure out a scale of rates of their own, and in some cases they have little or no knowledge of the costs incurred in handling different types of traffic. Careful cost studies might reveal some rates which were so low in relation to cost that it would be better to surrender the traffic to the railroads if public interest permitted, and they might reveal instances of rates which were lower than necessary to meet rail competition in the light of the superior service of the motor carrier.

There is evidence that this problem is engaging the attention of serious and responsible students. The Interstate Commerce Commission has given the problem of cost finding some thought, and the same can be said for certain elements within the motor transport industry. A third possible solution which suggests itself is the coordination of rail and motor service under unified management. It is reasonable to suppose that if such unification were achieved, management would not find it difficult to allocate to each agency those services which it could perform most economically and efficiently on the basis of costs. This matter is given further consideration in Chapter 33.

SUGGESTED READINGS

Britton, Lewis W., ed., *Transportation in 1948*. Washington: The Traffic Service Corporation, 1949. Also *Transportation in 1949*, 1950.

Board of Investigation and Research, *Federal Regulatory Restrictions Upon Motor and Water Carriers*, 79th Congress, 1st Session, Senate Document 78, 1945. A detailed account of restrictions on operating rights.

Department of Commerce, *Industry Report*, May-August, 1948. An evaluation of motor truck transportation.

Interstate Commerce Acts Annotated, Vols. 10-14. These volumes, together with the more detailed *Motor Carrier Cases* of the Interstate Commerce Commission, constitute the chief source of information for the material contained in this chapter.

Interstate Commerce Commission, *Federal Regulation of the Sizes and Weights of Motor Vehicles*, 77th Congress, 1st Session, House Document 354, 1941.

Locklin, D. Philip, *Economics of Transportation*, 3rd Ed. Chicago: Richard D. Irwin, Inc., 1947. Chapters 28 and 29.

Stocker, H. E., *Motor Traffic Management*. New York: Prentice-Hall, Inc., 1942.

Taff, Charles A., *Commercial Motor Transportation*. Chicago: Richard D. Irwin, Inc., 1950.

Part Four

DOMESTIC WATER TRANSPORTATION

22

Development and Economics
of
DOMESTIC WATER TRANSPORTATION

TYPES OF WATER TRANSPORTATION

Types of waterways. Domestic water transportation service, both inter-state and intrastate, is provided on navigable rivers and canals, principally by barges and towboats; on the Great Lakes by boats especially designed for handling bulk cargo which can be loaded and unloaded mechanically; and between various seaports of the United States by ocean-going ships. Each of these three types of water transportation has its own special features and problems, and for that reason it will be desirable to treat each type separately.

Types of carriers. Domestic water transportation is provided by three different types of carriers. Common carriers offer a for-hire service to all shippers who can use it. As in the case of motor carriers, common carriers by water may offer a general cargo service, or they may confine themselves to the movement of one or a few types of commodities. Contract carriers do not offer their service to the general public but make separate contracts with individual shippers. By its very nature contract carrier service is of a highly specialized nature, such as the movement of ore or coal or liquid petroleum products in specially designed vessels. Private carriers are operated by industrial or commercial concerns for the movement of their own products, usually in highly specialized vessels. A good example of private carriage is the movement of liquid petroleum products from the Texas Gulf coast to the Atlantic seaboard in tankers owned by the large oil companies.

When Congress placed the regulation of domestic water transportation in the hands of the Interstate Commerce Commission in 1940, it exempted a large number of carriers from regulation, including a number of common and contract carriers, and this has given rise to a fourth type of carrier called an exempt carrier. The exempt carrier does not offer a type of transportation service different from those described above, but its exemption from regulation gives rise to certain problems requiring special consideration.

DEVELOPMENT OF WATER TRANSPORTATION

RIVER AND CANAL TRANSPORTATION IN THE NINETEENTH CENTURY

Era of canal and river prosperity. The opening of the Erie Canal in 1825 marked the beginning of a period of great canal and river prosperity in the United States which lasted for some fifty years. Although most of the canals built between 1825 and 1840 proved to be unprofitable and soon declined in importance, the Erie Canal was a phenomenal success, and each year more and more freight was carried on its waters. On the Ohio, the Mississippi, the Missouri, and the Arkansas, and on numerous smaller rivers in the South, the commerce of the interior was carried by a great fleet of river steamboats. Some communities, isolated by dense forest or swamp areas, were completely dependent for contact with the outside world upon diminutive steamers crawling up and down tiny streams. Large quantities of timber, cotton, coal, and general freight moved up and down the rivers, and for a generation or more the river steamboat played a major role in the movement of passenger traffic.

Decline of river and canal transportation. With the passing of the years something happened to the great inland commerce by river and canal which had developed during the middle years of the nineteenth century. Traffic on the Erie Canal reached a peak of more than 6,500,000 tons in 1872, although the relative importance of the Erie Canal had been declining rapidly for a number of years. Even the removal of all tolls in 1882 could not halt the decline of traffic which had started in 1873. Complete statistics on the volume of traffic on the Mississippi River system were never collected, but it is believed that peak traffic came about 1889, and there is little doubt that the relative importance of river transportation began to decline much earlier than this. By the turn of the century river transportation had all but passed out of the picture except for the movement of coal on the Ohio River.

Basic causes of decline of river and canal transportation. The decline of river and canal transportation during the latter part of the nineteenth century was due almost wholly to the inability of the water carriers to compete with the growing network of railroads. The railroads, of course, had a very great advantage in the movement of high grade and perishable commodities where speed of delivery was an important consideration, but too much emphasis should not be placed on this point, for such traffic never had been a major source of revenue to the water carriers. It was the ability of the railroads to capture the lower grade heavy and bulky staple commodity traffic which brought ruin to the boat lines.

Railroad rates at first were too high to be attractive to shippers of lumber and cotton and coal and other similar products where low freight rates were more important than speed of delivery. As the railroad network expanded and keen competition broke out between rival railroads, however, freight rates began to fall. Keen competition also led railroad managements to search for new sources of traffic, and rates were lowered where necessary to attract river and canal traffic to the railroads. This proved to be a profitable undertaking, for anything which such rates brought to the railroad over and above the variable or out-of-pocket costs was all to the good.

Railroad rate reductions do not alone explain the decline in river and canal transportation. The inland waterways, unlike the railroads, could not provide shippers with an integrated system of lines over which traffic could move in all directions. As population expanded westward a predominantly east-west flow of traffic developed which the nation's principal river system could not serve. Shifts in industry and the disappearance of such typical water traffic as timber and its products from the banks of the rivers brought an inevitable decline in waterway traffic. The seasonal nature of water transportation in many parts of the country was a definite disadvantage once year round railroad transportation became available. Finally, water carriers were poorly organized to meet railroad competition, an especially serious drawback once the railroads began to cooperate instead of compete.

Much has been said by earlier writers about the destructive competitive practices followed by the railroads. They could and did haul water-competitive traffic at a loss if necessary. They bought up canals and river boat lines and subordinated them to their own interests. They obtained control of dock facilities and secured desirable water front property for freight yards, thus seriously handicapping the delivery of freight to and from water carriers. It was a common practice for railroads to refuse to interchange freight with water lines, a policy which limited the latter to the diminishing volume of traffic originating at and destined to points on the water. While this writer has no desire to minimize these practices, it is difficult to see how they could have altered the fundamental situation. They may have hastened the decline of river and canal transportation, but they did not cause it.[1]

RIVER AND CANAL TRANSPORTATION IN THE TWENTIETH CENTURY

Revival of interest in river and canal transportation. Toward the end of the nineteenth century there was a sudden revival of interest in water-

---

[1] In this connection it may be pointed out that canal interests were equally guilty of various tactics designed to hamper the development of early railroads.

ways and waterway transportation. By this time, however, many of the nation's inland waterways had fallen into disrepair as a result of lack of proper maintenance. In addition, there were long stretches of rivers which once had been navigated successfully by small boats, and it was recognized that these waterways could not hope to compete with the railroads as arteries of transportation unless their channels were widened and deepened sufficiently to accommodate large boats and barges. Hence the revival of interest took the form of a demand for river and canal improvements financed with public funds.

It is difficult at this late date to appreciate the extent to which waterway development had caught the public fancy. Numerous waterway conventions were held, and two waterway commissions were appointed by the Federal Government. In 1903 the people of New York State voted to rebuild the Erie Canal, and in 1911 Congress joined them by making the first appropriations for an Ohio River improvement program. This was but the beginning. In the one hundred years prior to 1890 the Federal Government spent approximately $214 million for waterway development, but in the years between 1890 and 1931, just prior to the era of depression spending, it spent about $1,370 million, exclusive of appropriations for flood control, hydroelectric projects, and the Panama Canal.[2]

Reasons for revival of interest. Great popular movements often are the result of a complex of factors, and this certainly was true of the demand for waterway improvements. To no small extent the agitation for waterway improvement was closely tied into the movement for the conservation of natural resources which also was an important issue at the time. A second major factor which influenced the demand for waterway improvements was the almost universal belief that transportation on improved waterways was inherently more economical than railroad transportation. A third major consideration back of the agitation for waterway improvements was a widespread public antagonism against the railroads brought about by rising freight rates, fear of monopoly, revelations of mismanagement, and the like. It was widely believed that government financed waterway improvements which would put the boats back on the water would protect the people from the consequences of railroad monopoly. Other considerations included flood control, water purification, development of hydroelectric power, and a belief that the railroad network was overtaxed.

While there were large numbers of sincere and enthusiastic advocates

---

[2] Harold G. Moulton and associates, *The American Transportation Problem.* Washington: The Brookings Institution, 1933, pp. 434-438.

of inland waterway improvements, there were others who had ulterior motives for supporting a waterways program, and their activities unquestionably played an important part in the movement. For years the rivers and harbors bill had been a major item of pork barrel legislation, and its enactment by Congress was the occasion for much log rolling. Every city and town in the United States was happy to have the Federal Government spend money on local improvements, and a good way for a congressman to please his constituents and get reelected was to introduce legislation involving river or harbor improvements of interest to the area he served. Few congressmen had sufficient influence to push such projects through Congress singlehanded, but it was relatively simple for a number of them to get together, and by agreeing to vote for each other's projects, to get them all adopted. No doubt, too, individuals who might stand to gain financially from waterway construction work played a part in the enactment of rivers and harbors legislation.

Failure of traffic to develop. In spite of the widespread enthusiasm for waterway improvements, traffic on the nation's major waterways continued to decline, reaching its lowest point at about the time the United States entered the First World War. The funds appropriated by Congress did not achieve immediate results, partly because of the length of time it takes to complete a major waterway project and partly because the pork barrel nature of much early rivers and harbors legislation led to a dissipation of funds over numerous disconnected and unrelated local projects. Furthermore, investors did not share the public's enthusiasm for water transportation to the extent of risking their capital in barge line operations. The railroads were not disposed to interchange traffic with water carriers, and it is difficult to see how the latter could move any substantial volume of traffic as long as they were confined to traffic which originated at and was destined to waterway points only.

Impact of World War I. The transportation crises which followed upon the entry of the United States into World War I led business interests in New Orleans and St. Louis to make an effort to expand water transportation facilities on the Lower Mississippi, but they were unable to obtain the material to build the necessary tugs and barges. In 1918, however, the United States Railroad Administration commandeered privately owned boats and barges on the Mississippi River and the Warrior River, arranged for the construction of new equipment, and took over water operations on these rivers. But the war was over before any appreciable expansion of inland waterway service could be made.

Progress during the 1920's. The Federal Government's water transport facilities on the Mississippi River and the Warrior River were turned over to the War Department in 1920, following the termination of federal control, and they were operated directly by the War Department until 1924. In that year they were transferred to the Inland Waterways Corporation, the stock of which was subscribed for and owned by the United States Government, which carried on subsequent operations. Throughout the 1920's federal expenditures on waterway improvements continued apace, and the Ohio River project was formally opened in 1929. The progress made in river improvements during the 1920's was influenced to no small extent by Herbert Hoover who was interested in the program as an engineer and who, first as Secretary of Commerce and later as President, was in a position to do something about it.

Influence of depression. The waterway improvement program commended itself to the powers behind the New Deal, and activities were stepped up sharply during the 1930's, partly for pump priming purposes and partly to provide work relief. Several major projects were brought to completion or virtual completion during this period, principally on the Mississippi River system. In the ten years, 1931-40, Congress appropriated $1,164,241,000 for rivers and harbors which was more than double the amount appropriated during the preceding decade and came close to equaling the total appropriations of $1,558,982,000 covering the entire period from 1791 to 1930.[3]

Present status of river and canal transportation. During World War II river improvements were, of course, subordinated to the war effort, but after the war the river improvement program was resumed. It has been estimated that total public aid to waterways had risen to $4,121,199,097 by the end of 1949, with $451,000,000 estimated for fiscal 1950 and 1951.[4] Table XVIII shows the composition of the inland waterway system as reported in congressional hearings in 1950.

The effect of the stepped-up program of waterway improvements, plus government policies designed to encourage the movement of goods by water, is reflected in Table XIX showing the growth of traffic on the Mississippi River and its tributaries. The figures themselves are not too significant because they include a substantial tonnage, particularly of sand and gravel, which would exist even though no waterway improvements had been made, and also a certain amount of nonpermanent traffic resulting from the actual work of improvement. Nevertheless, the increase in traffic is significant.

---

[3] Board of Investigation and Research, *Public Aids to Domestic Transportation,* 79th Congress, 1st Session, House Document 159, p. 326 (1945).

[4] *Domestic Land and Water Transportation,* 82nd Congress, 1st Session, Senate Report 1039 (1951), pp. 31, 72.

DEVELOPMENT OF WATER TRANSPORTATION

Table XVIII

LENGTH AND DEPTH OF INLAND WATERWAYS IN THE UNITED STATES [5]

River or River System	Under 6 feet	6 to 9 feet	9 to 12 feet	12 feet and over	Total
Mississippi River System:					
Mississippi River			1,586	226	1,812
Illinois River and Waterway			327		327
Missouri River	1,474	767			2,241
Ohio River			981		981
Monongahela River, Pa. and W. Va.		37	91		128
Allegheny River, Pa.	153		72		225
All other Mississippi tributaries	3,741	1,864	754		6,359
Total, Mississippi River System	5,368	2,668	3,811	226	12,073
Atlantic coast rivers	2,470	1,026	539	1,799	5,834
Gulf coast rivers	2,729	610	637	24	4,000
Intracoastal waterways	78	660	163	2,065	2,966
St. Lawrence River to Canadian boundary				62	62
Pacific Coast rivers	803	256	97	222	1,378
All other waterways (miscellaneous)	260	539			799
Great Lakes and connecting channels				1,479	1,479
Grand total	11,708	5,759	5,247	5,877	28,591

Table XIX

TRAFFIC ON THE MISSISSIPPI RIVER SYSTEM [6]

Year	Ton Miles	Year	Ton Miles
1925	4,504,041,000	1938	10,977,156,000
1926	5,880,126,800	1939	12,369,098,000
1927	5,553,911,687	1940	13,934,427,000
1928	5,662,742,961	1941	17,037,435,000
1929	4,982,630,693	1942	16,498,840,000
1930	5,172,389,380	1943	16,765,204,000
1931	5,507,976,047	1944	20,381,558,000
1932	5,083,119,420	1945	19,595,193,000
1933	6,990,028,257	1946	18,358,220,000
1934	5,872,777,385	1947	23,479,053,000
1935	8,654,457,000	1948	27,923,751,000
1936	10,044,061,000	1949	27,399,055,000
1937	10,703,687,000		

[5] *Domestic Land and Water Transportation*, 82nd Congress, 1st Session, Senate Report 1039 (1951), p. 28.
[6] *Annual Report of the Chief of Engineers, U.S. Army*, various years. Ton mile statistics not available prior to 1925.

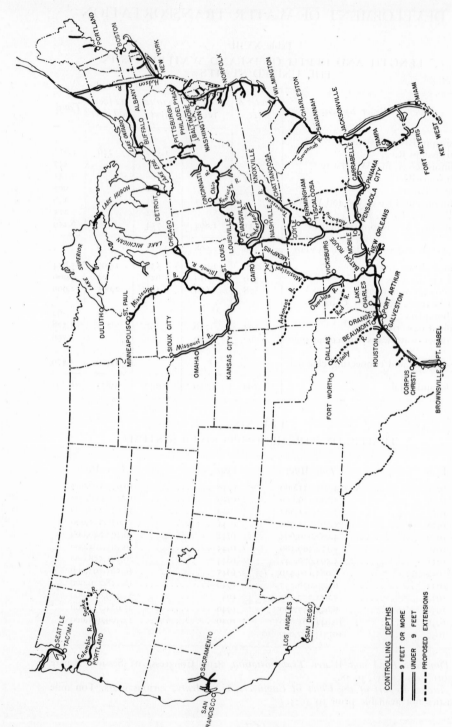

FIGURE 6. *Inland and Intracoastal Waterway System, March 1950.* (Adapted from map, courtesy of American Waterway Operators, Inc.)

CONTROLLING DEPTHS

—— 9 FEET OR MORE

—— UNDER 9 FEET

---- PROPOSED EXTENSIONS.

DEVELOPMENT OF WATER TRANSPORTATION

COST OF RIVER AND CANAL TRANSPORTATION

Rivers not natural waterways. There is a tendency to look upon rivers like the Mississippi as natural waterways in the sense that they can be navigated on a commercial scale in their natural state, and much faulty thinking about the economy of inland waterway transportation has resulted from a lack of knowledge of the fact that it takes large sums of money for the construction and maintenance of dams, locks, and channels in order to make and keep a river navigable. No river of any consequence in the United States would be navigable for any distance in its natural state by modern commercial vessels.

Right-of-way costs. Since the typical United States river is not suitable for modern navigation in its natural state, it must be improved to make it navigable, and it must be maintained continuously to keep it navigable. A channel of suitable width and depth must be dredged or blasted out of the river bed. It is necessary to construct locks around rapids or falls, revetments to hold banks in place, wing dams to direct the flow of water, and larger dams upstream behind which water may be impounded for release during dry seasons. Silting of channels with sand and mud and the tendency of rivers to shift their channels make necessary continued maintenance to keep a channel navigable. In the case of canals a ditch must be excavated directly from the earth and locks must be provided to overcome variations in ground levels. Except for a very limited amount of state activity, all of this work has been and is being done by the Federal Government.

Terminal costs. In a large number of cases the cost of constructing and maintaining water front terminal facilities, including docks and warehouses, has been met by the municipalities where these facilities are located, or by agencies of the Federal Government. These publicly-owned water front terminal facilities are available for use by river and canal boats, sometimes free of charge and sometimes with a payment required for their use. According to the Board of Investigation and Research none of the public agencies assessing user charges derived sufficient revenue in this way to cover the costs incurred.[7] In addition to the publicly-owned water front properties, large shippers frequently provide their own water front facilities, either for use by their own vessels or by carriers for hire which serve them.

Transportation and other costs. The cost of providing and maintaining boats and barges must, of course, be met by the companies engaged in

---

[7] *Public Aids to Domestic Transportation*, p. 381.

providing service by water. So also must these companies meet the cost of operating their vessels. And they must meet various freight handling expenses, the cost of traffic solicitation, and all of the general and administrative expenses which are characteristic of any business organization, including income taxes and state and local taxes on property owned. An exception must be made in the case of the Inland Waterways Corporation which in a quarter of a century of operations has incurred substantial deficits from operations, and such deficits must be met by taxpayers in general. More is said about the operations of the Inland Waterways Corporation in a later chapter.

Importance of considering all costs. The cost of providing and maintaining improved channels and terminal facilities is just as much a part of the cost of river and canal transportation as is the cost of providing, maintaining, and operating the boats and barges which use these facilities. As pointed out above, channels are improved and maintained by government, principally by the Federal Government, and they are provided *free of all tolls* to all who wish to use them. To a considerable extent, too, terminal facilities are provided by local governmental bodies. Some of these are available to users without charge, and none earn sufficient revenue from user charges to cover all costs. This means, then, that barge line operators pay little more than those costs which are incident to the actual movement of goods over the water. Under the circumstances it is not surprising that their rates are low and that those shippers who are in a position to use river and canal transportation find it quite economical to do so.

The fact that water carriers pay nothing for the use of improved channels and make only a partial payment for the use of publicly owned terminals, does not eliminate the cost of providing these facilities, for the cost is there and must be met by someone if river and canal carriers are to operate. What happens, of course, is that a substantial part of the cost of river and canal transportation is shifted onto the shoulders of the taxpayers. This shifting of costs might not be so objectionable if any large part of the public benefited, directly at least, from river and canal transportation, but the principal beneficiaries are those small segments of the population located on or near navigable waterways. It is true that combined water and rail movements extend at least a part of the benefit of low water rates to nonwater points, and it is true that water rates exercise some influence on railroad rates at nonwater points, but for the most part these benefits are restricted to a limited number of commodities and are apt to disappear rapidly as distance from the nearest waterway increases.

Hypothetical taxes. Since water carriers make use of waterways and terminal facilities owned by governmental bodies, they are relieved of the burden of right-of-way taxes which they would have to pay if waterways were privately owned. The railroads pay every tax of consequence which is paid by water carriers and, in addition, contribute a substantial sum each year to state and local governments in the form of taxes on owned right of way. Consequently they bear a substantially heavier tax burden than do the river and canal carriers.[8] This fact is important for two reasons. In the first place, to the extent that railroad traffic is diverted to tax free rivers and canals, it becomes that much more difficult for railroads to pay property taxes on their own right of ways, and in the last analysis this may result in state and local governments being deprived of an important source of tax revenue. And in the second place, differences in relative tax burdens are important in making true comparisons between different types of transportation, because variations in the tax burden introduce a purely artificial factor into the cost picture. It is important not to confuse this argument with another sometimes made to the effect that tolls should be levied against the users of rivers and canals to help pay for the upkeep of waterway and terminal facilities. The taxes involved here are those taxes which are expected of all business concerns to help defray the costs of government and not charges made for the use of public property.

COST AS RELATED TO INDIVIDUAL WATERWAYS

Need for relating costs to specific projects. There are such wide differences in the cost and utility of different waterway projects that over-all studies of the cost of river and canal transportation are rather meaningless. One waterway may handle such a large volume of traffic that improvement and maintenance costs may be quite small per unit of traffic moved, while on another waterway the cost per unit of traffic moved may be exorbitant. Under such circumstances studies of the cost of water transportation take on significance only as they are related to specific projects, and that is the procedure followed here. Since there are hundreds of small waterway improvement projects scattered over the United States, however, consideration can be given only to those of major significance.

Techniques employed. Major river improvement programs commonly are designed to serve more than one purpose, and the cost of non-

---

[8] In this connection see figures on page 384.

navigation improvements must be excluded from any study of the true cost of inland waterway transportation. The first step, then; is to calculate what it has cost to make a given waterway navigable. Here emphasis usually is placed on expenditures made during the modern period because many of the expenditures made during the nineteenth century contributed little or nothing to the needs of modern commerce by water. Having determined the cost of the navigation improvements, their expected life is estimated, and with this information it is then possible to calculate the annual charge necessary to amortize the Government's investment. Interest on capital investment,[9] maintenance costs, and possibly a charge covering hypothetical taxes are added to the annual amortization charge, and the result is the cost per year of the navigation facilities.

Having determined the full cost of providing the navigation facilities, the cost of performing the actual transportation service is added, and the total is divided by the number of ton miles of traffic moved during the year in question. The result is the full economic cost of the service per ton mile of traffic moved. In the case of a new project it may be desirable to make an estimate of ton-mile costs on the basis of anticipated traffic if a reasonable basis exists for measuring the traffic potential of the waterway.

Waterway studies. Both the Federal Coordinator of Transportation and the Board of Investigation and Research made studies of public aid to water transportation, the former as of about 1936 and the latter as of 1940.[10] The Board's study is too limited in scope to be suitable to the purpose at hand, and only occasional references will be made to it. The Coordinator's study, to which frequent reference is made, is based on the annual cost method described above. Cost estimates employed include the cost of the improvements, interest on investment, and depreciation, but an effort is made to avoid some of the more controversial issues by presenting costs on three different bases. Basis 1 includes the total volume of traffic moved regardless of its nature and excludes hypothetical taxes. Basis 2 is like Basis 1 except that traffic which does not require the improvements made is excluded. Basis 3 excludes traffic which does not require waterway improvements and adds hypothetical taxes. The Co-

---

[9] It has been argued that interest on investment is not a cost, at least to the extent that public works projects are financed from tax revenues, because the Government does not actually make the interest payments. This overlooks the fact that a taxpayer's money has alternative uses, and if the Government had not taxed him to provide the waterway in question, he could have invested the funds involved and received interest on them.

[10] *Public Aids to Transportation,* Vol. III, and *Public Aids to Domestic Transportation,* Chapter V.

ordinator's study also attempts to show what it would cost to move water traffic by railroad. Unfortunately, at the time the Coordinator's study was made, a number of waterway projects were only partially complete, and since that time there have been additional expenditures and substantial increases in traffic. A more recent study would be desirable, but none is available.

MISSISSIPPI RIVER SYSTEM

Ohio River. The great bulk of the traffic on the Ohio consists of coal, sand and gravel, petroleum products, and iron and steel products. These alone have been estimated to comprise more than 95 per cent of the traffic. The Federal Coordinator calculated the cost per ton for an average haul of each of these items, with the exception of sand and gravel, by water and by rail, and his figures are shown in Table XX.

Table XX

COST OF MOVING CERTAIN COMMODITIES BY RAIL AND WATER [11]

Commodity	Cost Per Ton			
	Water			Rail
	Basis 1	Basis 2	Basis 3	
Coal	$0.76	$0.79	$0.83	$1.22
Iron and Steel	4.53	4.67	4.99	3.32
Petroleum Products	2.73	2.84	3.00	2.88

The above figures show a substantial advantage in moving coal by water and a substantial advantage in moving iron and steel products by railroad, with neither type of transportation having an outstanding advantage in the movement of petroleum products. Coal made up more than one-half the tonnage moved on the Ohio River in 1936, and since much of it moved short distances in the Pittsburgh area, a reasonable conclusion from the Coordinator's study would be that Ohio River improvements in the general Pittsburgh area have made possible a real saving in transportation costs. Over the major portion of the river, however, it would be hard to reach a similar conclusion on the basis of 1936 figures. Since 1936 Ohio River traffic, including sand and gravel and freight moved in connection with river improvement work, has increased as shown in Table XXI.

---

[11] *Public Aids to Transportation,* Vol. III, p. 87.

DEVELOPMENT OF WATER TRANSPORTATION

Table XXI

TRAFFIC ON THE OHIO RIVER [12]

Year	Ton Miles	Year	Ton Miles
1936	2,652,870,080	1943	5,996,346,526
1937	2,671,926,225	1944	7,004,056,443
1938	2,578,824,818	1945	6,064,698,999
1939	3,360,454,251	1946	4,999,559,560
1940	3,852,508,298	1947	5,746,075,544
1941	5,197,440,060	1948	6,585,854,082
1942	5,299,846,755	1949	6,904,147,229

Since the major part of the Ohio River work was completed at the time of the Coordinator's study, these traffic increases suggest the need for further study of the economics of river transportation on the Ohio River.

Ohio River tributaries. There are a number of streams flowing into the Ohio River which have been improved to varying depths for navigation. These include the Monongahela, the Allegheny, the Kanawha, the Tennessee, the Cumberland, and others. In general, the Coordinator's study indicated that the full cost of water transportation exceeded the cost of rail transportation, sometimes by very substantial amounts. An outstanding exception was the Monongahela where the cost of moving coal was placed at 37¢ as compared with a rail cost of $1.03.[13] Traffic on Ohio River tributaries reached a peak about 1941 or 1942, and since then it has tended to decline on most of the rivers.[14]

Upper Mississippi River. Because of differences in channel depths and differences in the nature and volume of traffic, it is convenient to divide the Mississippi River into an upper and a lower portion. Unless otherwise stated, the Upper Mississippi is here considered to include that part of the river between Minneapolis and the mouth of the Missouri River near St. Louis. A nine-foot channel is maintained on this part of the river. Studies of the comparative cost of rail and water transportation in the Upper Mississippi River region are not available, but the Federal Coordinator estimated that the cost of the Upper Mississippi River improvements, as of 1936, ran from 45.07 mills to 60.69 mills per ton mile depending upon the basis used.[15] These figures do not take into account the greater distances freight must move by water, but even if this factor is disregarded, the cost per ton mile of providing an improved channel

---

[12] *Annual Report of the Chief of Engineers*, various years.
[13] *Public Aids to Transportation*, Vol. III, p. 90.
[14] *Annual Report of the Chief of Engineers*, 1950.
[15] *Public Aids to Transportation*, Vol. III. Table 37, facing p. 78.

was four and a half to six times the average revenue of 9.74 mills per ton mile derived by the railroads for hauling all kinds of freight in all parts of the country in 1936. If consideration were given to the shorter rail line distances and the much lower revenue derived from water competitive freight, the difference would be much greater.

Traffic on the Upper Mississippi has increased considerably since 1936 as shown by the figures in Table XXII but there also has been a substantial increase in the Government's investment on the Upper Mississippi since 1936. In view of the very considerable cost disadvantage existing in 1936 it seems unlikely that water transportation on the Upper Mississippi is paying its way today.

Table XXII

TRAFFIC ON THE UPPER MISSISSIPPI RIVER [16]

Year	Ton Miles	Year	Ton Miles
1936	154,129,683	1943	858,042,916
1937	342,758,636	1944	979,501,053
1938	458,573,005	1945	1,014,868,144
1939	536,536,232	1946	1,604,032,741
1940	832,600,100	1947	1,583,934,563
1941	1,064,707,656	1948	1,691,094,015
1942	1,054,679,328	1949	1,854,080,202

Illinois waterway. This waterway is made up of the south branch of the Chicago River, the Chicago Sanitary and Ship Canal, the Des Plaines River, and the Illinois River, and provides a minimum nine-foot channel between Chicago and the Mississippi River. The improvements made at the Chicago end were designed originally for sewage disposal purposes and their cost can be assigned only in part to navigation. The improvements made on the Des Plaines River and the Illinois River, however, were largely for navigation. The original improvements were made by the Chicago Sanitary District and the State of Illinois, but the project was turned over to the Federal Government in 1928. The Federal Coordinator's study estimated the annual cost of the improvements to run from 20.91 mills per ton mile to 28.45 mills per ton mile, depending upon the basis used. Ton miles moved since 1936, including sand and gravel, are shown in Table XXIII. As in the case of the Upper Mississippi River, considerable money has been spent by the Federal Government on the Illinois Waterway since 1936, and it would be difficult to pass judgment on the economy of this project at the present time.

---

[16] *Annual Report of the Chief of Engineers,* various dates.

DEVELOPMENT OF WATER TRANSPORTATION

Table XXIII

TRAFFIC ON THE ILLINOIS WATERWAY [17]

Year	Ton Miles	Year	Ton Miles
1936	141,102,419	1943	925,274,878
1937	289,622,634	1944	1,041,252,292
1938	393,988,943	1945	1,048,789,931
1939	597,378,218	1946	1,087,350,501
1940	761,364,345	1947	1,699,362,963
1941	943,662,066	1948	2,080,771,249
1942	945,625,613	1949	1,963,407,299

Missouri River. In the early years of the nineteenth century the Missouri River was a favorite means of access to the West and Northwest and was much used by hunters and trappers and explorers, but to make it usable for present day commercial transportation involves problems of great magnitude. Its banks are composed of alluvial materials which are subject to extensive erosion. It has unstable channels, and navigation is plagued by shifting sand bars. Water falls to a very low level at certain seasons of the year, while at other seasons there are destructive floods. Its lower reaches are closed to navigation for three and a half months during the winter, and its upper reaches for longer periods. Modern improvements began in 1912, and a nine-foot channel has been approved between the mouth of the river above St. Louis and Sioux City, Iowa. The actual depth varies from three and one-half feet to six feet or more. The cost of construction and annual maintenance have been heavy, and traffic, other than that generated by the improvement work itself, has been insignificant.

At the time of the Coordinator's study practically all Missouri River traffic consisted of materials used in the improvement work itself, and no attempt was made to determine ton-mile costs.[18] According to the Board of Investigation and Research the Government had spent approximately $260 million as of 1940 to provide a six-foot channel from Sioux City, Iowa, to the mouth of the Missouri, and the project was still incomplete at that time. This was more than double the Government's investment in the Ohio River and almost as much as the investment chargeable to navigation for the entire Mississippi River, both of which rivers have a minimum channel depth of nine feet.[19] As late as 1949 less than 600,000 tons of commercial freight moved on the Missouri River. A conflict of interests exists between farmers in the upstream areas, who need water for irrigation pur-

---

[17] *Annual Report of the Chief of Engineers,* various years
[18] *Public Aids to Transportation,* Vol. III, pp. 42-44.
[19] *Public Aids to Domestic Transportation,* pp. 365-366.

poses, and navigation interests who want water to maintain a navigable channel downstream during the dry seasons. In addition, power production and flood control also are involved, and there are possibilities of conflicts developing between all of these interests. A great deal of traffic will have to develop in order to justify the cost of this project.

Lower Mississippi River. A nine-foot channel has been maintained on the Lower Mississippi for many years, and from Baton Rouge south sufficient depth is maintained to permit navigation by deep water vessels. A large part of the cost of the improvements is chargeable to flood control and the prevention of bank erosion, but substantial annual maintenance expenditures are necessary to keep the channel navigable. The Federal Coordinator's staff estimated the full economic cost of the average haul on this part of the river to be $5.48 on Basis 1, $5.97 on Basis 2, and $6.37 on Basis 3, as compared with a rail cost of $3.81 per ton for a comparable haul.[20] A part of this cost differential is attributable to the winding nature of the Lower Mississippi which makes for water distances some 60 per cent greater than rail distances. Some idea of the growth of traffic since 1936 may be obtained from Table XXIV.

Table XXIV

TRAFFIC ON THE LOWER MISSISSIPPI RIVER [21]

| | Ton Miles | |
Segment	1936	1949
Mouth of Missouri to Mouth of Ohio........	279,727,451	1,314,455,703
Mouth of Ohio to Baton Rouge	2,322,207,621	8,409,630,608
Baton Rouge to New Orleans:		
Foreign (Oceangoing)		167,360,797
Coastwise (Oceangoing)	882,863,098	644,923,867
Inland domestic		1,222,062,883
New Orleans to Mouth of Passes:		
Foreign		1,099,997,812
Coastwise	2,052,193,083	1,328,149,662
Domestic		233,089,951
Total	5,536,991,253	14,419,671,283

OTHER WATERWAYS

Warrior River system. The Warrior River system is made up of parts of the Warrior, the Black Warrior, and the Tombigbee, and provides a nine-foot channel from a point west of Birmingham to the junction of the Tom-

[20] *Public Aids to Transportation*, Vol. III, p. 86.
[21] *Annual Report of the Chief of Engineers*, 1937, 1950.

bigbee with the Alabama forty-five miles above Mobile Bay. Its principal function is to provide a water route between the mining and manufacturing area surrounding Birmingham and the Gulf coast at Mobile Bay. The principal products moving over the system are coal, petroleum and its products, limestone, and iron and steel products. The Coordinator's staff estimated the full economic cost of the average haul to be $2.74 per ton on Basis 1, $2.83 on Basis 2, and $3.01 on Basis 3, as compared with a rail cost of $2.17 per ton.[22] Ton miles moved on the Warrior River system since 1936 are shown in Table XXV. It will be observed that the increase has not been impressive.

Table XXV
TRAFFIC ON THE WARRIOR RIVER SYSTEM [23]

Year	Ton Miles	Year	Ton Miles
1936	301,842,689	1943	280,514,389
1937	429,112,502	1944	240,431,701
1938	402,195,059	1945	235,375,451
1939	378,637,078	1946	259,412,611
1940	393,435,213	1947	349,535,655
1941	454,456,500	1948	392,989,000
1942	334,905,434	1949	421,324,060

New York State Barge Canals. Traffic on the Erie Canal and the Lake Champlain branch declined from a peak of 6,500,000 tons in 1872 to 3,346,000 tons in 1900. Rehabilitation was undertaken and completed, for the most part, in 1918. Known now as the New York State Barge Canals, the new system cost the State of New York something in excess of $176 million. During the period of rehabilitation traffic continued to decline, reaching a low of 1,159,000 tons in 1918. Although some increase in traffic followed upon the completion of the project, the results were disappointing, and a movement developed to convert it into a ship canal which would permit an uninterrupted movement of ships between Great Lakes ports and the Atlantic coast. The U.S. Engineers, however, concluded that prospective savings in freight charges were insufficient to justify the cost.

The Coordinator's study gives separate figures for moving various products between specified canal points, and an average of these figures shows that the typical canal shipment involved an over-all cost of $3.86 per ton on Basis 1 and $4.25 on Basis 3. These figures compare with an average cost of $2.65 for hauling the same goods between the same points by railroad.[24] Since the Coordinator's study was made traffic on the canals has suffered a

---

[22] *Public Aids to Transportation,* Vol. III, p. 87.
[23] *Annual Report of the Chief of Engineers,* various dates.
[24] *Public Aids to Transportation,* Vol. III, p. 90.

substantial decline, which is in sharp contrast with traffic trends on other waterways. Under the circumstances it would appear that the New York State Barge Canals provide an unduly costly form of transportation.

Intracoastal Waterways. The Intracoastal Waterways consist of two independent and unconnected segments, the Atlantic Intracoastal Waterway and the Gulf Intracoastal Waterway. The Atlantic Intracoastal Waterway provides a protected water route from Massachusetts Bay to Miami, Florida, a part of which can be navigated by ships and a part of which is open only to barges and small boats. For the most part it consists of sounds, bays, and rivers, connected where necessary by canals. The Gulf Intracoastal Waterway extends from Carabella, Florida, near the Florida-Alabama line, to Brownsville, Texas. Between Carabella and New Orleans the route is based mostly on existing waterways. Between New Orleans and Freeport, Texas, the improvements consist largely of canals, but south of Freeport a series of long lagoons provide the basis of the waterway. The last section of this waterway, extending from Corpus Christi to Brownsville, was opened in 1949. There has long been agitation for a channel across the Florida peninsula which would connect the two waterways and provide a single sheltered route all the way from the Mexican border to New England, but as yet this project has not been approved.

Existing cost studies of the Intracoastal Waterways do not mean much because of the various stages of incompletion of the projects at the time the studies were made. In 1949 the barge portion of the Atlantic section, running between Norfolk, Virginia, and the St. Johns River, Florida, accounted for only 5,775,190 ton miles of freight, an insignificant amount. Traffic on the Gulf coast section, however, was much heavier, with 4,592,284,691 ton miles moving in 1949. Most of this moved over the section between Corpus Christi, Texas, and the Mississippi River, and this in turn reflects a significant movement of petroleum and petroleum products from the coastal refining areas of Texas and Louisiana into the Mississippi River.[25] Opportunities for economical transportation appear to exist on the Gulf section, especially from Mobile Bay west and Corpus Christi north and east to the Mississippi River. It is too early at this time to pass judgment on the newly opened section between Corpus Christi and Brownsville.

ADVANTAGES OF RIVER AND CANAL TRANSPORTATION

Economy. The principal advantage claimed for river and canal transportation always has been that it is inherently more economical than land transportation, but those who make this claim generally fail to include in

---

[25] *Annual Report of the Chief of Engineers,* 1950.

their calculations the heavy cost of channel improvement and maintenance. It is sometimes contended that the savings which accrue to shippers who are able to take advantage of the low rates charged by water carriers will offset or more than offset the cost to government of providing and maintaining channel improvements, but at best this represents no more than wishful thinking since there is no up-to-date information on which to base such a contention. It may well be true of some waterways that savings in freight rates will offset or more than offset the cost of channel improvement and maintenance, but it is almost certainly not true of others.

Regulation of railroad rates. Occasionally it is said that waterway improvements are desirable in that they provide an effective means of regulating railroad rates. It was noted many years ago that railroad rates were lower wherever water competition existed, and it is easy to understand how this could be used as an argument for waterway improvements at a time when the Interstate Commerce Commission had no effective control over railroad rates. But for many years now the Commission has exercised such an overriding control over railroad freight rates that it would seem somewhat ridiculous at this late date to justify river and canal improvements as necessary for regulatory purposes. In this connection it is worth noting that water carriers often object strenuously when railroads seek to lower rates at water competitive points, an attitude which seems strangely inconsistent with the idea that river and canal transportation provides an effective means of regulating railroad rates.

About the only basis on which the rate regulation argument could be sustained today would be that water competition could do the job better and cheaper than it is now being done and so eliminate the need for the Interstate Commerce Commission. But it would be impossible to do away with the Commission because it exercises jurisdiction over a wide variety of matters not directly related to rate making. As a matter of fact it would not even be possible to do away with the Commission's rate-making activities. Water carriers could regulate railroad rates only at water competitive points and on water competitive traffic, and it would be necessary to provide some other means for regulating rates on noncompetitive freight and on all freight at the vast majority of points in the United States where water competition does not exist. Indeed, it would be necessary to have a commission to regulate rates at water competitive points, for without such control the railroads would soon run the water carriers out of business. Finally, a commission would be necessary to exercise jurisdiction over other forms of transportation. As to the relative costs of the two types of regulation, the Board of Investigation and Research estimated that the subsidy to domestic water transportation in the year 1940 amounted to about

$125 million,[26] but the annual appropriation for the Interstate Commerce Commission, which regulates domestic water carriers, motor carriers, and pipe lines, as well as railroads, was only $8,948,000 in that year.[27]

Waterway improvements and flood control. Waterway improvements are sometimes justified on the ground that they are incidental to flood control activities. For example, great dams have been built on the upper tributaries of the Mississippi, the Missouri, and the Ohio, behind which water is impounded during periods of heavy rainfall in an effort to prevent destructive floods on the lower reaches of these rivers; and these waters can be released to maintain navigable water levels during dry seasons.

Whether or not the construction of flood control dams will justify a navigation project depends upon two things. First, the dams themselves will not render a river navigable, and consideration must be given to the additional expenditures necessary to achieve this purpose. And second, consideration must be given to the transportation needs of the area which would be served. If there is a surplus of transportation facilities, providing additional facilities will do more harm than good.

It is also argued that some of the improvements made directly for navigation purposes may be of value in connection with flood control. A straight clean channel maintained for navigation purposes will aid in speeding up the runoff of water during rainy seasons, and dams built on certain rivers to maintain a given water depth have been justified as contributing to flood control. There is a considered opinion, however, that navigation dams are of little or no value for flood control purposes.

Waterway improvements and hydroelectric power. Dams which are built in connection with navigation projects sometimes may be useful for the production of hydroelectric power, and to the extent that there is a real need for the navigation project to begin with, the possibility of producing hydroelectric power at a low cost is certainly a factor to be taken into consideration. It has been argued that the location of the dams may have no relationship to the needs of the areas for additional power, but this argument becomes less significant as improved methods of long distance power transmission are developed. The possibility of producing hydroelectric power as a by-product of navigation improvements has injected into the waterway controversy the issue of public versus private power production, and at times this has beclouded the transportation aspects of the waterway problem.

Bank erosion and irrigation. It has been necessary to build revetments for many miles along the banks of the Lower Mississippi in order to pre-

---

[26] *Public Aids to Domestic Transportation*, p. 66.
[27] Interstate Commerce Commission, *Annual Report*, 1940.

vent bank erosion. These revetments are necessary to protect property and for flood control purposes, but they are also of value in the maintenance of navigable channels. It is apparently a matter of some uncertainty whether this work should be charged to flood control or to navigation, and some students have split the cost evenly between the two. Also, when great dams are built on the tributaries or headwaters of navigable rivers, the water impounded may be used for irrigation purposes as well as for maintaining water levels, but as already pointed out conflicts may arise over who shall have first claim to the water.

River and canal improvements and national defense. It is sometimes said that river and canal improvements are necessary for national defense because they provide needed additional transportation facilities in time of war. In this connection, it is interesting to note that traffic on the Mississippi River, including traffic carried by deep water boats, increased from 7,272,133,000 ton miles in 1940 to 10,087,100,000 ton miles in 1944, while the Illinois Central Railroad, which competes directly with Mississippi River barge lines, increased its traffic from 9,700,320,000 ton miles of revenue freight in 1940 to 21,451,213,000 ton miles in 1944. The Board of Investigation and Research estimated that navigation improvements on the Mississippi River represented an investment of about $150,000 per mile as of 1940 while the roadway investment of the Illinois Central came to $74,139 per mile in that year, and the difference in investment per mile is even greater when consideration is given to the greater distances by water.[28] In view of the high cost of providing waterway facilities and the slow speed and limited utility of water transportation, it would seem that a better case could be made for government subsidies to provide standby railroad facilities in the interest of national defense.

It has been pointed out that improved waterways made it possible to build smaller sized naval craft at many interior points during World War II, a procedure which may have eased somewhat the strain on railroads serving coastal ship building areas and which made possible the use of local labor rather than its transfer to distant points; but it is an open question whether these advantages are of sufficient importance to justify the expenditure of large sums of money on waterway improvements.

DISADVANTAGES OF RIVER AND CANAL TRANSPORTATION

Limited service. River and canal transportation suffers from numerous handicaps which limit the extent to which it can be used. In the first place, service can be offered to or from only a relatively small number of points.

---

[28] Based on data from *Public Aids to Domestic Transportation*, and *Statistics of Railways in the U.S.*, 1940, 1944.

DEVELOPMENT OF WATER TRANSPORTATION

Water service can be extended through the establishment of joint rail-water routes and rates, but there are practical limitations on the extent to which such routes and rates can be made available, or made available at rates which represent an appreciable saving to shippers. Not only are the points where service is practical somewhat limited, but also the number of commodities which can be moved is quite limited.

Irregularity of movement. Another limitation on river and canal transportation is irregularity of movement due to variations in water stages and freezing over of many waterways during the winter months. At times the railroads have expressed themselves rather bitterly on this aspect of river and canal transportation because they are expected to provide sufficient equipment to move all of the traffic when barges cannot operate and then side track this equipment during the season of navigation.

Effect on other carriers. River and canal improvements do not create new traffic to any extent but tend to divert traffic from existing transportation agencies. Because of the extent to which railroad costs are constant, any reduction in the volume of railroad traffic will bring a more than proportionate decline in profits, and may even lead to losses, and this in turn makes it more difficult to render satisfactory service at points where water competition does not exist, or it may necessitate charging higher rates at nonwater points and on traffic which cannot move by barge. Occasionally traffic may be diverted from the highways to water carriers, as in the case of the movement of new automobiles by barge, but in general motor and water carriers are noncompetitive.

Burden on shippers and taxpayers. Shippers who are in a position to use river or canal transportation benefit from reduced costs of transportation, but their gains are, in some measure, at the expense of shippers who must rely on railroad transportation. And taxpayers in general are called upon to shoulder the entire cost of river and canal improvement and maintenance. Even if it could be demonstrated that savings in freight charges offset or more than offset the cost of providing improved channels, the fact still remains that these savings are achieved at the expense of taxpayers in general.

TRANSPORTATION ON THE GREAT LAKES

History of transportation on the Great Lakes. Traffic began to develop on the Great Lakes after the Erie Canal was opened in 1825, but it was not until the 1850's, when rich iron ore deposits were opened up in the Lake Superior region, that the Great Lakes really came into their own. In due course the Lake carriers, like the river and canal carriers already discussed, found themselves in keen competition with the expanding network of railroads, especially in connection with the eastbound grain traffic, but the railroads were unable to destroy shipping on the Great Lakes, and traffic in substantial amounts continued to move by Lake boats long after it had all but disappeared on other inland waterways. The reasons for this are not hard to discover. The Great Lakes are big enough and deep enough to permit the utilization of large vessels which can carry substantial quantities of bulk freight for long distances at a very low cost, and the traffic is there to be moved. Furthermore, the direction of traffic on the Great Lakes is east and west in conformity with the general channel of trade in the United States, and the length of haul via the Great Lakes compares favorably with the length of haul by railroad. Indeed, between some points the Lake haul is shorter than the rail haul.

The railroads were not slow in getting into the Lake shipping business, and the big trunk line railroads succeeded in practically monopolizing east bound Lake traffic. This monopolistic control of Lake shipping was broken up in 1912 when Congress, in the Panama Canal Act, outlawed railroad ownership of competing boat lines except as it might be approved by the Interstate Commerce Commission. Satisfactory statistics showing ton miles of commerce on the Great Lakes in early years are not available, but the movement of traffic in recent years is shown in Table XXVI.

Table XXVI

TRAFFIC ON THE GREAT LAKES [29]

Date	Ton Miles
1925	83,716,742,000
1930	77,365,558,000
1935	54,690,214,000
1940	95,645,008,000
1945	113,028,096,000
1946	96,022,046,000
1947	112,165,321,000
1948	118,707,121,000
1949	97,503,348,000

Nature of traffic. The principal item of Great Lakes traffic is iron ore moved by railroad from mines in Northern Michigan, Wisconsin, and Minnesota to Lake Superior ports where it is loaded mechanically into special Lake boats. The iron ore is unloaded by mechanical means at the lower Lake ports for shipment to the great steel mills in Illinois, Indiana, Ohio, and Pennsylvania. The next most important item of traffic is coal, which moves from the eastern coal fields to Lake Erie ports by railroad for transfer to Lake boats which carry it westward to various Canadian ports and ports in the United States. The coal, like the iron ore, is handled in bulk

[29] *Annual Report of the Chief of Engineers,* various dates.

and is loaded and unloaded mechanically. Although not handled in as large quantities as iron ore and coal, there is a considerable movement of stone and grain, also handled in bulk. These commodities are moved almost wholly by private and contract carriers.

Before World War II a few companies offered a package freight service, but the volume of such traffic was insignificant as compared with the bulk movements discussed above. The package carriers faced keen competition from other forms of transportation and were operating at a loss before the outbreak of war. During the war, the boats used in this service were taken over by the Government, and it does not appear that the service can be resumed without the purchase of new and more efficient equipment. Because of prewar losses and wartime traffic diversion, the outlook for a resumption of this service does not appear to be bright.[30]

Cost of transportation on the Great Lakes. It has been necessary to provide artificial channels at only three points in the Great Lakes area. One of these is at St. Mary's rapids separating Lake Superior and Lake Huron where a ship canal less than a mile long was originally opened on the United States side in 1855. This was later improved and supplemented by a canal on the Canadian side built in 1895. The second point where channel work has been necessary is between Lake Huron and Lake Erie where it has been necessary to improve the St. Clair and Detroit rivers in order to make them navigable by Lake boats. The third point is at Niagara Falls where the original Welland Canal, built by the Canadian Government, was opened as far back as 1829. Government expenditures on terminal improvements have taken the form of deepening and otherwise improving harbors at numerous points on the Great Lakes. The cost of harbor work has varied widely between different harbors, both in absolute amount and in terms of tons of traffic handled.

Partly because of the relatively small sums of money spent on channel and harbor improvement and maintenance, and partly because of the large volume of traffic moved over the Great Lakes, the cost of public aid per ton mile has been very low. The Coordinator's staff estimated that public aid amounted to only .22 mills per ton mile in 1935.[31] Since the great bulk of traffic is not subject to Interstate Commerce Commission control, little information is available on the actual cost of conducting transportation operations on the Great Lakes. The Coordinator's staff estimated that in 1928 average ton mile revenues, including handling charges, ranged from .63 mills on coal to 1.11 mills on ore and 1.7 mills on grain.[32] From such

---

[30] For a discussion of the package freight problem see Department of Commerce, *Domestic Transportation*, December 1945-January 1946, pp. 21-28. See, also, p. 509.
[31] *Public Aids to Transportation*, Vol. III, p. 52.
[32] *Ibid.*, p. 72.

data, old and fragmentary as they are, it seems clear that the Great Lakes stand in a class by themselves when it comes to the economical movement of those bulk commodities which are best adapted to Lake transportation.

DOMESTIC COASTWISE AND INTERCOASTAL WATER TRANSPORTATION

Distinction between coastwise and intercoastal transportation. A coastwise shipment is one which moves by an ocean-going vessel between two United States ports, both of which are located on the same coast, or between Atlantic and Gulf coast ports. A movement between a United States port on the Atlantic or Gulf coasts and a United States port on the Pacific coast is called an intercoastal movement. There are many similarities between coastwise and intercoastal shipping, but there are differences in types of goods handled and to some extent in the economic problems faced.

The vessels used for coastwise and intercoastal shipping are similar to those used for handling goods moving to and from foreign ports, but there are wide differences between domestic and foreign trade shipping. The domestic carriers move a much smaller variety of products and are regulated by a different agency and to a somewhat greater extent than is true of foreign trade carriers. Another very important difference is found in the fact that the law does not permit boats of foreign registry to operate in coastwise or intercoastal service. While coastwise and intercoastal carriers are protected from foreign competition they face keen competition from land carriers, particularly the railroads.

The volume of traffic moved, both coastwise and intercoastal, in various years is shown in Table XXVII.

Table XXVII

GROWTH OF COASTWISE AND INTERCOASTAL TRAFFIC [33]

Date	Tons of 2000 pounds
1925	105,090,000
1930	117,821,000
1935	115,442,000
1940	156,831,000
1941	155,857,000
1942	73,977,000
1943	59,789,000
1944	70,784,000
1945	90,691,000
1946	138,526,000
1947	153,098,000
1948	174,081,000
1949	161,431,000

[33] *Annual Report of the Chief of Engineers*, various dates.

DEVELOPMENT OF WATER TRANSPORTATION

Coastwise shipping before World War II. For many years coastwise shipping played a dominant role in the movement of goods between Atlantic coast ports and between ports on the Atlantic and Gulf coasts. As the railroad network spread over the East and South, keen competition developed between the rail and water carriers, but the railroads were unable to put the boat lines out of business. In many cases, however, the railroads bought up and operated their own boat lines. Pacific coastwise shipping was never as important as on the Atlantic and Gulf coasts because there are few natural harbors on the Pacific and because the economic development of the West came at a much later date. After the passage of the Panama Canal Act railroads were forced for the most part to give up their boat lines, but it was only a few years until the First World War brought coastwise shipping to a standstill. Once the war was over the service was resumed with vessels built by the Government and purchased at favorable prices. From then on there was a steady if not spectacular increase in traffic up to the beginning of World War II.

Prior to the dislocation of trade brought about by World War II the principal item of traffic moved in coastwise service was petroleum and its products. Liquid petroleum products in particular were moved in very large quantities in tankers from the Gulf coast region to the centers of population on the Atlantic coast, mostly in tankers owned by the large oil companies. The next most important item of traffic was coal moved by railroad from the coal fields in the West Virginia area to tidewater and then north by boat to New York and New England. Other products carried in minor amounts included sand and gravel, fertilizer, sulphur, and food products, including citrus fruits. Almost all of this traffic was moved either by private or by exempt carriers. Common carrier operations, such as they were, were not particularly profitable, with common carriers doing little more than breaking even in the ten years preceding World War II.

Intercoastal Shipping before World War II. For many years water transportation between the East and the Pacific coast was slow and expensive, but it was the only means of transporting goods in quantity. The construction of railroads across the Isthmus of Panama and the Isthmus of Tehuantepec and their use in conjunction with Atlantic and Pacific coast steamers made possible a substantial reduction in the time and cost of the movement, but this route, of course, was not as satisfactory as the all-rail routes that developed. When E. H. Harriman started to build up his railroad empire in the West in the late nineteenth and early twentieth centuries, he made use of his control of the Pacific Mail steamship line to discourage transportation by way of the Panama route, and the result was a sharp decline in the volume of traffic moved by water between Atlantic and Pacific coast ports. It was hoped that the opening of the Panama Canal, together with the absolute prohibition of the ownership of boats using the canal by competing railroads, would lead to a revival of intercoastal shipping, but this revival was retarded by slides in the canal and the disruption of shipping brought about by World War I.

After World War I intercoastal operations were undertaken by a number of companies, with much use made of boats obtained from the Government. Intensive competition between numerous operators for a relatively small volume of traffic, however, made the business unprofitable. This condition was aggravated by the highly unbalanced nature of the traffic, with eastbound tonnage being almost double westbound tonnage. Before World War II the largest single item of traffic was eastbound lumber, with eastbound petroleum and products, westbound iron and steel and products, and eastbound fruits and vegetables following in order. Most of the tanker tonnage moved in boats owned by the large oil companies, but the bulk of the traffic, constituting some 85 per cent of the total, was moved by common carriers. It is interesting to note that a number of the common carrier lines were owned by industrial concerns. These lines carried the products of the parent company in one direction and competed for general cargo on the return haul, and for this reason they were able to make a somewhat better financial showing than the independent carriers.

Effect of World War II. Shortly after the United States entered World War II enemy submarine activities and the diversion of boats to foreign service brought about an almost complete cessation of commercial coastwise and intercoastal shipping. It may be noted in passing that the owners of requisitioned vessels fared very well financially from government use of their boats. The end of the war brought a resumption of normal peacetime operations by many of the private and exempt carriers, particularly in the case of tanker movements between the Atlantic and Gulf coasts. Common carriers, however, have been beset with many difficulties, and it will take heroic measures to revive this service.

Cost of coastal and intercoastal service. It is not possible to arrive at any specific cost figures for coastal and intercoastal water transportation. The improvement activities of the Federal Government involve for the most part harbor work and the construction of a few deep water channels, but all of these improvements are used extensively by ships operating in foreign trade as well as by those operating in domestic commerce. The Panama Canal, of course, represents a heavy investment, but its cost is chargeable in full to national defense, and commercial vessels are required to pay tolls for passage. Ship owners have received some financial assistance in connection with the construction of new vessels, but for the most part this is supposed to be limited to the national defense aspect of coastwise and intercoastal vessels. For a brief period after World War II coastwise and intercoastal shipping was carried on by the War Shipping Administration and later by the United States Maritime Commission, which bodies absorbed the resulting deficits, but operation by the Maritime Commission ceased in 1947. On the whole, it would appear that public aid to coastwise and intercoastal shipping as it exists today is not a factor of major importance.

Far more important than public aid in determining the economy of coastwise and intercoastal water transportation are the high operating costs encountered in the trade. These high costs reflect various considerations, including the use of slow and obsolete vessels, high labor costs, and unbalanced traffic. Furthermore, the railroads have been able to haul much of the competitive traffic at rates which have proved unremunerative to ship operators. Only in such special cases as the tanker movement of liquid petroleum products have the water carriers been able to show a distinct cost advantage over the railroads.

National defense. No discussion of coastwise and intercoastal water transportation would be complete without some mention of the defense aspects of the service. It has been recognized for a long time that the maintenance of an adequate fleet of cargo vessels is essential in case of war, and since a boat built for operation along the coast need not have the speed and heavy construction required for wartime service, the policy of having the Government pay for defense features incorporated in new boats seems sound. Losses incurred by ship owners as a result of high operating costs present a different problem, but it is one which must be faced if a privately owned merchant marine is to survive. The operation of merchant vessels engaged in foreign commerce is subsidized by the Government, but these subsidies have not been extended to companies operating in the coastwise and intercoastal trade. While such subsidies would be valid from the point of view of national defense, their possible effect on other agencies of domestic transportation raises problems of an entirely different nature. This matter is considered further in Chapter 32.

SUGGESTED READINGS

Association of American Railroads, *Transportation in America*, Washington, 1947. Chapter XIX. Presents the railroad point of view but at the same time gives what appears to be a reasonably objective account of operations and operating problems.

Board of Investigation and Research, *Carrier Taxation*, 79th Congress, 1st Session, House Document 160 (1945). Comparative tax burdens.

Board of Investigation and Research, *Public Aids to Domestic Transportation*, 79th Congress, 1st Session, House Document 159 (1945). Chapter V and Appendixes E to Z inclusive.

DEVELOPMENT OF WATER TRANSPORTATION

Chief of Engineers U.S. Army, *Annual Report,* various years. This is the primary source of statistics on inland waterway costs and traffic.

Department of Commerce, *Domestic Transportation,* December, 1945-January, 1946.

Federal Coordinator of Transportation, *Public Aids to Transportation,* Vol. III, 1939. This is the most comprehensive study made to date of the costs of domestic water transportation in relation to railroad costs.

Interstate Commerce Commission, *Annual Report,* 1945-1948.

Johnson, Emory R., Grover G. Huebner, and Arnold K. Henry, *Transportation by Water.* New York: D. Appleton-Century Company, 1935. Largely descriptive of water carrier operations.

Moulton, Harold G., *Waterways Versus Railways.* Boston: Houghton Mifflin Company, 1912. A courageous critical analysis of waterway costs written at a time of widespread clamor for waterway improvements.

—— and associates, *The American Transportation Problem,* Part V. Washington: The Brookings Institution, 1933. Considers subsidization but is now largely out of date.

23

Regulation
of
DOMESTIC WATER TRANSPORTATION

REGULATION PRIOR TO 1940

Act to Regulate Commerce. Federal regulation of domestic water transportation began in a small way in 1887 with the adoption of the original Act to Regulate Commerce, the provisions of which were made applicable to common carriers engaged in the transportation of passengers or people in interstate commerce partly by railroad and partly by water, provided that both were used under a common control, management, or arrangement for continuous carriage or shipment in interstate or foreign commerce. The purpose of this provision was not to regulate water transportation but to strengthen the hand of the Commission in connection with its railroad regulatory activities. If the Commission had no jurisdiction over railroad-owned or controlled boat lines, the railroads could use the water portion of a through rail-water haul to manipulate rates to suit themselves, to practice place and personal discrimination, and in other ways to evade the intent of the law.

Hepburn Act. In 1906 the Hepburn Act authorized the Interstate Commerce Commission to require rail and water carriers to establish through routes and to prescribe the maximum joint rates applicable thereto, providing the carriers in question refused or neglected to establish such routes and rates and no other reasonable or satisfactory through routes existed. There can be little doubt that this provision was a reflection of the widespread public demand for a revival of water transportation which existed at the time the law was passed. Generally speaking the railroads had refused to interchange freight with independent water carriers, and if they could be required to establish through routes with water carriers, it would give the latter some much needed additional traffic and at the same time extend the benefits of low water carrier rates at least in part to nonwater points. Obviously the purpose of the law was promotional rather than regulatory, but its effectiveness in promoting water transportation was limited by the fact that rail-water routes could be established only in the event that no other reasonable or satisfactory route existed. Also, there appears to have been some uncertainty about the extent of the Commission's power to prescribe the division of joint rates, and the water carriers experienced some difficulty in getting the railroads to agree to divisions which would leave them enough to make the operation profitable.

Mann-Elkins Act. In the Mann-Elkins Act of 1910 Congress took additional steps to promote and protect water transportation. The provision that a rail-water route could be required only when no other satisfactory route existed was eliminated, although a railroad could not be required to share traffic which it could haul the entire distance itself. Furthermore, the law provided that whenever a railroad in competition with a water route reduced a rate to or from a water competitive point, it could not subsequently raise that rate simply by showing that water competition had been eliminated. This provision was intended to discourage the railroads from running water carriers out of business by fixing rates at water competitive points so low that the water carriers could not survive.

Panama Canal Act. The Panama Canal Act prohibited the ownership of common carrier boat lines by interstate railroads with which they might compete. In the case of lines using the Panama Canal the prohibition was absolute, but elsewhere the Interstate Commerce Commission could make exceptions. The Panama Canal Act also authorized the Commission to require the establishment of dockside track connections under certain conditions and to determine the terms and conditions of their construction and operation. Without dockside track connections the cost of interchanging freight between rail carriers and water carriers might be so high as to be prohibitive, and the railroads were not inclined to do anything to facilitate such interchanges. Obviously the Panama Canal Act was another promotional and protective measure.

Shipping Act, 1916, and Merchant Marine Act, 1920. The Shipping Act, 1916, created the United States Shipping Board which was to function both as a promotive and as a regulatory body in connection with deep water shipping. The 1916 act was amended in certain respects by the Merchant Marine Act, 1920, and no attempt will be made here to separate the provisions of the two laws. A good deal of the Shipping Board's work related to vessels operating in foreign commerce and is not germane to the present discussion. Insofar as domestic commerce was concerned the Board's jurisdiction was limited to regular route coastwise, intercoastal, and Great Lakes common carriers. The law contained various provisions designed to prevent discriminatory practices by these carriers, and the Shipping Board was given the power to fix the maximum rates they charged. It had no control over river and canal carriers, but this was of no consequence because they accounted for only an insignificant amount of traffic. Far more important was the fact that it had no jurisdiction over the large volume of domestic commerce moved on the high seas and the Great Lakes by contract and private carriers. Limited as the Shipping Board's control was, however, it represented the first serious attempt to apply economic regulation to domestic water transportation.

Transportation Act, 1920. The Transportation Act, 1920, contained several provisions intended to promote the development of domestic water transportation. It was declared to be the intention of Congress to promote, encourage, and develop water transportation, and to foster and preserve in full vigor both rail and water transportation. Furthermore, the Commission was now authorized to require the establishment of a through rail-water route even though the rail carrier was in a position to haul the traffic the entire distance itself. Finally, by giving the Interstate Commerce Commission power to fix minimum rates, Congress removed the last weapon possessed by the railroads in fighting water carriers.

Inland Waterways Corporation Act. The Inland Waterways Corporation Act, adopted in 1924, created the Inland Waterways Corporation to conduct the Federal Government's barge line operations on the Mississippi and Warrior rivers. In 1928 it was amended in various respects by the Dennison Act, and the scope of the Dennison Act was expanded by further amendments in 1934 and 1935. Earlier legislation had *authorized* the Commission to establish through routes and joint rates by rail and water, but the railroads had been most uncooperative, and the effect of this legislation was to *compel* the establishment of rail-water routes and rates on certain rivers to the extent that the water carriers wanted them.

NEED FOR MORE EFFECTIVE REGULATION

Promotional nature of legislation. Throughout most of the period before 1940 Congress seems to have been interested primarily in legislation designed to promote and protect water transportation by restricting the ability of railroads to compete and by legislation designed to divert rail traffic to water routes. At the same time the Government was actively promoting water transportation in other ways. Although ship subsidies presumably were intended to assure the construction of vessels adapted to wartime usages, administrative bodies appear at times to have been rather liberal in their interpretation of what is necessary for war purposes. Of greater importance, as far as domestic water transportation is concerned, was the provision of improved waterways without direct cost to the users. Congress not only provided free waterways, but also through the Inland Waterways Corporation provided a subsidized common carrier service to operate on them. Finally, Congress was quite liberal in the sale of war-built merchant vessels to private operators.

REGULATION OF WATER TRANSPORTATION

Problem of dual jurisdiction. Brief mention may be made of the problem of dual jurisdiction which arose out of the fact that common carrier boat lines owned by railroads were subject to regulation by the Interstate Commerce Commission, while competing independent common carriers by water operating in interstate commerce on the high seas or on the Great Lakes were subject to regulation by the United States Shipping Board. Not only were the regulatory authorities different, but so also was the degree of regulation applied, with those carriers subject to the Interstate Commerce Commission being regulated to far greater extent than was true of those coming under the jurisdiction of the United States Shipping Board. To make matters worse, if an independent common carrier by water on the Great Lakes or on the high seas was a party to a through movement by rail and by water, it was subject to regulation by both bodies, with the Interstate Commerce Commission regulating its activities in connection with through movements by rail and water and the Shipping Board regulating its port-to-port activities. Such a situation was satisfactory neither to the public nor the carriers.

Financial status of carriers. In spite of legislation designed to protect and promote domestic water transportation, the operations of for-hire carriers were not on the whole profitable even before the stock market crash in 1929. Although the railroads continued to compete keenly, one of the principal difficulties faced by water carriers was a destructively low rate structure brought about by competition between the water carriers themselves. The original Shipping Act, 1916, authorized water carriers, with the approval of the Shipping Board, to organize conferences or associations to fix rates, pool traffic or profits, and cooperate in various other ways to limit competition; but since the Shipping Board had no control over minimum rates, water carrier conference agreements commonly suffered the same fate as early railroad pools and rate agreements. No restrictions were placed on the right to operate, and the Government's policy of selling surplus ships on favorable terms made it relatively easy for new carriers to enter the field. Thus with more boats being operated than could be supported by the available traffic, it is not surprising that competition assumed ruinous proportions. Further contributing to the financial difficulties of the for-hire carriers were the activities of private carriers which, when they had surplus cargo space available, offered it to shippers at rates which common and contract carriers could not meet.

Move for more effective regulation. The depression which followed the stock market crash of 1929 magnified the difficulties of the water carriers, and the early 1930's brought demands from various sources for more effective regulation. The larger and more responsible water carriers, and particularly the common carriers, recognized the need for regulation as a means of bringing an end to suicidal rate cutting. Many shippers favored regulation as a means of stabilizing rates and cutting down discrimination. Both the United States Shipping Board and the Interstate Commerce Commission went on record as favoring more effective regulation.

For the most part the advocates of further legislation concerned themselves primarily with the regulation of common carriers. There appears to have been some support for the regulation of contract carrier rates, but many contract carriers were opposed to such regulation. It is interesting to note, too, that the demand was confined to the regulation of shipping on the Great Lakes and in the coastwise and intercoastal services, there being no widespread interest at this time in the regulation of river and canal transportation.

Regulatory changes during the 1930's. The depression years saw a halting advance in the field of domestic interstate water carrier regulation. The duties of the United States Shipping Board were transferred to the Shipping Board Bureau of the Department of Commerce in 1933 and then to the United States Maritime Commission in 1936. By 1938 the Maritime Commission had authority to fix maximum and minimum rates for intercoastal common and contract carriers, maximum and minimum rates for coastwise common carriers, and maximum rates for Great Lakes common carriers. The Commission exercised no control of any kind over river and canal carriers or over private carriers anywhere. New carriers were free to go into business without regard to the need for additional service and the available traffic. Control over accounting procedures was inadequate, and there was need for some control over the financing of water carriers.

With competing carriers subject to different degrees of regulation and many not subject to regulation at all, and with jurisdiction still divided between two different agencies, conditions were satisfactory neither to the carriers nor to the shipping public. In addition, the railroads were complaining bitterly about the competitive advantages enjoyed by water carriers arising out of a lesser degree of regulation. They were particularly outspoken with regard to the absence of any effective regulation over competing river and canal carriers. Congress recognized the unsatisfactory nature of the existing regulatory setup, and instead of attempting further to amend existing legislation, it incorporated a completely new regulatory procedure in the Transportation Act of 1940. The new legislation, which made interstate commerce by water subject to the jurisdiction of the Interstate Commerce Commission and which closely followed the pattern of railroad and motor carrier regulation, was made Part III of the Interstate Commerce Act.

REGULATION OF WATER TRANSPORTATION

Scope of authority. Part III of the Interstate Commerce Act applies to the transportation of persons or property by water by common and contract carriers operating in interstate commerce and vests regulatory control over such transportation in the Interstate Commerce Commission. Interstate commerce is defined as encompassing movements between points in different states within the United States, including the District of Columbia. A movement between a point in the United States and one of the territories or possessions of the United States cannot be considered as interstate commerce within the meaning of the act. The provisions of Part III apply in part to lessors of vessels, but they do not apply to private carriers.

Transportation by water between United States ports and points outside of the United States comes under the jurisdiction of the Federal Maritime Board in the Department of Commerce, successor to the United States Maritime Commission. If passengers or property are moved partly by water and partly by railroad or motor vehicle between a place in one state and a place in another state, and if this movement takes place partly outside of the United States, the Interstate Commerce Commission has jurisdiction over that part of the transportation which takes place within the United States. If persons or property are transported between United States points and points outside of the United States with a transshipment taking place at a United States point, the Interstate Commerce Commission has jurisdiction over that part of the movement taking place within the United States.

Rights of the states. The jurisdiction of the Interstate Commerce Commission over the intrastate activities of water carriers is severely limited. The law specifically provides that the various states are to have the exclusive right to regulate intrastate commerce by water, and the Interstate Commerce Commission may not prescribe or regulate intrastate rates or service for the purpose of removing discrimination against interstate commerce or for any other purpose. Because of the characteristically long haul nature of most water transportation, intrastate transportation by water is not too important, and no further reference will be made to it.

Protection from foreign competition. Although vessels of foreign registry have been excluded from domestic coastwise and intercoastal service for many years, domestic carriers are not entirely free from the competition of such lines. Thus boat lines operating out of Canadian and Mexican ports compete with boat lines operating out of nearby United

States ports in the movement of goods and persons to and from various United States points. Since the activities of boat lines operating between United States ports and ports outside of the United States are not subject to Interstate Commerce Commission control, the law permits the Commission to relieve domestic carriers of the provisions of Part III to the extent necessary and for the time necessary to overcome any undue disadvantage which may arise as a result of this competition. This particular provision of the law has been of no significance up to the present, and no further reference will be made to it.

Other general provisions. The provisions of Part III are made applicable to carriers owned or controlled by the United States in the same way as they are applied to carriers generally. Thus the activities of the Inland Waterways Corporation are subject to the same regulatory control as are the operations of independently owned common carrier barge line companies. As in the case of motor transportation, the Commission is authorized to establish reasonable classifications of carriers, both common and contract.

PART III AS IT RELATES TO COMMON CARRIERS

Certificates of public convenience and necessity. The right to operate as a common carrier is conditioned upon the issuance of a certificate of public convenience and necessity by the Interstate Commerce Commission, and before such a certificate may be issued, the Commission must find that the applicant is fit, willing, and able to perform the service in question and that its proposed service is required by the present or future public convenience and necessity. A certificate must indicate the route or routes or the ports to be served and contain such conditions or limitations as the Commission may impose. The Commission may modify the terms of certificates, but it may not restrict the right of the carrier to add to its equipment or facilities, nor may it restrict the right of the carrier to extend its operations over uncompleted portions of waterways once these portions are completed. Certificates are transferable, subject to such rules and regulations as the Commission may prescribe. To make possible the provision of service for which there is an immediate and urgent need to a point or points or within a territory where there is no carrier service capable of meeting such need, the law permits the Interstate Commerce Commission to grant temporary authority for such service without hearings or other proceedings.

Grandfather operations. As in the case of the Motor Carrier Act, 1935, Part III contains a so-called "grandfather clause" entitling common carriers in bona fide operation by water on January 1, 1940, to a certificate of public convenience and necessity upon application within 120 days of the effective date of this provision.[1]

Dual operation. A single concern may not operate both as a common and as a contract carrier unless the Commission finds that such operation is consistent with the public interest and with the national transportation policy. This provision is somewhat more restrictive than the similar provision in Part II since the prohibition on dual operations by motor carriers is limited to operations over the same territory. The reasons for prohibiting dual operation are the same as those discussed in connection with motor transportation.

Individual rates, fares, and charges. It is the duty of every common carrier by water subject to Part III of the Interstate Commerce Act to provide such transportation upon reasonable request therefor, and to establish just and reasonable regulations and practices relating thereto. If after a hearing, the Interstate Commerce Commission is of the opinion that a rate, fare, charge, regulation, practice, or classification is or will be unjust or unreasonable or otherwise in violation of the act, it may determine the exact rate, fare, or charge, the maximum or minimum, or the maximum and minimum to be used. Similarly, it may determine the lawful regulation, practice, or classification where these are found to violate the act.

Through routes and joint rates. Common carriers by water must establish reasonable through routes with each other and with common carrier railroads for the transportation of persons or property, and they must charge reasonable through rates, fares, or other charges, provide reasonable facilities, including facilities for the interchange of traffic, and make reasonable rules and regulations with respect to such joint movements. Similarly, through routes and rates may be established with motor common carriers, but the law does not require either party to enter into such arrangements. Where joint rates are established, it is the duty of the carriers involved to work out equitable divisions of such rates.

The Commission may, after a hearing, fix the maximum, minimum, or exact rates on joint movements and also determine the lawful regulations, practices, or classifications applicable thereto. In the case of a joint rail-water rate the Commission is directed to prescribe such reasonable differentials as it may find to be justified between the all-rail rate and the joint rail-water rate. In other words, the Commission determines how much less the rail-water rate will be than the all-rail rate between the points involved. In the case of joint rates the Commission may prescribe equitable divisions between the parties involved.

---

[1] Ultimately fixed as February 1, 1941.

REGULATION OF WATER TRANSPORTATION

Rate-making directives. In determining the justness or reasonableness of any rate, fare, or charge the Commission is directed not to consider as an element of value of carrier property either good will, earning power, or the value of the certificate under which the carrier is operating. Part III also contains a rule of rate making which is the same as the railroad rule of rate making. The Commission, in the exercise of its power to prescribe just and reasonable rates, fares, and charges, is directed to give due consideration, among other factors, to the effect of rates on the movement of traffic by the carrier or carriers for which the rates are prescribed; to the need, in the public interest, of adequate and efficient water transportation service at the lowest cost consistent with the furnishing of such service; and to the need of revenues sufficient to enable water carriers, under honest, economical, and efficient management, to provide such service.

Discrimination. It is unlawful for any common carrier by water subject to Part III to make, give, or cause any undue or unreasonable preference or advantage to any particular person, place, region, or description of traffic. This is not to be construed, however, as applying to discrimination, prejudice, or disadvantage to the traffic of any other carrier of whatever description. The provisions of Part I relative to the granting of passes, free transportation, and transportation at reduced rates are made applicable to common carriers subject to Part III, and the same is true of the long and short haul clause. Although violations of the long and short haul principle were not a serious problem it appeared to be only equitable to make the clause applicable to water as well as rail carriers.

Tariff regulations and rate suspension powers of the Commission. Common carriers by water are required to file their tariffs, print them, and keep them open for public inspection; and they must not depart from the provisions of such tariffs. Thirty days' notice is required for any change in rates or classifications or in any regulation or practice, but the Commission may permit such changes to go into effect on shorter notice for good cause shown. The Commission may order a public hearing on any proposed change in rates, fares, charges, classification, regulations, or practices, and it is authorized to suspend the effective date of any such change for a maximum of seven months beyond the time when it would otherwise go into effect. If the matter has not been decided at the end of the suspension period, the proposed changes go into effect, but nothing is said about requiring the carriers to keep records for possible refunds.

Intercorporate relationships. The provisions of Part I of the Interstate Commerce Act relative to pooling, acquisition of control, unification, and other aspects of carrier intercorporate relationships are made applicable to common carriers by water subject to Part III. It will be recalled that under the Shipping Act, 1916, water carriers had been permitted to enter into pooling arrangements and other types of cooperative activity in an effort to bring an end to ruinous competition, and a continuation of such arrangements as were lawfully in effect was permitted, but the Commission could, after a hearing, outlaw any arrangement which was not in the public interest or which would unduly restrain competition. The provisions of the Panama Canal Act, prohibiting railroad ownership of competing boat lines operating through the Panama Canal and prohibiting railroad ownership of competing boat lines elsewhere except as the Commission might find such operation to be in the public interest, are continued in effect.

Accounts and reports. The Interstate Commerce Commission is authorized to require annual, periodical, and special reports in accordance with such form and in such detail as it may prescribe. It may prescribe a uniform system of accounts, and all accounts and records must be kept open for inspection by the agents of the Commission. The Commission also may require a carrier by water to file a true copy of any contract, charter, or agreement between it and any other carrier or person in relation to matters affected by the provisions of Part III.

Unlawful operation. Any water carrier or representative thereof knowingly and willfully offering, granting, or giving an unlawful concession, or knowingly and willfully assisting in obtaining such a concession is subject to a fine of not more than $5,000 for each offense. Persons who knowingly and willfully solicit, accept, or receive unlawful concessions are subject to the same penalty. Carriers or their representatives willfully failing or refusing to make reports as required, or failing to keep records and reports as prescribed, or falsifying reports or accounts, are subject to a fine of $5,000 for each offense. Willful violations of other provisions of the law are subject to a fine not to exceed $500 for each offense, with each day of such violation constituting a separate offense. In all cases a conviction must be obtained through the usual judicial channels. It is unlawful for a carrier or its agents to divulge information with regard to a shipper's or consignee's business which may be used to the shipper's or consignee's detriment or which may improperly disclose the shipper's or consignee's business transactions to a competitor. The maximum fine for such offenses is fixed at $2,000.

Matters not covered. It will be noted from the above discussion that the law for the regulation of domestic common carriers by water is patterned very closely after the provisions of Part I and Part II of the Interstate Commerce Act. There are, however, certain conspicuous omissions which are worth noting. Although the right of entry is made subject to Interstate Commerce Commission approval, the Commission cannot prevent the abandonment of service. Furthermore, while Part II authorizes the Commission to revoke a motor carrier certificate for good cause shown, Part III gives it no such authority, an omission which has created certain problems which will be discussed presently. The Commission has no control over water carrier service, but competition is often sufficiently keen to assure shippers reasonably satisfactory service. Finally, the Commission has no jurisdiction over the issuance of securities by water carriers.

PART III AS IT RELATES TO CONTRACT CARRIERS

Definition. A contract carrier by water, like a contract carrier by motor vehicle, does not hold itself out to serve all who may apply for its services, but provides transportation for hire on the basis of individual contracts or agreements. In addition, furnishing for compensation a vessel to a person or firm other than a carrier subject to the Interstate Commerce Act, to be used by that person or firm in transporting its own property, is considered to constitute, in regard to the vessel so furnished, engaging in transportation as a contract carrier by water. The Commission may, however, exempt such lessors from regulation if it feels that regulation is not necessary to effectuate the national transportation policy. This provision of the law recognizes the long standing practice of permitting an individual or a firm to charter a boat for one or more voyages for its own private use.

Permits. The right to operate as a contract carrier by water is conditioned upon the issuance by the Interstate Commerce Commission of a permit, and before such a permit may be issued the Commission must find that the applicant is fit, willing, and able to perform service as a contract carrier, to conform with Commission requirements, and that the proposed operation is consistent with the public interest and the national transportation policy. The permit, if issued, must specify the business covered thereby, and such conditions as the Commission may deem it necessary to attach. The Commission may modify the terms of a permit, but it may not restrict the right of the carrier to substitute or add contracts or to add to its equipment or service in order to take care of additional business within the scope of its permit. Permits are transferable, subject to such regulations as the Commission may prescribe. Provision also is made for granting temporary operating authority where an immediate and urgent need for contract carrier service exists. The act includes the customary "grandfather clause" entitling carriers in operation on January 1, 1940, to a permit upon application within a specified time.

Rates and schedules. Contract carriers must establish and observe reasonable minimum charges, and regulations applicable thereto; and schedules of charges must be filed with the Commission, published, and kept open for public inspection. Any new rate or charge, or any proposed change which will result in a reduction in rates or charges, must be filed thirty days in advance of its effective date, but the Commission may permit the proposed tariff to go into effect sooner for good cause shown. It is unlawful for a carrier to furnish facilities or service at a lower price than would result from the use of the rates and charges filed with the Commission. The Commission is given discretionary authority to grant relief from the provisions noted above to such extent and for such time and in such manner as is, in its judgment, consistent with the public interest and the national transportation policy.

If after a hearing the Commission finds that a minimum rate or charge or any rule or regulation affecting the value of the service contravenes the national transportation policy or some provision of Part III, it may prescribe a just and reasonable minimum charge or regulation. The charge or regulation prescribed must not give any advantage to contract carriers in competition with common carriers by water subject to the Commission's jurisdiction which is undue or inconsistent with the public interest and the national transportation policy. In determining minimum rates or charges or rules and regulations the Commission is to give due consideration to the cost of the service rendered by contract carriers and to the effect of the rates and regulations prescribed on the movement of traffic by such carriers. The Commission is authorized to suspend the effective date of any schedule proposing a charge for a new service or a reduction in existing charges for a maximum period of seven months beyond the time it would otherwise go into effect. If at the end of that time a decision has not been reached, the new charge or regulation goes into effect, but no provision is made for possible refunds. The burden of proof is placed on the carrier to justify the proposed new charge or reduction.

Other provisions. Contract carriers by water are subject to the same provisions as common carriers with reference to dual operation and penalties for violations. There is no specific prohibition against pooling, but otherwise contract carriers are subject to the same provisions with reference to intercorporate relationships as are common carriers. They are subject to the same provisions as common carriers with reference to accounts, reports, filing of contracts, and the like; but the Commission may not make public any contracts between carriers and shippers except as a part of the record in a formal proceeding where it considers such action consistent with the public interest. If it appears that a contract fails to conform with the carrier's published schedules, however, the Commission may make public such provisions of the contract as it considers necessary to disclose such failure and the extent thereof. Contract carriers by water, like motor contract carriers, are permitted to discriminate in their rates and charges provided that they do not charge less than the minimum charges filed with the Commission. As with common carriers, the Commission has no jurisdiction over abandonment of operation, service, or the issuance of securities.

EXEMPTIONS UNDER PART III

Unconditional exemptions. The law does not apply to the transportation of commodities in bulk when the cargo space of the vessel used is not being used for the transportation of more than three such commodities. The commodities involved must not be wrapped or in containers of any sort and must be received and delivered by the carrier without mark or count. This provision has the effect of exempting from regulation practically all of the freight moved by carriers for hire on the Great Lakes where the mechanically loaded and unloaded bulk cargo vessel has reached a high degree of perfection. Similarly, the transportation of liquid cargo in bulk in vessels designed exclusively for such use is exempted from regulation.

A contract carrier handling goods in bulk in a non-ocean-going vessel is exempt, providing not more than three such commodities are handled and the vessel passes within or through international waters. Also exempted is transportation by contract carriers which, because of the specialized nature of the equipment used or for some other reason, is not actually and substantially competitive with transportation by any common carrier subject to the Interstate Commerce Act. If the Commission finds that a water carrier is engaged solely in transporting the property of a person which owns all or substantially all of its voting stock, the Commission must issue a certificate exempting such carrier from the provisions of Part III. A certificate of exemption may be revoked, however, if, after a hearing, the Commission finds that the carrier is no longer entitled to exemption.

Terminal and ferry service incident to other transportation. Transportation by water by a railroad or motor carrier, if incidental to railroad or motor transportation, is not subject to Part III provided that the water carriage is necessary to perform service within terminal areas or for the performance of lighterage, floatage, car ferry, or towage. Such transportation is subject to the provisions of either Part I or Part II of the Interstate Commerce Act. Similarly, transportation by water by any person, either as an agent or by contractual arrangement, for a railroad, express company, motor carrier, or a water carrier subject to the jurisdiction of the Interstate Commerce Commission is regulated under whatever part of the act is applicable, when such transportation is performed as a part of the major carrier's terminal service or in the performance of lighterage, floatage, car ferry, or towage service.

Conditional exemptions. The law authorizes a number of conditional exemptions, some of which have already been mentioned. Thus the Commission may exempt lessors, domestic carriers if necessary to enable them to compete with carriers serving foreign ports, and it may relieve contract carriers from the necessity of filing and posting and charging reasonable minimum charges. In addition, the law provides certain other conditional exemptions. Except to the extent that the Commission shall find regulation necessary to carry out the national transportation policy, Part III does not apply to transportation in interstate commerce by water solely within the limits of a single harbor or between places in contiguous harbors, when such transportation is not a part of a continuous through movement of traffic; nor does it apply to transportation by small craft of not more than one hundred tons carrying capacity or not more than one hundred indicated horsepower, or to vessels carrying passengers only and equipped to carry no more than sixteen passengers, or to ferries, or to the movement by water carriers of contractors' equipment employed in construction or repair for such water carrier, or to the operation of salvors.

Cruise exemptions. A number of steamship lines conduct pleasure cruises beginning at one American port and ending at the same or another American port, with stops scheduled at various foreign ports. These lines contended that they were not engaged in transportation in the ordinary commercial sense, and the Interstate Commerce Act was amended in 1948 to exempt vacation cruise travel of the type described from regulation.

Extent to which water transportation not subject to regulation. Perhaps one of the most striking features of Part III of the Interstate Commerce Act is the extent to which domestic water transportation is exempt from economic regulation. The exemption of private carriers and of transportation for hire of commodities when not more than three commodities are hauled removes the great bulk of water transportation on the Great Lakes from Interstate Commerce Commission control. Almost all of the traffic on the Ohio River is moved in vessels owned or operated by private industries and so not subject to regulation. A substantial volume of traffic moves on other parts of the Mississippi River system in private vessels or in barges handling no more than three commodities in bulk, and this traffic is not subject to regulation. In the case of the coastwise and intercoastal service, Interstate Commerce Commission regulation is more significant, but even here there is an important volume of traffic moved by private carriers and by tankers which is not subject to economic regulation. Because of these various exemptions, only a small percentage of total domestic water traffic is subject to control by the Interstate Commerce Commission.

ACCOMPLISHMENTS OF INTERSTATE COMMERCE COMMISSION

Attitude of Interstate Commerce Commission. Shortly after the enactment of the Transportation Act of 1940 the Interstate Commerce Commission expressed the opinion that the provisions of the newly added Part III would not be likely to justify either the expectations of its more ardent friends or the foreboding of its foes. Neither would it cripple water transportation nor would it greatly aid the railroads. The Commission did believe, however, that Part III should help to stabilize and improve competitive conditions in transportation.

Bureau of Water Carriers and Freight Forwarders. Over the years the Interstate Commerce Commission has created within its organization a number of bureaus which administer the various provisions of Part I of the Interstate Commerce Act. When the Motor Carrier Act, 1935, was adopted a Bureau of Motor Carriers was created to handle administrative matters relating to interstate highway transportation, and this bureau was given a large part of the responsibility for administering the provisions of Part II. After the enactment of Part III, a Bureau of Water Carriers was organized and when the regulation of freight forwarders was undertaken in 1942, administrative duties relating to both water carriers and freight forwarders were combined in a single Bureau of Water Carriers and Freight Forwarders. In 1948 administration of the provisions of the Reed-Bulwinkle Act relating to rate bureaus were added to the duties of this bureau.

The duties of the Bureau of Water Carriers and Freight Forwarders, insofar as they relate to water carriers, are quite limited. It handles such things as exemptions, certificate and permit applications, classifying carriers, extending relief because of competition, granting temporary operating authority, and the like. Other aspects of administration, however, and particularly those related to the conduct of formal hearings, are handled by the various bureaus which function in connection with the administration of Part I. The Commission has given various reasons why it did not establish a water carrier bureau with the same status as the Bureau of Motor Carriers. In the first place, the regulatory ground covered under Part III is much less extensive than under Part II. Second, the number of water carriers subject to Commission jurisdiction is small, the carriers themselves better organized, and in general more accustomed to regulation. Finally, the Commission always has exercised limited jurisdiction over domestic water carriers, and its existing bureaus have some familiarity with water transportation.

The failure of the Commission to establish a Bureau of Water Carriers with broad administrative duties has led to the complaint that it is neglecting water transportation. No doubt, too, the combining of freight forwarders with water carriers for administrative purposes contributed to the feeling of neglect, although the virtual disappearance of coastwise and intercoastal shipping during World War II considerably reduced the administrative burden in connection with water transportation. The addition of the administration of the provisions of the Reed-Bulwinkle Act in 1948 suggests that the Bureau of Water Carriers and Freight Forwarders has become, at least temporarily, a sort of an administrative catchall.

Accomplishments. As of October 31, 1951, the Commission reported that 2,043 applications had been filed for authority to continue, extend, or institute water carrier operations, or for exemption from regulation.[2] Vessels used by the carriers coming under the jurisdiction of the Commission have been classified into five groups, as follows: (1) self-propelled vessels, (2) sailing vessels, (3) non-self-propelled vessels with use of separate towing vessels (barge line services), (4) towing vessels, and (5) vessels furnished to persons other than carriers for use by such persons in the transportation of their own property. These classifications apply to the operations of both common and contract carriers, with the exception of the last classification which is restricted to contract carriers. For statistical purposes water carriers have been divided into three classes. Class A includes all carriers with operating revenues exceeding $500,000; Class B, carriers with operating revenues in excess of $100,000 but not more than $500,000; and Class C, carriers with operating revenues of $100,000 or less. Tariff, accounting, and reporting regulations have been prescribed, but the accounting regulations are imposed only on carriers having average operating revenues in excess of $100,000.

---

[2] Interstate Commerce Commission, *Annual Report*, 1951, p. 127.

REGULATION OF WATER TRANSPORTATION

SUGGESTED READINGS

Not a great deal has been written on the subject of the regulation of domestic water transportation. The following readings, however, will prove useful for further reference.

Federal Coordinator of Transportation, *Regulation of Transportation Agencies*, 73d Congress, 2nd Session, Senate Document No. 152 (1934).

Johnson, Emory R., Grover G. Huebner, and Arnold K. Henry, *Transportation by Water*. New York: D. Appleton-Century Company, 1935. Useful in connection with the development of regulation up to the date of publication.

Sharfman, I. L., *The Interstate Commerce Commission*, Vol. II. New York: The Commonwealth Fund, 1931. Interstate Commerce Commission regulation prior to the enactment of Part II.

24.

Some Problems and Policies

of

DOMESTIC WATER TRANSPORTATION (I)

INTRODUCTION

A word of warning. It should be kept in mind in connection with the discussion which follows that the Interstate Commerce Commission's jurisdiction over domestic water transportation is limited to a very small portion of the total volume of traffic which moves by water in this country. This means that certain of its policies, while they may be quite significant insofar as regulated water transportation is concerned, are of little or no significance so far as water transportation as a whole is concerned. It is possible, therefore, to make serious errors of judgment if Commission policies established in connection with regulated carriers are projected to cover the whole field of domestic water transportation.

Characteristic features of carriers subject to Commission regulation. Although the law provides for regulating contract carriers, relatively few of the carriers subject to the jurisdiction of the Interstate Commerce Commission are of this type, probably because of the exemption of carriers of bulk commodities when no more than three such commodities are moved in a single vessel. Since this is the sort of cargo which has proved most profitable to water carriers, it naturally attracts the contract carrier type of operator. Most of the carriers subject to Commission jurisdiction are common carriers, and the amount of traffic they move is small relative to the total volume of water traffic and the total volume of traffic moved by all types of common carriers. To no small extent, regulated common carriers by water are devoted to moving commodities in bulk, usually in large quantities. Their tonnage is made up mostly of coal, petroleum and petroleum products, ore, grain, iron and steel products, and other similar heavy or bulky commodities. Manufactured products and small merchandise shipments of the kind moved extensively by railroads and motor carriers move by water only to a limited extent.

THE RIGHT TO OPERATE: GRANDFATHER OPERATIONS

Bona fide operations. The Commission's task in processing water carrier grandfather applications was simple compared with the task of processing similar applications from motor carriers. The number of applications was relatively small, 775 for water carriers as compared with 89,568 for motor carriers.[1] Also, the number of routes and points served by existing carriers was small, simplifying the verification of previous operations. Furthermore, the Commission did not have to concern itself with numerous attempts to undertake new operations solely to secure grandfather rights as was the case with motor carrier applications. This was because the number of individuals capable of navigating commercial vessels was small compared with the number of individuals able to operate a commercial trucking business and because the cost of acquiring equipment was considerably greater. Also, while there appeared to be good opportunities for profit in the trucking business, the same could not be said for water transportation.

Service limitations. In motor carrier cases the Commission generally restricted applicants to routes or points served on or about the critical date, but a much more liberal policy was followed with water carriers. Thus in one case it granted grandfather rights to serve sixty-nine Pacific coast ports, nine of which had been served in 1938 or 1939 but not between those dates and the critical date of January 1, 1940, and twenty-seven of which had not been served since before 1938. In this case the ports were along the route or routes usually traversed and the carrier had actively solicited traffic even though none was obtained.[2] Occasionally the Commission restricted water carrier applicants to the commodity or commodities or types of commodities handled on the critical date,[3] but more often it authorized common carriers by water, but not contract carriers to any extent, to handle commodities generally without too much regard to services actually performed on or about the critical date.[4] Grandfather rights also have been limited to the type of service performed by the equipment in use by the applicant. Thus an applicant using barges pulled by tugs had grandfather rights to perform service by barges and tugs,[5] and operators using other types of equipment were granted grandfather rights to provide the services peculiar to their equipment. The purpose of this policy was to control competition among water carriers operating different kinds of equipment.[6]

---

[1] Interstate Commerce Commission, *Annual Report,* 1950, pp. 99, 128.

[2] *Pope & Talbot, Incorporated,* 250 I.C.C. 117 (1941); *Central Barge Company,* 260 I.C.C. 329 (1944); see, also, *James McWilliams Blue Line, Incorporated,* 260 I.C.C. 673 (1945).

[3] *Phillips Packing Company, Incorporated,* 260 I.C.C. 297 (1944).

[4] *Russell Bros. Towing Co., Inc.,* 250 I.C.C. 429 (1942); *Wisconsin & Michigan Steamship Co.,* 250 I.C.C. 99 (1941); *Ohio River Company,* 260 I.C.C. 500 (1945).

[5] *Eastern Transportation Company,* 250 I.C.C. 505 (1942).

[6] *A. L. Mechling Barge Line,* 250 I.C.C. 77 (1941).

Conclusion. Two points in particular are worth noting in connection with the application of the grandfather principle to water carriers. Although the grandfather provisions of Part II and Part III of the Interstate Commerce Act are substantially the same, the Commission was just about as liberal in its application of these provisions to water carriers as it was restrictive in applying them to motor carriers. In part this may be due to the fact that the typical water shipment is large, and at numerous small ports along water carrier routes only an irregular and infrequent service can be offered. If an existing carrier stood ready to offer service when, as, and if traffic were available, no good purpose would be served by denying it grandfather rights simply because it had not actually rendered service at a given port for several years or had not rendered service at all.

There is the hint of another reason for greater liberality in a statement made by the Commission that it is proper to authorize the widest scope of operations compatible with the circumstances of an applicant's situation because it is desirable that improved waterways be utilized to benefit the greatest number of people.[7] It has been noted, too, that motor carrier and water carrier grandfather applications have been handled by different divisions of the Commission. Another suggestion has been that the greater relative size of the small operators in the water carrier field enabled them to present their cases better than was true of the typical operator in the motor carrier field.[8] Finally, the more liberal attitude toward water carrier grandfather applications may reflect in some degree the sharp criticisms of the highly restrictive policy followed by the Commission in motor carrier grandfather applications.

One other point worth noting is the fact that by far the largest number of applications submitted to and approved by the Commission have involved operations under grandfather rights. As of October 31, 1949, the Commission had processed about five times as many grandfather applications as it had applications for new operating authority, and it had approved 575 grandfather applications as compared with only 154 applications for new operating authority. This fact has tended to limit somewhat the Commission's control over the right of entry into the field of domestic water transportation, which is one of the major purposes of legislation in this area. As will be noted presently, however, many water carriers have gone out of business as a result of World War II and its aftermath, and should there be a major revival of domestic water

[7] *Upper Mississippi Towing Corporation,* 260 I.C.C. 85 (1943).
[8] Board of Investigation and Research, *Federal Regulatory Restrictions Upon Motor and Water Carriers,* 79th Congress, 1st Session, Senate Document 78, p. 266 (1945).

transportation in the future, control over the right of entry may be more significant than it has been up to the present.

EXTENSIONS AND NEW OPERATIONS

General. Because of the disruption to shipping caused by World War II most of the Commission's decisions involving the issuance of certificates or permits for extensions or new operations date from 1946. The recency of these decisions, the relatively small number of cases involved, and the present uncertain status of some types of domestic water transportation, suggest the need for caution in interpreting Commission policy with regard to extensions and new operations.

Fit, willing, and able. The law requires that an applicant be fit, willing, and able to perform the proposed service and conform with Commission regulations. Many of the leading cases have involved applications from existing carriers to extend their service or applications for grandfather rights made after the 120 day period allowed for filing such applications had expired. In these cases the fact that an applicant has operated successfully in the past is accepted as evidence of his ability to meet this particular requirement.[9]

Need for proposed service. Obviously the need for a given service is a factor which must enter into all decisions in certificate and permit cases. Indeed, in the case of common carrier applications the law requires a showing that the proposed operation is required by the present or future public convenience and necessity. Here, again, many of the leading cases involve shipping companies already in existence, and the fact that they are operating successfully is considered as evidence of a need for their services.[10] The possibility that a need for service might develop, however, does not constitute a showing of public convenience and necessity.[11]

Competition. It is, of course, the duty of the Commission to observe and consider the rights of existing water carriers in connection with applications for certificates and permits. But the Commission also has a duty to provide the public with the best possible service, and these two duties sometimes conflict.[12] The question of the effect of new

---

[9] *J. D. Orrell,* 250 I.C.C. 67 (1941); *West Coast Steamship Company,* 250 I.C.C. 235 (1942); *Foss Launch & Tug Co. Extension,* 260 I.C.C. 525 (1945); and others.

[10] *John L. Goss Corp.,* 250 I.C.C. 101 (1941); *Choctaw Transportation Co.,* 250 I.C.C. 106 (1941); and many others.

[11] *Foss Launch & Tug Co. Extension,* 260 I.C.C. 525 (1945); *Commercial Barge Lines, Inc., Extension,* 260 I.C.C. 701 (1946).

[12] *Upper Mississippi Towing Corporation,* 260 I.C.C. 292 (1944), protecting the carrier; *Commercial Barge Lines, Inc., Extension,* 260 I.C.C. 555 (1945), authorizing new service.

water carrier operations on other transportation agencies comes up from time to time, and here the position of the Commission has been quite definite. Even though there is adequate service by rail and highway, the Commission has questioned whether that fact alone warrants denial of a water carrier application. The Commission is of the opinion that there are certain inherent advantages in transportation by water,[13] and in a number of cases it has held that communities and shippers are entitled to adequate transportation service by water as well as by rail.[14]

Towage. On inland waterways it is common to transport goods in barges which are pulled or pushed by separate towing vessels. A carrier transporting goods by barge may employ the services of an independent towing company, in which case each company must have the proper authority to perform its particular service.[15] A carrier, however, may be permitted to tow its barges with its own towing vessels under a single certificate. Such a carrier may not conduct a separate towing business, but it may tow barges belonging to shippers provided the charges made for the service are based on the commodities carried, with a reasonable allowance made for the shippers' vessels. Obviously, without some such arrangement the door would be opened wide for discrimination against shippers who did not own their own barges.[16]

Seatrains and trailerships. An interesting development of modern times has been the use of special types of vessels to move railroad freight cars and motor truck trailers in what might be called a line-haul service. Seatrain Lines, Inc., was organized in the 1930's by the Missouri Pacific Railroad and the Texas and Pacific Railroad and operates partly under grandfather rights and partly under a certificate issued in 1942. Its vessels carry loaded and empty freight cars between various points, including New York City and the Gulf coast ports of New Orleans and Texas City, and also carry liquid cargo in bulk in tanks. More recently the Commission has authorized a somewhat similar service in connection with the movement of truck trailers. In this connection it has pointed out that road hazards and delays incident thereto can be avoided by transporting motor truck trailers by water.[17] These developments are interesting in that they constitute an attempt to combine the economy of long distance large volume movements by water with the greater flexibility of railroad and motor carrier service.

[13] *Commercial Barge Lines, Inc., Extension,* 260 I.C.C. 701 (1946).

[14] *Pan-Atlantic Steamship Corporation Extension,* 265 I.C.C. 169 (1947); *Inland Waterways Corporation Extension,* 265 I.C.C. 207 (1947); and others.

[15] *Southern Transportation Company,* 250 I.C.C. 453 (1942).

[16] *Eastern Transportation Company,* 250 I.C.C. 505 (1942); 250 I.C.C. 635 (1943).

[17] *Trailerships, Incorporated,* 265 I.C.C. 140 (1947); *H. E. Savage, Jr.,* 265 I.C.C. 157 (1947); *Chester D. and David C. Bintliff,* 265 I.C.C. 256 (1947).

Power to revoke certificates. The certificate issued in 1942 to Seatrain Lines, Inc., authorized that carrier to transport commodities generally between specified points, but in 1945 the Commission cancelled this certificate, issuing a new one limiting the carrier to the transportation of liquid cargo in bulk and to the transportation of empty and loaded freight cars received from and delivered to railroad carriers.[18] This action of the Commission was rejected by the Supreme Court in 1947, the Court noting that Part III of the Interstate Commerce Act does not authorize the Commission to revoke water carrier certificates.[19]

Since this decision the Commission has urged Congress to amend the law in order to give it authority to revoke water carrier certificates or permits. It has pointed out that there are a substantial number of certificates and permits outstanding which are not now being used. In some important trades the present service is far below that existing before World War II, but individuals who might be interested in undertaking new operations in these trades are deterred from doing so by the existence of unused operating rights which can be revived at any time. The existence of unused rights also makes it difficult for the Commission to determine to what extent it should approve applications for new operating authorities which duplicate ones not now being used.

Dual operations. Operation both as a common and as a contract carrier has been approved in several cases where the two services were not competitive or closely related. In one case the Commission permitted the applicant to operate a contract carrier service by sailing vessels and a general common carrier towage service using tugboats.[20] In another case it permitted operation as an intercoastal common carrier of general commodities along with operation as a contract carrier of lumber and lumber products on the Pacific coast.[21] If the common and contract carrier operations are competitive and conducted in substantially the same territories, however, dual operation will not be permitted.[22] The general prohibition against dual operation also applies to grandfather operations.

EXEMPT OPERATIONS

Bulk cargo carriers. The exemption from regulation of carriers of cargo in bulk when not more than three commodities are being hauled has necessitated a number of Interstate Commerce Commission rulings.

---

[18] *Seatrain Lines, Inc.,* 260 I.C.C. 430 (1945).
[19] *United States* v. *Seatrain Lines, Inc.,* 329 U.S. 424.
[20] *John L. Goss Corp.,* 250 I.C.C. 101 (1941).
[21] *Sudden & Christenson,* 260 I.C.C. 643 (1946).
[22] *Hyer Towing Company,* 250 I.C.C. 631 (1943); *American Barge Line Company,* 260 I.C.C. 783 (1946); and others.

If several barges are included in a single tow, not more than three bulk commodities may be handled in the entire tow if the exemption is to apply. The Commission has ruled that the term "in bulk" commonly refers to a loose mass which is poured or thrown into a vessel without regard to order and which is restrained during transportation only by the bottom and sides of the carrying vessel and its bulkheads. Commodities which are stowed in an orderly arrangement are not commodities in bulk.[23] And when bulk commodities are handled in the same vessel or in the same tow with nonbulk commodities, the transportation of the bulk commodities is not exempt from Commission jurisdiction.[24]

Noncompetitive contract carriers. Contract carriers offering services which are not actually and substantially competitive with transportation by common carriers subject to Parts I, II, or III, are exempt from regulation. Most of the exemptions approved have involved towing dredges and derricks and other types of floating equipment not designed or used to carry passengers and property.[25] Exemptions also have been granted where special types of equipment are necessary to handle certain commodities.[26]

Transportation by small craft. The Commission may remove the exemption of small craft if necessary, and in a few cases it has done so. It found that unregulated transportation by small craft in connection with motor carriers made it possible for a carrier to discriminate unjustly as between shippers, and the provisions of Part III were applied in cases of this kind.[27] It also discovered that when the same or similar services were performed between the same points or territories with both large and small craft, the regulation of each was necessary in order to eliminate the possibility of unjustly discriminatory practices.[28]

Ferry service. Ferry boats operate all over the United States at points where it is impractical to build bridges or where the volume of traffic does not warrant the expense of bridge construction. Many of these ferry operations technically are interstate in nature although the transportation service rendered often is of a purely local type, and no good purpose would be served by subjecting them to regulation by the Commission. A different situation arises, however, where ferries move railroad freight cars and truck trailers between distant points. For

---

[23] *John L. Goss Corp.,* 250 I.C.C. 101 (1941); *Ohio River Company,* 260 I.C.C. 501 (1945).

[24] *John J. Mulqueen,* 250 I.C.C. 436 (1942); *American Barge Line Company,* 265 I.C.C. 231 (1947); and others.

[25] *Tennessee Valley Sand & Gravel Company Exemption,* 250 I.C.C. 48 (1941).

[26] *Atwacoal Transportation Co. Exemption,* 250 I.C.C. 33 (1941).

[27] *Application of Part III to Transportation by Small Craft,* 260 I.C.C. 155 (1943).

[28] *Ibid.; Waterman Towing Company,* 260 I.C.C. 185 (1944); and others.

example, it is physically possible to move freight cars and truck trailers by ferry across Lake Michigan between Michigan and Wisconsin in what amounts to a through haul. The Commission has held that this is not ferry service in the ordinary sense of the word and is, therefore, subject to regulation.[29] The same principle has been applied to the transportation of passengers and their vehicles in what amounts to a line-haul service between distant points.[30]

The American Trucking Associations, Inc., argued that the ferries operated by the Delaware-New Jersey Ferry Company formed a connecting link between highways making up a route over which a substantial volume of interstate commerce moved along the Atlantic seaboard, and that it was the duty of the Commission to exercise its option to regulate ferries in order to see to it that the rates and charges were held at a reasonable and economical level. The Commission found, however, that Congress intended that such ferry operations should remain free of federal regulation unless interstate commerce was so affected as to make the application of Part III necessary. It found that the ferry company's revised rates for transporting tractor-trailers, which were the basis of the motor carrier complaints, were not excessive and refused to remove the exemption.[31]

OPERATING PROBLEMS: RATES AND RATE MAKING

Water carrier costs. Wherever reference is made to water carrier costs in the following discussion of rates and rate making, the costs involved are those which are incurred by the operating companies in providing a transportation service and do not include anything by way of a charge to cover the cost of improving and maintaining waterways for navigation purposes. In any proper analysis of the *economy* of water transportation, waterway improvement and maintenance costs must be taken into consideration, but since the waterways are furnished free of all toll by the Government to all who may wish to use them, their cost does not enter into the actual determination of water carrier *rates*. The cost of providing municipal terminal facilities is included to the extent that water carrier user charges cover these costs.

Constant costs and variable costs. Water carriers are relieved of a heavy burden of constant costs because they are not required to provide

---

[29] *Ann Arbor Railroad Company,* 250 I.C.C. 490 (1942); *H. E. Savage, Jr.,* 260 I.C.C. 603 (1945).

[30] *Ann Arbor Railroad Company,* 250 I.C.C. 490 (1942); *Pere Marquette Railway Company,* 260 I.C.C. 206 (1944).

[31] *Application of Part III to Transportation by Delaware-New Jersey Ferry Company,* 265 I.C.C. 337 (1948).

their own rights of way, and to the extent that they make use of public and shipper-owned terminal facilities they are relieved of an additional burden of constant costs. The principal item of constant cost in water transportation is interest on investment in ships, tugs, and barges. In terms of carrying capacity this need not be large as compared with rail or motor transportation because of the smaller number of units required to move a given tonnage. In terms of ton miles of traffic moved, however, the comparison is not as favorable because higher rail and motor speeds make for a more efficient use of equipment.

Where water carriers offer a regularly scheduled service, their operating expenses exhibit some of the characteristics of constant costs because they must be met regardless of the volume of traffic carried. Since speed is not usually a primary consideration in water transportation, however, operators will seek to adjust their sailings to avoid moving under a partial load, and where this can be done operating expenses tend to vary with the volume of traffic. It would appear, then, that to the extent that water carriers can adjust their sailings to the volume of traffic available, their costs show a substantial degree of variability.

Terminal and line-haul costs. Water carrier terminal costs vary widely, depending largely upon the nature of the freight being handled. Terminal costs are high where a merchandise or package freight service is offered because of the handling costs involved. On the other hand, they may fall to a very low level where bulk cargo which can be loaded and unloaded mechanically is involved. It is not by chance that barge operators tend to limit their service to bulk freight moving in bargeload lots although a few do handle some package freight.

Because of the very large carrying capacities of ships and barges, line-haul costs per unit of traffic moved are characteristically low, assuming that cargo is available to fill the vessel to reasonable capacity. There appear, however, to be wide differences in cost depending upon the vessels used, with those of deep draft and great carrying capacity having the lowest unit costs.[32] The location of the operation is a factor affecting line-haul costs, also. Thus many of the Great Lakes operators navigate over almost straight line distances while intercoastal carriers operate over an extremely roundabout route. And barge line operators must follow the winding courses of rivers which adds to their operating costs. Finally, carriers offering a shipload or bargeload service will have a lower line-haul cost per unit of traffic moved than carriers offering a scheduled

[32] Board of Investigation and Research, *Comparison of Rail, Motor, and Water Carrier Costs*, 79th Congress, 1st Session, Senate Document 84 (1945).

merchandise or package freight service. This is because the former are more likely to operate under full load.

Wherever both line-haul and terminal costs are low, the cost of moving goods by water becomes less than by any other means of transportation. In this connection, special attention should be called to the transportation of bulk commodities on the Great Lakes. The routes followed are extremely direct and the freight is carried in shipload lots in vessels of large carrying capacity. Add to this the mechanical handling of such commodities as iron ore and coal at terminals, and the result is an extremely low cost transportation service.

Rule of rate making. The water carrier rule of rate making, which directs the Commission to take into consideration, among other things, the need of the carriers for revenues sufficient to provide an adequate and efficient service, does not mean a great deal in the light of the present day highly competitive conditions in transportation. The fact that the bulk of domestic water transportation is completely free of economic regulation puts the regulated water carriers at a disadvantage in attempting to obtain cargo at remunerative rates. And the keen competition of railroads is a significant factor in determining the profitability of the rates a water carrier can charge. It is true that some regulated carriers, particularly those which are able to limit their service to bulk shipments of heavy loading commodities, have operated profitably, but many others have had to go out of business.

Rates on particular commodities. A large number of common carriers by water operating in domestic commerce are parties to the Consolidated Freight Classification, but it must not be supposed that they carry all or even a large number of the commodities listed in that publication. The Interstate Commerce Commission stated in a 1949 report involving movements between Atlantic and Gulf coast points that ship lines were choosing traffic and applying a Class 25 rating as a minimum, even though lower rates were applicable.[33] Not many barge lines offer a service which is adaptable to the transportation of a wide variety of items, and there are, of course, a great many items in the Consolidated Freight Classification which would not move by water even if service were offered. As might be expected a large volume of freight moves under commodity rates. The principles of freight classification and the factors entering into the determination of commodity rates were discussed in Chapter 11 and need not be repeated here.

Rates on particular hauls. Common carrier port-to-port rates are generally related to railroad rates between the points involved and must be lower

---

[33] *Traffic World*, November 5, 1949, p. 40.

than railroad rates to compensate for the inferior service. In many cases on the Mississippi River a differential of 20 per cent under the railroad rate has been applied. Elsewhere differentials tend to vary with the nature of the commodity, the length of haul, and the extent of competition. Water rates, like railroad rates, follow the tapering principle, although in a number of cases ports have been blanketed over rather wide areas. In Chapter 21 a question was raised about the economic validity of basing motor carrier rates on railroad rates since the two industries operate under very different cost structures, but the same criticism cannot be made of the relationship of water and railroad rates. In a study published in 1945 the Board of Investigation and Research concluded that barge transportation of bulk freight was cheaper than rail transportation for all distances and was cheaper than rail transportation in the movement of package freight for distances of 500 miles and over.[34] The distances are rail distances and allow for the greater circuity of river transportation.

PROBLEMS OF POSTWAR READJUSTMENT

Barge lines. During the early years of World War II, a number of inland waterway operators suspended or discontinued all or part of their prewar services, and operations on inland waterways were largely shifted from normal routes and services to transportation incidental to the prosecution of the war. Large quantities of sulphur and petroleum and its products were moved by barge during the war, and various new movements of traffic were handled. After the war a number of barge line operators were successful in reestablishing peace time operations and even improved their financial status in spite of large increases in costs. In general, it may be said that the barge line operators fared better than other water carriers subject to Interstate Commerce Commission jurisdiction.

The success of the barge line operators in adjusting themselves to postwar conditions may be ascribed to various factors. Some of the operators acquired new floating equipment of the most modern type and installed labor-saving devices to offset increased labor costs. On the Mississippi River system rates have increased less than railroad rates and no doubt this has resulted in the shift of some traffic to barge lines. Finally, the barge lines have concentrated as much as possible on large shipments of heavy loading and bulk commodities which involve relatively low terminal-handling costs. It is probably this last consideration as much as anything which has contributed to the success of barge line operators. It is worth noting

---

[34] *Comparison of Rail, Motor, and Water Carrier Costs,* 79th Congress, 1st Session, Senate Document 84 (1945), p. 9.

that the Inland Waterways Corporation, the only barge line operator offering a regular service in handling small package shipments, has operated at a loss for a number of years.

Great Lakes. A large part of the Great Lakes traffic is moved in bulk by private and contract carriers not subject to the jurisdiction of the Interstate Commerce Commission. These carriers were not adversely affected by World War II, and since that war they have operated much as usual. The regulated water carriers operating on the Great Lakes had to make drastic changes in their operations in compliance with the requests or orders of government agencies, and some vessels subject to Interstate Commerce Commission jurisdiction were requisitioned by the Government. Following the close of the war the regulated carriers were affected by adverse economic conditions and by costly labor-management differences.

In its annual report for 1949 the Commission reported that the more specialized Lake carriers subject to its jurisdiction were experiencing substantial increases in business. Other carriers, however, have continued to experience difficulties. In September, 1950, Congress made available ten fast merchant ships from the government reserve fleet for purchase by operators interested in reestablishing the package freight service which existed before World War II, and applications were not long in coming in. It was said that the buyers would get ships which cost $4,400,000 each for an eventual investment of $165,000 per ship.[35]

Coastwise and intercoastal shipping. Practically all of the ships operating in the coastwise and intercoastal services were withdrawn for use by the Government during World War II, and after the war their owners faced the difficult task of restoring physical operations, reestablishing contacts with shippers, and making a supreme effort to regain traffic which had been lost to other transportation agencies. The Interstate Commerce Commission stated in 1948 that it was keenly mindful of the problems and needs of these carriers and the important defense role which the vessels of some of them had played. It also said that it had taken and would continue to take such steps as were within its power to help them in regaining the ground lost, although it recognized grave limitations on what could be done for them.[36]

Throughout the period in which the coastwise and intercoastal carriers were attempting to restore service they were faced with strikes and work stoppages involving both water front and vessel personnel, and strikes and threats of strikes naturally had an adverse effect on the development of traffic. Furthermore, operating costs had risen to the point where it was

---

[35] Reported in *Traffic World*, September 23, 1950, pp. 46-47.
[36] Interstate Commerce Commission, *Annual Report*, 1948, p. 6.

difficult for water carriers to maintain rates sufficiently below those of other carriers to make up for their poorer service. Successive increases in railroad rates have helped some by enabling the boat lines to raise their rates, but the financial picture has deterred many prewar carriers from resuming operations, and some have given up after short periods of operation at a heavy loss.

Pleas for higher railroad rates. In March, 1946, the War Shipping Administration, which operated a coastwise and intercoastal service for a brief period following the end of World War II, requested the Interstate Commerce Commission to investigate the lawfulness of railroad rates and practices to the extent that they were competitive with domestic water carriers. It was urged that the railroad rates in question were lower than necessary to meet water competition, that they were excessively lower than normal rates, and that they were not reasonably compensatory. Without attempting to pass judgment on the validity of these contentions, it is pertinent to point out another and perhaps more basic issue involved. If private enterprise were to resume water carrier service, rates would have to be raised to cover the greatly increased costs of operation. But water carrier rates must be differentially lower than railroad rates or shippers will not use the service. Hence if water carrier rates were to be raised, an increase in railroad rates would be necessary. This constitutes a significant reversal of earlier competitive conditions under which low water carrier costs forced the downward adjustment of many railroad rates.

Some of the railroad rates at issue constituted departures from the long and short haul clause which originally had been sanctioned by the Commission because of water competition. The Commission reopened a considerable number of these cases, and in most instances the relief formerly granted the railroads was rescinded or modified. Water carriers also have urged increases in many other railroad rates which, while they did not constitute departures from the long and short haul clause, were claimed to be lower than they otherwise would be because of water and highway competition. It hardly can be denied that interagency competition has exercised considerable influence, either direct or indirect, on railroad rates all over the country, but the Commission was reluctant to undertake an investigation of such magnitude as would result. It has, however, undertaken several somewhat limited investigations, two of which led to an upward revision of railroad rates and the elimination of all departures from the long and short haul clause made as a result of water competition in the Pacific coast area. Water carriers, however, continue to place considerable emphasis on the need for higher railroad rates.

The extent to which the Interstate Commerce Commission is justified in raising the rates charged by one agency of transportation in order to keep another agency in business is a problem to which there appears to be no simple solution. Before the enactment of the Transportation Act of 1940, with its declaration of a national transportation policy, the Commission rejected the contention that it could order an increase in railroad rates to enable motor carriers to participate in certain traffic at a profit.[37] Since the adoption of the national transportation policy, however, it has said that the effect of railroad rates on the ability of water lines and other transportation agencies to compete with rail carriers must be considered in determining lawful rates. But the Commission also recognizes that the interests of competing carriers are only one of many factors which the law requires it to consider. Railroad rates are the backbone of all transportation rates, and many delicate balances have been built up over the years. As a result, a radical upward adjustment of certain rates can have far-reaching effects of a sort which have nothing at all to do with water transportation or with interests directly concerned with the maintenance of water transportation.[38]

Suppose, for example, that a given commodity is produced at different points in the United States and that railroad rates have been adjusted to enable producers at these points to compete in distant markets. Now suppose that at some of these points the railroad freight rate is raised in order to enable water carriers to participate in the traffic at a profit. The shippers located at these points who have been using rail transportation will have to pay higher railroad rates or use the less satisfactory service provided by water carriers. Concerns not located at water points will continue to ship at their old rates, however, thus giving them a competitive advantage. Of course, the competitive balance could be restored by raising the railroad rates at nonwater points, but carried to its ultimate conclusion this might result in a countrywide upward revision of rates. Not only are the rates on this one commodity involved, but also the rates on competing commodities, on the products from which they are made, on other commodities made from these products, and so on. Motor carrier rates also might have to be raised. It is not intended to imply that all of this would happen as a result of a single rate increase, but it is illustrative of the possible consequences of increasing the rates charged by one carrier in order to keep another in business.

RAIL-BARGE ROUTES AND RATES

General. Although the Interstate Commerce Commission was authorized as far back as 1906 to order railroads and water carriers to establish through

---

[37] *Petroleum and Petroleum Products from California to Arizona,* 241 I.C.C. 21 (1940).

[38] Interstate Commerce Commission, *Annual Report,* 1948, pp. 49-52.

routes and joint rates, not much was accomplished along this line until after 1928, primarily because of the unwillingness of the railroads to co-operate. In 1928 Congress passed the Dennison Act which, in effect, com-pelled railroad cooperation, and the through route and joint rate provisions of the present Part III of the Interstate Commerce Act are simply a re-enactment on a broader base of the similar provisions contained in the Dennison Act. The Commission is *required* to order common carriers by railroad and water to establish through routes and joint rates whenever it deems it necessary or desirable to do so in the public interest. In addition, it is empowered to fix the applicable joint rates, the divisions of revenues between the participating carriers, and reasonable differentials between the all-rail and the rail-water rates. It may be noted in passing that many of the present policies of the Commission relative to through routes and joint rates by rail and water were developed under the Dennison Act and al-ready were in effect at the time of the adoption of Part III.

There are three specific types of rail and water movements, which may be described as rail-barge, rail-Lake, and rail-ocean. Each of these three types displays certain distinctive characteristics and problems, and so each must be considered separately. Since the establishment of rail-barge routes and rates has given rise to major problems of public policy, however, most of the discussion which follows is confined to this type of movement. In most cases through movements by rail and water follow one of four route patterns, which may be described as rail-water, rail-water-rail, water-rail, and water-rail-water. For convenience, and in order to avoid awkward repetition, the term rail-water—or the terms rail-barge, rail-Lake, or rail-ocean—will be used to refer to all four types of routes.

Need for proposed rail-barge route. As previously noted, the Commis-sion is required to establish through routes and joint rates between common carriers by rail and barge line *when it finds it necessary or desirable to do so in the public interest.* One of the first issues to arise in this connection was the question of whether it was necessary or desirable to establish a through route and joint rate which would result in a diversion of traffic from existing railroads and which would displace tonnage from producing districts served by all-rail routes. The Commission very early refused to recognize such traffic diversions and tonnage displacements as constituting a valid reason for refusing to authorize the establishment of through routes and joint rates by rail and barge.[39] Obviously if the Commission had held otherwise, few if any such routes and rates could have been established.

In the limited number of cases in which the Commission has refused to

---

[39] *Through Routes and Joint Rates between Ohio & Mississippi Transit Company and Other Common Carriers*, 156 I.C.C. 724 (1929).

sanction the establishment of a proposed through route and joint rate, its decisions have been based primarily on the fact that the route would be unduly circuitous as compared with the all-rail route. It is to be expected, of course, that almost any rail-barge route will be more circuitous than the competing all-rail routes, but the Commission has held that this does not justify the establishment of all possible rail-barge routes, however circuitous and wasteful.[40] The Commission has developed certain formulas, involving a comparison of rail and water mileages, to help it in determining whether or not a proposed rail-barge route is unduly circuitous. In general, it may be said that these formulas are of such a nature as to justify the establishment of through rail-barge routes, even though a rather substantial degree of circuity is involved.[41] It should be noted, however, that the Commission has declined to order the establishment of rail-barge routes where the water part of the haul was so short that the cost of interchange would offset the assumed lower cost of water transportation.[42]

Division of joint rates. The rail-barge rate between two points must be lower than the all-rail rate or shippers will not use the service, and this means a smaller total amount of revenue to be divided among the participating carriers. On this point the Commission has held for many years that railroads should not be penalized for participating with barge lines in the through movement of freight, and it has adopted the principle that a participating railroad should receive the same amount of revenue for its services as it would have received from a comparable all-rail movement. In other words, if the joint rail-barge rate is lower than the joint all-rail rate, the resultant loss of revenue must be absorbed by the barge line and not by the participating railroads. And any added cost of interchange of freight between the railroad and the barge line must be borne by the water carrier.[43]

---

[40] *Carroon & Company, Incorporated,* v. *Arkansas & Louisiana Missouri Railway Company,* 178 I.C.C. 703 (1931). An extreme example of circuity is found in an early proposal of the Inland Waterways Corporation for the establishment of a through barge-rail route between Mobile, Alabama, and Columbus, Georgia, which would involve the movement of freight by barge some 400 miles north from Mobile to Birminghamport, and from there to Columbus by railroad. When the barge line portion of the proposed route was completed at Birminghamport, the freight would have been farther away from its destination than it had been before it left Mobile. Under the circumstances it is not surprising that the Commission was unable to find any justification for this route. (*Inland Waterways Corporation* v. *Alabama Great Southern Railroad Company,* 151 I.C.C. 126 (1929).)
[41] *Through Routes and Joint Rates between Inland Waterways Corporation and Other Common Carriers,* 153 I.C.C. 129 (1929); 167 I.C.C. 385 (1930); 172 I.C.C. 525 (1931).
[42] *Eastern Class Rate Investigation,* 164 I.C.C. 314, 453 (1930).
[43] *United States War Department* v. *Abilene and Southern Railway Company,* 77 I.C.C. 317 (1923); *Rail and Barge Joint Rates,* 270 I.C.C. 591 (1948).

Rail-barge rate differentials. When the Director General of Railroads undertook barge line operations during the period of federal control, he realized that shippers would not use the service unless it were offered at rates lower than those charged for railroad service. He decided to make the port-to-port barge rates 80 per cent of the rail rates between the same ports, this being the method of rate computation used by a barge line which had operated between Kansas City and St. Louis from 1911 to 1918. In order to prevent opposition to barge transportation on the part of commercial interests at nonriver points, it was decided to publish joint rail-barge rates to and from interior points. Since port-to-port barge rates were based on 80 per cent of the comparable rail rates, that part of the joint through rate covering the barge portion of the combined haul was based on 80 per cent of the rail rate between the points to and from which barge transportation was used. This gave a through rate for the rail-barge haul which was below the all-rail rate by something less than 20 per cent.

The Director General's method of computing joint rates set a pattern which was followed in a general way by the Interstate Commerce Commission until 1948.[44] In that year, after hearings, it prescribed differentials stated in terms of cents per hundred pounds and applicable between a large number of key points and via various river gateways. Thereafter the rail-barge rate between any two points was to be determined by deducting the prescribed differential from the all-rail rate applicable between the points in question.[45] The Commission indicated in its report and order that the differentials prescribed were largely a matter of judgment and complicated and difficult to explain, although it has been said that the system of rates adopted was much the same as had been suggested during the hearings by the Inland Waterways Corporation.[46] The railroads attacked the order largely on the ground that the Commission had failed to prove that the lower rates resulting from the prescribed differentials were justified by a lower cost of service, but on January 2, 1951, the Supreme Court sustained the Commission, holding that the law did not require proof that the rail-barge haul cost less than the all-rail haul.

Justification for lower rail-barge rates. Before the adoption of Part III the Commission had held that the differentials between rail-barge rates and all-rail rates must be reasonably fair to both railroads and barge lines. Furthermore, they should not be designed to divert traffic from one or the other but should reflect differences in the cost and in the value of the serv-

---

[44] In practice the port-to-port barge rate was deducted from the all-rail rate in effect between the ports involved, and this difference was then deducted from the direct line all-rail rate from origin to destination to get the joint rail-barge rate.

[45] *Rail and Barge Joint Rates,* 270 I.C.C. 591.

[46] Lewis W. Britton, ed., *Transportation in 1949,* p. 95.

ice performed.[47] Since the adoption of Part III, however, the Commission appears to have given little consideration to relative cost of service, and it has approved lower rail-barge rates on the ground that shippers will not otherwise use the service.

The Commission's decision to fix rail-barge rates somewhat on the basis of what the traffic will bear rather than on cost is significant, more particularly since it was made in the face of conclusions reached by its own rate experts that, in general, the cost of combined rail-barge movements was greater than the cost of all-rail movements. The higher cost of rail-barge movements was attributed in part to the high cost of barge line terminal operations and the higher cost of rail-barge interchanges as compared with all-rail interchanges. It should, perhaps, be pointed out that the costs referred to were operating costs, and nothing was included to cover the cost to the people of providing the waterways over which the water carriers operated. The decision to minimize cost considerations appears to have been strongly influenced by the effect that rates based on cost might have on the Inland Waterways Corporation's Federal Barge Lines. Congress, said the Commission, considered the Federal Barge Lines to be performing a pioneering function in the belief that a combined rail-barge service eventually would prove economical, and that it had no right to take action which would bring that experiment to an end.[48]

Decline in through traffic by rail and barge. The cost studies made by the Commission's staff were based on the period 1933-38, and it might be argued that they are too old to be of significance today. The experiences of barge line operators themselves, however, would seem to indicate that the conclusions with regard to the high cost of rail-barge movements is still valid. The principal barge line common carriers are the privately-owned Mississippi Valley Barge Line Company and the American Barge Line Company, and the publicly-owned Federal Barge Lines, operated by the Inland Waterways Corporation. The Mississippi Valley Company began operations in 1930 as a carrier of package freight, much of which was interchanged with the railroads, but it found these operations such a drain on its revenues that it placed embargoes on rail-barge traffic and concentrated on the movement of bulk freight on a port-to-port basis. By 1947 rail-barge traffic constituted less than 2 per cent of its tonnage. In the same year rail-barge traffic constituted less than 2/10 of 1 per cent of the tonnage of the American Barge Line Company. Both companies have been operating at a profit, but their profits have come from the port-to-port movement of heavy loading commodities in bulk.

---

[47] *Application of American Barge Line Company,* 190 I.C.C. 177 (1932).
[48] *Rail and Barge Joint Rates,* 270 I.C.C. 591 (1948).

The Inland Waterways Corporation which runs the Federal Barge Lines is the largest operator on the rivers. It was organized in part to demonstrate that a rail-barge service could be operated at a profit, and such a service always has constituted an important phase of its activities. But even in the case of the Federal Barge Lines the trend away from rail-barge traffic is evident. In 1930 joint traffic with the railroads made up 68 per cent of its total tonnage, but by 1947 this had fallen to 17 per cent. Over the years it has operated at a substantial loss and is presently in poor financial condition.

Shipper interest in through routes and joint rates. The principal demand for a continuation of rail-barge rates differentially lower than all-rail rates comes from Mississippi Valley shippers and from organizations such as the Mississippi Valley Association which are interested in promoting the welfare of the Valley region. Many shippers do not find it practical to use water transportation, but those who can are keenly interested in the saving in transportation charges which results from the rail-barge differentials. Furthermore, rail-barge routes and rates lower than all-rail rates have been extended to many parts of the country, and their continued existence enables Mississippi Valley interests to count on the support of shippers in areas remote from the river itself for continued maintenance and improvement of navigation facilities.[49]

Conflicts of law and policy. The Transportation Act, 1920, included a statement that it was the policy of Congress to promote, encourage, and develop commercial water transportation. In 1924 the Inland Waterways Corporation was organized to provide a pioneer barge line service, and when the railroads proved reluctant to aid the barge line by establishing through routes and joint rates, Congress passed the Dennison Act which compelled them to do so. Also, during the 1920's and 1930's the Federal Government was spending large sums of money on waterway improvements for navigation purposes. Under the circumstances it is not surprising that the Interstate Commerce Commission felt some obligation not to do anything which would retard the development of barge transportation.

But there is another side to this picture. The 1920 statement of policy declared it to be the policy of Congress to foster and preserve in full vigor rail transportation as well as water transportation. This declaration sounds quite impressive and eminently fair, but unless one of the two types of transportation happens to be carrying more traffic than it was designed to handle economically, which ordinarily has not been the case, it is difficult

---

[49] For an elaboration of this proposition see Charles L. Dearing and Wilfred Owen, *National Transportation Policy*, Washington: The Brookings Institution, 1949, pp. 237-240.

to understand how a policy of forcing the diversion of traffic from one type of carrier to the other, can function to foster and preserve *both* types in full vigor.

Attention also may be called to the national transportation policy adopted in 1940 which states in part that it is the policy of Congress to provide for the fair and impartial regulation of all forms of transportation subject to the act; so administered as to recognize and preserve the inherent advantages of each; to promote safe, adequate, economical, and efficient service; to foster sound economic conditions in transportation and among the several carriers; and to encourage the establishment and maintenance of reasonable charges without unjust discriminations, undue preferences, or advantages. Just how has Commission policy in establishing through routes and joint rates by rail and barge which are below the all-rail rates squared with this declaration of policy?

This question is largely rhetorical in nature. Impartial studies made in the 1930's showed rail-water movements to be more costly than all-rail movements, a conclusion which was still valid in later years if the experiences of the barge operators themselves are any criterion. Consequently, the Commission's policy of fixing joint rail-barge rates which are differentially lower than the all-rail rates, to the extent that it has been effective, has resulted in the substitution of high cost transportation for low cost transportation, a policy which on its face is economically unsound. In terms of the national transportation policy it has resulted in regulation which is neither fair nor impartial, which does not recognize and preserve the inherent advantages of each form of transportation involved, which does not promote economical and efficient service, which does not foster sound economic conditions in transportation, but which is unjustly discriminatory and unduly preferential to those shippers who are in a position to take advantage of water transportation. Much has been made of the fact that barge transportation may exercise a depressing effect on railroad rates over a rather wide area, but if the railroads are to survive, depressed rates in some areas on some commodities necessitate higher rates in other areas and on other commodities.

It would be useless to criticize the Interstate Commerce Commission for the actions it has taken. It is faced with irreconcilable policies and it must choose between them. From the point of view of the economy of the country as a whole it would have been better, perhaps, if it had chosen to follow the national transportation policy, for it is economically unsound to encourage the use of high cost transportation when lower cost transportation exists. This is more particularly true when the low cost agency is one of large constant costs, for the more traffic that is taken from such an agency the higher must be the rates charged on its remaining traffic and the more difficult it becomes for it to survive as a private enterprise. Thus the end result of a policy of encouraging high cost transportation may be the destruction of the low cost agency. But the Interstate Commerce Commission is an agent of Congress, and in all probability the course of action it took was the one which most nearly fit the wishes of Congress.

Sooner or later Congress must face the problems raised by these and other irreconcilable elements of policy, but one of the consequences of the Commission's choice of the promotional policy has been to put off this day of reckoning. The proponents of barge transportation are highly articulate and if the Commission had discouraged rail-barge routes by adopting rates based on cost, it is quite possible that Congress would have come down upon it like the proverbial ton of bricks, and the issue would have been squarely joined. By contrast, its failure to follow the national transportation policy has caused no significant outcry. It is doubtful that more than a very small fraction of the people of the United States is aware that any such thing as a national transportation policy exists. The chief complainants have been the railroads and a few shippers. But shipper complaint has been insignificant, and the railroads never have had too much success in stirring up public support for their cause.

RAIL-LAKE AND RAIL-OCEAN ROUTES AND RATES

Rail-Lake routes and rates. Through routes and joint rates involving railroads and common carriers operating on the Great Lakes were in existence long before the revival of barge line transportation, and the Commission had exercised jurisdiction over such routes and rates for many years. At the present time, however, only an insignificant amount of traffic is moved on the Great Lakes by common carriers subject to the jurisdiction of the Commission, most of the tonnage being moved in bulk by private carriers or carriers otherwise exempt from the provisions of Part III. Nevertheless, it is an inescapable fact that practically all of the bulk commodity traffic moved by the Lake boats, consisting primarily of iron ore and coal, is transported to or from, or to and from, Lake ports by railroads in what amounts to a through movement. Thus iron ore is moved from the mines by railroad to Lake ports where it is dumped into bins and then into boats, and at the lower Lake ports it is unloaded from the ships into railroad cars for movement to the great steel producing areas. Conversely, coal is moved by railroad from the coal fields to lower Lake ports where it is dumped into the holds of Lake boats which then move it to destinations in the United States and Canada. In the absence of joint rates the Commission has, in numerous cases, sanctioned so-called proportional railroad rates to and from Lake ports. These proportional rates apply only to traffic which has had or will have a water haul and are lower than the rates which would otherwise apply.

Rail-ocean routes and rates. As in the case of rail-Lake traffic, the Commission has exercised jurisdiction over rail-ocean routes and rates for many years. Before World War II, freight moved under joint rail-ocean rates between the northeastern states, including states as far west as Ohio, and points in Southern, Southwestern, and Western Trunk Line territories, and sometimes even farther. In addition, through routes and joint rates have been in effect between points in the Pacific coast states via Pacific coastwise steamships, and also through routes and rates between states in the Mississippi Valley region and the West coast via Gulf ports and the intercoastal lines. Some of the rates prescribed by the Commission were made specific differentials under existing railroad rates, but others were not. Because of the uncertain status of coastwise and intercoastal common carrier transportation, there would seem to be little point in attempting to describe the details of these rate structures.

SUGGESTED READINGS

Board of Investigation and Research, *Comparison of Rail, Motor and Water Carrier Costs*, 79th Congress, 1st Session, Senate Document 84 (1945).

———, *Federal Regulatory Restrictions Upon Motor and Water Carriers*, 79th Congress, 1st Session, Senate Document 78 (1945). Chapter VIII discusses Interstate Commerce Commission policy with regard to certificate and permit restrictions.

Interstate Commerce Commission, *Annual Report*, various dates. A useful brief source of information on recent developments.

———, *Interstate Commerce Acts, Annotated.*

———, *Reports.* These three publications constitute the principal source of information on much of the material in this chapter.

Traffic World. An almost indispensable source of information on current developments.

25

Some Problems and Policies
of
DOMESTIC WATER TRANSPORTATION (II)

INLAND WATERWAYS CORPORATION

Significance. The Inland Waterways Corporation, an instrumentality of the Federal Government, operates a common carrier barge line service over a large part of the Mississippi River system under the name of the Federal Barge Lines. It played a major role in the modern revival of river transportation and in the establishment of through routes and joint rates by rail and barge, with rates differentially below the all-rail rates. The continued existence of this publicly-owned corporation in a field otherwise dominated by private enterprise gives rise to some fundamental problems of public policy which are important to the public at large as well as to those shippers using the services provided.

Origin and development. As previously mentioned, the Federal Government undertook barge line operations on the Mississippi and Warrior rivers during World War I, and when wartime control of transportation was terminated in 1920, the Secretary of War was directed to continue the barge line service. In 1924 the Government's barge line operations were turned over to the newly organized Inland Waterways Corporation. All of the stock of this corporation, initially amounting to $5 million but increased in 1928 to $15 million, is owned by the Federal Government. Originally the Secretary of War was named president ex officio, but in 1939 the Corporation was transferred to the Department of Commerce, and since then its operation has been under the jurisdiction of the Secretary of Commerce.

Reason for creation of Inland Waterways Corporation. Recognizing the public demand for inland waterway transportation, Congress had embarked on a river improvement program, but private enterprise had shown little interest in providing a common carrier barge line service on such streams as were navigable. Therefore, proponents of barge line transportation concluded that it was up to the Government to demonstrate to private enterprise that such transportation could be made to pay. Unfortunately, the War Department's barge line service had been conducted at a loss, and this was no way to prove to private enterprise the error of its ways. It was claimed that the War Department was not organized to conduct a business venture for profit, however, and it was believed that if the service could be established on a sound business basis and operated in the same way as a private transportation company, it would be successful. Hence the Inland Waterways Corporation was organized to demonstrate that a common carrier barge line service organized on a sound business basis could be operated profitably.

Provisions for disposal. It was not the intention of Congress to stay in the barge line business indefinitely, and the original law specified that the Inland Waterways Corporation was to develop a barge line service to the point where it could be transferred to private enterprise to the best advantage of the Government. The conditions under which such a transfer might take place were not outlined, and no specific provisions were made for liquidation in the event of failure, but those who framed the measure contemplated that success would come within five years, after which the Government would dispose of its properties to private enterprise and withdraw from the field.[1]

After four years of operation, the progress made by the Inland Waterways Corporation toward demonstrating the success of barge line transportation could best be described as microscopic, and the Dennison Act was passed in an effort to improve the situation by compelling the railroads to establish through routes and joint rates with barge lines. The Dennison Act also spelled out in rather precise terms the conditions under which the Government's barge line operations might be terminated. This part of the Dennison Act is still in effect and declares it to be the policy of Congress to continue the operation of the Inland Waterways Corporation until (1) adequate terminals and channels have been completed in the rivers where the Corporation operates, (2) terminal facilities for joint rail and water service have been provided, (3) joint rates with rail carriers have been made available, and (4) private enterprise engages or is ready to engage in common carrier service on the rivers served by the Corporation.

In the event that these requirements are met, the Secretary of Commerce is authorized to dispose of the facilities by sale or lease provided (1) they must not be disposed of to railroad interests, (2) the purchaser or lessee is willing to continue a service substantially similar to that rendered by the Corporation, (3) the Interstate Commerce Commission has determined the fair value of the facilities, and (4) the sale or lease is approved by the President of the United States. No time limit was placed on the life of the

---

[1] See report of the Committee on Interstate and Foreign Commerce to the House of Representatives, 68th Congress, 1st Session, H.R. 375 (1924).

Corporation and no provisions made for its termination in the event of failure to prove the success of the operation.

Financial results. Between 1924 and the end of 1938 the Inland Waterways Corporation showed a book profit in ten of the fifteen years involved. After 1938, however, it experienced continuous annual deficits except for a small book profit in 1943. The cumulative deficit as of June 30, 1950, was somewhere in the neighborhood of $7 million. For the year ending June 30, 1951, the Corporation showed a book loss of $526,770 on its waterway operations, but this was offset by a book profit of $608,505 earned by its railroad line running from Port Birmingham to Birmingham. Book figures overstate profits and understate losses because the Corporation receives the benefit of free postage, legal service, and office space; obtains reduced rates on telegrams; and does not have to pay taxes as would a private enterprise.

The Federal Coordinator of Transportation made a study of the Corporation's operations for the years 1924-35, charging the Corporation with interest on its investment, value of the services provided by the Government, certain other items, and taxes. On this basis the Coordinator concluded that the Corporation had failed by $15,138,839.14 to earn a return large enough to make the enterprise attractive to private capital.[2] For the years in question the Corporation's book profit came to $1,032,075.77.[3] The Board of Investigation and Research made a similar study for the years 1936-41 and concluded that during this period the Corporation had failed to earn a return sufficient to attract private capital by $8,246,151.81.[4] This figure compares with a book profit for the same period of $1,147,349.96. Neither the Coordinator nor the Board included in their calculations any charge for the use of the waterways provided by the Government.

Reasons for poor financial showing. Even on the basis of its own figures the Inland Waterways Corporation cannot be said to have demonstrated the success of the type of operation it is carrying on, and the reasons for its poor financial showing are of some interest. To some extent its losses

---

[2] Federal Coordinator of Transportation, *Public Aids to Transportation*, Vol. III, pp. 211-298. The Coordinator calculated that shippers had made a direct saving of $24,146,000 through the use of the Corporation's services, plus a large indirect saving in the form of reduced railroad rates. As he pointed out, however, a private enterprise cannot operate at a loss in order to save shippers money. It might appear that the Corporation could have raised its rates enough to cover the loss and still leave a saving to shippers, but obviously any increase in rates would have been accompanied by a diversion of traffic to the railroads.

[3] For the derivation of this figure see Lewis W. Britton, ed., *Transportation in 1948*, p. 146.

[4] Board of Investigation and Research, *Public Aids to Domestic Transportation*, pp. 792-793.

have been augmented by factors not related to the service itself. Poor management and political pressures are said to have contributed to the Corporation's difficulties until quite recently, and presumably these difficulties would be eliminated under private management. During World War II the barge lines were used in such a way as to create a badly unbalanced flow of traffic, necessitating the downstream movement of slack-loaded barges. The war also resulted in a substantial diversion of traffic to other agencies of transportation because of the urgent need for speed in the delivery of war materials. In recent years large increases in the cost of labor and supplies have helped to swell the deficit.

Among those causes of the Inland Waterways Corporation's poor financial showing which have a direct bearing on the basic issue of the success or failure of the barge line experiment, mention may be made first of the traffic moved under joint rail-barge rates. As indicated previously, the difference between the all-rail rate and the lower rail-barge rate comes out of the water carrier's share of the through rate, and the water carrier must bear the additional cost of rail-barge interchanges. The experiences of the privately-owned barge lines would seem to indicate that this business is unprofitable, but the Inland Waterways Corporation cannot withdraw from it because it is one of the Corporation's functions to demonstrate that a rail-barge service can be operated profitably. It cannot resolve this dilemma by demanding that the railroads accept a smaller share than they would receive from the division of an all-rail rate because this would mean railroad subsidization of barge line operations and would largely destroy any claimed economy of the service. Nor can a solution be sought in higher rail-barge rates because of the danger of diverting traffic to the railroads.

A second basic cause of the Inland Waterways Corporation's difficulties is its small shipment service. The privately-owned common carrier barge line companies do not attempt to handle small shipments and as a result their service is of value only to a limited number of large shippers. But in order to justify its existence a publicly-owned barge line must offer its services to as large a number of users as possible, and under the law anyone interested in purchasing the barge lines must agree to continue to provide substantially the same service. The Inland Waterways Corporation is the only common carrier providing a package service to small shippers, and there is ample evidence that the cost of handling these shipments at terminals is excessive. The operators of the Corporation recognize this difficulty, but whether sufficient traffic can be developed to make the installation of more efficient terminal facilities worth while is a matter of some uncertainty. In any event, it is clear that the package freight service has contributed to the losses experienced by the Corporation.

A third basic difficulty relates to the number of points served by the Inland Waterways Corporation. It provides service at numerous small river ports and this service has been expensive for the Corporation and for the municipalities which have provided terminal facilities. The number of ports served has been reduced considerably over the years, but there are limits to the extent that service can be reduced. In the first place, the Corporation is supposed to serve as many shippers as possible, including small shippers as well as large, and every reduction in service means a reduction in the number of shippers served. And in the second place, the communities and shippers affected by service reductions are in a position to bring political pressure to bear to bring about a restoration of service regardless of the effect on the Corporation.

There is evidence that some segments of the routes served by the Inland Waterways Corporation are more productive of losses than others. This appears to be particularly true of the Warrior River operation and of operations on the Missouri. The cream of the Warrior River traffic, consisting of steel and oil, has been taken over by private carriers, and there does not seem to be any prospect of carrying on this service except at a loss. But strong opposition develops to every proposal that it be abandoned. Private operators consider navigation on the Missouri unfeasible, and so people in this area demand that the Inland Waterways Corporation continue and expand its Missouri River service in order to prove that it can be carried on profitably. Relatively high railroad rates in the Missouri River area have been another factor contributing to the demand for continued operation.

There remains for consideration one other factor which has bulked large in recent discussions of the future of the Inland Waterways Corporation. Because of continued deficits extending over a long period of years, the Corporation has been unable to replace obsolete and worn-out equipment. Use of this equipment has meant poorer service to shippers, increased loss and damage claims, and a heavy drain on the Corporation's earnings in the form of maintenance costs. New equipment and complete rehabilitation of such equipment as is still usable appears to be essential to continued operations, but in view of the inability of the Corporation to earn enough in the past to replace and maintain its equipment, some doubt has been expressed about the wisdom of making the necessary investment.

Proposals to rehabilitate. After World War II, with money obtained from the sale of additional stock to the Government, the Inland Waterways Corporation built and put into operation an experimental integrated tow, consisting of the towboat *Harry Truman* and a series of barges operated as a unit. On the basis of results achieved with this new unit the officers of the Corporation expressed the belief that with new equipment and improved handling of freight at terminals they could operate the Corporation at a profit sufficient to attract purchasers. A number of bills have been introduced which would increase the capital stock of the Corporation and permit its rehabilitation, but as of early 1952 none had been adopted.

Objections to rehabilitation. The railroads, of course, do not want additional money put into the Inland Waterways Corporation. Opposition also has been expressed by some shippers and shipper organizations, including the nationwide National Industrial Traffic League. Some coastal ports have opposed rehabilitation on the ground that it will continue to give New Orleans what they say is an unfair freight rate advantage. The operators of privately-owned common carrier barge lines have been particularly opposed to any legislation which would permit the Corporation to expand its bulk cargo and bargeload operations in competition with private enterprise. The people of the United States are committed, in general, to the principle that governments should not engage in business enterprises, and this objection is raised from time to time in connection with continued operation of the Inland Waterways Corporation. It would appear, however, that more often the real issue involved is the effect of continued operation on the economic self-interest of the objectors.

Support for rehabilitation. Rehabilitation has been supported by Mississippi Valley interests and by Missouri Valley interests who believe that barge operations will afford them relief from high railroad freight rates. River communities and shippers who can use the service naturally have supported rehabilitation. Support has come from some individuals who feel that the Corporation can, if provided with modern equipment, still demonstrate the success of the operations it has been conducting. There also is some feeling that without the Inland Waterways Corporation, only large shippers will be able to use the river improvements made by the Government, and that small shippers are entitled to use of these facilities even if the operation has to be subsidized.

Proposals to sell. Since the inception of the Inland Waterways Corporation, its eventual disposal to private enterprise has been contemplated, but private enterprise has not been interested, the principal stumbling block being the requirement that the purchaser or lessee must continue to provide essentially the same services as are now being offered. The first real opportunity to dispose of the barge lines came on January 12, 1950, when a group of privately-owned barge line companies made an offer to lease the facilities, exclusive of terminal operations, for five years, with the right to renewal and an option to purchase. Secretary of Commerce Sawyer rejected the proposal on the ground that it did not make adequate provision for necessary rehabilitation of the properties, and because the proposal would still leave the Government encumbered with the terminal operations.

Later in 1950 the Tennessee Coal, Iron and Railroad Co. offered to purchase the Warrior River segment, together with its railroad connection between Port Birmingham and the Birmingham area. This company was contemplating the construction of its own railroad facilities to the Warrior River where it already operated a contract carrier barge line service, and as an alternative it proposed to take over the Warrior River segment and operate the facilities as a common carrier and to guarantee adequate service at reasonable rates for all shippers. This appeared to be an excellent opportunity to dispose of a segment which had been operated at a loss since its inception, but it was impossible to consummate the sale because the law prohibited sale to a railroad.

On September 13, 1951, the president of the Inland Waterways Corporation and thirteen members of his staff addressed a letter to Secretary of Commerce Sawyer in which they expressed belief that the failure of Congress to provide for rehabilitation of the system condemned the Corporation to death if it remained within the Government. They proposed, therefore, to purchase the facilities of the Inland Waterways Corporation for cash at its Interstate Commerce Commission value, with a guarantee that a substantially similar service would be maintained. Secretary Sawyer rejected this offer, stating that continued operation of the line could not be accomplished successfully by employees who were giving their attention to the possibility of winding it up. He further stated that he would not consider a sale to any of the Corporation's employees, past or present.[5]

Conclusion. The Inland Waterways Corporation was established in 1924 to demonstrate that a comprehensive common carrier barge line service could be carried on at a profit sufficient to attract private enterprise into the field. It has been demonstrated that port-to-port movements of goods in large quantities can be conducted at a profit by private enterprise, but the Corporation has failed completely to demonstrate that the type of service it offers can be conducted profitably. After more than a quarter of a century of operation, it has lost a substantial sum of money even by its own accounting standards. With its equipment worn out and most of its capital gone, the Corporation's supporters want Congress to put up as much as $18 million for rehabilitation so that it may continue its efforts to demonstrate that the type of operation it is carrying on can be performed at a profit. On its face the request appears to be somewhat less than logical.

Attention is called to the large sums of money which the Government has spent in improving the rivers for navigation purposes and which will be lost to small shippers if the Inland Waterways Corporation is liquidated. They will not, of course, be lost to large shippers who are able to move their own goods in their own boats or who can arrange for the transportation of their goods by privately-owned common and contract carriers de-

---

[5] For an editorial comment on this action see *Traffic World*, October 6, 1951, p. 5.

voted to the movement of freight in large lots. But small shippers were told time and again in the past of the benefits which would accrue to them from a program of government-financed waterway improvements, and if they cannot receive the benefit of cheap water rates on their shipments, they will have to turn to agencies with higher rates, and they will be worse off than they were before to the extent that they may compete with concerns large enough to be able to use water transportation. Hence it might be argued that the Government has an obligation to see to it that small shippers as well as large enjoy the benefits of waterway improvements, even if it has to provide service at a loss. In any event, the support of the small shipper is necessary if existing waterways are to be maintained and new ones improved.

There can be little doubt that the fight for the continued operation of the Inland Waterways Corporation, as well as the whole question of waterway improvements, is closely tied into the long struggle of the South, and of the Middle West to a lesser extent, for a greater industrialization of these areas. Leaders in the South and Middle West saw in river improvements and cheap water transportation an opportunity to attract industry, and now that they have this transportation they are not going to give any of it up without a struggle. In other words, the barge line question reflects the same issue which led to the charges of railroad freight rate discrimination and the demand for equalization of class rates between the South and the Middle West on the one hand and the East on the other.

Finally, mention should be made of another and broader issue which involves the economy and the interests of the country as a whole. Proponents of continued operation of the Inland Waterways Corporation, and of barge line transportation in general, have repeatedly emphasized the salutary effect of river transportation in forcing a reduction in railroad freight rates in the immediate area of competition and often at points remote from the rivers. But from the point of view of the whole economy this is no proper way to achieve lower freight rates. If railroad freight rates are too high in some parts of the country as compared with others, then public pressure should be brought to bear on the Interstate Commerce Commission, even as has been the case, to bring about an equitable adjustment. Subsidized transportation is a costly, inefficient, and inequitable method of adjusting freight rates.

ST. LAWRENCE SEAWAY AND POWER PROJECT

Nature of project. For many years people in the United States and Canada have been intrigued with the idea of a deep water connection between the Great Lakes and the Atlantic Ocean by way of the St. Lawrence River.

Existing channels now permit ocean boats to navigate the St. Lawrence as far inland as Montreal, but between Montreal and Lake Ontario a 14 foot minimum channel depth limits navigation to shallow draft vessels. On the Great Lakes the 27.6 mile Welland Canal, connecting Lake Ontario and Lake Erie, has a depth of 25 feet. The 88 mile channel between Lake Erie and Lake Huron in the Detroit area also has a 25 foot depth, as has the 63 mile St. Mary's River connection between Lake Huron and Lake Superior.

The proposed St. Lawrence Seaway and Power Project would provide a minimum channel depth of 27 feet from the Atlantic Ocean to Duluth, Minnesota, at the western tip of Lake Superior. The project would require an increase of two feet in the minimum depth of the 180 miles of connecting channels on the Great Lakes, plus the deepening of harbors to accommodate ocean-going vessels. The major problem, however, would come on the 184 mile stretch of the St. Lawrence River between Montreal and Lake Ontario where the controlling depth is now 14 feet. Channel improvement work in this area would include the construction of dams which could be used in part for the generation of large amounts of hydroelectric power. Hence the project involves both navigation and power production.

Legislative history. Attempts to establish a deep water connection between the Great Lakes and the Atlantic by way of the St. Lawrence River date back to 1895 when the United States and Canada appointed a Deep Waterways Commission which subsequently reported favorably on the feasibility of the project. Since that time other commissions and boards of engineers have studied the project, and construction proposals have been before Congress on various occasions. In recent years an active campaign has been waged to secure congressional approval for a seaway to be built jointly by the United States and Canada, but an active campaign also has been waged against the project. Current proposals differ in one major respect from previous proposals in that they provide for the imposition of tolls which, it is claimed, will make the Seaway self-liquidating and self-supporting.

Public power issue. As suggested, sharp differences of opinion exist over the desirability of the St. Lawrence Seaway and Power Project, and one important cause of this conflict of opinions is the fact that the project involves the production of hydroelectric power as well as navigation facilities. While the following discussion is confined to the navigation aspects of the proposal, it is well to keep in mind that the public versus private power issue will play a part in its ultimate approval or rejection.

Divergent points of view. Joined together in supporting the Seaway are the states bordering the Great Lakes, the Great Lakes ports, and various commercial and manufacturing interests in the Great Lakes area. Support also comes from the northern tier of western grain growing and raw material producing states which hope to gain from anticipated lower export freight rates. In addition, there is considerable advocacy of the Seaway as necessary for national defense.

In general, the states on the Atlantic seaboard and in the Gulf coast area are opposed to the project out of fear that its completion would divert export traffic from eastern and Gulf coast ports. Opposition also has been expressed by Mississippi Valley interests because of the possibility of a diversion of export grain and other traffic from the Mississippi River to the Seaway. Similarly, opposition has come from groups and individuals who are anxious to have the Missouri River project completed. The Chicago Association of Commerce and Industry is opposed to the construction of the Seaway. Railroad and Lake carriers have fought the project because of a possible diversion of traffic. Coal operators and miners have opposed it, primarily because of the possibility of producing large quantities of hydroelectric power which might reduce the demand for coal. Numerous individuals and interests opposed to public power production are against the Seaway. Finally, there has been some opposition on the ground that building up Canadian ports at the expense of United States ports, which may result if the Seaway is built, is contrary to the public interest.

An evaluation of a project like the St. Lawrence Seaway involves unusual difficulties because there are few facts available on which conclusions can be based. To make matters worse there are no other waterways in existence which are sufficiently similar to the St. Lawrence project to make comparisons possible. The views of many of the most articulate proponents and opponents of the project are highly colored by self-interest, and it is often difficult to determine which of two diametrically opposed arguments or sets of figures is the more reasonable. This is particularly true of cost studies and traffic surveys. A few studies of the Seaway made by government agencies and other presumably impartial bodies are available, but most of these studies are old and of uncertain value today, and in some cases it is not always clear that they are completely free of bias. An attempt will be made to evelute some of the arguments pro and con, but for the most part the reader will have to draw his own conclusions.

Inadequacy of existing facilities. The difficulties encountered by the railroads in moving freight during and immediately after World War I led to rather widespread support for construction of the Seaway on the ground that the railroad network was inadequate to meet the needs of commerce. During the 1920's, however, the railroads worked out a system of cooperation which made possible large increases in carrying capacity, and the development of alternative means of transportation during the 1930's added tremendously to the transportation facilities of the nation.

In view of the remarkable accomplishments of the railroads in handling freight during World War II and in view of the development of alternative means of transportation, the inadequacy of present railroad facilities is no longer a major issue in the campaign for the Seaway.

Reduced cost of transportation. Until recently the principal argument advanced in favor of the Seaway has been that it would result in a substantial reduction in transportation costs, with special emphasis on benefits to farmers accruing from lower grain rates to Europe. Some of the estimated savings have been unduly optimistic to say the least. For example, a savings of from 5¢ to 8¢ and even 12¢ a bushel has been claimed at times when grain was being shipped via the Great Lakes from Duluth to Montreal and placed in the holds of ocean-going vessels for a total charge of 5½¢. Some saving in transportation charges should result from a through movement, however, and the question becomes one of determining whether or not this saving will offset or more than offset the cost of providing the channel. If the Seaway can be made self-liquidating by the imposition of tolls or user charges as its present advocates claim, then a genuine reduction in transportation costs will result. If it cannot be made self-liquidating, transportation will not be as cheap as is claimed.

Possibility of use of Seaway by ocean-going vessels. Some of the early Seaway studies questioned the willingness of the operators of ocean-going vessels to send their ships into the Great Lakes.[6] Attention was called to the difficulties and delays encountered in navigating large ocean-going vessels in narrow bodies of water, to the problem of what to do with ships regularly plying the St. Lawrence when the river was closed by ice, and to the problem of obtaining cargo in both directions. It has been pointed out, also, that most ocean-going boats would find it impossible or economically impractical to operate on a 27 foot channel. More particularly, this apparently would exclude a large part of the vessels of United States registry from use of the Seaway. In recent years, however, considerable emphasis has been placed on the possibility of using Lake boats to move foreign iron ore up the Seaway and into the Great Lakes, and these boats can navigate a 27 foot channel more economically than ocean-going boats.

Exhaustion of iron ore reserves. World War II and the postwar boom which followed caused a considerable drain on the deposits of high grade iron ore in the Lake Superior region, and it is estimated that they will be exhausted by 1970 or sooner. New sources are being developed in South America and Africa, but the people of the Great Lakes area naturally are

---

[6] See, for example, Harold G. Moulton, Charles S. Morgan, and Adah L. Lee, *The St. Lawrence Navigation and Power Project,* Chapter IV. Washington: The Brookings Institution, 1929.

fearful that if reliance is had on ore from overseas points, the steel industry will move to the Atlantic coast. The large ocean-going oreboats now in use could not navigate the proposed Seaway, but its advocates believe that if it were built, the ore could be transferred to smaller boats at Montreal and moved into the Lakes for substantially less than the cost of moving it by railroad from the Atlantic coast to the interior.

The Seaway movement has received a new lease on life as a result of the discovery of high grade iron ore in Labrador and Quebec in what might prove to be one of the largest and richest deposits in the world. A 350 mile long railroad will move this ore to the Gulf of St. Lawrence and if the Seaway is built, the ore can be moved directly into the Great Lakes by Lake boats. In this connection it should be noted that present traffic via the Great Lakes and the existing 14 foot St. Lawrence River channel is badly unbalanced, with by far the larger portion of the traffic moving down stream. If the Labrador deposits materialize, and if the same boats can be used to move both upbound and downbound traffic, substantial savings in costs should result from the better balance of traffic.

On the other side of the picture attention has been called to the existence of enormous deposits of a low grade ore called taconite in the Lake Superior region. Experiments are being carried on in an effort to find a way to make this ore usable in American blast furnaces, but the processes developed so far are too costly to be practical. Continued experimentation may result in the development of an economical method of utilizing taconite, but the investment required to achieve volume production is so large that fear has been expressed that further development would cease if low cost foreign ores were introduced into the Great Lakes by way of a St. Lawrence Seaway. Hence the United States would become dependent upon foreign sources for iron ore when potential supplies of ore are available, a consideration of major importance in both peace and war.

National defense. At the present time construction of the Seaway is being advocated as being necessary to national defense. For one thing, it is said that it would provide needed additional transportation in time of war. On the other hand, it is said that the service would be too slow to be useful because of the difficulty of navigating vessels of deep draft in restricted channels and locks. Opponents of the Seaway also have argued that the great need for ocean shipping in time of war would make it impractical to navigate the St. Lawrence Seaway with deep-water vessels.

The Seaway is said to be necessary for national defense in order that the steel producing centers in the Great Lakes area can be sure of an adequate supply of iron ore in time of war. If war came immediately, use could be made of existing supplies of ore in the Lake Superior region, and the development of processes for utilizing taconite could be pursued vigorously. If war came later, then the Seaway might prove very valuable in bringing foreign ore into the Great Lakes area. Opponents have argued, as noted previously, that development of the Seaway would tend to discourage further experimentation with taconite. Also, dependence upon foreign ores other than those coming from Labrador would make it absolutely essential for the United States and its allies to control the sea lanes. Attention has been called to the vulnerability of the Seaway to air attack via Arctic air routes. A single bombing attack on the locks and dams in the St. Lawrence or in the Welland Canal could put the Seaway out of commission for months and bottle up large numbers of ships in the Great Lakes.

Finally, it is said that development of the Seaway would make it possible to utilize the shipbuilding facilities and potentialities of the Great Lakes in the construction of war vessels and cargo boats. A substantial number of smaller war vessels were built on the Great Lakes during World War II and a 27 foot channel unquestionably would enable Great Lakes shipyards to build bigger boats. In view of the vulnerability of this whole area to air attack, however, there is some uncertainty over the extent to which it could be used for shipbuilding. Not only would the shipyards themselves be subject to possible attack, but also if the Seaway were put out of commission, completed vessels could not reach the ocean.

Cost. Over the years various estimates of the cost of the St. Lawrence Seaway and Power Project have been made by United States and Canadian engineers. On the basis of 1948 prices the over-all cost has been estimated as $966,763,000, of which $164,197,000 represents the cost of existing improvements which would be utilized as a part of the Seaway. Deducting the cost of existing improvements, the cost of new construction necessary to complete the project comes to $802,566,000.[7] Since this is a combined navigation and power project, it is difficult to determine the cost of the navigation project alone, but as a rough estimate probably something more than half of the total cost can be charged to navigation.

Of the $164 million representing the cost of work already completed, about $133 million represents improvements made by Canada. Canada would pay the cost of new work necessary on that part of the river which lies solely within its borders, while improvements on the section of the river which forms the boundary between the United States and Canada would be met jointly by both Governments, with the United States paying three-quarters of the cost. Of the $802,566,000 necessary to complete the project, the United States would pay $573,463,000.

Estimates of this sort are always open to criticism as being too high or

[7] See statement of Senator Wiley in *Traffic World*, February 18, 1950, p. 54.

too low. It has been pointed out, for example, that nothing is included in them to cover the cost of deepening harbors in the Great Lakes, which would be necessary to maintain a minimum 27 foot navigation depth. Another consideration which cannot be overlooked is the fact that engineering estimates of the cost of improving waterways now completed often have been notorious for their understatement of the actual costs incurred.[8] One recent study places the cost of the improvements, including necessary harbor improvements, at somewhere in the neighborhood of $2,500 million.[9]

Traffic estimates. All sorts of estimates have been made of the volume of traffic which would or might move over the Seaway. After examining a number of such estimates, running all the way from a low of 10 million tons per year to a high of 84 million tons, and after studying sharply conflicting estimates of the capacity of the Seaway, the author of this volume finds himself engulfed by a feeling of complete frustration. There appears to be so much uncertainty over the amount of traffic which would develop that an average of all estimates probably would be no more reliable than the individual estimates themselves.

Tolls. The more recent Seaway proposals call for the imposition of tolls or user charges to make the project self-liquidating. Secretary Sawyer has testified that tolls will bring in from $36,500,000 to $49 million per year, which he concludes will be about double or more than double the amount necessary for maintenance and amortization. Since projects such as the St. Lawrence Seaway commonly have cost a great deal more than the original estimates and since there appears to be little evidence to support the belief that tonnages up to 84 million per year would develop, or could be handled by the proposed Seaway if they did develop, it is simply impossible to draw any conclusions whether the Seaway could or could not be made self-liquidating.

A thirty-foot seaway. Objections made to the Seaway on the ground that a 27 foot channel could not accommodate modern ocean-going vessels, and that the United States would be paying the major part of the cost of providing a channel which could not be used by the ships of its own merchant fleet, were answered by Chairman Fleming of the United States Maritime Commission in the first part of 1950. Chairman Fleming testified

---

[8] In an adverse study of the Seaway the following figures are cited: Chicago Drainage Canal, estimated cost, $16 million, actual cost, $53 million; Suez Canal, estimated cost, $30 million, actual cost, $80 million; Welland Canal, estimated cost, $114 million, actual cost, $128 million; Panama Canal, estimated cost, $160 million, actual cost, $375 million. (B. D. Tallamy and T. M. Sedwick, *The St. Lawrence Seaway Project.* Buffalo: Niagara Frontier Planning Board, 1940, p. 32.)

[9] Chicago Association of Commerce and Industry. Quoted in *Traffic World,* September 8, 1951, p. 18.

that only 10 or 12 per cent of United States merchant vessels could navigate a 27 foot channel if loaded to 100 per cent draft but that almost every type of vessel in this fleet could operate on the Seaway under 75 per cent loads, a load which he considered profitable. At these same hearings Major General Pick, chief of the Army engineers, recommended consideration of the advisability of making provision for increasing the channel depth from 27 to 30 feet, and Chairman Fleming estimated that with such a channel about 80 to 85 per cent of the United States merchant fleet could be accommodated with little or no restrictions.[10] No data are available on what such a channel would cost, the extent to which it would be used by ocean-going boats, or the traffic potentials.

Conclusions. On the basis of such data as are available it seems to be impossible to draw any very definite conclusions with reference to the desirability of the navigation aspects of the St. Lawrence Seaway and Power Project. Excepting for the moment the possible up-river movement of iron ore, existing transportation facilities are fully capable of handling available traffic, and if any sharp increase in traffic is expected, they could be expanded to meet the need at a much lower cost than would be the case with the proposed Seaway. There seems to be some doubt that ocean-going boats would use the Seaway if it were constructed, partly because of channel depth, partly because of other navigation difficulties, and partly for economic reasons. A 30 foot channel might eliminate the first of these difficulties.

There is not much doubt that completion of the Seaway would result in lower freight charges on those commodities which could be moved over it. But this does not mean that there would be an over-all benefit to the nation as a whole because some consideration must be given to the effect of possible traffic diversion on other carriers and because the cost of providing the channel must be offset against the lower freight charges resulting from its use if proposed tolls proved to be inadequate. Where traffic is diverted from existing agencies of transportation, and more especially from the railroads, it may be necessary for them to raise the rates on traffic which cannot use the Seaway, or tax revenues may have to be used to help them, either through direct subsidies or through government operation at a loss. It is easy, however, to overemphasize this contingency because much of the traffic anticipated for the Seaway would be new traffic. If a large upbound movement of iron ore were to develop, it would not hurt the railroads because they do not now handle long haul ore. Some grain and other items of traffic would be lost to the trunk line railroads, and loss of grain traffic might also be important to barge lines operating

[10] *Traffic World,* May 6, 1950, p. 59.

on the Mississippi River system. Some concern has been expressed about the effect of the Seaway on the traffic of existing St. Lawrence River carriers.

Of greater significance is the cost of the proposed Seaway as compared with the saving in freight charges. On the basis of past experience in estimating the cost of projects of such magnitude, there is a real possibility that the cost of the Seaway will greatly exceed present estimates. Estimates of potential traffic, ranging from a low of 10 million tons to a high of 84 million tons, appear to be quite meaningless. There is some reason to believe that the latter figure exceeds the practical capacity of the proposed Seaway unless an enlargement of the Welland Canal is undertaken. Estimates of the amount of revenue which might be derived from tolls are as meaningless as the traffic estimates. Optimistic estimates of toll receipts are useful in obtaining support for the project, but it must be remembered that if the Seaway is built and it does not prove to be self-liquidating, there is no way in which the investment can be recovered. Indeed, it is conceivable that it might not even be self-supporting, let alone self-liquidating, in which event it would be a permanent expense, for it is extremely unlikely that once constructed it would be abandoned simply because it could not pay its way.

The anticipated exhaustion of the Lake Superior iron ore reserves offers a somewhat more tenable basis for construction of the Seaway. Assuming that the Labrador deposits are as rich as they are hoped to be, it is possible that the low cost of shipping ore by water might justify the cost of improving the Seaway, although the savings would have to be substantial in view of the very considerable cost of construction and maintenance which is involved. The national defense aspects of this proposed ore movement are not so clear. Because of the vulnerability of the Seaway and of the whole Great Lakes region to air attack and the possibility of both cutting off the ore supply and bottling up shipping in the Great Lakes, the Seaway could be as much of a liability as an asset to national defense. If the Seaway is built, some consideration certainly should be given to improving the rather extensive railroad facilities which exist from Quebec and Montreal down into the Great Lakes region, and at all costs work should continue on present efforts to find an economical method of utilizing the low grade iron ore deposits in the Lake Superior region.

SUGGESTED READINGS

Note: Much of the information available on the Inland Waterways Corporation and the St. Lawrence Seaway and Power Project is of a propagandistic nature or at least slanted in a particular direction. Numerous pamphlets have been and are being distributed by both proponents and opponents of the Seaway, all of which should be read with caution.

Association of American Railroads, *The Great Delusion*. Washington, 1946. Pamphlet in opposition to St. Lawrence Seaway.

——, *The St. Lawrence Project*. Washington, 1946. Pamphlet in opposition.

Board of Investigation and Research, *Public Aids to Domestic Transportation*, 78th Congress, 1st Session, House Document 159 (1945).

Britton, Lewis W., ed., *Transportation in 1948*. Washington: The Traffic Service Corporation, 1949. Contains some factual information on Inland Waterways Corporation.

——, ed., *Transportation in 1949*. Washington: The Traffic Service Corporation, 1950. Same as the preceding reference.

Department of Commerce, Industry Report, *Domestic Transportation*, August-November, 1947. Very favorable to construction of the St. Lawrence Seaway and Power Project.

Federal Coordinator of Transportation, *Public Aids to Transportation*, Vol. III.

Johnson, Emory R., Grover G. Huebner, and Arnold K. Henry, *Transportation by Water*. New York: D. Appleton-Century Company, 1935. Contains some information on the earlier history of the Inland Waterways Corporation.

Moulton, Harold G., Charles S. Morgan, and Adah L. Lee, *The St. Lawrence Navigation and Power Project*. Washington: The Brookings Institution, 1929. Generally not too favorable.

Tallamy, B. D., and T. M. Sedwick, *The St. Lawrence Seaway Project*. Buffalo: Niagara Frontier Planning Board, 1940. In opposition to the Seaway.

Traffic World. A major source of information on current developments in all forms of transportation.

Part Five

AIR TRANSPORTATION

26.

Development
of
AIR TRANSPORTATION

DEVELOPMENT OF FLYING

General. The possibility of human flight has intrigued mankind since ancient times, the first speculations and experiments antedating the Christian era by several centuries. It was not until the late eighteenth century, however, that the first successful balloon ascension was made by a human being, and it was not until December 17, 1903, at Kitty Hawk, North Carolina, that the Wright Brothers had the honor of making the first successful flight in a self-powered man-carrying airplane. During World War I the aviation industry was born and turned out large numbers of planes. At the same time many pilots were trained and numerous improvements were made in the planes they flew.

In the years immediately following World War I surplus planes were purchased by stunt flyers, and the airplane soon took the place of the balloon ascension at county fairs. Throughout the 1920's and 1930's numerous improvements were made in flying equipment and in training pilots, and one flying record after another was broken. Also during this period commercial air transportation was born, and by the outbreak of World War II it had become an accepted form of long distance mail and passenger transportation. Developments in the field of aviation during World War II were so extensive that it would be impossible even to list them in the space available. Special mention should be made, however, of the remarkable development of electronic devices for taking off, navigating, and landing which have helped in the reduction of early flying hazards.

AIRPORTS

Development. The first flying fields were nothing more than conveniently located flat surfaces from which local flights could be made. After World War I, however, a campaign was pressed to provide airports which would make point-to-point and long distance flying possible. The development of an air-mail service by the Post Office Department also contributed to the construction of airports, and by 1920 mail was being flown coast to coast over a system of municipally-owned airports. Airport construction was seriously affected by the depression which began in 1929, and by 1933 building had all but ceased. In the latter year, however, the Federal Government began to spend considerable sums on airport construction and improvement, at first as part of its work relief program, and up to the end of 1944 it had spent $740,705,171 on civil airport improvements. The Federal Airport Act of 1946 provides for a $1 billion airport improvement program, with $500 million of federal funds to be matched by an equal amount by other governmental jurisdictions. As of June 30, 1950, $142,-597,000 had been appropriated for projects within the continental United States under the provisions of this law. Taxpayers of the United States are said to have an investment of about $1,500 million in civil airports.[1]

Classification of airports. Airports may be classified in various ways. The Civil Aeronautics Administration has classified airports from Class Sub I through Class IX, primarily on the basis of the length of landing strips and runways, with Class Sub I airports having landing strips up to 1,800 feet in length and Class IX airports having landing strips of 9,700 feet or more in length. Modern commercial transport planes use airports of Class III or larger. Airports may also be classified in accordance with the principal use to which they are put, including private flying, fixed base operations of a local nature, scheduled airline service, and facilities for the armed forces. In smaller communities a single field will provide facilities for all users, but in some of the larger cities scheduled airline service has become so heavy that it is necessary to provide separate facilities for different types of activities. Finally, airports may be classified according to their ownership and administration as private airfields, privately-owned commercial airports, municipal airports, and airports owned and operated by various agencies of the Federal Government.

Importance of municipal ownership. There has been a strong trend in the United States toward municipal airport development. All over the United States aviation enthusiasts have been able to convince public officials that an adequate airport is essential to the development of the community, and since almost all airports are money-losing ventures, the only way a municipality can be sure of getting an adequate airport is to construct one itself. Furthermore, federal funds are restricted to public projects, and the only way in which the people of a given community can assure themselves of a share of this federal money is to make airport construction and improvement a public venture.

It is impossible to make any broad generalizations whether or not the

---

[1] Stanley Berge, "Subsidies and Competition as Factors in Air Transport Policy," *Journal of Air Law and Commerce,* Vol. 18, No. 1, Winter, 1951.

intangible benefits accruing to a community from its airport offset the cash losses incurred in construction and operation. In the larger centers of population these benefits are real enough, since direct air-mail service and the rapid transportation of passengers and goods can be used to advantage by a substantial number of people and industries. And it seems reasonable to suppose, also, that the large city without adequate airport facilities will lose business and prestige to rival cities having such facilities. In the smaller communities, and more particularly the large numbers of such communities which do not have, and are not likely to have, regularly scheduled commercial service, the case for spending public funds on airports is not so clear.

Legal aspects. Under the early English common law there evolved the principle that he who owned the soil owned everything above and below, from the heavens to the center of the earth. After flying became common, however, the courts took the realistic view that property owners have the right to exclusive possession of such airspace as they reasonably need or use, and that the use of airspace by airplanes above a reasonable altitude does not constitute an actionable trespass. What constitutes a reasonable altitude will, of course, vary with circumstances.[2] The right to use the airspace does not, of course, release the owner of an airplane from liability for actual property damage caused by his plane as, for example, in the case of a crash or forced landing.[3]

In addition to cases involving the law of trespass there have been a number of complaints that the operation of airports constitutes a nuisance against which property owners should be protected. Such complaints involve such things as fright caused to cattle and people by low flying airplanes, dust and air disturbances from flying fields, noise, searchlights, and the like. In general, the courts have held that the consequences of the ordinary and necessary operations incident to carrying on business at an airport do not constitute a nuisance. If it can be shown that noise and dust are excessive or greater than necessary, however, or if it can be shown that it is possible for planes to operate at higher altitudes, a nuisance does exist, and the courts will order its abatement.[4]

A somewhat different legal problem arises in connection with obstructions or structures on private property near airports which constitute a

---

[2] Leading cases include *Smith* v. *New England Aircraft Company,* 170 N.E. 385 (1930); *Burnham* v. *Beverly Airways, Inc.,* 42 N.E. (2) 575 (1942).

[3] *Rochester Gas & Electric Corp.* v. *Dunlop,* 266 N.Y.S. 469 (1933). For a discussion of the law of trespass see Gerald O. and Lillian G. Dykstra, *The Business Law of Aviation,* Chapter VI. New York: McGraw-Hill Book Company, Inc., 1946.

[4] *Ibid.,* Chapter VII.

flight hazard. Where such structures serve no useful purpose, having been purposely built to constitute a nuisance, the courts have ordered their removal,[5] but they have not required the removal of such necessary structures as power lines existing adjacent to an airport.[6] High structures in an airport area constitute a real problem because large modern planes and newer methods of navigation require a rather long approach at a low level for landing and takeoff operations, and the purchase of all the land necessary to assure a free approach may involve a prohibitive investment. The most common attempt at a solution of this problem is regulation of the use of the land surrounding a large airport, and most states now have airport zoning statutes. Great care must be taken in applying zoning ordinances to specific situations, however, in order to prevent unreasonable infringements on the rights of property owners. It also has been suggested that the right to use airspace at low levels might be purchased from owners of property adjacent to large airports.

AIRWAYS

Civil airways system. In simple terms an airway is a designated path through the air between two airports, usually covering a route over which a substantial volume of traffic moves. A civil airway, which is available for all types of flying, is designated by connecting two points on the earth's surface by a straight line called a center line. The airway consists of the airspace for five miles on either side of the center line, thus giving it a horizontal dimension of ten miles. Vertically the airway extends up to the maximum flying height. Ground markers of various types are located along the route, and on lighted airways the Federal Government maintains rotating beacons at intervals of from ten to fifteen miles. The Government also maintains intermediate landing fields for emergency landings, and frequent information on weather conditions is provided. Numerous air traffic regulations have been established to prevent collisions along the airways and in landings and takeoffs.

In recent years various electronic devices have been developed which enable the pilot of a plane equipped for instrument flying to maintain his course without reliance on ground markers. As these devices are developed it will be possible for more planes to operate safely over heavy traffic lanes and in poor weather. It is probable that with progress along these lines such things as rotating beacons will pass out of existence except at landing fields. Unfortunately, satisfactory electronic systems for airway

---

[5] *Tucker v. Iowa City*, 1936 U. S. Av. R. 10.
[6] *Capital Airways, Inc. v. Indianapolis Power & Light Co.*, 18 N.E. (2) 776 (1939).

and airport traffic control are quite expensive, and they can be provided only at government expense.[7]

COMMERCIAL AIR TRANSPORTATION

Development. Probably the first use of the airplane for commercial transportation arose when some local operator was approached and agreed to carry an individual or a light weight shipment of goods on an emergency flight. Airplanes also were used occasionally for transportation purposes as an advertising device. Out of these early beginnings there has developed a system of commercial air transportation which now links every important population center in the United States, operates to a large extent on regular schedules, and carries passengers, mail, express, and freight as a matter of course.

Concentration of control. There has been a strong tendency for the business to be concentrated in the hands of a few large companies. This in turn has been the result, to no small extent, of the conscious policies of Congress and the federal agencies which at one time or another have been charged with the development of commercial aviation. Although there are numerous airlines in operation today, approximately 80 per cent of the domestic business is carried on by the five largest operators—American Airlines, United Airlines, Eastern Airlines, Transcontinental & Western Air (Trans World), and Northwest Airlines. These lines compete keenly with each other and with other airlines at numerous points, but at many other points they enjoy a monopoly of air transportation service. The present government policy is to permit competition where practical but to prohibit the excesses of unrestrained competition. Government regulation also protects the public at noncompetitive points from undue exploitation.

Scheduled versus nonscheduled operators. Scheduled airline service, as the name implies, is offered over fixed routes, between specified terminals, and in accordance with regularly published schedules. All of the major airlines operate in this way today. All are common carriers, although some charter and contract carrier activities are carried on along with the regular common carrier service. In addition to the scheduled airlines there are numerous companies which provide what is known as a nonscheduled service. Some offer their services over a fixed route between specified termini, but they are not supposed to operate on a fixed schedule, at least insofar as interstate commerce is concerned. Other nonscheduled oper-

---

[7] For a discussion of airway and airport traffic control see John H. Frederick, *Commercial Air Transportation*, 3rd ed., Chicago: Richard D. Irwin, Inc., 1951, pp. 46-55.

ators provide an irregular service, undertaking to serve various points in a given area rather than confining their activities to a fixed route or routes. Nonscheduled operators may offer a common carrier service or they may operate on a contract carrier basis. In some cases a charter service is offered in which exclusive use of a plane is provided.

Certificated and noncertificated carriers. In the Civil Aeronautics Act of 1938, to be discussed, Congress established a comprehensive system of regulating common carriers by air operating in interstate commerce. This act includes, among other things, a requirement that no common carrier by air may engage in interstate air transportation without first obtaining a certificate of public convenience and necessity. However, the regulatory commission created by the act, now known as the Civil Aeronautics Board, initially exempted nonscheduled operators from this and other provisions of the law, an action which has given rise to a distinction between certificated and noncertificated carriers. It has also given rise to the same kind of problems found in surface transportation when unregulated or partially regulated carriers are permitted to compete side by side with fully regulated carriers. This matter is considered further in Chapter 28.

Intrastate carriers. While the great bulk of air commerce is handled by the big interstate carriers, there are a number of smaller companies which operate exclusively in intrastate commerce under the exclusive jurisdiction of state regulatory authorities. Some of these carriers provide a regularly scheduled passenger service, but others operate irregularly as traffic becomes available. None are certificated by the Civil Aeronautics Board, nor can any of them carry mail or otherwise operate in interstate commerce.

Without doubt the best known of the intrastate carriers are those which provide passenger service between Los Angeles and San Francisco and certain other important California points. This service was pioneered by California Central Airlines which began operating between Los Angeles and San Francisco on January 2, 1949, transporting passengers at a rate of about 3¢ a mile. This was slightly less than half the rate then charged by the certificated airlines, but by concentrating its activities along dense traffic routes, California Central made money, and other intrastate operators entered the business. At least one of the certificated airlines complained that the intrastate operators cut corners on safety and that they used poorly trained and low paid help. Intrastate carriers like California Central, however, were given a clean bill of health by both federal and state authorities, and the big operators have been forced to cut their rates to meet this competition.

Classification of carriers by areas served. Domestic airlines may be classified into four groups according to the nature of the areas they serve. The first group is made up of the transcontinental lines which provide a coast-to-coast service, and which include Northwest Airlines, operating over the northern route; United Airlines, operating over the central route; Transcontinental & Western Air, operating a south central route; and American Airlines, operating the southern route. A second group is made up of those carriers operating intersectionally but not on a transcontinental scale. These include Braniff Airways, operating between Chicago and points in the Midwest and Southwest; Chicago and Southern, operating between Chicago and Detroit on the one hand and New Orleans and Houston on the other; Delta Air Lines, operating between Chicago and points in the South and Southwest; Eastern Airlines, operating between various points in the East as far west as Chicago and St. Louis and points in the South and Southwest; Capital Airlines, operating between points in the East and South; National Airlines, operating along the Atlantic and Gulf coasts and serving New York, Florida points, and New Orleans; and Western Airlines, operating between California Pacific coast points and points west of the Rocky Mountains. A third group of lines consists of those operating wholly or largely within a single section of the country. These include Colonial Airlines, operating in the Northeast; Continental Airlines, operating primarily in the Southwest; Mid-Continent Airlines, operating north and south between North Dakota and Louisiana; and Northeast Airlines, operating in New England. (See folded map at rear of book for routes served by these carriers.)

Toward the end of 1951 arrangements were under way which, if approved by the Civil Aeronautics Board, will result in Colonial being taken over by National Airlines. Also contemplated was a merger of Braniff Airways and Mid-Continent Airlines.

The three groups of carriers named above are known collectively as the trunk line carriers, all of them providing a long distance through transportation service as well as transportation over shorter distances. A final group of carriers is composed of smaller lines offering a short haul local or feeder service. Some of these lines carry mail and operate under certificates issued by the Civil Aeronautics Board. Others, like California Central Airlines, operate exclusively in intrastate commerce under the jurisdiction of state bodies.

AIR-MAIL TRANSPORTATION

Development. Experimental movements of mail by air in the United States go back as far as 1911, but it was not until several years later that the Post Office Department was able to get funds to provide a regular air-mail service. The first regular air-mail route was put in operation between

New York and Washington in 1918 under the joint sponsorship of the Post Office Department and the War Department. In a few months, however, the Post Office Department assumed entire responsibility and subsequently developed a transcontinental air-mail route. The Post Office Department pioneered in developing planes especially designed for carrying mail, in obtaining adequate weather information, in developing the necessary ground service and facilities, and in night flying. It had never been intended that the Post Office Department would fly the mail as a permanent venture, however, and by 1925 the service had developed to the point where it could be turned over to private enterprise. In 1926 several new air-mail routes were established under contract arrangements with commercial carriers and in 1927 the Post Office Department withdrew from the field entirely. Since that time the air-mail service has expanded all over the United States, with several hundred cities having direct mail service and thousands having a combination of air and surface carrier service.

Air-mail contracts. Initially the arrangements with commercial carriers were made under the terms of the Contract Air Mail Act of 1925, which provided for awarding mail transportation contracts on the basis of competitive bidding. In 1930, however, the Postmaster General successfully eliminated competitive bidding by the use of techniques of questionable propriety, and as a result the mail contracts were granted to a few selected carriers. The Postmaster General had been instructed by Congress to aid in the unification of a large number of airlines, and this appears to have been his intent in eliminating competitive bidding. All of these contracts were canceled in 1934 on the ground of collusion, and the Army was directed to fly the mail until other arrangements could be made. The Air Mail Act of 1934 provided for new contracts on the basis of competitive bidding, but in 1938 this system was abandoned in favor of the present arrangement under which airlines with mail rights advise the Post Office Department what points they wish to serve and what schedules they propose to fly. Once the schedules are established the Department may send the mail by any scheduled plane.

Payment for carrying mail. Under the Contract Air Mail Act of 1925 the carriers were to receive not more than 80 per cent of the air-mail postage on the mail they carried, but this was changed in 1926 to provide a maximum rate of compensation of $3.00 per pound for the first 1,000 miles and 30¢ per pound for each additional 100 miles or fraction thereof. In 1930 the Watres Act again changed the method of compensation, this time in such a way as to help the weaker lines and to encourage the development of air passenger transportation. Payments were made on the basis of so much per space-mile regardless of whether the space was utilized or not, and under the formulas employed space-mile compensation increased with the passenger carrying capacity of the planes employed. The Air Mail Act of 1934 provided for competitive bidding on the basis of so much per airplane mile, with subsequent adjustments in rates to be made by the Interstate Commerce Commission. Under this provision carriers made ridiculously low bids in order to get air-mail contracts, expecting that later the Commission would revise the rates upward to a compensatory level. In one case a bid of zero cents was made. Under the Civil Aeronautics Act of 1938, the Civil Aeronautics Board was directed to fix the amount of compensation for carrying mail at an amount sufficient, together with all other sources of revenue, to enable the air carriers to operate, in effect, at a profit. The effect of this provision was to use the air-mail payments to subsidize airline operations.

Growth. Satisfactory figures on the growth of the volume of air mail in terms of ton miles are not available prior to 1934, but the figures from 1934 on are shown in Table XXVIII. The postwar decline in traffic was to be expected, but the figures show a steady increase from the postwar low.

Table XXVIII

MAIL TON MILES HANDLED BY DOMESTIC SCHEDULED AIRLINES [8]

Year	Ton Miles	Year	Ton Miles
1934	2,237,175	1943	36,061,868
1935	4,132,708	1944	51,139,973
1936	5,741,436	1945	65,092,921
1937	6,698,230	1946	32,953,307
1938	7,449,246	1947	33,086,175
1939	8,610,726	1948	37,509,922
1940	10,117,858	1949	40,874,188
1941	13,118,015	1950	46,314,753
1942	21,162,102		

Whether or not there will be any very substantial increase in the volume of air-mail traffic in the future will depend primarily upon two things—the expansion of feeder lines to provide air-mail service to smaller communities, and a reduction in postage rates. A system of feeder lines has been developed in certain parts of the country in recent years, but it is at least an open question whether the benefits derived will justify the subsidies necessary to make such operations worth while.

[8] Figures for 1934-47 inclusive from Civil Aeronautics Administration, *Statistical Handbook of Civil Aviation*, 1948, p. 71. The 1934 figure does not include 224,236 ton miles flown by the Army. Figures for 1945-47 do not include mail carried under special contract or foreign mail. Figures for 1948-50 from Air Transport Association of America, *Air Transport Facts and Figures*, 1951, p. 4.

DEVELOPMENT OF AIR TRANSPORTATION

It has been proposed from time to time that all first class mail be moved by air at first class postage rates. If adopted, this proposal would result in an enormous increase in the volume of mail moved by the airlines, but whether the advantages of such a service would outweigh its cost is another matter. In 1946, for example, the Government paid the airlines $26,788,000 for moving 23,509,000 pounds of mail, while in the same year the railroads received $22,106,000 for handling 396,426,000 pounds of nonlocal first class mail, this latter figure not including franked and penalty mail on which the Post Office Department derives no revenue. The payment made to the railroads included rental for use of post office cars in which mail is sorted en route, a type of service not provided by the airlines.[9]

It should be pointed out that the average haul on nonlocal first class mail is considerably less than the average haul for air mail, being somewhere in the neighborhood of 500 miles as compared with 1,400 miles for air mail. Also, since 1946 there have been substantial increases in railroad mail pay, although these increases have been offset in part by a shift to highway transportation of mail on shorter hauls. But even when these factors are taken into consideration there still is a very wide difference in cost. In addition, it would be necessary to continue to handle the large volume of other than first class mail by ground carriers, and it is unlikely that there would be a proportionate reduction in the cost of this service with the elimination of first class mail. Furthermore, the present useful method of sorting mail en route in post office cars would have to be abandoned with an attendant increase in post office sorting costs and possible delay. Finally, the movement of all first class mail by air would require an expensive expansion of airports and airport mail-handling facilities.

It is doubtful that the movement of all first class mail by air would be of any great benefit to the general public. On first class mail moving relatively short distances there would be no advantage at all. Indeed, it is difficult to see how the airlines could even handle this traffic. For longer movements speed of delivery would be increased considerably, and the extension of direct air-mail service to small communities would be of some benefit. But judging by the enormous volume of first class mail as compared with air mail, even between points which have direct air-mail service, it would appear that in most cases there is no great demand for an expedited service. The conclusion seems to be inescapable that the movement of all first class mail by air would be of primary benefit only to the airlines and the aviation industry.

---

[9] Association of American Railroads, *Air Transportation*, Washington, 1947, pp. 57-58. Source of data given as Post Office Department cost ascertainment reports.

DEVELOPMENT OF AIR TRANSPORTATION

AIR PASSENGER TRANSPORTATION

Development. Prior to 1926 there was no regularly scheduled air passenger transportation service in the United States. Passage of the Contract Air Mail Act of 1925, however, provided a backlog of revenue which made it possible for the air-mail carriers to offer a passenger service, and the formulas used in determining air-mail pay under the Watres Act provided something of an incentive for the companies to operate planes of larger seating capacities. Finally, the method of air-mail compensation prescribed in the Civil Aeronautics Act of 1938, which had the effect of underwriting operating losses, encouraged the development of air passenger transportation in areas and over routes which would not otherwise have been able to support a passenger service. The remarkable growth of air passenger transportation is shown in Table I on pages 21-22.

Factors influencing growth of air passenger transportation. There can be little doubt that government policy has played an important part in the development of air passenger transportation. In addition to the financial encouragement contributed by the Post Office Department, municipalities have provided airports, and the Federal Government has provided airways and has promoted air transportation in various other ways. All of these things have made it possible for the airlines to offer an attractive service at rates which are lower than would otherwise be the case. But while subsidies are important, they do not alone account for the phenomenal increase in travel by air, and some consideration of other significant growth factors is in order.

Managerial initiative. Until the rapid rise of highway passenger transportation had cut sharply into railroad passenger traffic, railroad management had not been noted for its energy in improving passenger accommodations and service. While this situation has changed considerably in recent years, there are those who believe that imagination still is needed in tackling the railroad passenger decline. By contrast, airline management has been most active in developing and promoting travel by air. Many airlines have sought to develop good will by prohibiting employees from accepting tips, providing free meals, free writing materials, and even decks of cards for passengers in flight. Continuous improvements are made in the equipment utilized, innovations such as reduced rates for family travel are tried out, and big city travel bureaus are paid commissions for selling air transportation to their clients.

The fact that the airlines have been more energetic than the railroads in promoting passenger traffic, at least until recently, may be attributed to a combination of circumstances. For one thing, air transportation is a new type of service, and as such it has probably attracted individuals into managerial ranks who have the pioneer spirit and the will to try new things. Again, because it is a new type of transportation, airline management and airline employees are not handicapped by the heavy hand of tradition. Then, too, airline management from the beginning has had to battle to get travelers away from existing forms of transportation. At the outset it was handicapped by public fear of air travel, by last minute flight cancellations resulting from bad weather, and by a high level of rates. But these and other handicaps only sharpened the determination of airline management to overcome them. In this connection, too, it is worth noting that the airlines until recently had nothing to sell directly to the public except passenger transportation, whereas the railroads sold both passenger and freight transportation, principally the latter. Hence energetic solicitation of passenger traffic was immediately more important to the airlines than it was to the railroads.

Separate mention must be made of one other factor which has been of help to airline management, and that is governmental policy. The Government has actively promoted the development of air transportation by providing airways and airports, by granting profitable mail contracts, by promoting the use of air mail, and by various other devices and policies. There can be little doubt that this promotional policy, quite irrespective of its merits, has proved discouraging to railroad management. Indeed, in some respects it would seem that government policy tends to discourage rather than encourage the further development of railroad transportation.

Extraneous events. Although commercial air transportation enjoyed a steady growth in the United States before World War II, its real development came during and after the war years. During the war, time was of the essence, and many businessmen and government officials were introduced for the first time to the advantages of air travel. There can be little doubt that these wartime travel experiences contributed importantly to the growth of commercial air transportation. At the same time hundreds of thousands of young men and women who had had little or no previous contact with commercial transportation of any kind were closely associated with aviation during the war. To them, flying became a commonplace, and in this way there was created a large and entirely new potential source of business for the commercial airlines.

Characteristics of air passenger transportation. While government policy, managerial efficiency, and extraneous events have had an important effect on the development of air passenger transportation, in the long run the success of any form of transportation depends upon the public demand for the type of service it has to offer. With this in mind an attempt may be made to assess the future of air passenger transportation by giving some consideration to the factors which influence the individual traveler in his choice of transportation. Among the more important of these are speed, economy, safety, comfort, dependability, frequency of service, and scope of service. No one means of transportation enjoys superiority in all of these characteristics, which means that each prospective traveler must strike a balance between them in deciding how he will travel. Obviously, the weight given to each of these characteristics will differ with individuals and with circumstances.

Speed. Because modern commercial passenger planes maintain cruising speeds of about 300 miles per hour, make few stops, and fly in straight lines, passenger transportation by air has an overwhelming advantage whenever speed is the primary consideration. There are, however, two minor qualifications to this statement. For short trips surface transportation may be faster than air transportation because of time lost going to and from airports remote from business districts. Also, wherever overnight Pullman service between two cities is available, the railroad may have an advantage since by traveling as he sleeps the traveler loses no time at all. No doubt the bulk of travel by air today is traceable to the speed factor, but the airlines cannot rely on speed alone to bring about any considerable increase in air travel, unless it be assumed that people in general will be in a bigger hurry in the future than they are today. The speed advantage of the airplane, however, *along with other considerations,* can and no doubt will, contribute to a substantial increase in air travel.

While railroads have been successful in speeding up the schedules of their through trains they cannot hope to meet airline speeds. In 1951, for example, a commercial jet plane was operated by the British across the North Atlantic at speeds in excess of 600 miles per hour.

Economy. In general, airline passenger fares are about the same as first class railroad fares, including Pullman accommodations, especially where competition is keen. Reductions are made in both types of service for round trips and for carrying children under twelve years of age. Mention may be made, too, of the free meals and no tipping policy which reduces somewhat the comparative cost of air travel. Hence it would appear that in this sphere the airlines are directly competitive with the railroads.

For the economy minded, however, the situation is different. Railroad coach fares, varying from 2.5¢ to about 3.375¢ per mile, are substantially lower than airline fares, which averaged 5.72¢ per mile in 1950. In a few cases airlines have sought to invade this field by cutting out free meals and other frills and offering an air coach service at fares somewhat comparable with those charged by the railroads. Of necessity air coach service has been confined to heavily traveled routes because maximum loading is essential to its success. Obviously great care must be taken to prevent air coach accommodations from siphoning off standard airline traffic. Generally speaking it does not appear that the airlines, except on a limited number of routes, can attract any appreciable amount of the rail coach traffic. One point in this connection which does not seem to have attracted much attention is the fact that much of the growth in air passenger travel has taken place during a period characterized by economic prosperity and relatively high individual incomes for a large number of people. Should this situation be reversed the wide difference between standard airline and rail coach fares might become a serious matter for the airlines.

Safety. Although fear of death in an airplane crash is not as important as formerly, there probably are still a great many people who are afraid to travel by air. In this connection it will be useful to compare the relative safety records of different modes of transportation. Table XXIX shows a

Table XXIX

REVENUE PASSENGER FATALITIES PER 100,000,000 REVENUE PASSENGER MILES TRAVELED [10]

Year	Passenger Cars and Taxicabs	Domestic Commercial Airlines	Bus Lines	Railroads
1941	4.0	2.32	.24	.14
1942	2.7	3.66	.23	.20
1943	2.7	1.32	.22	.30
1944	2.9	2.09	.22	.26
1945	2.9	2.14	.17	.16
1946	2.5	1.20	.19	.18
1947	2.3	3.21	.21	.16
1948	2.1	1.3	.18	.13
1949	2.0	1.3	.20	.09
1950		1.2		.56

wide difference between the safety record of passenger cars and airlines, on the one hand, and bus lines and railroads on the other. Passenger automobiles, including taxicabs, show the worst record, except for the years 1942 and 1947 when the domestic commercial airlines topped the list. The best record is that of the railroads, except for the years 1943 and 1944 when the bus lines had a slightly lower death rate.

An interesting fact about the airline figures is the extent to which they fluctuate from year to year.[11] This is probably due to the fact that when

---

[10] Air Transport Association of America, *Air Transport Facts and Figures*, 1951, p. 8. 1950 figures are estimated.

[11] The airline safety record shown above is much better than the record for the 1930's. The ratios for the 1930's show the same rather marked fluctuations, varying from a high of 28.57 to a low of 1.20.

an airplane crashes practically everyone aboard is killed, thus bringing about a close correlation between the number of crashes and the number of passengers killed. This is not nearly so true in the case of surface transportation wrecks. In many railroad wrecks, for example, the only casualties are among the members of the train crews. In wrecks where passenger fatalities do occur there are often more people hurt than killed, and generally most of the passengers are not hurt at all.

As far as the future of air passenger transportation is concerned the figures given in Table XXIX are not as important as is the use to which they may be put. The railroads, for example, can publicize the fact that in 1949 air passengers took 19 times the risk of getting killed as did railroad passengers, which is true. At the same time, however, it can be argued that a record of 1.3 fatalities per 100 million passenger miles flown indicates that air transportation is a pretty safe way to travel, and that there is less chance of getting killed in a commercial transport plane than there is of getting killed in an automobile, all of which also is true. The airlines are at some disadvantage because of the extensive newspaper publicity which accompanies airplane accidents. Furthermore, because of the extent to which prominent people travel by air, there is a greater likelihood of the death of some widely known person with attendant unfavorable publicity. The airlines and the Government are working continuously to improve flying safety, but it probably will be a long time before fear is completely eliminated.

Comfort. Since space in an airliner is at a premium, the airlines cannot allow too much space per passenger, whereas the railroads can and are providing more and more spacious accommodations. On the other hand, travel time by air is so much shorter than by rail that this probably is not a factor of any consequence.

Dependability. All carriers offering regularly scheduled services seek to maintain their schedules as nearly as possible. All realize the irritations caused by long delays in departure and the even greater irritations and ill will caused by missed connections, failures to meet appointments, and the like. The problem of delay is particularly important to the airlines because of the great emphasis they place on fast service. In addition, the airlines have the further problem of flight cancellations caused by adverse weather conditions. If the cancellation comes too late for a reservation holder to make other arrangements for transportation, he is caused an unreasonable and perhaps expensive delay. Airline managements realize the ill will caused by flight cancellations, and with better weather information available, efforts are made to inform reservation holders of the status of a given flight in time to enable them to make other arrangements. Nevertheless, the canceled flight still remains a problem, especially during the winter months.

Frequency of service. By nature the railroad is a producer of mass transportation, and it can operate economically in the passenger field only to the extent that it can depend upon a large number of passengers per train. This means that a railroad cannot afford to offer service at frequent intervals except between a limited number of points where a large volume of traffic exists. Airlines, on the other hand, can offer more frequent service if traffic is available because of the limited carrying capacity of the airplane. The airlines tend to concentrate their activities between points where a considerable volume of traffic exists, however, and since these are the same points where railroad service is best, frequency of service probably is not as much of an advantage as it might appear to be.

Scope of service. As suggested above, commercial airlines tend to limit their services to the larger cities, making few stops en route, and this means that for the people of thousands of communities air passenger transportation is of limited utility. In recent years considerable interest has been shown in the development of feeder airlines to offer service at points intermediate between major trunk line stops and at points off the major airline routes. A number of such lines using small planes have been established, and if they can be operated generally and without too much reliance on air-mail subsidy, they will be of real benefit to the public. The major airlines will benefit, too, from the increased traffic resulting from interchanges with feeder lines.

Highway travel as a potential source of airline traffic. In the preceding discussion of the factors entering into the determination of the choice of a means of transportation, primary consideration was given to the relative merits of air and rail transportation. Obviously the airlines are not competitive with highway vehicles for short hauls. To what extent can they expect to attract any of the long distance passenger traffic now moving by highway? There does not seem to be any possibility of attracting any long distance bus traffic because they could not even remotely approach the low fares which are about the only reason why people travel long distances by bus. They have, however, attracted some traffic which formerly moved over the highways in private automobiles. Salesmen, government employees, and the like, who formerly traveled from point to point in their own cars, are finding increasing use for airline service as a means of conserving their time. Some salesmen operate automobiles in areas where stopping points are close together or where airline service is unavailable, but fly to and from more distant points. Mention may be made, too, of plane-auto service, providing automobiles for the use of airline patrons at various destination points.

DEVELOPMENT OF AIR TRANSPORTATION

Development. The American Railway Express Company made an experimental shipment of express by air in the winter of 1919, using a four-engine bombing plane for the purpose, but the plane was damaged en route and the experiment discontinued. The establishment of commercial airlines operating on regular schedules stimulated the company to re-enter the field, and it contracted with four major airlines to transport express by air. These contracts, which were later extended to other airlines, provided that the express company would solicit the business and perform a pickup and delivery service. In 1929 the railroads took over the assets of the American Railway Express Company, and thereafter its air express activities were carried on by the railroad-owned Railway Express Agency. A number of independent air express operations were undertaken at one time or another by various airlines, but none were successful. In 1932 seven major airlines organized General Air Express to offer an independent service, but it was unsatisfactory, and by 1937 all had returned to the Railway Express Agency. One difficulty with General Air Express was that it could offer service only at major population points. Also, its ground handling facilities were inferior and more costly than those of the Railway Express Agency.

Railway Express Agency interest in air express. There has been a good deal of argument pro and con about the desirability of the somewhat anomalous situation brought about by the fact that solicitation and at least partial control of the air express business is in the hands of an agency of the railroads. It is claimed by some that this arrangement tends to stifle the development of air express because the Railway Express Agency will be more interested in developing rail express than air express. On the other hand, the Railway Express Agency offers at least a partial air express service at every city and town in the United States and in this way originates some air express traffic which an independent air express service could not get. Furthermore, it is in a position to forward air express shipments by rail in the event of a flight cancellation, a service which can be of decided advantage. Finally, the Railway Express Agency has at its disposal an extensive pickup and delivery system which can be utilized for handling air express at very little additional cost. Apparently the airlines have concluded that the advantages of utilizing the Railway Express Agency outweigh its possible disadvantages.

For a number of years the relationships between the Railway Express Agency and the various airlines were governed by contracts which included, among other things, an agreement on the part of the airlines to accept express business only from the Railway Express Agency, an agreement by the Railway Express Agency to deal only with the contracting airlines, and an agreement that air express rates were not to be reduced to less than twice the railroad express rates except with the approval of the Railway Express Agency. In principle this last provision was objectionable, but in practice it was of no importance because the airlines themselves held air express rates at more than twice the rail level. In 1943, after an investigation by the Civil Aeronautics Board, new contracts were adopted eliminating all three of the above provisions. Under the new arrangement the Railway Express Agency deducts the expenses it incurs in soliciting and handling air express from gross air express revenues, and the balance is divided 87½ per cent to the airlines and 12½ per cent to the Railway Express Agency.

Air express traffic. One of the most important items of air express traffic consists of machinery and machine parts. When a machine breaks down and the necessary repair parts are not available locally, they can be obtained quickly by means of air express. Similarly, a rush order or sudden increase in demand may necessitate the prompt acquisition of a new machine or machines, and this can be accomplished by utilizing air express. Other important items of traffic moved by air express include style goods, particularly women's clothing; printed matter, including newspapers and advertising material; legal documents, securities, and the like; newspaper electrotypes; moving picture films; cut flowers; drugs; jewelry; and various other items. In general, it may be said that air express falls into three groups: emergency shipments, goods of high value in relation to bulk, and perishables which can stand a high transportation charge.

Ton-mile figures showing the growth of air express and air cargo traffic are given in Table XXX. Separate figures are not available before 1946, but the scheduled airlines handled very little goods traffic except by air express before the end of World War II. The figures show a steady growth before the war, and then a sharp increase during the war years. The continued increase after the war probably reflects in part a continued high level of business activity, in part an increasing recognition of the value of air express service, and in part the effect of rate reductions instituted during the war and immediate postwar period.

Future. The future growth of the air express service is difficult to forecast. Between many important express points the railroad express service is fast enough for most business purposes and much cheaper. Of course, on long hauls air express has a very real advantage over surface carriers, but on these longer hauls the new and rapidly growing air cargo service can offer a service almost as good as air express and at considerably lower rates.

DEVELOPMENT OF AIR TRANSPORTATION

Table XXX

EXPRESS AND FREIGHT TON MILES FLOWN BY DOMESTIC SCHEDULED AIRLINES [12]

Year	Express and Freight	Express	Freight
1935	1,097,602		
1936	1,865,798		
1937	2,162,488		
1938	2,182,420		
1939	2,713,099		
1940	3,476,224		
1941	5,258,551		
1942	11,901,793		
1943	15,139,359		
1944	16,991,598		
1945	22,196,852		
1946		23,788,392	14,822,325
1947		28,766,659	35,911,554
1948		29,768,883	70,437,811
1949		27,329,361	94,189,591
1950		36,629,167	113,809,786

AIR CARGO

Nature of air cargo service. Air cargo, or air freight as it is sometimes called, may be distinguished from air express in several ways. In the first place, the service is rendered directly by the airline itself. Second, shipments moving by air cargo do not always receive the expedited service available by air express. Where air cargo is moved by ordinary transport planes, mail, express, and passenger traffic have priority in the allocation of available space, and where shipments are made in separate cargo planes, freight may be accumulated until sufficient tonnage is available to justify the flight. Third, larger shipments are accepted as air cargo than are accepted by the air express service. Fourth, minimum weights per shipment are higher. And last and probably most important, the rates charged for air cargo service are substantially below air express rates.[13]

Development. The first serious step toward developing a scheduled commercial air cargo service in the United States was taken in 1941 and 1942 when all but one of the major airlines joined together in sponsoring Air Cargo, Inc., which conducted an extensive survey and study of the

---

[12] Civil Aeronautics Administration, *Statistical Handbook of Civil Aviation,* 1948, p. 71 for data before 1948. Figures for 1948-50 from Air Transport Association of America, *Air Transport Facts and Figures,* 1951, p. 4.

[13] Air cargo rates vary roughly from 14¢ to 20¢ and higher per ton mile as compared with air express rates which will average roughly 60¢ per ton mile.

possibilities of developing a regular air cargo service. In October 1944, American Airlines established an air cargo service, but lack of equipment and other wartime handicaps made it of somewhat limited value. After the war, other major airlines went into the air cargo business, although they did not push the service vigorously at first.

The real boost to air cargo transportation came as a result of the experiences of the armed forces with cargo shipments during World War II. The armed forces were, of course, concerned primarily with the rapid movement of war cargo, and their experiences provided no criterion on the profitability of commercial operations, but they did demonstrate that a wide variety of goods could be handled by air over long distances at high rates of speed. The end of the war brought demobilization of thousands of young men with aviation experience and a war-born love for flying, and many saw an opportunity to earn a living by purchasing surplus military planes and going into the air cargo business. As in the case of the early activities in the field of motor truck transportation, some of these new enterprisers knew nothing of business methods, cut rates to the bone, failed to allow for depreciation, cut corners on safety, and ended up in the business graveyard. A number, however, survived and their businesses have grown to respectable proportions. As might be expected this development stimulated the regularly scheduled airlines to renewed activity in the field, and they are now engaging increasingly in air cargo transportation.

Air cargo traffic. The kinds of goods moving by air cargo are essentially the same as those moving by air express except that air cargo handles goods of greater bulk and lower value. Documents, securities, and the like, still go by air express. To some extent goods now moving as air cargo would otherwise move by air or rail express, but there also is a substantial volume of air cargo which represents entirely new traffic. Such traffic includes flowers, certain fruits and vegetables, seafoods, and other perishables which cannot by their nature be shipped long distances by surface transportation or which cannot be sold at destination at prices sufficient to cover air express charges. Satisfactory data on the growth and present volume of air cargo traffic are not available, the figures in Table XXX showing only the traffic handled by the scheduled airlines. These figures, however, indicated pretty clearly that the volume of goods moving by air cargo is increasing rapidly.

All sorts of forecasts have been made of the future of air cargo transportation. There are some who believe that the air cargo service will in time cut into the higher grades of traffic now moving by railroad and motor carrier, and some who believe that it will eventually take over even the lower grades of freight. Such beliefs would seem to be unduly optimistic, and it should be said that those in charge of air cargo operations do not seem to be thinking in such terms. Only a small fraction of the total volume of freight traffic needs to move at aircraft speeds, and low freight rates are far more important than speed as far as the great bulk of freight is concerned. Even in the case of high grade railroad freight there would have to be a considerable reduction in air cargo rates before much of it could be diverted to air carriers.[14] Furthermore, any substantial diversion of surface traffic to the air would require a very large investment in land for airport and terminal facilities, an investment which would, in terms of units of traffic handled, be out of all proportion to the investment required by surface carriers for terminal facilities. This need for greatly expanded airport facilities to handle an expanded volume of air cargo, and the possible effect of acquiring and maintaining these facilities on air cargo costs, seems to have been overlooked by many writers on the subject.

All of this is not to say that there is no future in air cargo transportation. On the contrary, the service fills a real need, and the volume of traffic should grow steadily. In all probability there is an air cargo potential of substantial size which has not been exploited simply because shippers are not aware that they can make advantageous use of an air cargo service. No doubt much of this potential can be developed through advertising and energetic traffic solicitation. Expansion of air cargo transportation to serve more points, either directly or by means of joint rates with surface carriers, will generate additional traffic. If a sufficient volume of traffic can be developed to justify the operation of specialized cargo planes operating on frequent schedules, the lower air cargo rates will undoubtedly attract traffic now moving by air express. If operating costs can be reduced sufficiently, it should be possible to divert additional traffic from the railway express and parcel post services. And unless the railroads can further speed up the movement of less-than-carload freight, the higher grades of this freight may be diverted to the airlines.

PUBLIC AID

Nature of public aid. The public aid granted to commercial air carriers is similar in nature to that granted to inland waterway transportation. The civil airways system is provided in its entirety by the Federal Government without cost to the users. Airports are usually provided by municipalities, with financial assistance from the Federal Government, and commercial users pay only a fraction of their share of the full cost of construction and

---

[14] Railroad less-than-carload and motor carrier freight rates will average somewhere in the neighborhood of 5¢ per ton mile and over-all railroad freight rates something more than 1¢ per ton mile. These figures compare with air cargo rates running approximately from 14¢ to 20¢ and more per ton mile.

maintenance. In addition, the Government subsidizes, or stands ready to subsidize, the operations of the certificated airlines. The Federal Government provides various other aids to commercial air transportation, but they are minor compared with those mentioned above.

Extent of public aid. No recent study of the extent of public aid to commercial air transportation is available, the latest being that made by the Board of Investigation and Research as of 1940. The Board concluded that public aid to domestic scheduled airlines for 1940 amounted to $22,528,248, made up of $4,272,467 as a fair share of airway costs, $3,780,111 as the excess of airport costs over payments, and $14,475,670 as air-mail subsidy.[15] These figures are, of course, very much out of date and of little practical value today. Since 1940, the Federal Government has embarked on a $1 billion airport expansion program, and large sums have been spent in other ways in aid of air transportation. On the other hand, air-mail payments per unit of traffic handled have been reduced substantially since 1940, at least for the major airlines, and the great expansion of air traffic in recent years suggests that if figures were available, they would show a decline in the amount of public aid per unit of traffic handled. In the absence of a current over-all study, a brief consideration of recent developments in each of the major areas of public aid mentioned above may be instructive.

Airways. The Board of Investigation and Research found the total cost of domestic airways to be $111,881,934, for the period 1925 to 1941. It felt that 31.1 per cent of this amount was chargeable to domestic scheduled airlines, 36.8 per cent to governmental functions, and 32.1 per cent to other flying. Expenditures on airways during World War II and during the postwar years have been very large, making total federal airway expenditures through 1949 of $478 million, with additional expenditures of $100 million estimated for 1950 and $136 million for fiscal 1951.[16] In addition, a system of electronic aids has been proposed which, if approved, is estimated to cost $1,113 million. The Civil Aeronautics Administration has proposed a 1½¢ tax on high octane gasoline beginning in 1953 as a step toward making the airway system self-supporting.

Airports. The Board of Investigation and Research placed the total capital expenditures on publicly-owned airports at the end of 1940 at $352 million, of which amount more than $270 million was spent on airports used by domestic scheduled airlines. The annual airport cost was placed at $124,217,996, of which $27,445,225 was charged to the airlines. From

---

[15] Board of Investigation and Research, *Public Aids to Domestic Transportation,* pp. 78-80.

[16] Burton N. Behling, "Subsidies to Transportation," Library of Congress, Legislative Reference Service, *Public Affairs Bulletin, No. 86,* August, 1950, pp. 42-43.

this figure the sum of $5,102,819 was deducted to cover payments made by the airlines for use of airport facilities, leaving a net airport subsidy of $22,342,406. Or, in other words, airline payments equalled 18 per cent of their share of airport costs.

In 1946 Harvard University published a study of the financing of terminal airports, the type of airport at which commercial airline activities tend to be concentrated. The capital investment represented by these airports was estimated to be approximately $775 million and full annual cost of operation, including interest on investment, was placed at $58 million. It was also estimated that within ten years from 1945 the investment in this type of airport might equal $2 billion and annual costs reach $190 million.[17] The study showed that revenues derived from all aviation users, including private flyers and fixed base operators as well as scheduled and non-scheduled commercial lines, varied widely from airport to airport. The principal factor in assessing user charges seems to be that of bargaining power, with cities which were anxious to obtain service offering extremely favorable terms, while strategically located cities were able to assess somewhat higher user charges. Disregarding extremes, the study reached the conclusion that at representative intermediate and limited stop airports, aviation user payments equalled 7/10 per cent on the investment and at major terminals, 1 per cent.[18] Since these figures are for all aviation users, it will be seen that the commercial airlines' contribution toward the cost of supplying airport facilities was extremely modest.

Air mail. For many years the cost to the Post Office Department of providing an air-mail service, including ground handling costs as well as payments to carriers, exceeded air-mail postage revenues. Indeed, payments made to the carriers, alone, exceeded postal revenues throughout most of the period up to 1941. More recently air-mail postal revenues have exceeded payments made to carriers by substantial amounts, and during the war years, 1943-46 inclusive, postal revenues were in excess of total costs.[19] The difference between air-mail postage revenue and the payments made to mail carriers has been used at times as a measure of the amount of air-mail subsidy or as a measure of the amount of Post Office Department "profit" on air mail. But neither of these calculations has any meaning since no consideration is given to the costs incurred by the carriers in

[17] Lynn L. Bollinger, Alan Passen, and Robert E. McElfresh, *Terminal Airport Financing & Management.* Boston: Division of Research, Graduate School of Business Administration, Harvard University, 1946, pp. 168-169.

[18] *Ibid.*, pp. 139-140.

[19] Detailed figures for the years 1918-47, inclusive, are given in Civil Aeronautics Administration, *Statistical Handbook of Civil Aviation*, 1948, p. 80.

rendering the service. Only by comparing the payments made to carriers with the cost of providing the transportation service under honest, economical, and efficient management can the degree of subsidy, if any, be determined.

Since 1938, however, the provision of air-mail payments based on the need of a carrier as well as on cost of service has resulted in a definite subsidization of scheduled airline operations. While some of the larger lines have been able to operate at times without subsidy, others never have been able to do so. This is especially true of the smaller lines providing a so-called local or feeder service. According to one study trunk line mail payments contained 57.6 per cent subsidy in 1948, and the $9,501,953 paid to feeder lines in that year represented 96 per cent subsidy.[20] In 1951 the Civil Aeronautics Board estimated that of mail payments of $457 million made since the passage of the Civil Aeronautics Act of 1938, $270 million represented subsidy—approximately 57 per cent of the total.

Justification of public aid. The preceding discussion of the extent of public aid to commercial air transportation, while admittedly inadequate, is sufficient to indicate that public aid has been and still is an important factor in the success of commercial air transportation. Perhaps the principal justification for the policy of public aid is that it is in line with the long-established policy of the Government in providing assistance to promising forms of business enterprise during their developmental stage, a policy which dates back to the protective tariffs established very early in the history of this country. After all, the policy of public aid to air transportation is no different from the policy of aiding railroads, motor carriers, and water carriers.

Another justification of public aid relates to the importance of air transportation to the national defense. At the outbreak of the last war the armed forces took over a good many planes owned by commercial air carriers, and commercial air transportation played an important part in wartime transportation. There seems to be some difference of opinion on the importance of commercial aviation as a means of training personnel for the armed forces. It would seem, however, that a rather strong argument could be made for the support of commercial aviation on the ground that it provides a means of maintaining in active operation an aircraft industry ready to be expanded to meet the needs of war. It is interesting to note that a proposal to charge a part of the airline subsidy to national defense was criticized by former Secretary of Defense Early who felt that other forms of transportation also were essential to the national defense. He also stated

---

[20] M. George Goodrich, "Air Mail Subsidy of Commercial Aviation," *Journal of Air Law and Commerce*, Vol. 16, Summer, 1949, p. 259.

that service to the national defense was counterbalanced by national defense expenditures which conferred positive benefits on civil aviation.[21]

Criticisms of public aid. Two principal criticisms of public aid to air transportation are usually voiced. There are those who do not object to helping a new industry during its development stages but who are acutely aware that policies of public aid build up vested interests, and once started they are difficult to bring to an end. Some people believe that commercial air transportation has been in existence long enough to prove its worth and that government policy should be reoriented to put the industry on a self-supporting basis as rapidly as possible. Members of the economy bloc in Congress have questioned the wisdom of continued extensive support to air transportation without a careful survey of the need for such support. And some municipalities, burdened with the heavy cost of maintaining expensive airport facilities, are beginning to feel that the users of these facilities should be willing to contribute more than they do at present. The other principal criticism of public aid to air transportation is that the policy has been carried on without any regard to its possible effect on other carriers and on the transportation system as a whole. This, of course, is a criticism which has been leveled at public aid to all modern forms of transportation. It will be considered further in the concluding section of this book.

SUGGESTED READINGS

Behling, Burton N. "Subsidies to Transportation," Library of Congress, Legislative Reference Service, *Public Affairs Bulletin, No. 86*, August, 1950.

Board of Investigation and Research, *Public Aids to Domestic Transportation*, Part VI. 79th Congress, 1st Session, House Document 159 (1945).

Lynn L. Bollinger, Alan Passen, and Robert E. McElfresh, *Terminal Airport Financing and Management*. Boston: Division of Research, Graduate School of Business Administration, Harvard University, 1946.

Civil Aeronautics Administration, *Statistical Handbook of Civil Aviation*, 1948.

Department of Commerce, *Industry Report, Domestic Transportation*, August-September, October-November, 1946. On air passenger and air cargo problems.

Dykstra, Gerald O., and Lillian G. Dykstra, *The Business Law of Aviation*. New York: McGraw-Hill Book Company, Inc., 1946.

Frederick, John H., *Commercial Air Transportation*. Chicago: Richard D. Irwin, Inc., 1946. Good general discussion.

Journal of Air Law and Commerce.

Puffer, Claude E., *Air Transportation*. Philadelphia: The Blakiston Company, 1941. Excellent general discussion of the problem up to date of publication.

---

[21] *Traffic World,* February 4, 1950, p. 59.

DEVELOPMENT OF AIR TRANSPORTATION

Smith, Henry Ladd, *Airways*. New York: Alfred A. Knopf, Inc., 1942.

Wilson, G. Lloyd, and Leslie A. Bryan, *Air Transportation*. New York: Prentice-Hall, Inc., 1949. Includes good summary of early development of aviation.

Wolfe, Thomas, *Air Transportation, Traffic and Management*. New York: McGraw-Hill Book Company, Inc., 1950.

27

Regulation
of
AIR TRANSPORTATION

EARLY FEDERAL LEGISLATION

Air Commerce Act of 1926. The Air Commerce Act of 1926 was enacted to promote civil aviation, and such regulatory provisions as it contained also contributed to that end. The Secretary of Commerce was instructed to foster air commerce by studying the possibilities for its development, by establishing a civil airways system, by working with other departments and agencies of government to improve navigation facilities, and in other ways aiding in the development of air commerce. Jurisdiction over existing airways, then exercised by the Post Office Department, was placed in the hands of the Secretary of Commerce. The law also gave the Secretary of Commerce jurisdiction over the safety aspects of civil flying. He was authorized to require the registration of civil aircraft, to examine and rate pilots and mechanics, and to promulgate air traffic rules and regulations.

Need for regulation of commercial air transportation. Commercial air transportation was just being born at the time the Air Commerce Act of 1926 was adopted, and there was no need for its regulation at that time. But in a few short years this situation had changed completely. Sired by the Air Mail Act of 1925, nurtured by subsequent air-mail legislation, and fostered by the activities of the Department of Commerce as prescribed by the Air Commerce Act of 1926, commercial air transportation grew rapidly, and by the 1930's the need for regulatory legislation had become apparent.

Legislative action of some sort also was indicated by the unsatisfactory way in which the Government's promotional and regulatory activities were scattered over different agencies. The Department of Commerce was charged with promoting air transportation and regulating the safety aspects of civil aviation. The Post Office Department awarded air-mail contracts and was able to regulate the routes and service of air-mail carriers in this way. Finally, the Interstate Commerce Commission exercised some regulatory authority as a result of its power to fix rates of compensation for carrying the mail. This divided authority was ineffective and made it hard on commercial air carriers who had to respond to the demands of three different masters.

Legislative history of the Civil Aeronautics Act of 1938. During the middle 1930's strong support developed for the economic regulation of air transportation, but there were sharp differences of opinion whether the industry should be placed under the jurisdiction of the Interstate Commerce Commission or under an entirely separate regulatory body. By 1937 Congress appears to have been pretty well agreed on legislation which would have placed the regulation of air transportation in the hands of the Interstate Commerce Commission in line with a recommendation by President Roosevelt, but this legislation failed of enactment. Its failure was attributed to jealousies among the departments then exercising some degree of control over commercial air transportation.

Subsequently, President Roosevelt expressed support for the idea of a separate commision to regulate all phases of aeronautics, and bills were drafted along this line. In the hearings on these bills the United States Maritime Commission entered the fray, arguing that it be given control over the overseas phase of air transportation, but it was unsuccessful in getting this split in control approved. In the spring of 1938 each House of Congress agreed upon a separate regulatory measure, a conference committee was appointed, and its report was accepted. The measure then went to President Roosevelt who signed it on June 23, 1938. Thus the Civil Aeronautics Act of 1938 became law.

CIVIL AERONAUTICS ACT OF 1938

Multiple organization. The Civil Aeronautics Act of 1938 created a five-man Civil Aeronautics Authority to exercise legislative and judicial functions in connection with the regulation of the economic and safety aspects of civil aeronautics, its duties and powers being much the same as those of the Interstate Commerce Commission. The law also provided for an office of Administrator within the Civil Aeronautics Authority. Briefly stated, the function of the Administrator was to exercise those powers and duties formerly exercised by the Department of Commerce with respect to the promotion of civil aeronautics, the development of airways and aids to navigation, and the like. Finally, the law created within the Civil Aeronautics Authority a three-man Air Safety Board to investigate accidents, report the facts and probable causes of accidents, and make recommendations to prevent similar accidents in the future.

All of these various officials were to be appointed by the President by and with the advice and consent of the Senate. Members of the Authority were appointed for six-year terms and could be removed only for inefficiency, neglect of duty, or malfeasance. No term of office was specified for the Administrator nor were any limitations placed on his removal. Members of the Air Safety Board were appointed for six-year terms, but no conditions were specified for their removal. Thus the Administrator and the members of the Air Safety Board, but not the members of the Authority, were subject to removal at the will of the President.

Reorganization Act of 1939. The purpose of this tripartite organization was to place responsibility for all aspects of civil aviation within a single organization in such a way that administrative functions would be subject to control by the executive branch of government without, however, the executive branch exercising any control over legislative and judicial functions. The Reorganization Act of 1939 provided for an extensive reorganization of numerous federal departments and agencies, presumably in the interest of greater efficiency, and among the agencies affected was the Civil Aeronautics Authority. Reorganization of the Civil Aeronautics Authority was effected in 1940. The Air Safety Board was abolished and a new Civil Aeronautics Authority, composed of the Civil Aeronautics Administration and the Civil Aeronautics Board, was created within the Department of Commerce. Actually the Civil Aeronautics Authority exists only as a name, since all of the functions of the Civil Aeronautics Act are exercised by the Civil Aeronautics Administration and the Civil Aeronautics Board.

Civil Aeronautics Administration. The Civil Aeronautics Administration, headed by the Administrator of Civil Aeronautics, functions within the Department of Commerce. It is responsible for the construction, maintenance, and operation of the civil airways system and engages in various promotional activities along the same lines as those formerly conducted by the Administrator under the original provisions of the Civil Aeronautics Act of 1938. In addition, it is charged with enforcing the civil air regulations established by the Civil Aeronautics Board. In this connection it examines and inspects aircraft and aircraft equipment, pilots, flight schools, and the like, and in general performs all of those duties involving the administration of safety regulations formerly performed by the Civil Aeronautics Authority.

Civil Aeronautics Board. The Civil Aeronautics Board carries on the legislative and judicial functions associated with the economic regulation of air transportation, and it promulgates rules and regulations in connection with matters relating to safety, in the same manner as was formerly done by the Civil Aeronautics Authority. In addition, it carries on the investigative functions formerly performed by the Air Safety Board. As mentioned previously, however, actual enforcement of the various safety rules and regulations is now in the hands of the Civil Aeronautics Administration. Although the Civil Aeronautics Board has been placed within the Department of Commerce for "housekeeping" purposes, the law provides that it will perform its rule making, adjudicative, and investigative functions independent of the Department of Commerce.

PROVISIONS OF CIVIL AERONAUTICS ACT RELATING TO
ECONOMIC REGULATION

Introductory remarks. The following discussion of the provisions of the Civil Aeronautics Act is subject to certain qualifications which should be noted carefully. First, the discussion does not follow exactly the terms of the original act but takes into consideration the changes effected by the Reorganization Act of 1939. Second, since this volume is concerned with transportation in the United States, primary emphasis has been placed on the regulation of *domestic* air transportation. The regulation of overseas and international air transportation is an integral part of the work of the Civil Aeronautics Board, however, and it is included to the extent necessary to give a complete picture of the nature of the Board's work. Finally, many of the provisions of the law relating to economic regulation have been drawn almost word for word from the Interstate Commerce Act, particularly from Part II, and no attempt will be made to explain these provisions in detail. To do so would simply mean a repetition of matters covered in earlier chapters. Emphasis, therefore, is placed on those regulatory provisions which are peculiar to air transportation as such.

Definitions. The Civil Aeronautics Act starts out with a long series of definitions, some of which introduce concepts not heretofore encountered. An *air carrier* is defined as any citizen of the United States [1] who undertakes, either directly or indirectly, or by a lease or any other arrangement, to engage in air transportation. *Air transportation* means interstate, overseas, or foreign air transportation or the transportation of mail by aircraft. *Air commerce* means interstate, overseas, or foreign air commerce or the transportation of mail by aircraft or any operation or navigation of aircraft within the limits of any civil airway or any operation or navigation of aircraft which directly affects, or which may endanger safety in interstate, overseas, or foreign air commerce. Air commerce seems to cover the whole range of civil aviation, including intrastate air commerce to the extent that it may endanger the safety of other types of commerce.

Interstate air commerce means the carriage by aircraft of persons or property for compensation or hire, or the carriage of mail by aircraft, or the operation or navigation of aircraft in the conduct or furtherance of a

---

[1] A citizen of the United States is defined as an individual citizen of the United States or its possessions, a partnership made up of such individuals, or a domestic corporation owned or controlled by individual citizens.

business or vocation, in commerce between points in different states, between points in the same state through airspace over any place outside of the state, or between points within any territory or possession of the United States. The term *interstate air transportation* covers the same kind of movements but is confined to common carriers for hire or the carriage of mail by aircraft. *Overseas air commerce* and *overseas air transportation* refer to movements between the United States and its territories or possessions. *Foreign air commerce* and *foreign air transportation* refer to movements between the United States and points outside the United States.

Declaration of policy. In the exercise and performance of its powers and duties the Civil Aeronautics Board is to consider, among other things: (a) The encouragement and development of an air transportation system properly adapted to the present and future needs of the foreign and domestic commerce of the United States, of the Postal Service, and of the national defense; (b) The regulation of air transportation in such a manner as to recognize and preserve the inherent advantages of, assure the highest degree of safety in, and foster sound economic conditions in, such transportation, and to improve the relations between, and coordinate transportation by, air carriers; (c) The promotion of adequate, economical, and efficient service by air carriers at reasonable charges, without unjust discriminations, undue preferences or advantages, or unfair or destructive competitive practices; (d) Competition to the extent necessary to assure the sound development of an air transportation system properly adapted to the needs of the foreign and domestic commerce of the United States, of the Postal Service, and of the national defense; (e) The regulation of air commerce in such manner as to best promote its development and safety; and (f) The encouragement and development of civil aeronautics.

This declaration of policy sounds very much like the declaration of a national transportation policy subsequently included in the Transportation Act of 1940, but there are fundamental differences between the two. In the first place, the declaration of policy in the Civil Aeronautics Act of 1938 applies to air transportation alone whereas the various statements contained in the 1940 declaration of policy refer specifically to rail, motor, and water transportation. Second, the declaration of policy in the Civil Aeronautics Act is a specific directive to the Civil Aeronautics Board whereas the national transportation policy is stated to be a declaration of congressional policy. It is true that the declaration of a national transportation policy does state that the provisions of the Interstate Commerce Act are to be applied with a view to carrying out that policy, but in certain respects the national transportation policy conflicts with other congressional policies, and it will take further action by Congress to make it fully effective.

A third outstanding difference between the two declarations of policy is found in the goal to be achieved. The policies outlined in the national transportation policy are to be carried out "all to the end of developing, coordinating, and preserving a national transportation system by water, highway, and rail, *as well as other means. . . .*" [2] whereas the goal prescribed in the Civil Aeronautics Act is quite frankly that of promoting civil aeronautics. In the one statement Congress declares, in effect, that its purpose is to develop, coordinate, and preserve a national transportation system, and in the other it directs the Civil Aeronautics Board to encourage and develop civil aeronautics without reference to its place in or effect upon a national transportation system. As long as air transportation remains in a developmental stage this procedure probably is wise, but eventually these two conflicting policies will have to be resolved.

Exemptions. The Civil Aeronautics Board is authorized to exempt any air carrier or any class of air carriers from economic regulation, either in whole or in part, if it deems such regulation would constitute an undue burden and is not necessary in the public interest. The law contains one or two minor limitations on this right which are not important to the present purpose, and it should be emphasized that exemptions from safety regulation are not sanctioned. As will be noted, the Civil Aeronautics Board made extensive use of this power of exemption, freeing all but the scheduled airlines from economic regulation.

At first thought it would seem that the broad power of exemption granted the Civil Aeronautics Board, and especially the extent to which it has utilized this power, ignores completely earlier experiences in connection with the regulation of surface transportation. The evils which arose in the past out of situations in which regulated carriers found themselves in competition with unregulated ones have been pointed out, as have the difficulties of regulation where such situations still exist. Comprehensive economic regulation was applied to air transportation at an earlier stage in its development than was true of other types of transportation, however, and it probably was wise to allow the Civil Aeronautics Board considerable freedom of action to permit exemptions in areas where regulation might prove to be unnecessary or undesirable. And there is something to be said for the flexibility provided by the Civil Aeronautics Act as compared with such absolute exemptions as are found in Part III of the Interstate Commerce Act. The Civil Aeronautics Board presumably can apply the provisions of the Civil Aeronautics Act to unregulated carriers at any time it feels such action is desirable in the public interest, but the Interstate Commerce Commission has no similar power to assume jurisdiction over the large segment of domestic water transportation not now regulated.

---

[2] Italics added.

REGULATION OF AIR TRANSPORTATION

Certificates of public convenience and necessity. No air carrier may engage in air transportation without a certificate of public convenience and necessity issued by the Civil Aeronautics Board. The Board must find the applicant fit, willing, and able to perform the service properly, able to conform with the law and the Board's rules and regulations; and that the service is required by the public convenience and necessity. A certificate, if issued, must specify the points to be served and the nature of the service, and the Board may attach such reasonable conditions as the public interest may require. It may, after notice and hearing, change or suspend a certificate, and a certificate may be revoked for failure to perform service for a period of ninety days. Intentional failure to comply with the law or with the Board's rules and regulations is good cause for revocation of a certificate, but a certificate may not be revoked for this reason unless the holder fails to comply with an order to obey within a reasonable time. Certificates may not be transferred without the approval of the Civil Aeronautics Board. Provision also is made for granting temporary certificates.

The foregoing certificate requirements are essentially the same as those required in connection with the issuance of surface carrier certificates. In addition, the Civil Aeronautics Act provides that a certificated air carrier may not abandon a route or a part of a route without the approval of the Civil Aeronautics Board, and certificated carriers are required to comply with the provisions of the Railway Labor Act in handling labor disputes. Air carriers holding certificates authorizing the transportation of air mail are obligated to provide necessary and adequate facilities for such transportation, and the Civil Aeronautics Board may grant new certificates or amend existing ones when the Postmaster General certifies that additional service is necessary.

Grandfather clause. The law contains a typical "grandfather clause" entitling air carriers which had operated continuously from May 14, 1938, to the effective date of this particular provision, August 22, 1938, to a certificate by virtue of such operation. Interruptions beyond the control of the carrier were to be disregarded, but if the carrier's service was shown to have been inadequate and inefficient, the Board could refuse to issue a certificate. A grandfather certificate authorized a carrier to handle all classes of traffic for which authority was sought, except mail, between points continuously served between May 18, 1938, and the effective date, August 22, 1938. In order to secure grandfather rights, application for such rights had to be made within 120 days after the date of enactment of the law, June 23, 1938.

Permits. Foreign carriers engaged in transportation between foreign points and the United States are required to obtain a permit from the Civil Aeronautics Board before they may engage in such transportation. The

Board may issue such a permit if it finds the carrier fit, willing, and able properly to perform the service, to conform with the provisions of the law and the rules and regulations of the Board; and that such transportation will be in the public interest. The Board may prescribe the duration of a permit, attach reasonable conditions, and it may, after notice and hearing, change, suspend, cancel, or revoke a permit upon finding that such action is in the public interest. Permits issued to foreign air carriers should not be confused with the permits required for operation as a contract carrier by highway or water.

Tariff regulations. Carriers are required to file their tariffs with the Civil Aeronautics Board, to print them, and keep them open for public inspection. The rates, fares, and charges must be collected as shown, and no rebates or special concessions may be given. An exception to this last provision is made to permit air carriers to give free transportation or transportation at reduced rates to officers and employees and to certain other special groups, including relief in the case of accidents or disasters. No change may be made in any rate, fare, or charge, or any classification or regulation affecting such rates, fares, or charges, without thirty days' notice being filed, posted, and published. The Board may, however, permit a change to go into effect on shorter notice, and it may otherwise modify tariff regulations in particular or special cases.

Duties of carriers with reference to rates and service. It is the duty of every air carrier to provide safe and adequate service of the type specified in its certificate and upon reasonable request therefor, at just and reasonable rates, fares, charges, and so forth, and without discrimination. A certificated air carrier must provide reasonable through service in connection with other air carriers at just and reasonable joint rates, fares, charges, and the like. In the case of through service the participating carriers must establish just, reasonable, and equitable divisions of the charges collected, and these divisions must be filed with the Civil Aeronautics Board. This particular section of the law further specifies that there must be no discrimination with respect to persons, ports, localities, or descriptions of traffic.

Powers and duties of Civil Aeronautics Board with reference to rates. The Civil Aeronautics Board may, upon complaint or upon its own initiative, and after notice and hearing, prescribe maximum, minimum, or maximum and minimum rates, fares, charges, classifications, and so forth. Whenever a tariff, other than an initial tariff filed by an air carrier, is filed which involves a new or changed rate, fare, charge, classification, and the like, the Board may suspend the operation of the tariff for a period of ninety days pending a hearing, and may from time to time apply further suspensions, providing the aggregate period of suspension does not exceed 180 days beyond the effective date of the tariff. In the event that a decision has not been reached within this period the proposed rate, fare, charge, and so forth, goes into effect.

Through air transportation service and rates. The Civil Aeronautics Board has the power to require the establishment of through service and joint rates by two or more air carriers, and the maximum, minimum, or maximum and minimum rates applicable thereto. Likewise it may prescribe just, reasonable, and equitable divisions of such rates.

Rule of rate making. In exercising and performing its powers and duties with reference to rates for the carriage of persons or property, but not for mail, the Civil Aeronautics Board is to take into consideration, among other things: (1) the effect of such rates upon the movement of traffic; (2) the need in the public interest of adequate and efficient transportation of persons and property by air carriers at the lowest cost consistent with the furnishing of such service; (3) such standards respecting the character and quality of service to be rendered by air carriers as may be prescribed by or pursuant to law; (4) the inherent advantages of transportation by aircraft; and (5) the need of each air carrier for revenue sufficient to enable such air carrier, under honest, economical, and efficient management, to provide adequate and efficient air carrier service. It will be observed that this rule is essentially the same as the rules prescribed for surface carrier rate making except that it is applied to individual air carriers as well as to air carriers in general.

Transportation of mail. Holders of air-mail contracts under the Air Mail Act of 1934 had grandfather rights as noted above, and their contract rights were incorporated in their certificates. Air carriers are required to file with the Civil Aeronautics Board and the Postmaster General the schedules they maintain on the routes served, and the Postmaster General may designate any such schedule for transporting mail between points where the carrier is authorized to transport mail. Furthermore, the Postmaster General may require the establishment of additional schedules for transporting mail between these points. Such actions of the Postmaster General are subject to review by the Civil Aeronautics Board.

Rates for transporting mail. The Civil Aeronautics Board is empowered and directed to fix fair and reasonable rates of compensation for transporting mail by air, the facilities used and useful therefor, and the services connected therewith. The law permits the Board to fix different rates of pay for different carriers or classes of carriers and for different classes of service. In determining the rate in each case the Board is to take into consideration, among other things, (1) the fact that air-mail carriers are obligated by their certificates to provide necessary and adequate facilities and service for handling mail, (2) that they must conform with certain standards respecting the quality and character of the service to be rendered, and (3) "the need of each such air carrier for compensation for the transportation of mail sufficient to insure the performance of such service, and, together with all other revenue of the air carrier, to enable such air carrier under honest, economical, and efficient management, to maintain and continue the development of air transportation to the extent and of the character and quality required for the commerce of the United States, the Postal Service, and the national defense."

It is this last provision which makes it possible to use the air-mail service to subsidize the operation of air-mail carriers. It is interesting to note that the rules of rate making found in the Interstate Commerce Act specify that the Interstate Commerce Commission, in fixing reasonable rate levels, is to take into consideration the need of the carriers for revenue sufficient to enable them to provide adequate and efficient service. In the nature of the case, the revenue in question must come from the users of the transportation service involved, but since the rules of rate making also specify that the Commission must give consideration to the effect of rates on the movement of traffic, it is not always possible to prescribe a level of rates sufficient to yield the carriers adequate revenues. In the case of air-mail carriers, however, the law enables the Government itself to make up any deficiencies in revenue resulting from the inability or unwillingness of users to pay charges high enough to cover their full share of a carrier's operating costs.

Intercorporate relationships. The law outlines in some detail various types of intercorporate relationships involving air carriers which are declared to be unlawful unless approved by the Civil Aeronautics Board. An air carrier may not, without approval, consolidate or merge its properties with those of other air carriers or with those of any other common carrier. Nor may it acquire control of another air carrier through purchase, lease, contract to operate, or in any other way whatsoever. And it may not acquire control by purchase, lease, or contract to operate the properties of anyone engaged in any phase of aeronautics other than as an air carrier, except that this last provision does not prohibit an air carrier from having an interest in such terminal and ground facilities as are reasonably necessary for the performance of its service.

Common carriers other than air carriers may not consolidate or merge their properties with those of an air carrier; nor may they acquire control of any air carrier by purchase, lease, contract to operate, or in any other way whatsoever. Foreign air carriers may not acquire control in any manner of any United States citizen or business engaged in any phase of aeronautics. And persons engaged in phases of aeronautics other than air transportation may not consolidate or merge their properties with those of an air carrier. Nor may they acquire control of any air carrier by purchase, lease, contract to operate, or in any other way whatsoever.

It should be emphasized that these are not absolute prohibitions. The Civil Aeronautics Board is authorized, after notice and hearing, to give its approval to any of the arrangements mentioned above, with certain limitations. If it finds that any given proposal will result in creating a monopoly and thereby restrain competition or jeopardize another air carrier, it must not give its approval. And if the applicant is a carrier other than an air carrier, the Board must find that the transaction proposed will promote the public interest and will not restrain competition before it can give its approval.

In addition to the control exercised over consolidations, mergers, and acquisitions of control, the law further specifies that interlocking directorates, whether achieved by direct or indirect means, are unlawful when they involve an air carrier and another common carrier or an air carrier and anyone engaged in any phase of aeronautics. The Civil Aeronautics Board, however, may approve such interlocking directorates if they do not adversely affect the public interest. If the Board finds, after notice and hearing, that an air carrier is engaged in unfair or deceptive practices or unfair methods of competition, it is directed to order such practices or methods stopped. Pooling arrangements of various sorts are permitted subject to approval by the Civil Aeronautics Board. The merger of international air transportation companies is subject to final decision by the President of the United States.

These various provisions relating to carrier relationships were not designed by Congress to discourage combinations and cooperation between carriers. Rather their purpose is to bring all such relationships within the jurisdiction of the Civil Aeronautics Board so as to make it possible to permit such cooperation as will eliminate destructive competition without doing away with the more desirable features of competition. The prohibitions against combinations, acquisitions of control, and interlocking directorates involving air carriers annd other aspects of the aviation business make it possible for the Board to prohibit undesirable tieups between equipment manufacturers and air transportation companies. The various restrictions on tieups between air carriers and other common carriers obviously are intended to prevent railroad control of airlines in such a way as to be detrimental to the further development of air transportation. The special provision requiring the Board in these cases to find that the transaction proposed will promote the public interest and not restrain competition is reminiscent of similar provisions in the Interstate Commerce Act relating to combinations of railroads and motor carriers.

Other provisions. The Civil Aeronautics Board is authorized to classify carriers and to establish reasonable rules and regulations for each group. It has the usual powers over accounts, records, and reports, as discussed in connection with the regulation of surface carriers. Penalties consisting of fines, prison sentences, or both, are provided for violations of the law, including such acts as forging of certificates, interfering with air navigation, granting rebates, failing to file reports, falsifying records, refusing to testify, and violating safety and postal regulations. Conviction, of course, must be in a court of law. The Civil Aeronautics Act also provided for the repeal of various parts of earlier legislation involving matters now placed under the jurisdiction of the Civil Aeronautics Board, as well as provisions for handling administrative and judicial proceedings which were pending at the time the law was passed.

Joint boards. Air carriers are authorized to establish reasonable through service and just and reasonable charges with common carriers other than air carriers, and to handle matters of this type the law directs the chairman of the Civil Aeronautics Board and the chairman of the Interstate Commerce Commission to appoint an equal number of members to serve as a joint board to consider and pass upon such matters as may arise out of a combination of such services.

International aspects of regulation. The powers and duties of the Civil Aeronautics Board extend to the regulation of the overseas and foreign operations of United States air carriers. These powers and duties, together with its authority to grant or deny permits to foreign air carriers desiring to provide service to United States points, give rise to problems not encountered in connection with the regulation of other forms of domestic transportation. Perhaps the most serious problem here is the possibility that decisions of the Civil Aeronautics Board may conflict with the international relations and foreign policy of the United States. With this in mind the law provides that applications from United States carriers involving certificates relating to overseas and foreign operations, and applications involving permits from foreign carriers to provide service to and from United States points, must be transmitted to the President before hearings are held, and all decisions relating to such certificates and permits must be submitted to the President before publication. All matters relating to such certificates and permits are subject to the approval of the President. Provision also is made for the Secretary of State to advise and consult with the Board concerning the negotiation of agreements with foreign governments for the establishment or development of air navigation, including air routes and services.

Differences between air and surface carrier regulation. A number of differences between air carrier regulation and surface carrier regulation have been mentioned. The Civil Aeornautics Board is directed to exercise its functions so as to encourage and develop civil aeronautics without regard to its place in or effect upon a national transportation system. The Board has broad powers to exempt air carriers from economic regulation. And the Government stands ready to make up any losses resulting from the inability or unwillingness of other users to pay rates or fares sufficiently high to cover the cost of operation.

Aside from these differences, certain other differences may be pointed out. The detailed regulations relating to the relationships between air carriers and other branches of the aviation industry have no exact parallel in the Interstate Commerce Act. Likewise the control which the Civil Aeronautics Board can exercise over unfair or deceptive practices or unfair methods of competition is not spelled out specifically in the Interstate Commerce Act. It is mentioned in the national transportation policy, however, and such practices can be limited to a great extent by the Interstate Commerce Commission through the exercise of numerous other regulatory powers.

On the other side of the picture, certain important provisions of the Interstate Commerce Act are not found in the Civil Aeronautics Act. The act defines the regulatory power of the Civil Aeronautics Board in terms which limit its jurisdiction to common carriers insofar as economic regulation is concerned, and the Board has urged Congress to extend its jurisdiction to include contract carriers. Airline security issues are subject to the regulations of the Securities Exchange Commission rather than of the Civil Aeronautics Board, whereas railroad and motor carrier securities are regulated by the Interstate Commerce Commission. Here, again, the Board has asked Congress to extend its jurisdiction. The Civil Aeronautics Act does not include a long and short haul clause, but this is an omission of no great significance. The long distances between stops and high operating costs would make such discrimination costly unless the rates to the shorter points were very high, and the need for fostering air transportation makes it desirable to keep these as low as possible. Furthermore, it is on the relatively short hauls that surface carriers are best able to compete. In any event, the rate-making powers of the Civil Aeronautics Board are adequate to prevent such discrimination should it be attempted.

The Interstate Commerce Act provides that when the Interstate Commerce Commission is unable to reach a decision on a rate change within the seven-month suspension period, the new rate may go into effect, but the carriers must keep records and make refunds in the event the change is not approved. The Civil Aeronautics Act makes no provision for refunds of this sort. More important than this is the fact that the Interstate Commerce Commission has authority to award reparations when shippers are injured as a result of charging rates held to be unreasonable or unlawful, a power which the Civil Aeronautics Board does not have. The need for developing traffic probably makes this a matter of minor significance today, but it could become important later.

STATE REGULATION

Safety regulation. As in the case of other forms of transportation, the states were the first to enter the field of air transport regulation. In some cases this was the result of the existence of public utility laws which covered all forms of transportation and so automatically were applied to air transportation when it made its appearance. In other cases, regulation was the result of legislation especially enacted to cover aviation activities. For the most part this early state legislation was designed to protect the public by requiring licensing of pilots and aircraft in order to assure public safety and to assure the public some protection from loss and damage resulting from the operation of aircraft. It also was designed to some extent to promote the development of aviation by taking steps to increase the safety of flying. In general, this legislation applied to all types of flying and was not limited to air transportation as such.

As soon as the Federal Government began to regulate the safety aspects of civil aeronautics some invasion of the rights of the states was inevitable, for the intrastate operation of aircraft under one set of safety regulations could not help but result in interference with aircraft operating interstate in accordance with a different set of regulations. Since this problem obviously fell within the zone of concurrent powers, it was inevitable that the courts would insist that state laws give way before federal action. The Air Commerce Act of 1926, among other things, made it the duty of the Department of Commerce to promulgate air traffic rules, and in 1929 it was held that all or nearly all of the air traffic rules established by the Department of Commerce applied to intrastate as well as interstate flying.[3]

The Civil Aeronautics Act gives the Civil Aeronautics Board the power to establish rules and regulations necessary to promote safety in air

---

[3] *Neiswonger v. Goodyear Tire & Rubber Company,* 35 F(2) 761 (1929).

commerce, including the navigation of aircraft within the limits of any civil airway, and the courts have held that intrastate operators using the civil airways must conform with the Board's rules and regulations.[4] As a matter of fact the Board's authority extends to any operation directly affecting or which may endanger safety in interstate, overseas, or foreign air commerce. Thus, as a result of the very great increase in air traffic following upon the outbreak of World War II, the Civil Aeronautics Board issued an order requiring federal certification of all pilots and aircraft without reference to use made of the civil airways, and this order was upheld by the courts.[5]

These various decisions do not deny to the states the right to enact legislation having to do with the safety of intrastate air traffic. They do mean that such legislation must not be of such a nature as to conflict with federal laws or the regulations of the Civil Aeronautics Board. In effect, however, the states actually have lost to the Federal Government their major rights to regulate the safety of intrastate commerce by air.

Economic regulation. While efforts of the states to exercise jurisdiction over the safety aspects of flying are almost as old as aviation itself, the states made little effort to extend their activities to the field of economic regulation. Thus by the time of the passage of the Civil Aeronautics Act, only ten states had adopted legislation which even touched on economic regulation.[6] Probably the reason for this lack of interest in economic regulation is to be found in the fact that there was not enough intrastate air commerce in existence to make regulation worth while. It is significant that railroad and motor carrier transportation developed first on a local basis from which it later expanded into the field of interstate commerce. In the case of air transportation, on the other hand, the development was reversed. By its very nature air transportation always attracted long haul traffic, and except in a few areas, long haul traffic is almost certain to be interstate in nature. Hence effective economic regulation was undertaken first by the Federal Government. Unlike safety regulation, the economic regulatory provisions of the Civil Aeronautics Act are not worded to apply specifically to intrastate commerce, and the Civil Aeronautics Board did not attempt to apply them to intrastate operations.

Demand for uniform economic regulation. In recent years the great expansion of commercial air transportation, together with new develop-

---

[4] *Rosenhan* v. *United States,* 131 F(2) 932 (1942).
[5] *United States* v. *Drumm,* 55 F.S. 151 (1944).
[6] Association of American Railroads, *Air Transportation,* Washington, 1947, p. 115.

ments in aviation, has led to an increasing interest in the development of short haul and feeder service which is essentially intrastate in nature, and this field of activity has been growing. This in turn has led to a growth of state legislation which has for its purpose the economic regulation of intrastate commerce by air. Considerable alarm has been expressed in connection with this development, and legislation has been proposed which would give federal authorities exclusive jurisdiction over the economic regulation of all air commerce.

Among the supporters of the idea of uniform economic regulation may be mentioned the Air Transport Association of America, which represents the certificated airlines, the Civil Aeronautics Board, and the Civil Aeronautics Administration. One of the principal reasons for the demand for uniform regulation is a probably well founded fear that it will be difficult for civil aeronautics to develop as contemplated if it is subject to forty-eight different sets of state regulations as well as to federal regulation. There also seems to be some fear that state regulatory bodies will be influenced by the needs of surface carriers and might even permit surface carriers to engage in air transportation.

The demand for uniform regulation gives rise to the constitutional question of the extent to which the Federal Government can exercise jurisdiction over intrastate commerce in the field of air transportation. The decisions of the Supreme Court in the Shreveport and Wisconsin Passenger Fare cases, however, have given the Interstate Commerce Commission almost unlimited jurisdiction over intrastate railroad rates and fares and other matters which may interfere with interstate commerce, and there is no reason to believe that the precedents established in these cases would not apply as well to air transportation.

Case for state regulation of intrastate commerce. Opposition to legislation which would place all economic regulation of commercial air transportation, intrastate as well as interstate, in the hands of the Civil Aeronautics Board has come from the states, from advocates of states' rights, and from the National Association of Railroad and Utilities Commissioners. This opposition stems in part from those individuals who are opposed as a matter of principle to encroachments by the Federal Government into any area not specifically delegated to it by the Constitution. More specifically, they are opposed to further encroachments in the field of transportation. They were successful in retaining state control over intrastate motor transportation, but unfortunately for the advocates of states' rights, the peculiar characteristics of motor transportation which led Congress to protect state authority—including the essentially local nature of much of this transportation, the existence of a large number of small scale operations, and state ownership of the highways—do not exist in the field of air transportation. From the point of view of transportation characteristics the Shreveport doctrine would seem to be fully applicable to air transportation.

Opposition to federal control over intrastate air commerce does not stem alone from a desire to preserve the doctrine of states' rights. As pointed out above, air transportation originated as an interstate operation and it is still largely interstate in nature. But since the end of World War II, increasing interest has been shown in the possibility of developing local service of an intrastate nature, and fear has been expressed that the development of local air transportation will be retarded if all economic control over it is placed in the hands of the Civil Aeronautics Board. There are two main reasons for this fear. In the first place, it is maintained that the right to operate intrastate, together with the nature of the service rendered and the rates charged, is of local significance only, and local interests can be protected and promoted better by local control than by centralized control which is hundreds or even thousands of miles away. And in the second place, it is believed that under federal control local service will be dominated by the big interstate airlines and will not be developed by them to promote local needs.[7]

Conclusion. The principal argument in favor of a single federal regulatory body which would exercise jurisdiction over the economic regulation of both interstate and intrastate commerce by air is based on the fear that a national system of transportation by air cannot be developed adequately if the same carriers are to be subjected to a multiplicity of laws and regulations. In an attempt to overcome this objection numerous uniform state aviation laws have been proposed, but it is difficult to see how such laws could solve the problem. There is no way in which all of the states can be compelled to accept a uniform law, and even if they did adopt such a law, the multiplicity of jurisdictions still would exist.

As far as states' rights are concerned, it is now well established that Congress has the power to exercise control over intrastate commerce which interferes with interstate commerce, either directly or indirectly. Furthermore, it seems reasonable to suppose that local or short haul operators would want to accept goods and passengers moving in interstate commerce in order to make maximum use of their facilities, while many will want to obtain air-mail rights. Either of these situations would subject them to considerable control by the Civil Aeronautics Board. Whether or not the development of local air transportation will be

---

[7] See, for example, statement by Judge John D. Biggs in Association of American Railroads, *Air Transportation*, Washington, 1947, pp. 116-117.

retarded if subjected to the jurisdiction of the Civil Aeronautics Board is uncertain. The Board has received a good many requests for permission to offer local services involving interstate commerce or mail carriage, and it is true that it has approved only a few of these, and then only for limited periods of operation.

The fact that the Civil Aeronautics Board has been sparing in its certification of local operations does not necessarily mean that it is discouraging the development of local air transportation or that it is holding this field open for the scheduled airlines when as and if they wish to provide service. It does mean that the Board has not been convinced in many cases that a traffic potential sufficient to justify successful operations exists. Past history has demonstrated that local authorities have been inclined to give their blessings to new transportation ventures without too much concern for the possibilities of success, and a too rapid expansion followed by numerous failures can be just as discouraging to the development of local air transportation as a policy of undue caution. The history of railroad construction prior to 1920 is replete with examples of lines which were built on enthusiasm, many of which were subsequently abandoned with unhappy results for all concerned.

ACCOMPLISHMENTS OF CIVIL AERONAUTICS BOARD

Administrative procedures. In order to handle the various aspects of its duties, the Civil Aeronautics Board has established a number of bureaus and offices within its organization, including a Bureau of Air Operations, Bureau of Safety Regulations, Bureau of Investigation, Bureau of Hearing Examiners, Office of General Counsel, Office of Enforcement, and Office of Administration.[8] The procedure followed in handling applications, investigations, and other matters is the same as that followed by the Interstate Commerce Commission. The Board itself may hold a hearing, but many hearings are conducted by examiners in various parts of the country. After concluding a hearing, the examiner prepares a written report which sets forth his findings and includes his recommendations on what should be done. If exceptions are taken to the examiner's report by any of the parties at interest, the Civil Aeronautics Board gives them an opportunity to be heard, after which it presents its findings and issues an order similar to the orders issued by the Interstate Commerce Commission.

Nature of applications received. Table XXXI gives the nature and total number of cases heard under the Civil Aeronautics Act from August

---

[8] Civil Aeronautics Board, *Annual Report*, 1951, p. 4. The Board's organization has gone through several revisions.

22, 1938, to July 1, 1950. For several years the Civil Aeronautics Board showed the disposition of cases in its annual report, but it no longer provides this information.

Table XXXI

STATUS OF FORMAL DOCKET OF CIVIL AERONAUTICS BOARD [9]

(Cumulative total from August 22, 1938, to July 1, 1950)

	Cases Opened	Cases Reopened	Cases Closed	Cases Pending
Applications for Certificates of Public Convenience and Necessity: Grandfather:				
Domestic	58	3	60	1
Alaskan	33	0	33	0
Foreign and/or overseas	5	0	5	0
New routes and amendments:				
Domestic	1,781	72	1,491	362
Alaskan	139	5	113	31
Foreign and/or overseas	465	20	333	152
Foreign Permits	159	0	113	46
Rates for Transportation of Mail	156	41	135	62
Interlocking Relationships	373	5	366	12
Miscellaneous	1,319	22	1,074	307
Total	4,488	168	3,683	973

Exemption of nonscheduled carriers. The Civil Aeronautics Authority exempted nonscheduled carriers from economic regulation pending completion of studies with respect to this type of transportation, and this exemption was continued in effect by its successor, the Civil Aeronautics Board. An investigation of nonscheduled transportation was instituted by the Board in 1944, and the large increase in this type of activity following World War II made at least some control essential. Consequently, effective June 10, 1947, the Board created two new classes of carriers called noncertificated irregular air carriers and noncertificated cargo carriers. An irregular air carrier was defined as one which engages directly in interstate or overseas air transportation of persons and property, or foreign air transportation of property only, but which does not hold itself out to operate between designated points regularly or with a reasonable degree of regularity. All irregular air carriers were to be issued letters of registration as evidence of their authority to engage in air transportation, and the larger carriers were required to file their tariffs and were made subject to the various provisions of the act relating to intercorporate relationships. Subsequently the general exemption under which these letters of registration were issued was terminated as far

---

[9] Civil Aeronautics Board, *Annual Report*, 1950, p. 56.

as the larger carriers were concerned, and each was required to file application for individual temporary exemptions, thus bringing them under closer control.

The 1947 regulation defined a noncertificated cargo carrier as any air carrier directly engaged in interstate or overseas air transportation of property only which, on May 5, 1947, did not possess a certificate of public convenience and necessity, but which did have on file with the Board an application for such a certificate, and which was actively engaged in the business of carrying property by air for compensation. Noncertificated cargo carriers were required to obtain letters of registration and to conform with economic regulations along the same line as provided for the irregular carriers. These letters of registration were temporary in nature and were good only until sixty days after the Board disposed of each carrier's application for a certificate. As of October 31, 1947, twenty-three carriers had filed applications for letters of registration, and of these, twelve were granted. Of the twelve, one was surrendered by the carrier, and no operations were carried on under three others. Four cargo carriers were granted five-year certificates of public convenience and necessity for the transportation of property by air, the certificates to become effective August 12, 1949.

Safety regulation. An important phase of the work of the Civil Aeronautics Board has to do with the investigation of accidents and with the promulgation of rules and regulations designed to improve the safety of flying. This work accounts for a relatively larger part of the activities of the Civil Aeronautics Board than is true of the safety work carried on by the Interstate Commerce Commission because aircraft safety regulations are necessarily far more extensive and detailed than those required in connection with railroad and motor carrier transportation. Furthermore, airline equipment and operational practices are backed by a much shorter history than is the case with the railroads, and so they are subject to continuous improvement and change. Finally, the Civil Aeronautics Board is responsible for private as well as for commercial flying. For the year ending June 30, 1950, there were 181 air carrier accidents reported, of which the Board investigated 156. But in the same period there were 4,622 noncarrier accidents, and the Board investigated 1,189 of these. The rules and regulations promulgated by the Board and the details of some of its investigations are of a technical nature, and no attempt will be made to explain them here.

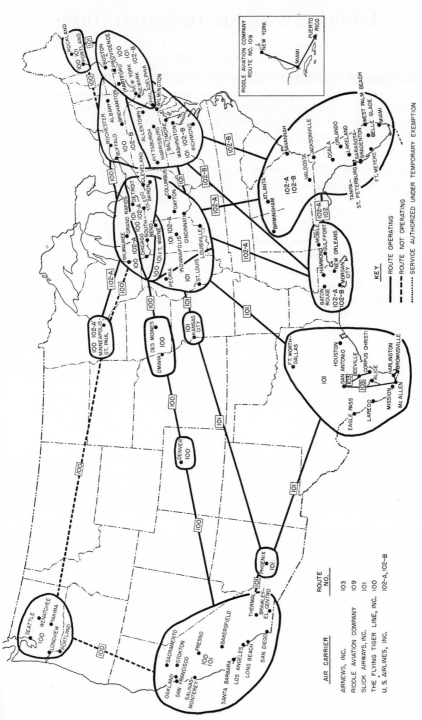

FIGURE. 7. *Certificated Limited Period Property Carrier Routes, September 1951.* (Adapted from map, courtesy of Civil Aeronautics Board.)

REGULATION OF AIR TRANSPORTATION

SUGGESTED READINGS

Association of American Railroads, *Air Transportation,* Washington, 1947. Chapter XII contains an account of the arguments for and against federal regulation of intrastate commerce. This is about the only readily available publication which even attempts to give the states' side of the controversy.

Civil Aeronautics Authority, *Annual Report,* 1939-1940.

Civil Aeronautics Board, *Aeronautical Statutes and Related Material.*

Civil Aeronautics Board, *Annual Report,* 1941 and later.

Dykstra, Gerald O., and Lillian G. Dykstra, *The Business Law of Aviation.* New York: McGraw-Hill Book Company, Inc., 1946. Chapter II includes major cases relating to federal control over intrastate air navigation.

Frederick, John H., *Commercial Air Transportation.* Chicago: Richard D. Irwin, Inc., 1946. Part II contains an extended discussion of regulation and regulatory problems.

Locklin, D. Philip, *Economics of Transportation,* 3rd Ed. Chicago: Richard D. Irwin, Inc., 1947. Chapter XXXIII.

Rhyne, Charles S., *Civil Aeronautics Act Annotated.* Washington: National Law Book Company, 1939. Useful as a source of congressional history of aviation regulation up to and including the Civil Aeronautics Act of 1938.

Wilson, G. Lloyd and Leslie A. Bryan, *Air Transportation,* Part III. New York: Prentice-Hall, Inc., 1949.

Wolfe, Thomas, *Air Transportation, Traffic and Management,* Part II. New York: McGraw-Hill Book Company, Inc., 1950.

28.

Some Problems and Policies
of
AIR TRANSPORTATION (I)

THE RIGHT TO OPERATE: GRANDFATHER OPERATIONS

Nature and purpose. As in the case of interstate motor carriers, Congress recognized the necessity of protecting the rights and investments of those air carriers which had been in actual operation prior to the adoption of the Civil Aeronautics Act. Hence it made it possible for such carriers to obtain an operating certificate without proof of public convenience and necessity. In the nature of the case, most of these applications were made in the early months of the law's existence and were handled by the Civil Aeronautics Authority before it gave way to the Civil Aeronautics Board.

Proof of citizenship. Since by definition an air carrier must be a citizen of the United States, citizenship was the first consideration of the Civil Aeronautics Authority in passing on grandfather applications. In the case of a corporation the applicant had to show that its president and two-thirds or more of its board of directors and managing officers were citizens of the United States and that at least 75 per cent of the voting stock of the corporation was owned or controlled by United States citizens. Such information is not easily obtained where stock is widely held or actively traded, and difficulties are encountered when all or a part of the stock of one corporation is owned by another corporation. The Civil Aeronautics Authority very early adopted a realistic and practical approach to this requirement of the law.[1]

Inadequate and inefficient service. An unusual feature of the Civil Aeronautics Act is the power it gave the regulatory body to deny grandfather rights to an applicant whose service was inadequate and inefficient during the test period, May 14 to August 22, 1938. In one case the Civil Aeronautics Authority denied a certificate on the ground that the applicant had given poor service and failed to satisfy an existing demand for transportation.[2] The fact that a given service was operated

---

[1] For example, see *Pan American Airways Company (of Nevada)*, 1 C.A.A. 214 (1939).
[2] *Airline Feeder System, Inc.*, 1 C.A.A. 167 (1939).

at a loss or at a relatively high cost and without adequate capital, however, was held not to be controlling where the service was reasonably satisfactory.[3]

Service limitations. An air carrier, once its grandfather rights had been established, was entitled to carry all classes of traffic, other than mail, for which it sought authorization, between all points served continuously during the test period. If it was a mail carrier, it was entitled to carry the mail and all other classes of traffic for which authorization was sought between all points authorized by the Postmaster General prior to August 22, 1938.

The Civil Aeronautics Authority, in issuing grandfather certificates covering the carriage of mail, operated on the assumption that Congress intended it to do no more than to replace the previous mail authorizations of the Postmaster General with identical authorizations of its own.[4] If an applicant did not seek to have a given point or points included as intermediate stops in its certificate, this was all right as far as traffic other than mail was concerned, but if its air-mail authorizations provided for stops at these points, it could not avoid the obligation of providing mail service simply by failing to request authorization to serve them.[5] By the same token, if the Postmaster General annulled or abolished certain air-mail stops, such stops could not be included in an applicant's certificate.[6] In some cases carriers which flew more than one route sought to combine all their routes into a single system and provide direct service between points on different routes, but the Civil Aeronautics Authority refused to recognize such direct operations as coming within the intent of the grandfather provisions of the law.[7]

NEW SERVICE

Issues involved. During the first year in which the Civil Aeronautics Act was in force, many applications for new routes were filed with the Civil Aeronautics Authority, some by existing air carriers, some by newly organized companies, and some by companies engaged in other forms of transportation. Collectively, these applications involved 30,653 route miles as compared with the 36,533 route miles then in existence,

---

[3] *Marquette Airlines, Inc.,* 1 C.A.A. 301 (1939).
[4] Civil Aeronautics Authority, *Annual Report,* 1939, p. 18.
[5] *Northwest Airlines, Inc.,* 1 C.A.A. 18 (1939).
[6] *American Airlines, Inc.,* 1 C.A.A. 105 (1939).
[7] Civil Aeronautics Authority, *Annual Report,* 1939, pp. 18-19; *Transcontinental and Western Air, Inc.,* 1 C.A.A. 190 (1939).

or a total of 19,126 new route miles after eliminating duplicating applications.[8]

These new service applications confronted the Civil Aeronautics Authority with a number of knotty problems which it had to solve promptly and without benefit of precedent. The law required that an applicant be fit, willing, and able to offer the service proposed, but few if any applicants could meet this requirement unless they received aid in the form of air-mail subsidies. Such subsidized ventures could be justified on the ground that the Authority was supposed to promote the development of civil aviation, but if the Authority were to approve all operations without regard to the prospects of success, an unjustifiable waste of public funds might well result. Again, the law stated that competition was to be encouraged, but a duplication of service without regard to available or prospective traffic might well lead to disaster for all or to an unnecessary burden on the Government. Finally, the Authority, if it decided not to permit all applicants to serve a given route, had to decide which applicant or applicants should be granted authority. This last was a problem of some magnitude since as many as five applicants had filed for substantially similar routes.

In its annual report for 1940 the Civil Aeronautics Authority outlined the policy it had adopted in disposing of applications for new service. It said that in reaching a decision on such an application the questions to be considered were "(a) whether the new service would serve a useful public purpose; (b) whether this purpose can and will be served adequately by existing lines or carriers; (c) whether it can be served by the applicant without impairing the operations of existing carriers contrary to the public interest; and (d) whether the cost of the proposed service to the Government will be justified by the benefit which would accrue to the public from the new service." [9] The Civil Aeronautics Board, as successor to the Civil Aeronautics Authority, has followed a similar policy in its decisions on new service applications.

New routes. In analyzing the policies of the Civil Aeronautics Board in connection with new service applications, it is necessary to make a distinction between those applications involving services over new routes and those which will duplicate existing services. Where a new route application is involved, the first point to be decided is whether or not the proposed route is required by the public convenience and necessity. In reaching a decision on this point, the Civil Aeronautics Board must consider the relationship of the proposed route to the whole national

---

[8] Civil Aeronautics Authority, *Annual Report*, 1939, p. 19.
[9] p. 5.

air transportation picture because the term public convenience and necessity has been defined as referring specifically to the *national* public convenience and necessity.[10] In addition, it must give consideration to the economic characteristics of the communities proposed to be served, the extent to which existing traffic can be diverted from surface carriers, and the cost to the Government of establishing the proposed route.

Characteristics of communities to be served. Some need can be shown for almost any proposed service, but the Civil Aeronautics Board is not inclined to authorize service at points which can generate only a paucity of traffic.[11] A careful study must be made of the traffic potential, and here one of the most important considerations is the nature of the economic activity characteristic of the various communities along the proposed route. Some types of industrial and commercial activity are known to be good potential sources of traffic, while others are likely to provide little or no traffic. Established merchandise distributing points can be expected to generate much more traffic than essentially agricultural or one-industry communities. Political centers also are good potential sources of traffic. Such things as bank clearings, number of telegrams and long distance telephone messages, volume of first class mail, and volume of traffic moved by surface carriers are all useful in determining the traffic potentials of communities.[12]

Extent to which traffic may be diverted from surface carriers. Although airlines create new traffic, they must depend to a greater or lesser extent upon traffic diverted from surface carriers. Hence it becomes necessary to give consideration to the availability and quality of surface transportation between the points which would be served by a proposed new route. If hauls are typically short and the terrain favorable for surface carrier operation, the prospects of diverting passenger traffic to the air will not be good. On the other hand, if hauls of some length are involved, or if surface transportation service is poor, the prospects will be much better. In the case of freight and express movements, the same factors must be considered, although here the distances over which surface carriers can compete successfully are greater than is true in the case of passenger transportation. Thus where surface carriers can offer overnight or second day service, the time saved by air is insufficient for almost all commercial purposes to justify the higher charges which must be paid.

---

[10] *American Airlines, Inc., et al.,* 1 C.A.A. 480 (1939).

[11] *Pennsylvania-Central Airlines,* 2 C.A.B. 207 (1940).

[12] For a more detailed discussion see John H. Frederick, *Commercial Air Transportation,* (1946 ed.) pp. 282-285.

Cost to Government. The Civil Aeronautics Board must balance traffic prospects and the public need for a proposed new route against the cost to the Government of establishing and maintaining a new airway and of covering the operating losses of the carriers using it. In some cases the cost of a new airway may be justified by the needs of national defense and the postal service,[13] but operating subsidies are another matter. A new operation cannot be expected to pay its own way at the outset, and there is always the possibility that it may never be able to do so. Hence the Board must decide what weight, if any, it should give to future prospects as compared with present needs in determining whether or not the cost to the Government is justified. In general, its policy has been to balance costs against immediate needs and benefits,[14] although some are of the opinion that this attitude is much too conservative.[15] Certainly some weight should be given to traffic prospects as well as present needs, but traffic prospects should be based on something more than mere optimism and enthusiasm. There is little sense in throwing the people's money away simply in the hope that success may be achieved at some uncertain time in the future.

Choice of carrier. If the Civil Aeronautics Board decides that service over a new route is required by the public convenience and necessity, it is often faced with the additional problem of determining which of a number of applicants should be permitted to provide the service. Perhaps the most significant action of the Board in this connection was its early decision to encourage the development of new routes by existing carriers rather than by certificating new lines.[16] Since that time a number of new carriers have been certificated to provide local or feeder service, and a few certificates have been issued to air cargo carriers. But every one of the big trunk line airlines operating today was in operation at the time the Civil Aeronautics Act was adopted. In this field, which accounts for the great bulk of airline traffic, the Board never has issued a certificate to a new operator.

Since there is nothing in the law which even remotely suggests that Congress intended to limit the field to those carriers possessing grandfather rights, the Board's policy has come in for a good deal of criticism. There is much to be said, however, for a policy of favoring existing carriers when new routes are opened up. In many cases it is better to

---

[13] *Mid-Continent Airlines, Inc., et al.,* 2 C.A.B. 63 (1940).

[14] *Continental Air Lines, Inc.,* 1 C.A.A. 598 (1940); *Braniff Airways, Inc., et al.,* 2 C.A.B. 288 (1940).

[15] For example, John H. Frederick, *Commercial Air Transportation,* (1946 ed.) p. 290.

[16] *Delta Air Corporation, et al.,* 2 C.A.B. 447 (1941).

treat a new route as an extension of an existing route because of the opportunities for providing through service between distant points. There are enough major airlines in operation today to permit competition on many hauls, and the number of points between which competition has been permitted is increasing. In any event, an existing carrier has an advantage over a proposed new line if for no other reason than that it is a going concern with a number of years of experience in air transportation operations, and if its past operations have been successful, it is reasonable to suppose that it is a better risk than a new company would be. Of course, if the new applicant is an existing nonscheduled carrier, this last argument loses much of its force.

The Civil Aeronautics Board is faced with a difficult decision when two or more existing certificated carriers seek permission to operate over a proposed new route. If one carrier can make more effective use of the route in rendering a through service than can another, this will be a factor in its favor.[17] On the other hand, routes also have been awarded in such a way as to permit the integration of regional carriers.[18] Sometimes an applicant has maintained that it should be awarded a route because its application was the first to be filed, but this has little bearing on the real test of public convenience and necessity.[19] An interesting and important development has been the tendency of the Board to favor the smaller or weaker lines over the larger ones where it is practical to do so.[20] In view of the difficulties encountered by Congress in attempting to solve the strong and weak line problem in the field of railroad transportation, there is something to be said for reducing disparities in the size of the major carriers by air. It should be kept in mind, however, that an extension of the route miles of a small line is not as significant as the earnings which may be derived from such a route extension.

Competition with existing air carriers. The discussion up to this point has dealt with the policy of the Civil Aeronautics Board in connection with applications to provide service over new routes. What, now, of the Board's policy in disposing of proposals which would duplicate in whole or in part existing transportation facilities and services? The very fact that certificates of public convenience and necessity are required as a prerequisite to operation implies a desire on the part of Congress to limit competition, but at the same time the Civil Aeronautics Act makes

---

[17] *Braniff Airways, Inc., et al.,* 6 C.A.B. 169 (1944).

[18] *Northeast Airlines, Inc., et al.,* 4 C.A.B. 686 (1944).

[19] *Continental Air Lines, Inc., et al.,* 1 C.A.A. 88 (1939).

[20] *Continental Air Lines,* 4 C.A.B. 1 (1942); *Mid-Continent Airlines, Inc., et. al.,* 6 C.A.B. 253 (1945).

it clear that competition is not to be eliminated. Rather it is to be preserved as fully as is consistent with the public interest.

At first the Civil Aeronautics Board was reluctant to approve applications which involved services which would duplicate those of existing carriers, a policy which undoubtedly was wise at a time when airline traffic was thin. The tremendous increase in traffic generated during and since World War II, however, led to a change in the Board's attitude, and competitive services have been approved in a number of cases.[21] Approval of competing services has been based in part on the "presumption doctrine" first enunciated in 1943, the Board then stating in part that " ... since competition in itself presents an incentive to improved service and technological development, there would be a strong, although not conclusive, presumption in favor of competition on any route which offered sufficient traffic to support competing services without unreasonable increase of total operating cost.[22]

The desire of certain carriers to provide through service from and to important points on their routes and important points on the routes of other carriers also has contributed to the extension of competitive services. Under the sectionalized route patterns which developed in this country, through service between a number of pairs of important points was not offered for the simple reason that the same carrier did not serve both points. In order to provide for through service the Board permitted a number of carriers to extend their routes to points which formerly could be reached only by transferring from one line to another, a procedure which had reduced somewhat the airlines' speed advantage.

The expansion of competitive services permitted by the Civil Aeronautics Board during the middle 1940's has been criticized on the ground that it went too fast and too far. The presumption that competition is desirable on any route where traffic is sufficient to support competing services without an unreasonable increase in total operating costs has been challenged in a recent study which holds that service improvement is subject to diminishing returns in places where more than two carriers have been permitted to provide service.[23] And it appears that on certain route segments the Board has permitted operations by more carriers than the available traffic justified.

---

[21] *Eastern Air Lines, Inc., et. al.,* 4 C.A.B. 325 (1943); *Transcontinental & Western Air, Inc., et. al.,* 4 C.A.B. 373 (1943); *Northwest Airlines, Inc., et. al.,* 6 C.A.B. 217 (1944); *Mid-Continent Airlines, Inc., et. al.,* 6 C.A.B. 253 (1945).

[22] *Transcontinental & Western Air, Inc., et al.,* 4 C.A.B. 373 (1943).

[23] Frederick W. Gill and Gilbert L. Bates, *Airline Competition,* Boston: Division of Research, Graduate School of Business Administration, Harvard University, 1949, pp. 630-631.

Of course, no one can question the desirability of providing a through service between important points, wherever the volume of traffic will permit, but the consequences of providing this service by means of route extensions have not always been happy. One carrier has a part of its route duplicated, and not only does it lose the interchange traffic it formerly enjoyed, but also it is faced with competition for traffic along the duplicated portion of its route. A route extension may bring a weak carrier the right to operate over a short but dense route segment over which it cannot operate profitably with existing equipment and high terminal costs; and where a relatively weak carrier is permitted to extend its operations over a route served by a strong line, it may find it difficult to compete effectively with the strong line.

Recently the Civil Aeronautics Board has given tacit recognition to the fact that it may have gone too far in granting route extensions in certain areas.[24] In some cases it has granted route extensions which permit the holder to offer a through service between points on the extension and points on its old route, but which are restricted in one way or another so as to limit or prohibit competition with existing carriers for local traffic on any duplicated route segments. This device will, of course, protect existing carriers on a given route segment from excessive competition and at the same time provide for through service, but the practice of issuing restricted operating rights is one which should be used with caution. If carried too far, such restrictions can lead to uneconomic operations and to evils worse than those they were designed to correct. One need only look to the restrictions placed on motor carrier operating rights to observe the difficulties involved.

Certificate restrictions are not the only way in which this problem can be attacked. In some cases unification may be the answer, and there have been some such unifications. Similarly, one carrier may purchase a part or all of the operating rights of another. Or arrangements may be made to permit one carrier to operate over a part of the route of another. Still another possibility is the interchange of equipment so as to permit through service by a single plane from an origin point or points on the route of one carrier to a destination point or points on the route of another. The Civil Aeronautics Board has looked with favor on this latter solution and has repeatedly urged carriers to utilize it where appropriate. A few such interchange arrangements have been approved, although in these cases it is necessary that the cockpits of the planes used by the two companies be standardized to avoid any operating difficulties

---

[24] Civil Aeronautics Board, *Annual Report,* 1948, p. 9.

which may result from the unfamiliarity of one company's crews with the other company's planes.

Is competition excessive? Professor Berge has raised an interesting question with reference to the problem of airline competition. He argues that the largest part of the investment in an airline consists of aircraft, an extremely mobile form of capital, and that a substantial part of airline costs are variable rather than constant. Hence, in the absence of restrictions on the right of entry, air transportation would more nearly exhibit the characteristics of an ordinary business enterprise than those of a public utility. Professor Berge suggests the possibility of substituting responsible free competition for present restrictive policies but recognizes that responsible free competition cannot succeed as long as the solvency of all competitors is guaranteed by the Government. Perhaps the problem is not one of too much competition but one of too much subsidized competition, and if commercial air transportation were not subsidized, and particularly if marginal operations were not subsidized, it actually might be possible to have more competition.[25] While such a position obviously will not receive much support from airline enthusiasts, responsible free competition without subsidy has much to recommend it as a means of developing a sound air transportation industry.

SCHEDULED V. NONSCHEDULED CARRIERS

Nonscheduled cargo transportation. Following the end of World War II there was a spectacular growth in the number of companies offering a nonscheduled air cargo service, these operations being carried on under the blanket exemption from economic regulation originally issued by the Civil Aeronautics Authority. It was not long before the certificated carriers saw the possibilities in this field, and they proceeded to make a strong play for the business. Since their existing cargo rates were substantially higher than those charged by the nonscheduled carriers, the first step was to reduce rates, and in August 1947, they published a consolidated tariff quoting rates which were considerably lower than those formerly charged. Furthermore, some of the scheduled airlines published special commodity rates as low as 12¢ per ton mile, an unprecedentedly low figure for carrying cargo by air. Later some of the scheduled carriers proposed to extend the list of items to which commodity rates were applicable and to make a further general reduction in cargo rates.

The nonscheduled carriers claimed to see in these actions an attempt

---

[25] Stanley Berge, "Subsidies and Competition as Factors in Air Transport Policy."

on the part of the scheduled airlines to take over the cargo business. It was argued that the certificated carriers were in a position to establish cargo rates which were below cost because they could apply for increased mail payments to cover any losses, thus putting the Government in the position of aiding in the destruction of the nonscheduled lines.

Seeing a destructive rate war in the offing, the Civil Aeronautics Board acted to maintain the status quo and suspended certain of the proposed rate changes. This was followed by a general investigation of the air cargo problem in which the Board found that the suspended rates were noncompensatory, and on May 22, 1948, it established minimum rates for both scheduled and nonscheduled carriers of 16¢ per ton mile for the first 1,000 ton miles in a single shipment and 13¢ for each ton mile in excess of this amount. As previously noted, the Board also took action to require nonscheduled carriers to file their tariffs, and recently it has certificated a few of the larger cargo carriers for regular operation.

Nonscheduled passenger transportation. Nonscheduled passenger transportation antedated the inauguration of scheduled service by a number of years. After the passage of the Civil Aeronautics Act, it was continued under the blanket exemption from economic regulation, the Civil Aeronautics Board looking upon this form of service as complementary rather than competitive with the regular scheduled services of the certificated carriers. In this connection the Board has said that the scheduled carriers serve a fairly uniform, average, and predictable demand, while nonscheduled operators complement this fixed pattern by providing services which are accommodated to unforeseeable demands and needs which fluctuate according to quantity, time, and place.[26]

After World War II nonscheduled air passenger carriers began to develop a degree of regularity of service which went considerably beyond the bounds of what would ordinarily be considered a nonscheduled type of operation. Several reasons may be cited for this development. In the first place, a nonscheduled passenger carrier, unless its passenger-carrying activities are incidental to cargo carrying or to some other form of activity, is not likely to succeed on the basis of the casual or occasional transportation of passengers. Second, the large increase in air travel during and immediately after World War II attracted new operators to the field, but the Civil Aeronautics Board consistently refused to grant any of these operators the right to offer a scheduled service. Finally, the blanket exemption from economic regulation created possibilities for carrying on business free of rate control and other aspects of economic regulation. Of course, nonscheduled operators could not publish schedules or advertise to

---

[26] *Standard Air Lines, Inc., et al.,* 9 C.A.B. 583 (1948).

the public that their services were available at specified times, but in some cases they got around these difficulties by making arrangements with ticket agents who contacted prospective passengers and sold space on nonscheduled planes.

The activities of certain nonscheduled carriers in offering what amounted to a regular service became a thorn in the side of the scheduled airlines because the "nonscheds" generally charged lower fares and attracted a substantial amount of business which might otherwise have gone to the scheduled carriers. Ostensibly their fares were lower because they offered a simplified service, but there were other reasons besides this. Of these the most important, no doubt, was the fact that the nonscheduled operators tended to provide service only between points where air travel was heavy. They avoided light traffic routes, and they did not bother with the more costly intermediate service on the routes they served. Furthermore, they enjoyed some economies through not being subject to certain of the regulatory requirements of the Civil Aeronautics Board. The principal points served were New York and San Juan, Puerto Rico; Seattle and Alaska; and New York and the Pacific coast. Indicative of the size of these activities is the fact that some of the carriers operated equipment of the same size and quality as the certificated airlines.

As early as 1944 the Civil Aeronautics Board undertook an investigation of the activities of all noncertificated carriers. In 1946 it found that Page Airways, a contract carrier, had operated a number of flights between Rochester, Washington, and Miami, Florida, that the number of passengers it carried under contract was small as compared with the number of general public passengers carried, and that no member of the public was denied accommodations as long as space was available. Page made use of travel agencies and hotel employees in procuring passengers and cargo. In this case the Board ordered the carrier to cease and desist from operations which it held violated the law and the Board's regulations.[27]

In 1947 the Civil Aeronautics Board created an irregular air carrier classification, such a carrier being defined in part as one which directly engages in interstate or overseas air transportation of persons and property, and which does not hold itself out to the public, expressly *or by a course of conduct,* that it operates one or more aircraft in air transportation between designated points regularly or with a reasonable degree of regularity. Such carriers were required to obtain a letter of registration, and those operating large planes were required to file their tariffs, make flight reports,

---

[27] *Page Airways, Inc.,* 6 C.A.B. 1061 (1946). See also, *Trans-Marine Airlines, Inc.,* 6 C.A.B. 1071 (1946).

and were subject to those provisions of the law relating to intercorporate relationships.

The foregoing action of the Board placed those large nonscheduled carriers which had been doing a more or less regularly scheduled business in a difficult position. In order to continue to operate they had to apply for letters of registration as irregular carriers or for certificates of public convenience and necessity as scheduled airlines. Since they knew that the latter would not be granted, they had to apply for the former. But in applying for and receiving letters of registration as irregular carriers they were subjecting themselves to a definite prohibition against rendering service with any degree of regularity, the very life blood of their business.

A substantial number of the larger irregular carriers sought to comply with the intent of the new regulations and to provide an irregular service as contemplated by the Civil Aeronautics Board, but some continued to perform what amounted to regular operations. Arrangements were worked out with ticket agents who solicited business between specified points on a regular or frequent basis, and who arranged with the carriers for transportation in such a way that first one carrier and then another was used. In this way each individual carrier maintained a semblance of irregularity although the whole operation provided a frequent and regular service. In a further effort to prevent continued violation of the intent of its regulations the Board in 1949 withdrew the blanket exemption from economic regulation insofar as large irregular carriers were concerned, and it required each of them to apply for individual exemptions. New and more stringent controls were placed on their activities, and in several cases the Board revoked letters of registration for continued violation of the law.

More recently the Board in its battle to control the activities of large irregular carriers established a rule limiting irregular air carriers to three flights per month between eleven specified pairs of points and only eight flights per month between any other pairs of points.[28] Two large irregular air carriers, however, obtained a permanent injunction against the application of this rule. The court's ruling was appealed by the Civil Aeronautics Board.[29] The irregular carriers also have petitioned Congress, and at least some members of Congress have expressed concern over the policy followed by the Civil Aeronautics Board in attempting to restrict the activities of irregular operators.

Freight-forwarder problem. A freight forwarder accepts small shipments which he consolidates with other small shipments into large lots for transportation to various destinations by existing carriers, deriving his profit

---

[28] *Traffic World*, March 10, 1951, pp. 46-47.
[29] *Ibid.*, June 9, 1951, p. 53; July 7, 1951, p. 50.

from the spread between the small shipment rates paid to him by shippers and the volume shipment rates which he pays to the carriers. The boom in air cargo traffic following World War II brought with it numerous applications for authority to operate air freight forwarder services, and some seventy-eight cases were consolidated for hearing in 1948.

Forwarder applications were opposed by the certificated airlines, these lines arguing the irresponsibility of operators and that forwarders, by holding shipments until a sufficient quantity of cargo had accumulated to make a volume shipment worth while, would slow up the air cargo service. On the other hand, it was argued that there was a need for the service and that the scheduled airlines opposed its development simply because they were opposed to anything which might affect the monopolistic position they enjoyed. In September 1948, the Civil Aeronautics Board granted a five-year exemption from economic regulation and letters of registration to fifty-six applicants for air freight forwarder rights. The temporary exemption from economic regulation was granted because the Board felt that the industry needed time to develop. It also felt that it would be necessary to have some operating experience in the field before determining just what its permanent policy should be toward air freight forwarding. Applications from forwarding companies owned or controlled by railroads were denied.

The regulations established by the Civil Aeronautics Board in 1948 permitted freight forwarders to use the services of any type of air common carrier in legal operation, including irregular carriers operating under letters of registration. Early in 1949 the certificated carriers protested this regulation on the ground that it made possible a tieup between freight forwarders and irregular carriers which would permit the establishment of a new regular air transportation service. It was pointed out that forwarders could make use of the services of different irregular carriers in rotation and so provide a regular service without violating the law. In June 1949, the Board took cognizance of these possible operations by issuing a notice of rule making which would prohibit air freight forwarders from making use of irregular carriers in conducting a forwarding business.

INTERCORPORATE RELATIONSHIPS

Equipment interchange. In several cases the Civil Aeronautics Board has approved arrangements for interchanging equipment to make possible through service between points served by two different carriers. Of course, in such cases consideration must be given to the possibility that an equipment interchange may result in the establishment of a new competitive service between points already served by a single carrier.

Acquisition of air carriers by other air carriers. From time to time the Civil Aeronautics Board receives applications involving the consolidation or merger of two existing airlines or the acquisition of control of one airline by another, but so far these applications have not involved any unique decisions. The principal determinant seems to be whether or not the proposal will lead to monopoly or otherwise unduly restrain competition, and in a few cases the Board has denied its approval on this ground.[30] In other cases it has approved proposals on the ground that they would simplify corporate structures,[31] reduce uneconomical duplications, and provide more dependable service,[32] and the like.

Acquisition of air carriers by surface carriers. It will be recalled that the Civil Aeronautics Act provides that when a carrier other than an air carrier makes application to acquire control of an air carrier the Civil Aeronautics Board must find that the transaction will promote the public interest by enabling the surface carrier to use aircraft to public advantage in its operations and will not restrain competition. The Board has interpreted this statement in such a way as virtually to exclude surface carriers from air transportation, the reason for its position being well stated in a 1946 decision which reads in part as follows:

... It would be expecting too much to assume that a transportation company engaged in both air and sea transportation would be in a position to provide vigorous competition between its air transportation and its surface transportation on this route.... Any assumption that an automatic competition between two forms of transportation, conducted by the same management and operating over the same route, could develop would be an assumption at war with the realities of business experience and of human nature. In such circumstances the transportation activities offering the larger investment interest may be expected to dominate in any competitive conflict between the two. We believe, therefore, that the maximum development of air transportation on the proposed route cannot be assured under a plan which carries the inherent danger, in the event of a conflict of interest, that the air transportation may find itself a captive of the surface transportation interest.[33]

Applications of surface carriers to carry on new operations. The Civil Aeronautics Act imposes no special restrictions on applications by surface carriers for certificates to carry on new airline operations, and it would appear that such applications would have to be considered on their merit and without regard to the fact that the applicant was a surface carrier. In

---

[30] See, for example, *United Air Lines Transport Corporation—Acquisition of Western Air Express Corporation*, 1 C.A.A. 739 (1940); *Acquisition of Cordova Air Service, Inc., by Alaska Airlines, Inc.*, 4 C.A.B. 708 (1944).

[31] *Pan American Airways, Inc., et al.*, 2 C.A.B. 503 (1940).

[32] *Marine Airways, Alaska Air Transport, Inc.—Consolidation*, 3 C.A.B. 315 (1942).

[33] *Additional Service to Latin America*, 6 C.A.B. 857, 903-904 (1946).

practice, however, the Civil Aeronautics Board has denied a number of applications on the ground that the applicants were surface carriers, without regard to the merits of the applications themselves. For a time the Board held that it was required to consider the restrictive provisions of the acquisition of control section of the law in passing on surface carrier applications.[34] Later, however, it appears to have recognized that this position was untenable, and more recently it has held that it would continue to limit the entry of surface carriers into air transportation unless it could be shown that the public interest required service by a surface carrier regardless of the circumstance that it was a surface carrier.[35] Nevertheless, the attitude of the Board is not such as to suggest that any major change in policy is to be expected.[36]

The railroads have been quite bitter about the attitude taken by the Civil Aeronautics Board, and an amendment to the Civil Aeronautics Act has been urged as necessary to change what they refer to as the Board's discriminatory policy against surface carriers.[37] If the issue is confined to those provisions of the law relating to the certification of new operations, then there is some basis for the railroad complaint, but it must be kept in mind that one of the duties of the Civil Aeronautics Board is to *promote* the development of air transportation, and it is by no means clear that a railroad controlled air transportation service would accomplish this purpose.

Interlocking relationships. Over the years a large number of requests have been filed for permission to establish or continue interlocking relationships between air carriers, between air and surface carriers, and between air carriers and other branches of the aviation business. Interlocking relationships between air and surface carriers have been approved where no competition existed between the two or where there was no significant degree of conflict of interest present or foreseeable.[38] In cases where the two carriers were in direct competition, however, the Board has refused to permit interlocking relationships.[39] An interlocking relationship between a feeder airline and persons engaged in the sale and service of personal type aircraft was approved since this type of aircraft was not suitable for use by the airline.[40] An interlocking relationship between an airline and a

---

[34] *Additional Service to Latin America*, 6 C.A.B. 857 (1946).

[35] *American President Lines, Ltd., et al.*, 7 C.A.B. 799 (1947).

[36] See Lewis W. Britton, ed., *Transportation in 1948*, p. 172.

[37] For a statement of the surface carrier position see Association of American Railroads, *Air Transportation*, Washington, 1947, pp. 119-121.

[38] *Interlocking Relationships, Walter S. McLucas, et al.*, 6 C.A.B. 399 (1945).

[39] Civil Aeronautics Board, *Annual Report*, 1946, p. 17. See also, *Traffic World*, December 9, 1950, pp. 57-58.

[40] Civil Aeronautics Board, *Annual Report*, 1948, p. 29.

manufacturer of helicopters was denied because there appeared to be some prospect of the airline making use of helicopters,[41] but in another case a similar relationship was approved on the ground that helicopters were not suitable for the operations conducted by the line.[42]

Contracts and agreements. A large number of contracts and agreements between airlines have been filed with the Civil Aeronautics Board in accordance with the requirements of the law. Some of these are of a routine nature, involving such things as joint use of airports and other ground facilities. Some involve necessary joint arrangements in connection with the interchange of traffic, issuance of passes, uniformity of rules, contracts with the Railway Express Agency, rate agreements, agreements with motor carriers for pickup and delivery service, negotiations with employees, and other operating problems. For the most part these agreements have been approved because they result in substantial economies without restricting competition unduly. Still other agreements have involved the establishment of trade associations like the Air Transport Association of America and other similar cooperative agencies.

FEEDER LINES

Nature of problem. Air transportation tends to be offered only between larger centers of population. This situation is unsatisfactory from the public point of view because the people living and working in the thousands of communities not within the orbit of regular airline service contribute through tax payments to the maintenance of an air transportation system which is of only limited value to them. Nor is this situation conducive to the further development of air transportation or to the expansion of the business of existing airlines. If a community is reasonably close to a major airline stop, a combination of surface and air transportation may be practical, especially if a fairly long movement by air is contemplated. But between many nonairline points surface transportation is as fast as or faster than a combination of surface and air transportation. And since the surface transportation is likely to be cheaper than a combination movement, particularly where goods shipments are concerned, the situation doubly militates against the use of air service. Furthermore, even where possibilities of combining the two services do exist, the airlines are at a disadvantage in that they usually do not have facilities for soliciting off-line traffic.

The obvious solution to the above shortcoming is to establish feeder or

---

[41] *A. Felix du Pont, Jr.—All American Aviation, Inc.*, 8 C.A.B. 672 (1947).
[42] Civil Aeronautics Board, *Annual Report*, 1948, p. 29.

local service airlines. Such airlines, utilizing small planes and simplified operating facilities and techniques, could serve to funnel traffic to and from the trunk line air carriers and also to provide a local service between points not now served by air. Unfortunately, even small planes are expensive to operate in terms of carrying capacity, and in a great many parts of the country the volume of traffic available is not yet adequate to make such operations possible without heavy government subsidies. Furthermore, the necessity of making frequent stops in order to serve the maximum number of points in a given area tends to reduce the speed advantage enjoyed by air carriers over surface carriers.

Feeder line investigation. In the early years of its history the Civil Aeronautics Board received a large number of applications for authority to provide local and feeder service, and on March 22, 1943, it initiated a general investigation of local and feeder line service. Hearings were held all over the United States, and widespread support for an expansion of air transportation service was expressed at these hearings; but there were sharp differences of opinion over how this expanded service should be provided. The existing airlines supported an expansion of service but were opposed to the entry of new companies into the field, while new applicants felt that feeder line operations and services were different from those already in existence and that the development of feeder lines should not be limited to the major airlines.

On July 11, 1944, the Civil Aeronautics Board issued an opinion with regard to policy matters relating to the development of local and feeder airline service, and its subsequent actions have been based largely on the policy outlined in this report.[43] The Board recognized that the air traffic potential at small cities was not encouraging, that the airplane used in short haul transportation would face keen competition from surface carriers, and that the fares which could be charged would not be such as to make short haul operations self-sustaining, at least for a time.

The Board recognized that it was expected to encourage the development of an air transportation system, however, and so it felt justified within limits in giving qualified applicants an opportunity to translate their plans and estimates into the results of experience. Because it felt that the services established would be largely experimental and because it did not want to saddle the Government with an extended financial liability in the form of mail payments, the Board decided to issue temporary certificates to feeder lines covering a period of three years only. Thus if a particular feeder line proved to be so unsuccessful as to necessitate excessive govern-

---

[43] *Investigation of Local, Feeder, and Pick-Up Service,* 6 C.A.B. 1 (1944).

ment support, the Board could refuse to renew its certificate and so terminate its operations.

Development of feeder and local service. In expanding the air transportation system to provide service to smaller communities the Civil Aeronautics Board has in some cases permitted existing trunk lines to extend their operations, and in some cases it has permitted the establishment of new companies to provide an exclusively local and feeder service. As of September 30, 1951, there were twenty-one feeder lines authorized to conduct operations on a temporary basis, most of these operations being concentrated in the Atlantic coast area, along the Pacific coast, in the Texas-Oklahoma area, in the area just west and southwest of Lake Michigan, and in the Rocky Mountain region. In granting certificates for feeder line operations the Board has adopted certain principles which are worth noting briefly. It has, for example, not looked with favor upon feeder lines skipping intermediate points along their routes in such a way as to provide what is essentially a trunk line operation in competition with existing trunk line carriers. And in some cases it has withheld the issuance of a certificate until a satisfactory showing had been made within a reasonable period of time regarding the adequacy of airport facilities at intermediate points.[44]

The Board has followed a stated policy that, in general, where a feeder carrier's route is duplicated by a trunk line carrier, and the route is not necessary to the trunk line carrier's operation, such route should be served by the feeder line alone. Similarly, it has proposed in several cases involving feeder route extensions, that certain points on feeder lines served by trunk lines should have the trunk line service suspended. On the other hand, where a route is a necessary and integral part of a trunk line carrier's system, and essential to its economical operation, then such route should not be served by a feeder carrier. In brief, competition between feeder lines and trunk lines is discouraged.[45]

With the approach of the expiration dates of temporary certificates issued to feeder lines, the Civil Aeronautics Board issued show-cause orders to determine whether, in the light of a carrier's record and conditions in its area of operation, its certificate should be extended or terminated. In general, certificates have been extended for five-year periods, although in a few cases extensions of particular route segments have been denied or made for one-year periods only. In the case of Florida Airways, Inc., which had applied for a five-year extension of its temporary certificate, the Civil Aeronautics Board was unable to find that the service could develop to the

---

[44] *North Central Case,* 7 C.A.B. 639 (1946).
[45] Civil Aeronautics Board, *Annual Report,* 1949, p. 12.

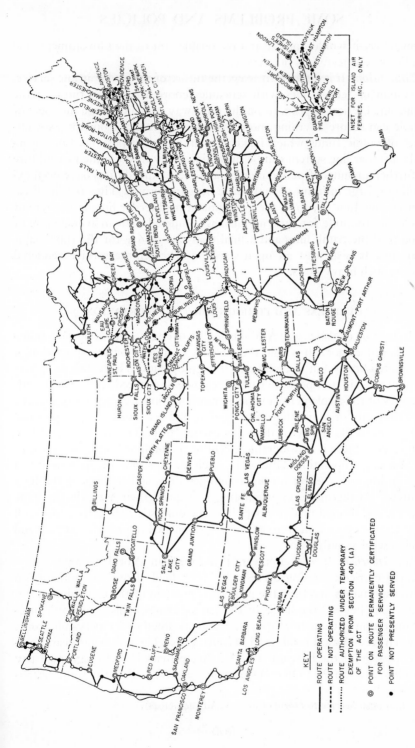

FIGURE 8. *Feeder Airline System, September 1951.* (Adapted from map courtesy Civil Aeronautics Board.)

KEY

—— ROUTE OPERATING

----- ROUTE NOT OPERATING

········· ROUTE AUTHORIZED UNDER TEMPORARY
EXEMPTION FROM SECTION 401 (A)
OF THE ACT

◎ POINT ON ROUTE PERMANENTLY CERTIFICATED
FOR PASSENGER SERVICE

● POINT NOT PRESENTLY SERVED

INSET FOR ISLAND AIR
FERRIES, INC., ONLY

point where it would operate at a reasonable cost to the Government, and the line's certificate was not renewed.[46]

Conclusion. It is difficult to assess the future of the feeder airline service. A system of feeder lines with schedules coordinated with those of the trunk line carriers appears to be the only way in which large numbers of people can secure anything more than minor benefits from the expenditures of public funds which make air transportation possible. But apparently a feeder line system can be maintained only through the expenditure of further amounts of public money, and these expenditures have been exceedingly large in terms of immediate benefits derived. Thus for the fiscal year ending June 30, 1950, the government paid feeder lines at the rate of $28.65 per ton mile for carrying mail as compared with an average rate of $1.09 paid the trunk lines and a final mail rate of 63¢ for the four major operators. It is at least an open question whether the service rendered justifies such heavy costs.

OVERSEAS AND FOREIGN AIR TRANSPORTATION

A word of explanation. A discussion of overseas and foreign air transportation does not fall within the purview of a book on transportation in the United States, but overseas and foreign operations have had an impact on domestic air transportation which cannot be ignored entirely. The advantages of the airplane for overseas transportation are even more marked than they are for domestic transportation, and since there are no physical limitations to the ability of domestic carriers to provide overseas and foreign service, there is considerable incentive to combine both types of service in a single operation. Obviously, such an expansion of operations can have an important effect on domestic operations and services of the lines involved. Furthermore, in attempting to expand their activities into the overseas and foreign field of operations, the domestic airlines have met with considerable opposition from an airline certificated to provide overseas and foreign services only.

Pan American World Airways. Pan American World Airways, a certificated carrier operating exclusively in the field of overseas and foreign air transportation, has been the principal opponent of the expansion of domestic lines beyond the limits of the United States. This company's original operation got under way in 1927 and consisted of a ninety-mile route between Key West, Florida, and Havana, Cuba. The following year, however, passage of the Foreign Air Mail Act provided for foreign mail pay subsidies, and the Post Office Department awarded all of the routes estab-

---

[46] *Additional Service to Florida Case,* 9 C.A.B. 444 (1948).

lished to Pan American. These air-mail contracts enabled Pan American to extend its activities into the West Indies, to Mexico, and to Central and South America; and further expansion resulted from subsequent exclusive mail contracts.

The Pan American monopoly is said to have been fostered by the Postmaster General who believed that a single carrier was to be preferred over a multiplicity of carriers operating in the foreign field. Be that as it may, Pan American continued to expand, and until 1944 it was practically the only United States carrier receiving air-mail payments for flying mail to countries outside of North America. Although a number of United States lines are operating in the overseas and foreign field at the present time, Pan American has grown to be the world's largest airline, operating 127,930 route miles as of December 31, 1950, with additional mileage operated by subsidiary and affiliated companies.[47]

Chosen instrument doctrine. During World War II the Civil Aeronautics Board issued temporary certificates to certain domestic carriers to provide foreign air transportation service, and several of the domestic lines gained considerable experience in this field as a result of contract flying operations carried on for the Army and Navy. It is not surprising, therefore, that domestic airlines soon began to file applications for permanent certificates to operate in overseas and foreign service, arguing that competition was desirable in this field. It was also pointed out that to permit one company to enjoy a monopoly of foreign air transportation would place that company in a position of tremendous power and that it might interfere with the implementation of United States foreign policy. In 1945 the Civil Aeronautics Board concluded that competition would be desirable [48] and granted operating rights to domestic companies.

Pan American, together with various individuals both in and out of Congress, has opposed the expansion of domestic carriers into the international field. The principal argument for its so-called "chosen instrument" doctrine has been that most of the countries providing international service do so through the use of a single government-owned or government-subsidized company and that the only way in which the United States can compete with foreign lines is to adopt a similar policy. Bills to effectuate such a policy have been introduced into Congress from time to time, but so far all have been defeated.

Pan American, concerned with the expansion of domestic lines into the international field, made application for authority to establish eight domes-

---

[47] *Air Transport Facts and Figures,* 11th edition, Washington, Air Transport Association of America, 1950, p. 15.
[48] *Northeast Airlines, Inc., et al.,* 6 C.A.B. 319 (1945).

tic routes serving thirteen major cities in the United States. It proposed to offer direct service between these points and points on its overseas and foreign routes, offering newer planes, higher speeds, and lower rates than prevailed at the time it made its application. Hearings began late in 1946 and the proceedings dragged out until August 1, 1950, on which date the Civil Aeronautics Board refused its approval.[49]

SUGGESTED READINGS

See references for Chapter 29.

---

[49] *Traffic World*, August 5, 1950, p. 13; January 13, 1951, p. 46.

29

Some Problems and Policies
of
AIR TRANSPORTATION (II)

RATE AND OPERATING PROBLEMS: AIRLINE COSTS AND REVENUES

Nature of airline costs. Airline costs may be divided into capital costs, operating expenses, and tax accruals. Capital costs include interest on funded debt, interest on bank loans, and payments made in connection with the purchase of equipment. Operating expenses are divided into two groups, aircraft operating expenses and ground and indirect expenses. Aircraft operating expenses include the direct costs incurred in operating an airplane, direct maintenance of flight equipment, and depreciation on flight equipment. Ground and indirect expenses include a variety of ground expenses, various selling expenses, and general and administrative expenses. Tax accruals include amounts due in the form of property taxes, income taxes, and the like.

Constant v. variable costs. An analysis of airline operations suggests that constant costs are of some significance in commercial air transportation, although not as important as in the railroad business. One of the reasons why they are less important than in railroad transportation is found in the fact that the fixed charges are smaller relative to total costs. Interest on funded debt, an important cost in the railroad business, was practically nonexistent in air transportation up to 1944, although since 1944 long-term debt has increased substantially. Airlines have no expensive right-of-way investment, nor do they have any large investment in airports. Fees paid for the use of landing and takeoff facilities might be said to represent in some measure a charge similar to interest on investment in railroad terminal facilities, but these fees are small relative to the cost of providing the facilities, and they are only partially constant since they vary with the number of landings and takeoffs. The airlines must, of course, meet the cost of providing flying equipment, but this is said to be small relative to total costs.

Aircraft operating expenses, including fuel, wages of crew members, direct maintenance, and depreciation, vary with the number of flights made but tend to be constant per airplane mile flown. If it could be assumed that airplanes were always flown with a full pay load of passengers, mail, and goods, then these costs would be variable because the number of planes could be increased and decreased to meet varying quantities of traffic. For various reasons which are discussed presently, however, planes very often are not fully loaded. Hence there is an element of constant cost involved here, and it is not insignificant. In the case of ground and indirect expenses there will, of course, be some variations in cost with variations in volume of traffic, but there is a hard core of constant cost in the form of minimum maintenance forces and equipment, station personnel, sales forces, and the like. Airline property taxes and other state taxes have been nominal, but federal income taxes have grown considerably in recent years. These taxes, to the extent that they can be looked upon as costs, tend to increase the variable aspect of airline costs.

As far as the present writer is aware, the extent to which airline costs are constant or variable has not been given much consideration. From what has been said above it will be apparent that constant costs arising out of fixed charges are relatively small today but are becoming more important. On the other hand, because it is necessary to operate many planes at only partial capacity, there is a substantial element of constant cost found in aircraft operating expenses, and ground and indirect expenses also exhibit important elements of constant costs. Hence, while constant costs probably are not as significant in air transportation as they are in railroad transportation, they are nevertheless a factor of some importance.[1]

Terminal v. line-haul costs. The cost of handling passengers and goods at terminals is not as large relative to line-haul costs for air carriers as it is for railroads. It has been pointed out that terminal-operating costs as shown by the Civil Aeronautics Board do not take into consideration landing and takeoff operations which are expensive and essentially a part of terminal operations. This consideration probably is not too important at the present time, however, since air carriers tend to concentrate on the long hauls, thus minimizing landing and takeoff operations. Because terminal costs are low relative to plane-operating costs, total operating costs per ton mile do not follow the tapering principle to the same extent as railroad costs.

Social costs. The above discussion of airline costs refers only to those costs which are met by the carriers themselves. Air carrier costs do not include the cost to society of providing the necessary airways nor do they cover more than a part of the cost of providing airport facilities. Some day the air carriers may be required to pay their share of these costs through

---

[1] This characteristic of airline costs is discussed in Chapter II of Claude E. Puffer, *Air Transportation.* Philadelphia: The Blakiston Company, 1941. Professor Puffer's data are drawn from the experiences of the 1930's. He concludes that air transportation is subject to decreasing costs both in the short and long run.

Table XXXII

OPERATING EXPENSES AND REVENUES OF DOMESTIC TRUNK LINE AIR CARRIERS [2]

(Fiscal years ending June 30)

	1942	1943	1944	1945	1946	1947	1948	1949	1950
Operating revenues:									
Passenger	$75,876,084	$77,594,541	$94,089,870	$140,879,885	$211,406,179	$291,193,233	$319,268,199	$363,844,734	$390,948,417
Express	} 4,287,308	} 8,169,487	7,360,177	} 10,308,643	7,649,835	11,036,575	9,866,435	9,430,864	9,918,297
Freight			1,810,473		1,658,668	6,187,359	11,015,498	16,309,495	19,893,413
Excess baggage	969,229	1,610,227		2,152,121	2,252,561	3,165,565	3,808,325	4,153,123	4,497,557
Nonscheduled transport	336,442	24,157	5,424	62,599	501,917	1,548,026	1,048,023	1,979,253	3,542,001
Other nonmail revenue	1,007,405	1,340,131	977,818	799,656	1,080,867	2,558,529	1,647,878	1,839,730	2,507,564
Total nonmail revenue	82,476,468	88,738,543	104,243,762	154,202,904	224,550,027	315,689,287	346,654,358	397,557,199	431,307,249
U. S. mail revenue	23,393,159	21,981,568	27,489,105	34,918,577	27,335,433	23,967,417	37,690,530	47,824,307	45,436,902
Total operating revenue	105,869,627	110,720,111	131,732,867	189,121,481	251,885,460	339,656,704	384,344,888	445,381,506	476,744,151
Total operating expenses	91,860,493	80,778,749	105,279,609	146,415,298	236,482,440	359,504,418	390,403,259	428,286,742	448,523,957
Operating profit	$14,009,134	$29,941,362	$26,453,258	$42,706,183	$15,403,020	$19,847,714 (loss)	$6,058,371 (loss)	$17,094,764	$28,221,094

[2] Civil Aeronautics Board, *Annual Report*, 1950, p. 45.

the assessment of user charges, but as long as the present system of operational subsidies prevails not much would be gained by assessing user charges, at least as far as the scheduled airlines are concerned.

Airline revenues. Some idea of the nature of airline revenues today, as compared with the revenues of earlier years, may be gleaned from Table XXXII which shows airline revenues from different sources as compared with operating expenses. It will be observed that passenger revenues have increased substantially in recent years, and this increase has been accompanied by an over-all decline in the ratio of mail to nonmail revenue. The rapid growth of air freight should also be noted, along with the fact that it has outstripped by far the air express revenues. The losses incurred in 1947 and 1948 in the face of rapidly rising revenues are explained in part by higher costs and in part by declining load factors, a consideration to which attention may now be directed.

LOAD FACTORS

Revenue passenger load factor. The revenue passenger load factor is the ratio of revenue passenger miles flown to the total number of seat miles available and is an index of the extent to which plane carrying capacity is being utilized. Thus an annual revenue passenger load factor of 70 would mean that on the average 70 per cent of the seats available were occupied by paying passengers. Since the cost of operating a passenger flight is about the same whether the plane is practically empty or filled to capacity, a certain minimum load factor must be maintained if the carrier is to break even on its operations, and variations above and below this break-even point determine whether operations are conducted at a profit or a loss. The size of the load factor necessary to break even is not, of course, a constant but varies substantially with changing conditions. It will rise with an increase in costs of operation or with a reduction in passenger fares, and it will fall with a decline in operating costs or an increase in passenger fares. Also, since passenger planes generally carry mail, express, and cargo, as well as passengers, variations in the volume of traffic and revenues derived from these sources will influence the size of the load factor necessary to break even.

Load factors achieved by domestic trunk line air carriers in recent years are shown in Table XXXIII, together with airline profits for these years. It will be observed that in 1938 planes were operated at less than 50 per cent of their passenger carrying capacity and that the 1938 load factor was insufficient to enable the domestic trunk lines to break even on operations. During preparations for war and with the advent of World War II itself the load factor increased rapidly, approaching 90 in fiscal 1944. As might be expected, the break-even point also increased as operating expenses rose, but it did not rise as fast as the load factor, and a substantial excess of revenues over expenses was the result. With the close of the war, load factors began to fall rapidly and operating profits turned into operating losses for a brief period.

Table XXXIII

REVENUE PASSENGER LOAD FACTORS AND OPERATING PROFITS OR LOSSES OF DOMESTIC TRUNK LINE AIR CARRIERS [3]

(Fiscal years ending June 30)

Year	Load Factor	Operating Revenues Expressed as Percentage of Operating Expenses	Excess of Revenues Over Expenses
1938	49.08	96.39	−3.61
1939	53.03	103.45	3.45
1940	58.56	111.90	11.90
1941	56.48	104.77	4.77
1942	64.29	115.25	15.25
1943	82.20	137.07	37.07
1944	89.48	125.13	25.13
1945	88.60	129.17	29.17
1946	85.96	106.51	6.51
1947	71.29	94.48	−5.52
1948	62.20	98.45	−1.55
1949	58.52	103.99	3.99
1950	59.10	106.29	6.29

Maximum practical load factors. The high load factors achieved by the domestic trunk line air carriers during World War II were the result of unusual wartime conditions which hardly could be expected to be duplicated in time of peace. Early in 1942 the airlines were called upon to relinquish more than half of their transport planes for use by the United States and other countries, which in turn meant handling an ever increasing volume of passenger traffic with only about half as many planes. Applications for space reservations exceeded space available on many flights, and this practically guaranteed capacity operations even on days of the week normally not popular for travel. In order to maximize the use of equipment it was necessary to schedule stops at hours which were inconvenient to the traveling public, but people were willing to put up with this inconvenience in order to obtain space. Some normally light traffic routes were suspended and the equipment concentrated on routes of heavy travel. Under the circumstances it is not surprising that load factors rose to very high levels and operating profits rose with them.

With the end of World War II there was a decline in the over-all de-

---

[3] Civil Aeronautics Board, *Annual Report*, various years.

mand for common carrier passenger transportation. At the same time the end of the war released airline equipment utilized by the Government, and it became possible for the airlines to obtain new equipment. Keen competition developed between airlines and surface carriers for the declining total volume of traffic, and competition increased between the airlines themselves as more equipment became available. In order to attract traffic it was necessary to establish more frequent flights and at hours which were convenient to the traveling public. Also, service was reestablished on light traffic routes which had been suspended during the war. But while airline passenger traffic increased, the growth in traffic was accompanied by an even greater growth in available seat miles. Hence load factors declined, and operating profits dropped sharply from wartime peaks. It seems to be well agreed that the high load factors achieved during the war cannot be duplicated under peacetime operating conditions, and it has been said that a load factor of between 65 and 70 is the maximum feasible where competition requires that the public be provided with reasonably adequate service at convenient hours.[4]

Feeder lines. Feeder line load factors are available only for recent years. For 1946 the load factor was 57.29 but in 1947 it fell sharply to 29.80 and to 27.18 in 1948. A slight rise to 27.92 took place in 1949, and in 1950 the load factor stood at 28.88. These low load factors help to explain the very high rates of mail pay received by feeder lines. Again a question may be raised as to the desirability of supporting a branch of the airline industry which is so poorly patronized by the public.

Possibility of increased load factors. Some airlines, of course, enjoy load factors sufficiently large, and operating costs sufficiently low, to make their operations profitable, but this has not been true of others. If the airlines are ever to operate free of operating subsidies, not to mention subsidy in the form of airports and airways provided at public expense, they must increase their load factors, decrease their operating costs, or both. Where competition between airlines exists, elimination of this competition would no doubt bring some increase in the load factor, although in many cases surface carrier competition places limitations on the extent to which service can be reduced in this way. Then, too, it is not at all clear that a complete elimination of airline competition is in the public interest. However, if excessive competition exists, then some reduction might be desirable, and there is evidence that the Civil Aeronautics Board is aware of this possibility.

In 1948 reduced rates were inaugurated for families traveling as a unit

---

[4] Department of Commerce, *Industry Report, Domestic Transportation,* August-September, 1946, p. 27.

on the first three days of the week, these being days of light traffic, but by the middle of 1951 there was some feeling that this device for boosting load factors no longer was necessary. The growth of air freight in recent years offers some opportunities for offsetting light load factors on certain runs. Air cargo does not require the expeditious handling necessary in the case of air mail and air express, and where good service requires the operation of several flights, air cargo can be handled on those planes where the volume of passenger traffic is the lightest.

Reductions in operating costs. Since the necessity of offering frequent service at hours which are convenient to the traveling public places a more or less definite limit on attainable load factors, considerable attention has been devoted to the possibility of reducing operating costs as a means of improving operating profits. Long distance nonstop flights have been increasing in recent years because of the saving in time realized through the elimination of frequent stops and interchanges. Such flights also result in a reduction in cost through a reduction in landing and takeoff operations, but on the other hand, long distance flights require additional fuel supplies which tend to reduce the pay load which can be carried. Progress has been made in recent years in reducing operating costs per seat mile by building larger and more efficient planes, but while increased seating capacity reduces costs per seat mile, it intensifies the load factor problem.

RATES

General level of rates. The Civil Aeronautics Act directs the Civil Aeronautics Board to fix rates for the carriage of passengers and goods which will move the traffic and at the same time enable each carrier to earn enough, under honest, economical, and efficient management, to provide adequate and efficient service. As long as the Government stands ready to cover deficits arising out of the over-all operations of a given carrier, however, it is hard to see how a general rule of rate making applied to goods and passenger transportation can have much meaning. If at some future time, the subsidy element is eliminated, either as a result of improved earnings or a change in public policy, then the rule of rate making may take on some significance.

Rates on specific commodities. Because space in an airplane is at a premium, a space-weight system of air cargo rate determination has been adopted. If the over-all size of a shipment is not in excess of 300 cubic inches per pound of weight, it is charged for on the basis of actual weight, subject to a minimum weight of 25 pounds; but if the shipment exceeds 300 cubic inches in bulk per pound of weight, then each 300 cubic inches of bulk is considered to be equal to one pound in computing the charge.

A few airlines offer lower rates for shipments exceeding 16,000 pounds, but generally the rate is fixed at so much per pound regardless of the size of the shipment. In some cases specific commodity rates are published to attract desirable traffic to the airlines or to assure a lading where a directional unbalance of traffic exists. The space-weight system is also used in computing air express charges. In addition, air express is subject to a minimum charge which has the effect of reducing the rate per pound charged on heavier shipments.

Fares and rates between points. Airline passenger fares are based on the distance principle but are strongly influenced by competitive conditions. Where airline competition exists, all of the carriers involved will charge the same fare regardless of differences in route mileage. Fares tend to be higher where airline competition is lacking than where competition exists. Fares also are influenced by the effectiveness of the competition offered by surface carriers. Express charges are based on a block system with a uniform rate per block. Again, however, the use of a minimum charge has the effect of reducing somewhat the cost per mile as length of haul increases. Air cargo rates in general have been the same per unit of distance regardless of length of haul. In the spring of 1950, however, the Civil Aeronautics Board permitted the establishment of reduced rates, below the minima established in 1948, on air cargo from the West and South to the North and Northeast in an effort to overcome a directional lack of balance of traffic; and these rates are tapered to provide a lower charge per mile as length of haul increases.[5]

AIR-MAIL COMPENSATION

Congressional directive. The Civil Aeronautics Act directs the Civil Aeronautics Board to fix the compensation to be paid to the airlines for carrying United States mail. No specific rate-making techniques are set forth in the law other than the general directive instructing the Board to take into consideration, among other rate-making elements, the need of a carrier for mail compensation sufficient, together with all other sources of revenue, to enable it under honest, economical, and efficient management, to maintain and continue the development of air transportation. Or, to put the matter more plainly, mail compensation should be sufficient to cover any operating losses and enable the carrier to obtain a satisfactory return on its investment. Actually the law provides the Civil Aeronautics Board with two measuring sticks for determining the rate of compensation for carrying the mail. One of these is the amount which would constitute a

---

[5] *Traffic World*, April 15, 1950, p. 47.

reasonable payment for the service rendered, and the other is the need of the carrier to earn a return on its investment.

Early policy. At the time the Civil Aeronautics Act was passed the air transport industry was in poor financial condition, and numerous applications were filed for fixing rates of mail pay in accordance with the terms of the law. In deciding these early cases no great departures were made from earlier methods of determining rates of compensation. As nonmail traffic began to increase, however, some of the larger carriers, who were still being paid pretty much in accordance with rates established in an earlier period of light traffic, began to make substantial profits, and the Civil Aeronautics Board began to order reductions in mail pay. This gave rise to the question of whether or not the new rates should be made retroactive to recapture past excessive profits, but the Board decided against such a policy.[6] Its reason for doing this was that the carriers had consistently plowed earnings back into the business and had not paid them out in excessive dividends. Also the Board concluded that accumulated earnings were not excessive when viewed in the light of the full period of operations. It did indicate, however, that the carriers should not pay dividends from the excess profits they were permitted to retain and that such profits would not be considered in the rate base.

Route v. carrier concept. In an early case a carrier opened up a new route over which it sustained losses for a short time before the route was designated as a mail route and funds appropriated for mail service, and a question was raised whether such losses should be met by the Government. The conclusion of the Board on this point was that air-mail compensation was to be based on the need of the carrier as a whole, after taking into consideration other revenues, regardless of conditions on any particular geographical division of its operations.[7]

Rate base. In exercising its rate-making functions, the Civil Aeronautics Board declared in 1943 that it had consistently declined to measure the reasonableness of rates in terms of the fair return on fair value doctrine, certainly a wise decision in the light of the earlier experiences of regulatory commissions with this doctrine. The Board has held that the rate of return should be predicated upon funds actually and legitimately invested in the transportation business. Consistent with this decision it has declined to make any allowance for going concern value unless it can be shown that the amounts claimed represent amounts actually and legitimately expended. In numerous cases, too, the carriers urged that extension and developmental expenses should be included as legitimate operating expenses in determin-

---

[6] *Pan American-Grace Airways, Inc.—Mail Rates,* 3 C.A.B. 550 (1942).
[7] *Chicago and Southern Air Line Mail Rates,* 3 C.A.B. 161 (1941).

ing fair and reasonable mail rates, but the Board has held that the burden of proof is on the carriers to show the reasonableness and propriety of such expenditures. It condemned such expense items as gifts, dinners, and other entertainment, designed to secure local public support in regulatory proceedings.[8]

Service v. need rates. As the volume of nonmail traffic increased, the earnings of some of the larger lines reached a point where they were no longer dependent upon air-mail subsidy payments to maintain profitable operations, and the Civil Aeronautics Board found it necessary to make a distinction between the rate of compensation paid to these carriers and the rates paid to carriers which still needed government support. For those carriers which had attained self-sufficiency, in the sense that operating revenues balanced or more than balanced operating costs, the Civil Aeronautics Board established rates based on cost of service insofar as it could be determined, but for the other carriers it continued to authorize rates based on the needs of the individual lines.

In 1943 the service rate, the term used for a rate based on cost of service, was fixed at 60¢ per ton mile, and as of June 30, 1944, eleven of the sixteen domestic trunk line carriers were being paid service rates. In the following year this rate was reduced to 45¢ for the four largest carriers, American, United, Eastern, and Transcontinental and Western, carriers which handled 86 per cent of the domestic ton miles of mail flown in the year ending June 30, 1945. Unfortunately the self-sufficiency which had been achieved by most of the domestic certificated carriers during the war years was followed by postwar financial difficulties, and for a time the Civil Aeronautics Board found it necessary to allow them substantial increases in mail pay to help overcome operating deficits. In one case it refused a request for additional mail pay on the ground that the carrier had unnecessarily overexpanded its facilities, an action which should not be underwritten with mail compensation.[9] Subsequently a number of service rates were established again.

Retroactive mail pay. In some of the air-mail pay increase cases the carriers urged that increases should be made retroactive to cover losses incurred during a period before the institution of the proceedings for higher rates of pay. As noted previously, the Board had refused to make reductions in rates of mail pay retroactive, and it now held that it had no legal power to review final mail rates which were in effect and not questioned before the institution of new rate proceedings. In other words, an increase in the rate of mail pay could not be allowed to cover losses incurred prior to the

---

[8] Civil Aeronautics Board, *Annual Report*, 1943, p. 18.
[9] *Traffic World*, May 7, 1949, p. 52.

institution of a proceeding for higher rates. This matter was taken to the courts by the carrier involved, but in 1949 the Supreme Court upheld the contention of the Civil Aeronautics Board that it could not make rate increases retroactive to cover past losses.[10]

Separation of subsidy payments. Several recent developments have led to an increasing demand in Congress for a separation of subsidy payments from payments made for carrying the air mail. In the first place, when the Civil Aeronautics Board refused to make retroactive mail pay increases, the airlines immediately filed for substantial increases in mail pay so that any subsequent losses would relate back to the time of filing, a procedure which would, in effect, assure them retroactive mail pay increases. Second, the Board ordered substantial lump sum mail payments to several large carriers to help cover losses in the period following World War II, and the size of these payments attracted considerable attention to the policy of practically guaranteeing the profits of scheduled airlines. Third, the Board issued a show-cause order in which it proposed an increase in mail pay for a carrier which had not requested an increase, and in another case it proposed an increase larger than the carrier had asked. Without attempting to evaluate these actions of the Board, it is easy to see how they caused some members of Congress to wonder if an unnecessary waste of public funds was involved in mail payments. Some criticisms also have been directed at the amounts of mail pay subsidy being granted to maintain feeder lines.

The practice of burying airline subsidies in Post Office Department appropriations puts Congress and the people of the United States in the position of paying out money to subsidize private business enterprises without knowing how much money is involved or whether or not the payments are necessary. A number of bills have been introduced to separate subsidies from mail payments, and the Civil Aeronautics Board has undertaken to make such a separation on its own account. This will have the advantage of eliminating, or at least bringing to light, any possibly excessive subsidies, and it may be discovered that the amount of subsidy necessary to support certain carriers is not justified by the service they render.

A BASIC PROBLEM OF PUBLIC POLICY: SINGLE VERSUS DUAL REGULATORY AUTHORITY

Nature of problem. The Interstate Commerce Commission was created to regulate the interstate operations of the nation's railroads, and when Congress assumed jurisdiction over interstate highway transportation in

---

[10] *Transcontinental & Western Air, Inc.* v. *Civil Aeronautics Board,* 336 U.S. 601 (1949).

1935 and expanded its control over domestic water transportation in 1940, the regulation of these forms of transportation was placed in the hands of the Interstate Commerce Commission as a matter of course. But when Congress undertook the regulation of commercial air transportation in 1938 it created an entirely new and independent regulatory body to exercise jurisdiction over the nation's airlines. Before the adoption of the Civil Aeronautics Act there had been considerable support for placing the airlines, along with other interstate agencies of transportation, under the jurisdiction of the Interstate Commerce Commission, and a good many students still believe that all forms of transportation should be regulated by a single agency. There is involved here a basic issue of public policy which is of considerable importance, for the future if not for the immediate present. It will be useful, therefore, to examine some of the pros and cons of the question of single versus dual regulatory control.

CASE FOR SINGLE REGULATORY AUTHORITY

Equal regulation. It is sometimes said that the demand for a single regulatory commission arises out of the belief that surface carriers, and specifically the railroads, are subjected to unregulated competition from the airlines and that it has been demonstrated time and again that competition between regulated and unregulated carriers is neither equitable nor desirable. Stated in this way the argument is, of course, ridiculous. It is true that competition between regulated and unregulated carriers can be inequitable and contrary to the public interest, but it hardly can be said that airlines are unregulated. Considering the short history of air transportation, Congress has done a pretty extensive job of regulating this segment of the transportation industry.

A variation of the above argument is that regulation by a single body is necessary to assure equal regulation of all carriers, the implication being that airlines are not regulated as extensively as surface carriers. Obviously, when one carrier is subjected to more complete regulation than another, the problem differs only in degree from that which arises when one carrier is not regulated at all; but is it true that airlines are not regulated as extensively as surface carriers? The railroads are subjected to a wider variety of economic controls than are air carriers, but air carrier safety regulation is much more comprehensive than is true in the case of the railroads. A point may be made of the fact that all railroads are subject to regulation while a good many air transportation concerns have been exempted at least partly from economic regulation, but at the same time it is well to note that the bulk of air traffic is handled by carriers which are subject to economic regulation.

SOME PROBLEMS AND POLICIES

The operating rights of motor carriers are much more severely restricted than is true of airlines, but motor carrier safety regulation is insignificant as compared with air carrier safety regulation. It seems reasonable to suppose that a much larger volume of traffic is free of economic regulation in the case of motor carriers than in the case of air carriers. And, of course, a very large volume of domestic water transportation remains unregulated. As a matter of fact, there is less difference in the degree of regulation applied to airlines as compared with railroads, than there is between the railroads and domestic water carriers, both of which are regulated by the same body. Under these circumstances it is obvious that differences in degrees of regulation have no bearing on the question at hand.

If equality of regulation were desirable, then a good case could be made for a single regulatory body, but equality of regulation is neither desirable nor possible. While many of the regulatory problems encountered in air transportation are identical with those found in surface transportation, consideration must be given to the fact that each type of carrier has its own peculiar problems which necessitate some differentiation in the nature and degree of regulation to apply. Furthermore, some consideration must be given to the stage of development in which a given type of transportation finds itself, for too much regulation during the early stages of development can stifle a new form of transportation and thus be worse than no regulation at all.

Equitable treatment of all carriers. Arguments that a single regulatory agency is necessary to prevent the inequities which arise when one carrier is regulated while another carrier is unregulated or only partly regulated are indefensible, but they should not be permitted to draw attention from an outwardly similar but basically different argument in favor of a single commission. The real objections to dual commission regulation arise out of the difficulty of achieving equity in the treatment of different types of carriers under such a setup, and the impossibility of developing a national transportation system when different carriers are regulated by agencies completely independent of each other.

The Interstate Commerce Commission has no direct obligation to consider the effect of any of its decisions on the airlines,[11] and the Civil Aeronautics Board has no obligation at all to consider the effect of its decisions on any form of transportation other than air transportation. Thus even though both air transportation and surface transpor-

---

[11] In a sense it may be said to have an indirect obligation since the national transportation policy refers to the development, coordination, and preservation of a national transportation system by water, highway, and rail, *as well as by other means.*

tation are regulated, the fact that they are regulated by separate and independent agencies leaves the door wide open for possible inequities. With the Civil Aeronautics Board responsible for promoting the well-being of air transportation and the Interstate Commerce Commission responsible for promoting rail, motor, and water transportation, no one is responsible for protecting the public in the event of a conflict between these two promotional policies. And obviously a sound national transportation system will be difficult to evolve as long as the carriers composing this system are not subject to a single control.

OBJECTIONS TO INTERSTATE COMMERCE COMMISSION JURISDICTION OVER AIR TRANSPORTATION

Interstate Commerce Commission railroad minded. If the idea of regulation by a single agency were adopted, it is possible that Congress might see fit to create an entirely new regulatory authority to exercise jurisdiction over all forms of transportation, but the usual presumption is that regulation by a single agency would mean regulation by the Interstate Commerce Commission. Hence most of the objections to regulation by a single agency appear to be objections to granting the Interstate Commerce Commission jurisdiction over air transportation.

Perhaps the most common objection to Interstate Commerce Commission control arises out of the fear that the Commission would regulate the airlines in the interest of the railroads. This same objection was raised to giving the Interstate Commerce Commission control over motor and water carriers, but the fears expressed proved to be groundless. As pointed out in earlier chapters, the Interstate Commerce Act contains a national transportation policy which may be interpreted as a directive designed to protect motor and water carriers from discriminatory treatment, and the Commission has shown little inclination to discriminate against these carriers in favor of the railroads. On the contrary, some might claim that water carriers in particular have been favored by the Commission at the expense of the railroads.

Application of surface carrier regulation to air transportation. It is believed by some that the Interstate Commerce Commission has regulated surface carriers over such a long period of time that it has established numerous precedents which would be used in regulating air transportation whether they were applicable or not. While earlier precedents have been followed to some extent in regulating motor and water carriers, the Commission has said on various occasions that these forms of transportation have their own peculiar characteristics and problems, and it has guided its actions accordingly. It is, of course, impossible to say to what extent the Interstate Commerce Commission would be guided by precedent if it were charged with regulating air transportation, but the Commission is composed of intelligent men who should be able to take cognizance of differences between different kinds of transportation.

Unfamiliarity with air transportation problems. Another objection is to the effect that the Interstate Commerce Commission is unfamiliar with the problems of air transportation. This objection has been countered with the contention that it was not familiar with motor and water transportation problems but managed to overcome this weakness without difficulty. The two cases, however, are not parallel. Motor and water carriers are surface carriers, and in many ways their problems are more like those of the railroads than is the case with the airlines. Although the Commission may not be familiar with air transportation as such, it is more familiar with transportation regulation than any other body, and it would be no more difficult to establish a Bureau of Air Carriers within the Commission, staffed by experts in the field, than it was to establish similar bureaus in connection with motor and water transportation.

Interstate Commerce Commission overworked. Still another objection has been that the Interstate Commerce Commission already has more work than it can handle effectively. To an ever increasing extent the Commission has had to turn over its functions to examiners who hold hearings and render proposed reports, while the members of the Commission confine themselves to major issues and to complaints arising from proposed reports of examiners. There is little doubt that the Commission does have more work than it can handle effectively, and this has resulted in extended delays in connection with certain major decisions.

Safety problem. It will be recalled that at one time responsibility for the control and development of civil aeronautics was scattered among several different government agencies, and one of the reasons for the adoption of the Civil Aeronautics Act was to bring these various activities under the jurisdiction of a single agency. Without doubt one of the most important governmental functions in connection with civil aviation has been that of promoting safety, for there is no mode of transportation where the exercise of every precaution is so vital. The need for regulation to assure maximum safety, however, is not confined to commercial air transportation but is essential to private flying as well. Not only must private operators be protected from the consequences of their own carelessness, but also public lives and property must be protected. Since in many ways the same safety rules apply to both commercial and private flying, it is sound policy to have both regulated by a single body. Furthermore, since private flying often will be interstate in nature and since private flyers use the same airways and to a considerable extent the same airports as are used by interstate carriers for hire, regulation must be by a national body.

The need for having a single body responsible for safety in all types of flying created something of a dilemma for the early advocates of regulation by the Interstate Commerce Commission. The Commission was established originally to regulate commercial transportation, and it had never attempted to extend its regulatory activities into the field of private transportation except to a very limited extent in connection with the interstate operations of private motor carriers. To have turned the regulation of air transportation over to the Interstate Commerce Commission would have made it necessary for that body to extend its activities into a field which was completely foreign to its history. Furthermore, the Commission had made it clear that it wanted no part in the regulation of private flying.[12]

There is no doubt that the problem of safety regulation played a part in the final decision to establish a separate regulatory body for air transportation. This factor is not as important now as it was in 1938, however, because the Reorganization Act of 1939 placed the administration of safety regulations in the hands of the Civil Aeronautics Administration, leaving the Civil Aeronautics Board only with the responsibility for making rules and regulations.

Promotion of civil aeronautics. Perhaps the most compelling reason for placing the regulation of commercial air transportation in the hands of a separate body has to do with implementing the declared policy of Congress to promote the development of civil aeronautics. The original Civil Aeronautics Act placed the promotion and regulation of civil aeronautics within the confines of a single agency, although since that time it has been found desirable to make a separation between regulation and broad promotional programs. Inasmuch as the regulatory and promotional programs are now separate it might be argued that regulation could be carried on by the Interstate Commerce Commission as well as by the Civil Aeronautics Board, but the objections to such an arrangement are obvious.

Even though such promotional activities as airway construction and aid to airports are carried on by the Civil Aeronautics Administration, the Civil Aeronautics Board functions in some degree as a promotional as well as a regulatory body. Among other things, the Board is charged with carrying on its activities in such a way as to promote civil aero-

---

[12] Charles S. Rhyne, *The Civil Aeronautics Act Annotated.* Washington: National Law Book Company, 1939, p. 58.

nautics, whereas if the Interstate Commerce Commission had been given jurisdiction over air transportation, it appears reasonable to suppose that it would have been directed to promote rail, motor, water, and air transportation without favoring one over the other. In view of the pioneer nature of air transportation it is believed by many that it should be given special consideration, at least until such time as it comes of age. And it seems clear that this policy can be accomplished better by a separate agency than if the regulation of air transportation had been turned over to the Interstate Commerce Commission.

CONCLUSION

Self-interest. There has been a great deal of argument pro and con with regard to the relative merits of separate regulatory bodies as against a single agency, and as is often the case some of the argument has generated more heat than light. Various interests have a stake in the question of single as against dual regulation. The aviation industry and the air transportation industry no doubt feel that they will get more favorable treatment from the Civil Aeronautics Board than they would from the Interstate Commerce Commission, and in this they probably are correct. Probably railroad interests object more to the promotional aspects of government policy than they do to the existence of separate regulatory bodies as such. Regulation of air transportation by the Interstate Commerce Commission might be considered more favorable to the railroads since the Commission probably would not engage in promotional activities, but this would still leave the Civil Aeronautics Administration to carry on its work, and there is no reason to believe that a unification of regulatory control would be accompanied by the elimination of the Civil Aeronautics Administration and its promotional activities.

Conflicting purposes. Aside from any special financial considerations which may be involved, there are many sincere proponents and opponents of the single commission idea. It appears probable that their differences arise largely out of a fundamental difference in point of view concerning the purpose of regulation. Those who are opposed to the single commission are thinking in terms of promoting *civil aviation* without regard to the over-all transportation picture. Indeed, some of them appear to have little or no understanding of transportation economics as such. On the other hand, those who favor the single commission are thinking in terms of promoting a *national transportation system* without regard to the importance of developing civil aviation. And it may be said that some in this group appear to have little or no understanding of the importance of civil aviation as such.

To the present writer it appears that Congress was wise in establishing a separate regulatory body which could encourage the development of air transportation during its formative stages. It also seems obvious that a strong system of civil aviation is essential for national defense. But in the long run a sound national transportation system cannot be developed unless by legislation or regulation each form of transportation is utilized on the basis of its own clear economic advantage and not as a result of continued artificial stimulation. If air transportation ever develops to the point where it can fly on its own wings, there will be much less argument for a separate regulatory body and greater reason for bringing all forms of transportation under a single jurisdiction.

SUGGESTED READINGS

Air Transport Association of America, *Air Transport Facts and Figures*, various years. Contains useful statistics covering the operations of scheduled airlines.

Association of American Railroads, *Air Transportation*, Washington, 1947. The railroad viewpoint on air transportation.

Civil Aeronautics Board, *Reports*. Decisions and orders of the Civil Aeronautics Board. Unfortunately there is no master index to these reports similar to *Interstate Commerce Act, Annotated*, prepared by the Interstate Commerce Commission, and it is necessary to examine the index of each separate volume for specific information.

Civil Aeronautics Board, *Annual Report*, various years. These reports contain useful summaries of important developments in the year covered.

Department of Commerce, *Industry Report, Domestic Transportation*, August-September, 1946, on air passenger transportation, and October-November, 1946, on air cargo transportation.

Frederick, John H., *Commercial Air Transportation*, Parts II and III. Chicago: Richard D. Irwin, Inc., 1946.

Gill, Frederick W., and Gilbert L. Bates, *Airline Competition*. Boston: Division of Research, Graduate School of Business Administration, Harvard University, 1949. An interesting and detailed study of the effects of competition on quality and price of service and airline self-sufficiency.

Puffer, Claude E., *Air Transportation*. Philadelphia: The Blakiston Company, 1941. A good general work although now out of date.

Traffic World.

Wilson, G. Lloyd, and Leslie A. Bryan, *Air Transportation*. New York: Prentice-Hall, Inc., 1949.

Wolfe, Thomas, *Air Transportation, Traffic and Management*. New York: McGraw-Hill Book Company, Inc., 1950. Useful data on rates and traffic patterns.

Part Six

OTHER TRANSPORTATION AGENCIES

30

Pipe Line Transportation

of

PETROLEUM AND ITS PRODUCTS .

DEVELOPMENT OF PIPE LINE TRANSPORTATION

Early pipe lines. Pipe lines as a means of transporting water have been in use since ancient times. The Chinese are said to have constructed water lines of bamboo some five thousand years before Christ, and the inhabitants of Asia Minor, Egypt, Greece, the Roman Empire, and other parts of the ancient world piped water and even sewage in lines built of burned clay, stone, and metal. But it is not with water pipe lines that this chapter is concerned. Water lines are operated almost entirely as adjuncts of municipal water supply systems and not as transportation agencies in the ordinary sense of the word. The real development of the pipe line as a transportation agency is part and parcel of the development of the petroleum industry, and it is with this type of pipe line that the present chapter is concerned.

Discovery of oil. Petroleum oil seepages had been observed by the Indians and early white settlers of northwestern Pennsylvania long before the first well was drilled, and some oil occurred as an unwanted by-product from salt wells. In the early nineteenth century it appears to have been used almost entirely as a medicine, but in the 1850's experimenters succeeded in distilling from it an illuminating oil similar to coal oil. Coal oil had become a popular source of illumination, but it was expensive, and it was clear that a huge potential demand existed for a petroleum illuminating oil provided some means could be developed for obtaining the petroleum in large quantities and at a nominal cost. In 1854 a man named Bissell noticed the picture of a salt well on the label of a bottle of petroleum oil sold as a medicine, and this is said to have given him the idea of securing oil by drilling wells below the level necessary to obtain salt. In 1859 E. L. Drake undertook a drilling operation in the Oil Creek area near Titusville, Pennsylvania, and in August he brought in the first producing oil well at a depth of 69 feet. In practically no time at all the country round about was in an unproar, and well after well was drilled and brought into production.

Early development of petroleum pipe lines. The fact that these early oil wells were drilled in a rather remote area immediately created a transportation problem. The first crude oil was transported by water down Oil Creek to the Allegheny River and thence to refining centers, but as new producing areas were opened up at points distant from the water, teamsters were employed to haul the oil in barrels to the nearest railroad. Extremely high wages, poor roads, and the necessarily limited carrying capacity of the wagons employed made this a rather unsatisfactory method of transportation, and it was inevitable that some better means of getting the crude oil to the railroads would have to be devised.

The possibility of moving oil by pipe line appears to have been suggested as early as 1860, and attempts to put this idea into practice followed shortly thereafter. Unfortunately, the early efforts of the pipe line builders were frustrated by the teamsters who correctly saw in the pipe line an end to their highly profitable activities, and they stole out during the night to rip up lines and smash pumps as fast as they could be built. But with the opening up of new producing areas, which spewed forth crude oil in such quantities that it was physically impossible to handle it by wagon, the pipe line became an absolute necessity, and although the teamsters continued their battle against the pipe lines, they could no longer prevent their construction and expansion.

Enter the Standard Oil Company. Once the success of the pipe line had been established a process of unification began to take place, and by 1872 the pipe line business was dominated by three companies, the Pennsylvania Transportation Company, the Pennsylvania Railroad's Empire Transportation Company, and the United Pipe Lines. At about the same time Rockefeller and his Standard Oil Company were engaged in a similar process of unification of oil refining facilities. Rockefeller was fully aware of the value of owning or controlling the pipe line systems as an important step in gaining control of the oil industry, and he set to work to build new lines, obtained an interest in United Pipe Lines, and rapidly assumed a major position in the pipe line business. There followed a bitter struggle with the Pennsylvania Railroad which ended in a Rockefeller victory and acquisition of the railroad's pipe line interests by the Rockefeller group.

Long distance pipe lines. All of the early pipe lines were what are known as gathering lines, extending from the wells to small local refineries or to nearby railroad sidings where the oil was transferred to railroad cars and moved to distant major refineries. The economy and efficiency of pipe line transportation of crude oil, however, soon led men to consider the possibility of constructing trunk lines which would take the oil from the gathering lines and move it across country in competition with the railroads. The first of these lines, sixty miles long, was built by the Columbia Conduit Company and was designed to connect the Pennsylvania oil fields with the Baltimore & Ohio Railroad at Pittsburgh. When Dr. Hostetter, the owner, learned that Rockefeller had whipped the Pennsylvania Railroad and taken over the Empire Transportation Company, he promptly sold out to the Rockefeller group.

Hostetter was not the only one who became alarmed at the news of Rockefeller's victory over the powerful Pennsylvania Railroad. The actual producers of crude oil were not happy about the prospect of having to sell their oil to Rockefeller at whatever price Rockefeller chose to pay, and they decided to support the construction of a trunk line from the Pennsylvania fields over rugged country to a connection with the Reading Railroad, the latter undertaking to complete the haul to refineries in the New York City area. Such a project was started in 1878 by the Tidewater Pipe Line Company, and while Rockefeller appears to have been skeptical of the success of this venture, he took no chances and made every effort to block its construction. Nevertheless, the line was completed in 1879, and it was a success.

Standard monopoly achieved. As soon as oil began to flow through the Tidewater line, machinery was set in motion to obtain control of this threat to the growing Standard Oil monopoly, and control finally was obtained in 1883. In the meantime the Rockefeller interests began building long distance pipe lines from the oil fields to the Atlantic coast, to the Great Lakes, and elsewhere. By the turn of the century Rockefeller controlled about 40,000 miles of pipe line, as compared with 550 miles controlled by his largest competitor. In addition, working arrangements with the railroads kept railroad rates on crude oil at a high level which made it difficult for independent refiners to obtain oil at a reasonable cost. Eventually, however, the Standard monopoly was broken as a result of determined court action, and its pipe line transportation activities were divorced from its refining activities.

Expansion of petroleum pipe lines. At the beginning of the present century, pipe line mileage was concentrated in the northeastern part of the country, but as great new oil fields were opened up in Texas, Louisiana, California, Kansas, Wyoming, Illinois, and elsewhere, long distance crude oil pipe lines were built to carry the oil from these fields to refineries all over the United States. Perhaps the crowning achievement came during World War II when the Government constructed the Big Inch, a 1,300 mile line with a 24 inch diameter, to connect the East Texas field with the North Atlantic seaboard. As of December 31, 1949, there were 63,639 miles of crude oil trunk pipe line and 47,212 miles of gathering line in operation in the United States.[1]

Gasoline pipe lines. If pipe lines can be used so effectively to transport crude oil, then it would seem reasonable to suppose that they also could be used for the movement of refined petroleum products. As a matter of fact, kerosene and other refined products were moved successfully, and in the same line, as early as 1893, but the movement of gasoline in pipe lines necessarily had to wait upon the development of the automobile and the great expansion in the demand for gasoline. The first movements of gasoline in pipe lines were for relatively short distances from refineries to tidewater ports, but since 1930 pipe lines have come into increasing use for transporting gasoline to domestic markets. As of December 31, 1949, there were 14,133 miles of gasoline pipe line in operation in the United States.

Effect of pipe lines on other carriers. The successful construction of trunk pipe lines marked the beginning of the end of railroad transportation of crude oil, but railroads have benefited greatly from a tremendous volume of tonnage of refined petroleum products. The movement of petroleum and liquid petroleum products by coastwise tank steamers and by river barges developed some time after the appearance of trunk pipe lines and proved to be quite economical. The tanker fleets generally are owned by the same large refiners who own or control the trunk pipe lines, and this assures the most efficient use of each. There never has been any amount of crude oil moved by truck.

The development of pipe lines for the movement of refined liquid petroleum products naturally has had some effect on the railroads, and this effect will become greater to the extent that pipe lines for handling refined products are expanded. Pipe lines are not likely to have any effect on water carriers of refined petroleum products for the simple reason that these products can be moved more cheaply in tanker vessels than by pipe line. Nor are pipe lines for carrying refined products likely to have any great effect on movements of these products in tank trucks since the latter are characteristically short haul movements into areas which hardly would support the cost of constructing pipe lines.

Pipe line operation. Modern crude oil pipe line transportation begins at the well or the well tank, from which point gathering lines carry the oil to the trunk line or lines serving a given field. The trunk lines, which take the oil from the field to refining centers, are laid underground, and at intervals of about forty miles pumping or relay stations are provided in order to keep the oil moving through the pipe. Tank storage farms usually

---

[1] Interstate Commerce Commission, *Statistics of Oil Pipe Line Companies,* 1950, p. 9.

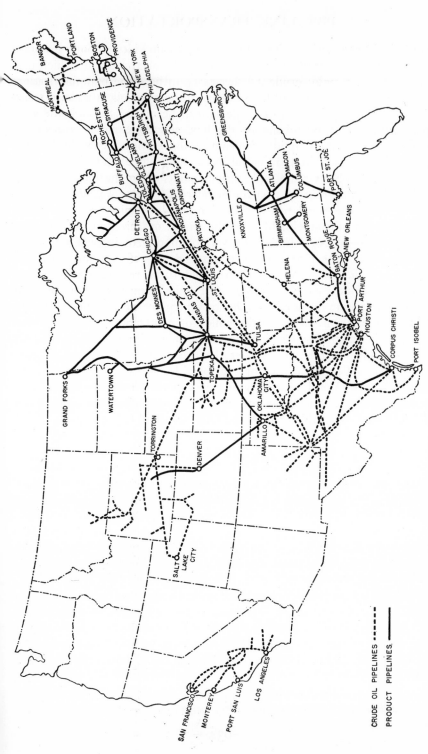

CRUDE OIL PIPELINES ------

PRODUCT PIPELINES ———

FIGURE 9. *Petroleum Pipe Line System.* (Adapted from map courtesy of American Petroleum Institute.)

are built in connection with relay stations to provide temporary storage when the movement of oil is heavy. In moving oil from fields which produce a heavy type of crude it is necessary to have the pumping stations closer together, and it may be necessary to heat the oil to make it transportable. Different grades of crude oil can be moved through the same pipe with very little mixing of the lots, and the same is true of the movement of refined liquid petroleum products. Movements through the pipe are controlled from a central dispatching office connected by telephone, telegraph, or radio with various points along the line.

Pipe line ownership. In 1911 the Standard Oil Trust was dissolved, and the stocks of the Standard's various pipe line companies were distributed ratably among the stockholders of the parent organization, the Standard Oil Company of New Jersey. Thus a community of interest was established between the pipe line companies and the refining and marketing companies, but the groundwork was laid for a real separation of the two groups. In the meantime large new refining companies were springing up, particularly in the newly developing oil regions west of the Mississippi, and these companies adopted the policy of constructing their own pipe lines. This integration of pipe line ownership with refinery ownership has continued to this day, and at the present time the great majority of pipe line mileage is owned or controlled by a few large refining companies. Before World War II, 90 per cent of the trunk pipe line mileage was owned by refiners, the other 10 per cent being owned by eight companies which had been divorced from Standard Oil in 1911.[2]

REGULATION

Demand for regulation. Some of the early pipe line companies operated as carriers for hire, accepting shipments of crude oil from producers and moving it through their lines for a given charge. Other companies, however, made a practice of purchasing the oil before putting it into their lines, and since they moved only their own property, they claimed to be what would be called today private carriers. Among those companies which operated as private carriers were those which were owned or controlled by the Standard Oil interests, and as the Standard's grip on the pipe line system tightened, it became increasingly difficult to get crude oil moved by pipe line on a normal for-hire basis. Producers found that they could not dispose of their crude on a free market but were forced to sell to Standard at Standard's price. Similarly, independent refiners

---

[2] American Petroleum Institute, *Petroleum-Industry Hearings Before the Temporary National Economic Committee*, New York, 1942, p. 16.

found it difficult to obtain supplies of crude oil by pipe line. Independent oil interests sought to avoid the Standard's grip by building their own pipe lines, but in almost every case the Standard either succeeded in blocking construction or was able to secure control of the line after it was built. Under the circumstances it is not surprising that independent oil interests turned to the Government for relief.

Hepburn Act. Although Rockefeller had succeeded in destroying nearly all of his competitors and had built up an almost complete monopoly of the oil business, at the turn of the century he found himself faced with a threat which he was unable to overcome—an aroused public opinion. The antitrust movement was in full swing, aided by the dynamic personality of President Theodore Roosevelt, and Standard Oil was a prime target. In 1906 the Bureau of Corporations submitted a report citing in detail countless examples of railroad rate discriminations which favored the Standard Oil Company and the difficulties encountered by independents seeking to transport crude oil by pipe line. Legislation was promptly introduced providing for the regulation of interstate petroleum pipe lines. Attempts were made to have the proposed legislation apply only to those pipe lines which were operated as common carriers, thus making it inapplicable to the Standard's far flung system, but this move was unsuccessful. Regulation of interstate petroleum pipe lines was included in the Hepburn Act of 1906, in which Congress declared all interstate pipe lines transporting oil or other commodities, with the exception of water and natural gas, to be common carriers, and as such subject to all of the applicable provisions of the Act to Regulate Commerce as administered by the Interstate Commerce Commission.

Present law. No good purpose would be served by attempting to trace the development of pipe line legislation since it is part and parcel of railroad legislation, but it may be useful to summarize briefly those provisions of the law as it stands today which are applicable to interstate pipe line transportation. Pipe lines are regulated as common carriers under Part I of the Interstate Commerce Act. As common carriers they are required to transport oil for all who are in a position to use their facilities, to do so at reasonable rates and without discrimination, to publish and file tariffs with the Interstate Commerce Commission, and to keep their accounts and make reports as required by the Commission. The Commission may suspend proposed rate changes for a maximum of seven months beyond the effective date. It is supposed to fix rates in accordance with the 1933 rule of rate making prescribed for the railroads, and it may fix maximum, minimum, and exact rates. Intercorporate relationships are subject to the jurisdiction of the Commission. It also determines the valuation of pipe line properties. The Commission has no control over pipe line security issues or over pipe line construction and abandonment, and the commodities clause does not apply to pipe lines.

Constitutionality of pipe line regulation. After the passage of the Hepburn Act, the pipe line companies, most of which were controlled by the Standard Oil interests, quite generally followed the practice of requiring producers to sell their oil before it was put into the lines. These companies took the position that they were not in fact common carriers and could not be regulated as such. In view of the general failure of pipe line companies to operate as common carriers, the Interstate Commerce Commission undertook an investigation of the pipe line business, and in 1912 it held that it had jurisdiction over all interstate petroleum pipe lines and ordered them to file tariffs as required by law.[3] This order paved the way for a judicial test of the law which came in 1914.

The Pipe Line Cases.[4] The central issue in *The Pipe Line Cases* was the right of Congress and the Interstate Commerce Commission to regulate pipe line companies which did not profess to offer, and which did not offer, common carrier service. Referring specifically to the Standard Oil Company's practice of insisting on the purchase of the oil before transporting it, the Court ruled that the Standard pipe lines were in reality common carriers because they provided the only practical means of transporting oil to market, and because they transported oil belonging originally to anybody. The lines were common carriers in substance, said the Court, and Congress had the power to require them to become common carriers in form as well.

The Supreme Court, however, ruled that the Interstate Commerce Commission had erred in classifying one company, the Uncle Sam Oil Company, as a common carrier because this company used its pipe line exclusively for transporting its own oil from its own wells in Oklahoma to its own refinery in Kansas. Although the Hepburn Act declared all interstate pipe lines to be common carriers, the Court held that the Uncle Sam Oil Company was not engaged in transportation within the meaning of the Hepburn Act, the transportation being merely an incident to the use of the oil at the end of the line.

Twenty-five years later the question of the common carrier status of an interstate pipe line was again before the Supreme Court.[5] The Valvoline Oil Company purchased oil from wells in Pennsylvania, West Virginia, and Ohio, and transported this oil through its own line to its own refineries in Pennsylvania. Thus, while it bought oil from independent

---

[3] *In the Matter of Pipe Lines,* 24 I.C.C. 1 (1912).
[4] 234 U.S. 548 (1914).
[5] *Valvoline Oil Co.* v. *United States,* 308 U.S. 141 (1939).

producers, it did not sell this oil at the other end of the line. The Court took cognizance of the fact that the Valvoline Oil Company bought oil from many producers and that it was in a position to control the price of crude oil at the wells if producers could not use its line as a common carrier. Under these circumstances the Court ruled that the Valvoline Company was subject to regulation by the Interstate Commerce Commission. The essence of this decision was the fact that there was a need for public regulation because of the existence of a monopolistic situation.[6]

In more recent cases involving the Champlin Refining Company, the Court appears to have placed a somewhat different interpretation on the law. Champlin owns a pipe line which it uses to transport gasoline from its refinery at Enid, Oklahoma, to points in Kansas, Nebraska, and Iowa, at which points the gasoline is delivered to jobbers and to the company's own bulk stations for resale. The company maintained that this line was a plant facility, that it had never held itself out to be a common carrier, and that it had never been asked to perform a common carrier service. In 1942, however, the Interstate Commerce Commission held that the company was operating an interstate pipe line and was by reason of that fact a common carrier subject to its jurisdiction. The Commission also gave weight to the fact that the company sold the gasoline at destination at a price which was determined, in effect, by adding the applicable railroad freight rate to the price at the refinery.[7]

The Commission ordered Champlin to provide certain data necessary for a valuation of its line, and this order was upheld by the Supreme Court.[8] Later the Commission also ordered the company to file reports, maintain a uniform system of accounts, and publish tariff schedules. In 1951 the Supreme Court held that the collection of information, and even the establishment of a uniform system of accounts, may have statistical significance and that it may expose or prevent practices which might involve a violation of the law. Hence it upheld this part of the Commission's order. But, said the Court, Congress did not intend to make common carriers for hire out of private pipe lines whose services were not used, not sought, and not needed by independent producers, and whose presence, as in this case, actually fostered competition. Therefore, it refused to sanction the Commission's requirement that Champlin publish tariff schedules.[9] Justice Black in a dissenting opinion expressed the belief

---

[6] Theodore L. Whitesel, "Recent Federal Regulation of the Petroleum Pipe Line as a Common Carrier," *Cornell Law Quarterly*, Vol. 32, No. 3, March, 1947, p. 343.

[7] Champlin Refining Company, *Valuation of Pipe Line*, 49 I.C.C. Valuation Reports 463 (1942).

[8] *Champlin Refining Company* v. *United States*, 329 U.S. 29 (1946).

[9] *Traffic World*, May 12, 1951, pp. 52-53.

that this decision made it uncertain whether the Commission could force any oil company to carry products for others as a common carrier.

State v. federal jurisdiction. In addition to the Federal Government, about half of the states regulate pipe lines as common carriers. Lines which operate solely in interstate commerce are subject to regulation by the Interstate Commerce Commission, and lines which operate solely in intrastate commerce are subject to regulation by state bodies in those states which provide for regulation. Lines which operate both as interstate and intrastate carriers are subject to regulation both by the Federal Government and by the states. The student of transportation will immediately observe the possibilities of conflict in this situation, but as yet conflicts between state and federal authorities have been few, and the jurisdictional issue has not been decided by the courts.[10]

FAILURE OF PIPE LINE COMPANIES TO ASSUME STATUS
OF GENUINE COMMON CARRIERS

Pipe line companies today not real common carriers. Although Congress declared interstate petroleum pipe line companies to be common carriers in 1906, an action which was sustained by the Supreme Court as long ago as 1914, the fact remains that pipe line companies today engage in common carrier transportation only to a very limited extent. As noted above, 90 per cent of the trunk pipe line mileage is owned by refiners, and in the hearings before the Temporary National Economic Committee it was determined that over 90 per cent of the crude oil moved by pipe line belonged to the line owners. In the case of gasoline lines it was stated that no independent refiner had ever tendered any gasoline to these lines.[11] In fact, if not in law, most pipe lines function as plant facilities rather than common carriers, and they have so functioned for many years. It will be worth while to analyze briefly some of the reasons advanced to explain this situation.

Minimum tender requirements. After the Supreme Court upheld the constitutionality of regulation in 1914, the pipe line companies filed tariffs with the Interstate Commerce Commission. But the companies required such large minimum shipments that use of the lines was effectively restricted to their owners. For example, the Federal Trade Commission found that the minimum quantity accepted for shipment in the Midcon-

---

[10] For a brief discussion of state regulation and the jurisdictional question see William Beard, *Regulation of Pipe Lines As Common Carriers.* New York: Columbia University Press, 1941, pp. 45-55.

[11] American Petroleum Institute, *Petroleum-Industry Hearings Before Temporary National Economic Committee,* New York, 1942, pp. 53-54.

tinent field varied from 25,000 to 100,000 barrels, whereas many refineries used less than 200,000 barrels of oil per year and many producers would have to accumulate oil for years before they would have 100,000 barrels. Hence these large minimum tender requirements sometimes functioned to prevent the use of pipe lines by small producers and refiners.[12]

It should be pointed out that there is nothing wrong with a minimum tender requirement because it is uneconomic to accept and dispatch over long distances a few barrels of oil at a time. Furthermore, when several different grades of oil are pumped through the same line, there is always a certain amount of mixing at the end of each column of oil, and the smaller the size of the individual shipments the greater will be the loss from intermingling and contamination. It also has been pointed out that acceptance of small shipments would have encouraged the development of small scale inefficient refineries. Thus the issue involved was not the requirement of a minimum tender but the reasonableness of the minima required.

This issue was first before the Interstate Commerce Commission in a case decided in 1922 which involved the movement of crude oil by the Prairie Pipe Line Company and connecting carriers from the Midcontinent field to two pipe line stations in Pennsylvania. On these shipments the carriers required a minimum tender of 100,000 barrels, and the complainant wanted the Commission to lower the minimum to 2,000 barrels. The Commission recognized that the pipe line carriers could not be expected to accept shipments "on a driblet basis," but it felt that the 100,000 barrel minimum was unreasonable. In this case it ordered a 10,000 barrel minimum tender established,[13] but this order proved to be ineffective. Although the Prairie Pipe Line Company reduced its minimum tender requirement to the amount specified, a survey made as of December 31, 1931, indicated that only twenty shipments of less than 100,000 barrels had been made over this route, and all of them were made by two large refiners. The Interstate Commerce Commission, in a later case involving a large number of interstate pipe lines, decided that a 10,000 barrel minimum tender was as large as it could find reasonable.[14]

Other service restrictions. Aside from the restrictive aspects of minimum tender requirements, pipe line companies at one time or another adopted various regulations and practices which made it difficult for outsiders to utilize their facilities. One early device was to locate intakes and outputs

---

[12] Federal Trade Commission, *Report on Pipe Line Transportation of Petroleum,* Washington, 1916, p. 20.

[13] *Brundred Brothers* v. *Prairie Pipe Line Company, et al.,* 68 I.C.C. 458 (1922).

[14] *Reduced Pipe Line Rates and Gathering Charges,* 243 I.C.C. 115 (1940).

in such a way as to make it impractical or impossible for those seeking common carrier service to make the necessary connections onto the main line. Also, when a pipe line was offered more product than it could move at a given time, it could discriminate against independents in accepting oil for shipment. Other restrictions have included unreasonable delivery requirements and unreasonable deductions made for shrinkage while oil was being moved. Several of the states have acted against such practices, but there appears to be only one instance in which the service issue was raised before the Interstate Commerce Commission.[15]

Alleged excessive rates. Ever since the Supreme Court forced the pipe line companies to assume the status of common carriers there have been repeated complaints that pipe line rates are excessive and that they discriminate in favor of the large refining companies which own or control the pipe lines. Obviously it would not make too much difference to a refining company if its pipe line subsidiary charged excessive rates since what it paid out in excessive rates it would get back in the form of pipe line profits. But to the independent refiner an excessive rate would constitute a real handicap in competing with integrated refiners. Similarly, independent producers might find it difficult to sell except to the refiner-owner.

Are pipe line rates excessive? Shortly after the first common carrier pipe line rates were filed the Federal Trade Commission sought to compare costs with rates charged by the pipe lines serving the Midcontinent field. On one haul it found that the rate represented a markup of 17½ per cent over cost but on other major hauls this markup increased rapidly, in one case coming to about 530 per cent.[16] Thus it would appear that the original rates filed with the Commission were clearly excessive.

Pipe line statistics have been accumulated by the Interstate Commerce Commission since 1921, and these statistics show earnings on depreciated investment rising from about 11 per cent in 1921 to 31 per cent in 1929. After 1929 the rate of return continued at a high level, although showing a generally downward trend. In recent years earnings have been low, coming to about 6.6 per cent on depreciated investment in 1949.[17] These figures are for all lines, and the returns of some companies have been very much higher. It would appear from the record that pipe line rates have

---

[15] *Crude Petroleum Oil from Kansas and Oklahoma to Lacy Station, Pa.,* 59 I.C.C. 483 (1920).

[16] Federal Trade Commission, *Report on Pipe Line Transportation of Petroleum,* Washington, 1916. Percentages computed from figures shown on p. 19.

[17] Interstate Commerce Commission, *Statistics of Oil Pipe Lines,* 1949, p. 4, and earlier years.

been excessive, but at the present time they do not on the whole yield an excessive return on investment.

Pipe line supporters always have maintained that pipe line construction and operation involves a degree of risk which necessitates higher rates of return than are enjoyed by other regulated enterprises. In some cases a new field is exhausted in a relatively short time, and this creates an element of uncertainty in pipe line construction which would seem to justify higher earnings, at least during the early stages of a development. The present policy of restricting production, however, plus the various techniques adopted to secure maximum recovery of the oil from each pool, operate to extend the prospective life of the trunk pipe lines, and so high rates of return are not as significant as was formerly the case. One other risk which must be taken into consideration is the possible discovery of new fields which are closer to major markets than those being served by existing trunk lines. Even though it may be possible to connect the new field with an existing line, it will be obvious that the usefulness of a part of that line will be reduced.

The practice of computing rates of return on investment also has been subject to criticism. In the past it appears that for one reason or another pipe lines were generally undercapitalized, and it is said that if rates of return were based on true worth, they would be very much less. In addition, the practice of computing the return on depreciated investment has been criticized as leading to an overstatement of earnings, although there is considerable difference of opinion on this point. The Interstate Commerce Commission has determined the value of the pipe lines, using a combination of the various valuation factors, and it was stated in 1939 that average pipe line net income would have been 13.6 per cent if the Commission's valuation figures were used as a base.[18] This compares with a rate of 21.7 per cent on depreciated investment in that year.

Attitude of Interstate Commerce Commission toward pipe line rates. With one minor exception,[19] the Interstate Commerce Commission did not concern itself with pipe line rates until 1934, at which time it undertook a general investigation on its own initiative. At about the same time it decided to institute pipe line valuation proceedings, a necessary first step to the determination of reasonable rates. These investigations required several years to complete, and in 1940 the Commission ordered thirty-seven lines moving oil out of the Southwest to reduce their rates so as not to yield a return in excess of 8 per cent of their value.[20] Later the 8 per cent rule was

---

[18] American Petroleum Institute, *Petroleum-Industry Hearings Before the Temporary National Economic Committee*, New York, 1942, p. 91.

[19] *Brundred Brothers* v. *Prairie Pipe Line Company, et al.*, 68 I.C.C. 458 (1922).

[20] *Reduced Pipe Line Rates and Gathering Charges*, 243 I.C.C. 115 (1940).

applied in connection with rates charged by a line serving the Wyoming fields.[21] In 1941 it ordered a substantial reduction in the rates charged by two gasoline pipe line companies serving the Middle West, but in this case the new rates were designed to permit a return of 10 per cent.[22]

Major company gasoline swapping. In the last case mentioned in the preceding paragraph the independents complained about the practice followed by the large integrated companies of trading gasoline with each other. A large oil company having a gasoline pipe line serving a given area will turn over gasoline to other large oil companies, which do not have gasoline lines in that area, in exchange for an equal amount of gasoline delivered to it by other companies in areas were it does not have pipe line facilities. In this way the large integrated companies avoid the necessity of paying the much higher railroad freight rates which would be involved if they had to transport their own gasoline in tank cars into areas where they do not have gasoline pipe lines. The smaller refining companies, since they do not own pipe lines, are not in a position to take part in this swapping arrangement and so they are placed at a competitive disadvantage. The Interstate Commerce Commission took the position that it was not the proper body to receive a complaint of this sort because it involved a marketing rather than a transportation practice.

Physical inability of independents to use pipe lines. It is sometimes argued that the failure of the major company pipe lines to transport oil for independent refiners is not due to alleged high rates or discriminatory practices but simply to the fact that the independent refineries are located in or near the oil fields and have no use for the pipe line facilities involved. This, however, gives rise to a rather nice question. Have the independents failed to make use of common carrier pipe line facilities because their refineries are located in the oil fields, or are their refineries located in the oil fields because they have been unable to make effective use of the major company pipe lines? After all, an oil field is not exactly an ideal place to locate a refinery since exhaustion of the field may necessitate removal of the refinery or its abandonment. Furthermore, while the refinery saves transportation costs on crude oil, it costs more to move its finished product to market.

---

[21] *Minnelusa Oil Corporation, et al.* v. *Continental Pipe Line Company, et al.,* 258 I.C.C. 41 (1944).

[22] *Petroleum Rail Shippers' Association* v. *Alton & Southern Railroad, et al.,* 243 I.C.C. 589 (1941).

PIPE LINE TRANSPORTATION

ATTEMPTS TO FORCE TRUE COMMON CARRIER STATUS
ON PETROLEUM PIPE LINES

Action through Interstate Commerce Commission. The paucity of Interstate Commerce Commission action with regard to pipe line rates and services is not easy to explain. It is true that almost no formal complaints have been filed with the Commission, and this has been interpreted by some as an indication that conditions are satisfactory, but there have been numerous informal complaints in and out of Congress which suggest that conditions are not as ideal as the absence of formal complaints might indicate. It has been suggested that the Commission, already overburdened with the problems of rail, motor, and water transport regulation, is not likely, in the absence of formal complaints, to devote any more time than it must to the regulation of pipe lines. Hence there are those who believe that steps should be taken to bring about a vigorous enforcement of the law.

Regulation through Elkins Act. In 1940 the United States brought suit against a number of major oil companies and their pipe line affiliates on the ground that their method of operation constituted a violation of the Elkins Act.[23] In essence, the Government's case rested on the contention that when refiners shipped oil to themselves through pipe lines which they owned or controlled, the dividends they received as pipe line stockholders constituted rebates within the meaning of the Elkins Act. Under the terms of a consent decree the major oil companies agreed not to receive dividends on their pipe line stock in excess of what would amount to their share of a 7 per cent return on the value of the line as determined by the Interstate Commerce Commission. In the event that a pipe line company earns more than a 7 per cent return, the resulting surplus can be used for debt retirement or for improvements, but if improvements are made out of such surplus funds, they may not be included in the valuation on which dividends are based.

As noted previously, the Interstate Commerce Commission has permitted rates to yield a return of 8 per cent on oil and 10 per cent on gasoline pipe line valuations, which means that the pipe line companies are in a position to earn more than they can turn over to their shipper-owners in the form of dividends. The only way in which the shipper-owners can recover any resulting surpluses is through the ultimate sale of their interest in the lines, but this they do not want to do. Under the circumstances it would seem that an incentive would exist to lower pipe line rates to the point where they will not yield a return greater than 7 per cent on value, in the expec-

---

[23] See Chapter 6.

tation that the lower pipe line transportation charges will increase their refining profits, and there is no doubt that this was one of the hopes of those who backed the prosecution. On the other hand, to the extent that independent refiners are in a position to use the facilities, the large integrated companies may not want to lower pipe line rates.

Proposed application of commodities clause. In the congressional debate which preceded the adoption of the Hepburn Act it was proposed that the commodities clause be made applicable to pipe line companies, but this was not done. Since that time the idea of a complete divorce of pipe line transportation from the business of petroleum refining has been broached periodically in the hope that such a move would open up the pipe lines to wider use. It also has been argued that when an integrated common carrier pipe line company transports oil or gasoline for independent operators, the inevitable result is a rebate to the refiner-owner, and this is true even though the rates charged are reasonable. Not only does the refiner-owner receive a rebate on every barrel of oil shipped for its account, but it also receives a drawback on every barrel of oil shipped over its line by competing refiners.

To the extent that pipe line rates are higher than they need to be, there is obvious validity in this contention, but if pipe line rates are reasonable or can be made reasonable by regulatory authorities, then the argument is not so clear. It has been argued, too, that pipe line rates were so high in the past that the owning companies recovered their investments long ago, and so any present dividend payments constitute rebates and drawbacks. It should be kept in mind, however, that the large returns received by refiner-owners in the past were the result of the high rates which they themselves paid.

Various objections have been raised to a policy of divorcement. Considerable doubt has been expressed about the willingness of private capital to invest in existing pipe lines or to build new lines to be operated free of any association with the large refining companies. It is said to be much too risky to build and operate a crude oil pipe line unless the builder owns producing wells at one end and refining and marketing facilities at the other, all of which will assure a steady volume of traffic. Similarly, it is said not to be worth while to build a gasoline pipe line unless the builder has a source of supply at one end and a market at the other.[24] If pipe lines were independently owned, refiners would have no particular incentive to use the facilities of any given carrier, and as new and cheaper sources of supply were developed, they would shift their purchases to these newer

---

[24] American Petroleum Institute, *Petroleum-Industry Hearings Before Temporary National Economic Committee*, New York, 1942, p. 55.

sources as soon as pipe line connections were available. This, it is said, would make it too risky to operate pipe lines as independent common carriers.

It also has been pointed out that when a large refining company operates a pipe line connecting its refineries with a given field, the operation constitutes a rather effective commitment to producers that they will continue to have a market for their oil. Obviously an integrated company will not abandon its investment in a given line until the available supply of crude declines to the point where it is quite impractical to continue operations. Spokesmen for the major companies have stated that independent producers as a class were opposed to divorcement of the pipe lines from their present ownership. They also have stated that a majority of the independent refiners opposed divorcement, either because they were satisfied with existing conditions or wanted to be free to build their own lines.[25] Another argument against divorcement is that when a new field is opened up, one or more major companies promptly lay pipe to it, thus assuring producers a market for their oil, whereas an independent pipe line company could not afford to lay pipe until it was assured of sufficient oil and of an adequate market to make the operation profitable.

CONCLUSION

Failure of regulation to achieve results anticipated. When Congress declared pipe lines to be common carriers, it hoped that this step would open up the lines to small independent operators and enable them to compete with the Standard monopoly. Today, Standard no longer has a monopoly, but the industry is dominated by a few large integrated companies, each of which owns its own lines which it uses almost exclusively to transport its own products. Thus the small independent refiners are not much better off today than they were in 1906 in so far as obtaining the benefits of cheap pipe line transportation are concerned.

There are those who believe that pipe lines can be made common carriers in fact as well as in form by vigorous enforcement of existing laws, especially with reference to a reduction in rates and minimum tender requirements. But even if this were done, would there be any substantial increase in the use of pipe lines by companies other than their owners? Obviously the move would not benefit those refineries located in or near the oil fields. The benefits would have to accrue to refiners presently located in the general market areas served by the pipe lines or who might

---

[25] American Petroleum Institute, *Petroleum-Industry Hearings Before Temporary National Economic Committee*, New York, 1942, pp. 54-55.

desire to build new refineries in these areas, but here they would have to compete with the large and highly efficient refining and marketing mechanisms of the established companies. Thus it would appear that it would require something more than a vigorous enforcement of the law to bring about any substantial increase in the use of pipe lines by the nonintegrated companies. Nor is it at all clear that divorcement of ownership would achieve satisfactory results.

Pipe lines as plant facilities. Some students believe that it is a mistake to look upon pipe lines as common carriers or to attempt to regulate them as such. They argue that pipe lines are nothing more than plant facilities operated as a part of a vertically integrated business enterprise. It also has been argued that if pipe line facilities could be operated in such a way as to make them available to small refiners, the result might well be a considerable growth of small inefficiently operated refineries serving local areas and wasting a valuable and limited natural resource. Maximum economy and efficiency in the utilization of petroleum resources is achieved, it is said, when the entire process of production, from extraction of the crude oil to the disposal of the finished product, is carried on as a single integrated operation. Hence in recent years a school of thought has developed which would favor complete integration of the industry and then provide for the regulation of the various integrated companies as public utilities. Such a move may or may not be acceptable, but an evaluation of it is beyond the scope of this volume.

NATURAL GAS PIPE LINES

Development of natural gas pipe lines. In the frenzied oil prospecting which followed Drake's discovery in the Oil Creek area, prospectors often brought in gas wells rather than oil wells. These wells constituted quite a problem because the gas had no saleable value, the wells were a potential fire hazard, and if not plugged, their fumes could destroy vegetation and animal life and render the adjacent countryside uninhabitable. The late 1880's and early 1890's saw the first efforts to pipe the unwanted gas to nearby communities for household consumption, and this marks the beginning of the natural gas industry in the United States. Since then there has been a considerable expansion of natural gas pipe lines, and gas has found extensive industrial as well as domestic use. In 1945 there were 22,137.5 miles of natural gas transmission lines in the United States subject to regulation by the Federal Power Commission.[26] This figure does not include

---

[26] Federal Power Commission, *Natural Gas Company Cost Units*, p. 3.

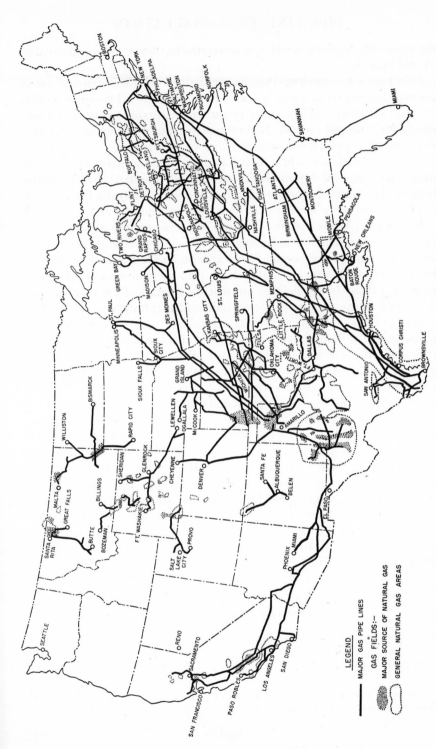

FIGURE 10. *Principal Natural Gas Pipe Lines, 1951.* (Adapted from map prepared by Ford, Bacon & Davis, Inc., New York.)

the 1,300 mile Big Inch which was converted to transport natural gas after World War II.

Effect on other carriers. Pipe lines constitute the only practical means for transporting natural gas, but they have had and will continue to have an effect on other carriers to the extent that natural gas is used as a substitute for coal and fuel oil. Natural gas is a much cleaner product than coal, and the supply is not subject to sudden disruption by strikes of coal miners. For this reason, wherever it is practical to do so, natural gas is being substituted for coal for industrial power and industrial and residential heating. This could become a matter of serious concern to the railroads, particularly to those serving important coal-producing areas.

Regulation. At the time the Hepburn Act was passed Congress was concerned with the pipe line only because of its close association with the oil monopoly, and natural gas pipe lines were specifically excluded from regulation. Nevertheless, even at that early date there was some interest in regulating them. It was pointed out that the owners of a natural gas pipe line could refuse to take gas from independent producers because they could tap wells on adjacent property and draw the gas from beneath the property of the independents, thus forcing them to sell their property or their gas at the pipe line company's own price. As the network of natural gas pipe lines grew, there was an increasing demand for regulation, and in a number of states these lines were classified as common carriers and regulated as such in so far as they operated in intrastate commerce.[27]

The sale of gas to ultimate consumers has been regulated for many years by the municipalities in which it is used or by state public utility commissions. As long as gas was produced artificially in local plants regulation created no particularly difficult problems, but when local gas distributing companies began to purchase gas from interstate pipe line companies, state commissions were handicapped by the fact that they could not control the price charged the local companies. This situation was remedied in 1938 when Congress passed the Natural Gas Act which gives the Federal Power Commission authority to regulate the transportation and sale of gas moved in interstate commerce by pipe line.

SUGGESTED READINGS

American Petroleum Institute, *Petroleum-Industry Hearings Before the Temporary National Economic Committee.* New York, 1942. The petroleum industry's point of view.

---

[27] William Beard, *Regulation of Pipe Lines As Common Carriers.* New York: Columbia University Press, 1941, p. 47.

PIPE LINE TRANSPORTATION

Beard, William, *Regulation of Pipe Lines As Common Carriers*. New York: Columbia University Press, 1941. A useful source of information.

Federal Trade Commission, *Pipe Line Transportation of Petroleum*. Washington, 1916. A document of considerable historical interest.

Flynn, John T., *God's Gold*. New York: Harcourt, Brace & Company, Inc., 1932. The story of Rockefeller and his times. Contains information on the discovery and development of crude oil and its transportation.

Stocking, George Ward, *The Oil Industry and the Competitive System*. Boston: Houghton Mifflin Company, 1925.

Whitesel, Theodore L., "Recent Federal Regulation of the Petroleum Pipe Line as a Common Carrier," *Cornell Law Quarterly*, Vol. XXXII, No. 3, March, 1947, pp. 337-377.

Wilson, Charles Morrow, *Oil Across the World*. New York: Longmans, Green & Company, 1946. A popular account of pipe lines and the pipe line business.

31

Transportation
by
INDIRECT CARRIERS

INTRODUCTION

Indirect carriers. There is available to the shipping and traveling public a number of specialized transportation services provided by transportation agencies which do not themselves engage in line-haul operations. Instead, these specialized agencies rely on rail, motor, water, or air carriers, or a combination of two or more of such carriers, to provide the line-haul transportation necessary to the conduct of their business. For lack of a better term these various agencies of transportation are designated here as indirect carriers. They include freight forwarders, the Railway Express Agency, the postal service, and the Pullman Company. There are, in addition, a number of private car companies which provide shippers and the railroads with specialized equipment, but these are not carriers in the sense that they provide a for-hire transportation service.

DEVELOPMENT OF FREIGHT FORWARDING

Nature of freight forwarding. Railroads generally charge substantially more per hundred pounds for hauling a given commodity in less-than-carload quantities than they do for hauling the same commodity in carload lots,[1] and freight forwarders take advantage of these rate differentials by soliciting small shipments, consolidating them into carload lots, and shipping these carload lots to themselves at various distributing points. When a car arrives at the distributing point, the forwarder unloads it and delivers the individual items to the true consignees. The individual shipper pays the forwarder an amount approximately the same as the less-than-carload rate, and the forwarder pays the railroad the carload rate. The difference between the less-than-carload rates paid by the shippers to the forwarder and the carload rates paid by the forwarder to the railroads constitutes the "spread," and it is out of this spread that the forwarder ex-

---

[1] The reasons for these differences are explained in Chapter 11.

pects to cover his cost of doing business and make a profit. Forwarders also make extensive use of motor carriers, although on a somewhat different basis as will appear presently.

There are several reasons why a shipper may prefer to use the services of a freight forwarder. Forwarders are able to offer a faster service on small shipments between many points than the railroads offer on less-than-carload shipments handled through their own freight houses. Also, forwarders provide a practical means of combining the services of two or more agencies of transportation, particularly rail and motor transportation, in a way which is profitable to them and beneficial to shippers. At one time freight forwarder rates were lower than railroad less-than-carload rates, but the tendency today is to emphasize service rather than rates. As a rule forwarder rates are now about the same as railroad rates.

Charges on mixed carload shipments. Freight forwarders accept different classes of freight for shipment, and a rate problem arises when it becomes necessary for a forwarder to load different classes of freight into a single car in order to make up the minimum weight required to obtain the benefit of a carload rate. Rule 10, Section 1, of the Consolidated Freight Classification provides that when more than one class of freight is loaded into a single car, the rate applicable to the highest rated item in the car shall be applied to the entire shipment. Furthermore, if the actual weight of the shipment is less than the highest carload minimum weight applicable to any item in the car, this minimum weight must be used in computing the charge.[2]

The possible unfavorable effect of the application of Rule 10, Section 1, on the freight forwarder business is shown in the following hypothetical shipment.

Commodity	Actual Weight	L.C.L. Rating	Carload Rating	Carload Minimum Weight
A	15,000 lbs.	1	3	30,000
B	5,000 lbs.	2	4	30,000
C	10,000 lbs.	3	6	36,000

Although the total weight of the shipment is only 30,000 pounds, and it contains freight rated as low as sixth class in carload lots, Section 1 of Rule 10 requires the assessment of charges on the basis of 36,000 pounds (highest minimum carload weight) at the third class rate (highest carload rating on any article in the shipment). Obviously the application of this rule

---

[2] Rule 10 provides certain alternative methods of calculating the charge for a mixed carload shipment, but all involve the same or similar difficulties.

greatly reduces the spread on which the forwarder relies to cover his costs and profits. In the above illustration, the spread on commodity C is completely eliminated, and if lower grades of freight were added, the spread on these items would become a negative quantity.

There are, however, two or three ways out of this difficulty. Many railroads publish what are known as all-commodity rates, which permit the movement of mixed freight under a specified minimum weight and a specified rating. Usually the minimum weight is fixed at 30,000 pounds and the carload rating at third class, but in some cases the rating is fourth class and may be even lower. Furthermore, many railroads which do not publish all-commodity rates have commodity rates which permit a liberal mixing of differently rated commodities. Also, many railroads today have adopted a modified form of Rule 10 which permits the use of the carload ratings applicable to each item in a mixed shipment.

Characteristics of forwarder traffic. Freight-forwarder traffic demonstrates certain characteristics which should be mentioned briefly. In the first place, freight forwarders tend to concentrate on the higher grades of freight because there is a greater spread in terms of cents per hundred pounds on high grade freight than on the lower rated items. Also, the application of Rule 10 makes it unprofitable to handle the lower grades of freight except insofar as they may be used to make up carload minimum weights. A second characteristic of freight forwarding is the necessity of concentrating the business between points or areas where the volume of small shipments is sufficient to make carload or truckload shipments possible. Finally, the freight-forwarder business is not well adapted to short haul traffic because the motor carrier can provide the same or faster service, and in some cases at lower rates. Also, the long haul business is more attractive to forwarders because the spread, again in terms of cents per hundred pounds, increases with distance.

Origin of modern freight forwarder. A form of freight forwarding developed in the earlier years of railroading before the railroads undertook the responsibility of handling through shipments which had to move over two or more different lines, but forwarding in its modern form is said to have originated in New York about 1908 when a New York broker consolidated a number of small import shipments destined for Chicago into a carload lot. He had this car shipped to himself at Chicago, paying the carload rate, and when it arrived the various items were delivered to their respective owners. The railroads attacked this procedure on the ground that the broker did not own the goods being shipped and that the transaction did not really involve the shipment of a carload lot. Both the Interstate Commerce Commission and the Supreme Court upheld the legality of the transaction, however, the Supreme Court holding that a forwarder was a shipper as far as the railroad was concerned.[3]

Prior to World War I freight forwarders confined their operations almost entirely to export and import business, but embargoes on less-than-carload freight during the war led shippers to request forwarding companies to consolidate less-than-carload freight into carload lots for shipment in domestic commerce. At first this service was restricted to freight moving between large centers of production and consumption, but in due course forwarders began to use motor carriers to bring freight from smaller communities to consolidation points from which it was shipped in carload lots to distributing or break-bulk points. At these points the process was reversed, with motor carriers delivering shipments to smaller communities in the area adjacent to a given distributing point. In addition, freight forwarders began to make some use of motor carriers for through hauls, particularly where the distances involved were relatively short.

Present status of freight forwarding. As of December 31, 1950, there were ninety-four freight forwarders reporting to the Interstate Commerce Commission.[4] They had total transportation revenues of $287,023,718 and purchased transportation in the amount of $218,210,502. The three largest forwarding companies, Acme Fast Freight and affiliated companies, Universal Carloading and Distributing Company, and National Carloading Corporation, accounted for 59.83 per cent of forwarder revenue in 1950; and the twenty-two largest companies accounted for 94.42 per cent of the revenue. The relative use made of different kinds of transportation in 1950 is indicated by the fact that forwarders doing an annual gross business of $100,000 or more paid $151,197,501 for railroad transportation, $34,564,043 for motor transportation, $2,653,655 for water transportation, $29,627,541 for pickup, delivery, and transfer service, and $167,762 for miscellaneous transportation.

FREIGHT-FORWARDER INVESTIGATION

Freight forwarding fostered by railroads. The growth of certain questionable practices led the Interstate Commerce Commission to institute an investigation into the relationships between railroads and freight forwarders, the results of which were made public in 1938.[5] The early failure of the

---

[3] *Interstate Commerce Commission v. Delaware, Lackawanna and Western Railroad Company,* 220 U.S. 235 (1911).

[4] All figures on freight forwarders are from Interstate Commerce Commission, *Selected Financial and Operating Statistics from Annual Reports of Freight Forwarders, 1950.*

[5] *Freight Forwarding Investigation,* 229 I.C.C. 201.

railroads to meet motor carrier competition gave the freight forwarders, some of whom also operated truck lines, an opportunity which they did not overlook. They offered pickup and delivery service on small shipments at rates below those charged by the railroads and obtained a substantial amount of business for concentration into carload lots. The railroads appear to have encouraged the freight forwarders to go after this business since it enabled them to retrieve indirectly a considerable amount of the traffic lost to trucks. Railroad managements generally have considered the solicitation and handling of less-than-carload freight to be an expensive operation, whereas carload freight is handled expeditiously and at a profit. Hence it was argued that the forwarder relieved the railroads of unprofitable less-than-carload traffic, for which it substituted profitable carload traffic.

Competition for forwarder traffic. It is characteristic of the freight-forwarding business that freight-forwarding companies tend to concentrate their traffic into as small a number of channels as practical. If several railroads offer service between two important cities, a given forwarder will tend to limit its shipments to just one of them. Obviously a forwarding company may not be able to accumulate enough small shipments to make it possible to load cars via several different railroads, nor does it wish to duplicate its facilities at railroad terminals unnecessarily. The railroads are not unaware of the value of the forwarder business especially since it is said that railroad revenue is greater per car on forwarder traffic than it is on carload freight generally, and they are anxious to get as much forwarder traffic as possible.

Railroad concessions to forwarders. In its investigation the Interstate Commerce Commission brought to light numerous concessions made to freight forwarders by the railroads, concessions which were not made to shippers generally or which were of such a nature as to make them of particular value only to forwarders. For example, the Commission found that freight forwarders generally handled traffic through railroad freight houses or other railroad facilities, in some cases occupied buildings or facilities which had been especially constructed or remodeled for them by the railroad, and often obtained these facilities free of charge. It found that these and other practices constituted an undue and unreasonable preference and advantage to forwarders and their traffic in violation of the Interstate Commerce Act.

The all-commodity rates mentioned earlier in this chapter, while published and available to all shippers, were found to have been especially designed for freight-forwarder use. Some carriers published exceptions to rules contained in the Consolidated Freight Classification which, while again not specifically limited to forwarder use, were of such a nature as to be more beneficial to forwarders than to other shippers. The Commission found certain railroads performing special services for forwarders which they did not perform for shippers generally or for which they charged forwarders less than other shippers. In some cases the Commission found the carriers and the forwarders engaging in subterfuge to evade the spirit of certain of its rules, and in a few cases there appeared to be direct violations of the rules. Where the Commission found that carrier rules and practices favored forwarders over shippers generally, and such rules and practices constituted violations of the law, it ordered them canceled.

Railroad control of forwarding companies. In its investigation of freight forwarding the Interstate Commerce Commission found that some of the major forwarding companies were controlled by specific railroads. The possible consequences of such control may be illustrated by taking the case of New York Central control of Universal Carloading and Distributing Co. Both the New York Central and Universal provided a pickup and delivery service on less-than-carload freight at a number of common points, and both might and frequently did move shipments between the same points in the same train. But the shipper who used the Universal service got a lower rate than a shipper who, perhaps unaware of the Universal operation, shipped directly via the New York Central. The Commission also introduced some evidence to suggest that the New York Central had used its control over the routing of Universal freight to influence other railroads. The Commission found in this and one other case that such control of freight forwarders constituted a violation of the Interstate Commerce Act, and trustees were appointed to hold the forwarder stock of the railroads involved.[6]

Possibility of eliminating independent freight forwarders. It was generally agreed that the forwarder method of operation was more efficient than existing methods of handling individual packages through railroad freight houses. The Interstate Commerce Commission also recognized that the forwarders had regained for the railroads considerable traffic which had been lost to the trucks, but at the same time it felt that the railroads had not benefited as much from this traffic as they might have because of numerous concessions made to freight forwarders. The Commission expressed the opinion that there were no persuasive reasons why the railroads, either by themselves or through one or more wholly owned and controlled agencies, could not provide an attractive less-than-carload freight service and retain the entire profit for themselves.

---

[6] Interstate Commerce Commission, *Annual Report*, 1939, p. 34.

INDIRECT CARRIERS

DEVELOPMENT OF DEMAND FOR REGULATION

Anomalous position of freight forwarders. For many years after its inception freight forwarding occupied an anomalous status. Freight-forwarding companies solicited their own business, collected their own charges, issued their own bills of lading, assumed responsibility for pickup and delivery of freight at origin and destination, were liable for loss or damage to goods entrusted to their care, and were the only transportation agency known to their customers. In addition, the courts held that freight forwarders were common carriers under the common law and so must assume the duties and obligations of common carriers.[7] On the other hand, in their relationships with the railroads whose services they utilized, they were shippers, and as such they possessed none of the rights and privileges of common carriers. Specifically, forwarders did not have the right to establish joint rates with railroads, nor did they enjoy the protection from destructive competition which has resulted from statutory regulation of common carriers.

Forwarder relationships with motor carriers. The use of motor carriers by freight forwarders in expanding the area of their operations preceded the adoption of the Motor Carrier Act, 1935, and since neither the forwarders nor the motor carriers were subject to statutory regulation insofar as their interstate operations were concerned, the forwarders made special contracts or agreements with individual motor carriers covering the amount to be paid by the forwarder for motor transport service. Thus, while forwarder traffic could not move by railroad at rates which were less than those available to all shippers, forwarders could and did secure motor transportation at less than the prices charged shippers in general. These arrangements could be justified on the ground that the cost of handling forwarder traffic was less to the motor carrier because the forwarder solicited the traffic, made up and collected freight bills, and provided its own pickup and delivery service. And where unbalanced traffic existed, forwarders sometimes were able to provide motor carriers with traffic to fill empty or lightly loaded trucks.

The adoption of the Motor Carrier Act, 1935, made a continuation of the special contract arrangements impossible. Some of the forwarders, however, took the position that they now were common carriers by motor vehicle, filed applications for authority to "continue" operations under the grandfather provisions of Part II of the Interstate Commerce Act, and filed tariffs with the Interstate Commerce Commission naming joint rates with

---

[7] See, for example, *Kettenhofen v. Globe Transfer and Storage Company*, 70 Wash. 645.

motor carriers. In most instances the motor carriers' share in the division of these rates was less than the rates published for general shipper use. In due course this matter came before the Commission which held that forwarders were not carriers subject to Part II of the Interstate Commerce Act, could not participate lawfully in joint rates with motor common carriers, and ordered the joint forwarder-motor carrier tariffs stricken from its files.[8] The Commission's position was sustained by the Supreme Court.[9]

The result of the Commission's action was to reduce forwarders to the status of ordinary shippers in their relationships with motor carriers. But if forwarders were required to pay the less-than-truckload rates on freight trucked into concentration points and out of distribution points, they would have to increase their charges, and doubt was expressed that they could hold the off-line traffic under such conditions. Fear was expressed, too, that the smaller communities would lose the forwarder service they had enjoyed since the advent of motor transportation, and so would be at a competitive disadvantage in comparison with the larger cities which enjoyed direct forwarder service. Several bills were introduced in Congress to relieve this situation, and pending the outcome of hearings on these bills, the Interstate Commerce Commission postponed from time to time the effective date of its order striking out the joint rates.

Legislative history of regulation. Congressional hearings on forwarder legislation were held in 1940 and 1941. Joseph B. Eastman, Chairman of the Interstate Commerce Commission and former Federal Coordinator of Transportation, prepared a draft bill which he presented to Congress in his own name. A majority of the Interstate Commerce Commission, however, took the position that the railroads could and should perform the service then being rendered by the forwarders. Freight forwarders favored regulation which would change their status. The American Trucking Associations favored regulation to prevent abuses, but some individual trucking companies opposed it. The railroads were sharply divided over the extent and nature of forwarder regulation. In general, shippers wished to retain the benefits of a forwarder service but recognized the desirability of regulation to prevent unlawful practices. On May 16, 1942, after extended discussion, freight forwarders were made subject to regulation by the Interstate Commerce Commission, the provisions of the law being incorporated as Part IV of the Interstate Commerce Act.

---

[8] *Acme Fast Freight, Incorporated, Common Carrier Application,* 2 M.C.C. 415 (1937); 8 M.C.C. 211 (1938); 17 M.C.C. 549 (1939); *Tariffs of Forwarding Companies,* 23 M.C.C. 95 (1940).

[9] *Acme Fast Freight, Inc., v. United States,* 309 U.S. 638 (1940); *United States v. Chicago Heights Trucking Co.,* 310 U.S. 344 (1940).

INDIRECT CARRIERS

REGULATION OF FREIGHT FORWARDERS UNDER PART IV
OF THE INTERSTATE COMMERCE ACT

Definition of freight forwarder. Part IV defines a freight forwarder as a person, other than a carrier subject to Parts I, II, or III of the Interstate Commerce Act, which holds itself out to the general public to transport or provide transportation of property for compensation in interstate commerce, and which (a) assembles and consolidates property and provides for breaking up consolidated shipments and distributing the items shipped, (b) assumes responsibility for transporting such property from point of receipt to point of destination, and (c) utilizes in whole or part the services of carriers subject to Parts I, II, or III. Freight-forwarder services involving the use of air carriers subject to the Civil Aeronautics Act, and services involving motor transportation used as an incident to air transportation, are specifically excluded from the provisions of Part IV. The utilization of air carriers by freight forwarders is, of course, subject to control by the Civil Aeronautics Board.

Permits. No freight forwarder subject to Part IV may operate without a permit issued by the Interstate Commerce Commission. Before the Commission may issue a permit, it must find that the applicant is ready, willing, and able to perform the proposed service, and that the service will be consistent with the national transportation policy. A permit, however, may not be denied solely on the ground that the service proposed will compete with the services of forwarders already possessing permits. Since forwarders make use of the facilities of existing carriers, increasing the number of forwarders will not result in an oversupply of transportation facilities, and a little competition between forwarding companies may help to offset the evils resulting from railroad competition for forwarder traffic.

The Commission may attach such reasonable terms, conditions, and limitations to a permit as are necessary, and it may subsequently suspend, change, or revoke a permit for willful failure to comply with the law or Commission orders. Before a permit may be revoked, however, the holder is entitled to a reasonable time in which to demonstrate compliance. Approval of the Commission is required for the transfer of a permit, for amendment or revocation at the request of the holder, and for abandonment of service when the forwarder is controlled by a carrier subject to Parts I, II, or III. Forwarder permits do not authorize the holders to conduct any direct railroad, water, or motor carrier operations, except that motor vehicles may be utilized in terminal service. No permit may be issued to a common carrier subject to Parts I, II, or III, but a corporation controlled by or under common control with such a carrier may not be denied a permit solely because of such relationship.

Exemptions. The law does not apply to cooperative associations as defined by the Agricultural Marketing Act of 1929, as amended, nor to the movement of ordinary livestock, fish, agricultural commodities, or used household goods. Individual shippers or associations of shippers operating on a nonprofit basis may consolidate or distribute freight for themselves without being subject to the law. And warehousemen or shippers' agents who confine their activities to terminal areas are exempted.

Grandfather operations. A forwarder in business as of the effective date of the act was permitted to operate for 180 days without a permit. If application for a permit was made within that period, the forwarder could continue to operate under such regulations as the Commission prescribed, and until otherwise ordered by the Commission. Thus the right of forwarders to continue to operate as they did before the law was passed is by no means absolute.

Rates and service. It is the duty of every freight forwarder subject to the act to provide the service which it holds itself out to perform at just and reasonable rates and charges, including just and reasonable classifications, regulations, practices, and the like. It is unlawful to give any undue or unreasonable preference or advantage to any person, place, or description of traffic, and there are the usual prohibitions against rebates and the like. The Interstate Commerce Commission, on its part, is authorized to establish reasonable requirements with respect to continuous and adequate service; to determine maximum or minimum or maximum and minimum rates and charges; and to determine lawful classifications, regulations, and practices. In any proceeding to determine the justness or reasonableness of a rate, the Commission is not to consider good will, earning power, or the value of the forwarders' permits as evidences of property value. The law contains a rule of rate making essentially the same as those provided for carriers subject to Parts I, II, and III.

Tariffs. All freight-forwarder tariffs must be filed with the Interstate Commerce Commission and kept open for public inspection. A tariff becomes effective only after thirty days' notice, but the Commission may, for good cause shown, permit a tariff to go into effect upon shorter notice. The Commission also has the usual power to suspend new rates, charges, classifications, regulations, or practices for a maximum of seven months beyond the effective date. If at the end of that time it has not concluded its proceedings, the new rate, charge, classification, regulation, or practice is permitted to go into effect.

Assembly and distribution rates. An assembly rate may be defined as a rate charged by a carrier subject to Parts I, II, or III for moving forwarder traffic from various origin points to the nearest concentration point, where individual packages are consolidated into carload or truckload lots and shipped to break-bulk or distribution points. A distribution rate is one charged by the above described carriers for moving forwarder traffic from distribution stations to off-line destinations. Part IV permits carriers subject to Parts I, II, or III to make assembly and distribution charges to forwarders, and others who utilize common carrier facilities under like conditions, which are lower than are paid by shippers generally, provided that the lower charges can be justified by differences in the conditions under which common carrier facilities are utilized. The law originally specified that this concession was not to apply to rates charged for the movement of forwarder traffic between concentration and break-bulk points, but this restriction was modified later as will be noted. It will be clear that the assembly and distribution rates were intended to enable freight forwarders to continue to offer forwarder service to off-line points, at least to the extent that they could show that forwarder traffic was more economical to handle than ordinary less-than-truckload traffic.

Adjustment period. In order to provide a reasonable period during which the new assembly and distribution rates could be put into effect, Congress provided that existing joint forwarder-motor carrier rates could remain in effect for a period of eighteen months. The adjustment period was extended from time to time until February 20, 1946, when Congress made substantial changes in this part of the law. Under the 1946 amendment the Interstate Commerce Commission was called upon to determine and prescribe a method for fixing the compensation to be paid by freight forwarders for the services of common carrier motor vehicles which would be in furtherance of the national transportation policy. Although the law relating to assembly and distribution rates was not repealed, the Commission was authorized to approve other methods of compensation. The new amendment also permitted the establishment of lower charges to forwarders on motor carrier hauls between concentration and distribution points, provided that the Commission found such lower charges justified because of conditions of use and the nature of the service performed.

Intercorporate relationships. Freight forwarders are not permitted, either directly or indirectly, to acquire control of carriers subject to Parts I, II, or III. Shippers whose business operations are such as to commonly call for the use of forwarder service may not engage in the forwarder business except to the extent that the Interstate Commerce Commission may find that such an arrangement is consistent with the public interest and the national transportation policy. It is not unlawful, however, for a common carrier subject to Parts I, II, or III to acquire control of a freight-forwarding concern.

Miscellaneous provisions. Freight forwarders, like motor carriers, are expected to file bonds, insurance policies, or the like, for the protection of the public using their services and for the same reasons that motor carriers have been required to follow a similar procedure. There are the usual provisions relating to a uniform system of accounts and the requirement of annual and periodical reports; and detailed penalties are provided for violations of the law, disclosure of information about shippers' business, and the like. In the event that intrastate regulations discriminate against interstate commerce the Interstate Commerce Commission is authorized to act to remove the discrimination. Except in the performance of terminal services, freight forwarders may not utilize any carriers other than common carriers by railroad, motor vehicle, or water, subject to the Interstate Commerce Act; express companies subject to the Interstate Commerce Act; and air carriers subject to the Civil Aeronautics Act. Certain minor exceptions of no particular significance are permitted.

INTERSTATE COMMERCE COMMISSION POLICY AND FREIGHT-FORWARDER PROBLEMS

Grandfather operations. The Interstate Commerce Commission has ruled that Part IV does not contain a true grandfather clause which entitles an applicant in business on May 16, 1942, to a permit solely because of that fact. Such an applicant, like any other, must show that it is ready, able, and willing to perform the proposed service, and that the service will be consistent with the public interest and the national transportation policy.[10] Obviously, however, the fact that an applicant was operating successfully on the date specified would react strongly in his favor in connection with an application to continue operations.

Shipper associations. It sometimes happens that individual shippers or associations of shippers have less-than-carload freight consigned to or being shipped from a common point, and in some cases they have found it worth while to pool their individual shipments into carload lots which move at carload rates. Such operations, when conducted on a nonprofit basis for the benefit of the members of the group, are specifically exempted from regulation under Part IV, although they serve essentially the same purpose and operate in essentially the same way as does freight forwarding.

Enactment of Part IV was followed by a material increase in the pooling of traffic by shippers, and bona fide forwarding companies began to complain that some of these shipper groups were soliciting desirable traffic from nonmembers at cut rates. In 1947 the Commission found in an investigation of the Pacific Coast Wholesalers' Association that nonmember

---

[10] *Republic Carloading and Distributing Co., Inc.*, 250 I.C.C. 670 (1943); *Acme Fast Freight, Inc.*, 250 I.C.C. 747 (1943).

consignors were selling goods to members on a delivered basis and paying the Association the less-than-carload freight rate for delivering the goods to its members. The Commission held that the difference between the less-than-carload rate received by the Association from nonmember consignors and the carload rate it paid the railroads represented profit and the Association was, therefore, operating on a for-hire basis.[11] The courts, however, held that the Association was serving no one other than its members, and the Commission's order was set aside.[12]

Permit policy. It sometimes happens that a group of forwarding companies is operated under common management and control, and where the several companies seek permission to perform substantially the same services, the Commission has refused to grant a permit to more than one company in the group. The issuance of more than one permit in a situation like this affords opportunities for discriminatory practices contrary to public interest.

Following the plain requirement of the law, the Interstate Commerce Commission has not refused to issue permits solely on the ground that competition with existing freight forwarders would result. The organized freight forwarders have argued that they are entitled to protection from excessive competition just as other regulated transportation agencies are protected, but it is hard to see how they can achieve such protection short of a change in the law.

In general, it may be said that the Commission has followed a rather liberal policy with reference to the nature of products handled and territory served by freight forwarders. Since there is a natural tendency for forwarders to prefer the higher rated commodities and the points where traffic volume is large, nothing much would be gained by attempting to place restrictions on the variety of goods handled or territory served.

Rates and practices. The Commission has recognized that rates may vary somewhat with the size of a shipment, but it has frowned upon the practice of granting special rates based on the amount of freight shipped over a period of time. It has held that such rates do not have any relevant bearing on the cost of handling individual shipments and are a device for favoring large shippers which cannot be permitted.[13]

Joint rates with motor carriers. The assembly and distribution rates which Congress provided in 1942 were not accepted generally as the solution to the problem of motor carrier compensation for handling forwarder

---

[11] *Pacific Coast Wholesalers' Association, Investigation of Status,* 269 I.C.C. 504 (1947).

[12] *Traffic World,* February 11, 1950, pp. 47-48.

[13] *Books, Drugs, and Cotton Goods from New York to Chicago,* 256 I.C.C. 85 (1943); *Forwarder Rates Conditioned Upon Aggregates of Tonnage,* 258 I.C.C. 635 (1944).

traffic, and they were published only in a few instances. The failure to establish such rates was attributed in part to the reluctance of motor carriers to establish assembly and distribution rates for forwarders which also would be available to shippers who could use the services in a similar fashion.

Congress recognized that the law was not working out as planned and subsequently directed the Interstate Commerce Commission to determine a reasonable method of compensation under which freight forwarders could utilize the services of motor carriers. The Commission instituted an investigation in which it found that motor carriers were able to make substantial savings in the cost of handling assembly and distribution traffic for freight forwarders, and so it approved forwarder-motor carrier compensation by agreement insofar as this kind of traffic was concerned. It pointed out, however, that forwarder traffic should bear its proper share of the cost of motor carrier service and prescribed the conditions under which the forwarder-motor carrier agreements were to be made.[14]

Terminal-to-terminal movements. Part IV, as amended in 1946, permitted lower charges on forwarder traffic when moved by motor carriers in truckload lots between concentration and distribution points, provided that the Interstate Commerce Commission found that the special conditions surrounding forwarder traffic justified such lower charges. The Commission, with three of its members dissenting and one not participating, concluded that there was little difference between the cost of handling forwarder and nonforwarder traffic insofar as these terminal-to-terminal movements were concerned, and so it ruled that forwarders must pay the established truckload rates on shipments between concentration and distribution points.[15]

The Commission had held consistently that freight forwarders were not common carriers in the ordinary sense of the word and that Congress had not intended to clothe them with a common carrier status when it adopted Part IV of the Interstate Commerce Act in 1942. In the eyes of the Commission they were shippers insofar as their relations with existing carriers were concerned, and they were not entitled to rates lower than those available to shippers generally except to the extent that it could be shown that the cost of handling forwarder traffic was less. There appears to have been substantial disagreement with the Commission's position that motor carriers could not handle forwarder traffic in truckload lots between concentration and distribution points at a saving, and on December 20, 1950, President Truman signed a bill giving freight forwarders the legal status of common

---

[14] *Freight Forwarders, Motor Common Carriers, Agreements*, 272 I.C.C. 413 (1948).
[15] *Ibid.*

carriers and permitting them to enter into contracts with motor carriers for terminal-to-terminal movements of forwarder traffic for distances less than 450 miles at rates below those available to other shippers.[16]

RAILWAY EXPRESS AGENCY, INC.

Origin and development of express business. There is a difference of opinion about who originated the express business, but credit usually is given to a New England railroad conductor by the name of William F. Harnden. Businessmen sometimes asked Harnden to carry small parcels or to perform services for them in communities along his route, and in 1839 he quit his job and went into business for himself, advertising a weekly express service between New York and Boston, partly by rail and partly by boat. Other men saw opportunities in this field, many express companies were organized, and the business expanded rapidly along with and beyond the expanding network of railroads. Most of these companies had a short life. In some cases there were ruinous rate wars which ended in combination, and there was a good deal of interlocking ownership among the major operators which led to a division of territory and a restriction of competition.

Organization of Railway Express Agency, Inc. During World War I the major express companies, Wells Fargo, American, Adams, and Southern, together with three minor companies, combined their operations under the name American Railway Express Company, and this arrangement was so satisfactory that it was made permanent after the war. The American Railway Express Company provided a single nationwide express service, except on the lines of the Southern Railway and its subsidiaries where a new company, the Southeastern Express Company, was organized to provide express service.

During the stage coach era and when mining camps were remote from railroad connections, there was some merit in separately incorporated express companies which could provide a through service on small packages, money, and other articles of great value. But with the expansion of the railroad network, domestic express companies came to operate exclusively by railroad, thus becoming a sort of wheel within a wheel. As a consequence the railroads got together and on March 1, 1929, took over the assets of the American Railway Express Company, replacing it with the newly created Railway Express Agency, Inc., a railroad-owned corporation. The Southeastern Express Company was merged into the Railway Express Agency, Inc., in 1938, and all express is now handled by this one organization.

---

[16] *Traffic World*, January 6, 1951, p. 17.

INDIRECT CARRIERS

Relationship with railroads. The stock of the Railway Express Agency is owned by seventy major railroads, but the Agency's operations are not confined to these railroads. It operates in conjunction with numerous short-line railroads, airlines, motor carriers, water carriers, and electric railroads. The relationships between the Railway Express Agency and the railroads over which it operates are governed by a standard form of arrangement. The railroads provide the Express Agency with station facilities and rolling stock and undertake to move express shipments in passenger trains or in special express or mail trains. The Railway Express Agency solicits traffic, collects charges, provides pickup and delivery service, and assumes liability for loss of or damage to express shipments. From its gross income the Agency deducts its operating expenses, taxes, and payments to carriers not parties to the standard form of agreement, and the remainder is divided among the individual contracting railroads approximately in proportion to the participation of each in total express traffic. Carload express traffic, which is relatively small, is paid for on a somewhat different basis. No net income accrues to the Railway Express Agency and no dividends are paid on its capital stock.

Nature of express traffic. Express traffic today is made up largely of shipments too small to be practical to handle as railroad less-than-carload freight, shipments requiring fast delivery, small shipments of explosives or other articles not accepted by the parcel post system, and such high value articles as money, documents, manuscripts, and art objects.

SOME EXPRESS AGENCY PROBLEMS

Regulation. Absence of effective competition between express companies had the inevitable results of high rates, arbitrary actions, and other abuses of monopoly power. When the Hepburn Act was adopted in 1906, Congress included express companies as common carriers subject to the provisions of the Act to Regulate Commerce. Today the Railway Express Agency is regulated by the Interstate Commerce Commission under the provisions of Part I of the Interstate Commerce Act, to the extent that the provisions of Part I have application to a carrier of this type.

Rates and rate making. The Official Express Classification provides for first class rates on articles not otherwise classified; second class rates on certain food products, perishables, and a few other items; and third class rates on certain types of printed matter. In addition, there is a so-called money classification covering money and articles of unusually high value. Commodity rates also are published to a limited extent. For purposes of rate making the United States has been divided into 950 numbered blocks, the lines of latitude and longitude constituting the block boundaries, and each of these blocks is divided into sixteen lettered subblocks. A directory of express stations provides the block and subblock for each station, while the actual rates are determined by reference to other tariffs. Block-to-block rates are used in calculating rates between points in nonadjacent blocks, and subblock rates are used between points in adjacent blocks or in the same block. The tapering principle discussed in connection with railroad rates is employed, which means that express rates do not increase proportionately with distance.

Present status. Before the establishment of the parcel post system in 1913, the predecessors of the Railway Express Agency enjoyed a monopoly on the movement of small shipments, but this is anything but true today. As the original highly restrictive parcel post weight and size limits were liberalized and insurance and C.O.D. privileges were established, a large amount of the highly important small package express traffic was diverted to the postal system. In addition to this, packages too large for the postal service to handle are moving increasingly by motor carriers, freight forwarders, expedited railroad less-than-carload freight services, and air freight. Increased costs of operation during and after World War II have made it necessary to raise express rates substantially, and while the rates charged by competing agencies also have gone up, the relative increases have not been too favorable to the Express Agency. This has been particularly true in the case of parcel post rates. On top of all this, wartime congestion in terminal areas and the necessity of employing inexperienced help resulted in a noticeable deterioration in the quality of express service.

As a consequence of the diversion of traffic to other agencies, and particularly to the parcel post system, the Railway Express Agency has been placed in a difficult position. According to a statement made by Representative Vursell in the Congressional Record of October 17, 1949, the Express Agency had vacated 30,000 jobs since 1946, while the Post Office Department found it necessary to add over 40,000 employees to its staff.[17] Since it does not compensate the railroads on the basis of an established scale of charges, there is no way to determine the extent to which the Agency is operating at a profit or a loss, but there does not seem to be much doubt that the railroads are handling express traffic at a loss.[18] Express company officials and employees have urged substantial increases in rates on parcel post on the ground that the latter service is carried on at a loss. In addition, reduction in the size and weight limits of packages acceptable for parcel post service have been advocated, reductions which it is

---

[17] *Traffic World,* October 22, 1949, p. 53.
[18] See Lewis W. Britton, ed., *Transportation in 1949,* p. 70.

believed would throw some traffic to the Express Agency. These proposals are discussed further in connection with the parcel post system.

POSTAL SERVICE

Development of parcel post system. A parcel post system had been advocated for many years before its establishment in 1913, but up to that time it had been fought successfully by the express companies and by small town businessmen who were afraid of competition from mail order houses. Many reasons may be cited for the demand for a parcel post system. In the first place, the monopoly enjoyed by the express companies led to practices which were irritating to many people, and these people saw in the parcel post system an answer to the express monopoly. Second, people residing on rural routes and in numerous small communities throughout the United States enjoyed mail service but could get express service only by making trips to and from the nearest town big enough to support an express agency. Finally, many European postal systems offered a parcel post service and there was an international parcel post system in operation, all of which was at variance with the practice in the United States. In this connection, however, it should be noted that the express service was a distinctively American development and was not found on railroads in other parts of the world.[19]

Before 1913, the maximum weight parcel acceptable for movement in the United States mail was four pounds, and the rate was one cent per ounce or fraction thereof regardless of distance. The parcel post system, inaugurated January 1, 1913, permitted the acceptance of packages weighing up to eleven pounds and having a maximum combined length and girth of seventy-two inches. A system of zones was established with rates increasing with distance by zones. Various restrictions were placed on the kinds of goods acceptable for shipment. The law authorized the Postmaster General, with the approval of the Interstate Commerce Commission, to change the rates from time to time, and the Postmaster General was given broad discretionary powers with regard to various other aspects of the parcel post system.

In the years following the enactment of the original law, many changes were made in the parcel post regulations, most of which were designed to make the service more attractive to small shippers. The maximum

---

[19] The absence of a parcel post system in the United States brought about an unusual contractual relationship in which a privately owned express company handled parcel post packages in the United States for the postal services of certain foreign governments. See Alden Hatch, *American Express*. Garden City, New York: Doubleday & Company, Inc., 1950, p. 104.

weight limit was increased over the years from eleven to seventy pounds, and the size limit from a combined length and girth of seventy-two inches to one hundred inches. Restrictions on the kinds of goods acceptable for shipment by parcel post were liberalized to the extent that even day-old chicks could move by parcel post. Shipments were insured in exchange for the payment of a small fee, and a C.O.D. service was made available. Rates have been changed both up and down on various occasions, but the general principle of rates increasing by zones has been retained. As of the beginning of 1951 parcel post rates were not too much greater than they were when the system was inaugurated in 1913, and in some cases they were actually lower.

Parcel post vs. express. A comparison of the parcel post and express services reveals that each has certain advantages over the other. The Railway Express Agency provides both a pickup and a delivery service whereas only a delivery service is available on parcel post. For business concerns the express pickup service represents a definite advantage, but for others it is almost always more convenient to take packages to the post office or to a substation than it is to call the express office and wait for a truck to pick them up.

The Express Agency gives a receipt to the shipper and requires a receipt from the consignee on all shipments, a practice which is not followed on ordinary parcel post shipments. All express shipments are insured automatically for a maximum of $50, or 50¢ a pound on shipments exceeding one hundred pounds in weight, whereas parcel post shipments are insured only upon request and upon the payment of an additional fee. Parcel post insurance is not provided in amounts in excess of $200 per package whereas the Express Agency regularly handles items of very high value for which it assumes full liability provided excess value fees have been paid.

Poisons, explosives, live animals, and certain other items which are not acceptable for shipment by parcel post are accepted as a matter of course for express shipment. Similarly, articles which exceed the maximum weight and size limits acceptable for parcel post are taken by express. It is often possible to make such shipments by parcel post, however, by making two or more packages of the shipment.

There are two principal advantages of the parcel post system. In the first place, the parcel post system provides a small package transportation service to millions of people living on rural routes and in communities which do not have railroad express service. The other big advantage of parcel post is, of course, the lower cost of the service to the shipper. As will be noted presently, however, the parcel post system has been operating at a loss, making the true cost of the service greater than the actual charges assessed.

SOME POSTAL SERVICE TRANSPORTATION PROBLEMS

Problem of payment for transporting mail. Originally the railroads carried mail under contracts entered into with the Postmaster General, subject to maximum limits fixed by law. In 1873 this method was abandoned in favor of a rather unique arrangement which permitted the Postmaster General, subject to certain limitations, to determine what the railroads would receive for carrying mail. Although this system of paying the carriers remained in effect for over forty years, it gave rise to several difficulties, not the least of which was the friction resulting from the fact that rates were not fixed by mutual agreement but by unilateral action on the part of the Post Office Department. A new method of compensation was authorized in 1916, and since that time the railroads have been paid on a space-mile basis, the rate varying with the size of the car space required and the nature of the equipment utilized. At the same time the Interstate Commerce Commission was given the power to determine fair and reasonable rates to be paid by the Post Office Department to the railroads for the service rendered.

Mail pay cases have been before the Commission from time to time, but no good purpose would be served by attempting to trace the various changes which have taken place. In February 1947, the railroads filed a petition for a 45 per cent increase in mail pay rates, last determined in 1928, and the Commission granted a 25 per cent increase pending a final decision in the case. Subsequently the railroads requested a minimum increase of 65 per cent, which request was later raised to 80 per cent, and still later to 95 per cent above the rates in effect in 1947. Late in 1950 the railroads and the Post Office Department agreed to an increase of about 48 per cent to cover the period from February 1947, to the end of 1950. Thereafter both parties filed suggested rate scales for the future, and in November 1951, the Commission prescribed new rates estimated to be about 95 per cent above the 1947 level. At the same time it noted that even this large increase would not cover increased costs unless the carriers were able to effectuate operating economies.

In recent years the Post Office Department has shown increasing interest in the movement of mail by truck, and a number of short haul mail truck routes have been established.

Parcel post charges. In the years following World War II a persistent demand developed in some quarters for substantial increases in parcel post charges. There are two rather obvious explanations of this demand. In the first place, the Post Office Department had been incurring rather substantial losses on its parcel post service, and the Department favored higher rates as one means of reducing the postal deficit. Also, a good many members of Congress, desirous of reducing unnecessary costs of government, favored a move which would reduce the postal deficit. The other reason for higher rates arose out of a desire to do something to aid the Railway Express Agency. Most of the small package business once handled by express had been diverted to parcel post, and it was believed that a substantial increase in rates would return some of this business to the Express Agency. This position was supported by the railroads, the Express Agency and its employees, and many of the nation's law makers who were opposed to government competition with private enterprise.

The demand for higher parcel post rates was accompanied by a demand for a drastic reduction in the maximum size and weight limits on packages accepted for shipment by parcel post. While it might be argued that such a reduction would result in a further decline in the postal deficit, the primary reason for it obviously was to aid the Railway Express Agency by making it impossible to ship numerous items by parcel post.

Considerable opposition was expressed to these proposed changes in the parcel post system. There were those who expressed doubt that it was socially desirable to operate the parcel post system at rates which would cover the full cost of the service. Shippers who made considerable use of the parcel post service were, of course, directly concerned. The attitude of the mail order houses was that they were not opposed to such rate increases as might be necessary to cover the cost of the service, but they objected to specific aspects of various proposals, and they questioned the methods employed by the Post Office Department in arriving at the cost of the parcel post service.

Shippers were definitely concerned about the proposals to reduce existing size and weight limits. Thus the Illinois Traffic League was quoted as saying:

The size and weight reductions were not included in the original bills, nor were they recommended by business or the mailing public. It appears that it could be asked, "Are these bills proposed for the benefit of the Postal Service and the public?" or is it intended "by legislation" to force this package delivery service back to the express agency or other transportation services not only at a greatly increased cost to the shipper, but with an inferior delivery service to the consignee? [20]

Opposition also was expressed by farm organizations because the substitution of express service for parcel post would leave people living on rural

---

[20] *Traffic World*, January 28, 1950, p. 51.

routes and in numerous towns where there was no express service without any convenient means for sending and receiving small shipments.

During 1951 substantial increases in parcel post rates were put into effect, and additional increases were adopted to become effective early in 1952. In October 1951, legislation was enacted lowering the maximum size and weight limits permissible for parcel post shipments. The new law reduced the maximum of 100 inches in length and girth to 72 inches. The severity of this reduction may be indicated by the fact that a box fifteen inches square becomes too large to ship by parcel post. Maximum weight limits were reduced from 70 pounds to 40 pounds in the first and second zones and 20 pounds in zones three to eight. These reductions do not apply to packages shipped to or from second, third, or fourth class post offices or rural routes, thus assuring a continuation of the existing service for those people who do not have express service available.

PULLMAN SERVICE

Development of Pullman service. Although crude sleeping cars are said to have been operated on the Cumberland Valley Railroad as early as 1836, there was little need for sleeping car service on the short lines operated by the early railroads. As longer journeys by railroad became possible more sleeping cars appeared, but these continued to be crude affairs by present-day standards. Credit for developing the modern sleeping car must be given to George M. Pullman who remodeled an Alton Railroad coach into a practical sleeping car in 1859 and in 1865 built the first modern car. It is not by chance that the terms "Pullman" and "sleeping car" are synonymous today. In 1867 Pullman organized his own company which for many years has produced sleeping cars, dining cars, parlor cars, and other specialized types of passenger train equipment for the railroads of the United States.

Pullman contract. For many years the Pullman organization owned and operated practically all of the sleeping and parlor cars used on railroads in the United States. Relations between the Pullman Company and the railroads were governed by individual contracts under which the Pullman Company agreed to supply an adequate number of cars, to provide bedding and other supplies, and to provide the necessary personnel to operate the cars. The railroads agreed to haul the cars, pay for running repairs, provide ticket quarters, and the like.

Of the revenues derived from the Pullman service, a certain minimum per car year went to the Pullman Company, with the remainder divided in one way or another between the individual railroads and the Pullman Company. The exact nature of this last arrangement varied widely from line to line, depending upon the ability of a given railroad to provide its own sleeping car service. In other words, if a railroad was in a position to perform its own service, it got better terms than a line which could not afford to do so. This arrangement was quite profitable to the Pullman Company, and it was satisfactory for the railroads as well because it relieved them of the necessity of investing large sums of money in expensive specialized equipment. On many lines, too, the demand for Pullman service was and is somewhat seasonal in nature, and operation of the cars by the Pullman Company made for maximum efficiency in the utilization of equipment, cars being shifted from line to line and from one section of the country to another to meet the seasonal needs.

The Standard Car Manufacturing Company, which built sleeping and other cars, and the Pullman Company which operated the sleeping car service were controlled by a holding company, Pullman, Inc. In 1946, as a result of an antitrust suit, the latter company was ordered by the courts to divest itself of one or the other of the two operations. Pullman, Inc., decided to dispose of its operating activities, and the Pullman Company was sold to the major passenger carrying railroads which continued the operation of the Pullman Company much the same as before. Many railroads today own their own sleeping and parlor cars, however, especially those used in conjunction with the streamlined high speed "name" trains.

Pullman charges. The charge made for sleeping car accommodations varies with the nature of the accommodations used and the length of time they are occupied, while parlor car seats are charged for on the basis of distance traveled. These charges are in addition to the railroad fare collected by the railroad from all passengers regardless of the accommodations they occupy. Because Pullman and parlor cars are heavier than ordinary passenger coaches and accommodate a much smaller number of passengers, the railroads feel that Pullman passengers should pay for their transportation at a higher rate per mile than is assessed against passengers in ordinary coaches. Beginning in 1920 Pullman passengers were required to pay a surcharge equal to 50 per cent of the price paid for Pullman accommodations, which sum went to the railroads to compensate them for the higher cost of moving Pullman passengers. In 1936 the Interstate Commerce Commission abolished the Pullman surcharge and established a "first class" fare for passengers occupying Pullman or parlor car equipment and a somewhat lower "coach" fare for other passengers. The first class fare is in addition to whatever charge is made for the special accommodations occupied.

INDIRECT CARRIERS

SUGGESTED READINGS

Beebe, Lucius, *U. S. West*. New York: E. P. Dutton & Co., Inc., 1949. A popular pictorial account of the early years of Wells Fargo.

Department of Commerce, *Industry Report, Domestic Transportation*, December, 1946-January, 1947. Deals with express service.

Harlow, Alvin F., *Old Post Bags*. New York: D. Appleton and Company, 1928. Story of postal systems.

————, *Old Waybills*. New York: D. Appleton-Century Company, Inc., 1934. An excellent account of the early history of the express business.

Interstate Commerce Commission, *Reports*. The best source of information on the freight-forwarding business.

Johnson, Emory R., *Transport Facilities, Services and Policies*. New York: D. Appleton-Century Company, Inc., 1947. Discussion of mail and express which is briefer than Miller but more up to date.

Miller, Sidney L., *Inland Transportation*. New York: McGraw-Hill Book Company, Inc., 1933. Contains an excellent brief discussion of the mail, express, and Pullman service up to the date of publication.

Traffic World. Best source of information on current developments.

Part Seven

NATIONAL TRANSPORTATION PROBLEMS AND POLICIES

32

Some Basic
NATIONAL TRANSPORTATION
PROBLEMS

NEED FOR A NATIONAL TRANSPORTATION POLICY

Expansion of transportation facilities. In the preceding chapters problems peculiar to each of the various forms of transportation have been considered in some detail. Attention must now be focussed on those broader problems arising out of the relationships of the different agencies to each other and to their place in and effect upon a national transportation system. Since 1920 the people of the United States have experienced a revolution in transportation as a result of the development of highway and air transportation and the revitalization of inland waterway transportation, a revolution the like of which has not been experienced since the steam railroad replaced horse-drawn vehicles more than one hundred years ago. As these new forms of transportation made their appearance, the railroads made little effort to utilize them in the performance of an integrated transportation service, and as a result each developed under independent ownership without reference to its effect on other forms of transportation or on the transportation system as a whole. In this connection it should be noted that the development of motor, water, and air transportation was made possible to no small extent by programs of public works and policies of direct financial support administered by various unrelated government agencies, and these programs and policies likewise were carried on without reference to each other or to their effect upon the transportation system as a whole.

There can be little doubt that the newer agencies of transportation enjoyed a much more rapid development under independent ownership and government assistance than would otherwise have been the case, and the public has benefited thereby. At the same time, however, the rapid increase in the total supply of transportation, together with the apparent failure to recognize the fact that all of these various agencies of transportation are parts of a national transportation system, has created problems, the solution of which will require a critical re-examination of present-day regulatory and promotional policies. That all is not well with transportation in the United States is a thesis which needs no defense among students, shippers, and practical transportation men, although the need for action has been obscured to some extent in recent years by an abnormal volume of traffic arising out of war and preparation for war.

The principal immediate cause for concern has been the generally inadequate earnings of the railroads, about which more will be said presently. For a good many years the railroads as a whole have been unable to earn a satisfactory return on their investment, except during times of war and preparation for war, and there are those who believe that the railroads are slowly drifting toward bankruptcy. Coastwise and intercoastal common carrier transportation generally is unprofitable. The Inland Waterways Corporation, attempting to provide a comprehensive barge line service, has been incurring substantial annual deficits in spite of the fact that it pays nothing for the use of the costly right of way on which it operates. Other barge lines are in better shape, but it is doubtful that they could survive for long if required to meet the cost of improving and maintaining the channels now provided for them without charge. Scheduled airlines have had to rely on direct financial aid in the form of mail subsidies, and they would have a most difficult time if they were required to pay their share of the cost of airway and airport improvements. It may be, of course, that the time will come when air and water carriers can operate without public assistance, but there does not seem to be much prospect of such a development in the near future. The case of the highway carriers is not so clear, with evidence being presented that they are and that they are not being subsidized.

A national transportation policy. The transportation system as it exists today, although it may appear to operate successfully during periods of abnormal traffic, is fundamentally unsound—as evidenced by the uncertain future of the railroads, the necessity for continued subsidization of air and water transportation, and a rather widespread popular belief that heavy trucks are destroying the nation's highway investment. While many reasons may be cited for this condition, the present writer is convinced that the basic cause of the difficulty is to be found in the policy of regulating and promoting the various agencies of transportation as more or less independent entities without much regard to their effect upon each other or to their proper place in a national transportation system. The nation needs to adopt a comprehensive national transportation policy which will regard each of the various agencies, not as independent modes of transportation, but as integral parts of a national transportation system. It must be recognized, of course, that the adoption of such a policy would meet with widespread opposition. Present transportation policies have resulted in the growth of vested interests, and these interests are sure to fight any changes in policy which may in any way deprive them of any of their present prerogatives.

NATIONAL TRANSPORTATION PROBLEMS

It may be objected that Congress already has adopted just such a policy as that proposed above, but this is not the case. The national transportation policy enunciated by Congress in the Transportation Act of 1940 is not all-inclusive, is inconsistent with other congressional policies, and is subject to widely different interpretations. At the outset it is declared to be the national transportation policy to provide for the fair and impartial regulation of all modes of transportation subject to the Interstate Commerce Act, a wording which automatically excludes air transportation, the great bulk of domestic water transportation, and a significant amount of highway transportation. The declaration also specifies that regulation is to be so administered as to recognize and preserve the inherent advantages of rail, motor, and water transportation; to promote safe, adequate, economical, and efficient service; and to foster sound economic conditions in transportation and among the several carriers. But it is difficult to reconcile a policy of preserving the inherent advantages of each type of transportation and of fostering sound economic conditions in transportation with other congressional policies which artificially stimulate or otherwise favor one form of transportation over another. And it is at least an open question whether regulatory bodies, in following a policy of severely limiting or altogether prohibiting railroad use of the newer forms of transportation, are following the declared national transportation policy or are protecting the vested interests of existing operators.

In the last analysis the basic goal of any sound national transportation policy should be to provide the people of the United States with the best possible transportation at the lowest possible cost, with due consideration being given to the needs of the national defense. The people of the United States now have available for their use more and better transportation than they have had at any time in their past history, but it is not clear that they are getting the best possible service from existing transportation facilities, and they are most certainly not getting that service at the lowest possible cost. Each agency of transportation claims that it is essential to the national defense, but not much thought appears to have been given to the rather obvious fact that the promotion of a healthy and economically sound peacetime transportation system is a first prerequisite to an adequate national defense.

In some measure the unhealthy condition of the transportation industry is traceable to carrier management and shipper self-interest, but it is difficult to escape the conclusion that the root of the trouble lies in the failure to adopt and put into effect a sound national transportation policy. The trouble with present day transportation policies is that they all have been adopted with the needs of some particular segment of the transportation industry in mind, and little or no consideration has been given to their impact on other segments of the industry or on the transportation system as a whole. A critical examination of the more important of these policies follows.

Subsidies pro and con. Subsidies, along with protective tariffs and other types of special concessions, are difficult to defend on economic grounds, and an economic defense is seldom attempted. Occasionally it is argued that the economic benefits, both direct and indirect, resulting from the use of subsidized transportation are greater than the cost of the subsidy to the Government, but such arguments invariably involve intangibles and sweeping generalizations which by their very nature cannot be measured and which often represent little more than wishful thinking. Subsidies are, however, quite commonly defended on social and political grounds, with the "me too" principle sometimes thrown in for good measure. An examination of these various aspects of the subsidy problem is now in order, with special reference to their effect on the development of a sound national transportation system.

Economic effects of subsidies. Where two or more agencies of transportation are competing for the same traffic, subsidies granted to some agencies but not to others create artificial advantages which lead to the substitution of high cost for low cost transportation. Suppose, for example, that the cost of performing an identical service, including a reasonable return on the investment, is $1.00 for Carrier A and $1.20 for Carrier B. Under the normal operation of a free economy Carrier B will be unable to compete with Carrier A, thus leaving the field to the carrier which can perform the service at the lowest cost.

But if the Government, either directly or indirectly, pays 20¢ of the cost of each service performed by Carrier B, then the latter can charge the same rates as Carrier A and compete on an even basis. While it is true that the total cost of the service performed by Carrier B is greater than that incurred by Carrier A, the rates charged by both are the same, and since shippers are more interested in rates than in costs, some will make use of the subsidized service. Other things being equal, the more efficient carrier will have to reduce its service, and the net effect will be an increase in the cost of transportation by the amount of the subsidy required to keep the less efficient carrier in operation. Actually it will be more than this because of the administrative expenses incurred by the Government in collecting the necessary tax revenues and distributing them to the subsidized carriers.

The above illustration oversimplifies the analysis in that it assumes that both types of carriers offer an identical service, an assumption which commonly is not in accordance with the facts. What will be the situation if

Carrier B is in a position to provide a service which is superior to that offered by Carrier A? Under the normal operation of a free economy those shippers who find it worth while to pay $1.20 for Carrier B's superior service will do so, while those unwilling to pay more than $1.00 will continue to patronize Carrier A. If there is enough traffic to support both carriers, both will survive. If there is not enough traffic, the one which shippers desire the most will survive.

But if the Government steps in and pays 20¢ of Carrier B's costs, Carrier B is in a position to offer a superior service at the same rate as that charged by Carrier A, and Carrier A is forced out of the field. Shippers, of course, will be better off since those willing to pay $1.20 for the superior service are getting it for $1.00, and those not willing to pay more than $1.00 are getting more for their money than formerly. As far as society is concerned, however, there has been a net loss as a result of the subsidy payments. Obviously those shippers willing to pay the higher cost of the superior service are getting the service at a lower rate only because society is paying the difference between what they pay and the true cost of the service. But more important than this is the fact that society is in the rather ridiculous position of paying the additional cost of providing a superior service for those shippers who were quite satisfied with the low cost service provided by Carrier A. Again it should be noted that the illustration understates the social cost because of the administrative expense involved in collecting taxes and paying them out in the form of subsidies.

It should be pointed out that a subsidy need not be so great as to equalize the rates charged by a subsidized carrier with those charged by an unsubsidized carrier, but if the subsidized carrier provides a superior service, the result still will be the substitution of a more costly service for an acceptable less costly one. If Carrier B can provide a superior service at a cost of $1.20, a subsidy of 10¢ will enable it to offer its service at a rate of $1.10 as compared with Carrier A's rate of $1.00, and some shippers will find it worth while to pay the extra 10¢ in order to get the superior service. Again society finds itself in the position of paying the additional cost of providing a service which shippers otherwise would find uneconomical to use. If there is not enough traffic to support both carriers, one of the two will cease operating. Since presumably it is the intent of the subsidy to keep the subsidized carrier in business, however, the chances are that further subsidies will be forthcoming to keep it, rather than the low cost carrier, in the field.

It does not follow necessarily that a subsidized carrier will provide a superior service to that which is provided by an unsubsidized carrier. In the case of river and canal transportation the subsidized carrier provides a service which is definitely inferior. Suppose, again, that Carrier A provides service at a cost of $1.00 while Carrier B can provide service only at a cost of $1.20, but this time suppose that Carrier B's service is inferior to that provided by Carrier A. Under the normal operation of a free economy no businessman in his right mind will attempt to offer an inferior service at a higher cost than other concerns in the field, except to the extent that these other concerns are unable to satisfy the demand, but a government subsidy will alter this situation. In this case, however, the subsidy will have to be large enough to cover the cost differential plus enough more to permit Carrier B to reduce its rates sufficiently to attract traffic from Carrier A. For example, Carrier B may find that, because of the inferior service, a rate of 80¢ is necessary to attract traffic from Carrier A, in which case it will have to have a subsidy of 40¢ to make operations possible. Here the effect of subsidy is to substitute a service which is inferior in quality and higher in total cost than the unsubsidized service, certainly a procedure difficult to defend on economic grounds.

Effect of subsidized competition on railroad transportation. The fact that the railroads perform the principal and possibly the only form of transportation which is not presently subsidized gives rise to a special problem which cannot be overlooked in connection with any study of the economic effects of subsidies on transportation. Since railroad transportation, according to most students, is characterized by high constant costs, any diversion of railroad traffic to a subsidized form of transportation will result in an increase in the per unit cost of handling the traffic which remains.[1] In an effort to compensate for these increased unit costs the railroads may be expected to attempt to increase their rates. Since, however, any general increase in freight rates can only result in a further diversion of traffic to subsidized carriers, the railroads will try to obtain the necessary additional revenue by increasing the rates on traffic which cannot be transported by other forms of transportation. Thus, in addition to the actual cost to the taxpayers of providing transportation subsidies, such subsidies may indirectly bring about an increase in the unit cost of transportation to those shippers who are unfortunate enough to be entirely dependent upon the railroads. Insofar as possible, these shippers will, of course, seek to pass on their higher transportation costs to the general public.

---

[1] This assumes that a railroad plant is not being used at optimum capacity. Should a railroad be handling traffic in excess of optimum capacity, its variable costs per unit of traffic handled will rise, and might ultimately reach a point where they exceed the savings achieved from the distribution of constant costs over the larger volume of traffic. In such a situation a diversion of traffic could result in lower unit costs and be advantageous to shippers and the public. While it may be true that railroads have at certain times operated in excess of optimum capacity, the condition is invariably a temporary one, and it may be doubted that it will ever become the rule rather than the exception.

As noted above, railroads cannot very well compensate for increased unit costs by raising the rates on competitive traffic. As a practical matter, there are also rather definite limits on their ability to increase the rates charged for the movement of noncompetitive traffic. In the first place, no traffic is noncompetitive in an absolute sense, and every rate increase is sure to be followed by some diversion of traffic. In the second place, a good deal of the noncompetitive traffic consists of low grade and relatively low grade heavy or bulky commodities, and on some of these commodities the rates already may be as high as the traffic will bear. And in the third place, such selective rate increases generally meet with strong shipper opposition and encourage decentralization of industry as a means of reducing transportation costs. Under these conditions it is not beyond the realm of the imagination that an unsubsidized type of transportation could be bankrupted and put out of business by subsidized transportation, a situation which would hardly commend itself to the economist.

Actually, of course, there is no likelihood of the railroads being put out of business, at least in the near future. Neither the motor carriers nor the airlines as presently organized are adapted to the movement of the large volume of relatively low grade heavy and bulky freight which now moves by railroad. They could handle it only at rates so high as to make its movement impractical, and some of it they could not handle at all. It is true that water carriers could handle this traffic, but they could provide service only at a limited number of points, and for most shippers water transportation without railroad transportation would be worthless. Since the nation is not yet in a position to junk its railroads, the only alternative to bankruptcy would be to subsidize railroad transportation, too, either directly or through government ownership and operation. Should this happen, even greater increases in the cost of transportation would result.

The above discussion is intended to demonstrate how subsidies to certain forms of transportation may adversely affect the presently unsubsidized operations of the nation's network of railroads. It is not intended as an explanation of what is actually happening, although there is some evidence that subsidies, along with other considerations, are slowly forcing the railroads into bankruptcy. The present status of the railroads is discussed in some detail at a later point in this chapter.

Infant industry justification of subsidies. Subsidies have been justified on the ground that it would have been impossible for the newer forms of transportation to develop in competition with the railroads without special assistance. This has been particularly true in the case of river and canal transportation which could never have reached its present status without the provision of free rights of way and the enactment of legislation designed to restrict railroad competition and to force the railroads to share their traffic with the barge lines. Subsidies also are justified on the ground that they promote the more rapid development of new types of transportation. The United States has long followed a policy of encouraging the development of promising new industries or services, either through direct pioneering as in the case of the air-mail service, or through subsidies, tariffs, or other devices. This was the purpose of the railroad land grants issued between 1850-70, and there is no doubt that the land grants were a major factor in the rapid expansion of the railroad network. Irrespective of the merits of the policy, it certainly is true that subsidies have been a major contributing factor to the rapid development of the newer forms of transportation.

This justification of the use of subsidies may be accepted as valid with, however, certain qualifications. In the first place, it assumes that a rapid development of additional transportation facilities is desirable, and this may or may not be true. Some students believe that the land-grant policy encouraged a more rapid development of railroads and of the West than was desirable. Certainly the financial difficulties encountered by some railroads over a long period of years can be traced in part to an overexpansion of the railroad network during the latter half of the nineteenth century. And recent subsidy policies have contributed to an increase in transportation facilities which at times has been quite distressing. On the other hand, a rapid increase in certain types of transportation may be desirable for noneconomic reasons, such as the development of civil aeronautics for national defense purposes.

A second qualification of the use of subsidies to develop new forms of transportation relates to the problem of whether or not the subsidized carrier will ever be able to operate without subsidy. Experience has shown that subsidies are more easily adopted than abandoned, and if a given operation proves to be economically unsound, there is danger that the people will be permanently saddled with its upkeep. The Inland Waterways Corporation may be an example of this danger. Finally, the decision to promote the development of a given form of transportation should never be made without reference to the effect of such a policy on the transportation system as a whole.

Social justification of subsidies. Although an economic justification of subsidies is difficult to make, subsidies are very often defended on social grounds. This has not been true, however, of transportation subsidies, the one outstanding exception being the defense of a subsidized postal service on grounds of social welfare. Since it is difficult to measure social welfare in terms of dollars and cents, opinions differ widely whether or not the value of any particular social service is equal to the amount of subsidy required to support it. In view of this fact, and in view of the fact that transportation subsidies are not ordinarily defended on social grounds, no further consideration will be given to the social aspects of the problem.

National defense. Transportation subsidies are often justified on the grounds that they are necessary for the national defense. Subsidies to airlines have been defended most often on the ground that the promotion of civil aeronautics is in itself a major contribution to national defense, and in addition the airlines provide an important high speed transportation service in time of national emergency. Subsidies to river and canal transportation also have been justified as being necessary for national defense, but the experiences of World War II cannot be said to have demonstrated the indispensability of this form of transportation. Although coastwise and intercoastal shipping is not subsidized, except for some aid in the purchase or construction of ships, subsidies can be defended on the ground that a strong merchant marine is essential in the event of an overseas war. Motor carriers may or may not be subsidized, but few would deny in this day and age that the motor carrier, or at least the motor *vehicle*, is essential to the conduct of war. The important role played by the railroads during World War II should not be overlooked either. Certainly an agency which handled better than 70 per cent of the goods traffic during the peak war years has established a claim to national defense indispensability.

The emphasis which is naturally and properly placed on the importance of aviation to the national defense very often results in a failure to realize that a healthy and economically sound peacetime transportation *system* is a first prerequisite to an adequate national defense. Attention has been called to the uncertain status of the railroads, and this constitutes a defense problem of the first magnitude. Obviously if peacetime earnings deteriorate to the point where plant and equipment cannot be maintained at a high level of efficiency and provision cannot be made for a surplus of freight cars, the railroads will be unable to carry the load expected of them in time of war. If subsidies to other forms of transportation are in any way responsible for the generally unsatisfactory condition of railroad transportation, then this fact should be taken into consideration in evaluating the need for subsidizing transportation in the interest of national defense.

Public aid to railroads. The railroads, of course, have been the most articulate critics of the policy of public aid to the newer forms of transportation, and it is often stated that this criticism comes with ill grace in view of the extensive land grants they received during their period of great expansion. There is an implication here that aid to railroads justifies aid to other forms of transportation, but a moment's reflection will reveal that this in itself is no sound basis for embarking on subsidy programs. A subsidy to any business can be justified only when the actual or potential benefits derived from it, intangible as well as tangible, exceed the cost to the people of providing the subsidy. Subsidies to the newer forms of transportation must be judged on their merits, not on what the Government did for the railroads 75 or 100 years ago. Quite apart from this, it will be recalled from the discussion in Chapter 3 that the land grants involved a *quid pro quo* in the form of reduced rates on government traffic, the savings from which probably were large enough to wipe the slate clean insofar as public aid to railroad transportation is concerned.

ROUTE AND COMMODITY LIMITATIONS

Motor carriers. Another factor which has contributed to inefficient and uneconomic transportation has been the issuance of motor carrier certificates and permits which place limitations, sometimes rather severe, on the operating rights of the holders. As pointed out in Chapter 20, some regular route carriers have been permitted to offer service between specified terminals but not at certain intermediate points, and vice versa. Some may offer a reasonably full service at certain points and a limited service at others. Some may offer service between two points but only over a roundabout and wasteful route. A great many motor carriers are authorized to carry only a limited number of commodities or classes of commodities, and some may haul only a single commodity or class of commodities. In some cases certain restrictions are placed on commodities hauled in one direction, while different restrictions are placed on what can be handled on the return haul. These and various other restrictions are not at all uncommon in the motor transport field.

Of course, motor carriers themselves often have requested limited rights, and where specialized equipment is used service limitations are inherent in the type of equipment used. But in many cases carriers are willing and able to perform a broader service than their operating rights permit. The result is an uneconomic utilization of truck space and unnecessarily long and expensive hauls by roundabout routes. Such restrictions tend to increase costs and reduce the quality of the service rendered to the public. These restrictions are traceable in part to the desire of the Interstate Commerce Commission to protect grandfather rights, and to some extent they are due to the need in the public interest of protecting existing carriers from excessive competition. But there is always the danger that the protection of existing carriers may come to be looked upon as an end in itself regardless of its effect on cost of service. Where several carriers with restricted operating rights are performing portions of a service which could be performed by a smaller number of carriers with broad operating rights, the public interest would seem to require that steps be taken to encourage or enforce a greater unification of operations.

Water and air carriers. As indicated in Chapter 24, the Interstate Commerce Commission has been quite liberal in issuing broad operating rights to domestic water carriers, a policy which has been traced in part to certain inherent characteristics of water transportation and in part to a suspicion that cognizance has been taken of the criticisms of its policy of issuing highly restricted motor carrier operating rights. The Civil Aeronautics Act specifically states that certificates issued to grandfather carriers are not to be restricted concerning the types of traffic handled, but recently the Civil Aeronautics Board has granted some route extensions which limit service at intermediate points.

Voluntary service limitations. Up to this point the discussion of route and commodity limitations has centered around the problem which exists when a carrier has been prevented, by virtue of limitations placed on its operating rights, from achieving maximum efficiency and economy in the performance of a transportation service. It should not be supposed, however, that all service restrictions are due to the restrictive actions of regulatory bodies. On the contrary, motor, water, and air carriers are not at all anxious to provide a complete transportation service. Motor carriers tend to concentrate on the higher grades of freight which move under relatively high rates, avoiding the heavy or bulky freight which can be moved only under very low rates. This may be accomplished by means of certificate or permit limitations, by providing poor service on unwanted freight, or by use of the rate stop device. Airline rates on goods movements are so high that they automatically exclude the great bulk of low grade freight. In addition, airlines limit their service as much as possible to points where they can get a substantial volume of traffic, and assume no responsibility for providing service at other points. Water carriers transport a considerable volume of low grade freight, mostly in bargeload or boatload lots, but generally they avoid small lot shipments.

Effect of service limitations on railroad transportation. From the point of view of the individual carrier a policy of limiting service to the more profitable traffic unquestionably contributes to economical and efficient operations. But from the point of view of the transportation system as a whole a somewhat different picture presents itself. This is because a policy of concentrating on profitable traffic only, no matter how desirable it may be from the point of view of the individual carrier, leaves quite unsolved the problem of how to move the very large volume of low grade traffic which the limited service carriers either cannot handle or do not want to handle. At the present time this traffic moves by railroad because the railroads, generally speaking, do not limit their service. In some cases the traffic which the limited service carriers do not want constitutes a lucrative source of revenue for the railroads, but in other cases it is hard to see how it can be particularly productive of revenue. Clearly a policy which permits the newer forms of transportation to pick and choose their traffic, while requiring the railroads to carry the burden of the unwanted traffic, may have serious consequences insofar as the transportation system as a whole is concerned.

Effect of service limitations on rates and rate structures. The service limitations which characterize the newer forms of transportation, and railroad objections to these limitations, can be understood only in terms of differences in cost structures and different philosophies of rate making. These differences are particularly significant in connection with the movement of heavy or bulky raw materials of considerable social utility which have a very low market value per unit of weight or bulk. If railroad freight rates were fixed on the basis of fully allocated costs, as is sometimes advocated, each commodity would have to bear a rate sufficiently high to cover its full share of all costs, but such a system of rate making would mean that the delivered price of certain low grade commodities would be too high to make their transportation and sale in quantity possible.[2]

In the case of some low value commodities, and particularly those which are subject to a considerable loss of weight in the manufacturing process, the transportation problem has been solved by establishing factories at the source of the raw materials and shipping out finished or semifinished products. It was learned a long time ago, however, that there were many commodities which would move to market or to manufacturing areas under rates sufficiently high to cover the variable or out-of-pocket costs plus some fraction of their share of the constant costs, and the railroads found that it was worth while to establish such rates, providing that they could count on sufficient volume and could charge high enough rates on the higher grade commodities to cover the balance of constant costs.

In this way there was established the practice of charging rates on low grade commodities which were less than would have been the case if they had been based on fully allocated costs, and of fixing rates on the higher grade commodities which were higher than if they had been based on fully allocated costs. It might be argued, of course, that this method of rate making was unfair to the buyers and sellers of high grade commodities, but on the other hand, whatever contribution the low grade freight made toward meeting constant costs reduced by that amount the burden borne by the high grade freight. But good or bad, the system made it possible for

---

[2] One important qualification must be made to this statement. If the volume of low grade traffic is sufficiently large, rates may be low enough to cover fully allocated costs and still permit the traffic to move. This is especially true where traffic of a particular type is large enough to permit the use of specialized equipment and operating techniques.

society to enjoy a wider variety of useful commodities than would otherwise have been the case.

The system of basing rates on "what the traffic will bear" worked well enough as long as the railroads had the field to themselves; but since the advent of the limited service carrier this time-honored system of rate making has been gradually disintegrating. It will be recalled that the motor transport industry is characterized by a high ratio of variable to total costs, which means that the out-of-pocket cost of handling any commodity by motor freight will much more closely approximate fully allocated cost than is true in the case of railroad transportation. Hence it is unprofitable for a motor carrier to establish a rate on any commodity which is very much below fully allocated costs except where an empty backhaul is involved. This explains why motor carriers are not enthusiastic about handling low grade freight. In order to handle such freight, motor carriers would have to establish rates which were competitive with those charged by the railroads, but since the railroad rates need not cover much more than out-of-pocket costs, it sometimes happens that the railroad rate on a given commodity is well below the actual cost of transportation by motor vehicle. On the other hand, to the extent that motor carriers are successful in avoiding the transportation of low grade freight at rail competitive rates, they are able to establish rates on high grade freight which are little if any greater than fully allocated costs; and this often gives them an advantage over the railroads in transporting high grade freight, either in the form of lower rates, better service, or both.

It would appear that variable costs are relatively more important in air transportation than in rail transportation, and wide differences in the rates charged for moving different commodities are not so common, at least where approximately the same service is involved. Since the airlines are not required to establish a scale of rates which will move all commodities, and since they are not required to serve light traffic points to any extent, they are able to provide service on high grade freight between heavy traffic points at rates considerably lower than would otherwise be the case. It is true that airline rates are substantially in excess of rates charged by surface carriers, but the high speed service for which the airlines are famous functions in some measure to offset these higher rates.

Common carriers by water, as previously noted, tend to concentrate as much as possible on the more profitable bargeload and boatload traffic, and to the extent that they are able to reject or minimize the small shipment service, they are able to establish lower rates on volume traffic than would otherwise be the case.

Conclusion. In some cases low railroad freight rates on heavy and bulky raw materials are made possible by the existence of a very large volume of one or a few types of such traffic. Aside from this, low rates on low grade freight are predicated on the existence of one or both of two conditions. One of these conditions is the ability of the carrier to handle as large a portion of the available traffic as possible, within the limits of the profitable use of its plant, so that constant costs can be distributed thinly over a large number of individual shipments. And the other condition is that the carrier will be able to handle the higher grades of freight at rates which exceed fully allocated costs. The rise of the newer forms of transportation has made it increasingly difficult for the railroads to maintain these conditions because the limited service carriers have been able to attract a substantial volume of railroad traffic as a result of their ability to provide better service, lower rates, or both, on a selective basis. This problem has been obscured by the abnormal volume of traffic attendant upon war and preparation for war, but it is there and cannot be ignored.

The situation outlined above has created something of a dilemma for the railroads, for the Interstate Commerce Commission, and for shippers entirely dependent upon railroad transportation, a dilemma presently postponed but not resolved. In the period of upward rate adjustments which followed World War II there was a natural tendency to emphasize rate increases on railroad traffic not subject to competition, but there is a practical limit to the ability of the railroads to raise the rates on much of this traffic. Proposals to make substantial increases in the rates on the lower grades of freight meet with strong shipper resistance, particularly in the case of agricultural products. At the same time substantial increases in these rates carry with them some threat of further traffic diversion which further aggravates the problem. Thus the railroads may find themselves caught in a vicious circle which could lead to bankruptcy and the possible loss of a cheap means of transporting low grade commodities.

On the other hand, it hardly seems reasonable to deprive those shippers who can make use of the newer forms of transportation of the many benefits derived from their services. Fundamentally, then, the problem is whether society can support in time of peace all available transportation services as presently organized. The fact that the newer forms of transportation cannot or will not transport a large volume of low grade freight at low rates does not eliminate the problem of what to do with this traffic, and if the railroads cannot haul it profitably, one of several things may happen. In the first place, it would be possible to abandon railroad transportation, a move which would require a complete revolutionizing of the existing economy. Second, the Government might subsidize railroad transportation with an attendant increase in the over-all cost of transportation. Third, the Government might take over operation of the railroads and continue to render the service, meeting deficits from taxation. A final alternative might be to streamline existing railroad transportation, eliminating light traffic lines and less-than-carload freight, and concentrating on the specialized movement of freight in large quantities.

UNECONOMIC INTERCARRIER COMPETITION

Advantages and disadvantages of railroad transportation. The development of motor, domestic water, and air transportation since 1920 has made available to the people of the United States a wide variety of transportation facilities each of which has certain unique qualities. The railroads are especially adapted to the economical movement of goods of all kinds in carload lots. Because of the operation of the tapering principle, they can transport freight over long distances at unusually low cost. And they stand ready to move many kinds of freight which other carriers cannot or do not want to handle. Because railroads are expensive to build and maintain, they are not suitable for providing transportation in light traffic areas. High terminal costs tend to make railroad transportation rather expensive for short haul movements. They are poorly adapted to the movement of short haul less-than-carload freight, and the service on such freight generally is poor and costly to the railroads. Local passenger service outside of commuter areas is poor as compared with bus service, and long haul passenger service, while superior to that offered by bus lines, is inferior to that provided by airlines.

Advantages and disadvantages of motor carriers. Motor carriers are especially well adapted to the short haul movement of goods in relatively small quantities and to short haul passenger transportation. They can operate economically in areas where the volume of traffic is too light to make railroad transportation practical. And they are unique among carriers in the flexibility of the service they provide. Because of limited carrying capacity and because of the necessity of requiring a separate power plant and driver for each truck or trucking combination, motor carriers cannot handle volume shipments as economically as can the railroads except on short hauls where low terminal costs give them an advantage. Because motor carrier costs do not follow the tapering principle to any appreciable extent, long haul transportation by motor vehicle is not as economical as railroad transportation. While it is true that motor carriers do handle long haul traffic, this service is mostly limited to high grade freight. This points up another disadvantage of motor transportation, the absence of a complete transportation service.

Advantages and disadvantages of water transportation. Water carriers are especially adapted to the transportation of bulk freight in large quantities where speed of delivery is less important than low transportation charges. They are not well adapted to the movement of freight in carload and less-than-carload quantities, to the movement of perishables, or to the movement of goods of high value. Furthermore, the number of points at which water carriers can provide service is strictly limited. Finally, barge line operators require costly right-of-way facilities which, apparently, can be provided only at public expense.

Advantages and disadvantages of air transportation. The airlines have a unique advantage in their ability to transport passengers and goods over long distances with a minimum of elapsed time. Rates charged for passenger transportation are comparable with those charged for the best railroad passenger service, but the rates charged for goods movements are extremely high as compared with those charged by surface carriers. The service is not so well adapted to short haul movements, and as a rule service is limited to those points which can assure the carrier a substantial volume of traffic. Finally, air transportation requires airways and airports, the cost of which must be borne for the most part by the public. In addition to providing airways and airports, the public also subsidizes the operations of air carriers where necessary.

Failure to utilize carriers to best advantage. Since each of the various agencies of transportation has certain unique advantages and disadvantages, the public interest would seem to demand that their services be coordinated in such a way as to make maximum use of the special qualities of each and at the same time minimizing their disadvantages. In actual practice, however, the possibilities of coordination scarcely have been scratched. Railroads compete with motor carriers for short haul traffic, and motor carriers compete with railroads for long haul traffic. The Inland Waterways Corporation continues to offer a small shipment service in spite of the fact that such a service is poorer in quality and higher in real cost than similar services provided by rail and motor carriers. And there can be little doubt that certain traffic now moving by water and by air would move otherwise if shippers were called upon to meet the full cost of the service.

Failure to control interagency competition. The evils of excessive competition in the field of railroad transportation were recognized many years ago, and in 1920 positive action was taken to bring competition under control. This same policy has been followed in connection with motor, water, and air transportation, at least insofar as common carrier operations are concerned. But while excessive competition has been brought under control within each of these various agencies of transportation, no similar policy has been applied to the transportation system as a whole. Two justifications for this attitude may be cited. In the first place, the entrance of a new form of transportation into a given field tends to force existing agencies to improve their services. And in the second place, it has been said that shippers should have an opportunity to enjoy the peculiar advantages of all forms of transportation. Both of these points are valid, but at the same time the very real danger of an overexpansion of transportation facilities must not be overlooked. Transportation facilities appear to have been expanded to the point where it is difficult for the transportation system as a whole to operate profitably except under abnormal traffic conditions.

In a free enterprise economy, competition is supposed to eliminate surplus facilities and provide the public with the best possible goods and services at the lowest possible prices. Thus if there are too many dry cleaning establishments, price and service competition is expected to eliminate the inefficient and at the same time hold the remaining operators in check to prevent exploitation of the public by monopoly. But competition does not function in quite the same way in the field of transportation. In the first place, for years transportation was not adequately competitive, and this is still true, although less so than formerly. Second, the contestants are not altogether free to compete on a price basis because transportation prices are subject to public control and competitive price cutting is not encouraged. Third, the policy of giving public aid to some agencies of transportation but not to others has made it possible for certain carriers to survive the competitive struggle and even to obtain an advantage over the unsubsidized. Finally, the policy of permitting some carriers to pick and choose their traffic while requiring others to provide a general transportation service creates an additional barrier to the functioning of the competitive principle.

REGULATED VERSUS UNREGULATED TRANSPORTATION

Problem stated. For a number of years the railroads complained that it was unfair to regulate their operations closely while permitting competing forms of transportation to operate without regulation, at least insofar as interstate commerce was concerned. Congress recognized the need for a more general application of transport regulation and subjected interstate highway transportation to regulation in 1935, air transportation in 1938, and domestic water transportation in 1940. In each of these cases, however, private individuals or business concerns were permitted to provide transportation for their own account free of economic regulation. Also, Congress applied a lesser degree of regulation to contract carriers than it did to common carriers by highway and by water, and made no provision at all for regulating contract carriage by air, even though in all cases contract carriers compete directly with other types of carriers. On top of this, Congress exempted certain types of operations, both common and contract, from regulation for reasons not related to transportation as such.

As a result of these various limitations, the railroads still find themselves subject to a considerable amount of competition from unregulated or partially-regulated carriers. Furthermore, the same situation which led the railroads to complain about the unreasonableness of subjecting their operations to regulation while permiting the newer forms of transportation to go unregulated now exists within each of these newer agencies. The continued existence of unregulated or partially-regulated carriers which compete directly with fully-regulated carriers has created problems which are hardly compatible with the operation of an economically sound transportation system.

Exempt carriers. The Motor Carrier Act, 1935, contained numerous exemptions from economic regulation, some absolute and some subject to the discretion of the Interstate Commerce Commission, but for the most part these exemptions were quite reasonable and have caused little or no trouble. The exemption of vehicles transporting fish, livestock, and agricultural commodities, but not including the manufactured products thereof, has created a difficult situation for regulated highway carriers and for the railroads. Presumably the intent of this provision was to help farmers and fishermen by exempting the transportation of agricultural products and seafoods in their natural state from points of origin to nearby primary markets or processing plants, but in practice the provision has led to the development of a startlingly large movement of agricultural products and seafoods over long distances free of all economic regulation.

The way in which the exemption has worked in practice is not in the interest of the development of a sound national transportation system. In the first place, there is no economic justification for exempting such a large body of carriers from regulation when they perform a transportation service which differs in no essential respect from the transportation services performed by regulated carriers. And in the second place, the more extensive exempt operations become, the more difficult it is to maintain an adequate common carrier service available at reasonable rates to all users.

Part III of the Interstate Commerce Act provides a number of exemptions, some absolute and some conditional, in connection with domestic water transportation. These exemptions are so sweeping that they remove a considerable part of for-hire transportation from Interstate Commerce Commission jurisdiction, and together with the exemption of private carriage, leave very little for the Commission to regulate. The exempt water carrier competes directly with regulated water carriers and with the railroads, and its exemption provides it with an artificial advantage which is not easy to justify.

The Civil Aeronautics Act leaves the power of exemption in the hands of the Civil Aeronautics Board. For many years the Board granted a blanket exemption to all carriers other than scheduled airlines, but in recent years it has found it increasingly necessary to restrict these exemptions. The Board has more authority in this respect than does the Interstate Commerce Commission, but as it limits exemptions the affected carriers appeal to Congress for relief.

Contract carriers. The motor contract carrier has an unusual advantage over the motor common carrier and the railroad in that only its minimum charges are subject to regulatory control. Since common carriers must make their schedules of charges available for public inspection, the contract carrier is free to examine these schedules and to offer its services at reduced rates in order to attract especially desirable traffic. The contract carrier is under no obligation to carry traffic which will not be profitable and does not do so. Furthermore, while common carriers are not permitted to offer special rates to shippers who can furnish a certain volume of traffic over a given period of time, a contract carrier may make favorable contracts with such shippers, thus obtaining a steady volume of profitable traffic. Much the same thing may be said for the contract carrier by water, with the additional comment that the provisions of Part III exempt many contract carriers from economic regulation altogether. Likewise, contract carriage by air is not subject to any economic regulation.

Opinions differ on the desirability of contract carrier transportation which permits the carrier to discriminate between shippers. Many people have argued that reduced rates to large shippers give them an unfair competitive advantage over the small shipper, while others have argued that large shippers are entitled to lower rates because of the savings or other advantages enjoyed by the carriers on such shipments. Be that as it may it is difficult to understand why it is all right for a contract carrier to offer selective rates but not all right for a common carrier to do the same thing. Indeed, quantity rates offered by a common carrier would have the virtue of being published and open for all to see whereas the contract carrier can make all sorts of arrangements without making them public. In any event it is doubtful that it is in the public interest to permit contract carriers to skim the cream of the traffic to the extent that common carrier transportation is endangered. It is interesting to note that when it comes to picking and choosing traffic, the contract carrier is in the same position relative to transportation as a whole as are the newer forms of transportation relative to the railroads.

Private carriers. Commissioner Rogers has estimated the number of private carriers by highway as 130,000 and the number of power units employed by them as 550,000,[3] both of these figures being considerably in

---

[3] *Traffic World,* March 11, 1950, p. 42.

excess of the combined totals for regulated and exempt highway carriers. A substantial part of the Great Lakes traffic is carried by private carriers. The same is true of tanker traffic out of Gulf coast ports, and of the great bulk of Ohio River traffic. It has been stated that inland waterway freight traffic totaled 630,228,874 tons in 1948, although in that year the Interstate Commerce Commission indicated that only 69,776,440 tons were moved by carriers subject to its jurisdiction.[4] The difference between these figures gives a good idea of the importance of private and exempt transportation on the inland waterways. Private transportation by air, at least insofar as goods movements are concerned, may be dismissed as insignificant at the present time.

The large volume of intercity traffic handled by private carriers gives rise to the question of whether or not this form of transportation is in the broad public interest. Industrial and commercial concerns which transport their own goods consider this to be nothing more than a legitimate extension of their primary business activities, and they believe that they have a right to enjoy the lower costs or better service they secure by providing their own transportation. On the other hand, it has been pointed out that the commodities clause effectively prevents railroads from engaging in commercial or industrial activities and then transporting their products over their own lines for sale. Why, it is asked, should a company providing railroad transportation services be prohibited from engaging in industrial or commercial activities when industrial and commercial enterprises are free to engage in transportation by highway or water? It is true that in the one case a general transportation service is being rendered while in the other case the transportation is restricted to the products of a single company, but in both cases the public is being served and the two are in direct competition with each other.

To some extent regulated carriers tend to look upon private transportation as an unwarranted invasion of their field by unregulated carriers. The motor carriers have been particularly critical of private transportation where a charge is made for the service, contending that this is transportation for hire subject to Part II of the Interstate Commerce Act. So far, however, they have been unsuccessful in impressing the Interstate Commerce Commission with this argument. It must be admitted that private transportation offers real advantages to those who are able to make use of it, and its abandonment is not seriously contemplated or anticipated. If, however, private transportation should ever grow to the point where it

---

[4] Testimony of W. L. Grubbs before a subcommittee of the Senate Interstate and Foreign Commerce Committee, April 25, 1950. *Traffic World*, April 29, 1950, p. 56.

threatened the existence of common carrier transportation, the small shipper would be placed in a precarious position.

PRESENT STATUS OF RAILROAD TRANSPORTATION

Problem stated. In recent years the nation has been faced with a number of knotty transportation problems, but none has caused more concern among students than the uncertain future of the railroads. For years the level of railroad earnings has been too low to maintain a healthy railroad transportation system in spite of rules of rate making, consolidation programs, and other legislative measures.[5] A peak in railroad traffic was reached in 1944, after which the railroads experienced a definite downward trend of traffic. Because of the importance of constant costs, a downward trend cannot continue indefinitely without more and more railroads facing disaster. Since the newer forms of transportation are in no position to shoulder the full burden of providing for the transportation needs of the country, at least as presently organized and developed, the reason for concern over the future of the railroads is obvious. While this difficulty may be obscured by abnormal traffic conditions, the problem is there and must be faced. In order to understand the condition of the railroads it will be necessary to review briefly the background of their difficulties.

Development of railroad transportation. The steam railroad, the first great development in land transportation since the discovery of the principle of the wheel, appeared in the United States about 1830, and during the next twenty years went through a period of experimentation and slow growth. By 1850, however, the railroad was beginning to emerge in something resembling its modern form. Ten years later railroad lines were spread over the East and South, and by 1870 the continent had been spanned and the railroad network was expanding over the country west of the Mississippi. From then on there was no stopping the railroad builders as enthusiasm for internal improvements, the westward movement of the population, land grants, and opportunities for speculative profits all combined to gridiron the nation with railroads. Peak growth was reached in 1916, and the decline in mileage which took place thereafter may be traced to earlier overexpansion, to such things as the exhaustion of natural resources, and to growing competition from newer forms of transportation.

Regulation. The demand for effective railroad regulation developed in the Middle West shortly after the Civil War. Farmers complained bitterly

---

[5] In this connection see Table V, p. 217. See also, Sidney L. Miller and Virgil D. Cover, *Rates of Return, Class I Line-Haul Railways of the United States, 1921-1948.* Pittsburgh: University of Pittsburgh Press, 1951.

of high and discriminatory freight rates; and such thi gs as financial manipulation, corruption of public servants, pools, and the sometimes arrogant attitude of railroad managements all contributed to the demand for regulation. The Granger laws, adopted in the 1870's, constituted the first serious attempt to subject railroads to public control, but they were of limited value because they could not be applied effective'y to interstate commerce. In an effort to remedy this situation Congress adopted the Act to Regulate Commerce in 1887, but this act in its original form was soon emasculated by the courts, and it was not until the amen nents of 1906 and 1910 that the Interstate Commerce Commission really became an effective agency of railroad regulation. Legislation since 1910 so extended the Commission's jurisdiction that it now exercises control over almost all aspects of the business of railroad transportation.

Background of present difficulties. The early years of the twentieth century were difficult ones for the nation's railroads. The overexpansion, overcapitalization, and financial manipulations of the late nineteenth and early twentieth centuries had left many of them with an excessive burden of fixed charges. In addition, a rising price level, coupled with the reluctance of regulatory bodies to allow rate increases commensurate with increased costs, made profitable operation increasingly difficult. These factors, together with certain conditions external to the railroad business, led to a drying up of railroad credit, and the railroads as a whole were in poor shape when the Government took them over during World War I. Wise men both in and out of Congress were acutely aware of the need for revamping regulatory policy in the interest of promoting a sound system of railroad transportation, and after a long period of discussion and debate Congress passed the Transportation Act, 1920—hailed by some as the solution to the railroad problem.

In order to prevent future overexpansion, the Interstate Commerce Commission was given jurisdiction over the construction of new lines and the extension of old ones. Similarly, it was given jurisdiction over the issuance of railroad securities in order to prevent overcapitalization and financial mismanagement. There was a growing feeling that excessive competition created evils which were greater than the advantages which might derive from competition, and to remedy this situation Congress gave the Commission power to fix minimum rates and directed it to work out a comprehensive plan for consolidating the railroads into a limited number of systems. In addition, Congress recognized that adequate earnings were essential to the maintenance of railroad credit and a sound transportation system, and to this end it adopted a rule of rate making which it was hoped would stabilize earnings at a satisfactory level.

The high hopes of those who looked upon the Transportation Act, 1920, as the solution of the railroad problem were not destined to be fulfilled. In only one year during the 1920's did the railroads come close to earning a fair return as defined by law, and the depression which began in 1929 destroyed all hope of their being able to do so. Indeed, numerous railroads soon found themselves in desperate financial straits, and by the end of 1938 almost one-third of the railroad mileage of the country was in the hands of receivers or trustees.

If the depression alone had been responsible for the condition of the railroads at the end of the 1930's, their situation would not have been so bad, for they could have looked forward to better earnings with a return of prosperity. But unfortunately for them the loss of traffic they had suffered was the result in no small measure of conditions of a more permanent nature. In varying degrees these losses reflected the growing tendency of industry to decentralize; the substitution of gas, hydroelectric power, and fuel oil for coal, and improvements in the utilization of coal itself; the substitution of such typically short haul products as cement for long haul products like steel and lumber; the decline of export and import traffic; and above all, the great increase during the depression years of competition from other forms of transportation.

World War II and after. It is difficult to speculate on what might have happened to the railroads had it not been for the outbreak of World War II. War brought with it a sharp increase in traffic and substantial improvement in earnings, and wartime earnings were used advantageously to reduce fixed charges by retiring funded debt and to finance a postwar program of plant rehabilitation and improvement. It was recognized that the war had created an abnormal traffic situation for the railroads, partly because much of the traffic was of such a nature that it could not be handled readily by the other forms of transportation, and partly because the newer forms of transportation were unable, for one reason or another, to expand their facilities sufficiently to maintain their prewar proportion of traffic. For these reasons it was not to be expected that the railroads would be able to maintain the high wartime level of traffic after the close of World War II, and they did not do so.

The figures in Table I on pages 21-22 reveal the expected decline in railroad freight traffic following the peak war year of 1944, but they also show a great deal more. Not only did railroad traffic decline after the 1944 peak, but it continued to decline steadily during the postwar years of peacetime prosperity and high production. Nor is it without significance that no similar decline in freight traffic was shown by other agencies of transportation. Motor carriers of freight enjoyed a continuous increase in traffic during the postwar period. Inland waterway carriers experienced a brief postwar slump, but by 1948 their tonnage exceeded that of their peak war year. The closing of the Big Inch and the resumption of tanker service brought an expected reduction in pipe line tonnage, although this traffic held up remarkably well. Goods movements by air, although accounting for only an infinitesimal amount of total tonnage, have shown a steady and continuous increase since 1937.

The passenger statistics tell a similar story, although the figures here have followed a predictable pattern. In addition to war-generated passenger traffic, all common carriers experienced a large increase in traffic as a result of limitations on the use of the private automobile, and the loss of much of this traffic was inevitable once gasoline rationing was terminated. It is worth noting, however, that the decline in motor bus traffic was quite modest in comparison with the decline in railroad passenger traffic, while airline passenger traffic increased both relatively and absolutely.

Explanation of postwar decline. In the years immediately following World War II the railroads found themselves faced with sharply increased costs of operation, due partly to a rising price level and partly to substantial increases in labor costs, and in order to meet these increased costs, they asked for and received a number of rate increases. It is true that other agencies of transportation also found it necessary to raise rates, but they were able to maintain their existing rate or service advantages over the railroads, and every increase in railroad rates brought with it some additional diversion of traffic to the newer agencies. Thus it would appear that under peacetime conditions shippers who can exercise a choice have shown increasing preference for the better service or lower rates afforded by motor, water, and air transportation. And passenger traffic, to the extent that it is not moved by private automobile, seems to be going to the motor bus and the airline rather than to the railroad. Hence it is not surprising that students of transportation and shippers who must use the railroads are showing considerable concern for the future of railroad transportation.

Responsibility of management. There are those who maintain that railroad management is responsible for railroad ills, and no doubt management must bear a part of the responsibility. It has been pointed out that opportunities for greater efficiency and economy can be achieved by means of railroad consolidations, very few of which have actually taken place. It is true that the unworkable provisions of the original law, outside pressures, and the lengthy periods of time required for railroad reorganizations have not been encouraging to consolidation, but if the will to consolidate had existed, more could have been done along this line. Failure of railroad management to anticipate the development of competition has been mentioned previously. There was a time when railroads could have made use of motor transport and even air transport, and they were even urged to do so, but for the most part management chose to ignore their possibilities, and these forms of transportation were developed by others.

Management is sometimes held responsible for the losses sustained from passenger train operation, including losses incurred in handling mail, express, and other "head end" traffic. Although some passenger trains have been made to show a profit, it is not a simple matter to place the blame for the over-all loss on this traffic. Probably many railroads would be better off if they could eliminate a part or all of their passenger business, but this is not easy to do. Indeed, in some cases state commissions have not even permitted the abandonment of individual trains on which substantial losses were being sustained. Railroad management also has been accused of being unimaginative in the introduction of more efficient equipment and operating techniques. Certainly, however, modern railroad management is much more alive to opportunities of this sort than was formerly the case. Furthermore, economies resulting from the introduction of labor-saving devices or operating procedures have met with strong opposition from railroad labor as noted in Chapter 17.

Responsibility of government. There can be little doubt that Government and parts of the shipping public must bear some responsibility for the present unsatisfactory status of railroad transportation. Public aid, which permits some carriers to offer better service or lower rates than provided or charged by the railroads, quite aside from the various justifications for such aid, unquestionably has been responsible for a diversion of traffic from the railroads. And certainly shippers who encourage such aid in order to get better service or lower rates must bear their share of the responsibility. Congressional and regulatory policy which permits interagency competition irrespective of the relative efficiency of the competing agencies in any given situation is also at fault. And the desirability of permitting certain carriers to pick and choose their traffic needs to be reexamined in the light of its over-all effect on the transportation system as a whole.

Are railroads the victims of technological development? It is sometimes stated that the railroads today are the victims of technological development. The wagon and stagecoach and the river and canal boat had to give way before the expanding network of railroads and now, it is said, the railroad has become outmoded and must give way before newer and more efficient methods of transportation. This argument fails to consider the fact that these newer forms of transportation exist and are able to compete at the present time largely because of public assistance. If they cannot exist without such aid, then they are not more efficient. On the other hand, it must be borne in mind that public aid may help them to reach a point where they can maintain themselves without help, in which event they may prove to be more efficient.

Nor does the argument take into consideration the fact that the newer forms of transportation do not provide a complete transportation service. It is perfectly possible for a limited service carrier to be more efficient than a railroad insofar as the performance of a *particular transportation service* is concerned, while at the same time the railroad is more efficient than the limited service carrier in the performance of a *complete transportation service*. If a situation were to arise in which the public found that its insistence on the former was bringing about the destruction of the latter and if the sum total of the services performed by the limited service carriers did not approach a complete transportation service, there can be little doubt about the nature of the choice it would have to make.

In the long run it is possible that the railroads may become the victims of technological progress. It is conceivable that atomic power and technological developments in the construction industry, in food processing, and the like, may ultimately eliminate the need for the long distance movement of coal, ore, steel, lumber, grain, and other heavy loading and bulky commodities, and so render railroads and water carriers obsolete. Certainly, once the need for transporting weight and bulk were eliminated the flexibility of the motor carrier and the airline would offer tremendous advantages. Such speculation, however, belongs to the future. For the present at least the nation is not prepared to do without its railroads.

33

Proposed Solutions

to

TRANSPORTATION PROBLEMS

GOVERNMENT OWNERSHIP AND OPERATION

Present status of government ownership. The transportation system of the United States is based on the concept of private ownership and operation. In a few cases in the past, railroads were built by state and local governments, but today the only important examples of publicly-owned and operated transportation services are the Inland Waterways Corporation and the 470 mile Alaska Railroad.[1] The highways, improved waterways, and airways are publicly owned, but publicly-operated transportation services are not provided over these facilities with the exception of those provided by the Inland Waterways Corporation. The emphasis on private ownership and operation reflects to no small extent acceptance of the traditional laissez faire philosophy that governments should not engage in business activities, although it also has an historical background. Some states suffered severe financial loss as a result of engaging in railroad building in the 1800's. Furthermore, private capital was readily available for railroad construction during the era of extensive internal improvements, and government construction was mostly unnecessary.

Throughout the rest of the world the great bulk of railroad mileage is publicly owned and operated, and the trend has been toward more rather than less government ownership and operation. Likewise many air transport systems are publicly owned or closely controlled by central governments. Little information is available on the general status of highway and inland waterway transportation, but in all probability private ownership and operation is somewhat more common than is true of rail and air transportation. Throughout most of the world the laissez faire philosophy apparently did not act as a bar to government entry into the field of transportation, and if economic development called for railroad construction and private capital was not available, governments stepped

---

[1] In addition, mention may be made of the 50-mile Panama Railroad, and the Warrior River Terminal Railroad, running between Port Birmingham and Birmingham, Alabama, which is a part of the Inland Waterways Corporation.

in as a matter of course. Political unification led some governments to build railroads, although in this country the same end was achieved by subsidizing private construction of the Pacific railroads. Public ownership of railroads in Germany and Russia was dictated in part by military considerations. In more recent years financial difficulties have led to the nationalization of railroads in several countries, and the British railroads were nationalized as a part of the over-all socialization program of a Labor government.

Early proposals of government ownership. Although the people of the United States have rejected government ownership and operation of railroads and other agencies of transportation, government ownership has not been without its supporters. Some states at one time actively engaged in railroad building, and there was substantial support for government construction of the Pacific railroad. The Windom Committee recommended in the 1870's that the Federal Government build one or more lines of railroad from the Atlantic to the Mississippi in order to provide competition with existing privately-owned lines. A number of minor political parties, especially those of the agrarian type which sprung up during the latter half of the nineteenth century, included government ownership of railroads as one of the planks in their platforms. During the congressional hearings on railroad legislation following World War I, railroad labor sponsored the Plumb plan under which the Government would buy the railroads from their owners and lease them as a unit to a corporation to be operated and controlled by its employees. Thereafter not much was heard about government ownership until 1948 when it was proposed once again by labor.

It is interesting to note that schemes for government ownership and operation are usually branded as socialistic and their advocates as socialists or communists, but demands for government ownership and operation of railroads in the United States are largely traceable to other considerations. Many of the early schemes for government ownership were the result of farmer irritation over highhanded railroad practices and what were considered to be excessive rates. It seems likely that the 1948 advocacy of government ownership by railroad labor leaders was directly related to the failure of railroad labor to obtain its demands of the moment. Furthermore, it is worth noting that the Inland Waterways Corporation, the one outstanding present example of government ownership and operation, was not hatched in Moscow or in the dingy halls of some indigenous left wing political party. On the contrary, its strongest advocates may be found among individuals who otherwise support the free enterprise system.

Early arguments in favor of government ownership and operation of railroads. The controversy over government ownership and operation of transportation services dates back to the period when the railroads had an almost complete monopoly over intercity transportation, and because of this fact much of the early debate on the subject has little meaning today. Government ownership and operation of railroads was, of course, advocated by the Socialists, but it may be doubted that their particular philosophy exercised an influence on any appreciable number of people. More important were the excesses of railroad management and the abuses of monopoly power which led many individuals and political groups to advocate government ownership.

There was no doubt, too, a strong feeling in some quarters that government ownership would lead to rate reductions. The Government, it was said, would not charge rates fixed on the basis of monopoly price, nor would it have to charge rates high enough to cover a profit to private owners. Furthermore, if the Government were to amortize the original cost of construction, it could eliminate a heavy cost in the form of interest on funded debt. By operating the railroads as a single system, the Government could avoid unnecessary duplication of facilities and the various costs of competition. And it could, were it deemed desirable, keep rates down by operating the railroads at a loss.

During the early years of the present century government ownership was proposed by some as a solution to the strong and weak line problem. With all railroads operated as a single system, there would be no problem of working out a method of regulation and rate making which would keep the weak in existence without unduly favoring the strong. Furthermore, the Government would be able to maintain a desirable weak line in existence in cases where it would be impossible to do so if it were operated by private enterprise. The inability of railroads to obtain capital for needed improvements and expansion would be resolved under government ownership since the Government could obtain funds on its own credit at low rates of interest. Finally, it was said that government ownership would eliminate the need for regulation, which was expensive both for government and for railroads and shippers subject to such regulation.

Aside from the above arguments, which are essentially economic in nature, government ownership has been supported as leading to certain desirable social ends. It has been said that the Government would undertake the construction of lines where there was an indicated social need but where the prospects for profits were slim, at least for some period of time. The history of railroad construction in the United States, however, hardly suggests the necessity of government ownership to serve such a purpose. Time and again railroad construction preceded settlement or followed right along with it, and numerous bankruptcies attest in part the willingness of promoters to extend lines into areas considerably in advance of the need for them. Government ownership might, however, have some advantage in that it could assure continued operation of a desirable weak line which could not continue to exist under private ownership. Finally, it is believed by some that the uncertainties attendant upon railroad strikes and threats of strikes would be eliminated if the railroads were owned and operated by the Government. It is said that labor would receive better treatment from the Government than from private employers and that labor would be reluctant to strike against the Government.

Arguments against government ownership and operation of railroads. Perhaps the most common argument against government ownership and operation of railroads is that it is not in accord with the philosophy of free enterprise. More specific criticisms usually are based on the belief that private enterprise, actuated by the profit motive, is more efficient than the Government in operating a business enterprise, plus the belief that this greater efficiency offsets or more than offsets the fact that the users of the service are expected to pay enough to bring the owners a profit. It is said, for example, that political considerations will lead to the appointment of officers and employees on the basis of political affiliation rather than ability, to the construction of new or improved facilities at points where political expediency dictates rather than where they are needed, and to the employment of more workers than are necessary.

It is also believed that governments have no particular incentive to introduce improvements such as the diesel locomotive and streamlined air conditioned passenger trains. In the absence of competition, there would be no need for replacing equipment until it wore out completely. Some people believe that if the railroads were owned and operated by the Government, railroad labor would be able to exercise considerable influence in its own behalf because of the large bloc of votes it would control. In this connection, however, it is worth noting that organized labor has done pretty well for itself politically even without government ownership.

Evaluation of case for and against government ownership and operation of railroads. If the matter were put to a vote, probably the great majority of the people of the United States would reject government ownership and operation of railroads as being contrary to the principle of free enterprise. The more specific pros and cons of the issue are not so easy to evaluate because in actual practice differences in the circumstances surrounding the operation of the two systems make comparisons difficult. For example, in some countries governments have been forced to take over lines which private enterprise was unable to operate at a profit, and to compare the results of government operation of such lines with privately-operated lines would not mean very much.

PROPOSED SOLUTIONS

Of the arguments offered in support of government ownership, the best would appear to be the possibility of solving the weak and strong line problem, but much could be achieved along this line by aggressively pressing a program of consolidation under private enterprise. Some savings might be achieved through the elimination or simplification of regulatory processes, but they would be minor in nature. On the other side of the picture, government ownership and operation would bring the ever present danger that transportation policies would be dictated by political rather than economic considerations. Furthermore, fear has been expressed that government ownership and operation of the railroads would be but the opening wedge in a program of socializing all industry. On balance, it is the present writer's opinion that government ownership and operation of the railroads should be accepted only as a last resort.

Possibility of government ownership and operation of railroads. There is no present demand for nationalization of the railroads, but the inability of the railroads to obtain outside capital, and their inability to earn a satisfactory return except during periods of abnormal traffic, could create a situation in which government ownership would be the only alternative to abandonment. This has happened in other countries and it could happen here. Indeed, that is what a good many students think will happen unless present trends are reversed. Should the railroads be nationalized it is not likely that the Government will permit other types of transportation to compete as private enterprises against the publicly-owned railroads, especially if it has to subsidize these other types of transportation to keep them in existence. Either it will severely limit their operations or, what is more likely, eventually take over part or all of their operations and provide a single national transportation system.

Government ownership and operation of a national transportation system. Would government ownership and operation of all forms of transportation provide a solution to present day transportation problems? Government ownership and operation would help to eliminate the present unsatisfactory situation arising out of the fact that road building, waterway improvements, and airway and airport construction are carried on by separate agencies which are independent of each other and of the regulatory bodies; and which function without regard to the effect of their programs on the transportation system as a whole. It would be possible to coordinate the different forms of transportation in such a way as to make the best or most economical use of each. Also, government ownership of all forms of transportation would eliminate the effect of subsidies on the financial status of unsubsidized carriers, and it might lead to a reduction in subsidies.

PROPOSED SOLUTIONS

On the other hand, government ownership and operation might just as easily result in an increase in subsidized transportation as shippers and communities brought pressure to bear to expand transportation services and facilities without regard to cost. There is nothing to justify a belief that a single unified transportation system would be operated any more efficiently under government ownership than would be the case with government operation of a nationalized railroad system. Clearly, government ownership and operation, either by default or by conscious policy, is no solution to the transportation problem.

ELIMINATION OR REDUCTION OF REGULATION

Elimination of regulation. It is occasionally suggested that the solution to the transportation problem lies in the abandonment of all transportation regulation, permitting the carriers to fight it out among themselves for supremacy. It is assumed that rate cutting would result in the least efficient being forced out of business with an attendant reduction in the total supply of transportation facilities, and since the public would no longer be faced with the necessity of paying rates sufficiently high to support a surplus of transportation facilities, rates in the long run would be reduced. The surviving carriers might all be of the same type, or there might be a division of the field with each agency of transportation confined to that particular area or service in which it has demonstrated a natural advantage. Or transportation companies, each offering a variety of services, might emerge. The idea of eliminating regulation necessarily assumes also the elimination of operating subsidies such as those received by the airlines since the competitive principle could not work if the Government stood behind one of the parties and made up its losses.

Consequences of eliminating regulation. In the rate wars which it is assumed would follow upon the abandonment of regulation the railroads would have a big advantage because of their greater financial resources. Probably the first thing they would do would be to expand their highway operations, and certainly not many independent motor carriers would have the financial resources necessary to outlive an all-out battle with the railroads. By cutting rates and refusing to interchange traffic, the railroads probably could bankrupt coastwise, intercoastal, and barge line common carriers, after which they could gain control of such operations as they considered worth while. It is hard to say what the status of the airlines would be in a free-for-all struggle. The railroads could not even remotely duplicate airline speeds, but if airline operating subsidies were removed, rates and fares would have to be raised, and this would return some airline traffic to the railroads. Some railroads might want to engage directly in air transportation, but others probably would find little advantage in such an operation.

If the railroads emerged victorious as a result of the abandonment of regulation, would shippers be deprived of the services of the newer forms of transportation? The railroads probably would find it desirable to substitute motor transportation for unprofitable branch line service and for handling short haul less-than-carload freight, and in this respect the shipper would not suffer. It is much less likely, however, that shippers would be able to make long haul shipments by truck at present rates. Coastwise and intercoastal common carrier service probably would disappear, as would much of the common carrier barge line service, but Great Lakes shipping would not be disturbed. It seems likely that air transportation would be set back, temporarily at least, by the elimination of subsidies.

Once the railroads had cleared the field, there is always the possibility that they might engage in a rate war among themselves. Certainly this possibility would arise in connection with railroad operation of highway vehicles, since the unregulated use of highway vehicles would enable one railroad to invade the territory of another. The railroads know the value of cooperation, however, and it is quite likely that they would combine or work out agreements to avoid suicidal competition. Hence the ultimate consequence of abandonment of regulation might well be the creation of an unregulated monopolistic control of the transportation system.

Abandonment of regulation would have other and more immediate effects on shippers. Place discrimination, including violations of the long and short haul principle, would reappear. Personal discrimination might be a very real threat because of the ability of large shippers to provide their own transportation facilities by highway or waterway. Railroad lines could be abandoned without restraint and without regard to the effect of such abandonments on the economy of the area involved. Absence of control over security issues would leave the door open for financial manipulations which might well be contrary to the general public interest. And while the general level of rates might not be any higher than under present regulation, if the railroads got together, it probably would be higher than necessary to bring them an adequate return.

Relaxation of regulation. Although a complete abandonment of regulation is no solution to the transportation problem, a better case can be made for a relaxation or reorientation of regulation. Perhaps one of the most valid criticisms of present regulatory policies is that many of them date back to the days when railroads had a transportation monopoly, and regulation designed to protect the public from monopolistic practices is not adapted to the highly competitive situation which exists today.

The railroads, with rare exceptions, are not permitted to establish reduced rates on multiple carload or trainload lots offered by a single shipper even if it can be shown that economies accrue to the carrier in handling such shipments. This principle was adopted to protect small shippers from competition by large shippers, since only large shippers could handle goods in multiple carload or trainload lots, and it may have had some merit when no alternative methods of transportation existed. Today, a large shipper, if he happens to be so situated that he can make use of water transportation, can ship his product in bargeload or boatload lots at rates lower than those provided for railroad carload shipments. In such a situation the establishment of a multiple carload railroad rate between water competitive points would do the small shipper no more harm than is presently the case, but multiple carload rates are rarely approved, and the railroads find it difficult at times to compete effectively for the traffic. The point has also been made that the railroad, although essentially a bulk carrier, cannot make bulk rates, but the contract motor carrier, essentially a small shipment carrier, can make rates for large shipments.

Curiously enough, when motor carriers sought to establish reduced rates on volume minimum weights which were in excess of the carrying capacity of a single truck, in order to compete with the railroads for carload freight, the Interstate Commerce Commission frowned upon the procedure *except to the extent that it could be shown that the cost per hundred pounds of multiple truckload shipments was less than for single truckload shipments.* Apparently a multiple truckload rate in competition with the railroad carload rates was acceptable to the Commission if it could be shown that the reduced rate was based on lower costs, but a multiple carload rate to compete with bargeload rates was questionable. It will be recalled that the Supreme Court rejected this particular decision on the ground that competition between the motor carriers and the railroads was a factor to be considered in determining volume rates. Thus competition is recognized as a valid reason for establishing a multiple truckload rate where motor carriers are trying to compete with railroads, but until recently it has not been recognized as a valid reason for establishing a multiple carload rate where railroads were trying to compete with barge lines.

A somewhat similar situation exists where a shipper can guarantee a certain large minimum quantity of traffic over a given period of time. Regulated common carriers are not permitted to establish special rates conditioned upon volume of traffic over a period of time, the Interstate Commerce Commission having held that such rates are not based on reduced costs and that they discriminate against small shippers. There is, no doubt, merit in the Commission's position, but it is weakened by the fact that shippers can make special contracts with contract carriers and accomplish exactly the same result.

Another hangover from the monopolistic days of railroad transportation is the commodities clause. This clause was established originally to prevent railroads from selling coal from their own mines at a lower price than it could be sold by independent coal mining companies, and it had some significance at a time when independent producers and other businessmen were completely dependent upon railroad transportation. Even more rigid restrictions were subsequently placed on airlines, although for somewhat different reasons. But no such restrictions are placed on highway and water carriers. A manufacturer today may transport his product to market in his own trucks or boats, and he may use these same facilities for the inward transportation of other materials, but a railroad may not manufacture a product and transport it over its own lines for sale. If a manufacturing concern can compete with a transportation company in this way, then perhaps there is something to be said for permitting the transportation agency to compete with the manufacturing concern in producing a product for sale.

At various times various individuals have proposed the relaxation of other regulatory provisions, or at least a more liberal and lenient interpretation of them. Some motor carriers would like to have operating rights liberalized. Private motor carriers would like to be able to handle pay loads on return hauls, although the for-hire carriers are opposed to such liberalization. Some students believe that the railroads should be permitted greater freedom in abandoning branch line mileage and in eliminating unprofitable passenger runs. Also, repeal of the long and short haul clause and greater freedom in rate making have been proposed. The Civil Aeronautics Board has been under attack repeatedly for its refusal to certificate any but grandfather operators to provide scheduled trunk line service. And there are those who would like to see a much greater degree of liberality in the certification of feeder line operations. Of course, it must be kept in mind that these various demands for relaxation of regulation are by no means universal in their appeal. Some come from special interests, and all of them are likely to meet as much opposition as support.

Expansion of regulation. While a relaxation of regulation may be desirable in some respects, a case also can be made for tightening it in other respects. It is difficult to justify the extensive movement of agricultural products and semiprocessed seafoods over long distances by motor carriers exempt from economic regulation. If regulated carriers are expected to operate in accordance with the law, then these presently-exempt carriers should either be regulated along with the others or forced to abandon operations. The situation is even worse in the field of water transportation where the exemptions are so widespread as to make a mockery of regulation. Mention should also be made of the contract carrier, both by highway and water. The contract carrier serves a useful purpose, but the lesser degree of regulation applied to this type of carrier gives it an artificial advantage over the common carrier which is sometimes hard to justify.

USER CHARGES

Abandonment of subsidies. As indicated in the preceding section, the proposal that all regulatory controls be removed of necessity carries with it the elimination of operating subsidies. Quite apart from this, however, railroad spokesmen and others have from time to time suggested eliminating all forms of subsidy as a first step toward establishing an economically sound transportation system. Operating subsidies would be eliminated by abandoning the Inland Waterways Corporation and by terminating all operating subsidies to airlines. In addition, user charges would be assessed against water carriers, private as well as for hire, sufficient at least to cover the maintenance of existing waterways, and sufficient to cover the full cost of all future improvements. Similar user charges would be assessed against all types of air carriers for the use of the airways, although here a part of the cost would have to be borne by private fliers and by the armed forces. Additional charges would be assessed against commercial airlines for the use of municipal airport facilities. Whether or not motor carriers would be subject to additional user charges would have to wait upon a satisfactory determination of the extent to which motor carriers do or do not pay their full share of highway costs.

Effect of abandonment of subsidies. What would be the effect on the transportation system as a whole if all forms of subsidy were abandoned? Proponents of barge line transportation sometimes assert that the savings made by shippers offset or more than offset the cost of waterway improvements to the Government, but there does not seem to be any logical reason why these costs should be met by taxpayers rather than users. Because of the slow and restricted nature of the service, the only possible excuse for barge line transportation is that it is cheaper than other forms of transportation, and for this reason every effort should be made to get at an honest appraisal of its true cost and require the users to meet this cost. No doubt this would mean the end of barge line transportation on some waterways, but it should be abandoned in these cases unless there is substantial evidence that it will be able to pay its way in the not too distant future.

Spokesmen for the airlines do not deny that air transportation is subsidized, but they insist that subsidies should be continued in the interest of the further development of air transportation and the national defense. If operating subsidies to scheduled airlines are to be continued, a careful study should be made of the present route pattern, with the possibility in mind of eliminating routes which have demonstrated that they cannot be operated except under very heavy subsidy. Air transportation probably would be set back for a number of years if it were required to pay its share of the cost of airway and airport improvements today, but there has been some talk in and out of Congress of the possibility of assessing user charges against the airlines within the next few years.

Whether or not additional user charges should be required of motor carriers is a matter of some uncertainty. If they are, motor carriers will no doubt suffer some loss of traffic as a result of the necessity of applying higher rates, but there still will be plenty of traffic to maintain a sound motor transport service.

COORDINATION

A coordinated national transportation system. There is a crying need today for greater coordination of the various agencies of transportation, coordination which will eliminate uneconomic competition and make it possible to take maximum advantage of the peculiar qualities of each agency of transportation. Coordination has been mentioned as one of the possible advantages of government ownership and operation of transportation facilities, but it should be possible to achieve coordination under private ownership and so avoid the objections to governmental activity in the transportation field. Just how would each of the various agencies of transportation fit into a coordinated national transportation system?

In order to justify barge line operations as a part of a national transportation system dedicated to the promotion of maximum economy and efficiency in transportation, the barge line companies must be prepared to pay user charges sufficient to cover the cost of maintaining existing waterways and the full cost of any future waterways which may be built. To the extent that this can be done they would continue to concentrate on long haul volume shipments of such freight as is adapted to movement by water. In view of the difficulties encountered by coastwise and intercoastal common carriers, it is not likely that their services would be continued except under very special circumstances, but the movement of cargo in bulk would continue on the Great Lakes in much the same manner as at present. The movement of small shipments by barge would be abandoned, and no attempt would be made to revive the Great Lakes package service. And, of course, wherever possible full advantage would be taken of through routes and joint rates by rail and water carriers.

PROPOSED SOLUTIONS

All volume shipments other than those which might move by water would be transported by railroad, with the exception of very short haul traffic. Small independent railroads and branch lines of larger railroads would be abandoned wherever insufficient traffic existed to justify continued operation, and their place would be taken by motor carriers. The railroads would not handle any less-than-carload freight through their own freight houses, and the railroad freight house would become a thing of the past. All short haul less-than-carload freight would be handled by motor carriers, and motor carriers would handle a good deal of freight in larger quantities over relatively short distances.

Long haul less-than-carload freight would be handled by freight forwarders operating much as they do today. In other words, forwarders would assemble less-than-carload freight into carload lots at assembly points and these carload lots would be transported by railroad to various distribution points. Long haul less-than-carload freight originating in smaller communities would be brought to the nearest assembly point by motor carriers, and at distribution points motor carriers would handle freight consigned to communities in adjacent areas. Insofar as possible, forwarder traffic would be handled in through freight trains operated under accelerated schedules. There is no fundamental reason why the railroads could not handle this traffic at higher speeds than are achieved today, and even if long haul service could not be offered at motor carrier speeds, the greater economy of railroad transportation would justify its use except in very unusual cases.

In connection with the coordination of railroad and highway facilities, special mention should be made of the possibility of moving loaded truck trailers on railroad flat cars. Under this arrangement the truck trailer would be loaded at the shipper's dock, hauled to the railroad yards, and there run onto a flat car, probably two trailers to a car. The truck trailers would then move to destinations by railroad, be unloaded, and moved to consignees by motor tractors. A similar arrangement could be made with water carriers in those cases where the water carrier was in a position to provide reasonably fast service. The truck trailer also would be adaptable for use in connection with the consolidation of less-than-carload freight at assembly points and its transfer at distribution points to final destination. Between important points where railroads have inaugurated high speed through freight service, loaded truck trailers could be handled by railroad as fast as or faster than they could be handled over the road by truck. Such a service also would be inherently more economical than over-the-road trucking, and it should aid materially in reducing traffic congestion on heavily traveled highways.

Air carriers would continue to provide the high speed service which has proved so useful, but sooner or later shippers and travelers would be required to pay their full fair share of the cost of such transportation. Air transportation probably would continue to be confined to service at major traffic centers, with coordinated feeder line service wherever such service could be made to pay a reasonable share of the cost. It would, of course, be essential to coordinate the high speed air service with ground handling by surface carriers. It seems likely that between many points such a coordination of trunk line air carrier service with ground carriers could provide a service almost as good as feeder lines could provide. An exception to this would be in rough country where surface routes were extremely roundabout.

Pipe lines would continue to render much the same service as at present. Express and parcel post services would be combined, either under the direction of a private company like the Railway Express Agency or under the direction of the Post Office Department, since it is clear that these two agencies cannot continue indefinitely to duplicate each others' services. Post Office control would have an advantage in rural areas where the delivery of small packages can be combined readily with the delivery of mail. On the other hand, postal facilities as they now exist are not well adapted to handling many kinds of express. Possibly some kind of a joint service could be worked out.

The coordination of passenger transportation facilities creates certain problems, especially with reference to the long haul air and rail services. If airline travelers were required to pay their share of the full cost of air transportation, it is possible that there might be room for a high speed high priced long haul air transportation service and a lower speed low cost long haul rail transportation service. If, however, a continuation of the present subsidy policy is believed desirable, or if airlines reach a point where they can provide an unsubsidized service at rail competitive rates, then it might be desirable to abandon railroad passenger service altogether. In this event it would be necessary to expand airline operations to provide service at points not now served, and it would be necessary to coordinate airline and motor bus schedules to provide a rapid through service to and from offline points. The motor bus would provide satisfactory short haul and local passenger service, and at the same time it would relieve the railroads of what is often a costly drain on their revenues.

Advantages and disadvantages. The advantages of a coordinated system of transportation are more or less obvious. It would eliminate uneconomic interagency competition which is costly to carriers and the public alike. It would make it possible to employ each agency of transportation in such a way as to assure over-all maximum efficiency of use. And it would enable the public to continue to enjoy the benefits of an unsubsidized railroad transportation service, at least until such time as it may be demonstrated that the nation no longer needs its railroads.

If the railroads can concentrate on the long haul and relatively long haul transportation of freight in carload lots, they will be concentrating on that form of transportation which they can handle most economically and most profitably. And motor carriers should do well enough by concentrating on the relatively short haul traffic. Should airline subsidies be removed there would no doubt be a decline in the volume of airline traffic, but if subsidies are retained, or if the airlines find they can reduce their costs sufficiently to pay their own way, they will be in as good a position as today with prospects of even better things to come. The status of water carriers is not so clear, but if they can demonstrate that water transportation really is economical by paying adequate user charges, they need have no fear of survival.

It must be recognized that coordination carries with it dangers as well as advantages. If all interagency competition were eliminated, then a major factor in the improvement of transportation service in recent years also would be eliminated. For example, the fast merchandise freights which handle less-than-carload freight, and which are now operated by the railroads between a number of important points, are a direct outgrowth of motor truck competition. If motor truck competition were eliminated between these points, what assurance would the public have that the railroads would maintain and improve this service? To some extent competition between the same kinds of carriers might solve this problem, although it should be kept in mind that, at least so far as the railroads are concerned, such competition has not always been too effective. Another case in point is store-door pickup and delivery. If the railroads withdrew from the less-than-carload freight business, could competition between motor carriers be expected to maintain the present extensive store-door pickup and delivery service which they originated? Similar questions may be raised about other aspects of the transportation business. Clearly, then, if coordination is attempted, steps must be taken to protect the public from the possible adverse effects of the elimination of interagency competition.

Coordination through regulation. If the advantages of coordination outweigh its disadvantages, and it is the belief of the writer that they do, how then is coordination to be achieved? Coordination through government ownership and operation of the transportation system has been mentioned, but it would seem possible to achieve a great degree of coordination by methods which would not destroy the present system of private ownership and operation. One obvious procedure which suggests itself is to bring about coordination through congressional action or through action of regulatory bodies to limit narrowly the areas in which each agency of transportation can operate.

One objection to coordination through regulation is that it would bring about a further expansion of regulatory controls at a time when many people believe that regulation already is overexpanded. The establishment of assembly and distribution points might create serious problems. Unquestionably the creation of new points would be opposed by motor carriers since it would shorten their hauls, while eliminating points would be opposed in many cases by the railroads. The procedure also would require the establishment and supervision of a very large number of through routes and joint rates with inevitable disagreements over the divisions of joint rates. Finally, a policy of delimiting areas of operation would tend to freeze the utilization of the various agencies of transportation into a given pattern, and it would tend to create vested interests which would make it difficult to change the pattern in order to take advantage of technological developments in transportation.

Coordination through the establishment of transportation companies. One other way of achieving coordination would be through the incorporation of transportation companies which would be permitted to combine various means of transportation under one ownership, utilizing each as a part of a single comprehensive transportation system. At the outset, at least, such a plan probably would be confined to surface carriers for reasons which will be mentioned presently. Such a plan need not contemplate a single nationwide transportation company, or even a single company for each region. On the contrary, provision could be made for several such companies in each region, which companies would compete with each other for traffic where a choice of routes was possible.

What would be the advantages of providing a coordinated system of transportation through the device of the transportation company? In the first place, it would not require a further expansion in the already extensive and rigid control now exercised over transportation by regulatory bodies. Indeed, in some respects it might well simplify the regulatory problem, since a much smaller number of carriers would be involved, and numerous interagency conflicts and problems which exist today would disappear. In the second place, it may be argued that private enterprise, operating under the incentive of the profit motive, would have a real incentive to work out and make effective the most efficient use of each type of transportation. Third, if technological changes dictated a change in the utilization of any given agency, private enterprise, again motivated by profit, would make the changes much faster than would be the case if the whole matter were left up to a regulatory body or to Congress. Finally, single company control would greatly simplify operations since it would eliminate the need for establishing an enormous number of through routes and joint rates, and it would eliminate the squabbles and pressures and inequities which arise out of attempts to work out acceptable divisions of joint rates.

Whether or not the service provided by a transportation company should include transportation by air is a matter of some uncertainty. Air transportation provides a unique high speed service of great value which surface carriers cannot hope to duplicate. Because of the very great emphasis on speed, a coordination of air and surface carrier transportation does not offer quite the same advantages as coordination of surface carriers, except where the haul by surface carrier is short. The network of airline routes is not nearly as extensive as highway and railroad networks which means that on many hauls it is just about as fast and a whole lot less expensive to use a direct surface carrier route than a combination of surface and air transportation. Attention should also be called to the fact that air transportation is still to some extent in the promotional stage, and if further promotion is decided upon as being in the public interest, no doubt such promotion can be handled better by an independent management than by one interested in a general transportation system.

The idea of establishing transportation companies which would utilize various agencies of transportation operated under a single ownership has been subject to some criticism, particularly from those closely associated with the newer forms of transportation. At the root of these criticisms probably lies the fear that if transportation companies were set up to perform all types of transportation, they would be dominated by the railroads. These fears probably are not without foundation, since railroad transportation would constitute the biggest single service offered by each company. Furthermore, the great financial strength of the railroads, as compared with the lesser strength of the smaller companies engaged in the newer forms of transportation, no doubt would stand existing railroad management in good stead in the organization of the new companies. There should be room in the new organizations for top men from all types of transportation, however, and the railroads might benefit from the introduction of this new blood.

Closely related to fear of railroad dominance is the fear that if transportation companies were established, dominant railroad interests would discourage the use of the newer forms of transportation. It will be recalled that the Civil Aeronautics Board expressed the opinion that if a company offered two types of transportation service, the transportation activities involving the larger investment would dominate, and partly on this basis it refused to permit a steamship company to provide air transportation service. Also, it has been pointed out that the railroads at one time were perfectly free to engage in motor and air transportation, but for the most part they made little or no effort to utilize these newer forms of transportation. It remained for others to develop the possibilities of the motor vehicle and the airplane for transportation purposes.

It must be admitted that the danger of railroad dominance of unified transportation companies, with the possible discouragement of the utilization of the newer forms of transportation, does exist, and some means would have to be found to remove this danger. One way to do this would be to make sure that competing transportation companies were established, and if steps were taken to make sure that these companies really were competitive, this would go a long way toward the promotion of the use of each agency to its best advantage.

REORGANIZATION OF PROMOTIONAL AND REGULATORY ACTIVITIES OF FEDERAL GOVERNMENT

Unorganized nature of promotional activities. Since the end of World War I Congress has appropriated billions of dollars for the development and promotion of transportation, including construction or aid in the construction of an extensive network of highways, waterways, airways, and airports. In addition, state and local governments have spent additional large sums of money in building highways, airports, and port facilities.[2] There are two things in particular about this developmental and promotional policy to which attention should be called at this point. In the first place, Congress has set up various agencies to develop and promote the growth of highway, waterway, and air transportation. Each of these agencies works independently of the others, and each is interested solely in promoting its particular kind of transportation. In general, they give little or no consideration to the effect of their promotional and developmental activities on other forms of transportation or on the transportation system as a whole. The result of this uncoordinated promotion and development has been a large increase in the total supply of transportation facilities, achieved without reference to the over-all demand, without reference to the real social cost, and above all, without reference to any plan whatsoever for the development of a sound national transportation system.

One other point with reference to the developmental and promotional policies followed by Congress must be noted, and that is the fact that

---

[2] The Brookings Institution has estimated that the Federal Government alone spent some $30 billion on transportation facilities and services in a little over thirty years, an average of about $1 billion a year. Charles L. Dearing and Wilfred Owen, *National Transportation Policy*, p. 353.

PROPOSED SOLUTIONS

Congress, while creating agencies to promote highway, waterway, and air transportation, has created no similar agencies to promote and develop railroad transportation. From one point of view this policy is understandable, since the newer forms of transportation probably would have been unable to survive a competitive struggle with the railroads without public assistance, and as a result shippers might well have lost their special services. On the other hand, with all emphasis placed on the development and promotion of highway, waterway, and air transportation, the potentialities of the railroad, either as an independent agency or as a part of a national transportation system, have either been ignored or taken for granted. Apparently railroad transportation, a sick industry even before the adoption of the various promotional policies, was to be permitted to sink or swim, although it is now recognized that the nation is a long way from being able to do without its railroads.

The lack of coordination in the national policy of development and promotion may be illustrated by taking note of a few of the more important government agencies having to do with transportation. The Bureau of Public Roads, in cooperation with the various state highway departments, is responsible for programming highway improvements. At one time its activities were directed toward the establishment of a national highway system, but its activities now extend far beyond that purpose. And it is not in any way concerned with a national highway system planned as an integral part of a national transportation system. Nor is it at all concerned with the effect which the construction of any particular highway will have on other forms of transportation. Oddly enough, too, the Bureau of Public Roads is responsible for highway construction, but it has nothing to do with the need for a given highway insofar as commercial carriers are concerned. On the other hand, the Interstate Commerce Commission, which is charged with regulating interstate highway transportation, has no voice in planning the highways to be used by interstate highway carriers.

Proposals for specific waterway improvements are presented to Congress by communities or shipper groups which will benefit from low water carrier rates. Since these improvements if made will be financed by the whole country, their advocates have a strong incentive to urge their adoption. Obviously, however, little or no thought is given to the over-all need for the improvements or to their place in or effect upon a national transportation system, even though lip service may at times be paid to such considerations. Traffic surveys and cost studies for proposed waterways are made by the Corps of Engineers of the United States Army. While obviously the services of existing carriers will have some influence on traffic estimates made in connection with a proposed waterway, if it appears that enough traffic may eventually develop to justify the cost, the project is likely to be recommended. It is believed that little attention is paid to the effect of construction on existing carriers or to the need for a given improvement as a part of a national transportation system.

A similar situation exists in air transportation. New airways are planned by the Civil Aeronautics Administration, and airport improvements are made by municipalities with federal aid. The Civil Aeronautics Board, on its part, certificates the carriers who will operate over the airways and into and out of the airports. All of the activities of these agencies are directed toward promoting and developing air transportation. They are not in the least concerned with the effect of their activities on the development and promotion of a sound national transportation system. Although this volume is confined to inland transportation, mention may be made of the Federal Maritime Board and its predecessors, similarly engaged in promoting overseas water transportation.

A Department of Transportation. The preceding discussion is not intended as a criticism of the activities of the government agencies involved. For the most part they are doing no more than carrying out the purposes for which they were established. Furthermore, the Interstate Commerce Commission is faced with the unenviable task of attempting to choose between irreconcilable statements of policy. The whole point of the discussion is to bring out the need for an over-all policy which will relate promotional programs to the development of a sound national transportation system which encompasses all forms of transportation.

In recent years various students have proposed the establishment of a Department of Transportation under a Secretary of Transportation with cabinet rank. One of the more recent of these proposals [3] provides for four assistant secretaries, one each for water, highway, air, and railroad transportation. The promotional, developmental, and subsidy aspects of highway, waterway, and air transportation would be handled within the Department, and presumably this would provide an opportunity for coordinating the work in the interest of a national transportation system.

The Brookings Institution proposal referred to above also would turn over various administrative duties now handled by regulatory bodies to the Department of Transportation. These would include safety matters, railroad car service, and railroad consolidations. This transfer of administrative functions is not unique to the Brookings Institution proposal but has been variously suggested in the past, and it will be recalled that an

---

[3] Charles L. Dearing and Wilfred Owen, *National Transportation Policy.* Washington: The Brookings Institution, 1949, pp. 387-405.

attempt was made to separate administrative and regulatory functions in the Civil Aeronautics Act.

Two reasons for the separation of administrative and regulatory activities are generally cited. In the first place, regulatory commissions function independently of the executive branch of government, which means that any administrative duties they perform are completely divorced from and beyond the control of that branch of government which was established for administrative purposes. The other argument is that with the expansion of regulation regulatory bodies are overworked and must have relief if they are to carry out their real function without interminable delay. Furthermore, the mass of administrative detail does not fit well with the judicial and legislative nature of the work they are supposed to do. On the other hand, objections may be raised to the removal of administrative functions from regulatory bodies on the ground that some of these functions are so closely related to their quasi-judicial and quasi-legislative activities that it is difficult at times to separate the two.

Regulation. Proposals have been made from time to time to transfer the regulatory bodies themselves to the executive branch of government, making them parts of existing government departments. All such attempts to make the regulation of transportation subordinate to a cabinet officer who is a political appointee have been vigorously opposed by students of transportation and government. Transportation is so closely related to the economic welfare of the nation that it should not be made subject to political control in any way. Furthermore, great injustices can be done to individual users and to different parts of the country if regulation is influenced by political considerations. It will be recalled that in 1940 the Civil Aeronautics Board was placed in the Department of Commerce for "housekeeping purposes," although it was to continue to function independently of the Department. It is not altogether clear just what major benefits are to accrue from this sort of an organization.

Perhaps the principal issue at the present time in connection with the reorganization of regulatory bodies has to do with the question of the substitution of a single regulatory body for the present dual regulation, or regulation by three bodies if the Federal Maritime Board is included. The arguments for and against a single regulatory body were discussed in connection with the regulation of air transportation and need not be repeated here. If the concensus of opinion is that air transportation requires further development and promotion, then something can be said for the continuation of the Civil Aeronautics Board as an independent regulatory body. If, however, Congress should some day decide to take steps to promote the development of a national transportation system designed to make most efficient use of all forms of transportation, then a single regulatory body would seem to be essential.

When and if the time comes to establish a single regulatory body, Congress will be faced with some extremely knotty problems. Not the least of these will be the need for streamlining the regulatory body's activities to the point where it can function effectively. It does not seem likely that a single body could handle effectively the many and diverse duties now carried on by the Interstate Commerce Commission and the Civil Aeronautics Board. Increasing the membership of the authority would make possible a division of the various functions among its members, but in so doing it might be difficult to retain the perspective required for the promotion of a sound national transportation system. Furthermore, the larger the regulatory body the more unwieldy it becomes, and the more time-consuming become its common deliberations.

The establishment of a single regulatory body probably would make it mandatory to transfer all promotional and administrative functions elsewhere, possibly to a Department of Transportation. In this event the regulatory body would devote its activities to such things as control over right of entry, rates and rate making, financial regulation, and carrier interrelationships. Should the separate transportation companies previously suggested come into being, this latter function would be relatively unimportant.

Finally, there would be the problem of deciding whether or not to transfer all regulatory activities to an existing body, probably the Interstate Commerce Commission, or to create an entirely new regulatory body. In favor of the former alternative it may be said that the Interstate Commerce Commission now has jurisdiction over the bulk of regulated transportation facilities, that it has had previous experience in expanding the scope of its activities, and that its present organization is set up in such a way that additional functions could be added with a minimum of reorganization. On the other hand, if administrative functions are removed and placed elsewhere, an extensive reorganization would be necessary anyway. Furthermore, the Interstate Commerce Commission's thinking always has been in terms of surface transportation and the Civil Aeronautics Board's thinking in terms of air transportation. If a single regulatory body is to do the job for which it is intended, it must think in terms of a national transportation system in which maximum use will be made of the special advantages of all forms of transportation. This suggests the desirability of creating an entirely new organization. The transition might be difficult, but in the long run it would be worth it.

Other regulatory problems. Whether a single regulatory body is established or not, there are other regulatory problems which must be faced and solved by Congress. One of these has to do with the conflict between the Interstate Commerce Commission and the Antitrust Division of the Department of Justice. For many years the railroads, and later the motor carriers as well, have followed a policy of handling rate making and other matters of common interest through what are known as rate bureaus. The Interstate Commerce Commission and shippers generally believe that these organizations are essential to the orderly handling of rates, but the Antitrust Division has maintained that as presently operated they constitute a violation of the antitrust laws, and it has continued to fight them even after Congress passed the Reed-Bulwinkle Act legalizing their activities.

Another problem has to do with speeding up the regulatory processes. It is desirable to give all parties at interest in any proceeding an opportunity to be heard, but this often results in long drawn-out hearings. This policy, along with the heavy pressure of handling numerous cases and duties, often leads to extended delays in handing down decisions on important matters. Thus it took the Civil Aeronautics Board four years to decide that it would not approve Pan American's domestic route application. There have been other extended delays which create a degree of uncertainty and make planning for the future difficult.

Perhaps most important have been the delays encountered by the railroads in obtaining rate increases from the Interstate Commerce Commission. The second application for a rate increase following World War II was made on July 3, 1947. Subsequently the Commission granted certain interim increases, but the final decision was not announced until July 29, 1948, more than a year after the original application was made. If carriers cannot adjust their rates promptly to meet increased costs during a period of rising prices, their earnings are bound to suffer. Yet if they cannot earn adequate profits during periods of heavy traffic such as existed immediately after World War II, they cannot make up for the low earnings of depression years and their solvency is threatened.

Finally, some more effective method of handling labor disputes must be found. The present Railway Labor Act does little more than provide a series of largely useless gestures which at best serve only to put off the evil day until some device of the moment is found for working out a temporary truce. The uncertainty surrounding railroad labor disputes is hard on labor, hard on carriers, and hard on the economy of the nation. Not only must some device be found for settling disputes amicably so that there can be no possibility of a stoppage of transportation, but also the device must be related in some way to the process of rate making. As it is now, the carriers cannot very well anticipate wage increases by applying for a rate increase in advance, but once a wage increase is granted, the carriers may have to wait six months or more to get a covering rate increase. And to make matters worse wage increases very often are made retroactive, but this is never the case with rate increases.

CONCLUSION

Prospect for congressional action. Enough has been said in the course of the preceding discussion to indicate that all is not well with transportation in the United States, even though the problem is obscured by abnormal traffic conditions. Fortunately, however, there is evidence that Congress is aware of the situation. On March 7, 1946, a national transportation inquiry was authorized, and since that time committees from both Houses of Congress have been engaged in holding hearings or in working on studies of transportation problems. The hearings have developed the usual clashes of interest, but they have served to bring out some of the major problems involved.

On August 30, 1949, President Truman requested the Department of Commerce to make a report outlining major policy issues which needed to be resolved in order to achieve maximum effectiveness and consistency of federal programs in the transportation field. This report was made on December 1, 1949, and indicates an awareness of the problem discussed above as well as various others.[4] In April 1950, the Interstate Commerce Commission issued an informal study of transport coordination and integration in the United States containing a considerable amount of factual material on the subject.[5] Mention should be made, too, of the work of a private nonprofit organization, The Transportation Association of America, made up of all sorts of individuals having an interest in transportation. The Association has been conducting forums and making studies designed to aid in solving transportation problems and is dedicated to the preservation of all forms of transportation.

Late in 1950 there was established within the Department of Commerce the office of Undersecretary of Commerce for Transportation for the purpose, among other things, of coordinating the promotional activities of the Department relating to transportation. The primary responsibility of the Undersecretary is policymaking and planning. He has no authority in connection with regulation. This is a step in the right direction, and the activities of the Undersecretary will be watched with interest.

From April to August, 1950, a Subcommittee on Domestic Land and Water Transportation of the Senate Committee on Interstate and Foreign

---

[4] Secretary of Commerce, *Issues Involved in a Unified and Coordinated Federal Program for Transportation*, 1949.

[5] Bureau of Transport Economics and Statistics, Interstate Commerce Commission, *Historical Development of Transport Coordination & Integration in the United States.*

PROPOSED SOLUTIONS

Commerce held extensive hearings at which carriers, shippers, and others were permitted to air their views on domestic transportation problems and policies. In October 1951, the subcommittee issued a progress report prepared by Senator Bricker of Ohio which, except for one or two omissions, constituted a rather remarkable summary of the transportation situation as it existed at the end of 1951.[6] On March 3, 1952, the Senate Committee on Interstate and Foreign Commerce began hearings on a total of thirty-six bills to amend existing transportation laws, which hearings were concluded on April 9. As might be expected, spokesmen for the various transportation agencies supported or opposed specific bills strictly along the lines of their own immediate self-interest. To a considerable extent, too, this was true of shippers, shipper groups, and communities having a stake in some particular form of transportation. However, the National Industrial Traffic League, a nationwide organization of shippers, and the United States Chamber of Commerce took a somewhat broader view of the problems involved. A brief review of some of the more important measures considered by the committee follows.

Among those bills specifically relating to railroads, S. 2518 attracted the most attention. The purpose of this bill was to permit the railroads to obtain general rate increases to meet rising costs without the costly delays they have experienced in recent years. While sympathy for the purpose of the bill was expressed in some nonrailroad quarters, considerable objection was raised to specific aspects of the bill itself. A closely related bill, S. 2519, would amend the rule of rate making to require the Interstate Commerce Commission, in connection with its power to prescribe just and reasonable rates, to consider such factors as the ability of the railroads to attract equity capital. This bill, also, would remove from the rule of rate making the requirement that the Commission, in prescribing rates, is to consider the effect of rates on the movement of traffic by the carriers for which the rates were prescribed. Some nonrailroad support was forthcoming for the first of these proposed changes but not for the second. S. 2754, which would eliminate the long and short haul clause, was supported by the railroads and opposed by water carriers. The National Industrial Traffic League expressed support for S. 2754 with some modifications.[7]

Numerous measures directly related to the motor carrier industry were discussed in detail. One of the most controversial of these measures was S. 2357 which would restrict exempt transportation of fish and agricultural products to fishermen and farmers. Farm organizations were outspoken in their opposition to this proposal. S. 2363 would establish maximum size

---

[6] *Domestic Land and Water Transportation*, 82nd Congress, 1st Session, Senate Report No. 1039.

[7] *Traffic World*, April 5, 1952, p. 18.

and weight limits for motor vehicles subject to the Interstate Commerce Act. This bill was opposed by spokesmen for both the railroads and the motor carriers. S. 2362, dealing with restrictions on the leasing of vehicles, proved to be particularly objectionable to spokesmen for private carrier interests. S. 2349, intended to make the long and short haul clause applicable to motor carriers, found little support. Among other bills directly related to motor transportation, S. 2360 would increase the amount of securities a motor carrier could issue without Interstate Commerce Commission approval, S. 2364 would authorize the Bureau of Public Roads to determine the amount and type of road taxes properly assessable against motor carriers, and S. 2752 would require contract carriers to publish the rates they actually charged.

S. 2364 would authorize the Interstate Commerce Commission to revoke or amend water carrier certificates or permits under certain circumstances, a type of legislation which the Commission had advocated for several years. S. 2743, which would require inland waterway carriers to pay tolls for the use of the waterways, was supported by the railroads but met strong opposition from water carriers and those shippers and communities having water carrier service. S. 2744, which called for the consideration of new waterway projects by the Interstate Commerce Commission, likewise was supported by the railroads and opposed by water carriers and associated interests. S. 2745 would, among other things, repeal the requirement for the establishment of differential rail-water rates, and this measure also was supported by the railroads and opposed by water carrier interests. S. 2742 provided for the dissolution of the Inland Waterways Corporation. In addition to railroad support, this measure was favored by the National Industrial Traffic League [8] and the United States Chamber of Commerce.[9] It was opposed by Mississippi Valley interests.

S. 2712 provided that freight forwarders be issued certificates of public convenience and necessity rather than permits, thus acknowledging their status as common carriers. S. 2713 was designed to place certain restrictions on the operation of private forwarder services by shipper groups. Freight forwarders declared that this legislation was necessary in order to avoid evasion of Part IV, but shipper groups asserted that it would sound the death knell of forwarding by shippers.

Considerably broader in its application than any of the preceding bills was S. 2351 which would require the Interstate Commerce Commission, in passing on proposals for new or extended operations by rail, motor, or water carriers, to consider the adequacy of other types of transportation

---

[8] *Traffic World*, April 5, 1952, p. 18.
[9] *Ibid.*, p. 20.

providing a similar service. This measure was supported by the railroads and opposed by motor and water carriers and by some shipper groups. Also, of more general interest were two bills which would provide for certain changes in Commission organization and procedure.

It will be observed that most of the measures discussed above are pro-railroad in the sense that, if adopted, they would improve the competitive position of the railroads over motor and water carriers. Hence it is not surprising that railroad spokesmen supported most of the bills while major opposition came from motor and water carriers. Shipper groups, other than those closely associated with a particular type of transportation, supported some measures and opposed others. While it appears likely that some legislation may come out of these hearings, it is doubtful that a sound national transportation system can be achieved by such a piecemeal approach to the problem.

INDEX

INDEX

INDEX

B

Baltimore & Ohio Railroad, 38-39
Bankruptcy Act, Section 77, 313-322
Bankruptcy, railroad, Chapter 15
Barge lines (see River and canal transportation; Inland Waterways Corporation)
Barker case, 419
Barriers to interstate commerce, 428-431
Basing point system of rate making, 249-251
Big Inch, 631
Blanketing principle of rate making, 252-253
Board of Investigation and Research:
  nature and purpose, 165
  studies of public aid to:
    air transportation, 560-561
    highway transportation, 385-386
    railroad transportation, 59-66
    water transportation, 462
Boiler Inspection Act, 192
Bond ratio, railroad, 294-296
Bonds:
  as source of permanent railroad capital, 292-296
  types, 291
  (see also Equipment obligations)
Brokers, motor transport, 403
Buck v. Kuykendall, 392, 394
Burden of proof in rate cases, 123, 164-165
Bureau of Motor Carriers, 405
Bureau of Public Roads, 369, 386
Bureau of Water Carriers and Freight Forwarders, 495-496
Bus transportation (see Motor passenger transportation)

C

Canal transportation (see River and canal transportation)
Canals:
  early, 32-36
  modern, 568-569
Capital stock, 290
Capitalizable assets, 301
Car, railroad:
  distribution, 326, 328-329
  pools, 327-328
  service, 225-229
  shortages, 326, 328-329
Certificates of public convenience and necessity:
  airline, 571

Certificates of public convenience and necessity (continued):
  motor carrier, 397
  railroad, 144-145
  water carrier, 487, 503
Champlin Refining Company case, 637-638
Chandler Act, 320
Chosen instrument doctrine, 607
Civil Aeronautics Act of 1938:
  C.A.B. policy, Chapters 28-29
  declaration of policy, 569-570
  international aspects, 575, 576-577
  legislative history, 566
  provisions, 566-577
Civil Aeronautics Administration, 567
Civil Aeronautics Authority, 566, 567
Civil Aeronautics Board, 567-568
Civil Airways, 542
Class Rate Investigation, 1939, 230-231, 277-278
Classification of freight:
  cost as a determinant, 234-237, 244-245
  demand as a determinant, 237-241, 243-244
  motor carrier, 438-441
  railroad, 222-241
Class rates:
  effect of unequal on industrialization, 279-280
  equalization of, 275-279
  in Mountain-Pacific Territory, 272
  in Official Territory, 266-268
  in Southern Territory, 268
  in Southwestern Territory, 271-272
  in Western Trunk Line Territory, 269-271
  interterritorial, 272-275
  motor carrier, 438-441, 442-445
  nature of, 220-221
  railroad, 222-241, Chapter 13
Coastwise and intercoastal shipping, 476-479, 509-511
Commerce Court, 123, 125
Commission Divisions Act, 127
Commodities clause, 119-120, 121, 644-645, 711
Commodity rates:
  in general, 221, 241-243
  motor carrier, 440
  railroad, 221, 241-243
Commodity restrictions, 687-691
Common carriers:
  duties and obligations, 92
  freight forwarders as, 663-664
  regulation of:
    air, Chapters 27-29

—732—

INDEX

INDEX

INDEX

R

INDEX

INDEX